Public
Administration
in America

PUBLIC ADMINISTRATION IN AMERICA

GEORGE J. GORDON
Illinois State University

ST. MARTIN'S PRESS · NEW YORK

Acknowledgments

Table 1-1 From Thomas D. Lynch, "A Context for Zero-Base Budgeting," *The Bureaucrat*, Vol. 6, No. 1 (Spring 1977), p. 6. Copyright © 1977 by Transaction, Inc. Reprinted by permission of Transaction, Inc.

Figure 1-3 From *New York State: A Citizen's Handbook*. Reprinted by permission of The League of Women Voters of New York State.

Eisenhower statement on governmental administration excerpted from Joseph Bower, "Effective Public Management," *Harvard Business Review*, March-April 1977.

Table 2-1 From Harold M. Barger, "Images of Bureaucracy: A Tri-Ethnic Consideration," *Public Administration Review* (May/June 1976). Reprinted from *Public Administration Review*. Copyright © 1976 by American Society for Public Administration, 1225 Connecticut Avenue, N.W., Washington, D.C. 20036. All rights reserved.

Figure 3-1 The Gallup Poll as reported in John E. Mueller, "Trends in Popular Support for the Wars in Korea and Vietnam," *American Political Science Review*, LXV (1971), and Gallup Opinion Index (March 1971 and February 1973). Reprinted by permission of the American Political Science Association and of the Gallup Poll, Princeton, New Jersey.

Acknowledgments and copyrights continue at the back of the book on pages 455–456, which constitute an extension of the copyright page.

TO THE MEMORY OF
ROSCOE C. MARTIN
SCHOLAR, MENTOR, GENTLEMAN, FRIEND

PREFACE

This book is designed as a basic, comprehensive text for use in public administration courses. It is *basic* in the sense that the reader is assumed to have some background knowledge of government and politics in the United States, but not necessarily specific information about administrative politics or government bureaucracy. Consequently, terms and concepts are defined and explained as they are introduced throughout the text. It is *comprehensive* in that it provides coverage of the subjects most public administration textbooks include—such as decision making, budgetary processes, and organization theory—and also of some areas not always discussed in other books—such as federalism and intergovernmental relations, government regulation, and administrative leadership.

The formal study of public administration is hardly new, but academic interest in the field has grown tremendously in recent years as the need for professionally trained administrators at all levels has become increasingly urgent. As a result, a great deal of new information and analysis has transformed what used to be regarded as a rather one-dimensional subject into a very complex one that continually challenges us to comprehend its intricacies. Few aspects of public administration can properly be viewed in isolation; the closer one looks, the more the interrelationships among seemingly disconnected facts and concepts become apparent. I have attempted to alert the reader to such interrelationships throughout the book.

The book has two principal emphases. The first is on the central importance of public administration in modern government. With literally thousands of separate public programs and billions of dollars spent each year in managing them, the scope of administrative operations at all levels of government is immense. The second emphasis is on the role of politics and political influence in shaping public administration. Undoubtedly this emphasis will make the book more attractive to some instructors than to others. However, unquestionably there are political elements and implications in what bureaucracy is and does, and students should be aware of the numerous ways in which political interests and administrative organization and practice are intertwined. Nor does this book take the position that it is necessarily wrong or harmful that politics plays such a prominent role. The discussion of politics in every instance is explanatory rather than moralizing; "pros" and "cons" of issues such as government regulation are carefully presented and examined; and the reader is left—indeed, encouraged—to draw independent conclusions.

I owe many debts of gratitude for assistance with the preparation of this book. Illinois State University and its Department of Political Science granted time for research and, in the fall of 1977, a sabbatical leave so that I could devote full energy to completing the manuscript. Thanks are due especially to Hibbert Roberts, chairman of the department, for his support and encouragement. Graduate students at Illinois State who supplied invaluable research assistance included the late Mary Bilyeu, Thom Bilyeu, Joan Bortolon, Cindy Colella, Mary Ann Collins, and Rod Meyer. Colleagues who suggested very useful ideas and perspectives included Michael Colella, Thomas Droleskey, Thomas Eimermann, Ann Elder, George Kiser, Alan Monroe, and Richard Payne. Glenn Cowley and Bert Lummus of St. Martin's Press provided thoughtful guidance as the manuscript took shape, and Carolyn Eggleston greatly enhanced the final product by her careful copy-editing. The consulting editor, Frederick Lane of the City University of New York, worked tirelessly to strengthen the text; his suggestions were invariably perceptive and beneficial. Alberta Carr was a thoroughly competent typist, and much more; her devotion to her task and an unerring eye for style and detail contributed tremendously. My wife, Myra, provided invaluable assistance in preparing the glossary; she also made it possible for me to devote countless hours to writing, and patiently sustained my spirits. These people deserve much of the credit for whatever strengths are present in the book; mine alone is the responsibility for its weaknesses.

This book is dedicated, with respect and affection, to the memory of Professor Roscoe C. Martin, who first awakened my interest in public administration.

George J. Gordon

CONTENTS

Public
Administration
in America

PART ONE
INTRODUCTION

Our chief concern in this opening section is to explore essential facts and concepts in public administration. Chapter 1 focuses on the approach that will be used throughout the book, one which emphasizes the political setting of public administration and the impacts of politics on administrative decisions. Basic terms are defined and discussed, and the most common structural arrangements of executive-branch agencies are described. Traditional conceptions of how bureaucracy "ought" to function are discussed, then compared with the broad realities of American bureaucracy—and the differences are important. Finally, public administration as an academic field is described, particularly its evolution from a relatively uncomplicated field of study in the early 1900s to a highly complex, rather unsettled academic discipline today.

Chapter 2 deals with underlying values in administrative practice. Of central importance are the tensions between *political* values, such as individual liberty, representativeness, and popular control, and *administrative* values stressing bureaucratic efficiency, economy, and political neutrality. In addition, the impacts of social change and controversy over values are analyzed, with emphasis on the turbulence of modern times.

CHAPTER 1
Approaching the Study of Public Administration

Public administration in America today is a large enterprise encompassing the daily activities of literally millions of government workers, and touching many aspects of the daily life of virtually every American. The growth of government activity and public bureaucracy, at all levels, is one of the most significant social phenomena of recent years. It has become the subject of much sober-minded discussion among scholars and practitioners. At the same time, it is a "hot" political topic, debated in highly emotional terms by politicians as diverse as George Wallace, Ronald Reagan, Jimmy Carter, and Hubert Humphrey, each of whom has had something different to say about "the Washington bureaucracy." For that matter, other politicians in other places have also run, with some success, "against" the bureaucracy.[1] It is safe to say that terms such as "bureaucracy," "efficiency," "coordination," and "red tape" are very much a part of America's organizational vocabulary, for better or for worse. It has even been suggested that the language ("jargon") of bureaucracy has had a negative impact on the English language as a whole.[2] In any event, the subject of public administration and bureaucracy is, for most Americans, not brand-new; in one way or another, most of us are familiar with it.

Our consciousness of bureaucracy obviously varies with the situation. We may be vividly aware of it when we fill out a federal income tax return (especially when we pay additional tax on April 15!), apply for a government loan to finance our college education, hear a TV news story on the latest congressional investigation of the CIA or FBI, or deal directly with that most visible of public administrators if we have to explain why we don't deserve a speeding ticket (police officers are, technically, bureaucrats, though not many of them—or us—would put it exactly that way).

We may be far less aware of the role and impact of bureaucracy under other circumstances. This is so either because bureaucratic decision making is obscure (which it frequently is) or because it is just not very salient (directly meaningful) to us. An example of the former might be the procedures followed by President John F. Kennedy and his advisors in resolving the Cuban missile crisis of 1962. These included secret photographic flights over Cuba and secret messengers carrying notes back and forth to Soviet diplomats. For an example of the latter, we might note the fight over the health hazard warning on cigarette packages, which the tobacco industry and its friends resisted vigorously, but which for most people—including most smokers—was not an exciting issue.[3]

Whatever our awareness of particular bureaucratic activities or decisions, there are apparently strong feelings about the institution of bureaucracy among millions of Americans. In the 1960s and 1970s the usual response to any mention of "the bureaucracy" has been negative; bureaucrats are not very popular people in the eyes of many whom they supposedly serve. Bureaucracy has become a favorite "whipping boy" for a good many of society's current ills. There are several reasons for this venting of discontent on bureaucracy: it is clearly influential; it is increasingly visible; we don't elect our bureaucrats (in all but a handful of cases); and it is a convenient target. We hear a great deal about the growing power of bureaucracy and bureaucrats, the arbitrary nature of many decisions, a lack of accountability, impersonal treatment—even about "pointy-headed bureaucrats who don't carry nothin' in those briefcases of theirs except their sack lunch," to quote George Wallace.

All in all, the public's regard for public administrators is at a low ebb, far below what it was thirty or forty years ago.[4] First in the Great Depression of the 1930s, then during and after World War II, which the nation largely supported, public administrators and their organizations enjoyed far greater public confidence than seems currently to be the case. The general public, through their elected officials, looked to the administrative apparatus of government to take on increasing programmatic responsibility. Congress, state legislatures, city councils, presidents, governors, and mayors alike delegated growing amounts of discretionary power to administrative officials, and in effect directed them to make the day-to-day choices involved in applying laws enacted through the formal legislative process. This is not to say that some great national referendum was held on the question: "Shall bureaucrats be given more responsibility?" It *is* to say that public acceptance of greater governmental involvement in a wider range of societal activities outweighed opposition to growth of government generally, and government bureaucracy in particular.[5] Table 1–1 illustrates governmental expansion from 1949 to 1976.

Thus, the trends of growth begun during the New Deal of Franklin D. Roosevelt and consolidated under Harry Truman and, significantly, under Dwight Eisenhower's Republican administration rested on a foundation of popular legitimacy that only recently has begun to deteriorate. This weakening of legitimacy seems to have developed as a reaction against

TABLE 1-1
AN ELASTIC YARDSTICK FOR MEASURING
THE GROWTH OF AMERICAN GOVERNMENT

	1949	1976	Percent Change from 1949 to 1976
Dollar Expenditures (in billions)			
Federal	41.3	390.6	845.7
State-Local	18.0	185.0	927.3
Total	59.3	575.6	870.7
Public Expenditures as a Percent of GNP			
Federal	16.0	23.2	45
State-Local	7.0	11.0	57.1
Total	23.0	34.2	48.7
Public Sector Employees (in millions)			
Federal	2.075	2.850	37.3
State-Local	3.906	12.229	213.1
Total	5.981	15.079	152.1
Public Sector Employees per 1,000 Population			
Federal	13.9	13.2	-5.1
State-Local	26.1	56.8	117.6
Total	40.0	70.0	75.0

Source: Adapted from Thomas D. Lynch, "A Context for Zero-Base Budgeting," *The Bureaucrat* (Spring 1977), 3–11, at p. 6.

particular governmental behavior—enforcement of civil rights laws, the Vietnam War, and the Watergate scandals—and against a government widely viewed as becoming too distant from the people it was designed to serve.

This book is concerned with describing, analyzing, and evaluating the wide range of governmental and political activities we refer to as "public administration." But first we should lay some groundwork. Thus, in this chapter we shall define a number of key terms and concepts; survey formal administrative structures of national, state, and local governments; review some long-standing conceptions of bureaucracy's relationship to the larger governmental system; and discuss key features of public policy making in American government, particularly administrative policy making.

Defining Basic Terms and Concepts

It is already evident that we are concerned with public administration in the broader context of American government and politics. *Politics* may be defined in a number of ways, but any definition should cover a multitude of situations and behaviors. Various definitions have been suggested: (1) the pursuit and exercise of power, (2) competition and conflict over scarce resources, (3) the authoritative allocation of resources, (4) the process of deciding "who gets what, when, how."[6] Out of these definitions—all of which help us "zero in" on the idea of politics—a number of major points emerge.

First, politics seems to be a process concerned with the acquisition of some desired objective: elective office, a policy favorable to one's interests or the interests of one's friends, or power to influence events. Second, power and other useful resources, such as money and influence, are available only in limited quantity compared to the demand for them, thus generating intense political conflict. As just one example, consider the tremendous number of candidates for political office compared to the much smaller number of offices to be filled. Third, politics can be said to permeate most, if not all, of the important processes of government decision making, in concept as well as in practice. What does government do if not decide "who gets what, when, how"? Similarly, isn't government the broad institution which makes "authoritative allocations" of various commodities—government contracts with private industry or universities, tax rules favoring this income group or that one; tight or not-so-tight regulations regarding automobile exhaust emissions? In short, politics and government, if not identical, are close relatives indeed. More to the point, much of what goes on in the government arena is related to political conflict over the resources government is in a position to pass around.

Another term has cropped up in this discussion. We have spoken of "power" as one of those commodities over which political conflict can and does occur. *Power* may be defined as an ability to cause other persons or groups to do something they might not otherwise do. Note that this definition, as with those of "politics," would fit a wide variety of situations: political party politics, military conflict, interpersonal relationships, administrative rule making—right on up to the forceful exercise of power by totalitarian governments.

Power implies that whatever the circumstance, one person or group can motivate other persons or groups to behave as the former wants them to behave. Two basic methods can be employed, either singly or in combination: (1) *incentives/rewards* ("if you do what is asked, this good thing will happen to you, or this bad thing will not happen"); and (2) *sanctions/punishments* ("if you do not do what is asked, this bad thing will happen to you, or this good thing will not happen"). How much power it takes to bring about the desired behavior depends to a considerable extent on the willingness of those on the receiving end to obey—logically enough. But the simple fact that this statement is logical should not obscure its importance, especially in a governmental system that rests upon "consent of the governed" instead of brute force. Such a government depends fundamentally upon a large measure of virtually automatic willingness on the part of the people to be governed by the government; that is, to obey those in power.

By referring to *government power*, we have narrowed the field of discussion somewhat. There is obviously something different about the power of a government, or any part of a government, when compared to power exercised by other organizations or by individuals. The differences are twofold. First, government possesses *authority*, that is, power defined according to a legal and institutional framework and vested in a formal structure. "Authority" implies definition of the legitimate uses of power. It implies further that power exercised under "proper authority" is validly used and appropriately directed toward agreed-upon societal objectives. Second, government itself is distinguished from all other organizations in society by its ability to take certain actions which would violate the law if executed by private citizens, including a government monopoly on the legal use of force. Within limits government officials may, for example, search a private residence; for the rest of us, that's burglary. A police officer may point a revolver at another individual and order him to halt; for the private citizen, such an act would be assault with a deadly weapon. Also, a government agency may issue regulations setting minimum prices for some kinds of goods sold in the private marketplace; if business firms do that, they can be prosecuted for conspiracy to fix prices. Subject to the limits imposed by the Constitution, courts, and public opinion, government can exercise greater legal power than any other group, organization, or individual.

One other concept enters into the discussion at this point, that of *legitimacy*. The legitimacy of any social institution which exercises power, including government, depends on the acceptance and the standing accorded it by the people over whom it is said to hold authority. Thus, legitimacy breathes life into authority, since it paves the way for willing acceptance of authority. Without legitimacy, even legally established authority has to resort more and more to direct force to secure compliance, and it becomes more a case of raw power than of respect for authority. If we proclaim the rule of law as a fundamental aspect of our governmental system, then the continuing legitimacy of our social and political institutions is a key to our ability to maintain that. In the wide variety of negative, even hostile, comments about bureaucracy cited earlier, we see some evidence of diminished legitimacy of bureaucratic institutions. We will have occasion to deal with this subject further in subsequent chapters.

What does all this have to do with public administration? There are several important connections. Administrative agencies and personnel have power, authority, and significant legitimacy in the overall political scheme of things. They allocate resources, exercise power, and have a great deal to do with determining who gets what. They are part of the legal and institutional framework of power, major participants in the structures and processes of governing America. All in all, we find that public administration stands squarely in the middle of a great many political and governmental currents.

What Is Public Administration?

Public administration may be defined as *all processes, organizations, and individuals (the latter acting in official positions and roles) associated with carrying out laws and other rules adopted or issued by legislatures, executives, and courts.* This definition should be understood to include considerable administrative involvement in formulation as well as implementation of legislation and executive orders; we will discuss this more fully later. Public administration is also a field of academic study and professional training, from which substantial numbers of government employees currently are drawn.

Note that the first definition does not limit the participants in public administration to administrative personnel, or even to people in government. It can and does refer to a varied assortment of individuals and groups with an interest in the consequences of administrative action. That certainly includes, perhaps foremost, administrators themselves. But it also includes members of the legislature, their staffs, and legislative committees; higher executives in the administrative apparatus of government; judges (somewhat less directly); political party officials whose partisan interests overlap extensively with issues of public policy; leaders and members of interest groups seeking from the government various policies, regulations, and actions; mass media personnel, particularly in their "watchdog" role over actions and decisions of public officials; and members of society at large, who can have some impact, even when not well organized, on the directions public policy follows. Furthermore, public administration involves all of those mentioned in shifting patterns of reciprocal (mutual) relationships, which are central to our study of the area. Again, this comes back to politics and the quest for power and influence, in state and local governments as well as Washington, and in national-state-local relations.

The politics of administration involves agency interactions with those *outside* the formal structure as well as interactions among those *within* administrative agencies; we are concerned with both. But before considering the dynamics of administrative politics, it would be useful to review briefly formal administrative structures, beginning with the national executive branch and then comparing those with state and local administrative arrangements.

Principal Structures of the National Executive Branch

The Constitution of the United States is virtually silent on the subject of public administration, except to refer to the president's responsibility to "faithfully execute the laws." The structures we have are the product of congressional action, as are many of the procedures followed within administration. The national executive branch is organized primarily into five major types of agencies; there are four formal bases, or foundations, of organization, and two broad categories of administrative employees. These are deserving of brief consideration because they have some impact on the way administrative machinery functions and on the content of policies it helps enact.

Questions of organizational structure may not appear at first glance to carry many political overtones. But formal organizational arrangements do not just happen, and they are not politically neutral in their consequences.[7] The choice of organizational structure may both reflect and promote some political interests over others. The reflection of political interests stems from a particular structure being the product of decisions reached through the political process by a particular majority coalition, whether directly (as through congressional action) or indirectly (as when the president proposes executive reorganization). Those who organize or reorganize an agency in a certain way obviously have reasons for doing so, one of which is usually promotion and protection of their political and policy interests. As one example, the new Department of Energy gives the president greater control over previously scattered agencies in the energy policy field, such as the Federal Power Commission and Federal Energy Administration.

The principal types of agencies are (1) cabinet-level departments, (2) independent regulatory agencies, (3) government corporations, (4) various units of the Executive Office of the President, and (5) other independent agencies (see Figure 1–1). These agencies can be organized according to function (general area of policy concern), geographic area, clientele, or work process. The two broad categories of employees are specialists and generalists, although these are not the only ways to categorize administrative employees. Let us consider each of these in turn.[8]

Cabinet-level departments (or just "departments") are the largest and usually the most visible of national executive organizations; this is also true in most states and localities. As of late 1977 there were twelve departments in the national government, including the Department of State, Department of Defense (DOD), Department of Health, Education, and Welfare (HEW), the Departments of Commerce, Interior, Labor, and Transportation, and the Department of Energy, established in late summer of 1977. Each department is headed by a secretary and a series of top-

Figure 1–1 Major Agencies of the United States Government

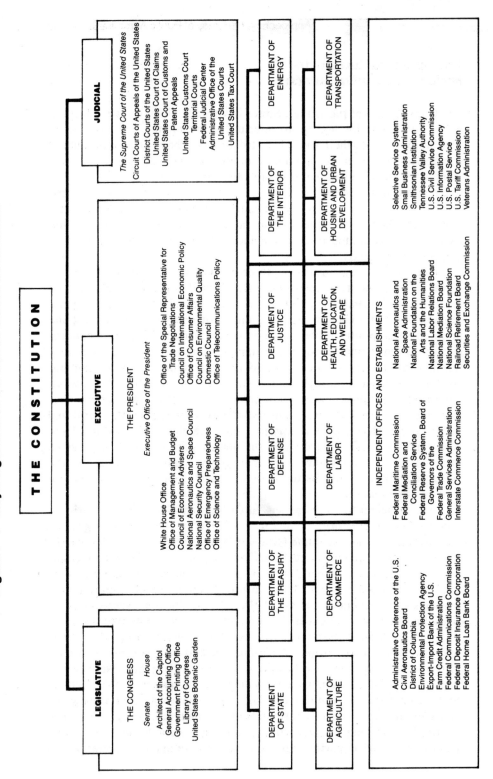

THE CONSTITUTION

LEGISLATIVE

THE CONGRESS

Senate   House

Architect of the Capitol
General Accounting Office
Government Printing Office
Library of Congress
United States Botanic Garden

EXECUTIVE

THE PRESIDENT

Executive Office of the President

White House Office
Office of Management and Budget
Council of Economic Advisers
National Aeronautics and Space Council
National Security Council
Office of Emergency Preparedness
Office of Science and Technology

Office of the Special Representative for
  Trade Negotiations
Council on International Economic Policy
Office of Consumer Affairs
Council on Environmental Quality
Domestic Council
Office of Telecommunications Policy

JUDICIAL

The Supreme Court of the United States
Circuit Courts of Appeals of the United States
District Courts of the United States
United States Court of Claims
United States Court of Customs and
  Patent Appeals
United States Customs Court
Territorial Courts
Federal Judicial Center
Administrative Office of the
  United States Courts
United States Tax Court

DEPARTMENT OF STATE

DEPARTMENT OF THE TREASURY

DEPARTMENT OF DEFENSE

DEPARTMENT OF JUSTICE

DEPARTMENT OF THE INTERIOR

DEPARTMENT OF ENERGY

DEPARTMENT OF AGRICULTURE

DEPARTMENT OF COMMERCE

DEPARTMENT OF LABOR

DEPARTMENT OF HEALTH, EDUCATION, AND WELFARE

DEPARTMENT OF HOUSING AND URBAN DEVELOPMENT

DEPARTMENT OF TRANSPORTATION

INDEPENDENT OFFICES AND ESTABLISHMENTS

Administrative Conference of the U.S.
Civil Aeronautics Board
District of Columbia
Environmental Protection Agency
Export-Import Bank of the U.S.
Farm Credit Administration
Federal Communications Commission
Federal Deposit Insurance Corporation
Federal Home Loan Bank Board

Federal Maritime Commission
Federal Mediation and
  Conciliation Service
Federal Reserve System, Board of
  Governors of the
Federal Trade Commission
General Services Administration
Interstate Commerce Commission

National Aeronautics and
  Space Administration
National Foundation on the
  Arts and the Humanities
National Labor Relations Board
National Mediation Board
National Science Foundation
Railroad Retirement Board
Securities and Exchange Commission

Selective Service System
Small Business Administration
Smithsonian Institution
Tennessee Valley Authority
U.S. Civil Service Commission
U.S. Information Agency
U.S. Postal Service
U.S. Tariff Commission
Veterans Administration

Source: Adapted from the U. S. Government Organization Manual.

level subordinates, all of whom are appointed by the president with the approval of the Senate (such approval is rarely withheld). They serve "at the pleasure of the president," meaning that the president can dismiss them for reasons of political disloyalty without having to explain why (legally, that is—political repercussions are another matter).

Departments are composed of many smaller administrative units with a variety of titles such as bureau, office, administration, and service. Within HEW, for example, one finds the Office of Child Development, the Social Security Administration, and the Public Health Service, among many others (see Figure 1–2). The fact that these are located within the same departmental structure does not necessarily mean they work cooperatively on any one venture; in fact, conflict among agencies within the same department is not uncommon. Where they are formally "located" has little practical bearing on patterns of cooperation or conflict within the administrative apparatus. Finally, departments and their subunits generally are responsible for carrying out specific operating programs enacted by Congress; they have, and attempt to maintain, fairly specific program jurisdictions (programmatic areas of responsibility) and often some apparently concrete program objectives.

Independent regulatory agencies are a second major type of administrative entity, usually identified as a "commission" or "board." Among such agencies are the Federal Trade Commission (FTC), Civil Aeronautics Board (CAB), National Labor Relations Board (NLRB), and Interstate Commerce Commission (ICC). They differ from cabinet-level departments in a number of important ways. First, they have a different function, namely, to oversee and regulate activities of various parts of the private economic sector. Second, their leadership is plural rather than singular; that is, they are headed by a board or commission of several individuals (usually five to nine) instead of a secretary. Third, they are designed to be somewhat more independent of other institutions and political forces than are departments. Members of these agencies are appointed by the president with Senate approval (as are senior department officials) but are better protected legally against dismissal by the president; in addition, they normally serve a term of office longer than that of the appointing president. In relation to Congress, these agencies are supposedly somewhat freer to do their jobs than are departments and their subunits; while this is questionable in practice, the design does have some impact. Finally, agencies are designed to regulate private-sector enterprises in a detached and objective manner, with some expectation of effectiveness in preventing abuses, corruption, and the like.

Rising criticism of regulatory agencies in recent years makes it clear that there are at least some people and groups who are not satisfied with the job that has been done. Critics claim that the agencies are not sufficiently independent from those whom they regulate, creating a gap

Figure 1–2 U. S. Department of Health, Education, and Welfare

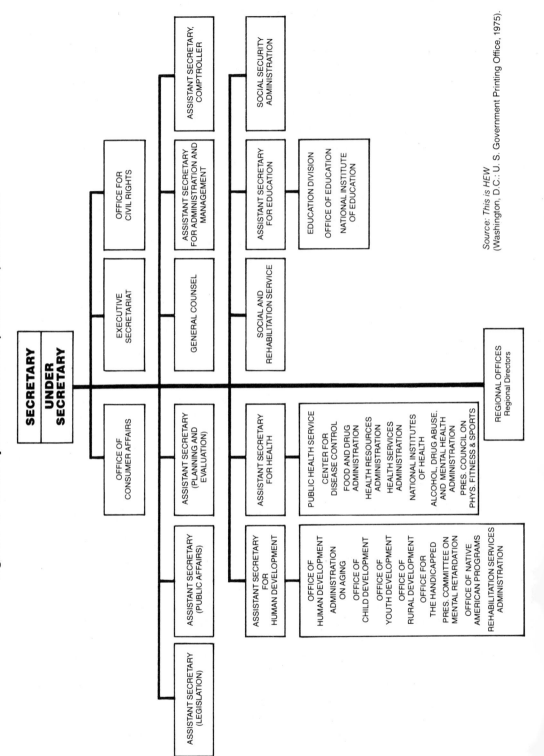

Source: *This is HEW*
(Washington, D.C.: U. S. Government Printing Office, 1975).

between design and actual performance in regulation. One vocal source of such criticism has been Ralph Nader, but he is not the only one.[9]

Government corporations are national, state, or local government agencies identical to private corporations in most of their structures and operations, but government-owned. Also, while some (such as Amtrak and local public utilities) seek to make a profit, others (such as the Federal Savings and Loan Insurance Corporation and the Lower Colorado River Authority of the state of Texas) do not.[10] These agencies are constituted as corporate entities for a number of reasons. Their legislative charters permit somewhat greater latitude in day-to-day operations than is the case with other agencies; they have power to acquire, develop, and dispose of real estate and other kinds of property, acting in their own name rather than that of the national, state, or local government; and they have power to bring suit in a court of law—and liability to be sued—also in their own name. They are headed by a board of directors, much as private corporations are, and are engaged in a wide variety of governmental activities. Three of the newest such entities are the National Rail Passenger Service Corporation (Amtrak), the Corporation for Public Broadcasting, and the U.S. Postal Service; two of the oldest, both founded in the 1930s, are the Federal Deposit Insurance Corporation (FDIC) and the Tennessee Valley Authority (TVA).[11]

The *Executive Office of the President* (EXOP) is now nearing its fortieth year, but it has become newly important in the 1960s and 1970s. The Executive Office is a collection of administrative bodies physically and organizationally housed close to the office of the president and designed precisely to work for the president. Several EXOP entities are especially prominent and important. (1) The White House Office is located at 1600 Pennsylvania Avenue and consists of the president's key staff aides and staff directors.[12] (Richard Nixon's White House Office included H. R. Haldeman, John Ehrlichmann, John Dean, Jeb Stuart Magruder, and other Watergate figures; current White House Office personnel are less well known.) (2) The Office of Management and Budget (OMB) assists the president in assembling budget requests for the entire executive branch and forwarding them to Capitol Hill as the president's annual Budget Message, as well as in program coordination, development of high-quality executive talent, and supervision of management processes throughout the executive branch. (3) The Council of Economic Advisors (CEA) is the president's principal research arm for economic policy, and it frequently influences the president's economic thinking (not surprisingly, since presidents usually appoint economists to the CEA who generally reflect their own economic philosophies).[13] (4) Agencies such as the National Security Council and Domestic Council, which we might label broad overview forums, consist of the president and vice-president together with key cabinet secretaries and other officials. The purpose of these councils is to assess the overall condition of broad administration policies. They become directly involved in policy making to a greater or lesser degree according to the president's inclinations. Dwight Eisenhower, for example, made far greater use of the National Security Council (NSC) than did either John F. Kennedy or Lyndon Johnson. This was due in large part to pressing "cold war" policy development needs during the 1950s, combined with Eisenhower's greater inclination to rely on his executive staff. The NSC has also played a vital role in dealing with specific crises (such as the Cambodian seizure of the U.S. freighter *Mayaguez,* which took place off the coast of Cambodia shortly after Gerald Ford became president in 1974) and in broader, yet still crucial, policy decisions (such as cancellation of the sale of concussion firebombs to Israel by the Carter administration early in 1977). Much of the councils' routine activity is devoted to evaluating existing policy and its impacts, but the potential does exist for them to fulfill more systematic policy-making roles.

Finally, there is a collection of miscellaneous agencies which we might call *other independent agencies*—those that have no departmental "home" but fit no other category we have discussed. Included in this category would be the U.S. Civil Service Commission (USCSC), which oversees the federal personnel system (acting partially in the name of the president but with considerable independence from him); the General Services Administration (GSA), the government's office of property and supply; the Environmental Protection Agency (EPA); the Nuclear Regulatory Commission (NRC); and the Appalachian Regional Commission (ARC), among others.

The foundations of organization referred to earlier were function, geographic area, clientele, and work process. The most common organizational foundation is *function*, indicating that an agency is concerned with a fairly distinct policy area and one not limited to a particular geographic area. Organization according to *geography* indicates that an agency's work is in a specific region; examples include TVA, Pacific Command of the Navy, Alaskan Command of the Air Force, and ARC. The other two foundations of organization are less visible.

Clientele-based agencies are those which appear to address problems of a specific segment of the population, such as the Veterans' Administration (VA) or the Bureau of Indian Affairs (BIA). Two comments are in order regarding this apparent focus. First, *every* agency has a clientele of some kind, a group in the general population on whose behalf many of its programs are conducted—for example, farmers and the Department of Agriculture, skilled and semiskilled laborers and the Labor Department, and coal interests and the Bureau of Mines. The label "clientele-based agency" may be misleading for that reason; it is not only those agencies that have administrative clienteles.

The label may be misleading for a second reason: these clienteles may not always be satisfied clienteles (this is true universally in administrative politics, for that matter). The two examples cited above—the VA and BIA—are, in fact, excellent illustrations of agencies whose clienteles have gotten up-in-arms about some aspect of agency performance. In 1975 various veterans' groups and individual veterans complained vigorously about the VA's alleged shortcomings in awarding and processing veterans' benefits, to the point that a virtual sit-in took place in the office of the VA director. As for the BIA, it has been a principal target of dissatisfaction, expressed by the American Indian Movement and others, with government management of Indian problems on and off the reservation. In both instances the clientele was the most dissatisfied group, which is not uncommon in bureaucratic politics.

Finally, *work process* agencies engage predominantly, if not exclusively, in data gathering and analysis for some higher-ranking official or office, and rarely if ever participate formally in policy making (though their work can have policy implications). Agencies such as the Economic Research Staff of the Department of Agriculture, the Economic Studies Division of the Federal Power Commission, and the Soils Research Staff of the U.S. Geological Survey fall into this category.

Individual administrators occupying the multitude of positions in the various agencies can be categorized several different ways. For example, most federal administrators are *merit employees*—those who are hired and presumably retained and promoted because they have the skills and training necessary to perform the duties of their particular jobs. Of approximately 2.5 million full-time civilian employees of the national government, 90 percent work under a merit system of some kind. The remaining 10 percent include unionized employees not under a merit hiring procedure—for example, blue-collar workers in shipyards and weapons factories—as well as *political appointees*, some of whom can be removed by the president. In the latter group, numbering some 2,200 individuals, are the highest-ranking officials of the executive branch—cabinet secretaries and undersecretaries, regulatory agency commissioners, and Executive Office of the President personnel, among others.

Another way of viewing administrative employees is in terms of their being *specialists* or *generalists,* categories which generally correspond to the merit and political designations discussed above. The term "specialist" refers to employees at lower and middle levels of the formal hierarchy whose responsibilities center on fairly specific programmatic areas. The term "generalist" is used to describe those in the higher ranks of an agency whose responsibilities cover a wider crosssection of activities within the agency, involving some degree of supervision of various specialists in the ranks below.

While some administrators are clearly generalists (for example, an undersecretary of Health, Education, and Welfare for Legislation, or the attorney general) and others are just as clearly specialists (a research chemist in the Food and Drug Administration, an economist with the Economic Development Administration in the Department of Commerce, or a nuclear physicist with the Energy Research and Development Administration in the Department of Energy), it is not always easy to distinguish one from another. How does one classify, for instance, the chief of the Wildlife Division in the Fish and Wildlife Service in the Interior Department if that individual has spent his entire career in the division and worked up through the ranks to the chief's office? The Wildlife Division itself is a middle-level bureaucracy, yet the chief heads it up; is there a clear definition here? Similar questions could be raised about countless other bureaucrats whose agency positions leave them in something of a hybrid situation.

One broad distinction that has been suggested involves the types of decisions a bureaucrat makes. Specialists are said to deal more with the merits of a question in technical terms, generalists more with agency political needs and the political implications of particular policies and decisions. Another distinction suggested is between primary sources of political support, specialists being said to derive major backing from legislative and interest-group allies (see chapter 3), with generalists' support coming more from administrative superiors in the formal chain of command. A third distinction is one of formal rank in the hierarchy: generalists are identified as those in the top three federal personnel grades (GS–16, –17, and –18) plus political appointees, and specialists are all those below. Yet none of these distinctions is entirely adequate; criteria for decisions, sources of support, and personnel grade are not invariably associated with only one type of administrative decision maker. One's role as a generalist or specialist appears to depend much more on how the duties of a job are formally defined and carried out, and on the needs of the particular situation, than on any universally applicable set of bureaucratic criteria.

The national executive branch, then, is organized primarily into five major types of agencies, with four formal bases of organization (function being the most common) and two broad categories of administrative employees. The picture in state and local government, while similar, varies somewhat from the national government and is worth considering briefly for the same reasons we have examined the national executive branch: the structure has some impact on the way the machinery functions and on the content of policies it helps enact.

State and Local Executive Structures

In general, states and larger local governments resemble the national government in composition and organization of their executive-branch agencies. Most states now have numerous cabinet-level departments which stand in much the same relationship to the governor as do national departments to the president; states also have a wide variety of regulatory agencies, some government corporations, and miscellaneous agencies. (Figure 1–3 illustrates New York State's executive-branch organization.) Many governors, though not all, have fairly strong executive office staffs responsive to the governor's leadership (see chapter 4).

Some state agency structures reflect past or present influences of particular interest groups more than those in Washington do. One example is Pennsylvania's powerful Department of Mines and Mineral Industries, indicative of the role played in the state's economy by coal mine owners over the years. Another is Illinois' Department of Aging, created in the mid-1970s in response to the emergence of a growing constituency with common problems of "senior citizenship." So-called special interests have "their" agencies in the national government, of course, but a pattern found in many states is creation of somewhat higher level agencies in response to constituency pressures. Another distinctive feature of state executive structures is greater legislative control over some individual agencies' budgets and personnel compared to Congress's hold over federal agencies. This varies, however, from state to state, so that no single pattern may be said to exist.

Larger cities such as New York, Chicago, Houston, Philadelphia, Boston, and Miami (to name only a few) have bureaucratic arrangements not unlike those in state and national governments. (Figure 1–4 shows Houston's government organization.) There is a fair amount of administrative specialization, a directly elected chief executive (mayor) with a highly developed executive office staff, and similar bases of organization. There are, however, some differences. Local party politics frequently play a more prominent role in shaping municipal policy making—for example, in Chicago, Boston, and New York. Local public employee unions have a great deal of influence in communities such as New York and San Francisco (see chapter 9). And the nature of government activity is much more heavily oriented to provision of essential services such as water, sewage disposal and sanitation, and police and fire protection, than to broader policy concerns such as long-term welfare reform or mass transit development.

In many smaller communities, as well as in most counties and townships, bureaucratic structures are not very numerous or sophisticated. This can also mean (though it does not always) that professional expertise in local government is inferior to that found in many state governments and the national government. Lack of expertise is often reflected in the limited quantity and quality of programs enacted by many local governments, a pattern visible particularly in most county governments (except the very largest), many smaller towns and villages, and most special districts.[14] Many local governments, as noted earlier, concentrate on providing basic urban services, with less emphasis placed on the sorts of operating programs and regulatory activities which

Figure 1–3 Organization of the Executive Branch, State of New York*

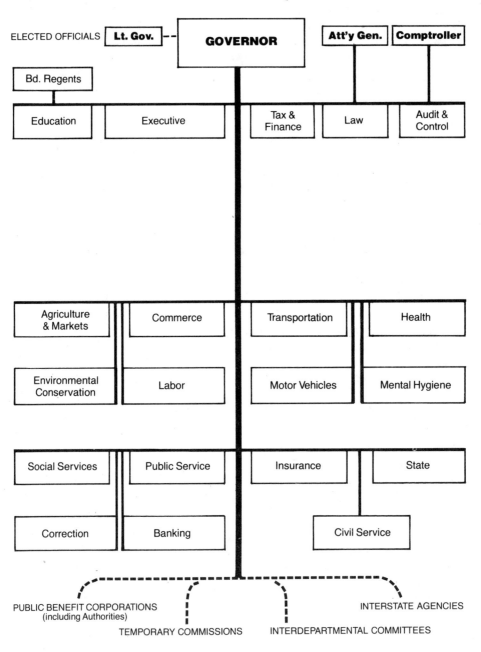

ELECTED OFFICIALS

| Lt. Gov. | GOVERNOR | Att'y Gen. | Comptroller |

Bd. Regents

| Education | Executive | Tax & Finance | Law | Audit & Control |

| Agriculture & Markets | Commerce | Transportation | Health |
| Environmental Conservation | Labor | Motor Vehicles | Mental Hygiene |

| Social Services | Public Service | Insurance | State |
| Correction | Banking | | Civil Service |

PUBLIC BENEFIT CORPORATIONS (including Authorities)

TEMPORARY COMMISSIONS

INTERDEPARTMENTAL COMMITTEES

INTERSTATE AGENCIES

*Does not include quasi-independent agencies within departments.

Source: New York State: A Citizen's Handbook (New York: League of Women Voters of New York State).

Figure 1–4 Government Organization—City of Houston

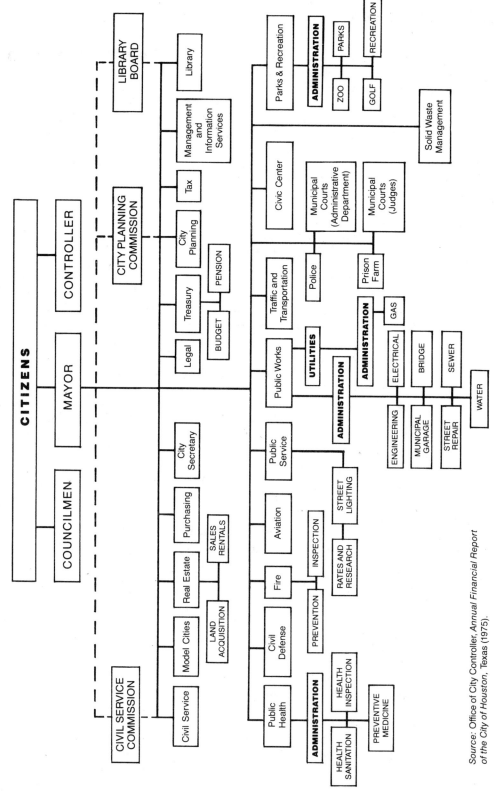

Source: Office of City Controller, *Annual Financial Report of the City of Houston, Texas* (1975).

characterize state and national administration. The larger the unit of local government, the more likely its bureaucracy will resemble state and national administrative agencies.

There are, however, aspects of public bureaucracies other than formal structure which bear more directly on their manner of operation. Traditional conceptions of how bureaucracy *should* function influence what it does. The way public policy is made in the United States also has an important impact. We turn now to these facets of public administration.

Traditional Conceptions of Bureaucracy in Government

Bureaucracy has traditionally been conceived in terms of implementing, or carrying out, directives of other institutions of government, as a servant of political forces external to it but not a political force in its own right. This notion of *bureaucratic neutrality* is central to an understanding of the way executive-branch bureaucracies have been designed to function in Western governments for nearly a century. A number of companion assumptions have also been evident in administrative practice and are worth brief examination.

First, bureaucratic behavior is assumed to follow the intent of the legislature, as that is translated into legislative enactments and guidelines for implementation. With legislative intent as a principal guiding force, bureaucracy's responsibility to the legislature is clearly established. It relies on the legislature for substantive policy direction and financial and political support. The legislature, in turn, looks to the bureaucracy for faithful and competent administration of the laws enacted through the legislative process.

Second, there is a legitimate function of legislative oversight, or supervision, of bureaucratic behavior that is a logical complement to legislative intent. The legislature, in other words, is expected to oversee the work of the bureaucracy to insure conformity with legislative intent. Present in both assumptions is the expectation that bureaucracy is distinctly subordinate in the political process to the will and initiative of other parts of the government. In no way did traditional conceptions of bureaucratic activity allow for significant autonomy (independence), discretion (freedom to make choices), or direct political involvement.

Third, bureaucratic behavior is assumed to be subject to direction by the chief executive of the government. The apparent contradiction between chief executive direction and legislative direction of the bureaucracy stems from the fact that these traditional assumptions were derived from parliamentary forms of government, in which the chief executive and top-level ministers were themselves members of the legislature. The chief executive (prime minister or premier) was usually leader of the majority party in the legislature (parliament), thus creating a situation in which bureaucratic responsiveness to the chief executive and to the legislature were one and the same thing. There is, however, a real contradiction—and often, political conflict—between chief executive and legislative control of the bureaucracy in a system such as ours. Here, the chief executive and top-level executives are independent of the legislature—indeed, they are constitutionally prohibited from serving in Congress at the same time that they hold executive office. We shall deal more directly with this topic in the next section.

Finally, it was traditionally assumed that the bureaucracy would be a neutral, professional, competent structure staffed by specialists in both general administrative processes and their respective specific policy areas.

The notion of a competent bureaucracy, responding in a politically neutral manner to initiatives of executives and legislators external to it, seems to be the image of administration held by many Americans, and it has had a powerful influence on administrative design and practice in this country. That this image is not altogether accurate, however, is the focus of the next section.

Dynamics of Policy Making in America

Under parliamentary forms of government there is little question about how authority is exercised, by whom, and through what channels. Most questions of that type can be answered simply by examining the makeup of the parliament and learning the identity of key executives. In the United States, however, such questions take on importance because there are no similarly convenient answers. Government power and authority in America are highly fragmented and scattered. This is by design, for the framers of the Constitution feared nothing so much as concentrations of power. They did all they could, therefore, to see to it that power was divided among the different branches of the national government, and gave each branch various means of checking the power of the other two. Examples include the president's power to veto an act of Congress (and Congress's power to override a presidential veto by a two-thirds majority) and the requirement that the Senate must confirm the great majority of presidential appointments to executive and judicial positions. Such a division of power within national, state, and local governments places bureaucracy in a very different position from the one it occupies in parliamentary systems.

The making of public policy in the United States and the participation of bureaucracy in that process are characterized by a number of major features. First, the process lacks a centralized mechanism that "directs traffic'' comprehensively, as already implied. There are, rather, many centers of power scattered throughout the executive and legislative branches, including the bureaucracy.

Second, this lack of centralization produces a great deal of "slack" in the decision-making system. That is, in the absence of tight legislative or executive control, there are many opportunities for lower-ranking executives to make decisions affecting implementation of—and sometimes sabotaging—a law. This phenomenon of *administrative discretion* is widespread, arising not only from structural separation of powers but also from frequent political conflicts and tensions which characterize executive-legislative relations.

Third, it follows that there are many "power vacuums" randomly scattered through the decision-making process. Where power is splintered, in other words, there will be some exercise of it that is not clearly defined and is therefore "up for grabs." This is the basis for some, but not all, of the conflict between the president and Congress, and between many governors and their legislatures. It also means that others in the decision-making process can compete for small amounts of power, increasing their influence (if they can) a little bit at a time. And among the most active contenders for these small quantities of power are interest groups and bureaucratic agencies, both of which seek to dominate the making of policy in the areas of greatest concern to them.

It is not only formal governmental power that is fragmented and scattered in American politics. So also is the ability to influence policy making in specific subject-matter areas. In other words, there is no one overarching policy process in which the same top government officials make all decisions and take responsibility for them. Rather, the policy-making process is broken into many little parts, with responsibility over each part determined by a combination of structural, functional, and political factors. In such a setting, it is not uncommon for public administrators to become significant "players" in the political game, for them to assume a stance that is *not* neutral, for them to take policy initiatives in small ways that nonetheless influence the long-term development of policies and especially specific programs under their jurisdiction—for them, in short, to be "politicians."

Thus, bureaucracy in American government differs from traditional notions of bureaucracy in important ways. First, it functions in a system in which power is neither centralized nor coherent. Second, bureaucracy has at its disposal a great deal of discretionary power in making day-to-day decisions, as well as in dealing with broader policy questions. Third, bureaucratic accountability is enforced through multiple channels and without a great deal of effectiveness due to the fragmentation of higher political authority.

How does all this affect behavior of public administrators? It would be impossible to answer that question entirely in a few well-chosen words, but two general observations suggest the nature of the bureaucratic environment. First, political scientist Graham Allison, in his analysis of the 1962 Cuban missile crisis, noted that top executives are not in a position of *commanding* the bureaucracy to act; rather, "government leaders can substantially disturb, but not substantially control, the behavior of these organizations."[15] This clearly implies that bureaucracies have independent momentum with which political leaders must interfere if they are to influence bureaucratic activity—hardly the conditions suggested by traditional conceptions. Second, the focus of bureaucratic activity is predominantly on the respective areas of agency jurisdiction, and a bureaucracy will usually contest any significant change in the policy area over which it has jurisdiction.[16] Both of these phenomena indicate the nonneutral condition of the American bureaucratic environment. This is one of the most important differences between American bureaucratic practice and any ideal model of bureaucracy against which it might be measured.

Public Administration as a Field of Study

The principal focus of public administration as an academic field of study has changed more than once since it first emerged in the late 1800s. Changing and overlapping conceptions of the subject sometimes reflected and sometimes preceded evolution in administrative practice in the "real world" of government, and cross-fertilization of ideas between practitioners and academics has remained a prominent feature of the profession throughout the twentieth century. Because so many public administrators were trained in formal academic programs, thus promoting the impact that academic disciplines have had on government administrative practices, it is useful to review major emphases which have characterized and helped shape the academic field.[17]

In the earliest period, from roughly 1887 to 1927, public administration was viewed as distinct and separate from politics, more akin to business and business methods than to anything political. Woodrow Wilson, in his classic essay "The Study of Administration," wrote that administration "is removed from the hurry and strife of politics. . . . Administrative questions are not political questions. Although politics sets the tasks for administration, it should not be suffered to manipulate its offices."[18] The concept of a dichotomy between politics and administration was widely accepted during this period, based not only on the writings of Wilson but also on the first textbook in the field, by Frank Goodnow, entitled (significantly) *Politics and Administration* and published in 1900. According to Goodnow, the bureaucracy was to administer—impartially and nonpolitically—the programs which the legislative branch enacted, subject only to judicial interpretation.[19] The dichotomy between politics and administration was reinforced by publication of Leonard D. White's *Introduction to the Study of Public Administration* in 1926. White captured the conventional wisdom of administrative theory: politics and administration were separate; management could be studied scientifically to discover the best methods of operation; public administration was capable of becoming a value-free science; and politically neutral administration should be focused on attainment of economy and efficiency in government, and nothing more.[20]

The next phase in development of the discipline was the movement toward discovering "principles" of public administration. This was an offshoot of the "scientific" approach to administration and was based on the belief that there existed certain permanent principles of administration which, if they could only be discovered and applied, could transform the performance of administrative tasks. Publication in 1927 of F. W. Willoughby's *Principles of Public Administration* marked the beginning of a decade in which identifying and correctly applying these principles was the predominant concern of many in and out of academic circles. Luther Gulick and Lyndall Urwick's *Papers on the Science of Administration*, published in 1937, defined seven principles that have become professional watchwords: planning, organizing, staffing, directing, coordinating, reporting, and budgeting (known by the acronym POSDCORB). Gulick and Urwick reemphasized the importance of these administrative principles, declared their applicability to almost any human organization regardless of what the organization was or why it existed, and stressed the fundamental desirability of efficiency as underlying administrative "science."[21]

Even as Gulick and Urwick wrote, however, the dominant themes of public administration were changing. Beginning in the late 1930s, the politics-administration dichotomy came to be questioned, and more significantly, critiques appeared which asked whether it had ever been possible to wall off one from the other. Part of this was due to the New Deal, in which a strong president (Franklin Roosevelt) had demonstrated, in political scientist Alan A. Altshuler's words, "that patronage might be of great value in aiding a vigorous President to push through programs of social and economic reform."[22] Politically neutral "efficiency" considerations, viewed in terms of their effect on presidential leadership, could constitute a hindrance to meaningful social reforms supported by many academics. Part was also due to the emerging belief that the POSDCORB principles were logically inconsistent.[23]

These principles, which had been considered so lofty and significant, became the subject of repeated and intensive analysis which led to a twofold conclusion: (1) that some of them were at least potentially contradictory, and (2) that the principles themselves gave no direction concerning how to choose the one most appropriate for particular situations. For example, one principle held that for purposes of control, workers should be grouped according to *either* function, work process, clientele, or geography. There is nothing here that suggests standards for using one instead of another, nor whether these are mutually exclusive categories.[24] (But as we have seen, these four categories are still used in government bureaucracy.) Critiques of this sort came from many scholars in the field, but most notably from Herbert Simon, whose *Administrative Behavior* (1947) did the most to pry the discipline loose from its attachment to the "principles" approach.

No comparable set of values replaced the POSDCORB principles, but different concerns in public administration began to emerge. Through the 1940s and into the 1950s, public administration found its relationship to political science—its parent discipline—one of growing uneasiness. Political science itself was undergoing significant change in the post–World War II period, most of it in the direction of developing far more sophisticated, empirical (including statistical) methods of researching political phenomena, but always on the assumption that objectivity in research methods was of the highest importance.

The problem for public administration in this "behavioral" era was that many functions and processes of administration do not lend themselves to the same sorts of quantitative research as do, for example, legislative voting patterns, election data, and survey research of public opinion. As Altshuler points out, administrative decision making is frequently informal; many decisions are made in partial or total secrecy; the exact values of administrators and the alternatives they consider in making a decision are difficult, at best, to identify and analyze; and traditional emphasis on efficiency (which has by no means disappeared) contrasts sharply with the core concerns of modern political science.[25] As a consequence, public administration became (again quoting Altshuler) a "rather peripheral subfield of political science," with many academics in and out of public administration questioning its place in the larger discipline.

Another related development was the growth following World War II of research into administrative and organizational behavior that sought to examine all sorts of organizations, not only, or even necessarily, *public* entities. This movement worked from the assumption that the social psychology of organizations made less important the question of precisely what kind of organization was to be studied, and sought to integrate research from not only social psychology but also sociology, business administration, and information science. This field, known currently as "organizational behavior," represents an attempt to synthesize much of what is known about organized group behavior within the boundaries of formal organizations.

Altshuler questions whether this direction—as valuable as it has been in furthering our understanding of human behavior in an increasingly organized society—has resulted in research findings that have *political* relevance, that is, relevance to the research directions of contemporary political science.[26] Nicholas Henry goes further, asserting that public administration has begun to declare its intellectual and institutional independence from political science and business-administrative science, moving instead toward establishment of autonomous departments or programs. He cites data that indicate a strong trend developing in this direction, including sharp increases in both undergraduate and graduate enrollment in public administration courses, and in the number of separate academic units at universities around the country which focus on public administration, urban affairs, and public policy.[27]

Public administration as an academic field of study, then, is not and has not been a settled discipline. There are somewhat blurred boundaries between it and other fields, a few loose ends in terms of what to study and how, a history of some conflict with its parent discipline (that is, political science), and growing controversy over just where public administration "belongs," intellectually and institutionally. It is within this setting that we take up our study, seeking in this book to emphasize the political environment, involvement, and significance of America's public administrative agencies.

SUMMARY

Public administration has become a prominent and influential force in American government and society, especially in recent years. Most of us have some familiarity with bureaucracy, and many of our most pressing current political issues are related to administrative agencies and actions. There has been some decrease in public approval of, and support for, government bureaucracy when compared to thirty or forty years ago.

Definition of basic terms is appropriate. Politics is concerned with acquiring something desirable from and through the governmental process; it suggests relatively limited supplies of those desirable things, compared to the demand for them; and political processes such as conflict, negotiation, and compromise are important in decisions made by formal governmental institutions. Power refers to the ability to cause others to behave in ways they otherwise might not; this might be accomplished through a system of incentives and punishments, in a wide variety of situations. The powers exercised by government are different in important respects from powers of any other group or individual: (1) governmental power is defined as legal authority to take certain actions which are valid and appropriate, and (2) government possesses *sole* power over particular actions and functions which would be illegal if done by private citizens or groups. The legitimacy accorded institutions and decisions of government makes possible the assertion of authority with a minimum of coercive force; the continuing legitimacy of government is important to its operation and effectiveness. Public administration is a part of all this because government agencies exercise power and legal authority; they take part in allocating resources, which is central to politics; and their effectiveness depends to some extent on their legitimacy in the eyes of the public.

Public administration is the set of processes, organizations, and individuals associated with implementing laws and other rules enacted by legislatures, executives, and courts. This includes administrative agency involvement in formulation of many such rules as well as their application. Public administration is also an academic field of study and training. Those who actively participate in public administration include administrators themselves, legislators and legislative staffs, higher executives, judges, political party officials, interest group leaders and members, mass media representatives who "cover the news," and the general public. These participants encounter one another in different patterns of mutual relationships in the politics of administration, and examples of each can be found at all levels of government and in national-state-local relations. Public administration and its politics involves interactions both internal and external to the formal agency structure.

Public administration in the national government is characterized by several different types of agencies, a number of methods of agency organization, and several ways of categorizing administrative employees—each of which may affect what agencies do and how they do it. The principal agencies are cabinet-level departments, independent regulatory agencies, government corporations, divisions of the Executive Office of the President, and other miscellaneous agencies. These can be organized according to function (the most common basis of organization), geographic area, the clientele served, or work process (research and other informational services). Administrative personnel can be classified according to whether they were hired by merit procedures or through political appointment, and whether they are specialists or generalists, though distinctions between these two categories are not always clear. Suggested means of distinguishing between generalists and specialists include differences in the aspects and consequences of problems with which each is primarily concerned, in their main sources of political support, and in general hierarchical rank. While useful, such distinctions are not sufficient to account for all administrative offices or all possible combinations of functions and duties.

The organizational structure of state and local executive branches is generally comparable to that of the national government. Most states and larger localities have departmental organization and executive office staff support for the chief executive similar to that in Washington. In certain respects, however, state executive structures differ from federal ones—for example, in exhibiting stronger structural representation of group interests and more direct legislative control over some agencies' operations. In larger local governments, some essentials of organization are the same as at the national and state levels—for example, administrative specialization, chief executives with some degree of staff support, and similar bases of organization. But local political parties, employee unions, and the nature of government activity all represent differences on the local scene as compared with the national government. Smaller local governments differ much more sharply in their less extensive bureaucratic development and, not uncommonly, less professional expertise. The larger a local government, the more likely its bureaucracy will resemble state and national bureaucracies in structure and program.

Traditional conceptions of bureaucracy and its role in government include the following: (1) political neutrality in carrying out decisions of other government institutions, (2) legislative intent as a principal guiding force for the actions of bureaucracy, (3) legislative oversight of bureaucracy as a legitimate corollary to legislative intent, (4) direction by the chief executive of activities of administrative agencies (which in a system of separation of powers creates the possibility of conflict over control of bureaucracy), and (5) professional competence in bureaucracy. These conceptions, while exerting a powerful hold on our beliefs, are not altogether accurate.

Because of the fragmented nature of the policy-making process in America, government administrators function in a political environment with these important features: (1) there is no central policy coordinator with total control capability; (2) there is, as a result, "slack" in the system, which allows administrators a considerable amount of discretion; (3) not all decision-making power or authority is clearly allocated, resulting in many small conflicts over fragments of power. In such a setting, public administrators are often active in political roles and take policy initiatives that are not neutral, thus departing from important traditional views about bureaucratic roles and functions. American bureaucrats are in a position to develop semiindependence from elected leaders. Furthermore, bureaucratic activity is organized around jurisdiction over particular policy areas, and bureaucracies seek to prevent changes in jurisdiction which might harm their political interests or those of their supporters.

Public administration as a field of study has been characterized by several major and partially overlapping schools of thought: (1) the politics-administration dichotomy, (2) the objectives of economy and efficiency as the keynote of public administration, (3) the search for principles of administration, (4) a tentative rejection of the "principles" approach, (5) a turning toward different perspectives on administrative behavior—for example, social and psychological factors in internal organizational processes, (6) a growing ferment regarding the links between public administration and its parent discipline of political science, and (7) developing trends that seem to carry the study of administration not only away from political science but also away from allied fields of administrative study and toward disciplinary autonomy. This book focuses on the interrelationships between politics and public administration.

NOTES

1. See, for example, "Big Government: Everyone Is Running against the Bureaucracy," *Congressional Quarterly Weekly Report,* 34 (October 23, 1976), 3036–3037.

2. A number of authors have recently commented on the relationship between the proliferation of bureaucratic jargon and the deterioration of the English language, some writing in a serious vein, others in a semiserious or humorous vein. For serious commentary, see, among others, Alvin M. Weinberg, *Reflections on Big Science* (Cambridge: M.I.T. Press, 1967), chapter 2, especially p. 54. For more jocular treatment of the subject, see James H. Boren, *When in Doubt, Mumble: A Bureaucrat's Handbook* (New York: Van Nostrand Reinhold, 1972); John Kidner, *A Guide to Creative Bureaucracy: The Kidner Report—A Satirical Look at Bureaucracy at the Paper Clip and Stapler Level* (Washington, D.C.: Acropolis Books, 1972); and Edwin Newman, *Strictly Speaking: Will America Be the Death of English?* (Indianapolis: Bobbs-Merrill, 1974).

3. Two observations about issue salience are in order. First, issues may have direct bearing on our lives without their being salient, due to our not perceiving the effect on us; this is why some policy matters become issues as their meaning is increasingly perceived. Secondly, to the extent that an issue *is* salient to us, we are more likely to ask questions about it, thereby challenging the pattern of obscured decision processes that prevails generally in bureaucracy.

4. There is some evidence of mixed feelings about bureaucrats—negative in the abstract, but more positive about individual, face-to-face contacts with them. See "Americans Love Their Bureaucrats," *Psychology Today,* 9 (June 1975), 66–71.

5. It should not be forgotten that there was organized, even intense, opposition to the expansion of government and bureaucracy—from Republican politicians and some Democrats, from those who supported the credo of "states' rights," and others. This opposition may have had some limiting effect, but it did not reverse bureaucratic expansion.

6. These and similar definitions can be found in any substantial text in an introductory American politics course. The last is taken from Harold Lasswell's classic *Politics: Who Gets What, When, How* (New York: McGraw-Hill, 1936).

7. See Harold Seidman, *Politics, Position, and Power: The Dynamics of Federal Organization,* 2nd ed. (New York: Oxford University Press, 1975).

8. A useful introduction to this subject is James W. Davis, Jr., *The National Executive Branch* (New York: The Free Press, 1970).

9. A generally critical overview of the regulatory process may be found in Louis M. Kohlmeier, Jr., *The Regulators: Watchdog Agencies and the Public Interest* (New York: Harper & Row, 1969). Two excellent studies of specific policy areas and regulatory politics are A. Lee Fritschler, *Smoking and Politics: Policy Making and the Federal Bureaucracy,* 2nd ed. (Englewood Cliffs, N.J.: Prentice-Hall, 1975); and Erwin G. Krasnow and Lawrence D. Longley, *The Politics of Broadcast Regulation* (New York: St. Martin's, 1973). See chapter 11.

10. See Roscoe C. Martin et al., *River Basin Administration and the Delaware* (Syracuse, N.Y.: Syracuse University Press, 1960), pp. 244–251.

11. TVA is perhaps the most extensively studied federal agency in the history of our nation. A partial listing of the literature includes David E. Lilienthal's spirited book *TVA: Democracy on the March* (New York: Harper and Brothers,

1944); Philip Selznick's critical study *TVA and the Grass Roots: A Study in the Sociology of Formal Organization* (Berkeley and Los Angeles: University of California Press, 1949); Roscoe C. Martin, ed., *TVA: The First Twenty Years* (University, Ala., and Knoxville, Tenn.: University of Alabama Press and University of Tennessee Press, 1956); Preston J. Hubbard, *Origins of the TVA: The Muscle Shoals Controversy, 1920–1932* (Nashville, Tenn.: Vanderbilt University Press, 1961); Victor C. Hobday, *Sparks at the Grass Roots: Municipal Distribution of TVA Electricity in Tennessee* (Knoxville: University of Tennessee Press, 1969); and Marguerite Owen, *The Tennessee Valley Authority* (New York: Praeger Publishers, 1973).

12. Since the Watergate scandals, the White House Office has been the object of considerable examination. One of the best analyses is Dan Rather and Gary Paul Gates, *The Palace Guard* (New York: Harper & Row, 1974). Significantly, a study of the White House Office written *before* the Nixon administration took office foresaw some of the possibilities that eventuated in the Watergate affair. See Patrick Anderson, *The President's Men* (Garden City, N.Y.: Doubleday, 1968). See also Carl Bernstein and Bob Woodward, *All the President's Men* (New York: Simon and Schuster, 1974).

13. See Edward S. Flash, Jr., *Economic Advice and Presidential Leadership: The Council of Economic Advisors* (New York: Columbia University Press, 1965).

14. John Rehfuss, *Public Administration as Political Process* (New York: Charles Scribner's Sons, 1973), pp. 64–68.

15. Graham Allison, *Essence of Decision: Explaining the Cuban Missile Crisis* (Boston: Little, Brown, 1971). This quote is taken from an earlier version of the book, which appeared as "Conceptual Models and the Cuban Missile Crisis," *American Political Science Review,* 63 (September 1969), 698.

16. See Matthew Holden, "'Imperialism' in Bureaucracy," *American Political Science Review,* 60 (December 1966), 943–951.

17. This section relies on Nicholas Henry, "Paradigms of Public Administration," *Public Administration Review,* 35 (July/August 1975), 378–386; Alan A. Altshuler, "The Study of American Public Administration," in Alan A. Altshuler and Norman C. Thomas, eds., *The Politics of the Federal Bureaucracy,* 2nd ed. (New York: Harper & Row, 1977), pp. 2–17; Dwight Waldo, *The Study of Public Administration* (New York: Random House, 1955); and Waldo, ed., *Public Administration in a Time of Turbulence* (Scranton, Pa.: Chandler Publishing, 1971).

18. Quoted by Altshuler, "The Study of American Public Administration," p. 2.

19. Henry, "Paradigms of Public Administration," p. 379.

20. Ibid.

21. Altshuler, "The Study of American Public Administration," p. 3; Henry, "Paradigms of Public Administration," pp. 379–380.

22. Altshuler, "The Study of American Public Administration," p. 3.

23. Henry, "Paradigms of Public Administration," p. 380.

24. Altshuler, "The Study of American Public Administration," p. 5.

25. Ibid., pp. 10–11.

26. Ibid., p. 13.

27. Henry, "Paradigms of Public Administration," pp. 384–385.

SUGGESTED READINGS

Charlesworth, James C., ed. *Theory and Practice of Public Administration: Scope, Objectives, and Methods*. Philadelphia: American Academy of Political and Social Science, 1968.

Davis, James W., Jr. *The National Executive Branch*. New York: The Free Press, 1970.

Flash, Edward S., Jr. *Economic Advice and Presidential Leadership: The Council of Economic Advisors*. New York: Columbia University Press, 1965.

Fox, Douglas M. *The Politics of City and State Bureaucracy*. Pacific Palisades, Calif.: Goodyear, 1974.

Lasswell, Harold. *Politics: Who Gets What, When, How*. New York: McGraw-Hill, 1936.

Martin, Roscoe C. "Political Science and Public Administration: A Note on the State of the Union." *American Political Science Review,* 46 (September 1952), 660–676.

Waldo, Dwight. "Public Administration." *International Encyclopedia of the Social Sciences,* 13. New York: Macmillan and The Free Press, 1968.

———. *The Study of Public Administration*. New York: Random House, 1955.

———, ed. *Public Administration in a Time of Turbulence*. Scranton, Pa.: Chandler Publishing, 1971.

Wilson, James Q. "The Bureaucracy Problem." *The Public Interest*, 6 (Winter 1967), 3–9.

CHAPTER 2
The Context of
Public Administration:
Values and
Social Change

Public administration does not exist in a vacuum, nor does the larger governmental system of which it is a part. Like all other human institutions, they have been shaped by public values and beliefs, both past and present, about what government "should" do and how. A major influence is the social setting of government—the society's basic values, the extent of agreement on those values, and how directly they relate to the conduct of government. Values about other institutions in society—business, education, religion—also play a part in shaping government and public administration by creating demands and expectations that may need to be met through government action. The public demands a national-level commitment to higher education, for example, and expects government to conduct its affairs in a "businesslike" way, with a high degree of "economy" and "efficiency."

Equally important to the context of public administration is change—in values about government, in administrative concepts, in general social values and public demands. On the one hand, modern bureaucracy is the result of cumulative evolution in theory and practice. Institutional change in general tends to be cumulative; that is, as patterns of behavior come and go, they leave behind carry-over effects, which then mingle with, and become indistinguishable from, the patterns that replace them. So it is with our administrative machinery, in which much of what we do today reflects lingering influences of the past. On the other hand, in contemporary America social values and established institutional patterns are subject to rapid, unpredictable, and turbulent change. Today, many basic values are changing—toward marriage and family life, sex roles, God and religion, the place of (and respect for) authority, material possessions, the environment, and "human rights," to name only a few. For traditional institutions, including bureaucracy, to respond to such social upheaval is a large order, and much recent criticism of bureaucracy focuses on its apparent failure to do so. This chapter is concerned with these new challenges to public administration in America today.

Political Values

Our discussion of political and administrative values has three purposes: (1) to understand the fundamental beliefs underlying American government and bureaucracy, (2) to recognize the impacts both sets of values have on public administration, and (3) to see the ways they conflict conceptually—and how that conflict affects the conduct of public administration.

The term "political values," as used here, refers to basic beliefs and assumptions not only about politics and the political system but also about what is appropriate in government's relationship to private activity, especially economic activity. The last falls under the heading of political values and has relevance to a discussion of public administration because of increasing governmental responsibility in regulating business and industry.

The United States has defined itself politically as a "liberal democracy," and economically as a capitalist system.[1] Two political concepts, popular sovereignty and limited government, are central to the notion of liberal democracy. *Popular sovereignty*—government by the ultimate consent of the governed—implies some degree of popular participation in voting and other political endeavors. While it does not necessarily imply mass or universal political involvement, America has moved steadily toward ever wider participation in voting and lately in other areas, including administrative decision making. The specific vehicle for popular rule has been representative government. Initially, Americans placed emphasis on legislative representation; the Constitution stresses that. More recently, concern has grown for representation and representativeness elsewhere in politics, notably in administrative organizations and processes. As the public grew dissatisfied with the degree of popular control over bureaucracy, greater representativeness in bureaucracy was seized upon as the solution. Political scientist Herbert Kaufman has gone so far as to suggest that "the quest for representativeness in this generation *centers primarily* on administrative agencies,"[2] indicating the paramount importance attached to increasing the public's voice in administrative decision making.

The second central concept, *limited government,* reflects the predominant view held by those who framed the Constitution that government posed a basic threat to individual liberties. In their experience, of course, their (British) government had in fact suppressed personal liberties, and they were intent on preventing that from happening here. Limited government was to be achieved through four devices working concurrently: (1) separation of powers among the executive, legislative, and judicial branches of government; (2) a system of checks and balances, whereby the exercise of even a fundamental power by one branch would require some involvement of a second branch (for example, the requirement of Senate approval of treaties negotiated by the president); (3) federalism, under which certain powers were allotted to the national government while others were retained by the states (political entities to some degree independent of control by the national government); and (4) judicial review, by which federal courts could invalidate, on constitutional grounds, laws and actions of other government entities. In addition to this multiple fragmentation of government powers, the Bill of Rights (the first ten amendments to the Constitution) established broad areas of protection for individual liberties against encroachment by official government actions.

Two related concepts widely reflected in American society are individualism and pluralism.[3] Our emphasis on the individual is evident in the complex of civil rights and liberties protections, but individualism also implies the right to participate meaningfully in the political process in pursuit of the goals one considers important. Pluralism, on the other hand, stresses the appropriateness of group organization as a means of securing protection for broad group interests in society. As political scientist Richard Page has put it:

> Pluralism, as a theory and practice, assumes that groups are *good*: that citizens have the right to organize to advance their interests; that groups with differing interests will bargain and compete; and that the result of bargaining and competition among group interests is the interest of the whole community or nation—the public interest.[4]

The right of citizens to "organize to advance their interests" links individualism and pluralism, suggesting that individual freedom includes the right to be a political "joiner" and to become active in organized interest groups.

Directly related to individualism and pluralism is the notion of political and economic competition, primarily among groups but also among individuals. Limited government, of course, suggests that competition will be loosely regulated by government; in theory, competition itself will establish boundaries of acceptable behavior among the competitors, and allocate the fruits of victory. This fits very comfortably with capitalist theories. These economic doctrines, geared to private profit and general economic growth, emphasize maximum freedom for private entrepreneurs (individuals) and minimal involvement of government in decisions and operations of the private economic sector. Two assumptions link capitalism to the political values of limited government, individualism, and pluralism: (1) the individual is assumed to be both self-sufficient and capable of self-governing, therefore minimizing the need for government; and (2) the individual is thought to be better off both politically and economically if government is restricted from interfering where it is not needed.

In the past century, government's relationship to the economy has changed dramatically, and what once was minimal involvement has become much more. Have limited government and capitalism, then, been lost? Some argue that they have. A careful reading of American political history suggests, however, that government programs for economic development and social welfare are not brand-new ideas, that a "governmental obligation to insure economic well-being and social justice is a Whig, Progressive, New Deal, and contemporary tenet [value]. But the dominant values have been liberal and capitalist, not radical and socialist."[5]

Government, in other words, has expanded upon earlier values in American politics, rather than establishing totally new directions, in pursuing modern economic and social programs. At the same time, these developments have been geared to basically capitalist themes such as sustaining economic competition in the private sector and reconciling the entrepreneur's right to reap the benefits of free enterprise with the buying public's right to good-quality products at a fair price. While these aims may be the subject of controversy, they are a long way from socialism. Also, it is apparent that demands by some powerful economic interest groups have resulted in increasing governmental protection for, rather than control of or interference with, those interests. That too represents a modification of capitalism. Finally, in the United States and other postindustrial nations, the industrial-growth economy so central to traditional capitalism has been gradually changing to a service-oriented economy. Instead of manufacturing durable goods and other products, more and more of our energies are now devoted to providing services in such areas as finance, insurance, real estate, health care, education, and child care. In short, the private sector itself is changing, as well as government's relationship to it.

It should be noted that our values generally emphasize *how* things are accomplished more than *what* is accomplished. Our political values stress the importance of means, not ends; the end does not justify the means; rather, procedures are valued for their own sake. Fair procedure lends legitimacy to what is done. Thus our commitment to "due process of law"—though there is some gap between ideal and reality. Our ideology does not attempt to define specifically what is "good" or "correct" public policy. We leave it to the political process to formulate policy, and concentrate on insuring that that process is characterized by some degree of public access to decision making and decision makers, some degree of equity in the distribution of political and economic benefits, and a great deal of competition. *How much* access (or equity or competition) exists is itself a matter requiring political resolution.

A major political value in America has been "democracy," and increasing emphasis has been placed on democratizing the political process. What that entails has not always been clear, however. Some elements of democracy are universally supported, or nearly so, while others are the subject of continuing controversy. Most would agree, for example, that *majority rule* and *minority rights* are fundamental. The former enables the political system to make and implement decisions through popular control, while the latter permits those not in the majority freedom to voice their political views and to otherwise be politically active. Directly related to these principles is the free exchange of political ideas—the freedom to speak, write, and publish political concepts and commentaries, including those out of favor with officials and the majority of citizens. Most of us would at least pay lip service to the expression of ideas.[6] Most would also agree that democracy requires widespread participation in the election of public officials, through the right to vote and to take active part in political campaigns.

Four ideas which some feel are essential to democracy are at the center of current controversy over the nature of American government. One, previously mentioned, is the intrinsic importance of procedure in democratic government—as a safeguard against arbitrary or capricious government action threatening individual freedom. Those who disagree with this value feel that as long as other essentials are present (such as majority rule), regularized procedures are not critical to democracy.

Far more controversial is the contention that true political democracy is impossible without economic democracy. Those who hold this view believe that *some* degree of equity in the distribution of economic benefits is not enough; there must be wide-ranging equality in the distribution of wealth. Many also believe that political democracy depends on social equality as well. These doctrines arouse controversy because they conflict with certain fundamental conventional values, such as individual initiative, free economic enterprise, and money as a measure of personal success. Conflict over these ideas has increased as they have been advocated more and more intensely in the 1960s and 1970s.[7]

The third element emphasized recently as essential to democratic government is direct participation in making and administering important decisions by those most directly affected. There has been considerable resistance to this idea both in the abstract and in practice, since it would require extensive reallocation of political resources and power. Nevertheless, calls for "participatory democracy" in general and "participative management" in particular have met with some positive response. Two examples, which illustrate the challenges raised and conflict generated, are the demand for decentralization of urban government decision making to give city residents, especially the poor, more voice in running their schools,[8] the location of public housing, construction of highways, and so on; and the provision for "maximum feasible participation" by the urban poor in community action agencies, as part of the War on Poverty in the mid-1960s.[9] Direct participation, if implemented, would have the effect of expanding the number of decision makers at the same time that it altered decision-making mechanisms and almost certainly the content of some decisions. Whether representative democracy requires direct participation on a wide scale is open to debate, but merely raising the question has already had an impact on our thinking about democracy as well as on the ways some government decisions are made.

A fourth idea, closely related to direct participation, is an expanded definition of what constitutes "representativeness" in our major social, economic, and political institutions. The claim is made, with some justification, that numerous groups in the population—women, blacks, and Spanish-speaking citizens in particular—have been regularly excluded from decision making in government, business and industry, religious hierarchies, labor organizations, and political parties, and consequently these institutions have not been sufficiently responsive to the needs, interests, and preferences of such groups. It is argued that this systematic exclusion from power must be corrected, and increased direct representation of these groups in key decision-making positions, in proportion to their respective percentages of the total population, has been advocated as the most appropriate remedy.

There are three important underlying assumptions made by proponents of this view. One is that traditional modes of representation are inadequate, since they have operated to sustain majority representation only, rather than to articulate and respond to views and values of those who for a variety of reasons have rarely been part of a majority political coalition.[10] A second assumption is that each of these groups has distinct and identifiable group interests requiring concentrated political activity. And the third assumption is that it is desirable or necessary to make more representative not only institutions of government but also economic, religious, and other social institutions, some of which historically have not viewed representativeness as a value of any great importance. Not surprisingly, considerable political tension has been generated over this issue, and whether this view of representativeness will become dominant remains to be seen. Since 1972 federal government guidelines for "affirmative action" have been laid down and compliance with them made a prerequisite for receiving federal financial aid in educational institutions, local police forces, collegiate athletics, and a host of other programs and institutions. But compliance has often been grudging at best, and has been accompanied only intermittently by fundamental change in the attitudes and values in question.

Public administration in America is profoundly affected by all this. Hardly mentioned in the Constitution, let alone defined as to structure or purpose in any detail, administrative agencies serve both legislative and executive masters, and are thus part of the system of checks and balances at the same time that they complicate that system. It is these agencies that carry out whatever mandates for public policy exist in Congress and the White House, but increasingly they both initiate many of the ideas that surface elsewhere and shape details of the policies themselves in their implementation. Also on the increase are court cases in which administrative actions are challenged on constitutional grounds under provisions of the Bill of Rights, such as the "reasonableness" of searches and seizures by law enforcement officials, or on grounds that agencies have violated legislative intent or procedural requirements. An example of the former is the raid by agents of national and state drug control offices on two homes in Collinsville, Illinois, in April 1973, after which the agents and their employers were accused of raiding the wrong houses. The agents were exonerated of any wrongdoing, but the residents' claim that their homes were the wrong targets was not disproved. An example of the latter is the proliferation of court cases arising out of the requirement under the National Environmental Policy Act of 1970 that federal projects be undertaken only after sponsoring agencies file adequate Environmental Impact Statements (EIS) with the President's Council on Environmental Quality, assessing environmental costs of the proposed project.

Other dimensions also link political values and public administration. One is the diversity of interest groups, which creates the potential for political alliances with those in positions of influence in the government (see chapter 3). Second, increased governmental regulation of the economy has been concentrated almost exclusively in activities of administrative (especially regulatory) agencies. Finally, renewed concern for democratic values poses new questions about control of and by bureaucracies. It is clear that if public administration had been shaped solely by changing political values and the interplay of political forces, it would have been altered considerably from its earliest forms and practices in the nineteenth century. However, administrative values have also figured prominently in its evolution. To these we now turn.

Administrative Values

American public administration is grounded in certain fundamental assumptions that have dominated administrative thinking for nearly a century. Chief among them are the following.[11] First, it has been freely assumed by many that "politics" and "administration" are separate and distinct. Political determination of broad policy directions and administrative management of public programs have been thought to be different processes, in different hands. Professional administrators viewed their role in the early twentieth century as subordinate and responsive to prevailing political majorities in Congress and the White House. Theirs was not to initiate, but to wait on initiatives from others. This conception of bureaucracy was not unlike that of a finely tuned machine, activated only when someone else pushed the button. Administration was to be not only neutral politically but also passive.

A second common assumption has been that partisan politics should not intrude upon processes of management itself, although political control of administration was considered entirely appropriate and, indeed, consistent with bureaucratic neutrality. Third, it was assumed in the early 1900s that administrative processes and functions could be studied scientifically. Fourth, that by such scientific examination it would be possible to identify various "principles" of administration to guide administrative conduct. And fifth, it was thought that the purpose of developing a "science" of administration, as well as the principal measure of administrative performance, was "economy and efficiency" in government, a standard adopted from business and industrial practice. Companion values have included job-related competence (merit) instead of political loyalty tests as the primary basis for personnel decisions, faith in the work ethic and in statistical evaluations of work performance, and a basic social consensus underlying the public administrative process.[12]

These values first emerged in a period of government reform—the late 1800s and early 1900s—following some fifty to seventy-five years in which politics and administration had been deeply intertwined. Political and administrative jobs had been bartered crudely in exchange for political favors and support, and the guiding principle in public personnel administration had been "to the victors belong the spoils of victory."[13] The reform effort was based on the belief that politics of all kinds could have *only* an adverse effect on administration, thus making necessary separation of the two.

Heavily politicized administration had indeed been wasteful and inefficient, and there had been undeniably negative effects on the quality and effectiveness of what government did. Thus there arose attempts to separate politics and administration which had as their ultimate goals economy and efficiency, and a companion concern with discovering "principles" of administration, stemming from a desire to hasten the attainment of economy and efficiency. It should be emphasized, however, that these were not merely "passing fancies." They held sway firmly in virtually all the major approaches to administration until after World War II and, significantly, among large segments of the general population even up to the present time. Some political reformers and others who seek to bring "better management practices" into government still cling to the doctrines of economy and efficiency almost as a matter of faith. And presidents from Teddy Roosevelt to Jimmy Carter (and other politicians as well) have found it politically advantageous to speak of improved economy and efficiency as a goal of their tenure in public office. There are, however, some problems posed by administrative values which stress separation of politics and administration while emphasizing efficiency.

CHIEF EXECUTIVES' ATTITUDES
TOWARD GOVERNMENTAL ADMINISTRATION

President Eisenhower in a letter to Henry Luce, the publisher of Time *magazine, who had called the presidency insufficiently aggressive, August, 1960:*

. . . the government of the United States has become too big, too complex, and too pervasive in its influence on all our lives for one individual to pretend to direct the details of its important and critical programming. Competent assistants are mandatory; without them the Executive Branch would bog down. To command the loyalties and dedication and best efforts of capable and outstanding individuals requires patience, understanding, a readiness to delegate, and an acceptance of responsibility for any honest errors—real or apparent—those associates and subordinates might make. Such loyalty from such people cannot be won by shifting responsibility, whining, scolding or demagoguery. Principal subordinates must have confidence that they and their positions are widely respected, and the chief must do his part in assuring that this is so.

Of course I could have been more assertive in making and announcing decisions and initiating programs. I can only say that I adopted and used those methods and manners that seemed to me most effective. (I should add that one of my problems has been to control my temper—a temper that I have had to battle all my life!)

Jimmy Carter, then Governor of Georgia, to the National Governors Conference, June, 1974:

On the campaign trail, a lot of promises are made by candidates for public office to improve economy and efficiency in government if they are elected. This pledge has a natural appeal to the financially overburdened taxpayer. But when the winning candidates take office, they too often find that it's easier to talk about economy and efficiency in government than to accomplish it. Entrenched bureaucracy is hard to move from its existing patterns. . . .

---

① First, they are not all consistent with the political values articulated by the Constitution. The framers did not seek to establish an extensive bureaucratic structure, nor (as far as we can tell) did they foresee one:

> They placed their faith in periodic elections, legislatures, and an elected chief executive rather than in a bureaucracy, however pure and efficient. There is nothing to suggest that they believed sound administration could compensate for bad political decisions. Redressing grievances and bad political decisions [was] the function of the political process, rather than of administrative machinery.[14]

Thus the dichotomy between politics and administration probably would

CHIEF EXECUTIVES' ATTITUDES TOWARD GOVERNMENTAL ADMINISTRATION

Immediately upon election, I began planning a program to keep my commitments. I knew that simple appeals for greater productivity in government were not the answer. Economy and efficiency must come from basic, subtle changes that slice across the complete spectrum of a government's activity. The two areas that seemed to offer greatest possibilities of success were budgeting and planning. Through tight budgeting, more services can be squeezed out of every tax dollar spent. Through planning, the groundwork can be laid for implementing new programs and expanding existing ones in ways that will avoid possible pitfalls and launch the programs directly towards their goal from the beginning.

As a citizen interested in government and as a former legislator, I had long believed that too many governmental programs are botched because they are started in haste without adequate planning or establishment of goals. Too often they never really attack the targeted problems. . . .

In budgeting, we initiated a new concept called zero-base budgeting to help us monitor state problems better and attain increased efficiency. In the area of planning, we merged the roles of planning and budgeting—which had previously operated completely independent of each other—so that they could work together in promoting more economy in government. At the same time, we clearly defined the various roles of planning and assigned the proper roles to the appropriate organizational unit.

The functions of planning and budgeting were merged in a broad reorganization program that completely streamlined the executive branch of Georgia's state government. Much of our success during the past three years in improving state programs is a direct result of reorganization.

Source: For Eisenhower's statement, Joseph Bower, "Effective Public Management," *Harvard Business Review* (March/April 1977); for Carter's statement, Carter Presidential Campaign office, Atlanta, Georgia.

have been seen by the framers either as undesirable, since government through the political process was central to the constitutional scheme, or as impossible.[15] It seems likely they would have regarded with suspicion any developments that had the effect of insulating important decision makers, such as administrators, from effective control by the voters or their elected representatives. Yet the administrative values we have discussed here suggest precisely that sort of insulation, although for reasons many thought laudable when they were first formulated.

Second, it has become clear from a substantial body of research since World War II that public administration is not merely machinery for implementing decisions made by other government institutions. As we saw in chapter 1, public agencies and administrators have both authority and the power of initiative to make a host of decisions—large and small—that have real impact on public policy. Protections against undue political manipulation instituted a century ago in response to unmistakable excesses have given rise to the possibility of administrative excesses, because control over policy making is more indirect and therefore more difficult for elected leaders and their immediate subordinates to exercise.

③ Third, there is some tension, if not outright conflict, between the major emphases of the Constitution (at least originally) and those of administrative values. The framers sought, perhaps above all else, to prevent the unchecked exercise of political power by any institution of government or by government as a whole. While they undoubtedly would not have advocated deliberate waste or wanton corruption, they were far more concerned with preventing the growth of concentrated political power, regardless of who wielded the power or with what degree of effectiveness (or efficiency). Thus they deliberately fragmented the formal powers of government so as to create a certain amount of inevitable—and calculated—inefficiency. Furthermore, as noted previously, the framers placed great reliance on the political process and on representative institutions (legislatures in particular) as devices for resolving political conflicts and representing the sovereign people. In sum, the framers contemplated a political system which could both tolerate and benefit from somewhat inefficient exercise of power—the benefit being that government would have greater difficulty infringing on individual liberties—and which would freely resort to the political process for making decisions and solving problems.

The values of administration, on the other hand, clearly point in the direction of efficiency not merely as a desirable feature of government operation but as a key standard for measuring and evaluating actual government performance.[16] The reformers who first sought to increase efficiency in government associated most forms of politics with inefficiency—in many instances, rightly so—and as a result were largely "anti-politics." Their values strongly inclined toward political neutrality as a key feature of both the composition and operation of public administrative agencies, and thus as the major remedy for inefficiency.

If the framers trusted political processes, efficiency-minded reformers clearly did not. The reformers concentrated their efforts on the administrative components of government, dealing only in a limited way with selection processes or operations of other public officials. They were intent mainly on reducing the number of administrative positions which were filled solely or largely according to political party service, loyalties, and connections. This they succeeded in doing to a considerable extent. They also succeeded in that they left behind them a strong legacy of values pertaining to the "proper" means of administering government. But their very success created inconsistencies between the two sets of values, political and administrative. The framers, in the public interest, wanted to keep government weak; the reformers, also in the public interest, wanted to make government more efficient. While both sets of values have continued to influence American government, inconsistencies between them have been difficult to reconcile—the notion of a weak *and* efficient government is a strange one, after all. And in a time of growing complexity and change in society at large, reconciling them becomes an even greater challenge.

Social Change and Public Administration

The social setting of public administration, like the context of values, has both direct and indirect impacts, and changes in that setting, like changes in values, carry with them potentially far-reaching implications. Several societal changes of the past half-century have been of particular importance in shaping contemporary public administration.

The most obvious change is population growth. We have become a nation of some 225 million inhabitants, from less than half that many a century ago and only two-thirds of that number (151 million) in 1950.[17] This striking growth in numbers has meant a parallel increase in demands for public services, demands directed more often than not at administrative agencies (especially at the state and local level, for example, police and fire protection, teachers and other educational personnel, sanitation, and health services). Complicating and intensifying this increased service demand is a second, related development: the continuing concentration of people in urban areas. During the 1950s and 1960s, the greatest population growth occurred in suburban rings around larger cities, mainly in the Northeast and Midwest. More recently there has been a general migration of people into newer, smaller cities (and *their* suburbs) of the "sun belt" states—especially Florida, Texas, New Mexico, Arizona, and California. Florida, in particular, is experiencing very rapid growth.

Metropolitan expansion spawned a host of government concerns. Some of these had been with us before in urban areas—for example, inadequate housing and overcrowding, poverty, unemployment, and sewage and sanitation problems. Others were relatively new—race-related problems, for example, have existed in a distinctly urban context only since World War II. And some objective conditions have only recently been defined as "problems," for example, environmental pollution and mass transportation needs. Combating urban problems has fallen largely to administrative entities, and paying for higher levels of services has increasingly called into play the combined fiscal resources of national, state, and local governments, changing the face of the federal system (see chapter 5). Population change, in sum, has called forth government responses to problems new in their complexity and scope.

Technological change has also been of crucial import to public administration. We have experienced nothing short of a revolution in electronic communications, both in terms of linking widely separated parts of the world virtually instantaneously via satellite, and in terms of mass communications capabilities whereby literally millions of people can witness an event simultaneously (as well as "live and in color"). Technology, in the form of automation and other mechanical advances, has also permitted mass production and distribution of durable goods on a scale never before known. The "knowledge explosion" is a further dimension of technological change, giving rise to both the education "industry" and expansion of scientific research supported by millions of dollars in government, and other, funds. Government regulation of, and participation in, increasingly complex technologies—for example, the space program, energy research, and pollution control—demands far more sophisticated and specialized bureaucracies. This drastic alteration in responsibilities has had a permanent effect on the nature and course of American public administration.

The need for increased specialization is evident throughout much of both public and private administration. As tasks and skills become more complex, mastering any one of them demands more of an individual's time and attention, thus hampering acquisition of broad skills. Specialization, of course, is one of the core values in traditional conceptions of public bureaucracy, and thus movement toward greater specialization represents extension of an existing feature rather than a new one. A very important consequence for public administration has been that specialists inside and outside of government have been able to be—indeed, have had to be—in closer working contact with one another as part of the policy-making process. This reinforces the dual patterns of more informed decision making, because of the knowledge resources that can be brought to bear, and less centrally directed decision making, due to top executives' limited ability to fully comprehend all the specialties of those in their organizations. Specialization is a major reason for fragmenting and compartmentalizing decision-making responsibility within a bureaucracy, permitting a specialized staff or organization considerable discretionary authority within its jurisdiction. To the extent that personnel systems are based on job-related competence, and "competence" is judged to include increasingly specialized knowledge, these tendencies are likely to be reinforced.

Political decisions to address new problems, that is, to identify certain conditions present in society as "problems," have also resulted in enlarged responsibilities for administrative bodies. Without being unduly cynical, this is to suggest that many of today's challenges—environmental pollution, civil rights, civil liberties, energy sources and conservation, and population growth and stability, to name only a few major ones— have actually been with us for some time in one form or another, and "discovering" them as problems is really a result of deciding as a society that to do nothing about them would be inviting trouble. In all the cases cited, and some others, changes in societal values about what is important, or constitutional, or right, preceded identification of the problems. Previously, they were not widely regarded as problem areas requiring public action. Although that has changed today, there is still debate over both the size and nature of particular problems and what governmental actions are appropriate to solve them. Administrative entities empowered to deal with these problems thus are drawn into controversies surrounding the nature of the problems themselves.

In sum, the combined effects on bureaucracy of population growth and geographic redistribution, vast changes in our knowledge and technological capabilities, specialization, and the rise of new, complex social problems have been profound and probably irreversible. Accompanied by changes in some of our most fundamental political and administrative values, change in American society has led to new, unforeseen, and complex pressures on our machinery of government at all levels.

The Changing Value Context and Bureaucracy Under Pressure

During the 1960s and 1970s a host of values—social, political, administrative—have been subjected to scrutiny, generating ongoing social change as well as resulting from it. Value change, however, is not a new phenomenon in this country; evolution of even fundamental values has been a continuing part of American history. One evolving value concerns limited government. Beginning in the late 1800s government has come gradually to be viewed more as a positive instrument of social change than as something to be guarded against, feared, or mistrusted. Increasing international involvements have prompted growth in our military and diplomatic machinery, and a growing conception of government as a *guarantor* of rights and liberties, and even economic well-being, has given rise to more governmental activity in a larger number of domestic policy areas. The image of government as provider and protector, rather than as threat to individual liberty, has become widely accepted (though far from universally). Perhaps most important, public expectations have changed, with more and more people looking to government for reasonable solutions to their problems.

The devices used to insure limited government—separation of powers, checks and balances, federalism, and judicial review—have reflected these changes. Federalism and separation of powers, in particular, gradually assumed a somewhat different character. Federalism was modified due to the national government's increasing role in domestic affairs relative to the states and localities.[18] Separation of powers was affected by the expanding role of the president and executive-branch agencies relative to Congress, notably in their ability to initiate public policy proposals. (Congress itself assisted in the growth of presidential power by delegating considerable legislative authority to the White House.) Change in the relative influence of the presidency also affected the concept of checks and balances.[19] Judicial review became more important in that the U.S. Supreme Court upheld the general trend of expanded federal power, especially after the late 1930s.[20]

The scope of these changes can be illustrated by enactment of a graduated income tax in 1914, following a constitutional amendment which overturned a Supreme Court ruling in 1896 banning such a tax; Theodore Roosevelt's early natural resource conservation efforts; Woodrow Wilson's League of Nations venture; Franklin Roosevelt's New Deal; and far-reaching White House initiatives of the past two decades. Most innovative presidents have called on existing bureaucracies and/or created new ones to assist them in implementing their programs, and Congress has sometimes pressured bureaucracy to follow *its* directives in opposition to presidential leadership. In any case, a considerable amount of new administrative activity has grown up as a direct result of our redefining the role government should play in our lives.

Government's relationship to the private economic sector has also been modified in response to changing views about government's general domestic responsibilities. In the early 1900s regulation of business and industry centered on preventing development of monopolies ("antitrust" efforts) and maintaining fair trade (business) practices, broadly defined. But as business and industry grew into nationwide—and then, international—enterprises, the scope of government regulation broadened as well, first geographically and later substantively: the quality of food and pharmaceuticals (Food and Drug Administration), pricing and other practices in the oil industry (Federal Power Commission), stock market regulation (Securities and Exchange Commission), and more recently, environmental quality (Environmental Protection Agency) and consumer protection (Consumer Product Safety Commission), to name a few. This is not to say that government regulation has always been effective, consistent, or even present on all occasions,[21] but it does indicate that government policy directions have changed markedly from earlier laissez-faire (hands off) attitudes. These patterns have been largely repeated in many state governments, where one also finds environmental protection agencies, consumer agencies, and intrastate commerce regulatory bodies. The relationship of government to private enterprise has clearly changed in the past fifty years, and here too the burden has fallen principally on administrative agencies.

Democratic values emphasized in our thinking have changed also. Demands for direct participation and greater representativeness have crucial administrative implications, and as bureaucratic decision makers have gained in influence, criteria for their selection (based on job-related competence) and methods used (competitive examinations) have come under increasing fire for having promoted unrepresentative and unresponsive public bureaucracies.[22] Similarly, the growing emphasis on promoting economic and social equality through government action has given rise in the profession to a movement known as the "New Public Administration," composed of both scholars and practitioners whose paramount concern in administering government programs is social equity, that is, a fairer distribution of the benefits available from government.[23] Considerations such as these have the effect of casting administrators into "advocacy" roles—actively pursuing particular policy goals while seeking to uphold well-defined sets of social-political values. Whether or not this is appropriate is a matter of opinion, but it is clearly not in the tradition of bureaucratic neutrality. Those who subscribe to the "New Public Administration" argue, however, that bureaucratic neutrality has been sacrificed extensively in the past to comfortable working arrangements with large and powerful political interests (see chapter 3). They maintain that representing the interests of those lacking substantial influence is not only politically and socially justifiable but also consistent with past bureaucratic behavior, which had favored different, stronger interests.

Administrative values have been both redefined and reordered in relative importance. Whereas we devoted considerable effort in this century to strengthening the merit system, which promoted politically neutral competence in public administration, the current emphasis seems to have shifted away from strictly merit principles and toward greater representativeness and participation. Herbert Kaufman has suggested that the values of political neutrality and representativeness pull us in different directions, that strengthening one means weakening the other. That is, emphasizing competence may produce a less-than-representative public service due to differences in opportunities to acquire and develop skills, while seeking greater representativeness means emphasizing personal characteristics not necessarily related to job qualifications.[24]

Kaufman has also noted that a third value—strong executive leadership—has been more popular during periods when representativeness was emphasized more than political neutrality. In practice, strong leadership is enhanced when the public expects political representativeness in government institutions, and is inhibited by pressures for merit reform.

It appears that during the decade since Kaufman's observations, we have been in the midst of a historical cycle in which disenchantment has grown with politically neutral bureaucracy, pressures for reform along representative lines have been generated, and (according to some survey data) there is renewed interest in stronger executive leadership.[25] (Table 2–1 compares conceptions about government officials and businessmen.)

TABLE 2–1
**IMAGES OF GOVERNMENT OFFICIALS COMPARED
TO BUSINESSMEN BY ETHNIC GROUPS OF
SAN ANTONIO HIGH SCHOOL STUDENTS**

	Mexican-American			Black			Anglo		
	Agree	Dis-agree	(N)	Agree	Dis-agree	(N)	Agree	Dis-agree	(N)
Government officials are as highly respected as private businessmen	44%	31%	(208)	29%	31%	(45)	35%	39%	(354)
Overall, I have a good opinion of government workers	46	25	(208)	33	29	(45)	50	26	(354)
Government officials are just as honest as most businessmen	20	46	(209)	13	47	(45)	26	40	(357)
Public servants are dedicated workers	41	29	(205)	22	36	(45)	43	24	(355)
Government officials are more idealistic than businessmen	28	30	(206)	24	33	(45)	28	38	(352)
Persons holding government jobs could also qualify for private business jobs	58	24	(209)	44	33	(45)	45	36	(355)
Most government officials could probably qualify for the same kinds of jobs in private business	51	26	(210)	47	22	(45)	54	23	(355)
Imagination and creativity are important . . .	42	33	(207)	29	27	(45)	26	49	(357)
Promotions in government jobs are usually based upon ability and achievement and not by pull	45	28	(209)	47	28	(45)	30	46	(353)

N = Total number of students responding to each question; percentage of students responding "no opinion" not included in table.

Source: Harold M. Barger, "Images of Bureaucracy: A Tri-Ethnic Consideration," Public Administration Review (May/June 1976). This reports a study of 645 San Antonio, Texas, area high school juniors and seniors.

Here as elsewhere, old values have not been totally discarded; rather, they have been modified and adapted to different needs in different times. Bureaucracies that have attempted to continue operating according to only the old values have encountered difficulty, yet it has not been possible for those seeking change to bring it about completely. This conflict of values largely explains the tension existing currently in and around the administrative process.

One final source of pressure on bureaucracy today is growing interest on the part of chief executives in national, state, and local government to reassert more effective control over the policy-making process. Presidents in this century, of both parties, have increasingly been frustrated in their attempts to gain regular support for their programs from well-entrenched administrative structures and personnel, and have either induced the bureaucracies to work with them or have bypassed them, often setting up rival centers of bureaucratic influence. None of these efforts has been completely successful. Administrative agencies have demonstrated both staying power and considerable political savvy in whittling down a president's ability to coerce them or work around them.[26] The result has been attempts by recent presidents (notably Nixon and Carter) to restore chief executive control by means of more deliberate setting of presidential priorities, agency reorganizations, and budget devices like "zero-base budgeting," which would require justification by an agency of every proposed expenditure in every year's budget (see chapter 10). President Carter in particular has enjoyed substantial public support in such efforts, reflecting the link noted by Kaufman between strong executive leadership and greater representativeness in government (meaning here, representation of the political majority that elected the chief executive).

In sum, then, bureaucracy is under pressure because the political insulation provided by the merit system has come to frustrate chief executives hampered in their efforts to set policy directions effectively, and citizens who have found professional bureaucrats inaccessible, unresponsive, or both. The administrative values of political neutrality and professional competence have therefore been challenged increasingly, and other values offered (sometimes forcefully) as alternatives. Bureaucracy is also under pressure because, in contrast to some earlier periods when it was viewed as a source of innovation and initiative, it is now seen as a major obstacle to needed change—even though we may not agree on what changes are desirable or necessary, which only adds to the pressure. Finally, it is possible (though not conclusively demonstrated) that the rather impressive "track record" of government agencies in years past may have raised public expectations unduly by creating the impression (often with help from agency public relations personnel) that even in more complex and difficult times the bureaucracy can cope, if not conquer.[27] Failure to meet inflated expectations may thus be a part of today's bureaucratic dilemma.

SUMMARY

Contemporary public administration has been shaped by past and present political values, administrative values, and social change. Politically, our system is a liberal democracy, and economically, a generally capitalist one. Key political values have included popular sovereignty, limited government, individualism, and pluralism. We have also emphasized individual liberty as a central objective of the political system, and stressed democratic principles. Widely supported democratic principles include majority rule, minority rights, and the free exchange of political ideas. More controversial are procedural safeguards against arbitrary government decisions, economic and social equality, direct participation, and a broadened definition of "representativeness" in decision-making institutions. Our political values have fit comfortably, for the most part, with the economic doctrines of capitalism; and government economic policies, while increasingly regulative, have sought to sustain competition and protect the rewards of competitive success.

Major administrative values have included separation of politics and administration, scientific development of administrative "principles," and attainment of economy and efficiency in government as the paramount objective of a politically neutral "science of administration." These values were the basis of administrative reform in the late nineteenth and early twentieth centuries, and were a reaction against practices of the previous fifty to seventy-five years. These values, in varying degrees, have had continuing popular appeal and have been used quite effectively as part of campaign oratory by candidates for the presidency and hundreds of other offices.

However, our political and administrative values are not entirely consistent with each other. The framers of the Constitution assumed there would be effective political control by the voters or their elected representatives over all important decision makers, while the reformers intended to insulate administration from direct political control. Such insulation has become cause for concern as administrators have assumed or been delegated ever greater policy-making responsibility and authority. In addition, one set of values is based on the assumption that individual liberty and the public interest are best served by keeping government relatively weak, and therefore unable to infringe upon our freedoms, while the other set of values is geared toward improving the ability of government agencies to operate efficiently—also in the public interest. Changes in particular values have served to intensify pressures already existing on administrative institutions, especially in recent years.

Public administration also has had to respond to rapid social change in the past fifty years: population growth and urbanization, tremendous technological advances, increased specialization, and the emergence of new, complex social problems.

Accompanying social change have been modifications in underlying values, both political and administrative, with direct and significant impact on public administration. Government, generally, has become more active, with the chief executive and the bureaucracy spearheading the expansion of its role in society. Government's relationship to the private economic sector has increasingly taken the form of concern for product quality, regulation of numerous business and industry practices, consumer protection, and environmental quality. The concept of democracy has changed, with greater concern for broad, direct participation and more representativeness. This has resulted in pressures for change in administrative agencies that would deemphasize political neutrality and job-related competence as all-important values and place greater weight on popular involvement and control. The quest for control over bureaucracy has centered on chief executives, who are seen as most likely to possess the resources necessary to exercise such control. Finally, high public expectations have affected government agencies to the extent that there is considerable dissatisfaction with many aspects of bureaucratic performance, and considerable pressure being brought to remedy the things thought to be wrong.

NOTES

1. This discussion is based on the excellent treatment by Richard S. Page in "The Ideological-Philosophical Setting of American Public Administration," in Dwight Waldo, ed., *Public Administration in a Time of Turbulence* (Scranton, Pa.: Chandler Publishing, 1971), pp. 59–73. See, in the same volume, Allen Schick, "Toward the Cybernetic State," pp. 214–233. For an "advocacy" treatment of "liberal democracy," see Harold W. Chase and Paul Dolan, *The Case for Democratic Capitalism* (New York: Thomas Y. Crowell, 1964).

2. Herbert Kaufman, "Administrative Decentralization and Political Power," *Public Administration Review,* 29 (January/February 1969), 3–15, at p. 5 (emphasis added).

3. Page, "Ideological-Philosophical Setting," p. 61.

4. Ibid. There are, however, other ways to view "the public interest." See Glendon Schubert, *The Public Interest* (Glencoe, Ill.: The Free Press, 1960).

5. Ibid., pp. 61–62. See also Louis Hartz, *The Liberal Tradition in America* (New York: Harcourt, Brace and World, 1955).

6. Numerous studies of public opinion suggest, however, that many of us are inconsistent in our willingness to allow free expression of unpopular ideas. Ideas about socialism or communism, tightening gun control, permitting elective abortions, or banning prayer in public schools can offend people to the point that they may be inclined to prohibit expression of those (and other) ideas. Free expression of *all* ideas, in short, is far from guaranteed.

7. See, among other sources, "The Port Huron Statement," adopted at the convention of Students for a Democratic Society (SDS), Port Huron, Michigan, June 11–15, 1962; Martin Luther King, Jr., *Where Do We Go from Here: Chaos or Community?* (Boston: Beacon Press, 1968); Theodore J. Lowi, *The Politics of Disorder* (New York: Basic Books, 1971); and Robert A. Goldwin, ed., *How Democratic Is America? Responses to the New Left Challenge* (Chicago: Rand McNally, 1971).

8. See, especially, Naomi Levine with Richard Cohen, *Ocean Hill–Brownsville: Schools in Crisis* (New York: Popular Library, 1969); Alan

Rosenthal, ed., *Governing Education: A Reader on Politics, Power, and Public School Policy* (Garden City, N.Y.: Doubleday, 1969); and Marilyn Gittell and Alan G. Hevesi, eds., *The Politics of Urban Education* (New York: Praeger Publishers, 1969).

9. See Daniel P. Moynihan, *Maximum Feasible Misunderstanding* (New York: The Free Press, 1969). The literature on community control includes, among others, Alan A. Altshuler, *Community Control: The Black Demand for Participation in Large American Cities* (New York: Pegasus, 1970); H. George Frederickson, ed., *Politics, Public Administration, and Neighborhood Control* (San Francisco: Chandler Publishing, 1973); Milton Kotler, *Neighborhood Government: The Local Foundations of Political Life* (Indianapolis: Bobbs-Merrill, 1969); Eric Nordlinger, *Decentralizing the City: A Study of Boston's Little City Halls* (Boston: Boston Urban Observatory, 1972); and Joseph Zimmerman, *The Federated City: Community Control in Large Cities* (New York: St. Martin's, 1972).

10. As noted previously, that *is* one aim of democracy as we have understood the concept. What is argued is that majority representation without full representation of the minority is no longer sufficient for a democracy.

11. This discussion is taken from Dwight Waldo, "Public Administration," *The Journal of Politics,* 30 (May 1968), 443–479, at p. 448, cited by Page, "Ideological-Philosophical Setting," p. 62. Waldo's *The Administrative State: A Study of the Political Theory of American Public Administration* (New York: The Ronald Press, 1948) is a valuable examination of the evolution of our thinking regarding public administration.

12. James J. Heaphey, "Four Pillars of Public Administration: Challenge and Response," in Dwight Waldo, ed., *Public Administration in a Time of Turbulence* (Scranton, Pa.: Chandler Publishing, 1971), pp. 74–94.

13. See chapter 9 for a fuller treatment of public personnel administration and its development.

14. Page, "Ideological-Philosophical Setting," p. 63.

15. It is also quite possible, however, that they would have objected equally to the *blatant* politicizing of administration that occurred during the mid-1800s.

16. Martin Landau, "Redundancy, Rationality, and the Problem of Duplication and Overlap," *Public Administration Review,* 29 (July/August 1969), 346–358.

17. The U.S. Bureau of the Census makes available, after each decennial (ten-year) census, many volumes of data that illuminate the changes in American society. This section relies on the excellent summary treatments of census data found in Theodore H. White's *The Making of the President 1960* (New York: Atheneum Publishers, 1961), chapter 8, "Retrospect on Yesterday's Future," and *The Making of the President 1972* (New York: Atheneum Publishers, 1973), chapter 6, "The Web of Numbers."

18. See Richard H. Leach, *American Federalism* (New York: W. W. Norton and Company, 1970); Michael Reagan, *The New Federalism* (New York: Oxford University Press, 1972); Parris N. Glendening and Mavis Mann Reeves, *Pragmatic Federalism: An Intergovernmental View of American Government* (Pacific Palisades, Calif.: Palisades Publishers, 1977); and chapter 5 of this book.

19. See Dorothy Buckton James, *The Contemporary Presidency,* 2nd ed. (Indianapolis: Bobbs-Merrill, 1974).

20. See, among others, Kenneth T. Palmer, *State Politics in the United States,* 2nd ed. (New York: St. Martin's, 1977), pp. 30–31.

21. See, for example, Robert C. Fellmeth, *The Interstate Commerce Omission: Ralph Nader's Study Group Report on the Interstate Commerce Commission and Transportation* (New York: Grossman Publishers, 1970); and Louis M. Kohlmeier, Jr., *The Regulators: Watchdog Agencies and the Public Interest* (New York: Harper & Row, 1969).

22. See Kaufman, "Administrative Decentralization and Political Power."

23. See Frank Marini, ed., *Toward a New Public Administration: The Minnowbrook Perspective* (Scranton, Pa.: Chandler Publishing, 1971); and H. George Frederickson, ed., "Social Equity and Public Administration: A Symposium," *Public Administration Review,* 34 (January/February 1974), 1–51.

24. Kaufman, "Administrative Decentralization and Political Power."

25. Louis Harris, "Confidence and Concern: Citizens View American Government," a study conducted under contract with, and printed by, the Subcommittee on Intergovernmental Relations, Committee on Government Operations, U.S. Senate (Washington, D.C.: U.S. Government Printing Office, 1974), at p. 36.

26. For an example of presidential inability to coerce the cooperation of bureaucracies—even in times of crisis—see Graham Allison, *Essence of Decision: Explaining the Cuban Missile Crisis* (Boston: Little, Brown, 1971).

27. Francis E. Rourke, *Bureaucracy, Politics, and Public Policy,* 2nd ed. (Boston: Little, Brown, 1976), especially chapter 4.

SUGGESTED READINGS

Altshuler, Alan A. *Community Control: The Black Demand for Participation in Large American Cities.* New York: Pegasus, 1970.

Chase, Harold W., and Paul Dolan. *The Case for Democratic Capitalism.* New York: Thomas Y. Crowell, 1964.

Frederickson, H. George, ed. *Politics, Public Administration, and Neighborhood Control.* San Francisco: Chandler Publishing, 1973.

Harris, Louis. "Confidence and Concern: Citizens View American Government." A study conducted under contract with, and printed by, the Subcommittee on Intergovernmental Relations, Committee on Government Operations, U.S. Senate. Washington, D.C.: U.S. Government Printing Office, 1974.

Heaphey, James J. "Four Pillars of Public Administration: Challenge and Response." In Dwight Waldo, ed., *Public Administration in a Time of Turbulence.* Scranton, Pa.: Chandler Publishing, 1971, pp. 74–94.

Kaufman, Herbert. "Administrative Decentralization and Political Power." *Public Administration Review,* 29 (January/February 1969), 3–15.

Marini, Frank, ed. *Toward a New Public Administration: The Minnowbrook Perspective.* Scranton, Pa.: Chandler Publishing, 1971.

Moynihan, Daniel P. *Maximum Feasible Misunderstanding.* New York: The Free Press, 1969.

Page, Richard S. "The Ideological-Philosophical Setting of American Public Administration." In Dwight Waldo, ed., *Public Administration in a Time of Turbulence*. Scranton, Pa.: Chandler Publishing, 1971, pp. 59–73.

Zimmerman, Joseph. *The Federated City: Community Control in Large Cities.* New York: St. Martin's, 1972.

PART TWO
THE POLITICAL SETTING OF PUBLIC ADMINISTRATION

The next three chapters deal with various aspects of the political environment within which public administration functions. Chapter 3 discusses key elements of politics and power in bureaucracy. The discussion focuses on the dispersal of power throughout government and what that means for public administrators, foundations of bureaucratic power, political implications of structure, bureaucrats as political actors, and problems of accountability with regard to bureaucratic politics. Bureaucrats are seen as active participants in political interaction, with considerable variety and complexity in the manner of their involvement.

Chapter 4 examines chief executives and their leadership of bureaucracy at national, state, and local levels. Similarities and differences among them are given careful attention, particularly with regard to leadership resources available to each. How chief executives interact with those in administrative agencies and what difference they make to bureaucratic operations are also discussed.

Chapter 5 deals with an aspect of American government of increasing importance to public administration—namely, the changing nature of federalism and intergovernmental (national-state-local) relations. Description of the formal federal setting is followed by examination of intergovernmental relations within federalism. Particular attention is given to fiscal and administrative relations among the different levels and units of government, and a recent effort to improve coordination among them is analyzed. Intergovernmental relations and public administration overlap extensively, and an understanding of their mutual impacts is essential.

CHAPTER 3

Bureaucratic
Politics and
Bureaucratic Power

In this chapter we resume our discussion, begun in chapter 1, of the politics of American public administration. Here we shall deal with four principal themes. First, the political environment in which bureaucracy functions will be described. Second, we shall examine foundations of bureaucratic power, chief among which are the ability to build, retain, and mobilize political support for administrative agencies and programs, and expertise in a particular field. Third, we will look at "subsystem politics," describing how bureaucrats enter directly into political alliances with others in and out of government in order to pursue programmatic and political objectives shared by members of the subsystem or, if not shared, are at least mutually compatible. Fourth, we shall discuss the political accountability of nonelected government officials (most bureaucrats are nonelected), identify several limitations on bureaucratic accountability, and assess the possibilities for overcoming those limitations.

The Political Context of Bureaucratic Power

Public administration, like all other government institutions, functions within a framework of widely scattered political power. Both the formal framework of governmental power and actual competition for power reflect this lack of centralization in the political system. The formal framework refers to structural arrangements of the Constitution such as separation of powers, checks and balances, federalism, and judicial review. Competition for power includes conflicts among the branches of government and within them (especially within Congress), factional conflict within the two major political parties, and continual jockeying for position and influence among interest groups. This dispersal of power is sustained and supported by the noncentralized nature of American society, with its strong cultural emphases upon individualism and pluralism, and the accompanying acceptance of individual and group competition as appropriate mechanisms for "getting ahead" in politics and many other pursuits.

Wide dispersal of political power creates both constraints and opportunities for political actors (individuals, groups, institutions). The major problem facing any group or agency is that the quest for influence over a particular policy area is usually keenly competitive, with many other groups and agencies also seeking to have their preferences adopted as public policy. A current example concerns government energy policy, an area of considerable interest to the petroleum industry, manufacturers of electrical appliances, environmental groups, the utility industry, and consumer groups. Others with a stake in energy policy include coal companies, labor unions whose members are or may be employed in energy-related work, and government agencies such as the national Department of Energy, state utility commissions, and state and national resource conservation agencies which have responsibilities affecting, and affected by, decisions on energy.

A somewhat more specific example revolves around the decision by the federal Food and Drug Administration (FDA) early in 1977 to ban saccharin from the market because of its suspected cancer-causing properties. Among those who sought to reverse the ban were manufacturers of saccharin and of a wide variety of low-calorie food products that contained saccharin, and an unexpectedly large number among the general public who needed or wanted to have saccharin available (diabetics and others on sugar-restricted diets, for example). Those supporting the ban, besides the FDA, included some members of Congress, consumer advocate Ralph Nader's public health research organization, and others fearful of increased incidence of cancer. Though the FDA acted on congressional authority in imposing the ban, it did not have the "last word" on the subject because of Congress's ability to modify the FDA's powers—a situation faced by many agencies and their allies.

Perhaps the key to why bureaucratic agencies must play political roles is the lack of cohesive political majorities within the two houses of Congress, and resultant fuzziness in programmatic mandates enacted by Congress. Political scientist Norton Long, writing nearly thirty years ago, observed that "it is a commonplace that the American party system provides neither a mandate for a platform nor a mandate for leadership. . . . The mandate that the parties do not supply must be attained through public relations and the mobilization of group support."[1] Long goes on to suggest that the parties fail to provide "either a clear-cut decision as to

---

COMMENTS ON THE RELATIONSHIP OF
PUBLIC ADMINISTRATION TO POLITICS

"The exercise of discretionary power, the making of value choices, is a characteristic and increasing function of administrators and bureaucrats; they are thus importantly engaged in politics."
—from Wallace S. Sayre, "Premises of Public Administration: Past and Emerging," *Public Administration Review,* Spring 1958.

"Economy and efficiency are demonstrably not the prime purposes of public administration. Mr. Justice Brandeis emphasized that 'the doctrine of separation of powers was adopted by the Constitution in 1787, not to promote efficiency but to preclude the exercise of arbitrary power.' The basic issues of federal organization and administration relate to power: who shall control it and to what ends?"
—from Harold Seidman, *Politics, Position, and Power: The Dynamics of Federal Organization,* Oxford University Press, 1975.

"Political science and public administration not only have a natural mutual affinity through interest in the same general subject matter area: they also have a mutual and reciprocal need for each other. Robbed of concern for a vigorous and vital administration, political science would become largely a thing of library and classroom, hardly worthy to treat of so buoyant a subject as government. On its part, administration cries for the intellectual stimulation which can come only from the thinker of general qualities of mind."
—from Roscoe C. Martin, "Political Science and Public Administration: A Note on the State of the Union," *American Political Science Review,* September 1952.

"A theory of public administration means in our time a theory of politics also."
—from John M. Gaus, "Trends in the Theory of Public Administration," *Public Administration Review,* Summer 1950.

---

what [administrative agencies] should do or an adequately mobilized political support for a course of action."[2] He continues:

> The weakness in party structure both permits and makes necessary the present dimensions of the political activities of the administrative branch—permits because it fails to protect administration from pressures and fails to provide adequate direction and support, makes necessary because it fails to develop a consensus on a leadership and a program that makes possible administration on the basis of accepted decisional premises.[3]

Thus administrative agencies cannot simply take orders from above. If they were to wait for clear-cut orders and accompanying political support for their implementation, they would wait a long time indeed.

Congress lacks cohesive political party majorities that can speak with a clear voice over a significant period of time; rather, it is characterized by shifting coalitions, whose composition varies from one issue, and one vote, to the next. In addition, the language of congressional legislation tends to be ambiguous, and thus not terribly instructive either to the general public or to administrators charged with implementing federal laws. On occasion this is deliberate: Congress may be unsure of what the final outcome of legislation *should* look like, and therefore provides a rough outline with the expectation that agencies and administrators will help determine appropriate programs as they work through their own problems on a day-to-day basis.

Presidents, who might be expected to provide leadership for bureaucracy from a solid base of political support, ordinarily lack the sort of political backing that would permit them to take unequivocal policy positions. Another observation by Long, though made during the Truman presidency, is still applicable today:

> The broad alliance of conflicting groups that makes up Presidential majorities scarcely coheres [around] any definite pattern of objectives. . . . The President must in large part be, if not all things to all men, at least many things to many men. As a consequence, the contradictions in his power base invade administration.[4]

At times, intense political conflict over some specific issue will force a president to be deliberately unclear about his policy preferences and therefore to *not* take the lead in giving direction to administrative implementation of public policy. For administrators there is both benefit and cost in such presidential "nondirection": benefit, in not having to follow every presidential dictate exactly; cost, in not being able to rely routinely on presidential power, influence, or prestige for political support. Presidents may lend their political backing to administrative agencies, but only on those occasions when supporting a given program is advantageous to their political interests.

Before discussing the principal political resources of administrative agencies, some other generalizations are in order concerning the political context of bureaucratic power. First, strictly formal definitions of agency power or responsibility are not likely to tell the complete story about actual power or influence. Second, although bureaucratic agencies generally occupy a power position somewhere between total independence from president and Congress and total domination by either or both, just how much independence they have in any specific situation is also heavily influenced by the particular power relationships they have with other political actors and institutions. Agencies with relatively low political standing may be dependent on the support of Congress or the president in order to function adequately, thus running the risk of allowing others to "call the shots." Those with high political standing, or with strong backing from other supporters, are better able to stand on their own in relation to Capitol Hill and the White House. These generalizations also hold true in state and local politics.

Third, acquisition and exercise of bureaucratic power are frequently characterized by conflicts among agencies over program jurisdiction—the area of responsibility assigned to an agency by Congress or the president. One study of bureaucratic "imperialism"—the tendency for agencies to seek expansion of their programmatic responsibilities—suggests that such expansionism arises "from the simple fact that, whatever the purposes of the administrative politician, his first necessity is to maintain sufficient power for his agency. *Power is organized around constituency and constituency around jurisdiction.*"[5] Bureaucratic agencies, in their quest for "sufficient power," will seek support from permanent and semipermanent coalitions of constituency groups, which in turn are organized to pursue particular policy objectives of their own. To have a chance of securing backing from such groups, administrative agencies must be legally responsible for managing government programs of interest to these potentially supportive constituencies. Thus administrative agencies are always desirous of obtaining control over programs that have strong support from influential constituencies.[6] Bureaucratic imperialism, however, is neither universal nor automatic; for example, an agency may deny (in its own political interests) that it has legal authority to exercise powers within some specified, and unpopular, area of jurisdiction. Thus in the 1940s the Federal Power Commission (FPC) denied that the Natural Gas Act of 1938 conferred on it powers of regulation over the oil industry which many outside the industry desired to see the FPC exercise, but which its political allies in the industry sought to curb. The point is not that agencies are inherently imperialistic or nonimperialistic; rather, that an agency's decisions regarding program jurisdiction usually take into account potential political repercussions. Thus conflicts over bureaucratic jurisdiction are serious contests for political power.

Finally, governmental institutions, including administrative agencies, have at least two roles to play in the exercise of power and decision-making authority—roles that overlap but are conceptually distinct and can sometimes conflict. On the one hand, they may act as unified entities, seeking to maximize their influence and their share of available political rewards and benefits.[7] On the other hand, they also serve (whether willingly or not) as arenas of political competition, within which various political forces contend for dominant influence in decision-making processes. This is especially evident in Congress, where rival political coalitions are frequently in noisy dispute over well-publicized issues. When it is reported that "Congress voted today to . . . ," what this really means is that a majority coalition was successfully formed on a given vote. At issue, also, every time "Congress makes a decision" is control of the way the question is presented, possible amendments, use of numerous tactics to speed up or delay consideration, and other tactical questions. There is far less visible conflict in the bureaucracy than in Congress, but this pattern of conflict resolution within the institution is much the same, complete with conflict over shaping the issue, moving it along or "foot-dragging," and so forth. The bureaucracy, like Congress, operates within a complex web of political forces and must respond in some manner to the external (and frequently internal) pressures brought to bear on the administration of government programs.

Ordinarily, administrative agencies try to strike a manageable balance between what they *can* and *want* to do to further their own programmatic interests, and what they *must* do to insure their survival and prosperity, however that is defined. Achieving such a balance requires a willingness to compromise, a sure instinct in deciding when to seek a larger or smaller share of the pie, and an ability to "read" accurately political forecasts for both the long and short run. In addition to those internal skills, however, an agency must first have and maintain the two crucial foundations or sources of bureaucratic power mentioned earlier: political support, and expertise in the subject matter of its program responsibilities. Let us consider each of these in turn.

Foundations of Power: Political Support

Political support for an administrative agency in national politics has a number of key dimensions. First and perhaps foremost, Congress is a major potential source of support which must be cultivated carefully and continuously. In most instances, an agency derives its principal backing from one part of Congress—a committee or subcommittee with authority to oversee the agency's operations—rather than from Congress as a whole. Rare indeed is the agency with anything close to universal support in Congress, though it does happen—witness the long-term high status of the Federal Bureau of Investigation (FBI) under the directorship of J. Edgar Hoover, to the point that many inside and outside Washington felt that Hoover had more effective influence in Congress than did his nominal superior in the Justice Department, the attorney general. But that is an exceptional case; most agencies are faced with the task of continually generating and holding support from committees, subcommittees, and even individual members of Congress.

A second source of political support is the executive branch, meaning both presidential support and that of other administrators and agencies lodged formally in the executive hierarchy. Presidential influence can be decisive in determining success or failure, and an agency will do what it can to win presidential favor in both the short and long run. An important corollary of presidential backing is favorable reviews of agency budget requests by the Office of Management and Budget (OMB), which molds the executive-branch budget proposals submitted to Congress each year. OMB does not itself allocate funds to the agencies, but its support means that an agency can concentrate on persuading Congress—which does hold the purse strings—to back its programs financially, without having to expend a great deal of time, personnel, or political resources on first convincing OMB of their worth. The best position for an agency to be in is one where its programmatic responsibilities occupy a high-priority place on presidential policy agendas year in and year out,[8] but as suggested earlier, few agencies achieve this kind of enviable support. Far more common is a pattern of agencies and their programs having to compete for presidential favor and having to settle for a "win some, lose some" record.

Another means of acquiring executive-branch support is by allying with another agency or agencies in quest of common objectives. Such interagency alliances tend to be limited in scope and duration. Since most agencies are very protective of their program jurisdictions (for reasons we shall soon consider more fully), and since there is an element of risk in that a cooperating agency might also be a potential rival, most agencies enter rather carefully into alliances with others, even though they may share limited objectives. An example of such bureaucratic alliance is the periodic joining of forces by the Army, Navy, and Air Force in support of defense appropriations, even as each is contending with the others for a share of the fiscal pie. Another illustration is the shared response of the Army Corps of Engineers and the Bureau of Reclamation—long-time rivals for water project construction dollars—to President Carter's attempt to cut over thirty projects from the fiscal 1978 budget, most of which were under the jurisdiction of the Corps of Engineers. Though Reclamation's interests were not directly affected, the general proposition put forward by the president—that some water projects were not worth pursuing—raised the specter that at some future time the axe might fall on the Bureau of Reclamation as well. But these are occasional alliances, brought about by specific and passing needs, which usually do not outweigh more enduring differences among agencies. In sum, although cooperation with other agencies may indeed be a means of acquiring support, it has its limitations. The agencies with which cooperation would be most logical in terms of programmatic interest are the very ones with the greatest potential for conflict over jurisdictional responsibilities.

A third major source of support, which is carefully cultivated, is constituent or clientele groups that look to the agency for satisfaction of their policy demands. Such groups come under the heading of "interest groups," as that term is commonly used, and represent an organized expression of political opinion by a portion (usually a small portion) of the general adult population.[9] They tend to be groups affected directly by the agency's operations, and therefore they have a tangible stake in its programmatic output and impact. The political relationship which usually develops between an agency and such a group is one of reciprocity, where each has some political commodity from which the other can benefit. The agency's greatest strength is its expertise and the control it exercises over particular government programs that are of interest to the group. The group in turn has political resources which it makes available to the agency in return for agency attention to its needs and desires. The group may provide channels of communication to other influential individuals and groups in the political process, help the agency "sell" its program to Congress and the president, or aid the agency in anticipating changes in the political environment that would present problems or provide opportunities.[10] Examples of such agency–clientele group relationships include, among many others, the Pentagon and defense contractors, various entities in the Department of Agriculture and the tobacco industry, the federal Maritime Administration and the shipping industry, state commerce commissions and private business associations, and both state and federal Departments of Labor and the labor movement.

Administrative agencies often have more than one constituent group, creating both advantages and disadvantages. A principal advantage is that with multiple sources of support, an agency can operate more effectively in the political process without having to rely too heavily on any one source of assistance. A corresponding disadvantage stems from the fact that various clientele groups often have differing sets of interests, which move them to demand different things from an agency, or demand the same things but not in the same order of priority. Not infrequently, an agency faces a situation where satisfying one preference or set of preferences will inhibit or prevent its satisfying other preferences.

An agency must also deal with Congress or a specific committee as though it were a clientele group—a group like any other with demands and expectations that must be satisfied. An agency is well advised to consider congressional "clientele groups" as being among its most important, especially when confronted with conflicting sets of demands. It is unwise, in other words, to regularly disregard demands coming from Congress, even if this means making other (private) clientele groups unhappy with a given decision. As we shall see later in this chapter, however, agencies have some means at their disposal to avoid being caught, most of the time, in a "squeeze" between their congressional and private clientele groups.

In state politics, agencies are frequently tied even more closely to private interest groups. Where the governor has somewhat limited formal powers or informal influence, or where the state legislature is relatively passive or weak, support from interest groups is often the greatest source of strength for an administrative agency, and sometimes the only source. Even where the governor and the legislature are strong (as in New York, California, Illinois, and Michigan), the support of key interest groups can benefit an agency significantly. For example, the Illinois Agricultural Association (the state component of the American Farm Bureau Federation) is a vital source of political strength for the state Department of Agriculture, and in California farm organizations help sustain both the Department of Agriculture and the Department of Water Resources. In return, of course, the agencies are expected to advocate and defend the interests of their supporters (for example, water for California's farmers), and these relationships often become at least semipermanent.

One other aspect of agency-clientele relationships is quite important. As noted earlier, administrative organizations cherish their control over particular government programs and try to maintain effective direction of them. Sometimes, however, an agency may have to yield some control over its programs to outside influences—legislators, a private clientele group, or some other group—in return for continuing political support. If this yielding of control is temporary, an agency loses little and may gain a great deal in the long run. If, however, the yielding of control proves to be permanent, the agency is said to have undergone *co-optation,* a process whereby a set of outside interests acquires the ability to influence the agency's long-term policies. Co-optation can mean that *all* of the agency's substantive policies are subject to influence, not just those of most direct concern to the outside group or groups.

Numerous examples of co-optation may be cited. One of the best-known academic studies of this process is sociologist Philip Selznick's *TVA and the Grass Roots,*[11] which asserts that the Tennessee Valley Authority allowed the making of its agricultural development policies to be taken over by a coalition of entrenched, politically conservative interest groups already dominant in agricultural politics in the TVA region.[12] Another example of the phenomenon concerns the relationship that developed between some urban community-action groups and municipal administrations—"city hall"—in the late 1960s.[13] City government leaders occasionally succeeded in co-opting a group's leadership by giving them some of what they wanted, plus greater political visibility, in exchange for moderating other demands. This occurred especially in communities with well-entrenched local political organizations, such as Chicago, where community-action groups chose to settle for "half a loaf" rather than risk forfeiting all chance to have some impact on the way decisions were made and resources allocated in the city government system. As these examples demonstrate, co-optation can work both ways. TVA illustrates the traditional conception of a government agency's being co-opted by stronger nongovernmental groups, while the fate of the community-action groups shows how strong government structures are capable of co-opting nongovernmental groups. Either way, co-optation involves a surrender by a weaker entity to a stronger one of some ability to shape the course of the weaker entity's long-term activities.

Co-optation can and does lead to agency behavior that runs counter to the agency's apparent purposes and to general public expectations about its responsibilities. More to the point, an agency can end up serving a set of political interests other than those it was designed to serve or is generally thought to be serving. A recent example, though only one of many that could be cited, is the Bureau of Indian Affairs (BIA), which the American Indian Movement (AIM) has accused of working on behalf of everyone *except* Indians. AIM leaders have claimed that majority (non-Indian) interests in western states co-opted the BIA, causing it to respond to *their* political preferences and not to those of the Indian minority.

A fourth source of political support for an administrative agency is the general public. The potential weight of the unorganized public is great; if mobilized and concentrated on a particular issue, public opinion can tilt the political balance of power decisively. The problem for any political actor is to successfully mobilize the public, no easy task. Most Americans ordinarily pay scant attention to public issues until and unless the issues develop considerable salience or controversy.[14]

Yet the public's attention can be directed and its feelings made manifest with regard to a pending major policy decision. The public can, in some instances, force a decision to be made. Consider the role that broad public opinion played in the withdrawal of American troops from the battle zones in Vietnam (see Figure 3–1), in governmental decisions to mount a far more concerted effort than previously to combat environmental pollution, and in the multitude of reforms in the wake of Watergate. Without broad public demand and backing, these policy directions—which represented significant changes from earlier policies—could not have been proposed or sustained through the political process. The general public, in short, can provide a valuable political foundation to strengthen the hand of those in government who feel that a given policy should be adopted or scrapped. As numerous studies of public opinion have suggested, when the general public has strong feelings on a matter of importance to large numbers of people, the governmental response is usually not inconsistent with those feelings.[15] An agency supported by broad public opinion can generate political support for itself and its programs if it takes advantage of the opportunity.

An agency's overall task, in political terms, can best be understood as maintaining control of its programmatic responsibilities while simultaneously maintaining adequate support for its operations, without making any of its clientele groups overly unhappy with the way it is performing its functions. This is far from easy, and it is the exception rather than the rule when an agency succeeds on all fronts. More frequent is the pattern of agency adaptation and accommodation to particularly strong interests, from which political backing can be obtained in sufficient quantity to outweigh any costs incurred, in terms of diminished program control or dissatisfaction among weaker clientele groups.

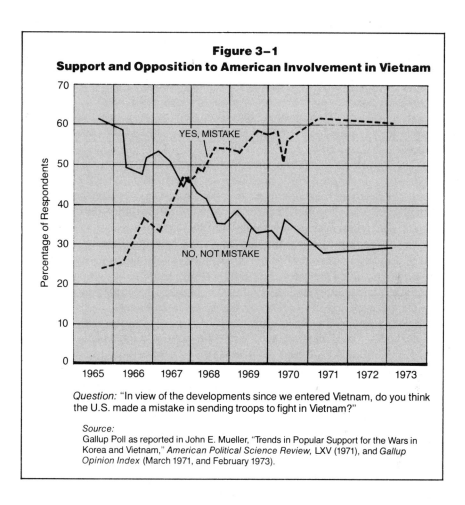

Figure 3-1
Support and Opposition to American Involvement in Vietnam

Question: "In view of the developments since we entered Vietnam, do you think the U.S. made a mistake in sending troops to fight in Vietnam?"

Source:
Gallup Poll as reported in John E. Mueller, "Trends in Popular Support for the Wars in Korea and Vietnam," *American Political Science Review,* LXV (1971), and *Gallup Opinion Index* (March 1971, and February 1973).

Foundations of Power: Bureaucratic Expertise

The other major foundation of bureaucratic power is the substantive expertise an agency can bring to bear on programs for which it is responsible. As society has become more complex and interdependent and technological advances have followed one another with astounding speed, people with "know-how"—the experts—have acquired increasing influence because of their specialized knowledge. Government is obviously subject to the same forces (particularly of technological change) as the rest of society, with the result that government experts now play a large and central role in numerous public policy decisions.

Political scientist Francis Rourke has suggested that the influence of experts rests on five major components, with a sixth lending credibility and prestige to expert performance.[16] The five principal components are (1) full-time attention by experts to a problem or subject-matter area, giving rise to both demand and opportunity for professionalism in public service; (2) specialization in the subject; (3) a monopoly on information in the subject area, which, if successfully maintained by only one staff of experts, makes them indispensable in any decision making involving "their" subject; (4) a pattern of increasing reliance on bureaucratic experts for technical advice; and (5) increasing control by experts of bureaucratic discretion.

The last three of these components deserve discussion. While a monopoly of information is desirable from a particular agency's point of view, it is rarely achieved in everyday practice. This is partly because no agency controls all governmental sources of information on any given subject, partly because government itself does not control all information sources in society, and partly because information—itself a source of power and influence—is the subject of intense interagency competition. Thus, where an expert staff has a monopoly on information relevant to making a given decision, its influence is greater. Conversely, influence can be more effectively contested where there is greater diversity of information sources.[17]

Reliance on expert advice, while on the increase, is not without limits; the influence of experts, therefore, is similarly constrained. Not every decision of an agency revolves around technical criteria or data. And even when an issue involves technical data, top-level administrators, for political or other reasons, may prefer a decision that is not the "best" according to technical criteria.[18] Thus expert advisors play a role in many agencies which, while important and influential, has its limitations.

As for experts' increasing control of bureaucratic discretion, there are two aspects worth noting. First, by exercising discretion, an expert maximizes the ability to decide just how vigorously or casually to implement public policies over which the agency has jurisdiction. Second, bureaucratic discretion enables agency experts to influence policy decisions by defining the decisional alternatives from which higher-level officials choose the course to be followed. To the extent responsible policy makers permit bureaucratic experts to define available alternatives, they strengthen the experts' influence, through what the experts choose to include and not include among the alternatives they present.[19]

Experts possess one more resource which has been useful in presenting a positive public image—their ability to employ the language as well as the tools of their respective trades, speaking in terms and concepts unfamiliar to most of us. This use of specialized language (some might say, jargon) has become a common phenomenon among experts in and out of government, posing problems for the layman who seeks to understand complex developments and issues. By using jargon, bureaucratic experts make it very difficult for others to challenge them on their own territory, so to speak; if we cannot fathom what it is they have proposed, how can we argue against it? This resource, moreover, has been greatly enhanced by the fact that, in countless cases, proposals put forward by experts have yielded very positive and beneficial results. As Rourke has noted, this combination of obscurity of means and clarity of results has helped consolidate the position, prestige, and influence of experts in government agencies.[20]

In recent years, however, the obscurity of means which previously was a source of strength for experts has contributed to growing public disenchantment with "big government," bureaucracy, and experts in general. With the increasing desire for broader public involvement in decision making (see chapter 2) has come greater unwillingness to "take the experts' word for it," and a more insistent demand that experts make clear to the general public just what it is they are doing, proposing, and advocating. In the long run, public reactions and attitudes may have more effect on the influence and power of government experts than any characteristic or action of the experts themselves.

The Politics of Organizational Structure

Another dimension of the political setting is the particular form of administrative organization. As noted briefly in chapter 1, structural arrangements can have political implications for administrative agencies. Here we shall take a closer look at the political meaning of structural arrangements, using as a principal illustration the Office of Economic Opportunity (OEO).

Organizational form can signify a number of things. First, a particular structure demonstrates commitment to some policy objectives and not to others. Establishment of OEO in the 1960s represented a policy commitment on the part of the Kennedy and Johnson administrations to combat poverty in the United States. That OEO was placed in the Executive Office of the President instead of, say, the Department of Health, Education, and Welfare was significant in that it demonstrated presidential commitment, not merely that of "the government" in a more ambiguous sense. However, it is not clear today whether Kennedy and Johnson were as comprehensively and consistently committed as some might have liked. There is some evidence suggesting that OEO's high-water mark was reached at its inception, and that it lost ground steadily in the late 1960s, particularly as hostilities in Southeast Asia absorbed more and more of President Johnson's attention. Congressional pressure to move operating programs out of OEO and into previously existing agencies also mounted during this period. Thus OEO may have been more of a symbolic than a real commitment, regardless of its institutional location.[21]

Second, a particular structure can signal adoption of a distinct policy direction by the government, either in a single policy area or more broadly in terms of general policy inclinations. OEO was an example of the former, even with the limitations noted. An example of the latter was reorganization of the federal Bureau of the Budget as the Office of Management and Budget (OMB) in 1970. This signified the emphasis President Nixon intended to place on improving and strengthening management processes in the executive branch, with OMB bearing primary responsibility for directing that effort. Management of national government programs had been one of Nixon's concerns in the 1968 presidential campaign, and this was organizational evidence that his concern had been genuine.

Third, a particular structure may serve to order political priorities, promoting some programs while relegating others to secondary status. The conflict over OEO demonstrates how well this is understood by those in Washington and by their respective clienteles. When President Nixon attempted in 1973 to break up OEO and redistribute its functions among traditional cabinet departments, the proposal was met by intense opposition. Various civil rights and antipoverty groups, together with a number of leading Democratic politicians (and some Republicans) felt the purposes served by OEO as it was then constituted would be shortchanged if it were reorganized as the president preferred. They feared that administrators who were not a part of the OEO staff and whose political ties were to other groups and interests might be hostile to the OEO constituency, comprised largely of the nonwhite poor. They achieved a stalemate with the Nixon administration, managing to prevent OEO's dissolution but not significant reductions in its funding and operations.[22] It is generally believed that the Nixon effort was in keeping with his attentiveness to the more conservative political constituency which had elected him president in 1968 and 1972, as well as being consistent with his own philosophy favoring a reduced government role in solving social and economic problems.

Fourth, a particular structure can provide greater access for some and less access for others to key decision makers in the government. We should recall in this connection comments made earlier about agency jurisdiction and how it relates to access and agency structure. Structure and jurisdiction are at least indirectly related, and while changes in jurisdiction may not necessarily be accompanied by a change in structure, any reformation of structure will almost inevitably mean some reallocation of program jurisdiction. Access and jurisdiction are also related. Clientele groups have meaningful access, at best, only to those administrators responsible for "their" programs. Changes in jurisdiction mean, at a minimum, that clienteles will need to reestablish lines of access, and such changes could well cause greater difficulties for these groups. Furthermore, clienteles normally much prefer to have all related programs clustered under one administrative roof, since that facilitates their having impact on the full range of programs. It is likely, also, that such an arrangement will be managed by administrators sympathetic to the programs for which they are responsible, whereas scattering the same programs among different agencies and administrators may result in more hostile treatment of both programs and clienteles. The programs may not be the *same* programs after restructuring, when all is said and done.

Our discussion has centered until now on the executive branch of the national government. However, these generalizations apply with equal force to other governments' executive branches, and to some other specific circumstances and issues in the politics of organization. Probably the clearest example that illustrates the same concepts in a different setting is the recurring struggle in cities and towns across the country over the form of local government structure to be adopted. This controversy has its roots in the late nineteenth and early twentieth centuries, when growing concentrations of European immigrants appeared in America's larger cities as well as some smaller ones, accompanied by more—and more powerful—political party organizations and their "bosses."

The effort to reform American municipal government, according to rhetoric of the time, was designed to bring about "economy and efficiency" in government, "take the politics out of local government," and promote government "in the interest of the whole community." Municipal reform usually involved (and still involves) one or more of the following structural arrangements: (1) the method of selecting the chief executive—whether to have a popularly elected mayor or a city manager chosen by and responsible to the city council; (2) the extent of the chief executive's powers, though this usually meant whether the mayor in particular was formally strong or weak;[23] (3) whether municipal elections were to have candidates selected by political parties or on a nonpartisan basis; and (4) whether members of the city council were to be selected to represent specific areas of the city (that is, by wards) or selected at-large.[24]

Political rhetoric aside, decisions about these fundamental arrangements carried with them major implications for the distribution of local political power. Citywide minorities, for example, had little chance of winning representation in at-large council elections, but a better chance in ward elections (provided ward boundaries were drawn up to reflect, rather than fragment, their population concentrations). Similarly, there were numerous instances where a chief executive elected under the strong mayor form was almost certain to be more favorable to ethnic or minority concerns in local politics than one chosen under a weak mayor or city manager form, because ethnic voters constituted the political majority in many such cities.

Leading proponents of structural reform in the late nineteenth century were almost entirely middle class and above, while the most vocal opponents were lower middle class and below. Historian Melvin

Holli has described the urban structural reform movement as "built upon a narrow middle and patrician class base and a business concept of social responsibility," and characterized by "zeal for efficiency and economy." The structural reformers also, according to Holli, "blamed the immigrant for the city's shortcomings," and devoted considerable effort to "exterminating lower-class vices, which they saw as the underlying causes of municipal problems."[25] Given this socioeconomic polarization, it seems clear that respective group preferences for or against structural reform did not happen by mere chance, but arose out of perceived group self-interest.

In sum, there are gainers and losers in this facet of politics as in all others. Organizational arrangements in many different settings reflect "values, conflicts, and competing forces . . . ."[26] They are, therefore, anything but neutral.

Bureaucrats as Politicians: Subsystem Politics in America

In this section we shall see how bureaucrats manage their political alliances, with regular collaboration often leading to establishment of semipermanent ties. These political roles are relevant to agency efforts to secure needed political support from interested clientele groups and various committees, subcommittees, and individual members of Congress.

We should begin by considering certain important parallels between the national government bureaucracy and Congress.[27] They have three features in common which are important in this context. First, within both institutions there is a well-established pattern of division of labor, that is, dividing the work to be done among numerous smaller, specialized units. In Congress this means the committees and subcommittees of each chamber; in the bureaucracy it refers to the multitude of bureaus, staffs, branches, and divisions that comprise larger executive agencies. Second, the divisions within both Congress and the bureaucracy are organized primarily according to function, dealing with a general area of policy concern such as housing, education, or defense. Third, in both institutions the specialized nature of these smaller units is the principal source of their influence in the policy-making process.

It is a pervasive rule of Washington political life that, all other things being equal, larger institutions defer to (that is, respect and follow) the judgments of their smaller, more specialized units. This pattern of regularized deference to smaller units means that in the great majority of cases these units tend to be focal points of important decision making. In Congress, though formal action by the full House and Senate is required for enactment of legislation, the proposals reported out of committees usually form the core of bills which eventually reach passage. Amendment of committee proposals is possible, but the initial form of legislation carries some weight, and key committee and subcommittee members are often influential throughout the entire process of deliberation in the full chamber.[28] In the bureaucracy specialized personnel (the experts described earlier) wield considerable influence in the formulation of proposals which make their way up the formal hierarchical ladder (and make their way to Congress as well), and in daily processes of program implementation.

In short, it is misleading to assume that influence is concentrated at the top of formal organizational structures in either Congress or the bureaucracy. The fine details of lawmaking, as well as of legislative oversight of administration, are the responsibility of subject-matter committees and subcommittees of Congress, each assigned jurisdiction over particular administrative agencies and their programs. Only infrequently do such matters engage the attention of the full House or Senate. Similarly, the "nuts and bolts" of administration normally are concentrated in the lower levels of organizations, not at, or even very near, the top. Thus, in the broad picture of policy making in Washington, there is a high degree of fragmentation, with many small centers of influence operating in their respective areas of expertise.

We have seen previously that bureaucratic expertise is a source of bureaucratic power. Members of Congress also seek to become specialized, for two reasons. First, they are encouraged to do so on the grounds that this is the best route to influence in Congress, and second, they quickly recognize that by becoming influential they can do more for their voters back home. For sound political reasons, most seek to join congressional committees that have jurisdiction over areas of public policy affecting their electoral constituencies. A representative from rural Kansas, for example, is likely to apply for membership on the House Agriculture Committee, hoping also to be on its subcommittee dealing with subsidies for wheat farmers, wheat export policies, and so on. A representative from a black and poor section of a large city would be likely to seek assignment to the Banking, Financing, and Urban Affairs Committee or perhaps the Education and Labor Committee—bodies that deal directly with problems of urban constituents. A senator from a state with a major coastal or inland port or a rail transportation center would cherish a position on the Interstate and Foreign Commerce Committee. And so it goes, all through Congress.

Not everyone gets his or her first choice of assignment, obviously. But in pursuit of their own electoral fortunes and policy objectives, members of Congress are attracted to those committee assignments in which they can have the most impact in policy areas of interest to them personally, and where they can maximize their political influence in support of constituency interests that could be decisive in their reelection bids.[29] This leads naturally to their having increasing contact with others interested in the same policy areas: administrators in agencies with jurisdiction over relevant programs; interest groups which, even more than legislators or bureaucrats, have specialized interests as the focal point of their existence and activities; and other members of Congress who have an interest in the same general area(s) of public policy.

What results from this complex of shared specialized interests, or what we might call *specialization in common,* is the potential for pooling political resources by individuals and small groups in different parts of the policy-making process in order to achieve common purposes. Hundreds of quiet, informal alliances have grown up in this manner,[30] with the term "policy subsystem"—or simply, "subsystem"—being used to describe them.

What is a *subsystem?* In general usage, the term refers to "a structure dependent upon a larger political entity but one that functions with a high degree of autonomy."[31] We define it here as any political alliance uniting some members of an administrative agency, a congressional committee or subcommittee, and an interest group with shared values and preferences in the same substantive area of public policy making. Subsystems are informal alliances or coalitions which link individuals in different parts of the formal policy structure. Their members usually have some influence in the policy-making process, due in part to their formal or official positions—bureau chief, committee or subcommittee chairman, or member. The essential strength of a subsystem, however, is its ability to combine the benefits of bureaucratic expertise, congressional leverage, and interest group capabilities in organizing and communicating to the government the opinions of those most concerned with a particular public issue. All subsystems have that potential to some extent; some, of course, are far more powerful than others.

One example of a very influential subsystem in Washington is the so-called military-industrial complex, composed at a minimum of civilian and military personnel in the Pentagon bureaucracy, key members of the House and Senate Armed Services Committees and each chamber's Appropriations subcommittee on armed services, and major government contractors for military hardware. The presence in this subsystem of large industries supplying military equipment expands the number of affiliated legislators significantly. By being located in New York state, for example, Grumman Aircraft can influence the votes of New York's congressional delegation, especially its two senators and the representatives from the congressional districts in which Grumman's plants are located; so also with Boeing in Washington state, McDonnell-Douglas in Missouri, and Lockheed in Georgia. Thus members of key congressional committees are not the only legislators who might belong to a subsystem; others may also belong due to their constituency interests.

Another good example is the highway subsystem, in which members of the House Public Works and Transportation Committee (among others), officials of the Bureau of Public Roads, and powerful interest groups such as auto manufacturers, auto workers' unions, tire companies and their unions, road contractors and their unions, and oil companies and their unions (plus members of Congress from their states) have a common interest in maintaining, if not expanding, automobile and highway usage. States represented include, among others, Michigan, Missouri, California, Texas, and Oklahoma; some key legislators come from those states. Little wonder that Congress has given ground so reluctantly on expansion of mass transit funding, or that it has defended using the Highway Trust Fund to pay only for new roads.

Still another example is the tobacco subsystem, which for years resisted all efforts to limit or regulate the sale of cigarettes and other tobacco products. They were successful mainly because tobacco is largely a southern crop, and congressional committee chairmen (including, notably, the chairman of the House Agriculture Committee) tended to be disproportionately from the South because of the seniority system. Supporting them were bureaucrats in the Agriculture and Commerce Departments. It was politically risky, if not foolish, for a member of Congress to challenge the united front of southern committee chairmen in what was, until the mid-1960s, a losing fight against tobacco. Significantly, when the Congress-based tobacco subsystem *was* successfully challenged, it was by another subsystem with its principal strength elsewhere—in the U.S. Public Health Service of the Department of Health, Education, and Welfare, and the Federal Trade Commission.[32]

Subsystem activity tends to be behind the scenes. Policy is made in a spirit of friendly, quiet cooperation among various interested and influential people, and many of their decisions turn out to be the key ones. Bureaucrats derive considerable benefit from such an arrangement because they can usually count on adequate political support from both within government (Congress) and without (interest groups). The three-sided relationship allows any one component of the subsystem to activate their joint effort toward common objectives with the willing cooperation of the others. Unless challenged from outside—by other subsystems, adverse publicity, or perhaps the president—a subsystem may well be able largely to dominate a policy-making area. It is rare, admittedly, that even a strong subsystem can ignore the possibility of rivals emerging and making it more difficult to operate. The cigarette controversy (over requiring a health warning on cigarette packages) is one illustration of that generalization; imposition of automobile exhaust emission controls over the objections of auto manufacturers is another. Under routine circumstances, however, subsystems—including their administrative participants—can enjoy decisive influence in the policy-making process.

The influence of similar informal alliances is often less extensive in state and local policy making than in national politics. There are several reasons for this. First, in many state legislatures individual committees do not have the same kind of independent standing or jurisdictional control over policy areas which congressional committees possess. Policy making is much more centralized in the hands of legislative leaders, making far less productive any interest group relationship with an individual committee. Second, in many states and localities the policy-making process is dominated by less diverse groups than is the case nationally and as a consequence lacks the intense competitiveness over access and influence characteristic of Washington politics. The necessity to develop close working relations with an individual committee or agency is therefore not as great. Third, especially in many local governments, the overall policy-making process is much more informal than at the national level. For many interest groups, particularly stronger ones, there is fairly regular opportunity for consultation on their policy preferences, and their influence is often felt throughout the whole of local government, not in just one part of it. Thus, though some elements of what we have called subsystem politics in national government also can be found in state and local governments, the general patterns identifiable in the national policy process do not operate to the same extent elsewhere.[33]

Bureaucratic Power and Political Accountability: More Questions than Answers

Having discussed the political context of bureaucratic power, key sources of that power, and the informal alliances through which much of that power is exercised, it is necessary now to consider to what extent bureaucracy is or can be made accountable for what it does or fails to do. It was suggested in chapter 1 that political accountability of the bureaucracy is enforced through multiple channels, both legislative and executive. As we have seen, political interests in the legislature and in the executive branch are frequently in conflict with one another, making it difficult to enforce accountability with consistency or effectiveness. The question is made more complex by the fact that most bureaucracies operate under authority delegated by both the chief executive and the legislative branch, and with considerable discretion to make independent choices, as a matter of law. The difficulty is further compounded by the hybrid systems of personnel management found in different parts of the executive hierarchy in the national government and in many states and localities. Frequently, top-echelon executives owe their positions to appointment through political channels, but the bulk of their subordinates are hired and usually retained through job-competence-related merit procedures, which some say have produced more job security for public employees than is healthy for the public service. In state and local government the mix of "political" and "merit" employees in a bureaucracy varies widely, and the presence of public employee unions raises other issues of bureaucratic accountability.

Another factor, referred to earlier, is the inability of top executives to command absolute responsiveness to their leadership from administrative subordinates. A substantial portion of the work of top executives is devoted to overseeing and monitoring activities of their underlings in an effort to bring about as much congruence as possible between executive directives and work actually done.[34] The essential point is that the bureaucracy, like the legislature, is far from a unified entity, even speaking in hierarchical (vertical organizational) terms, and that as long as this is the case, the task of holding bureaucracy accountable for what it does assumes formidable proportions.

The term *accountability* itself poses some problems. It can mean different things to different people. At a minimum, it suggests that bureaucracy, or any governmental entity, functions as part of a larger political system, not independent of it, and as a result must be subject to some controls that cause it to give a general accounting of and for its actions. The most it might mean is that there should be an accounting of each and every action taken by an administrator, with authoritative approval given or withheld, and adjustments in future behavior made accordingly. The latter, as an ideal type, seems to be what some mean by "accountability," but, as a practical matter, how much accountability we can realistically expect and strive for is far from a settled question.

Accountability implies several things. First, it implies that a political entity (in this case, the bureaucracy) is not beyond control of other entities in a checks-and-balances system or, ultimately, beyond reach of the consent of the governed. Second, it implies that to the extent such an entity exercises delegated authority and discretion in decision making, as our bureaucracy certainly does, it also has some responsibility to adhere to the broad will of the governed, however that will has been expressed. This also assumes it is possible to define the public will,[35] and to define the point at which accountability has been achieved and maintained. While in theory it may be possible to define these concepts and circumstances, in practice it is difficult to do so with certainty or finality. One approach is to interpret election results as representing the will of the majority, and to define bureaucratic accountability as accountability to the chief executive (president, governor, mayor), with his or her voice being dominant in setting policy directions and the standards by which subsequent administrative behavior will be judged. Opponents of a given chief executive or of executive power in general would resist such definition, however, looking instead to legislatures and sometimes to the judiciary to lay out broad guidelines for measuring bureaucratic accountability. Political conflict over criteria of accountability insures some fragmenting of the lines of accountability and less than complete adherence to whatever standards one may have.

In sum, it is not simply a matter of bureaucracy either being or not being "accountable." Rather, bureaucracy and all other institutions of government can only be "accountable *to*" officials or institutions outside themselves. Also, "the bureaucracy" cannot be viewed whole; its many subparts have institutional bases, lives, and priorities of their own. All these factors act as constraints on the political accountability of bureaucratic power.

Is it impossible, then, to speak in practical terms of accountability? No, it is not. Allowing for limitations such as those just outlined, it is possible not only to prescribe in theory but to describe in fact some forms and aspects of accountability that characterize political relationships between bureaucracy and other parts of the American polity.

First, both the president and Congress have some instruments of control at their disposal to bring to bear on bureaucratic behavior (governors, local executives, and state and local legislatures generally have parallel but less extensive powers over their respective bureaucracies). The president's arsenal includes (1) powers of appointment and dismissal which, although carefully restricted to the very top positions, give the president the ability to staff key leadership positions in the executive branch; (2) considerable, even crucial, initiative in lawmaking, which helps shape the legislative environment surrounding bureaucratic implementation of congressional enactments (this includes congressional delegation of authority to the president to formulate rules and regulations under which the bureaucracy functions); (3) the Executive Office of the President (EXOP), through which the president can make known his preferences and intentions to the bureaucracy, directly and indirectly; (4) specific entities of EXOP, notably the White House Office and the Office of Management and Budget, which carry the full prestige of the presidency when they interact with the bureaucracy and, in the case of OMB, can exert financial leverage that can be persuasive; (5) access to organs of the mass media, through which the president can generate favorable or unfavorable publicity; and (6) power to initiate bureaucratic restructuring, a course of action extremely unwelcome to most agencies,[36] though in the past it has been used sparingly. A shrewd president can make use of these instruments to bring about considerable responsiveness to his leadership, though the process requires a considerable expenditure of his political capital.

Congress also has some tools at its disposal with which to conduct legislative oversight of administration.[37] They include (1) appropriations power—the classic "power of the purse"—and the implied (sometimes real) threat that can represent to an agency's fiscal well-being; (2) power to conduct legislative postaudits of executive agency spending through the General Accounting Office (GAO) headed by the comptroller-general, which operates under the direction of Congress; (3) hearings before congressional committees in which bureaucrats may have to answer very specifically for their actions (most notably during budget hearings before appropriations committees and subcommittees); and (4) occasional devices such as senatorial confirmation of presidential appointees and special investigating committees such as the Senate Select Committee on Presidential Campaign Activities (more commonly known as the Senate Watergate Committee). These are not perfect control instruments, but they do afford Congress many opportunities to look into bureaucratic activities and keep some measure of generalized rein on the administrative apparatus.

Bureaucrats and bureaucracies are also held to account by the clientele groups they serve, perhaps more effectively than by either the president or Congress. An administrative agency is politically obligated to its allies in a subsystem, resulting in a pattern of mutually reinforcing accountability. But this is a highly noncentralized arrangement; the fact that an agency is held to account within its own subsystem is no guarantee that either the agency or subsystem is accountable in any meaningful way to anyone outside of it. In fact, some observers believe just the opposite, that this form of accountability is one of the least effective from the standpoint of the political system at large.[38] They hold that this pattern of exercising power is self-perpetuating to the point that political costs would be excessive for anyone, including the president, who sought to lessen subsystem influence on policy making. In this view, accountability to any but the most narrow constituencies is unlikely, thus fostering a growing alienation from the governmental process on the part of all those not adequately represented through subsystem politics. To the extent this view is accurate, it suggests a limited form of accountability based on previous political commitments, and exercise of power through very narrow political channels.

Bureaucracies are legally accountable to the federal courts for their observance of individual rights and liberties, whether in their investigative capacities (particularly pertinent in the case of regulatory agencies) or simply in the course of their routine activities. In this respect they differ hardly at all from the president and Congress, in that the courts have the ultimate say in defining acceptable legal boundaries of governmental behavior. It is perhaps symptomatic of the growth in the federal bureaucracy and in its impact on our national life that the most rapidly expanding area of federal court litigation has been in administrative law— cases arising out of administrative rules and regulations and their application to individuals, groups, and public and private enterprises of numerous types.

Bureaucratic agencies are also held to account by competing interest groups, the mass media, and the major political parties. Interest groups competing with agencies for political advantage, either individually or as part of rival subsystems, seek to monitor actions of bureaus and bureaucrats for reasons of self-interest, but in doing so they make it harder for activities and programs to be conducted out of public view. The news media's interest in bureaucratic activity is founded on a powerful ethic of

American journalism: that the press, acting in an adversary relationship to public officials, serves as a "watchdog" over what the government does. In particular, the investigatory potential of the news media makes bureaucracies wary. Part of an agency's political strength is good public relations, and adverse publicity resulting from a media investigation—even if unwarranted and even if successfully counteracted—can damage an agency's political standing. Thus the mere possibility of such an inquiry is enough to prompt most agencies to exercise some caution.

As for political parties, their organizational interest in winning elections overlaps numerous policy areas and brings them into contact with agencies responsible for administering those areas. Since agency actions can have a direct impact on the interests of the parties' various constituent groups, party officials have their own stake in trying to secure policies favorable to those groups. The impact of party leaders seems to be greater at state and local levels than at the national level, partly because state and local bureaucratic decision making is often more openly politicized and thus more susceptible to frankly political pressures, and partly because state and local party organizations are stronger than national party committees. But even in the national bureaucracy it is not uncommon for the views of party officials to be given some weight in agency deliberations. Thus, while political parties are not a major constraint on bureaucratic activity or a key means of insuring accountability, they do play their part.

Finally, there is some measure of bureaucratic accountability to the public. Although the general populace rarely has direct access to, or control over, a given bureaucratic entity, a widespread public outcry over bureaucrats' actions can have an effect. This ordinarily requires public pressure on other organs of government to get them to tighten the reins on an agency. Such pressure must be sustained over a sufficient period of time and with sufficient intensity to overcome political resistance from the agency and its supporters, but it can be done.

In sum, political accountability is a product of politics, and it must be achieved and maintained through the political process. An agency will be accountable to those with the power to make it so. Perhaps this fact, by itself, does much to explain why accountability is uneven and incomplete, yet is still present at many points in the political system.

SUMMARY

Bureaucratic power is exercised in the context of widely dispersed political power. Neither the legislature nor the chief executive has a power base that is sufficiently unified to permit decisive control over the bureaucracy. Administrative agencies are keenly interested in building political power bases of their own, and they seek to acquire program jurisdictions that bring with them constituency support for their activities.

Also, these agencies frequently are centers of political conflict, and must seek to maintain themselves through adaptation to pressures that are placed on them. How well they succeed can be important in determining their long-term well-being.

Bureaucratic agencies have two major foundations of power: (1) adequate political support, and (2) expertise in the programs they administer. Sources of political support include key legislative committees and sub-committees, chief executives and their staffs, other executive agencies (especially those directly under the chief executive), clientele groups who follow agency affairs because of their own interest in the same program areas, and the general public, which can occasionally be mobilized on behalf of particular agency objectives. The political impact of bureaucratic expertise stems from full-time attention to a specialized subject-matter area, a monopoly or near-monopoly on relevant information, a pattern of reliance on experts for technical advice, and experts' growing control of bureaucratic discretion. The experts' prestige has also helped consolidate the influence they wield in the government.

Organizational structure has political significance in a number of respects: (1) it demonstrates commitment, whether symbolic or substantive, to particular policy objectives; (2) it can signal adoption of specific policy directions; (3) it serves to order political priorities by emphasizing some programs over others; and (4) it can provide different degrees of access to decision makers—greater for some groups and interests, less for others. The OEO experience demonstrates the importance of organizational structure, including limitations on that importance. The politics of organization is also significant in settings other than executive-branch arrangements. A leading example is recurring conflict over the form of local government structures, a political struggle that has gone on intermittently in many cities and towns since the late nineteenth century.

Subsystem politics in America is built around coalitions which bring together interest group representatives and government officials with a common interest and shared preferences in a policy area. A subsystem ordinarily includes a congressional committee or subcommittee member, a representative of an interest group, and a bureaucrat from the responsible administrative agency; more than one of each (and others as well) may be a part of the subsystem. Because both Congress and the bureaucracy generally divide work among subunits, whose expertise they respect, quiet, informal alliances of specialists (subsystems) often dominate their respective policy areas. Bureaucrats contribute expertise to their subsystems and receive in return an opportunity to share control of a policy area. Similar patterns of political collaboration exist in state and local politics, but usually not in precisely this form nor to the same extent.

Promoting political accountability of bureaucratic power is not an easy task. Because the bureaucracy operates under delegated executive and legislative authority, tight controls from either are difficult to impose, and tight controls from both would be likely to conflict. "Accountability" generally suggests that bureaucracy is or should be answerable in a broad sense to other institutions and to the public for what it does, though it is difficult to put into practice because of the noncentralized nature of both government and bureaucracy. The president and Congress (and their state and local counterparts) each have methods of influencing bureaucratic behavior which, while effective to some degree, require continuing effort and vigilance. Bureaucracies are also accountable to their clientele groups, although it has been argued that this kind of bureaucratic accountability actually reduces accountability to the larger political system. Other interest groups, the news media, and political party organizations— each for its own reasons—also seek to hold bureaucratic agencies accountable by monitoring agency activities. The news media, in particular, have the ability to uncover and publicize information adverse to agency political interests. In addition, bureaucratic agencies have some accountability to the federal courts, in that their actions are limited broadly by legal guidelines laid down in judicial decisions. Finally, the general public can be mobilized either in support of or opposition to actions taken in the administrative process. All these instruments of accountability have some impact on bureaucratic behavior, but none is perfect. Agencies will be accountable to those with the power to make them so.

NOTES

1. Norton E. Long, "Power and Administration," *Public Administration Review,* 9 (Autumn 1949), 257–264, at p. 258.
2. Ibid., pp. 258–259.
3. Ibid., p. 259.
4. Ibid.
5. Matthew Holden, "'Imperialism' in Bureaucracy," *American Political Science Review,* 60 (December 1966), 943–951, at p. 951 (emphasis added).
6. While agencies usually lack dominant influence in settling questions of program jurisdiction, what influence they do have is ordinarily used to acquire jurisdiction that brings with it maximum political support.
7. Sometimes they are satisfied simply to "cut their losses"; that is, to lose as little as possible if that is the best they can do.
8. The FBI fit this description for close to fifty years.
9. For an introduction to the theoretical roles and political activities of interest groups in American politics, see David B. Truman, *The Governmental Process* (New York: Alfred A. Knopf, 1951); V. O. Key, Jr., *Politics, Parties, and Pressure Groups,* 5th ed. (New York: Thomas Y. Crowell, 1964), especially chapters 2 through 6; Lester W. Milbrath, *The Washington Lobbyists* (Chicago: Rand McNally, 1963); and L. Harmon Zeigler and G. Wayne Peak, *Interest Groups in American Society,* 2nd ed. (Englewood Cliffs, N.J.: Prentice-Hall, 1972).

10. It should be noted that an agency, especially a well-established and respected one, may perform these same sorts of functions on behalf of a clientele group or groups.

11. Berkeley and Los Angeles: University of California Press, 1949.

12. Selznick's study concentrated, in the words of the subtitle, on the "sociology of formal organization." He has been criticized in at least one later study for ignoring considerations of politics. See O. Ruth McQuown, "From National Agency to Regional Institution: A Study of TVA in the Political Process" (unpublished Ph.D. dissertation, University of Florida, Gainesville, 1961).

13. See James L. Sundquist, with the collaboration of David W. Davis, *Making Federalism Work: A Study of Program Coordination at the Community Level* (Washington, D.C.: The Brookings Institution, 1969).

14. See, among others, V. O. Key, Jr., *Public Opinion and American Democracy* (New York: Alfred A. Knopf, 1961); and Alan D. Monroe, *Public Opinion in America* (New York: Dodd, Mead, 1975).

15. See, for example, Warren Miller and Donald E. Stokes, "Constituency Influence in Congress," *American Political Science Review*, 57 (1963), 45–56; and Monroe, *Public Opinion in America*.

16. Francis E. Rourke, *Bureaucracy, Politics, and Public Policy*, 2nd ed. (Boston: Little, Brown, 1976).

17. See Anthony Downs, *Inside Bureaucracy* (Boston: Little, Brown, 1967), chapter 10, especially pp. 118–127; and Martin Landau, "Redundancy, Rationality, and the Problem of Duplication and Overlap," *Public Administration Review*, 29 (July/August 1969), 346–358.

18. See chapter 7 for elaboration of this point.

19. Graham Allison, in *Essence of Decision: Explaining the Cuban Missile Crisis* (Boston: Little, Brown, 1971), describes in detail John F. Kennedy's reliance on the Air Force and the Central Intelligence Agency (CIA) for intelligence information necessary in deciding how to respond to the presence of Soviet offensive missiles in Cuba in late 1962.

20. Rourke, *Bureaucracy, Politics, and Public Policy*, p. 84.

21. See John C. Donovan, *The Politics of Poverty*, 2nd ed. (New York and Indianapolis: Bobbs-Merrill, 1973), chapter 9. For another perspective on the war on poverty, see Daniel P. Moynihan, *Maximum Feasible Misunderstanding* (New York: The Free Press, 1969).

22. The effort merely to keep OEO in existence subsequently failed. Under Gerald Ford the agency was finally abolished and replaced by the Community Services Administration, a more traditional bureaucratic entity.

23. It is sometimes difficult to assess a mayor's strengths. For example, judging strictly by a reading of *formal* powers, one of the weaker mayors among America's big-city chief executives was Richard J. Daley of Chicago—one of the most powerful, in reality, for over twenty years locally, in the state of Illinois, and nationally, until his death in late 1976.

24. Robert L. Lineberry and Ira Sharkansky, *Urban Politics and Public Policy*, 2nd ed. (New York: Harper & Row, 1974), pp. 61–67.

25. Melvin G. Holli, "Varieties of Urban Reform," in Alexander B. Callow, Jr., ed., *American Urban History*, 2nd ed. (New York: Oxford University Press, 1973); the passages quoted appear on pp. 253–254. The selection appeared origi-

nally in Holli's *Reform in Detroit: Hazen S. Pingree and Urban Politics* (New York: Oxford University Press, 1969).

26. Harold Seidman, *Politics, Position, and Power: The Dynamics of Federal Organization,* 2nd ed. (New York: Oxford University Press, 1975), p. 14.

27. These parallels also exist at the state level, but usually to a lesser extent, and among some larger units of general local government (cities, counties, and townships). The pattern described is most pronounced in Washington politics, however.

28. The influence of committees and their members in the full chamber varies considerably, depending in large part on certain factors within the committees themselves. Richard Fenno describes and analyzes one powerful committee in "The House Appropriations Committee as a Political System: The Problem of Integration," *American Political Science Review,* 56 (June 1962), 310–324. An expanded study of the same committee is Fenno's *The Power of the Purse: Appropriations Politics in Congress* (Boston: Little, Brown, 1966).

29. Note that this implies *selective* attention to constituency interests, often focusing on objectives and preferences of influential friends and allies before—or at the expense of—objectives and preferences of others less powerful who live in the same constituency.

30. See Douglass Cater, *Power in Washington* (New York: Random House, 1964).

31. A. Lee Fritschler, *Smoking and Politics: Policy Making and the Federal Bureaucracy,* 2nd ed. (Englewood Cliffs, N.J.: Prentice-Hall, 1975), p. 4. The growing literature on subsystem politics, in addition to Fritschler's book, includes Ernest S. Griffith, *The Impasse of Democracy* (New York: Harrison-Hilton Books, 1939), and *Congress: Its Contemporary Role* (New York: New York University Press, 1961); Arthur Maass, *Muddy Waters: The Army Engineers and the Nation's Rivers* (Cambridge: Harvard University Press, 1951); J. Leiper Freeman, *The Political Process* (New York: Random House, 1965); and Emmette S. Redford, "A Case Analysis of Congressional Activity: Civil Aviation, 1957–58," *The Journal of Politics,* 22 (May 1960), 228–258, and *Democracy in the Administrative State* (New York: Oxford University Press, 1969), especially chapter 4.

32. Fritschler, *Smoking and Politics: Policy Making and the Federal Bureaucracy,* is an excellent case study of subsystem politics involving the cigarette-health controversy.

33. See chapter 5 for a discussion of how parallel functional interests among national, state, and local bureaucracies operate to influence policy in intergovernmental relations.

34. See Herbert Kaufman, with the collaboration of Michael Couzens, *Administrative Feedback: Monitoring Subordinates' Behavior* (Washington, D.C.: The Brookings Institution, 1973).

35. See Glendon Schubert, *The Public Interest* (Glencoe, Ill.: The Free Press, 1960).

36. See the comments earlier in this chapter regarding structure, jurisdiction, and clientele politics.

37. See Joseph P. Harris, *Congressional Control of Administration* (Washington, D.C.: The Brookings Institution, 1964).

38. For an articulate statement of the view that interest groups and their

allies dominate politics and policy making to the detriment of the larger political process, see Theodore J. Lowi, *The End of Liberalism: Ideology, Policy, and the Crisis of Public Authority* (New York: W. W. Norton, 1969).

SUGGESTED READINGS

Cater, Douglass. *Power in Washington*. New York: Random House, 1964.

Freeman, J. Leiper. *The Political Process*. New York: Random House, 1965.

Harris, Joseph P. *Congressional Control of Administration*. Washington, D.C.: The Brookings Institution, 1964.

Holden, Matthew. "'Imperialism' in Bureaucracy." *American Political Science Review*, 60 (December 1966), 943–951.

Kaufman, Herbert, with the collaboration of Michael Couzens. *Administrative Feedback: Monitoring Subordinates' Behavior*. Washington, D.C.: The Brookings Institution, 1973.

Long, Norton E. "Power and Administration." *Public Administration Review*, 9 (Autumn 1949), 257–264.

Miller, Warren, and Donald E. Stokes. "Constituency Influence in Congress." *American Political Science Review*, 57 (1963), 45–56.

Seidman, Harold. *Politics, Position, and Power: The Dynamics of Federal Organization*, 2nd ed. New York: Oxford University Press, 1975.

Selznick, Philip. *TVA and the Grass Roots: A Study in the Sociology of Formal Organization*. Berkeley and Los Angeles: University of California Press, 1949.

Truman, David B. *The Governmental Process*. New York: Alfred A. Knopf, 1951.

Zeigler, L. Harmon, and G. Wayne Peak. *Interest Groups in American Society*, 2nd ed. Englewood Cliffs, N.J.: Prentice-Hall, 1972.

CHAPTER 4
Chief Executives and Bureaucratic Leadership

American chief executives—presidents, governors, mayors, city managers, and county executives—stand apart from the executive-branch agencies they are said to lead. Unlike most modern bureaucrats, these leaders and their immediate subordinates obtain their positions through elections or are answerable directly to elected officials; presidents, governors, mayors, and county executives are in the first category, while their principal appointed assistants, cabinet secretaries and undersecretaries, and city managers fall into the second. These officials are responsible in the eyes of most of the public for the operations of the bureaucracies which comprise their respective executive branches, and historically they have taken much of the "heat" for bureaucratic failure. At the same time, however, they are not really a part of their bureaucratic structures, which are highly fragmented according to function and operate with a good deal of autonomy (see chapter 3) and which depend on chief executives for political support to only a limited extent.

Yet chief executives clearly are expected to provide the necessary leadership for the management of government agencies and programs. Certainly in the formulation of broad policy directions such leadership has been evident in national and state governments; in the past two decades presidential and gubernatorial policy initiatives have been commonplace and have come to be regarded as marking the "opening round" of policy deliberations on many issues. The influence of chief executives in the legislative process is considerable, especially that of the president, and they increasingly exercise powers delegated to them by their legislatures (sometimes even without asking for such grants of authority). Similarly, they are perceived by the public as the leaders with the greatest ability to activate the decision-making machinery and to deal effectively with difficult situations. The simple fact that they are more widely recognized by the public than other officials contributes to these perceptions.[1] Finally, there is little doubt chief executives enjoy superior access to the mass media, which enables them to advance their own political fortunes while simultaneously reinforcing the impression of chief executive power, prestige, and influence.

The ability of chief executives to significantly influence their bureaucracies, however, may bear little relationship to how much media coverage they receive or how popular they are generally with the electorate. Where the chief executive controls all or most of the key mechanisms of governmental and political party power—such as party nominations for office, patronage in government hiring, and awarding of government contracts—we can expect to find relatively responsive bureaucracies. Examples of such chief executives are Governor Huey Long of Louisiana during the 1930s, and the late Mayor Richard J. Daley of Chicago.[2] The degree of chief executive control over the bureaucracy may vary with the extent of these powers—comparisons among state governors are revealing in this respect[3]—but there are other factors involved as well.

Chief executives' control over the bureaucracy is frequently challenged by the legislative branch and others (such as opposition party spokesmen) who seek some voice in agency decisions. More importantly, in most instances their control is effectively challenged from within by bureaucrats themselves. For, as discussed in chapter 3, presidents (and most governors and many mayors) have diverse and frequently disunited coalitions of political support, which do not enable them to operate with a free hand or speak with a consistent voice. Bureaucracies, on the other hand, have a limited range of policy interests due to the need for specialization. By concentrating its efforts in one policy area, an agency can afford to develop its expertise and turn it into a political resource, and to nurture the support of those in the legislature and the public who seek favorable treatment of their interests by the agency. Thus agency responses to executive directives are usually calculated in terms of their effect on agency interests rather than on the interests of the chief executive. Since in most cases an agency is not beholden to the chief executive for its political survival and since the chief executive is unlikely to risk either political resources or political defeat every time an agency fails to follow orders from above, executive leadership is much more the product of political persuasion than of any clearly defined command authority.[4]

Presidential Leadership: Strengths and Weaknesses

The strengths of a president vary in relation to the specific constituency with which he deals, and some things that enhance his leadership in one set of circumstances may add little or even detract from his leadership at other times. A commonly noted source of strength, for example, is the fact that the president leads a powerful nation blessed with rich natural resources, an advanced technology, and a well-educated population, but this is considerably more important in the realm of international relations than in domestic or bureaucratic politics. Another general strength may be the particular character, personality, and style a president brings to the job, as well as his enjoyment of power, ability to cope successfully with the demands and pressures of his office, and his "aspiring to the moral leadership of the nation,"[5] that being a function we apparently expect of presidents.

A third source of strength, with potential impact in every aspect of leadership, is the president's ability to initiate a wide variety of ideas, proposals, and actions to which others must then respond. This power to initiate, in executive politics as elsewhere, provides an important advantage because the way a question or proposal is put forward to start with can significantly affect the outcome of the decision process.

A fourth source of strength is the capability of chief executives to respond to crisis situations, and that capacity is reinforced by public expectations that the chief executive will coordinate and direct governmental actions in the wake of floods, blizzards, droughts, outbreaks of violence, and other crises. The harsh winter of 1976–1977 provided numerous instances in which both the president and state governors in the East and Midwest declared fuel and other weather-related emergencies, while at virtually the same time governors of several western and mountain states were declaring drought emergencies. In one case, the New Jersey legislature gave Governor Brendan Byrne authority to declare it a crime, punishable by heavy fines, to keep home thermostats set higher than 65 degrees during that state's natural gas crisis in early 1977.

Presidential power has been called upon regularly in times of economic and military crisis—witness the invoking of wage and price controls by Richard Nixon (under authority delegated to him by Congress in historic legislation enacted in 1970), Lyndon Johnson's dispatching troops to the Dominican Republic in 1965, Dwight Eisenhower's sending the Marines into Lebanon in 1958, and Franklin Roosevelt's economic leadership during the Great Depression of the 1930s. As a rule, powers created or invoked to meet specific crises do not entirely disappear after the crisis has passed. Hence each time the president is called upon to deal with a crisis, the powers of the presidency are further enhanced.

There are some who argue that, especially in military matters, crises have sometimes been exaggerated in order that the incumbent president might secure additional power. The most vivid recent example concerns North Vietnamese actions against United States gunboats in the Gulf of Tonkin in 1965, which led to the passage of the Gulf of Tonkin Resolution authorizing President Johnson to make *any appropriate response* to military provocation by the North Vietnamese. The resolution passed unanimously in the House of Representatives and by a vote of 88–2 in the Senate, and the escalation of our involvement was shortly under way. Nearly a decade later, questions raised at the time were asked again, this time more insistently, about whether the attack had been as serious and provocative as we had been led to believe, or indeed whether there had even been an attack.[6]

A fifth source of strength is the legitimacy the institution of the presidency enjoys in the eyes of the public at large. The activism of modern presidents has been largely supported by public acceptance of those increased activities and initiatives that now characterize the office. It is also clear from most available survey data that a president attracts substantial public support and admiration simply by *being* president.[7] On the other hand, there is evidence that as part of a long-term decline in the prestige and legitimacy of American political institutions generally, the public standing of the presidency has also declined.[8] This decline dates back into the 1950s, with intensification of the opinion trend starting before either the Vietnam War or the Watergate scandal. But despite the downturn in public confidence, it is evident that there is still strong presidential influence on American life and politics.[9] Perhaps one measure of the presidency's intrinsic strength is the appeal Jimmy Carter's campaign had to a large segment of the electorate in 1976, especially in the Democratic primaries. His basic theme of believing again in the country, and in the presidency in particular, was responsive to what the Harris poll identified as a very real longing for a restoration of leadership in which the people could once again have confidence.[10]

While not unrelated to these sources of strength, a president's ability to direct the bureaucracy effectively depends more heavily on a different complex of factors within the governmental apparatus. One set of controls used by many presidents in the nineteenth century—extensive discretionary powers over appointment and dismissal of administrative employees—has been largely unavailable to twentieth-century presidents due to merit reform.[11] The president has the power to appoint some 2,200 executive-branch employees—most at or near the top of the hierarchy directly under the White House—out of a total of some 2.5 million. As a practical matter the president's power to appoint is more significant in the long-range composition of public policy than is his power to dismiss, since not all appointees are removable and those that are seldom find themselves actually fired. The president can direct quite effectively the activities of these appointees, but their impact on their respective bureaucracies is considerably more limited.

A far more potent instrument of presidential control is his role in the formulation of executive-branch budget proposals which go to Congress each year (see chapter 10). The president's programmatic and budgetary priorities form the guidelines by which the Office of Management and Budget—working directly with and for the president—evaluates each agency's request for funds, so that it is possible for the president to influence substantially how much money is included in his Budget Message to Congress for every agency in the executive branch. Congress, of course, is not bound by presidential recommendations for agency budgetary allocations. But it ordinarily appropriates to each agency a dollar amount not appreciably different from, although usually lower than, that requested by the president and OMB.[12] In the early 1970s another pattern developed where a Democrat-controlled Congress clashed with two Republican presidents over spending priorities and amounts, with the Senate especially inclined to vote larger sums than the president had asked. Under Richard Nixon this precipitated bitter conflicts over presidential vetoes and impoundment of funds.[13] In sum, the president has considerable influence over the amounts of money received by executive agencies, but his influence—and even his legal authority—cannot be said to be absolute. There is continual competition for control of executive agency funding, with the president having a major coordinating role.

A second function related to budgetary coordination emerged for OMB in the 1970s, chiefly at the instigation of President Nixon. When the old Bureau of the Budget (BOB), which had existed in the Executive Office of the President since 1939, was transformed into OMB in 1970, the change in title was not merely cosmetic. (Figure 4–1 shows the OMB organization chart.) It signaled Nixon's intent to gain greater mastery over operations and management practices of the sprawling bureaucracy. Other recent presidents had sought to exert greater control, but Nixon succeeded more fully than they in modifying management practices and in presidential monitoring of them. Nixon focused on making more rational the overlapping and duplicative system of federal grants-in-aid to states and local governments. This was to be accomplished by requiring federal agencies to coordinate similar programs, and by requiring grant applicants—particularly at the local level—to "touch base" with one another through a formalized review-and-comment procedure prior to submitting their applications to Washington. It was felt that these measures would improve intergovernmental communication and reduce duplication of specific grant proposals coming from local government.

OMB laid down the basic guidelines for this effort in Circular A-95, which implemented congressional directives calling for closer intergovernmental cooperation and more consideration by federal agencies of "state, regional, and local viewpoints"[14] in the formulation and execution of agency projects. But the mechanics of coordination were directed by the various grantor agencies more than by OMB. Since the agencies could be expected to have a greater interest in sustaining their own grant programs than in a "rationalizing" process that might result in elimination of some programs, the effectiveness of A-95 coordination was probably not what the Nixon White House sought. Hence, though the machinery for improving grant program coordination was in place (in the form of state, regional, and local "clearinghouses" operating under OMB's procedural guidance), it did not necessarily bring about improved program coordination. Once again, presidential control was offset to

Figure 4–1 Office of Management and Budget*

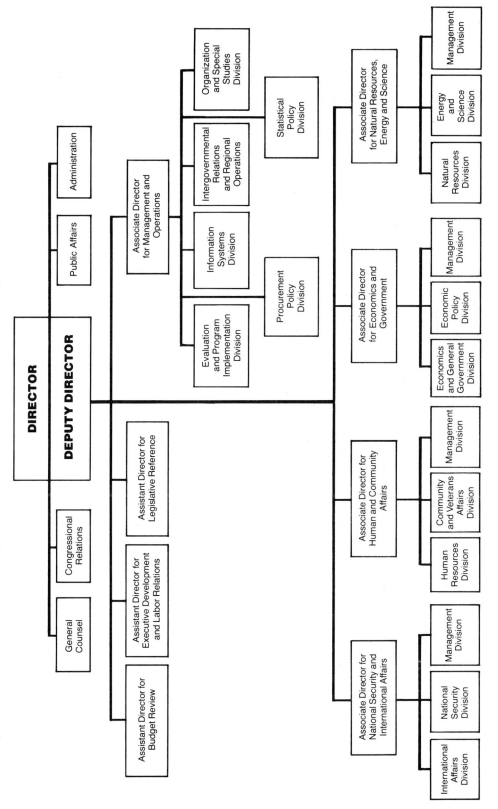

*Part of the Executive Office of the President. Chart is as of August, 1974.

some extent by the political autonomy of the agencies and their resultant ability to protect their programmatic interests ahead of those of the president. However, the ability of Nixon and OMB to partially reshape operating ground rules governing grant-in-aid procedures demonstrates the impact, in one form, of presidential influence, and the importance of this should not be underestimated.[15]

One other function of OMB in relation to bureaucratic agencies should be noted. When administrators seek to propose legislation for consideration by Congress, *central clearance* with OMB is required at least as a formality. This gives the president an opportunity to review possible proposals with an eye to their being consistent with his own legislative program. Here too, Congress may deal informally with agencies and their administrators regardless of the response of the president and OMB, but as a matter of routine most agencies seek clearance and do not openly work with Congress if clearance is denied, except in unusual circumstances.

Control over information represents a third broad approach to maintaining presidential influence over bureaucratic agencies, as well as general influence in the policy-making process. It is said that knowledge constitutes power, and in an era of intensive specialization, that holds true as never before. The president, of course, must deal with a highly specialized and expert bureaucracy (increasingly, inside as well as outside the presidential establishment itself).[16] How then is the president to gather the facts and figures necessary to informed decision making without being dominated by, or becoming excessively dependent upon, his sources of information?

To some extent the president is indeed dependent upon specialized bureaucratic agencies. There is reliance also on information supplied by the network of presidential advisory groups, both those within the Executive Office of the President (EXOP) and those having independent status.[17] The president's ability to keep his information network functioning adequately while avoiding dependence on any one source of information is crucial to his retention of political leadership and policy initiative. Franklin Roosevelt was perhaps the master of the art. He assured himself of a constant stream of facts, ideas, suggestions, and countersuggestions by (1) centralizing decision-making responsibility in the Oval Office, (2) delegating responsibility for proposing policy alternatives rather widely so as to involve large numbers of administrators in the process of "brainstorming" for ideas, (3) actively encouraging open debate and discussion among members of his administration, and (4) leaving just about everyone somewhat uncertain of whose ideas might be acted upon in any given situation. He also took care to follow suggestions from a variety of sources, thus demonstrating his intention to take useful ideas and follow them up irrespective of the source.[18]

Roosevelt's technique had the effect of generating more ideas than he could use, but it was to his advantage as a political leader to have that volume of information combined with the ability (which he carefully cultivated) to make the final choices himself. Presidents since FDR have had a far more difficult task in this regard due to the growth of virtually every major institution in the executive branch. There is more information than any one person can absorb and utilize; there are more competitors, both institutional and personal, for access to and control of information; and the greatly increased quantities of information generated by others for their own use and political advantage pose an obstacle to presidential policy direction that is difficult to surmount.

Recent presidents have tried to deal with their growing information needs by (1) increasing the information capabilities of EXOP; (2) enlarging the presidential establishment by making existing staffs bigger and by creating new ones, with corresponding increases in the political and programmatic responsibilities entrusted to them; and (3) delegating greater operating authority to EXOP personnel. These changes have produced quantitative and qualitative improvement in the president's information base for assessing alternatives and making choices, thereby creating something of a counterforce to the information generated in other parts of the bureaucracy and elsewhere. Furthermore, the proliferation of presidential staffs (see Table 4–1) has permitted more specialization within EXOP, thus strengthening the president's policy-making effectiveness vis-à-vis the expertise of the bureaucracy. Finally, by broadening the authority of assistants and staffs to speak and act in his name, the president has enhanced his ability to both transmit and acquire information through his immediate subordinates. This is important because presidents (and other chief executives) frequently encounter difficulty in transmitting and receiving accurate information through the bureaucratic hierarchy.

A major obstacle in transmitting information from one level in a hierarchy to the next is the tendency for a portion of the information to be screened out by those who receive it and in turn send it on. This may be deliberate, aimed at frustrating the will of the official sending the informa-

TABLE 4–1
PERSONNEL IN EXECUTIVE OFFICE OF THE PRESIDENT

Year	Number of Personnel
1945	853
1953	1,157
1963	1,538
1973	4,716

Source: Charles E. Jacob, "The Quest for Presidential Control: Innovation and Institutionalization in the Executive Branch," Paper prepared for the Annual Meeting of the American Political Science Association, Jung Hotel, New Orleans, Louisiana, September 4–8, 1973.

tion, or done without any particular motive—perhaps even unconsciously. Depending on how many levels there are in the structure, a great deal of information—as much as 98 percent under certain circumstances—can be distorted and even lost in this manner.[19] A chief executive, or any other top-level official, cannot casually assume that his or her communications—including instructions, statements of policy, or major program directives—travel down the hierarchy simply on the strength of their having been issued. There must be follow-up (sometimes repeated checks) to insure that communications have been received and accurately understood by those for whom they were intended.

Obtaining reliable information that gives a clear and complete picture of what is going on in the bureaucracy is the other side of the coin for the president. A truism of administrative practice is that unless there is some problem or disruption in the normal routines of administration, the chief executive does not have to be called in or informed about administrative activities. Such an assumption is justified on the grounds that the chief executive's responsibilities are broader than the activities of a single bureaucratic agency and that his or her attention should be directed to individual entities only if there is some special reason for doing so. In traditional administrative thinking, this assumption is called the *exception principle,* suggesting that only exceptions to routine operations merit involvement of the chief executive. But the exception principle does not always work well in practice. For one thing, there is a strong, if natural, reluctance to communicate "bad news"—such as the existence of a problem the agency finds hard to handle on its own—through the hierarchy, and least of all from an immediate subordinate to a superior official or agency. Also, for its own political reasons, an agency may prefer not to call attention to activities which are likely to be unpopular with its nominal superior. Therefore, for the president (or other chief executive) to have accurate and comprehensive information requires a successful effort to overcome or evade built-in resistance to a free upward flow of communication.

The president can facilitate the transmission of information from EXOP to the rest of the bureaucracy by maintaining regular follow-up checks for compliance and by requiring regular feedback from the agencies, though the formality of administrative feedback is much less difficult to establish than is useful substantive content.[20] Administrative agencies resist supplying feedback in the same way—and for many of the same reasons—that they resist other types of upward communication. Consequently, presidential (and other) monitoring of bureaucratic activity requires deliberate, concentrated action in order to have any chance of keeping some semblance of control from the top.

Among the ways of coping with problems in acquiring information are (1) making use of external sources of information (newspapers and other media, interest groups, and so on); (2) creating overlapping substantive areas of responsibility within or among bureaus, resulting in a measure of duplication of information sources and presumably more reliable information; (3) using informal channels to supplement formal ones; and (4) deliberately bypassing formal structures and intermediate layers of bureaucracy to contact directly the person or persons with the information being sought.[21] Franklin Roosevelt and John Kennedy, in particular, frequently telephoned lower-echelon bureaucrats to get from them information that was moving too slowly, or not at all, through formal hierarchical channels. Such a practice has two effects, both desirable from the president's point of view: it gets the particular information into his hands more quickly, and it signals to the rest of the bureaucracy that the president is prepared to bypass the usual channels when he deems it necessary. The latter is likely to reduce the time required to transmit communications through channels; the threat of being bypassed can motivate those responsible for forwarding information to the president to do so with a minimum of delay, outweighing any contrary motivations to obstruct or distort.

One other issue concerning presidents and control of information needs to be considered here. A president, by the simple expedient of withholding all or some information, can decisively influence the shape of internal deliberations, press reports, public debate, and even global confrontations. Three examples illustrate the impact of presidential control of information: (1) the Cuban missile crisis of 1962, when tight secrecy was essential for successfully negotiating the removal of Soviet missiles from Cuba, (2) the American buildup in Vietnam in the mid-1960s, when any information unfavorable to Lyndon Johnson's Vietnam policies was systematically withheld from the mass media and the public, and (3) the Nixon administration's secret (and illegal) domestic surveillance of anti–Vietnam War activists and civil rights organizers.

This device, however, has its limits, and failure to control information can also have major policy implications. A classic illustration involved President Kennedy's explanations of just what was promised to anti-Castro Cubans who wanted to invade Cuba at the Bay of Pigs in 1961. The invasion became a fiasco for the United States because, first, air cover promised for the landing on the beaches never materialized, and second, Kennedy's spokesmen—particularly a Pentagon press officer with years of experience on the job—denied any American involvement in either the planning or execution of the abortive invasion. These spokesmen followed up their denials, once they were known to be false, with claims that the national interest had both required and justified their giving out demonstrably false information! The documented falsehoods of the Nixon White House in regard to the Watergate affair also demonstrate the power of the president to influence, at least for a time, the course of public discussion, as well as the dramatic consequences of not maintaining complete information control. The essential points are these: (1)

presidents, through their control of information, can substantially affect debate and decision in and out of government, not to mention how others perceive the nature of public issues or the president's order of priorities; and (2) conflicts over access to, and use of, information involve crucial questions of political influence, with high stakes for the president and others in politics.

A president, on the other hand, can find himself forced to react to a situation in which *he* lacks crucial information. President Carter, less than a month after taking office in 1977, discovered that former President Ford's transition briefings had omitted mention of CIA cash payments to a number of foreign nations and heads of state, allegedly including Jordan's King Hussein. The allegations and their timing (on the eve of a visit to Jordan by Secretary of State Cyrus Vance) proved embarrassing to the Carter administration because of the negative image of "CIA money." The fact that the CIA was involved after that agency had already undergone extensive scrutiny by Congress and the executive only compounded the problem for the president.

Another instance in which a president lacked information vital to an impending decision—one of the highest magnitude—was the Cuban missile crisis. President Kennedy needed to establish beyond doubt that Soviet missiles had been installed in Cuba before deciding what actions to take. But despite the great urgency, he had difficulty obtaining the necessary (photographic) evidence, due to the time consumed by bureaucratic processing of the information and at least one interagency squabble—over whose pilots (Air Force or CIA) would fly whose planes over the western end of Cuba, where the missiles were ultimately spotted.[22] If presidents are not able to readily acquire information in the most extraordinary circumstances, even in a potential nuclear crisis, they clearly cannot depend on routine flows of information.

Just how effective, then, is information control in the total picture of presidential leadership? The answer is mixed. In terms of public and congressional leadership by the president, control of information can be a crucial instrument. But with respect to the bureaucracy, the president's leadership is subject to greater constraints, if for no other reason than that his control of information is less secure. The bureaucracy has more to do with shaping the available alternatives for presidential decisions—through provision of information—than any other institution or person.

In summary, presidential leadership rests on a base with the following components: (1) great public visibility and considerable fundamental respect for the presidency, though the latter has declined noticeably in recent years; (2) the president's own desire to provide leadership and the individual style of leadership he employs; (3) the power to initiate proposals, debates, and actions, to which others must then respond; (4) the ability to coordinate governmental responses to crisis, whether foreign or domestic; (5) the ability to make appointments to positions in the executive branch and the judiciary, though this is relatively limited; (6) authority to coordinate executive budget requests and to oversee implementation and management practices of executive agencies; and (7) control of information, though the president suffers from important weaknesses in this regard as well as benefiting from considerable institutional strength. Vitally important, of course, is the way a president makes use of each of these potential sources of strength, as well as how he copes with the weaknesses in his leadership base.

State Governors: "Chief" Executives?

The patterns of leadership found among American governors are predictably varied; while the fifty states do not display fifty different types of governor, there are important distinctions among the offices as well as their occupants. Some governors, notably in the larger urban-industrial states of the Northeast and Midwest, rather closely resemble the president in their public visibility, formal powers, the scope of their responsibilities, their institutional and staff resources, and the size and complexity of the bureaucracies with which they must contend. They are a minority, however. The majority of governors, especially those in states with more homogeneous economies, societies, and traditions, tend to have more limited grants of effective administrative authority and consequently a less active role in directing the implementation of state government policies. This is true even though most governors have acquired numerous additional powers (especially budgetary) under recent revisions in state constitutions and, in most instances, have exercised considerable influence in the proposing and development of state policy.

A major part of the variation among governors, in their formal powers as well as their actual leadership behavior, is traceable to differences in socioeconomic characteristics and political systems of their respective states. For example, states with large and diverse populations and economic activities seem to have, as a result of that diversity, a greater variety of problems, which require a strong chief executive to direct the state government's responses to those problems. Political scientist Kenneth Palmer has noted that as states more closely resemble the nation in their social heterogeneity, they must also "approximate the federal executive in their assignment of administrative authority to their governors."[23]

Another factor associated with strong governors is a competitive two-party system, as opposed to a situation where one party is dominant in most state elections. In many cases governors are acknowledged leaders of their parties, thereby strengthening the political leverage available in the exercise of policy leadership. Smaller states and states with one party dominant in their politics—groupings which may overlap—tend toward weaker formal powers in their governors' offices, although there are exceptions to that rule. Also, weak formal powers do not necessarily imply weakness in practice; informal bargaining, personal charm, and public relations can go a long way toward overcoming deficiencies in gubernatorial authority.[24]

Most governors, however, find their positions and capabilities defined—and often restricted to a greater or lesser degree—by legal and political factors that are formal in nature. For example, only eight of the fifty states have comprehensively rewritten their constitutions in the past twenty-five years—Michigan (1963), Connecticut (1965), Florida (1968), Illinois (1970), North Carolina (1970), Virginia (1970), Montana (1972), and Louisiana (1974)—while six others rejected proposed new state charters in the late 1960s and early 1970s (New York, Rhode Island, Maryland, New Mexico, Arkansas, and North Dakota).[25] A number of other states have partially revised their constitutions, focusing significantly on updating and strengthening the powers of the chief executive. Well over half the states, however, have governors operating under grants of authority dating back as far as the early 1900s, when the emphasis was on restrictive provisions on *all* government powers.

A related feature of many state constitutions (including some of those recently adopted) is the separate election of top-level executive officials, such as state attorney general, treasurer, and secretary of state. Forty-four states elect at least one of these officials entirely separately from the governor; a few even elect their lieutenant governors independently.[26] While estimates vary as to the impact of this executive fragmentation on gubernatorial leadership, there is no question that at least the potential exists for a governor's having to compete within his own official "family" for effective control and direction of state programs, budgets, and bureaucracies.

Even among governors with few competing elective officials, there are frequently limitations on powers of appointment and dismissal for subordinate executive-branch positions. While not even the president has unlimited authority in this respect, the authority of state governors seems to be considerably less extensive in comparison. In many states, for example, there are boards and commissions created by the legislature to which the governor cannot name members. In other instances appointees cannot be removed by the governor, except under the most extraordinary circumstances, once they have taken office. A 1971 study found that only thirteen governors could name as many as one-half of the appointees to key state agency leadership positions.[27] And most governors face the political necessity of at least tolerating appointees sponsored by political party or interest group supporters. In fact, in some rural states a bureau or department head might be selected by a committee made up entirely or in part of persons the agency serves; a common example of this is found in selection of many state agriculture department directors. Such committees are constituted independently of the governor and the private interests represented exercise at least a veto—and sometimes considerably more power than that—over appointments which appear to be under gubernatorial control.[28] The net effect is to reduce the leverage a governor has over subordinates, thus very likely frustrating efforts to develop and implement consistent policies.

A third constitutional feature found in many states is the specific mandating of programs and/or allocation of funds—requirements which reduce the ability of the governor (and everyone else) to make policy choices based on the best estimates of current societal and programmatic needs. Some states, for instance, have written into their constitutions very detailed budgetary allocations which would require a constitutional amendment to change (itself a difficult procedure in many states). As recently as the late 1960s Alabama's constitution effectively earmarked (reserved for specified uses) nearly 90 percent of its annual budget before the governor and legislature even began considering state priorities and spending.[29] Constitutional provisions elsewhere, if not as restrictive, nevertheless limit gubernatorial freedom of action beyond the usual constitutional and political checks and balances.

Another constraint on some governors' leadership resources is the fact that they serve a two-year term or a single four-year term without possibility of immediate reelection. As of 1976, forty-seven states had four-year gubernatorial terms, while forty-two states permitted their governors to serve at least two terms of office.[30] In the latter group were most, but not all, of the largest states; New York, California, and Illinois all permit unlimited reelection, for example, but Pennsylvania limits a governor to no more than two consecutive terms. Eight states—for example, Tennessee—do not allow a governor to hold office for even two consecutive terms.[31] This may seem a minor restriction compared to some others, but there is evidence to suggest that in the last year of a term where reelection is not possible, a governor has fewer policy options available and less effective control of political resources, because more attention is being paid to who the new governor might be than to the incumbent's identity or program leadership.[32]

Governors, of course, are affected to some extent by the nature of their states' bureaucratic structures and operations. Here too state constitutions play some part to the extent that they mandate the existence of specific agencies, commissions, and boards (in sharp contrast to the national Constitution's broad provisions). But more important than the constitutional framework are the dynamics of the relationships involving the chief executive and the bureaucracy. How extensive, for example, are the governor's powers of appointment and dismissal? We have already noted that these are often limited. Does the governor have broad or narrow authority to independently formulate and submit executive budget requests to the legislature? In twenty states the governor is required by law to collaborate in the basic steps of budget preparation with at least one other official, elected or appointed without any gubernatorial involvement in the selection; and in Arkansas the governor must collaborate with the legislature itself.[33] How effective is the state legislature as a political and policy counterweight to gubernatorial initiative? (Note that this question did not arise concerning Congress and the president.) In many states—even after legislative reapportionment and efforts to modernize operations—legislatures are still characterized by high rates of turnover in membership, part-time sessions, and woeful deficiencies in staffing and committee resources. Under these circumstances it might be assumed the governor has even more influence in the absence of effective legislative opposition and/or consultation, but in reality what frequently results is a legislature just effective enough to oppose and frustrate but incapable of coming up with its own serious policy alternatives.

The strength of the governor's own staff and executive office resources, including information capabilities, must also be assessed. In these areas many states have made considerable progress in recent decades, and much of the increase in gubernatorial effectiveness can be traced to these changes. Over two-thirds of the states have created a department of administration to assist the governor in directing the bureaucracy's operations,[34] and in a number of others the governor's personal staff has been expanded to include qualified subject-matter specialists, who strengthen the reservoir of expertise available in the executive office itself.

Two other formal powers that can augment the governor's position are the veto power over legislation and executive-branch reorganization authority. All but one of the governors have at least the same sort of veto power the president has (the exception being North Carolina's), and about half of the governors also have an *item veto,* which permits the governor to disapprove specific provisions of a bill while signing the remainder into law, a power the president lacks. In Illinois the governor has in addition an *amendatory veto,* empowering him not only to disapprove a provision but also to propose alternative language to the legislature; this could mean rewriting the content and even the intent of the legislation, if the legislature goes along. As for executive reorganization, there is a difference between being able to propose a "package" plan, subject only to legislative veto by one or both houses, and having to submit reorganization plans as part of the usual legislative process. Having to allow the legislature to amend, revise, and otherwise tinker with the proposals, even to the point of completely rewriting them, is a form—and a sign—of gubernatorial weakness compared to the "package" approach.

Finally, just how visible to the general public is state government, and how meaningful are its decisions and processes? Does the governor operate against a backdrop of highly visible agencies, programs, and politics, or does the "stage" of public opinion belong principally to the one office and its occupant?[35] To the extent that the governor dominates public visibility and public opinion regarding state government, his or her political leverage over all other parts of the formal structure is enhanced. But that is partly a matter of personality, as well as of formal powers or political strength.

From the governor's standpoint, a formula for greater effectiveness would appear to combine the following: (1) extensive personnel controls; (2) a central role in budget making for state executive-branch agencies; (3) considerable political strength in the legislature; (4) a competent and responsive executive office establishment with ample information resources; (5) at least minimal cooperation from independently elected executives; (6) some authority to reorganize the executive branch, subject only to legislative veto; (7) more extensive veto power; (8) a four-year rather than a two-year term and the ability to seek reelection; and (9) primary visibility before the public (which most governors have in any case). With state governors emerging in the 1960s and 1970s as important national political figures (for example, Jimmy Carter, Nelson Rockefeller, Ronald Reagan, George Wallace, and John Connally have all served as governors), and with public reawakening to the potential importance of the states themselves, the strength or weakness of governors is a matter of growing political importance as well as of central relevance to the making and implementing of public policy.

Mayors, City Managers, and County Executives: Variations on Recurring Themes

If it is difficult to generalize among fifty state governors, it is next to impossible to do so among the chief executives of American local governments. There are about 78,000 units of local government, of which fewer than half have chief executives separate from their legislative arms. There is considerable variation in the modes of election of these chief executives, as well as in the formal powers they exercise.

First, a word is in order about different types of local governments. Approximately 38,000 local governments are "general" or multiple-purpose governments, with responsibility and authority for providing local services such as police and fire protection, water supply, utilities, streets and roads, and sewage and sanitation facilities. Municipalities (cities, boroughs, some villages, and other municipal corporations), counties, and townships fall into this category. It is here that separate chief executives are found, such as mayors, city managers, and county executives, though not all general local governments are headed by a single chief executive (for example, townships and New England towns).

The other 40,000 local governments are single-purpose governments responsible for providing one governmental service (parks, schools, libraries, fire protection, water, mosquito control, airport service, and so on) to the public. These "special districts," as they are commonly known, are characterized almost without exception by a fusion of legislative, executive, and administrative functions under the direction of a board or commission, which appoints a professional administrator to manage the district's daily affairs. A common example is the local school district with its elected school board and appointed superintendent; about 40 percent of all special districts, in fact, are school districts.[36] Other prominent examples of special districts are the Port of New York Authority, with responsibility for a major portion of the transportation complex in and around metropolitan New York, including all three airports; the Chicago Park District; and a growing number of mass transportation districts in other major urban centers. Our discussion of local chief executives, however, will not include administrators of single-purpose districts; we will focus entirely on elected (mayors and county executives) and appointed (city managers) officials in municipal and county government.

Of these three types of local chief executive, the mayor is by far the most prominent. Yet mayors vary widely in their formal and practical strength in office; indeed, the terms "strong mayor" and "weak mayor" are commonly used to distinguish between different sets of mayoral powers. A *strong* mayor is one who (1) is the sole chief executive exercising substantive policy responsibilities, as opposed to a ceremonial mayor working in the shadow of a city manager's administrative role; (2) serves a four-year (rather than two-year) term in office, allowing for fuller development of executive policies; (3) has a central role in formation of the local government budget, usually with the assistance of a full-time city finance director and a finance department; (4) is influential in local politics, especially in party politics where local elections are partisan; (5) has both appointment and dismissal powers over other officials within the executive branch—the more extensive such powers, the greater the mayor's control; (6) has a veto power over legislation enacted by the city council; (7) has no limit on seeking reelection; and (8) can call upon an expert bureaucracy which is, nonetheless, generally inclined to follow the mayor's policy leadership. The more this description is applicable to a particular mayor, the stronger that mayor will be in local politics and policy making.

A *weak* mayor, by contrast, lacks some if not most of these powers, and is often found alongside a city manager who is the actual chief administrator of the community. A 1971 survey found that in 151 cities of 50,000 population with a formal mayor-council structure, only 39 had a strong mayor.[37] And according to the *1976 Municipal Yearbook,* two-thirds of all mayors lack a veto power, and a majority serve only a two-year term.[38] It can happen, of course, that a mayor lacking some powers can compensate by making skillful use of those that are available. For example, the city of Chicago—on paper—has a ''relatively weak mayor'' form of government, but the late Mayor Richard Daley's personnel control and his leadership in the Cook County Democratic party more than made up for any weaknesses in formal powers. Other resources which can help to overcome formal weakness include personal and political skills in relation to the local media and the electorate, and the political connections necessary to acquire significant sums of money from state and national government aid programs.

City managers, in contrast to mayors, are not directly elected by local voters for a fixed term of office. They are chosen by the city council and serve for as long as the council members approve of their performance. The original design of the city manager's position included the notion that the manager would be ''nonpolitical,'' administering policies agreed upon by the city council but taking no part in policy formulation.[39] In practice, however, city managers frequently exercise considerable leadership in city government, proposing a variety of actions to the council for their approval or disapproval and in general playing an initiator's role. One contributing factor is the manager's expertise and the legitimacy this provides; another is the fact that managers are full-time professionals and in many instances the mayor (ceremonial) and city council members are part-time. Also, the manager's staff resources ordinarily exceed those of either mayor or council.[40] Numerous studies have indicated not only that city managers are policy initiators and political actors in reality, but also that their fulfilling a policy-making role is quite consistent with the expectations held by others in local politics about the manager's job.[41] (Figure 4–2 illustrates the place of the executive function in local government structures.)

In the area of policy implementation, most mayors face problems not unlike those of many governors, in that the city bureaucracies are frequently highly professionalized and quite autonomous either in structure or in operation (or both). It requires a considerable investment of executive resources—assuming the mayor *has* such resources—to direct the implementation of local programs under the mayor's leadership. A weak mayor cannot do it; a strong one may be able to, but also may not. City managers may have some advantage here, in that many city charters specifically establish them as chief administrators endowed with the kinds of authority necessary to take charge of ongoing administrative responsibilities, subject always to the ultimate approval of the city council. Formal administrative powers seem to matter most to the city manager's exercise of leadership, if for no other reason than that the manager, by deliberate design, is not assumed to have access to party or other political resources, as many mayors do.

Different types of communities seem to be associated with the strong mayor form of government, on the one hand, and the city manager form, on the other. In general (though with some exceptions), the more

Figure 4-2
Place of The Executive Function in Local Government Structures: Some Illustrations

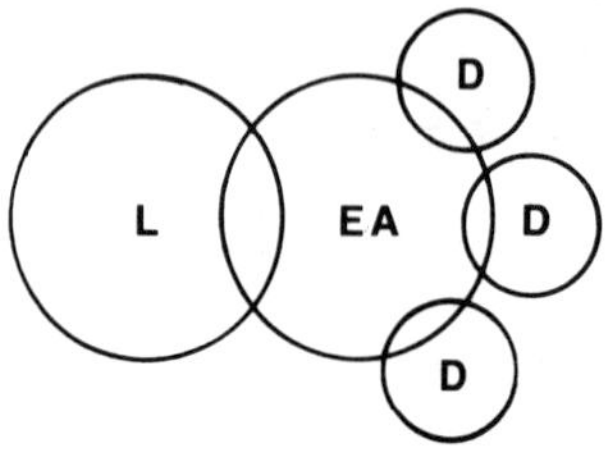

	Where both administrative and executive functions are performed by a strong mayor.	Municipalities outlined in the following section are categorized hereunder. The first three categories do not have a professional position. Those marked with an asterisk (*) are only tentatively placed in the category they most resemble.
	Where a weak mayor has some administrative responsibility, but departments also relate directly to the council.	
	The typical commission form where legislative, executive, and administrative functions are assumed by the commission.	

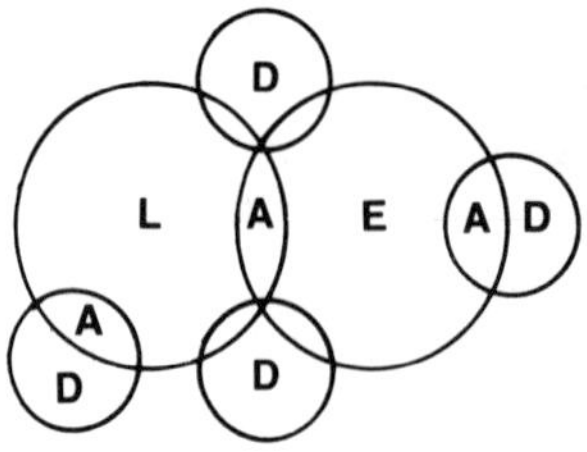

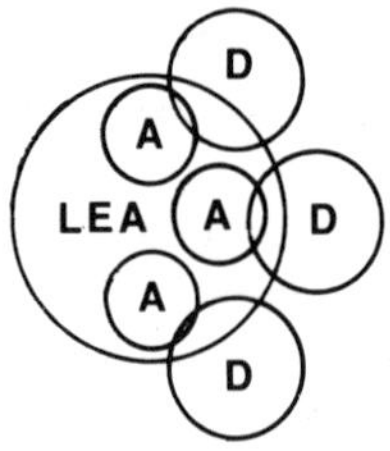

The various letters on the charts label basic functions.

L: The legislative function is primarily law-making. It involves oversight of the other functions by means of investigation and inquiry. It usually is performed by an elected council.

E: The executive function is focused on community leadership, consensus building, policy coordination and initiation, rulemaking, and interpretation of laws and the style of their enforcement. There is considerable variety in the assignment of this function in local governments.

A: The administrative function is concerned with overall implementation of policy, including control and feedback mechanisms between the legislative and executive functions on the one hand and departmental functions on the other. Like the executive function, there are a considerable number of ways local governments have provided for its conduct.

D: The departmental function is concerned with specific categories of activity and service; i.e., public works, human resources, utilities, etc.

	The council-manager plan with executive functions merged in the relation between the council and administrator (although the council ultimately holds them) and departmental functions consolidated under the administrator.	Ann Arbor, Mich.* Boulder, Colo. Columbia, Mo. El Cerrito, Calif. Phoenix, Ariz.
	Where a strong mayor performs executive func-tions, but departmental management is consoli-dated under an administra-tor.	Duluth, Minn. New Orleans, La. Trenton, N.J.
	Where a mayor with execu-tive authority and a separate administrator both have access to the council, but the depart-mental functions are con-solidated under the administrator.	Lee's Summit, Mo. Olympia, Wash. Seat Pleasant, Md. Troy, Ohio*
	Where a mayor has direct access and authority over all departments, but the administrator functions as administrative coordinator on a "first among equals" principle.	Allentown, Pa.

Source: Peter L. DeGroote, "Recognizing Professional Positions," *Public Management,* LV (March 1973), p. 7.

heterogeneous a community's economy and social composition, the more likely it is that the local chief executive will be a mayor rather than a city manager, with at least some features of the strong mayor form. Historically, the strong mayor first surfaced in larger cities where a substantial minority, if not a majority, of the population consisted of recent immigrants or their descendants from Ireland and from southern and eastern Europe (predominantly non-Protestant groups), and where strong local party organizations offered an avenue up and out of the ethnic ghetto. Such communities tended to develop in the path of the immigrants—on the Atlantic coast and inland as they traveled west. Thus Boston, New York, Philadelphia, Cleveland, and Chicago are (or have been) strong mayor cities, while other cities of similar size elsewhere (Los Angeles and Phoenix, for example) have not had strong mayors. As suggested above, however, one must not claim too much for the correlation between community composition and local executive form; there are significant exceptions to the rule as to community size, ethnicity, and location.

The office of county executive (or, as it is sometimes known, president of the county board) is a relatively new office of local government. County government historically has been among the more passive, nonpolicy-oriented governmental units, concentrating on administration of programs enacted at the state level (primarily agricultural and rural-related) and on maintaining a very few local services. Recently, however, there has been something of an awakening in county government as many counties have become steadily more urbanized, so that now county government is seen by some people as representing another potential governmental resource to be utilized in solving pressing social, economic, and service provision problems.

As was the case in other governments which grew more active, counties that have taken on more responsibilities have strengthened their policy-making capabilities, and some have placed central responsibility for policy formulation in the hands of a chief executive, separately elected by all the voters of the county. County executives tend to be found in counties with large populations—Nassau and Suffolk counties on Long Island (outside New York City), with a combined population approaching 2.5 million; and Cook County, Illinois (Chicago), with a population approaching 6 million. However, some smaller counties have at least considered establishing such an office—for example, Dane County in Wisconsin (Madison) in the late 1960s (population approximately 200,000 at the time).

There is still relatively little known about the dynamics of the role of county executives, but it appears their effective strength depends upon many of the same political, personal, and administrative resources that largely determine the leadership capabilities of urban mayors. Those possessing the necessary resources have been effective county executives and have had a major impact on government at the local level, including that of townships and municipalities within the county's borders. Two such officials were Eugene Nickerson, county executive of Nassau County in the 1960s, and George Dunne, president of the Cook County Board and successor to Richard Daley as Democratic county chairman in the late 1970s. Most counties, however, still do not have a popularly elected executive, and most of county government still is operated primarily by county boards, whose functions are legislative and whose powers are not well developed. The strong county executive is very much the exception, not the rule, among America's 3,000 counties.

Chief Executive–Bureaucratic Linkages

Interactions between chief executives and their administrative bureaucracies take various forms, but all have some impact both on the executive's political and policy fortunes and on bureaucratic behavior. Douglas Fox, in his study of city and state bureaucracy,[42] spoke of *policy development* and *policy implementation* as distinct phases of gubernatorial and local executive involvement with their respective bureaucracies. We shall use that approach in discussing these linkages, at those levels of government and in Washington (see chapter 12 also).

Development of policy in broad outline is probably what chief executives do best in their capacity as leaders of bureaucracy. Yet even executives with extensive formal and political power, such as the president and some governors, still must depend on professionals in the bureaucracy for program advice, and indeed for proposing new programs. The chief executive's dependence on experts varies among different policy areas. "The more technically complex the work of a bureau and the more structurally autonomous it is, the less impact he has on its policy development."[43] Policy areas such as energy conservation, public health, or transportation require more technical expertise than chief executives possess, with rare exceptions. Another factor affecting executive dependence on bureaucracy for policy development is the diversity of information sources within the chief executives' staffs, and among those that can be called upon outside government as well. Political considerations can often reduce dependence on experts; for example, economic recommendations on tax policy may be offset by judgments about public reaction. There may also be some choice as to *which* bureaucracy a chief executive relies on. But without question, *some* bureau or agency helps direct the course of policy development, in formative stages and often beyond.[44]

Policy implementation places chief executives in a position of even greater dependence on bureaucracies. Influence over implementation is generally limited to fairly broad-gauged actions (such as budget cuts and personnel measures) and related also to existing institutional resources. At the national level, for example, OMB has placed greater emphasis in recent years on management of federal programs, including introducing specific techniques into the bureaucracy and more management analysis by OMB personnel of what the bureaucracy is actually doing. This creates at least the potential for more effective presidential control over implementation. Similar developments have taken place at the state level, with management instruments such as departments of administration, new budget systems, and centralized planning increasingly available for gubernatorial use.

Local chief executives must rely on formal authority and perhaps party leadership to influence implementation, and even then the examples of successful mayors are few. Richard Daley in Chicago and Richard Lee in New Haven gained effective control of their city councils, boards of zoning appeals, and finance committees through adroit use of nomination to fill vacancies and through party patronage; Daley, in particular, was also successful in dealing with the city's public employee unions. But most mayors do not succeed in achieving this kind of control over major portions of their cities' policies. Lee himself wrestled with New Haven's police, education, and health bureaucracies, much as any other mayor would have, due to their professionalism and structural autonomy.[45]

In sum, most chief executives, including presidents, must contend with a dual difficulty. They must rely on bureaucratic expertise for much of the content of policy—especially in highly technical areas—at the same time they must seek agency compliance in implementing policy as they desire. A rising emphasis on program management, including strengthening the tools available to chief executives for coordinating and analyzing policy implementation, may bring some change, but for now most chief executives must induce cooperation from bureaucracy as they always have, rather than being able to count on it.

Commonalities and Differences in Leadership Resources

The institutional, legal, and personal factors which facilitate strong executive leadership seem to operate at all levels of government, though somewhat less clearly and predictably for city managers and county executives. Strong chief executives draw much of their strength from the following common features.

First, the power to initiate policy proposals and to follow them up politically is a key element of executive leadership. Legislatures at all levels ordinarily lack central policy formulation capabilities, so that a chief executive who wishes to influence the "public agenda" of issues which occupy government attention can do so in most cases. This assumes, of course, an executive leader who seeks to actively lead—an assumption that is usually, but not always, valid.

Second, a central role in executive budget making strengthens the overall influence and impact of the chief executive. If budgetary "central clearance" exists, executive agencies must pay heed to the preferences of the elected executive, at least during key stages of the annual (or, in some states, biennial) budget cycle.

Third, a key resource is control over personnel decisions in the executive branch. The more extensive the chief executive's authority to decide appointments and dismissals, the greater his or her political hold over actions of those whose tenure in office depends on pleasing their "patron" (hence the term "patronage"). Relatively few chief executives, at any level, currently enjoy that kind of personnel domination; thus personnel control is not a major contributor generally to the effective strength of chief executives.

Fourth, staff resources within the executive office constitute a major source of potential strength. This is a matter of institutional arrangements, where provision is made for adequate staff, and of the particular individuals who comprise the staff. A related factor is the information capability the staff creates. Here too there are institutional and personal factors involved, as well as considerations of information availability, transmission, and control.

Fifth, the ability to propose agency reorganizations enhances the chief executive's power, particularly if the legislature must accept or reject the proposals in toto. This power, however, is effective more as an implied threat or an occasional device, because reorganization is a major step and can be used only once in a great while. A chief executive who attempted more than one reorganization within a short time span would encounter either the likely defeat of the proposals and/or reduced credibility with the legislature. Reorganization authority is thus a political leadership resource of rather limited potential. Still, it is better to have it in reserve than to lack it entirely or have to subject any reorganization proposal to the normal legislative mill.

Sixth, the veto power is a useful tool, and executives who can exercise a veto have greater *potential* leverage over the legislature than those who cannot. The stronger the veto authority, the greater the leverage (as in the case of the governor of Illinois, who can veto an entire act, item veto, or amend legislation by the amendatory veto, subject to legislative override). Yet, as with reorganization, the veto should not be used indiscriminately. Veto power, in short, is not usually a "front-line" tool of positive executive leadership.

Seventh, a chief executive's political strength in the legislature, and as leader of a political party or faction, adds substantially to leadership capability in office. Research in congressional voting behavior, and to a lesser extent in state legislatures, suggests that there is considerable responsiveness on the part of many legislators to the initiative of the chief executive, particularly when party loyalty is invoked. While other considerations (such as policy preferences, constituency interests, and individual conscience) also play an important part in legislative decision making, many votes are cast strictly along party lines. If a governor is strong among legislators of his party—for example, Nelson Rockefeller through the 1960s in New York, Ronald Reagan (1967–1975) in California, and William Scranton (1963–1967) in Pennsylvania—it adds measurably to gubernatorial effectiveness. If, on the other hand, a governor must constantly labor to gain the support of his own partisans in the legislature, as was the case with (among others) Milton Shapp of Pennsylvania in his first term (1971–1975) and Dan Walker of Illinois (1973–1977), then leadership capability is a good deal more constrained.[46] The same general principle holds true for mayors and presidents with equal import. It is important to note, also, that strength in the legislature is usually tied to the amount of popular support that exists for the chief executive.

Some chief executives have particular advantages and disadvantages which should be noted. The president, for all his difficulties with semiautonomous bureaucracies, is better off than many governors and mayors by having fewer constitutional restrictions placed on his leadership. Many governors have a more flexible veto power (the item veto) than does the president, while many mayors lack veto power altogether. Both the president and the majority of governors are their party's acknowledged leaders, a situation many mayors can envy. Finally, most governors and city executives are limited in a broad sense by the fact that their governments' fiscal and administrative capabilities generally lag behind those of the national government, requiring them to depend in greater or lesser degree on federal grants-in-aid and revenue sharing for some proportion of their revenues. While this is an indirect impediment on executive leadership, in some ways it can have the most adverse effects on gubernatorial or mayoral policy initiatives and the ability to build for the long term, institutionally, at the state and local levels.

SUMMARY

American chief executives are highly visible to the public and are perceived as having the capability of providing political leadership and policy initiative in the governing process; they are also usually considered responsible for the operations of executive-branch bureaucracies. But most chief executives lack the specialization characteristic of bureaucracies and must rely on persuasion rather than on any command authority when dealing with them.

The strengths of a president start with those of the nation, his own leadership style and personality, and his ability to take the initiative in many matters of public policy. More substantial power lies in emergency powers which enable him to direct governmental responses to crises of various kinds (this is also a strength of governors); over time, residual powers originating in crisis situations tend to become part of the president's leadership resources. Another (indirect) resource is the legitimacy of the presidency in the public mind, even though this has declined somewhat over the past fifteen years.

The president's ability to successfully assume policy leadership depends on more tangible factors, such as personnel controls, a central role in the process of executive budget making and, more recently, in overseeing federal agency management processes, and (through OMB) a role in coordinating agency legislative proposals. A major factor is control over information—its acquisition in sufficient quantity and quality when needed by the president; sufficient resources in the White House and the Executive Office of the President for both gathering and organizing the necessary information; some means of overcoming the effects of "hierarchical distortion" in the transmission of information; and establishment of satisfactory monitoring of bureaucratic information and activities. Presidents have the ability to control the release of information in such a way as to affect significantly the course of public (and governmental) perceptions, debates, and decisions about public issues; but they can also be less than fully informed themselves, even after making every effort to acquire all necessary information.

Chief executive leadership at the state level is varied due to the diversity of state government bureaucratic structures. The position of governor in most states is stronger today than previously, but there are still numerous governors with limited formal ability to dominate the policy process in their state capitals. Stronger governors seem to be found in states which are socially and economically heterogeneous and two-party competitive. In terms of government structure and political factors, gubernatorial power is enhanced by personnel controls, budgetary influence, political strength in the legislature, strong staff resources, cooperation from other elected executives, power to reorganize the executive branch, veto power, a longer term of office, and public visibility. Many governors have some of these resources but few have them all, and policy development appears to be more susceptible to gubernatorial influence than does policy implementation.

Executive leadership at the local level is most prominent in general local governments—municipalities and counties (excluding townships)—and much less so in special districts. "Strong" mayors usually are the sole, substantive chief executive, serve for four years, direct budgetary decisions, play a significant role in local party politics, exercise control over personnel decisions, exercise a veto power, have no limit on reelection, and wield effective influence over the local bureaucracy. "Weak" mayors lack many or most of these formal powers and political resources. It is possible, however, for a few powers, skillfully utilized, to offset the absence of other powers. City managers are chief administrators with a tradition of remaining outside the role of political chief executive. Yet many are active initiators of policy proposals and directors of city administration. County executives are still relatively new and not very numerous. Most are found in urbanized counties with large populations, although some smaller counties have considered adopting the executive form. It appears that county executive leadership is dependent on many of the same factors that determine the extent of mayoral leadership in mayor-council municipalities.

Linkages between chief executives and bureaucracies come into play in policy development and policy implementation. In policy development, chief executives must depend on professionals in the bureaucracy for both general program advice and specific proposals. Executive dependency increases with program complexity and bureaucratic autonomy. In policy implementation, bureaucracies play an even greater role. For coordinating and analyzing implementation by the bureaucracy, chief executives must rely on broad-gauged actions (such as budget cuts and personnel measures) and on institutional capability in their executive offices. While it is possible for a chief executive to dominate implementation, that is rare at all levels of government.

Features facilitating strong executive leadership at all levels include policy initiative, a strong budget role, personnel controls, staff resources, reorganization power, veto power, and strength in the legislature and/or a political party. Each type of chief executive has some advantages and disadvantages that the others lack, besides the variations in leadership qualities which occur from individual to individual.

NOTES

1. See, among others, Fred I. Greenstein, *Children and Politics* (New Haven: Yale University Press, 1965); Robert D. Hess and Judith V. Torney, *The Development of Political Attitudes in Children* (Chicago: Aldine, 1967); and Kenneth P. Langton, *Political Socialization* (New York: Oxford University Press, 1969).

2. For an enlightening study of the Long years, see T. Harry Williams, *Huey Long* (New York: Alfred A. Knopf, 1969). Three useful, and contrasting, studies of Chicago's Mayor Daley are Mike Royko, *Boss: Richard J. Daley of Chicago* (New York: E. P. Dutton, 1971); Len O'Connor, *Clout: Mayor Daley and His City* (Chicago: Henry Regnery Company, 1975); and Milton Rakove, *Don't Make No Waves . . . Don't Back No Losers: An Insider's Analysis of the Daley Machine* (Bloomington: Indiana University Press, 1975).

3. See Coleman B. Ransone, Jr., *The Office of Governor in the United States* (University, Ala.: University of Alabama Press, 1956); Herbert Jacob and Kenneth N. Vines, eds., *Politics in the American States,* 2nd ed. (Boston: Little, Brown, 1971), especially "The Politics of the Executive," by Joseph Schlesinger, and "State Administrators in the Political Process," by Ira Sharkansky.

4. See Richard Neustadt, *Presidential Power: The Politics of Leadership, with Reflections on Johnson and Nixon* (New York: John Wiley and Sons, 1976).

5. The quote is from Emmett John Hughes, *The Living Presidency* (New York: Coward, McCann and Geoghegan, 1972). See also James David Barber, *The Presidential Character* (Englewood Cliffs, N.J.: Prentice-Hall, 1972); and Merle Miller, *Plain Speaking: An Oral Biography of Harry S Truman* (New York: Berkley Publishing, 1973).

6. An illuminating study of Vietnam-era decision making in the highest councils of the executive branch is *The Pentagon Papers* (Chicago: Quadrangle Books, 1971).

7. See Alan D. Monroe, *Public Opinion in America* (New York: Dodd, Mead, 1975), p. 164.

8. Louis Harris, "Confidence and Concern: Citizens View American Government," a study conducted under contract with, and printed by, the Subcommittee on Intergovernmental Relations, Committee on Government Operations, U.S. Senate (Washington, D.C.: U.S. Government Printing Office, 1974).

9. Survey data suggest that we have very mixed feelings about government and government officials, tending to support institutions while disdaining some of the people in them and some of the ways in which they operate. See Monroe, *Public Opinion in America,* pp. 164–165.

10. Louis Harris poll.

11. Frank J. Sorauf has pointed out that there are political limitations even on legal authority to appoint and dismiss political supporters and allies, since favorable treatment for some means disappointment for others. See *Party Politics in America,* 2nd ed. (Boston: Little, Brown, 1972).

12. See Richard Fenno, *The Power of the Purse: Appropriations Politics in Congress* (Boston: Little, Brown, 1966); Robert D. Lee, Jr., and Ronald W. Johnson, *Public Budgeting Systems* (Baltimore: University Park Press, 1973); and Aaron Wildavsky, *The Politics of the Budgetary Process,* 2nd ed. (Boston: Little, Brown, 1974).

13. "Impoundment" is the practice of the president's withholding final spending approval of funds properly appropriated by Congress in legislation the president has signed into law. For an account of the Nixon impoundment controversy, see chapter 10.

14. This is the language of Section 204 of the Intergovernmental Cooperation Act of 1968, the principal act of Congress which Circular A-95 was designed to implement.

15. See George J. Gordon, "Office of Management and Budget Circular A-95: Perspectives and Implications," *PUBLIUS: The Journal of Federalism,* 4 (Winter 1974), 45–68. Also, see chapter 5 of this text for discussion of the intergovernmental implications of the president's ability to dictate procedural guidelines for federal grant applications.

16. John C. Donovan, "The Domestic Council and the Politics of Presidential Leadership," paper presented to the American Society for Public Administration, New York, March 23, 1972, at p. 5. See also Donovan's *The Policy Makers* (New York: Pegasus, 1970), p. 48.

17. See Thomas E. Cronin and Sanford D. Greenberg, *The Presidential Advisory System* (New York: Harper & Row, 1969).

18. Arthur Schlesinger, Jr., *The Coming of the New Deal* (Boston: Houghton Mifflin, 1959), especially pp. 521–528 and 533–537. Those portions are reprinted in Francis E. Rourke, ed., *Bureaucratic Power in National Politics,* 2nd ed. (Boston: Little, Brown, 1972), pp. 126–138.

19. See Anthony Downs, *Inside Bureaucracy* (Boston: Little, Brown, 1967), pp. 116–118.

20. See Herbert Kaufman, with the collaboration of Michael Couzens, *Administrative Feedback: Monitoring Subordinates' Behavior* (Washington, D.C.: The Brookings Institution, 1973).

21. Downs, *Inside Bureaucracy,* pp. 118–126.

22. Graham Allison, *Essence of Decision: Explaining the Cuban Crisis* (Boston: Little, Brown, 1971), pp. 122–123.

23. Kenneth T. Palmer, *State Politics in the United States,* 2nd ed. (New York: St. Martin's, 1977), p. 101.

24. Ibid., pp. 101–102.

25. Ibid., p. 84.

26. Ibid., p. 98. The six states which do not have separate executive elections are Alaska, Hawaii, Maine, New Hampshire, New Jersey, and Tennessee.

27. Joseph Schlesinger, "The Politics of the Executive," in Herbert Jacob and Kenneth N. Vines, eds., *Politics in the American States,* 2nd ed. (Boston: Little, Brown, 1971), p. 227, quoted in Douglas Fox, *The Politics of City and State Bureaucracy* (Pacific Palisades, Calif.: Goodyear Publishing, 1974), p. 27.

28. Palmer, *State Politics in the United States,* p. 77.

29. Ira Sharkansky, *The Politics of Taxing and Spending* (Indianapolis: Bobbs-Merrill, 1969), p. 89.

30. Palmer, *State Politics in the United States,* pp. 105–106.

31. Tennessee had the experience in the 1950s and 1960s of two Democrats—Frank Clement and Buford Ellington—alternating occupancy of the governor's mansion because of this provision. (In 1978 the state amended its constitution to allow its governor two consecutive terms.)

32. Fox, *The Politics of City and State Bureaucracy,* p. 24.

33. Ibid., pp. 23–24.

34. Ibid., p. 29.

35. See Harmon Zeigler and Kent Jennings, "The Salience of American State Politics," *American Political Science Review,* 64 (June 1970), 523–536.

36. U.S. Bureau of the Census, *Statistical Abstract of the United States, 1973* (Washington, D.C.: U.S. Government Printing Office, 1973), p. 412.

37. Russell M. Ross and Kenneth F. Millsap, *The Relative Power Position of Mayors in Mayor-Council Cities* (Iowa City: Laboratory for Political Research, University of Iowa, 1971), cited in Douglas Fox, *The Politics of City and State Bureaucracy* (Pacific Palisades, Calif.: Goodyear Publishing, 1974), p. 31.

38. *1976 Municipal Yearbook* (Washington, D.C.: International City Management Association, 1976), p. 73.

39. This is a reference to the concept of separating "policy" and "politics" from "administration" which was quite prominent in the drive for municipal reform in the early 1900s. See chapter 2.

40. Fox, *The Politics of City and State Bureaucracy,* p. 34.

41. Ibid.

42. Ibid., chapter 2.

43. Ibid., p. 25.
44. Ibid., pp. 24–25.
45. Ibid., pp. 29–31 and 35.
46. See Sarah McCally Morehouse, "The State Political Party and the Policy-making Process," *American Political Science Review,* 67 (March 1973), 55–72.

SUGGESTED READINGS

Beyle, Thad L., and J. Oliver Williams, eds. *The American Governor in Behavioral Perspective.* New York: Harper & Row, 1972.

Cronin, Thomas E. *The State of the Presidency.* Boston: Little, Brown, 1975.

Fox, Douglas M. *The Politics of City and State Bureaucracy.* Pacific Palisades, Calif.: Goodyear Publishing, 1974.

Greer, Ann L. *The Mayor's Mandate: Municipal Statecraft and Political Trust.* Cambridge, Mass.: Schenkman, 1974.

Neustadt, Richard. *Presidential Power: The Politics of Leadership, with Reflections on Johnson and Nixon.* New York: John Wiley and Sons, 1976.

Palmer, Kenneth T. *State Politics in the United States,* 2nd ed. New York: St. Martin's, 1977.

Rakove, Milton. *Don't Make No Waves . . . Don't Back No Losers: An Insider's Analysis of the Daley Machine.* Bloomington: Indiana University Press, 1975.

Ransone, Coleman B., Jr. *The Office of Governor in the United States.* University, Ala.: University of Alabama Press, 1956.

Wildavsky, Aaron. *Perspectives on the Presidency.* Boston: Little, Brown, 1975.

Zeigler, Harmon, and Kent Jennings. "The Salience of American State Politics." *American Political Science Review,* 64 (June 1970), 523–536.

CHAPTER 5
American Federalism and Public Administration

One of the most widely recognized features of American government and politics is the arrangement we call the federal system. Federalism provides for national and state governments existing independently of each other in the same territory and commanding the loyalties of the same individuals as citizens of both state and nation.[1] The powers of both governmental levels are drawn from the same fundamental source—the sovereign people—and are exercised concurrently. The rationale for establishing a federal system in the United States was to prevent a concentration of power in a strong national government, with the states being viewed as counterweights and protectors of individual liberties against a central power. Yet the nature and operation of federalism have not always been agreed upon, and are not today. Indeed, this nation was torn by a civil war over the twin issues of slavery and the extent of the states' authority in opposition to the national government. With national supremacy confirmed by the outcome of that war, the past century has seen the emergence of new patterns within the federal framework. New questions and issues have arisen about the appropriate exercise of power by the different units or levels of government.

Public administration is at the heart of many of the questions and controversies that have characterized contemporary federalism. The two have had a reciprocal effect on one another. The administration of national government programs has required recognition of, and accommodation to, the existence, prerogatives, and preferences of states and localities which have their own decision-making apparatus and political majorities. At the same time, the growth of bureaucracy at all levels of government has helped reshape the federal system.

In this chapter our concerns will include (1) the definition of federalism and its formal setting in American government; (2) the growth of intergovernmental relations—that is, the multitude of formal and informal contacts among governmental entities throughout the federal system; (3) the tremendous expansion of intergovernmental financial assistance, particularly various forms of grants-in-aid and, more recently, general revenue-sharing disbursed by Washington to state and local governments; (4) intergovernmental administrative relations, a less visible but still important dimension of American government; and (5) some unresolved questions, both old and new, about the conduct of intergovernmental relations and the future of federalism.

The Nature of Federalism: The Formal Setting

The most elementary definition of federalism suggests that it is a constitutional division of governmental power between a central or national government and a set of regional units (such as the American states, Canadian provinces, Swiss cantons, Soviet federated republics, and so on); that under a federal arrangement both the national and regional governments have some independent as well as some shared powers over their citizens; that neither government owes its legal existence to the other (as local governments in the United States do to the states); and that as a matter of law neither may dictate to the other(s) in matters of structural organization, fiscal policies, or definition of essential functions. This definition clearly implies that the regional governments have substantial independence from the national government, but that both may exercise powers of government directly over their citizens. It leaves open, however, some pertinent questions about how authority is to be exercised *simultaneously* by different units of government sharing jurisdiction over the same territory and citizenry. Perhaps most important, this definition is a decidedly legalistic one, emphasizing the boundaries between levels of government far more than the potential for collaboration.

Political scientist Michael Reagan has drawn a distinction between two versions, or more accurately, two "generations" of federalism. "Old-style" federalism, according to Reagan, is a legal concept, defining and emphasizing the separate spheres of authority and division of functions between national and state governments. "New-style" federalism is "a political and pragmatic concept, stressing the actual interdependence and sharing of functions between Washington and the states, and focusing on the mutual leverage that each level is able to exert on the other."[2] According to this formulation, the principal concerns in federalism have shifted from questions about the proper legal boundaries between national and state authority and the relationship between national and state sovereignty, and have come to focus instead on the ways governments and government officials interact in the course of conducting the public's business. However, the earlier concerns have by no means disappeared. There are many citizens, as well as public officials and academics, to whom it matters a great deal which level or unit of government is most appropriate for handling particular functions.

In the early part of the nineteenth century, the U.S. Supreme Court defined some essential boundaries in national-state relations, with long-term implications for American federalism. The fundamental issue was the scope of the national government's authority, particularly when it overlapped and conflicted with state powers. Specific questions included, among others, whether states could tax national government agencies (they cannot,[3] and later rulings established mutual intergovernmental tax immunity); whether the national power to regulate interstate commerce (in Article I, Section 8, of the Constitution) superseded state regulatory actions setting up conflicting rules (it does, with some exceptions); whether the states could interfere in any way with national enforcement of national laws (they cannot); and whether the national Constitution's Bill of Rights restricted action by national officials only or governed state and local officials' actions also (originally, only national actions were covered;[4] in this century the Supreme Court has reversed that ruling, applying specific protections one case at a time to states and localities until the Bill of Rights now guards against infringement of most civil liberties by any instrument of government). Some other issues were resolved in Congress and by presidential action. The question of slavery, however, proved insoluble through the political system. This failure, coupled with irreconcilable differences (related to the slavery issue) over national versus state sovereignty, resulted in secession and the creation of a confederation of eleven states. The Civil War followed, culminating in a Union victory that was both military and political: slavery was ended, the Union preserved, and a federal rather than confederate system reaffirmed.

The national government emerged from the Civil War stronger than it was before, and the expansion of national powers came, to some extent, at the expense of state power and authority. Immediately after the Civil War and at the initiative of the Reconstruction Republican Congress, three amendments were added to the U.S. Constitution: the Thirteenth (1865) abolished slavery; the Fourteenth (1868) prohibited state actions which would deny "due process of law" or "equal protection of the laws" to any person (citizen or noncitizen) within the state's borders, or diminish the "privileges and immunities" enjoyed by citizens; and the Fifteenth (1870) granted full voting rights to former (male) slaves.

The addition to the national Constitution of provisions explicitly aimed at limiting official state behavior was a significant legal development, even though federal courts interpreted the provisions very narrowly at first. The importance of these amendments to the evolution of federalism was not to be felt until well after the turn of the century, when rulings of the U.S. Supreme Court made them (especially the "due process" and "equal protection" clauses) the basis for extending Bill of Rights guarantees to actions of state and local officials. Beginning in 1925, in a freedom of speech case,[5] the Court has set national standards for protecting civil rights and civil liberties, including among others the right to vote and freedom of speech and press.[6] Although movement in this direction has been very gradual and uneven over the past half-century, a trend is clearly evident toward "nationalizing" individual rights and liberties— requiring compliance by state and local government officials with nationally defined and enforced standards.

The early twentieth century was a time of transition between old-style and new-style federalism. Many basic decisions affecting the legal structuring of federalism were behind us, and as government generally became more active in dealing with problems of society, it became more common to find some form of joint or overlapping governmental activities. A number of new national programs combined participation by (especially) state governments and greater use of cash grants-in-aid from the national government to the states; examples include the Agricultural Extension Act of 1914, the Federal Aid Highway Act of 1916, and the Vocational Education Act of 1917.[7] Until the presidency of Franklin Roosevelt, old-style and new-style federalism coexisted, so to speak. Fundamental legal questions were receding in importance, but modern intergovernmental relations had not yet come into full bloom.

Intergovernmental Relations: The New Face of Federalism

Intergovernmental relations is a relatively new term which has come into common usage only in the past forty years. Synonymous with new-style federalism, it has been said to designate "an important body of activities or interactions occurring between governmental units of all types and levels within the [United States] federal system."[8] A distinction is immediately evident between formal federalism and intergovernmental relations (IGR); the structural framework of the federal system is the context within which IGR takes place, but there is more to IGR than the legal side of national-state or national-state-local relations. Intergovernmental relations embraces, in political scientist Deil Wright's words, "all the permutations and combinations of relations among the units of government in the American system."[9] These include national-state and interstate relations—the areas traditionally emphasized in the study of federalism—but also national-local, state-local, interlocal, and national-state-local relations. In addition there are a number of other key features of IGR worth noting.

First, strictly speaking there are no relations among governments as

such, only among officials of different governing units. "It is human beings clothed with office who are the real determiners of what the relations
between units of government will be. Consequently, the concept of
intergovernmental relations necessarily has to be formulated largely in
terms of human relations and human behavior . . ."[10] Both the content
and processes of IGR are shaped by individual interactions among public
officials.[11] Who the particular officials are, what roles they play in the
governmental process, what policy views they hold, and what interests
they seek to promote all have a bearing on the conduct of intergovernmental relations.

Second, the term IGR does not refer to one-time contacts, occasional
interactions, or formal agreements. Rather, it is "the continuous, day-to-
day patterns of contacts, knowledge, and evaluation of government officials."[12] IGR is concerned with informal, practical, and problem-
oriented contacts among government officials. Virtually all policy areas
have an intergovernmental dimension (including foreign policy, if one
notes the intergovernmental lobbying efforts of states and communities to
acquire military and other installations, attract international tourism, and
host conferences, exhibitions, and the like with international participation). Some domestic policies are almost totally the product of shared
intergovernmental policy formulation, implementation, and/or financing;
examples of such policies include public housing, vocational education,
airport construction and operation, agriculture (in a wide variety of programs), transportation, and education.[13] However, the fact that policy is
fashioned through intergovernmental processes does not mean that
government officials agree with one another on all or even most major
aspects of a policy; IGR can be cooperative or competitive/conflicting, or
some combination, and still be IGR.

A. Lee Fritschler and Morley Segal have defined four different types
of political relationships within IGR which in their view help explain the
variety of interactions referred to above.[14] The types of relationships
vary, they suggest, according to the identity and variety of the participants, the participants' attitudes toward one another, and the ways decisions are reached. The types are (1) joint policy making, (2) mutual accommodation, (3) innovative conflict, and (4) disintegrative conflict.

Joint policy making involves routine contacts among bureaucratic
agencies of different governments—agencies that share policy areas and
preferences in common—which result in cordial agreement on both the
general direction and specific activities in the policy area. Fritschler and
Segal suggest that this is most likely to occur when officials serve "nearly
identical client bases, such as the Department of Agriculture bureaucracy
and closely related county officials."[15]

Mutual accommodation normally involves a somewhat larger set of
participants—not only bureaus, but also legislative and interest group
participants, perhaps in the form of subsystems (see chapter 3), which

must resolve "important differences concerning how an intergovernmental program should be run and how financial technicalities should be
handled."[16] Examples are natural resource conservation efforts and
urban transportation programs, among others.

Innovative conflict occurs when one of the participants in a mutual
accommodation process tries to "manipulate the rules or structure of a
situation to his own advantage . . . ,"[17] putting other participants on the
defensive. Frequently, outside intervention is required to bring an end to
such stalemates and move the participants to negotiated bargaining to resolve their differences; "outsiders" might be White House staff
members, congressional committee figures, and/or their counterparts in a
state or local government. According to Fritschler and Segal, the national-state negotiations over law enforcement assistance provisions of
the 1968 Omnibus Crime Control and Safe Streets Act are a good example
of innovative conflict. "In this case the federal government refused to
consider state plans for the program until a number of conditions . . .
were included. Negotiations proceeded after these provisions had been
met."[18]

Disintegrative conflict results when one or more parties to a
disagreement refuse either to yield or negotiate, leading to a situation in
which the only way one can win is for the other(s) to lose. Examples of
this type of IGR are relatively infrequent, but the experience in school
desegregation, including national-local conflict over court-ordered busing, indicates the kinds of possibilities that do exist.[19]

Fritschler and Segal's categorization goes well beyond the simple
statement that intergovernmental relations can have cooperative or competitive elements, and helps distinguish among different policy areas and
their respective intergovernmental dimensions.

A third key feature of IGR is the involvement of public officials at all
levels of government. Clearly involved are chief executives and legislators in Washington, the state capital, the county seat, and city hall, since
theirs is the principal responsibility for enactment of the programs which
become a part of the IGR framework. In the past twenty-five years
another set of public officials—appointed administrators—has warranted
increasing attention in IGR. Administrative agencies at all levels of
government have assumed greater responsibility, and as IGR has
generally become more pervasive, intergovernmental *administrative* relations have taken on ever greater significance. (An issue of some importance in IGR, discussed later in this chapter, concerns the degree to
which influence in IGR has become concentrated in the administrative
arm of governmental levels without effective means of control by elected
officials.)

Fourth, IGR (unlike old-style federalism) is centrally concerned with
and rooted in the making of public policy. Questions of federalism tended
to focus on legal criteria for determining which level(s) of government

should take which actions on different policy matters. In contrast, IGR is not characterized by attempts to parcel out responsibility to only one level or unit of government. Furthermore, the criteria used in deciding on the particular mix of government activities in a given policy area are "chiefly political, economic, and administrative rather than legal."[20] That is, how to structure intergovernmental action depends upon the political setting, economic factors, and administrative needs and capabilities. What this suggests is that in the same way that many policy areas have an intergovernmental dimension, IGR and intergovernmental politics are distinctly policy-related. Among the most crucial policy questions are fiscal issues. These are sensitive matters indeed—the types and amounts of taxes raised by different governments, distributing the tax burden among wealthier or poorer taxpayers, purposes and amounts of government expenditures, intergovernmental aid, projected and actual benefits of government programs, and the different groups in society that benefit from those programs.

Richard Leach, writing in 1970, pointed out two other important aspects of modern IGR. First, "action in the American federal state is not confined to governments alone."[21] Although we speak of intergovernmental relations, many public purposes are accomplished through nongovernmental institutions and organizations. Thus intergovernmental relations, properly understood, also includes the public responsibilities and functions of organizations not formally part of any government (voluntary action groups, civic organizations, and so on).

Leach's second point is that action in the federal system is taken on parts of a general problem rather than on the total problem area; that is, action is fragmented rather than comprehensive. Governments are prone to act in response to relatively specific pressures for narrow objectives, and find it difficult and politically unprofitable to do otherwise. Thus government policies exist in such areas as water quality and noise pollution, but no *one* policy governs the nation's approach to environmental quality. Similarly, there are policies concerning urban mass transit and public housing, but there is no *one* overall urban policy. A major reason for this is the ability of literally hundreds of governmental agencies to act independently of one another, so that a policy emerges only in incomplete form and, in the majority of cases, lacking a centrally coordinated direction.[22] Thus when different governments *do* try to integrate their efforts through cooperative activity, their joint undertakings may well be built on a foundation of programs that are not consistent in intent, design, or execution. IGR is characterized both by this lack of central direction and by mounting efforts in recent years to overcome it.

Does all this mean that the legal side of federalism is no longer of any consequence? No, it does not. Legal issues, however, now tend to deal more often with sorting out parallel activities of different levels of government than with choosing which single level will be responsible for a given function. Environmental protection, where both national and state agencies have authority to set standards and regulate the quantities of pollutants discharged into the air and water, is a classic example. In two recent instances, state and national standards of environmental quality were in conflict, requiring judicial resolution. In California the state government imposed stricter automobile exhaust emission standards than had the national government and sought a court ruling which would permit states to go beyond federal requirements if they chose to do so. In Minnesota the state disputed federal safety standards regarding nuclear radiation and insisted on setting its own more stringent requirements. In both cases, the states won the right to act on their own, as long as their standards were no less strict than those of the national government.[23] In other areas of the law, as noted previously, some older issues are still "live ones"—for example, the constitutional requirement that criminal suspects be "given their rights" according to the Miranda rule.[24]

Just as old-style federalism has not completely disappeared, neither is IGR a purely twentieth-century phenomenon. Scholars disagree on the extent and significance of intergovernmental relations in the nineteenth century (and earlier), but some evidence of collaborative effort has been presented quite persuasively. Daniel Elazar and the late Morton Grodzins have been the leading proponents of the view that intergovernmental collaboration was common throughout the 1800s, and in some instances earlier. Elazar argues that even during periods when the rhetoric of "states' rights" and "dual federalism" (the separateness of national and state action) was at its peak, national, state, and local governments were actively cooperating with one another.[25] For example, the Army Corps of Engineers and various states and localities cooperated in the construction and maintenance of river and harbor improvements (including construction of the Erie Canal), and the national government reimbursed states for defense-related expenditures.[26]

Others argue, however, that areas of cooperation, while not trivial, were less significant than Grodzins and Elazar suggest. Historian Harry N. Scheiber, for one, contends that before 1860 the federal system was in fact dualistic, with intense interstate (and interlocal) rivalries, especially over economic development, quite common; and that after the Civil War the national government gradually took over major portions of numerous state and local responsibilities. Furthermore, according to Scheiber, where intergovernmental cooperation did exist before 1860, it was, in effect, unequal—and therefore not true cooperation—because the national government exercised predominant control.[27]

Whichever view of the past one holds, there is little question that in the latter part of the nineteenth century the national government did expand the scope of its activities due to rising demand for governmental action on several fronts. The war power grew as America's international involvement expanded. The tax power was enlarged with ratification of the Sixteenth Amendment, which permitted a graduated income tax, and subsequent enactment of such a tax. The power to regulate interstate commerce was employed far more liberally, as the emergence of a national economy spurred the growth of governmental machinery to monitor and regulate interstate business and industrial enterprises.[28] And on at least one point the Elazar and Scheiber schools of thought are agreed: some forms of intergovernmental cooperation became institutionalized during the early years of this century, with the New Deal period in particular marking a turning point in the development of modern IGR.

Leach and Elazar, among others, have emphasized one further point. The national government, for all its legal and political power to formulate broad policies and enact specific programs, is far from unified internally. Not only do the different branches fulfill their constitutional mission of checking and balancing one another (an inherently conflict-laden function), but also each branch is composed of individuals representing a wide spectrum of political opinion and issue preference. Leach cites, for example, frequent disagreements between the House and Senate, domination of both chambers by their respective committees, and lack of strong party-line voting (party discipline) among members of Congress. He also points out that Congress is constrained by presidential influence, Supreme Court rulings, and pressures from state and local constituencies (including government officials at those levels).[29] Finally, as discussed previously, the president and Congress must contend with an executive-branch structure in which most agencies have some degree of autonomy in their operations. Thus "the" national government is far from monolithic; there are many opportunities for those outside the formal machinery to influence what it decides and, more important, what it actually does.

Intergovernmental Fiscal Relations

Intergovernmental fiscal relations, or *fiscal federalism,* is central to contemporary IGR. While there have been some forms of financial aid from one governmental level to another throughout American history, the scope of such transactions in various forms has expanded rapidly and dramatically in the past forty years. The 1960s and 1970s especially have seen significant change in fiscal relations, accompanied by change in political, programmatic, and administrative relations as well. This applies to national government aid to states and localities and, to a lesser extent, state aid to local governments.

Intergovernmental aid has taken on greater importance for a relatively simple reason. State and local governments have weaker economic bases and less productive systems of taxation than the national government possesses, yet they provide the great bulk of public services in health, education, welfare, housing, highway construction, police protection, parks and recreation, conservation, and agricultural services. The national government, with far stronger fiscal resources, delivers *directly* only a few public services, such as Social Security benefits, veterans' payments, and farmers' subsidies.[30] This can be taken one step further: the national government, with the greatest tax resources, delivers the fewest services directly; local governments, with the narrowest and weakest tax bases, are frequently the most heavily laden with costly service obligations (police, fire, streets and roads, sewage and sanitation, water, utilities, and so on); the states fall between national and local governments in both respects.

There are two basic reasons for the revenue-raising disparity among different governmental levels. First, local and state governments have limited geographic areas—often dependent on one or two products or resources (for instance, coal in West Virginia)—from which to extract revenues. Only the national government has access to the full range of economic resources in the nation. A more diversified economy is a more stable and productive source of government income, and the national economy is by far the most diversified.

Second, different types of taxes yield different amounts of revenue from the same income base. The most productive, or "elastic," tax—showing the greatest increase in revenue for a given rise in taxable income—is the *graduated income tax* ("graduated" meaning that the rate of taxation rises as income increases).[31] Somewhat less elastic is the *sales tax,* where a flat rate of 4 or 5 or 6 percent (and sometimes more) is levied on the amount of purchase; some sales taxes are general, with few exemptions, while others are selective, applying to certain items only. Least elastic is the *personal property tax,* levied on real estate and other personal belongings. The national government is the principal user of the graduated income tax; states rely most extensively on sales and other excise taxes; and local governments, including special districts, depend most heavily on personal property taxes.[32]

Thus the government with the broadest tax base (the national government) also uses the most productive generator of revenue, while the governments with the narrowest and normally least diversified tax base (local governments) employ the least productive tax (with the states again falling between the two). The result, in Michael Reagan's words, is a "fiscal mismatch," not only between the service needs and fiscal capacities of different levels of government, but also among different governments at the same level in terms of their varying abilities to pay for needed public services (for example, rich and poor school districts). The rising service demands on government at all levels have placed a particular strain on those governments least able to rapidly expand their tax revenues (that is, local units). The consequence of all this has been increasing demand for aid from higher levels of government to help pay the costs of proliferating government services.

Grants-in-Aid

The growing needs of state and local government coincided with rising interest in Congress and the executive branch both in expanding and upgrading available public services, regardless of the specific government providing them. The stage was set, by the 1960s, for the national government (and some states, as well, within their own boundaries) to utilize financial assistance on a much larger scale as a means of providing not only more but also better public services. The principal device adopted to bring all this about was the grant-in-aid.

Grants-in-aid may be defined as "money payments furnished by a higher to a lower level of government to be used for specified purposes and subject to conditions spelled out in law or administrative regulation."[33] This form of cash transfer is used most widely by the national government, although states also make some use of it. At the time of John F. Kennedy's inauguration in 1961, some forty-five separate grant authorizations had been enacted by Congress (under each authorization, numerous allocations could be approved by the agency in charge of administering the particular program). But in the period 1965–1966, when Lyndon B. Johnson commanded decisive Democratic majorities in both chambers of Congress (295–140 in the House, 68–32 in the Senate), he took advantage of the opportunity to legislate a host of new grant programs as he pursued his vision of the "Great Society." By the time Richard Nixon entered the White House (only eight years after Kennedy had), the number of grants had mushroomed to just under 400—and another 143 were enacted in the first two years of the Nixon administration, bringing the total in 1970 to 530. Grants-in-aid financed state and local programs in nearly every major domestic policy area, such as airport construction, urban renewal, mass transit, air pollution control, construction of water treatment plants, model cities, and public health programs.[34]

Equally dramatic is the increase in dollar amounts appropriated under federal grant programs. In fiscal 1961, the figure was approximately $7 billion; by 1970, it had risen to nearly $24 billion; three years later, it was $41.3 billion; and by fiscal 1977, it was approximately $70 billion.[35] About 15 percent of federal grants go directly to local governments, while much larger amounts are passed through state governments to localities.[36] Figure 5-1 shows graphically the increase in federal grant assistance to state and local governments.

Federal grants-in-aid have been enacted to achieve certain broad purposes.[37] These include (1) establishing minimum nationwide standards for programs operating in all parts of the country, (2) equalizing resources

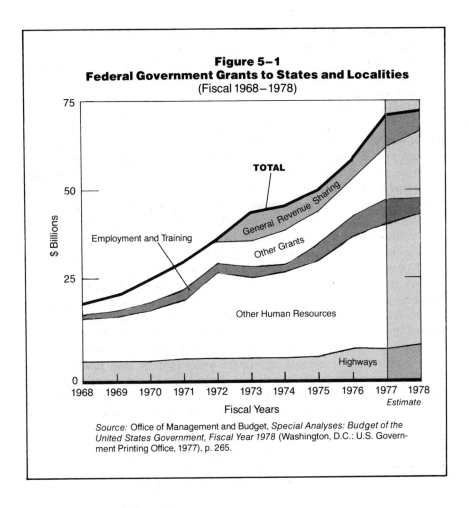

Figure 5-1
Federal Government Grants to States and Localities
(Fiscal 1968–1978)

Source: Office of Management and Budget, *Special Analyses: Budget of the United States Government, Fiscal Year 1978* (Washington, D.C.: U.S. Government Printing Office, 1977), p. 265.

among the states by allocating proportionately more money to poorer states (the "Robin Hood principle" of taking from the rich and giving to the poor), (3) improving state and local program adequacy, (4) making it possible to develop a coordinated effort to solve a particular problem (especially one that crosses government boundary lines, such as air pollution), and (5) increasing public services without enlarging the structure of the national government or its role in domestic politics. Other purposes have included improvements in the structure and operation of state and local administrative agencies (merit personnel practices, better planning, etc.), demonstration and experimentation in national policy, encouragement of general social objectives such as nondiscrimination in hiring, and provision of services to otherwise underserviced portions of the population. The importance of federal grants-in-aid in the total picture of domestic programs and administration is suggested by the fact that throughout the 1970s they provided approximately *one-fourth* of state-local revenues each fiscal year (see Table 5-1).

Federal grant programs were used in the 1960s to foster state and local planning activities where none had existed previously or where they were not systematic or well developed. Beginning with the Housing Act of 1954, some funding had been made available specifically to assist state and local planners in preparing proposals related to housing program grants, and this pattern was repeated in the host of new federal programs enacted in the years following. As national goals came to be stressed, Congress and the federal bureaucracy took this one step further, setting requirements for planning as a precondition for grant assistance. The Demonstration Cities and Metropolitan Development Act of 1966 (the "Model Cities Act") stipulated, in addition, that grant applications from local governments in metropolitan areas must first have been screened by an areawide comprehensive planning agency as to the project's relationship to overall area development, with the screening agency's comments (if any) accompanying the project application. Regional planning commissions (RPCs) and councils of government (COGs) were designated as the screening agencies for metropolitan areas; similar entities were formed for nonmetropolitan areas when the requirements were subsequently extended. Planning, along national operating guidelines, became a prominent emphasis within the grant system, and fulfillment of federal guidelines became a criterion for aid—and, not surprisingly, an occasional point of dispute between aid applicants and grantors. Significantly, most decisions in this area were in the hands of professional bu-

TABLE 5-1
FEDERAL GOVERNMENT AID TO STATES AND LOCALITIES
(In Relation to State and Local Revenues)

	Total Federal Aid	
Fiscal Year	Dollar Amount (in millions)	As a Percent of State-Local General Revenue from Own Sources
1954	2,967	11.4
1964	10,097	17.3
1969	19,421	20.4
1970	23,257	21.4
1971	27,121	22.8
1972	33,178	24.6
1973	41,268	27.3
1974	42,854	25.8
1975 est.	49,200	27.0
1976 est.	59,200	29.5

Source: Advisory Commission on Intergovernmental Relations, *Improving Urban America: A Challenge to Federalism* (Washington, D.C., ACIR, 1976), p. 85.

reaucrats and bureaucracies, with less direct involvement of either elected executives or legislators at any level of government.

The advantages of grants-in-aid are numerous. First, the national government affords a single focal point for bringing about a greater degree of concerted action on a policy problem (bearing in mind, of course, the diversity within the national government). Second, political minorities in states and localities have an opportunity to seek some measure of federal support for their policy demands, as blacks and other social-political minorities did in the mid-1960s. Third, grants-in-aid are an appropriate means of dealing with problems of nationwide scope; many policy questions are not only nationwide but also interrelated in terms of their impact, such as questions linking highways, urban transportation, and air pollution, or education, unemployment, poverty, and welfare. While a fully coordinated attack on such sets of problems has yet to be mounted (and is not likely to be), a greater degree of consistency is possible at the national level than among fifty separate states and 78,000 local governments.

Finally, and perhaps most importantly as a rationale, it has been suggested that federal funds assist states and localities with programs and projects which benefit citizens outside the borders of the recipient government. These "ripple effects"—or, as they are known more formally, *externalities*—justify national monetary support for state or local efforts because of the wider benefits realized. Three examples illustrate the point: (1) a state job training center, whose graduates may find employment in other states, (2) a state park system (such as Kentucky's, one of the best), which attracts tourists and vacationers from a much wider geographic area, and (3) local education systems, which, in a mobile society such as ours, are undoubtedly investing in the future productivity and contributions of individuals who will reap the benefits of their education elsewhere. Since the nation as a whole gains from such investments of state and local funds, there is good reason to add grant funding from the national treasury.

Grants-in-aid have taken several different forms. One way to distinguish among the various types is to ask how specifically the purposes or uses of the money are spelled out in the legislation and/or administrative regulations under which it is allocated. Another way is to determine whether the grant allocations are made according to a common formula or by national agency approval of specific project applications. Let us look at each of these in turn.

Categorical and *bloc* grants differ in that the former have narrowly defined purposes and the latter's purposes are much more broadly specified—in both cases, by the grantors. (A third variety of funding—revenue-sharing—is discussed separately, later in this chapter.) The principal difference is that the agency responsible for administering a categorical grant also has a great deal to say about the precise uses of the money, "leaving very little discretionary room on the part of a recipient government as to how it uses the grant."[38] Bloc grants, while also given out for use in a specific policy area (such as community development, public health, public safety, or manpower), leave a great deal more discretion and flexibility in the hands of recipient governments as to the use of the funds.

The specificity of categorical grants can be illustrated by two examples from the early 1970s; one deals with urban sewage treatment plants, the other with recreation.

> Under one program administered by the Farmers' Home Administration, cities of less than 5,500 population can apply for grants to finance sewage-collection systems. For cities with a larger population, collection systems are financed by the Department of Housing and Urban Development. In the case of interceptor sewers, which transmit the sewage from the collection systems to the treatment plants, financing is available from the Environmental Protection Agency (EPA). EPA will also finance sewage-treatment plants and sewer outfalls under the same grant programs as the interceptors, but these need not be financed under the same grant. The Economic Development Administration [in the Department of Commerce] also plays a role in financing sewage systems; for economically depressed areas, it will guarantee loans or make grants for any segment of a sewage system from collection to outfall sewer. Normally these grants or loans will finance the local contribution required by EPA, HUD, or FHA grants.
>
> · · ·
>
> A city that wants to buy open land for park purposes, build a swimming pool on it and operate an activity center for senior citizens, put in trees and shrubberies, and purchase sports equipment must make as many different grant applications as there are items mentioned in this sentence.[39]

With over 400 such grants currently in existence, the categorical grant business can be more than a little complicated. Bloc grants for sewage treatment plants might still differ according to size of city or type of sewer, but certainly recreation funds would be easier to obtain and put to use in bloc-grant form; this, in fact, is one of the most frequent arguments in support of bloc over categorical grants. The Ford administration took a significant step in 1974 by consolidating a large number of categorical grants for community development into a much smaller number of more flexible bloc grants. Whether this pattern will be extended to other policy areas is not yet clear; it will depend in large measure on the degree of ongoing support for categorical grant programs versus the growing pressures for change.

The second way to distinguish grant-in-aid types is by their allocation according to a formula or in response to individual applications. Of the 530 grants in existence in 1970, approximately 100 were *formula grants,* for purposes such as aid to the blind, an ongoing need and one common to many government jurisdictions; the remainder were *project grant* programs, available by application. The two illustrations given earlier are examples of project grants. Probably the best-known example is the complex of urban renewal grants available to local governments for a wide variety of purposes—low-rent apartments, commercial development, and so on—aimed at rejuvenating deteriorating core areas of central cities. Though project grants outnumber formula grants by about 4 to 1 in terms of separate authorizations, the amount of funding available was roughly equal at the start of the 1970s; the balance has swung somewhat in favor of project grants since then.

With grants-in-aid of all types, the proportion of total expenditure paid by the national government varies considerably. Congress defines some grants as representing important national initiatives and sets the federal government share at 100 percent. Other grants require dollar-for-dollar matching funds by the recipient government, which still doubles the total amount of money available to the recipient. Some other grant allocations require recipients to share the burden to some extent, but not fifty-fifty (sometimes as little as 1 percent of the total). The national share, then, is at least one-half, and can cover the total.

The expansion of grants-in-aid during the 1960s was accompanied by qualitative and administrative changes. First, project grants became far more numerous (the rapid growth in grants of the mid-1960s was primarily in this form). Second, there was an increased variety of matching-grant formulas. Third, it became possible to apply for multiple-function instead of single-function grants, though the number of these was small. Fourth, Congress broadened the eligibility of grant recipients and increased joint-recipient possibilities. Fifth, as part of President Johnson's "creative federalism" programs, aid was concentrated in large urban areas and directed to the urban poor in numerous new ventures. Sixth, there was increased national aid not only to governments but also to private institutions, including corporations, universities, associations of various kinds, and nonprofit organizations. Finally, the national government made funding available specifically to assist state and local jurisdictions in improving both their planning capabilities and their actual planning activities.[40] All of these changes grew out of an expanding emphasis on achieving *national* goals under the direction of the national government.[41]

The year 1960 marked something of a turning point in this regard. Prior to that time, federal aid had been used primarily to supplement policy actions of states and localities, but with the coming of the New Frontier under Kennedy and the Great Society under Johnson, presidential and congressional initiatives were couched more in terms of national purposes. Given this emphasis, it was deemed entirely appropriate to write into grant legislation substantive and procedural requirements which would promote those purposes.[42] Administration of these programs remained predominantly in the hands of state and local governments, but the national role in defining the uses of grant funds was clearly greater than before and, significantly, was decisive in determining general policy directions.

Political Reaction Against Grants

A number of problems developed and complaints began to be heard as a result of these changes in grant programs, especially in the mid-1960s. First, the proliferation of project grants ran counter to the objective of equalizing resources among recipient governments, because applying successfully for such grants required some professional skills (which became known as "grantsmanship") most likely to be found in states and communities which already had a fair amount of wealth.[43]

Second, it was alleged that the restrictions placed on the use of categorical aid resulted in distortion of state and local program priorities. Officials of state and local governments, it was argued, tended to apply for whatever grants were available, even if other needs were more pressing. This question of a forced reordering of state and local priorities was especially sensitive. If state and local autonomy were to mean anything, some said, it had to mean that states and localities could define their own high-priority problems, without allowing the availability of funding to skew those priorities. On the other hand, others argued that federal grants were designed precisely to induce state and local governments to become active in areas where they might not move on their own initiative, and that if national problems were to be solved in any sort of systematic way, they had to be tackled wherever they existed, even if local (including state) officials were not inclined to do so without financial incentives. This became both a political and philosophical battleground, and in many respects it still is.

A third problem, subtle yet potentially serious, was the possible yielding of policy initiatives by states and localities to aid grantors in the national government. There was some concern that as aid patterns became more established, and state and local officials grew more accustomed to congressional enactments leading to new infusions of money, a tendency might have developed among *some* officials to wait for national initiatives instead of pursuing their own. It is possible, too, that some federal officials came to feel that theirs was indeed the best view of national policy needs and that it was entirely appropriate for Congress and federal agencies to take the initiative through grant programs. Others argued, however, that the survival of states and localities as meaningful governing entities in the federal system depended on their continuing ability to generate ideas and actions within their own jurisdictions. To have the national government *substitute* for them instead of supplementing their programs was unhealthy in the long run, in this view.

Fourth, the national government did not aid all public services, so that in some cases greater inequality of available services resulted. Moreover, as Michael Reagan points out, governments that had to put up matching funds for aid that was available had a harder time meeting their other unaided service obligations.[44] This was particularly important in the patterns of aid to local governments in metropolitan areas. Some jurisdictions attracted considerable amounts of aid simply because the combination of public services they offered was covered extensively under federal programs, while other governments (mainly central cities) were responsible for services (such as fire protection and sidewalk maintenance) which the national government had not chosen to support through extensive grant funding.[45]

Fifth, many state and local officials objected to the mounting paperwork, considerable uncertainty, and frequent delays associated with applying for and receiving grants-in-aid. Many times a would-be aid recipient budgeted for a fiscal year on the assumption that the aid would be forthcoming; too often it arrived belatedly or not at all. The applications themselves were often complex and difficult to fill out, putting a premium on the "art of grantsmanship" referred to earlier. Reagan points out that grantsmanship often was tantamount to "gamesmanship"—that is, the ability to manipulate language on the application forms to please federal program administrators.[46] The mechanics of application, in short, became an issue in the growing controversy over grants.

Finally, due to the sheer number of grants and the variety of sources within the federal bureaucracy, there was an immense problem of grant coordination. The example of sewage system grants given earlier illustrates the availability of grants from different federal agencies for similar (and often overlapping) purposes, making it difficult to select the most appropriate grant program. Also, many general development projects in states and communities had component parts funded independently by separate federal agencies. As a result, a grant applicant was faced with applying separately for each part of the overall project (such as urban renewal or downtown business development), thereby running the risk of applications being approved for some portions of the project but not for others. Furthermore, most aid-granting agencies at the national level did not have much knowledge (if any) of what other programs were being funded by other agencies; and at the other end of the aid pipeline, most recipient governments knew or cared little about what other governments were receiving, or even applying for. Thus a rather chaotic situation prevailed. Grant applications were being reviewed and approved or rejected by federal agencies with no central instrument for keeping track of which states and localities were asking and/or receiving how much aid for what purposes. Nor was there provision for monitoring in any systematic way which agencies were responsible for programs with similar purposes or for determining the actual effects of grant funds. State and local officials, meanwhile, were chafing under what many considered unreasonable guidelines for spending grant money, in addition to the problems they were having in getting funding in the first place.

Revenue-Sharing

Out of these concerns grew considerable pressure for modification of the grant system, to deal somehow with the problems and complaints of aid recipients while continuing to make money available. (Many officials had, after all, begun to count on the availability of such funds in their routine budgetary calculations.) Two principal alternatives seemed most attractive: bloc grants, described previously, and the concept known as *revenue-sharing*.

The principle behind revenue-sharing is a simple one: a portion of federal tax revenues generated by the graduated income tax would be returned to states and to some (but not all) local governments in accordance with a prescribed formula defined by Congress and automatically followed each fiscal year. There would be, as proponents put it, "no strings attached" to revenue-sharing funds; recipient governments could use the money for almost any purpose. There would also be no need for a state or local government to apply for the funds; once the formula was determined, the money would be forthcoming with no uncertainty and no delay. Such an arrangement seems to respond directly to the sharpest criticisms of the grant-in-aid system, as they were made known to Congress and federal agencies during the course of the 1960s.[47]

The idea of revenue-sharing had first surfaced in the late 1950s when Representative (later Defense Secretary) Melvin Laird, a conservative Wisconsin Republican, introduced legislation in the House of Representatives, although the bill attracted little attention at the time and was never brought to a formal vote. Support for the idea also came from such liberal Democrats as Minnesota economist Walter Heller, who later (as chairman of the Council of Economic Advisors) pressed for adoption of the idea within the Executive Office of the President.[48] But little headway was made until after the political reactions against the course of federal grants-in-aid set in. More frequent calls were heard for both bloc grants and some form of revenue-sharing, based on their greater simplicity compared to grant funding and on the undeniable need for more money in a period when costs of government were rising across the board. It was not until Richard Nixon entered the White House, however, that serious effort was made to enact revenue-sharing legislation with full presidential backing.[49]

What made revenue-sharing so appealing to Nixon was that it allowed him to satisfy a number of political constituencies simultaneously at a relatively low cost (starting at $5.3 billion per year and rising to some $6 billion annually). As an alternative to grants, it held great appeal to disgruntled state and local officials, including a fair number of Democrats. These officials also welcomed the additional revenue that would supplement existing grants-in-aid. But revenue-sharing permitted Nixon to pay a large political debt as well to the electoral coalition which had put him in the White House. He had campaigned in 1968 for the votes of the "forgotten Americans," the "silent majority" comprising (in the words of some observers at the time) "the un-young, the un-poor, and the un-black." Much of Johnson's Great Society program had been explicitly addressed to the plight of the poor, especially in large central cities, and the ghetto violence of the mid- and late 1960s had led many to resent expenditures on programs aimed at aiding the urban poor, whom they blamed for the violence. Whether these public perceptions and attitudes were justified—and considerable evidence suggests they were not—is not the point. The heart of the matter was that Nixon was proposing a way whereby local political majorities—through their elected officials—could reassert their priorities in local (and state) spending, and not be bound to federal grant programs with which they disagreed more and more strongly on policy as well as procedural grounds.

Revenue-sharing also appealed to a good many Republicans on political-philosophical grounds. This was a way, Nixon suggested, to pass power back from the national government to the states and localities—as good a Republican doctrine as one can find. Nixon's program included limiting, if not reducing, the federal government's role in the life of the nation, and revenue-sharing was to be a first step in that direction. The appeal of this idea was not limited to Republicans, of course; quite a few Democrats and independents seemed sympathetic to any effort which would dilute the power of the "federal bureaucrats" and the national government generally.

Nixon, in fact, planned to phase in two different types of revenue-sharing, only one of which was actually adopted and implemented. *General* revenue-sharing, adopted in 1972, incorporated the themes described above in a program of allocations that operated over a five-year period (renewed for three years and nine months beginning January 1, 1977). Recipient governments (state, city, county, and township) could use the money largely as their executives and legislatures saw fit. States were permitted to apply their share to any program, of any type, without restriction; because single-purpose districts (including school districts) were excluded from receiving general revenue-sharing money, many states used the bulk of their money as state aid to education. Local governments were not entirely unrestricted, however. They were obligated to use their funding for operating and maintenance in eight "priority" categories: public safety, environmental protection, public transportation, health, recreation, libraries, social services for the poor or aged, and financial administration.[50] But it was left to their discretion how to define the composition of each category, and the majority of local functions were covered in any event. States and localities were also obligated to observe common procedural guidelines, such as complying with civil rights requirements, reporting the uses of revenue-sharing, and not using their revenue-sharing money as matching funds for grants-in-aid.

Of all the general revenue-sharing funds going into a state, one-third was allocated to the state government and the remaining two-thirds to the local governments mentioned above. The allocation formula took into account the population within a government jurisdiction (the more people, the higher the amount), the per-capita taxes already raised by that government (the greater the tax effort, the higher the amount), and the per-capita income of the population (the lower this figure, the higher the amount). When Congress approved an extension of general revenue-sharing in the fall of 1976, a few requirements were changed. The annual amount currently available is $6.65 billion, with the possibility of its being increased to $6.85 billion if income tax revenues rise sufficiently; local governments are no longer limited to spending in the eight "priority" categories; and it is now possible to use revenue-sharing money as matching funds.

General revenue-sharing was designed to supplement existing grant-in-aid funding, to help meet rising costs of government, and to build more discretion into the spending decisions of state and local officials. *Special* revenue-sharing, however, would have replaced the grant-in-aid structure, retaining the policy areas under which funds were allocated, but removing almost entirely federal agency and congressional guidelines for spending the money. This clearly would have placed the emphasis on state and local officials' judgments and preferences for the determination of most domestic policy, and would have effectively counteracted all the rationales and purposes of grants-in-aid. It would have (1) removed primary concern for national goals, standards, and policies; (2) substituted state and local political will for any sort of national perspective; and (3) defined state/local majorities rather than national majorities as the key electoral decision makers. Though special revenue-sharing was never enacted, general revenue-sharing embodies some of these same themes and does, in fact, build greater discretion for state and local officials into the intergovernmental fiscal system.

How that discretion would be used in spending general revenue-sharing funds was a major concern of some people in and out of government. In particular, those who had approved of national grants-in-aid for urban assistance, antipoverty programs, and federal programs in areas such as education, and as a means of fostering general social equality, feared the consequences of placing unrestricted funds in the hands of state and local officials. Two specific concerns stood out: (1) that revenue-sharing funds would be spent on programs and projects benefiting the relatively affluent majority in states and local communities instead of the poor, and (2) that the kinds of citizen participation increasingly mandated in federal grant programs would be lacking in decision making under the revenue-sharing system. The actual impacts of general revenue-sharing, then, merit brief consideration.

Impacts of Revenue-Sharing

Among the studies of revenue-sharing's effects, the work of Richard Nathan and his Brookings Institution associates has been most exhaustive.[51] The Brookings team studied the effects of the distribution formula, especially on urban centers and state governments; the purposes for which recipient governments spent the funds; and political effects, including participation in budgetary processes and impacts on intergovernmental relations.

The main findings concerning effects of the distribution formula were: (1) highly urbanized states, because of relatively high per-capita income, received less per capita than did some poorer states with high tax effort; (2) congressional intent to assist poorer states was fulfilled, perhaps to a greater extent than any other single aspect of the formula; (3) metropolitan central cities received considerably more funding per capita than did their suburbs—in some cases, twice as much—but did not fare as well as smaller communities elsewhere in the same state; and (4) heavily populated, highly urbanized counties received much less shared revenue than others, in relation to nonschool tax revenue raised locally.

Concerning use of revenue-sharing funds, a number of important features emerged. A fundamental finding was that *reported* and *actual* uses of the money may be different, due as much to difficulties in tracing specific dollar allocations and some misunderstandings about reporting requirements as to deliberate distortion. Within the constraints of uncertainty posed by that finding, however, some other conclusions were drawn. A central question was whether revenue-sharing funds would be spent for new programs or for substitution purposes, taking the place of other funds that were then put to other uses—such as offsetting a tax cut or replacing money that otherwise would have had to come from borrowing, a tax increase, or lowering general fund balances. "In general, the larger and harder-pressed local governments used proportionately more of their shared revenue to make ends meet and relieve fiscal pressure— that is, for substitution purposes. The smaller and financially better off jurisdictions used more of their money for new purposes."[52] Of the new spending—nearly 60 percent for local units of government and just over 33 percent for state governments in the Brookings sample—four-fifths was capital expenditures. Spending for construction of transportation facilities or sewage treatment plants was given higher priority than spending for social programs—a finding of some political significance. Perhaps equally important, many communities spent funds on new town halls, municipal golf courses, and other projects justified in terms of their general benefit rather than specific impacts.

Politically, revenue-sharing stimulated new activity, more competition, and more public interest in the budgetary process. Some communities (such as the city of Phoenix and Los Angeles County) set up revenue-sharing hearings that were widely publicized and drew substantial public response. This was not a universal phenomenon, however, so that any assessment of citizen participation must necessarily be inconclusive. As for intergovernmental relations, it appears that revenue-sharing money made possible joint efforts among two or more governments that otherwise would not have occurred. Seven states in the Brookings sample supervised fairly closely the expenditure of revenue-sharing funds by their local governments, though most of the seven had traditionally kept close watch over local finances and fiscal activity. Finally, townships were found to have received substantially more under revenue-sharing than the Brookings team felt was warranted, given a low level of per-capita expenditure. These and other findings were given attention in congressional debate over renewal of revenue-sharing, but major changes in the formula and in political requirements were few.

David Caputo and Richard Cole also examined the effects of revenue-sharing, confining their research to cities of over 50,000 population. Their principal findings were: (1) expenditures tended to be concentrated in a few categories—notably, law enforcement, fire protection, street repairs, and parks and recreation; (2) in large cities, poverty and its alleviation were not major spending targets; (3) funds tended to support existing programs rather than new ones; (4) tax rates were stabilized, not lowered; and (5) city officials seemed generally pleased with the revenue-sharing program.[53] Their findings coincide, for the most part, with those of Nathan and his associates.

In sum, revenue-sharing funds have been applied at the local level to problems of capital expenditure, tax relief, and, in some cases, upgrading or replacement of physical structures. States have used much of their funding for education, since school districts are not eligible (as noted previously). Social programs aiding racial minorities and other poor people have not received major emphasis under revenue-sharing. Determining exactly how revenue-sharing dollars have been spent, however, continues to pose some difficulties.

Intergovernmental Administrative Relations

Both before and during the 1960s, administration of funds under grant-in-aid programs was largely in the hands of individual agencies and their professional administrative personnel. As the aid system grew more specialized, agency personnel at the national level came to work more and more closely with their counterparts in state and local agencies, who had similar backgrounds, interests, and professional competence. "With each new category and subcategory of aid, a new crop of specialists and sub-specialists popped up at all levels of government to administer the wide variety of programs . . ."[54] Thus aid administrators in the national Department of Housing and Urban Development (HUD) developed ongoing working and fiscal ties with housing administrators in state and local governments; officials of the Bureau of Public Roads, with state and local highway department personnel; U.S. Office of Education administrators, with their counterparts in state departments of education and officials in the myriad local school districts; and Agriculture Department staffs, with state and county agricultural officials.

Some observers, noting the strengthening of these intergovernmental administrative linkages, cautioned that elected officials' lack of leverage within the bureaucracy would make it very difficult for them to hold administrators accountable for the way programs were implemented. The Advisory Commission on Intergovernmental Relations (ACIR) warned in 1969 of "vertical functional autocracies"[55] in referring to the problems encountered by chief executives and legislators in effectively overseeing the activities of their respective bureaucracies under national grants-in-aid.

In the early 1970s one observer wrote approvingly of some measures that had been taken in response to growing administrative autonomy, describing these measures as "curbing the 'new feudalists,' " a reference to the feudal system in the Middle Ages, which involved "strong contractual relationships between lord and vassal with a monarch at the top who reigned but did little ruling."[56] The measures to which he referred included reorganizations of the president's domestic policy staff, of congressional oversight capability and fiscal controls, and of federal agency field offices throughout the country; the Intergovernmental Personnel Act of 1970, which was designed to upgrade core management staffs of states and localities; and stronger state executive and legislative tools of administrative supervision.[57]

The development of intergovernmental administrative ties gave rise to a new label for the federal system. Whereas "dual federalism" was likened to a layer cake, with different levels of government clearly distinguished from one another, and whereas growing cooperation was likened to a marble cake, in which functions of different levels of government were intermingled, the new vertical administrative patterns prompted Deil Wright to coin the term "picket-fence" federalism.[58] Figure 5-2 illustrates Wright's conception of the federal picket fence. The bureaucratic officials within each of these "pickets," together with their clientele groups at all levels, do not always agree, of course, on the substance and procedures of programs they administer. But the responsibility for formulating many basic policies and resolving many of the conflicts that arise rests largely—and often exclusively—within the discretion of these functional groupings. How that situation can be reconciled with democratic values of public accountability and control is an important question, and one not easily answered.

Vertical administrative relations are not the whole story, however. There has also been a rapid growth in interstate and interlocal (horizontal) relations centering on administrative units and functions, as well as an

Figure 5–2 Picket-Fence* Federalism: A Schematic Representation

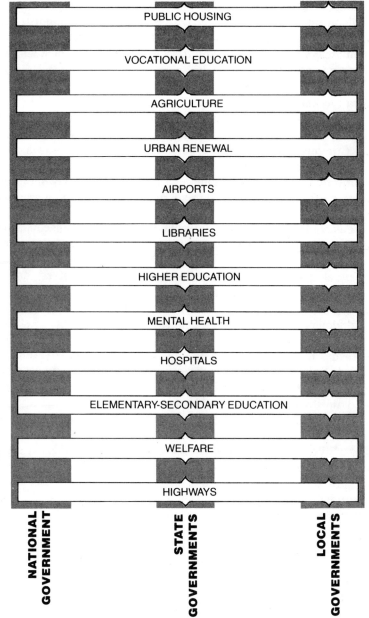

PUBLIC HOUSING

VOCATIONAL EDUCATION

AGRICULTURE

URBAN RENEWAL

AIRPORTS

LIBRARIES

HIGHER EDUCATION

MENTAL HEALTH

HOSPITALS

ELEMENTARY-SECONDARY EDUCATION

WELFARE

HIGHWAYS

NATIONAL GOVERNMENT

STATE GOVERNMENTS

LOCAL GOVERNMENTS

*Each picket represents the political and administrative ties among specialists in each policy area at all three levels of government.

Source: Adapted from Deil S. Wright, "Intergovernmental Relations: An Analytical Overview," *Annals* of the American Academy of Political and Social Science, 416 (November 1974), p. 15.

emerging emphasis on organizing functions on a regional basis, both within individual states and across state lines.[59] Local governments, which, historically, were restricted in many states from acting independently, have acquired substantial discretion in negotiating interlocal agreements, and now quite commonly collaborate on a variety of projects. Interstate compacts have also proliferated, many dealing with problems which clearly cross state lines, such as air pollution, water supply, water quality, and mass transportation. The New York Port Authority is an example of a mass transportation interstate compact.

Substate regions have been formed—mainly in response to national government encouragement—for a variety of purposes. These have included planning, economic development, water pollution abatement, manpower development, public health, review of grant applications, airport development, and air quality maintenance. Here again the "picket-fence" analogy is evident because national, state, and local administrative officials all have active roles in substate regional functions. Finally, interstate regional bodies—some of them the result of interstate compacts, others created through federal government action—deal either with water resource development, economic planning, or various aspects of both. Examples include the Delaware River Basin Commission, Appalachian Regional Commission, and Title V Commissions for Regional Economic Development (established in Title V of the Public Works and Economic Development Act of 1965).

One other entity of recent vintage is the Federal Regional Council, composed of the regional directors of major federal agencies in each of the ten federal government administrative regions. These bodies serve a coordinative role, seeking to integrate programs managed by the different agencies within their regions. This represents an attempt to foster coordination at an intermediate level between agency headquarters in the nation's capital and state and local levels, supplementing other efforts to improve the overall coordination of governmental activities.

OMB Circular A–95:
An Attempt at "Better Coordination"

The need for improving coordination among the hundreds of grant programs and the thousands of individual aid allocations was increasingly evident during the late 1960s. Congress and the federal agencies most deeply involved with grant funding began requiring some forms of areawide review of the aid requests local governments were making, especially in metropolitan areas. The aim was to weed out requests that could be met some other, better way; those which, if approved, would conflict with another approved grant proposal; and those which duplicated other allocations for similar or even identical purposes.

Several specific legislative steps were taken. Section 204 of the Model Cities Act of 1966, discussed earlier, stipulated that applications from local governments in metropolitan areas must first have been screened by an areawide comprehensive planning agency. Then, in 1968, Congress passed the Intergovernmental Cooperation Act, which contained three important provisions. Title IV of the act directed that more regularized evaluation-and-review procedures be set up for grant requests. Section 401(b) directed that the planning process take into consideration as fully as possible all national, state, regional, and local viewpoints which might be pertinent to the policy under consideration. And Section 401(c) made it national policy to seek maximum congruence (matching) between national program objectives and the objectives of state, regional, and local planning. These were lofty, if somewhat ambiguous, goals, but necessary in the face of widespread local (and state) unwillingness to consider effects of their own programs and planning on those of neighboring jurisdictions. Though interlocal cooperation was on the rise, as noted previously, there was still a good deal of hostility and competition, which made prior consultation about grant applications unsystematic at best. The 1966 and 1968 legislative acts were geared to forcing such consultation where it was not occurring voluntarily.

In July 1969 the Bureau of the Budget (now OMB) issued *Circular A–95*, which was designed to implement the evaluation-and-review provisions of the Model Cities and Intergovernmental Cooperation acts. The requirements laid down by A–95 were not the first effort to improve coordination; previous circulars had established standardized grant and audit procedures, and had designated various agencies as monitors of the grant system. But A–95 went further, requiring (1) all local aid applicants to forward their proposals to the areawide screening agency, (2) the screening agency to inform other governments in the area of a proposal's contents and to solicit reactions from those governments, (3) the local government to consider the responses received and to modify its own proposal if it chose to do so, (4) the screening agency to evaluate the proposal for consistency with existing state, regional, and local planning, and (5) the screening agency to forward the package of documents to the federal agency from which the grant would come.

This was clearly a more systematic process than any which had operated previously, one which required an aid applicant to "touch base" with other governmental jurisdictions that might be affected in some way by the applicant's receiving the grant. After one city had applied for a sewage treatment construction grant, for example, officials discovered that a neighboring jurisdiction was about to apply for the identical grant. Instead of both cities applying, the decision was made to collaborate on the project and apply for a single, somewhat larger grant—a better use of public funds. On another occasion, local officials discovered that a recreation development grant for a nearby lake wouldn't make much sense if the city on the other side of the lake received a grant for expanding its water supply—drawing its water out of the same lake! These illustrations suggest the possible benefits of prior "review and comment," and point up the sorts of problems that had existed.

Circular A–95 applied at the outset to some fifty government programs, most in planning and direct physical development managed by federal agencies. In April 1971 a major expansion of program coverage was instituted, bringing the total to about one hundred, including many social and human resource programs, such as facilities for the mentally retarded, law enforcement action grants, neighborhood development, education facilities, and manpower planning. In November 1973 OMB added thirty-five more programs, including health, adult and vocational education, job opportunity, and rural development. And in early 1976 coverage was again expanded, to some two hundred programs in all.

Smooth coordination is highly prized in American society, yet achieving it is often trickier than it might seem. Circular A–95 represents one approach to the problem. In effect, OMB ordered better communication and consultation among the governments at state and local levels. In political scientist James Sundquist's words, a central coordinator (OMB) "expedited, facilitated, and even coerced" better lateral coordination— that is, "consultation, sharing of information, and negotiation among equals." [60] Prior to 1969, the national government "chose to rely almost wholly upon systems of mutual adjustment [lateral coordination] rather than of central direction, upon what could be attained through negotiation among equals rather than through the exercise of hierarchical authority." [61] When that did not work adequately, the process of consultation was made a prerequisite for approval of aid applications—and that, not surprisingly, brought about more interlocal communication and a greater willingness to "touch base" with officials of neighboring government jurisdictions.

Circular A–95 has not been an unmixed blessing, however. While there have been undeniable positive effects, and while the review process is now very well established within the grant system, some problems remain. First, it is not clear that the "vertical functional autocrats" who are still largely responsible for administering grants-in-aid have cooperated more willingly than before at any level of government in the effort to secure a more rational, consistent grant system. Second, the state and local clearinghouses which refer proposals for review and comment vary considerably in how carefully they evaluate grant proposals, resulting in very uneven patterns of coordination. Third, local governments appear to be much more concerned with getting their aid applications approved than with more abstract matters of coordination (except when improving coordination will also work to their programmatic or fiscal advantage). Fourth, it is difficult to evaluate grant proposals for consistency with existing state or local plans when, as is sometimes the case, *no such plans exist*. Finally, there is some concern that the states and localities have been co-opted into the decision-making process of the national government via A–95, thus damaging the essential nature of the federal system. This concern is especially relevant since it was OMB, acting at the direction of the president, which issued A–95. If centralized authority was something to be avoided according to the original design of our national government, more recent designs seem in some respects to point the other way. Circular A–95 may be in this category, even though it has helped to reduce wasteful and duplicative spending and foster better overall cooperation among thousands of local governments.[62]

Circular A–95 is one prominent example of some recent steps taken in fiscal federalism, and it straddles the dividing line between intergovernmental fiscal and administrative relations. While it is possible to discuss these two dimensions of intergovernmental relations as separate topics, the operating realities of contemporary American federalism (as Circular A–95 illustrates) make them increasingly intertwined and inseparable. This development has important implications for administrative practice, to which we now turn.

Implications of IGR for Public Administration

The diffuse nature of federalism combines with growing intergovernmental ties in all directions to create a situation that is complex indeed. Public administration has been altered, perhaps permanently, by rapid change in intergovernmental relations.

We return to a comment made early in this chapter; namely, that intergovernmental relations has had a strong administrative component. Despite recent efforts to gain greater control of their bureaucracies, most chief executives have failed to stem the growth of vertical functional bureaucratic linkages—the "autocracies" referred to by ACIR. One reason for the inability of a president or governor to overcome the institutional strength of bureaucracies is precisely that the latter can call on political support from at least one other level or unit of government much more easily than a chief executive can. Intergovernmental administrative relations, in other words, has served to strengthen existing bureaucratic autonomy at *every* level of government.

A second area of serious concern for public administration resulting from the workings of the federal system is fiscal relations, and especially continuing financial difficulties of some American governments. Problems like those experienced in New York City in the mid-1970s may come to hound political leaders, administrators, and citizens in other communities, large and small, struggling to avoid fiscal chaos because of declining property tax bases and escalating service costs. Intergovernmental aid can do much to "bail out" a city here and a suburb there, but a real question exists whether costs imposed by inflation, rising service needs, and growing public employee union militancy can in fact be met over the long term by infusions of aid. The core of the problem is that recipient governments can easily develop a continuing dependency on such aid, whether national or state, and it is possible that needed aid will not always be there. Programs funded through intergovernmental aid, in whole or in part, could face sharp cuts or even curtailment if funding declined or ceased. For some, that is no longer just a hypothetical possibility: urban aid grants declined during the early 1970s, leaving a fiscal slack that was not taken up by revenue-sharing, and already hard-pressed central cities are worse off than before. Program cuts, efficiency, and priority-setting are relatively new concerns in public administration—in degree, if not in substance—arising out of the very real fiscal crunch enveloping this country and all of its governments.

A third area of concern is control over grants-in-aid and other funding. A stark reality of intergovernmental relations is bureaucratic—and "interbureaucratic"—controls on much of the money flowing from one level to another, raising questions about public accountability and about the ability of chief executives to effectively coordinate spending. Public administrators have a great deal of discretionary authority over public spending, and the age-old issue of fiscal responsibility and accountability has taken a new form as a result. A related concern is that some government institutions, such as state legislatures, lack any real access to key decision makers or impact on decisions regarding intergovernmental funding. Bureaucrats are, for the most part, "in the driver's seat" when it comes to grant funding, still by far the largest part of intergovernmental aid. Whether that is all to the good is an important question.

Finally, administrators themselves need to be alert to policies and programs in existence at other levels of government and to how these relate to their own activities. They need also to be conscious of their own roles in administrative relations, and of how they help shape programs managed by intergovernmental means. It is clear that in the relatively new setting of intergovernmental relations, political power is being exercised in news ways, with implications that are not yet fully understood.

SUMMARY

Federalism is a structure of government that divides power between a national government and regional units which have some independent standing in the governmental system. In a federal system governments may act separately, and may conflict over the proper boundaries between functions, or they may collaborate on shared ventures. American federalism emphasized separation of functions in earlier years and collaboration in more recent times.

Early in the nation's history some fundamental issues in national-state relations were resolved (for example, supremacy of national powers in regulating interstate commerce). However, the issue of slavery, plus deep differences over national versus state sovereignty, proved impossible to reconcile through the political process, and a Union victory in the Civil War was required to reaffirm a federal rather than a confederate system as our basic framework. The last third of the nineteenth century and the early years of the twentieth saw consolidation of national powers and the emergence of growing authority to regulate an evolving national economy. The Bill of Rights gradually was "nationalized," and intergovernmental collaboration became more frequent as the tasks of government grew more complex.

"Intergovernmental relations" refers to the varied activities and interactions involving all types and levels of government within the federal system. Strictly speaking, contacts among governments are contacts among their officials. It is assumed, also, that regular and informal contacts constitute the heart of intergovernmental relations. Such contacts may be competitive or cooperative, or some blend of the two. Fritschler and Segal suggest that joint policy making, mutual accommodation, innovative conflict, and disintegrative conflict may prevail at different times, depending upon the identity, variety, and attitudes of the participants and upon the ways in which decisions are made. Of growing importance in IGR is the complex of administrative relations which cross governmental lines.

The processes of making public policy are central to this "new-style" federalism. Action by nongovernmental institutions, and action on portions of policy problems rather than comprehensive approaches, are part of IGR. Legal issues, which once dominated federalism, still have some relevance; decisions about national versus state regulatory standards and about the application of Bill of Rights protections to actions of state and local officials are examples of current, policy-related legal questions.

There is disagreement about whether significant intergovernmental cooperation dates back to the earliest years of the nation, or whether it originated in its present form more recently. But the fact that the national government has become more active in this century is not disputed; and there is general agreement that the New Deal period marked a turning point in the development of contemporary IGR.

Intergovernmental fiscal relations, or fiscal federalism, is one of the most important aspects of current governmental activity. One government aiding another financially is not a new phenomenon, but the scope and variety of devices have expanded and become a principal feature of the federal system. A major factor in this expansion is the existence of a "fiscal mismatch." State and local governments have weaker tax bases and use less productive generators of revenue (that is, taxes) than the national government, yet they carry responsibility for delivering the bulk of public services. As a result, there has been rising demand for aid from the national government to state and local governments in the wake of public pressures for more—and more costly—public services.

The principal means of accomplishing this has been the grant-in-aid. Between 1961 and 1969, the period of greatest grant proliferation, the number of separate grant authorizations rose from 45 to about 400, amounting to over $20 billion in 1969 compared to $7 billion in 1961. In the 1970s grants-in-aid have accounted for about one-fourth of state/local revenues annually. Much grant funding was to be used for specific purposes, and proliferation of grant categories accompanied the other changes. An emphasis on state and local planning as a prerequisite for grant funding has emerged as a central part of the grant-in-aid system. Grants were supported because they afforded a single focal point for initiating action; they could be used to aid state and local political minorities; they were considered appropriate for dealing with problems of national scope; and many activities of state and local governments were said to have national impact, offering considerable benefits—such as recreation and education—to the nation as a whole.

The major forms of grants-in-aid are distinguished in terms of specific or general definitions of purpose, and by formula or project allocations. Categorical grants are used for very specific purposes, defined principally by the federal agency making the grant. Bloc grants may be used more flexibly by aid recipients, though still within a specified policy area. The great majority of grants during the 1960s were categorical; in the mid-1970s some movement toward bloc grants became noticeable. Formula grants are established for purposes common to a wide variety of recipients (such as aid to the blind). Project grants require separate application and approval, and involve a very complex set of procedural requirements. The national share of grant funding has varied from 50 to 100 percent of an individual grant.

In the 1960s the grant system changed in significant ways—more numerous project grants, more varied matching-grant formulas, multiple-function grants, wider eligibility of recipients, more direct aid to the urban poor, aid to private institutions, and increased attention to planning. Underlying these changes was a new emphasis on *national* goals and programs, with greater national influence in determining policy directions. But the grant system also had some problems—considerable overlap, duplication, and confusion; failure to equalize resources through grants because of proliferating project grants; allegations that state and local priorities were distorted by the availability of grants for some purposes but not for others; the possibility that policy initiative was being yielded to the national government; and failure to aid all services equally. Other problems included excessive paperwork, delay, and uncertainty for grant applicants, and problems of coordination involving different agencies and grants covering only parts of projects. Out of mounting concerns over these constraints came pressures for easing restrictions on federal aid, either in the form of bloc grants or of revenue-sharing.

First proposed in the 1950s, revenue-sharing was enacted in 1972 as a response to some of the problems of grants-in-aid. This device would have "no strings attached" (or at least very few); it would make more money available at a time when there was need for it; and it appeared to reduce the role of the national government relative to that of states and localities. General revenue-sharing, designed to supplement grants, was enacted with no restrictions on state use and few on local use of funds. It was renewed in 1976 with an easing of some of the original restrictions and somewhat more money allocated each year. Special revenue-sharing, which would have replaced grants, was never approved by Congress, though it appears to have been the ultimate objective of President Nixon in his efforts to reform fiscal federalism.

Actual impacts of general revenue-sharing include the following. More heavily urbanized states, local governments, and counties received less per capita in revenue-sharing funds than did less urbanized places. Local governments—especially those larger and harder-pressed—tended to use more of their revenue-sharing amounts for new programs than did states, concentrating on capital construction projects. Politically, more public participation seemed to be evident in some communities, particularly in decisions about how to spend revenue-sharing funds, and intergovernmental collaboration increased a bit as a result of disbursement of these funds. In large cities, expenditures were concentrated in a few areas (of which poverty was not one), and tax rates were stabilized, but not appreciably lowered. Overall, local use centered on capital expenditures, tax relief, and physical structures; states gave much of their funding to education; and neither stressed social programs. All this is said, however, keeping in mind that accounting for expenditure of revenue-sharing dollars is not an exact art.

Intergovernmental administrative relations grew along with fiscal relations due to the specialized nature of the grants process. As new categories were established, vertical linkages developed among national, state, and local bureaucrats who had common knowledge, backgrounds, and interests in the particular grant allocations. Some concern emerged about the inability of top executives and legislators to effectively control these "vertical functional autocracies," and steps were taken in the late 1960s and early 1970s aimed at counteracting the effects of specialized decision making and increasing specialists' accountability to the larger political system. Other administrative ties included horizontal relations and regionalism.

OMB Circular A–95—issued to implement the Model Cities and Intergovernmental Cooperation acts—was aimed at improving coordination of grants and the activities of programmatic specialists. It required all local aid applicants to submit their proposals to a "review-and-comment" procedure under the direction of an areawide screening agency (later known as a "clearinghouse"). A–95 led to more effective prior consultations among aid applicants, and its coverage was subsequently broadened so that it now includes some 200 programs. It represented a form of lateral coordination imposed by central direction. While beneficial in many respects, A–95 has not been without some persistent problems. Questions also have been raised concerning its impact on the federal system itself, especially since central (presidential) authority was the basis for the issuance of the circular. Finally, Circular A–95 demonstrates the growing intertwining of fiscal and administrative relations in contemporary federalism—a development of considerable significance.

Implications of increased intergovernmental relations for public administration include the following. First, IGR has had a strong administrative component, including (perhaps foremost) vertical functional linkages among bureaucrats, lending additional political weight to bureaucrats in charge of specialized programs. Second, fiscal relations— and especially fiscal difficulties—pose a serious problem for public administration. Intergovernmental aid may have created continuing dependencies at a time when a fiscal crunch has affected all governments. Third, bureaucratic control over grant funding raises serious questions about fiscal responsibility and accountability, though in a new form. The ability of top executives to coordinate spending is a related concern, as is the possibility that some government institutions—such as state legislatures—may be shut out of important intergovernmental decisions. Finally, administrators need to understand the key roles they play in an intergovernmental system where political power is exercised in ways not fully understood.

NOTES

1. Local government has no independent standing within the legal framework of federalism, though politically local governments possess considerable autonomy from their "parent" governments, the states.

2. Michael Reagan, *The New Federalism* (New York: Oxford University Press, 1972), p. 3.

3. *McCulloch* v. *Maryland,* 4 Wheaton 316 (1819).

4. *Barron* v. *Baltimore,* 7 Peters 243 (1833).

5. *Gitlow* v. *New York,* 268 U.S. 652 (1925).

6. See Henry J. Abraham, *Freedom and the Court: Civil Rights and Liberties in the United States,* 3rd ed. (New York: Oxford University Press, 1977).

7. W. Brooke Graves, *American Intergovernmental Relations* (New York: Charles Scribner's Sons, 1964), pp. 516–526.

8. William Anderson, *Intergovernmental Relations in Review* (Minneapolis: University of Minnesota Press, 1960), p. 3, cited by Deil S. Wright, "Intergovernmental Relations: An Analytical Overview," *Annals of the American Academy of*

Political and Social Science: Intergovernmental Relations in America Today, 416 (November 1974), 2. This discussion draws extensively on Wright's treatment.

9. Deil S. Wright, "Intergovernmental Relations: An Analytical Overview," *Annals of the American Academy of Political and Social Science: Intergovernmental Relations in America Today,* 416 (November 1974), 2.

10. Anderson, *Intergovernmental Relations in Review,* p. 4.

11. Wright, "Intergovernmental Relations: An Analytical Overview," p. 2.

12. Ibid.

13. Ibid., p. 15.

14. A. Lee Fritschler and Morley Segal, "Intergovernmental Relations and Contemporary Political Science: Developing an Integrative Typology," *PUBLIUS: The Journal of Federalism,* 1 (Winter 1972), 95–122.

15. Ibid., p. 106.

16. Ibid.

17. Ibid.

18. Ibid., p. 119.

19. Ibid.

20. Commission on Intergovernmental Relations, *A Report to the President for Transmittal to the Congress* (Washington, D.C.: U.S. Government Printing Office, June 1955), p. 33, cited in Deil S. Wright, "Intergovernmental Relations: An Analytical Overview," *Annals of the American Academy of Political and Social Science: Intergovernmental Relations in America Today,* 416 (November 1974), 4.

21. Richard H. Leach, *American Federalism* (New York: W. W. Norton, 1970), p. 59.

22. Ibid., pp. 61–63. See chapter 12.

23. See Daniel J. Elazar, *American Federalism: A View from the States,* 2nd ed. (New York: Thomas Y. Crowell, 1972), pp. 53–54.

24. *Miranda* v. *Arizona,* 384 U.S. 436 (1966). A conviction was reversed on the basis of the Miranda principle as recently as March 1977, demonstrating once again that state and local government behavior (in this case, by the police) under *national* standards is still a matter of some debate. *Brewer* v. *Williams,* 430 U.S. 387, 97 S. Ct. 1232 (1977).

25. See *The American Partnership: Intergovernmental Cooperation in the Nineteenth Century United States* (Chicago: University of Chicago Press, 1962). See also Morton Grodzins, *The American System: A New View of Government in the United States* (Chicago: Rand McNally, 1966).

26. See Parris N. Glendening and Mavis Mann Reeves, *Pragmatic Federalism: An Intergovernmental View of American Government* (Pacific Palisades, Calif.: Palisades Publishers, 1977), p. 120.

27. "The Condition of American Federalism: An Historian's View," A Study submitted by the Committee on Government Operations, Subcommittee on Intergovernmental Relations, U.S. Senate, 89th Congress, 2nd Session, 1966, reprinted in Mavis Mann Reeves and Parris N. Glendening, eds., *Controversies of State and Local Political Systems* (Boston: Allyn and Bacon, 1972), pp. 64–92.

28. See Allen Schick, "Toward the Cybernetic State," in Dwight Waldo, ed., *Public Administration in a Time of Turbulence* (Scranton, Pa.: Chandler Publishing, 1971), pp. 214–233, at p. 217.

29. Leach, *American Federalism,* pp. 28–35. Organized lobbying by state and local officials has become more prominent in recent years. See Donald Haider, *When Governments Come to Washington: Governors, Mayors, and Intergovernmental Lobbying* (New York: The Free Press, 1974).

30. Reagan, *The New Federalism,* pp. 31–32.

31. Since this taxes wealthier individuals proportionately more heavily than it does poorer ones, it also produces the most extensive redistribution of personal wealth.

32. Reagan, *The New Federalism,* pp. 36–42; Glendening and Reeves, *Pragmatic Federalism,* p. 150. States and localities both have made increasing use of sales and wage taxes in an effort to boost their revenues.

33. Reagan, *The New Federalism,* p. 55.

34. Ibid.

35. Ibid., p. 56; Office of Management and Budget, *Special Analyses: Budget of the United States Government, Fiscal Year 1978* (Washington, D.C.: U.S. Government Printing Office, 1977), p. 265.

36. Glendening and Reeves, *Pragmatic Federalism,* p. 152.

37. The following description relies on Reagan, *The New Federalism,* chapter 3.

38. Ibid., p. 59.

39. Ibid., pp. 60–61.

40. Elazar, *American Federalism: A View from the States,* pp. 70–77.

41. Ironically, it was under Eisenhower—a Republican president—that a systematic effort had been made to define broad national goals in the late 1950s. See President's Commission on National Goals, *Goals for Americans* (Englewood Cliffs, N.J.: Prentice-Hall, 1960). Nearly two decades later, this report still makes interesting reading.

42. See James L. Sundquist, with the collaboration of David W. Davis, *Making Federalism Work: A Study of Program Coordination at the Community Level* (Washington, D.C.: The Brookings Institution, 1969), pp. 3–6.

43. Reagan, *The New Federalism,* pp. 86–87.

44. Ibid., p. 88.

45. See Alan K. Campbell and Seymour Sacks, *Metropolitan America: Fiscal Patterns and Governmental Systems* (New York: The Free Press, 1967).

46. Reagan, *The New Federalism,* p. 86.

47. See, especially, *Creative Federalism:* Hearings before the Subcommittee on Intergovernmental Relations, Committee on Government Operations, U.S. Senate, 89th Congress, 2nd Session, on the Intergovernmental Cooperation Act of 1967 and related bills, November 1966 and February 1967 (Washington, D.C.: U.S. Government Printing Office, 1967).

48. Reagan, *The New Federalism,* p. 89. See also Paul R. Dommel, *The Politics of Revenue-Sharing* (Bloomington: Indiana University Press, 1974), and *Annals of the American Academy of Political and Social Science: General Revenue-Sharing and American Federalism,* 419 (May 1975).

49. It is probable that without the Vietnam War Lyndon Johnson would have made a greater effort to pass a revenue-sharing bill. Vietnam, in fact, may have had a more direct impact on the fate of revenue-sharing under Johnson; some observers have suggested that Heller pushed for its adoption in 1963–1964 be-

cause of an anticipated budget *surplus,* and administration economists were seeking a way to increase expenditures for public services rather than cut taxes! Vietnam, among its many other effects, removed any chance of a budget surplus—yet the idea of revenue-sharing lingered on. See David A. Caputo and Richard L. Cole, *Urban Politics and Decentralization: The Case of General Revenue Sharing* (Lexington, Mass.: D. C. Heath and Company, 1974), p. 27.

50. Michael A. Carroll, "The Impact of General Revenue Sharing on the Urban Planning Process—An Initial Assessment," *Public Administration Review,* 35 (March/April 1975), 143.

51. Richard P. Nathan, Allen D. Manvel, Susannah E. Calkins, and associates, *Monitoring Revenue Sharing* (Washington, D.C.: The Brookings Institution, 1975); the major findings are summarized in *The Brookings Bulletin,* 12 (Winter 1975), 1–3, and in *Brookings Research Report 139: Revenue Sharing in Operation* (Washington, D.C.: The Brookings Institution, 1975). See also Richard P. Nathan, Charles F. Adams, Jr., and associates, *Revenue Sharing: The Second Round* (Washington, D.C.: The Brookings Institution, 1977).

52. *The Brookings Bulletin,* 12 (Winter 1975), 1–3, at pp. 1–2.

53. David A. Caputo and Richard L. Cole, "General Revenue Sharing Expenditure Decisions in Cities over 50,000," *Public Administration Review,* 35 (March/April 1975), 136–142.

54. Advisory Commission on Intergovernmental Relations, *Improving Urban America: A Challenge to Federalism* (Washington, D.C.: ACIR, 1976), p. 5.

55. See *Urban America and the Federal System* (Washington, D.C.: ACIR, October 1969), p. 5.

56. David B. Walker, "Curbing the 'New Feudalists,' " *The Bureaucrat,* 1 (Spring 1972), 42–45, at p. 42.

57. Ibid., pp. 43–44.

58. Wright, "Intergovernmental Relations: An Analytical Overview," pp. 14–16. The metaphor of the picket fence was used by Terry Sanford in *Storm over the States* (New York: McGraw-Hill, 1967), p. 80.

59. See Richard H. Leach and Redding S. Sugg, Jr., *The Administration of Interstate Compacts* (Baton Rouge: Louisiana State University Press, 1959); Weldon V. Barton, *Interstate Compacts in the Political Process* (Chapel Hill: University of North Carolina Press, 1967); Martha Derthick, with Gary Bombardier, *Between State and Nation: Regional Organizations of the United States* (Washington, D.C.: The Brookings Institution, 1974); and Advisory Commission on Intergovernmental Relations, *Substate Regionalism and the Federal System,* 5 volumes (Washington, D.C.: ACIR, 1973 and 1974).

60. Sundquist, with Davis, *Making Federalism Work,* pp. 17–18.

61. Ibid., p. 19.

62. See George J. Gordon, "Office of Management and Budget Circular A–95: Perspectives and Implications," *PUBLIUS: The Journal of Federalism,* 4 (Winter 1974), 45–68.

SUGGESTED READINGS

Annals of the American Academy of Political and Social Science: General Revenue-Sharing and American Federalism, 419 (May 1975).

Annals of the American Academy of Political and Social Science: Intergovernmental Relations in America Today, 416 (November 1974).

Derthick, Martha, with Gary Bombardier. *Between State and Nation: Regional Organizations of the United States.* Washington, D.C.: The Brookings Institution, 1974.

Elazar, Daniel J. *American Federalism: A View from the States,* 2nd ed. New York: Thomas Y. Crowell, 1972.

Fox, Douglas M., ed. *The New Urban Politics: Cities and the Federal Government.* Pacific Palisades, Calif.: Goodyear Publishing, 1972.

Glendening, Parris N., and Mavis Mann Reeves. *Pragmatic Federalism: An Intergovernmental View of American Government.* Pacific Palisades, Calif.: Palisades Publishers, 1977.

Haider, Donald. *When Governments Come to Washington: Governors, Mayors, and Intergovernmental Lobbying.* New York: The Free Press, 1974.

Leach, Richard H. *American Federalism.* New York: W. W. Norton, 1970.

Nathan, Richard P., Charles F. Adams, Jr., and associates. *Revenue Sharing: The Second Round.* Washington, D.C.: The Brookings Institution, 1977.

Nathan, Richard P., Allen D. Manvel, Susannah E. Calkins, and associates. *Monitoring Revenue Sharing.* Washington, D.C.: The Brookings Institution, 1975.

Reagan, Michael. *The New Federalism.* New York: Oxford University Press, 1972.

PART THREE
DYNAMICS OF ORGANIZATION

This section focuses on organizational dynamics, addressing the subjects of organization theory, decision making, and administrative leadership. Chapter 6 reviews the evolution of organization theory, beginning with late nineteenth-century writings and following developments in theory up to the present time. Organization theory has moved from a formalistic, relatively "machine-like" view of organizations to more diverse and comprehensive concepts, reflecting growing complexity in approaches to organization and in organizations themselves. Emerging concern with *public* organizations is treated in the concluding section.

Chapter 7 examines administrative decision making—considerations which enter into decision processes and how decision makers deal with them. The impact of personal and organizational goals, factors involved in decisional choices, and the meaning of rationality in decision making are treated.

Chapter 8 deals with administrative leadership and its "tasks" within organizations. After a review of principal approaches to leadership, five tasks are discussed and leader roles examined carefully. While it is far from clear just what makes a "good" leader, certain characteristics and behaviors, as well as situational factors, appear to contribute to effective leadership.

CHAPTER 6
Organization Theory

Organization theory deals with the formal structures, internal workings, and external environment of complex human organizations. It has focused on prescribing how work and workers *ought* to be organized, and on attempting to explain actual consequences of organizational behavior (including individual behavior) on work being done and on the organization itself. The study of organizations—which spans business administration, sociology, economic theory, and psychology as well as public administration—has evolved over a period of nearly a century. It has had to contend with changing assumptions about men and women as workers in an organizational setting; with numerous and often contradictory hypotheses and research findings about what motivates workers and how motivation is affected by different types of tasks, employees, and situations; and with a variety of views, both past and present, regarding the reciprocal impacts of organizations and the environments in which they operate. As we proceed, some of the discussion will undoubtedly be familiar to anyone who has worked in an organization—which in our highly organized society means most of us.

Categorizing the major organization theories is no easy task. On one level, they can be distinguished according to whether they concentrate on needs, objectives, methods, and problems of management; on personal and social needs of workers within organizations; or on attempts by organizations to control their social, political, or economic environment. On another level, it is possible to identify a large number of specific theories, each with its own principal assumptions and emphases. Some of these theories overlap to an extent, sharing certain values and viewpoints while differing significantly in other respects. We shall examine four major areas of organization theory: (1) formal theories, (2) the human relations school, (3) the organizational humanism approach, and (4) modern organization theory.

Formal Theories of Organization

While formal organization theory as we think of it originated in the late nineteenth century, some formative thinking on the subject dates back many centuries. Such concepts of organization, in fact, were largely derived from the highly structured arrangements of most military forces throughout history and from relatively rigidly structured ecclesiastical organizations. Most notably, the idea of a *vertical hierarchy* (chain of command)—found in the great majority of contemporary organizations—springs from military and religious roots. Some other features of formal theory, such as the need for defining certain set procedures, also originated in very early organizations. However, the most prominent model of bureaucracy as an explicit form of social organization was formulated by German sociologist Max Weber (pronounced "vaber") late in the nineteenth century.

Max Weber and the Bureaucratic Model

The model set forth by Weber was intended to identify systematically the necessary components in a well-structured government bureaucracy. Weber prescribed the following key elements:

1. *Division of labor and functional specialization*—the work divided according to type and purpose, with clear areas of jurisdiction marked out for each working unit and an emphasis on eliminating overlapping and duplication of functions;
2. *Hierarchy*—a clear vertical "chain of command" in which each unit is subordinate to the one above it and superior to the one below it;
3. *Formal framework of rules and procedures*—designed to insure stability, predictability, and impersonality in bureaucratic operations, and thus equal treatment for all who deal with the organization, as well as reliability of performance;
4. *Maintenance of files and other records*—to insure that actions taken are both appropriate to the situation and consistent with past actions in similar circumstances;
5. *Professionalization*—employees who are (a) appointed (not elected) on the basis of their job-related skills, (b) full-time and career oriented, and (c) paid a regular salary and provided with a retirement pension.[1]

In addition to these explicit elements, two others should be mentioned. Weber obviously intended a government bureaucracy of the type outlined to be endowed with sufficient legal and political authority to function adequately. His model of bureaucracy, in fact, is based on both legal and rational authority[2] derived from a fixed central point in the political process, and is assumed to function under that authority.

The bureaucracy Weber envisioned may seem quite formalistic to modern observers, and lacking a number of important dimensions, such as informal lines of authority and communication or concern for the individual worker in the bureaucracy. Also, Weber himself indicated that the model was not meant to apply to all conceivable organizational situations, and that it represented only a broad framework rather than an all-encompassing model complete in every detail. However, despite these limitations, the Weber model has had a powerful influence on subsequent views of bureaucracy. His was the first effort to define systematically the dimensions of this new form of social organization, and prescribe or explain its operations in abstract and theoretical terms.

A comparison of the Weber model to contemporary American public administrative structures and operations illustrates simultaneously the attractiveness of the model as a yardstick against which to measure actual administrative arrangements and the limitations on its applicability to very different times and circumstances. American public bureaucracies operate within a formal framework of vertical hierarchy; extensive division of labor and specialization; specific rules, procedures, and routines; and a high degree of professionalization complete with extensive merit systems, career emphases, and salary and fringe benefits. Yet strong as these similarities with Weber's model are, there are equally prominent differences.

First, while it is true that there is a vertical hierarchy comprising the formal bureaucratic structure, it is also true that those within that hierarchy respond to commands, inducements, and decisions which arise from outside it. Thus the vertical hierarchy is often (sometimes at best) only one of the "chains of command" active in the bureaucracy.

Second, Weber's division of labor and specialization were designed to reduce functional overlap among bureaucratic units, so that functions performed by a given entity were the responsibility of *only* that entity. This, in Weber's view, was in the best interests of efficient operation. By contrast, American bureaucracy, though specialized, is shot through with functional overlap, reflecting among other things overlapping societal interests. As an example, a program for vocational training and rehabilitation could logically be placed under the jurisdiction either of the Labor Department (since the program is vocationally focused) or of HEW (since it emphasizes training and rehabilitation, which are HEW responsibilities in programs not related to labor). Furthermore, functional overlap is practically guaranteed in a federal system where separate governments organize their bureaucracies independently.

Third, the kind of professionalization foreseen by Weber has been achieved only partially in American bureaucracy. This is in one sense a matter of definition. Weber's "professionals" were so defined because they were making the bureaucracy their careers, were competent to perform the tasks for which they were hired, and were paid in the manner that other professionals were paid. American bureaucracy differs from this ideal in two respects. First, there is a wide variety of personnel systems, from the fully developed merit system in which job-related competence is the most important qualification for employment, to the most open and deliberate patronage system where political loyalty and connections are major criteria in personnel decisions. The U.S. Civil Service; such states as Minnesota, California, and Wisconsin; and many city-manager cities make personnel decisions largely or almost entirely on a merit basis. Patronage is found in many other states as well as numerous urban and rural governments throughout the country— sometimes even in personnel systems where a merit system appears to be operating.

The second departure from the Weber ideal of professionalism is found in the fact that more and more professions in the private sector— such as law, medicine, engineering, social and physical sciences, and administration—are represented among the legions of government employees. Whereas Weber seemed to be seeking a "professional bureaucrat," American experience has yielded "bureaucratic professionals," persons trained in various private-sector professions who find their careers in the public service. The difference between the two is more than of labeling or appearance. Weber's conception appears to be narrower than the American reality with regard to the scope and diversity of skills of his bureaucrats, as well as the variety of their professional loyalties.

A further implication of professionalization is that the employees of a Weberian bureaucracy would be judged by their *continuing* competence in their jobs. In this regard, American merit systems also diverge from Weber's model. In the majority of cases, those who secure a merit position need only to serve the necessary probationary period (usually six to eighteen months) before earning job security. How rapidly one rises through the ranks or how easily one can transfer to a new position may well be affected by periodic evaluations of competence, but it is the exception rather than the rule to find an employee dismissed from the public service solely for incompetence on the job.

Finally, Weber placed considerable emphasis on employment in a public bureaucracy as a career for the individual employee, but it is only recently (since 1955, to be precise) that the national government and some states and localities have attempted to structure their personnel systems so as to foster a career emphasis as an integral part of public-sector employment.

In summary, the Weber model's applicability to American public administration is limited in important respects, even though we have emulated much of this model. The fundamental importance of the Weber model lies in its defining bureaucracy as a structure of social organization and in paving the way for further theory, explanation, and prescription regarding the organization of human endeavors.

Frederick Taylor and "Scientific Management"

Frederick Taylor's theory of "scientific management"[3] marked the beginning of the managerial tradition in organization theory, and was designed to assist private-sector management in adapting production practices to the needs of an emerging industrial economy in the early 1900s. Prior to Taylor there was little systematic organization of work in private industry, and his writings became the principal source of ideas on the subject. Taylor differed from Weber in his focus (private industry) and in prescribing a "science" of management incorporating specific steps and procedures for implementation (Weber's more abstract model of bureaucracy did not specify actual operations). Both men, however, were formal theorists in that they gave major emphasis to formal structure and rules, dealt hardly at all with the employees' working environment, and directly or indirectly equated the needs of those at the top of the hierarchy with the needs of the organization as a whole.

The theory of scientific management rested on four underlying values. First was *efficiency* in production—obtaining the maximum possible from a given investment of resources. Second was *rationality* in work procedures—the arrangement of work in the most direct relationship to the objectives sought. Third was *productivity*—reaching and maintaining the highest levels possible. Fourth was *profit,* which Taylor conceived of as the ultimate objective of everyone within the organization. These values formed the framework within which the remainder of his theory was to be worked out.

Taylor made several other critical assumptions. He viewed authority within the organization as highly centralized at top management levels. He assumed a vertical hierarchy through which top management made its wishes known to those below. And he thought that at each level of the organization responsibility and authority were fixed at a central point. Taylor also believed that there was "one best way" to do any particular task,[4] that through scientific research the "one best way" could be discovered and applied, that the ideal method could be taught to workers responsible for the particular task, and that scientific selection of workers for their capabilities in performing the task(s) would be the most rational way to achieve the organization's overall objectives.[5]

What management needed to do to increase productivity, and thus profits, was threefold. First, the most efficient tools and procedures had to be developed. In this connection Taylor relied on so-called "time and motion" studies, which concentrated on identifying the most economical set of physical movements associated with each step of a work process. Taylor was a pioneer in time and motion studies, although he was only one of a number of researchers in this area. Second, in teaching the new techniques to workers, emphasis was to be placed on standardizing the procedures, to enable workers to discharge their responsibilities routinely yet efficiently. Third, there was need to develop and apply criteria for selecting workers that emphasized task-related capabilities. Note, again, that management was to be entirely responsible for successfully implementing this "science" of management.

As with any model or theory, there were shortcomings alleged in scientific management, particularly as it came to be applied in industry and, later, government. A theoretical difficulty which received considerable attention from later scholars was that the worker under scientific management was seen as merely a cog in the industrial machine, with motives and incentives that were purely financial and no other needs on or off the job worthy of incorporation in the theory. (Taylor viewed management, too, in rather one-dimensional terms, but critiques of his theory concentrated on the consequences of viewing workers so narrowly. Weber's model was criticized on much the same grounds.)

Taylor's theory ran into real trouble when American industry tried to put it into practice. Taylor had assumed management and labor would share the same objectives and that there would be no conflict over organizing to achieve them. Management would naturally seek efficiency, rationality, and productivity in order to maximize profits, and Taylor thought labor would support and work toward those same goals because, at the time, laborers were paid "by the piece" (that is, so much per item produced) and the greater the number turned out, the more money earned. Thus Taylor projected a united labor-management interest in implementing every aspect of his science of management. The problem was that this unity of interest was assumed without accounting for how it might be affected by the law of supply and demand. In the simplest terms, Taylor projected that demand for a product would always keep pace with supply, and thus that maximum productivity would always be a goal of both management and workers. In practice, however, production levels sometimes came to exceed public demand for a product. When this occurred, management laid off some workers, retaining only the number needed on the job for each to maintain maximum productivity without causing total output to exceed demand. This touched off vigorous opposition by workers who were laid off and their labor unions (then in their infancy). Most industrial managers had enough power to withstand labor's reaction, but Taylor's theory came under increasing fire.

Nevertheless, Taylor inaugurated a new direction in organization theory. Scientific management took hold not only in the private sector but also in public administration. For a time the values of efficiency, rationality, and productivity were virtually official doctrine in the federal bureaucracy, and an important body of theory in public administration evolved largely from Taylor's work. Scientific management has had lasting influence on organization theory—directly, as it has shaped values and structures in numerous private and public enterprises; indirectly, as other theories either followed from it or developed in reaction to it. In particular, scientific management is generally regarded as having had tangible impact on the "principles" approach to public administration.

The "Principles" and Other Early Writings

Leonard D. White, in his pioneering *Introduction to the Study of Public Administration* (1926), clearly borrowed from Taylor in asserting that management procedures could be studied scientifically to discover the best method of operation. This was not only White's view—it was commonly held by most students of public administration of that period. Together with the politics-administration dichotomy, the quest for economy and efficiency, and the notion of public administration as a value-free science, the scientific study of management practices was at the core of public administration theory.

Other elements of Taylorism appeared in the "principles of administration" approach, which became prominent in the 1930s. The very effort to discover "principles" was itself derived from the scientific approach to management, and individual principles reflected Taylor's continuing influence on the study of organizations, both public and private. The writings of Henri Fayol, F. W. Willoughby, and the team of Luther Gulick and Lyndall Urwick[7] set forth the essential themes of the "principles" approach.

In chapter 1 we referred to the set of seven principles known by the acronym POSDCORB—planning, organizing, staffing, directing, coordinating, reporting, and budgeting; these were formulated by Gulick and Urwick in 1937,[8] following from the writings of Fayol. But there were other important principles besides POSDCORB, resembling in most instances some aspects of Weber's and Taylor's thinking. The major ones were:

1. *Unity of command*—direction by a single individual at each level of an organization and at the top of the structure;
2. *Hierarchy*—the vertical ordering of superior-subordinate relations in an organization, with a clear chain of command implied;
3. *Functional specialization*—division of labor and subject-matter specialization as a main contributor to work efficiency;
4. *Narrow span of control*—each supervisor having responsibility for the activities of a limited number of subordinates, again in the interests of efficient and effective operation;
5. *Authority parallel with responsibility*—each responsible official endowed with the authority necessary to direct operations in the particular organizational unit; and
6. *Rational organizational arrangement*—according to function or purpose, geographic area, process performed, or people served (clientele)—the particular type (or combination) being selected with an eye to maximizing efficiency and effectiveness of performance.[9]

Later theories in public administration developed largely in reaction to the "principles" and paralleled what was happening elsewhere in the study of organizations—namely, the emergence of alternative formulations, especially about those who made up the work force of an organization. The human relations approach constituted the next major phase in the evolution of organization theory, and signaled the advent of the informal tradition.

The Human Relations School

The informal tradition differs from the formal in both major premises and assumptions and principal research directions. Whereas formal theories assumed that workers were "rational" in their actions and motivations, seeking to maximize their gains in economic terms, informal theories looked beyond economic motivations and viewed workers as having *non*economic needs on the job and being motivated (at least potentially) through satisfaction of those needs. Thus researchers in the informal school sought to determine what noneconomic factors in the work situation, broadly defined, might have impact—and what kinds of impact—on workers and their performance.

The Hawthorne Studies

The first major study in the human relations approach to organization was conducted at the Western Electric plant in Hawthorne, Illinois, in the late 1920s and early 1930s.[10] Elton Mayo and his associates at the Harvard Business School began the study in order to measure the effects of worker fatigue on production. But it was expanded over a period of five years, resulting in a set of findings about productivity and job-related factors other than economic reward. Specifically, the study centered on how workers reacted to actions of management, how variations in physical working conditions affected output, and how social interactions among workers affected their work. It is significant that Mayo did not initially intend to examine all these relationships; it became necessary to investigate some of them after early results did not turn out as expected.

In one experiment, male workers making parts of telephone switches were paid "by the piece" and, according to the Taylor theory, were expected as a result to try to maximize their production output. To the surprise of both Mayo and the management of Western Electric, production stabilized well below the expected level, primarily due to the workers' reluctance to increase it beyond a certain point. This appeared to be a result of their fear of layoffs, and nothing management did or said could change their attitude—or their level of productivity. This was totally unexpected and not explained by anything in the theory of scientific management.

Another experiment involved varying the physical surroundings of a group of female workers assembling telephone relays, and observing changes in output. It was assumed that improvements in working conditions would lead to greater output, and that changes for the worse would cause a drop in productivity. This same experiment was also run for the men making switches. The results, however, did not conform to expectations, on two accounts. First, production levels of the women went up after each change in working conditions, regardless of whether conditions had been improved (better lighting, bigger working area, more frequent rest breaks) or worsened. It appeared that the women were responding in part to being subjects of an experiment. More to the point, to the extent that management was paying consistent attention to them and their work, they seemed ready to produce at steadily higher levels. The second result that ran counter to expectations was that members of the male work group reacted entirely differently from the women—no matter what changes were made in working conditions, the men seemed to lag behind their previous level of productivity. Other findings also ran counter to the concepts of scientific management, suggesting that a new theory was needed to explain these phenomena.

Mayo and his associates concluded that within the formal organizational framework there was an *informal social structure* operating which tangibly influenced the behavior and even the motivations of the workers. Among the men, for example, there was pressure not to produce too much or too little, and not get too closely tied to management.[11] There was also, quite clearly, pressure to conform to the group's production target level, in preference to any set by management. And among both men and women there was group pressure to regard oneself as a group member and to react to management in those terms, rather than reacting strictly as an individual. This was very important in light of contrary assumptions made about workers by Taylor and other formal theorists. The work of the Mayo team also revealed the importance of noneconomic incentives and motivations on the job, in direct contrast to the "rational economic" assumptions of formal theorists.[12]

In sum, the Hawthorne studies opened the way to investigation of factors other than formal organizational structure and operations, and they established the importance of social structure and worker interaction. They became the basis for the human relations school of organization theory, which stressed the social and psychological dimensions of organizations, particularly the satisfactions workers derived from the work situation, and effective motivating forces on the job.

Leadership in Organizations

A major emphasis in the human relations school during the 1930s was the study of organizational leadership, and how—if at all—leadership affected workers' behavior and the organization's general performance. Two of the most important scholars in the area were Chester Barnard and Kurt Lewin. Barnard examined the nature of authority within organizations, concentrating on leader-follower interaction, while Lewin studied different leadership styles and the effects they had on subordinates.

Chester Barnard spent his professional life in executive positions in the private sector (e.g., as president of the New Jersey Bell Telephone Company). Writing on the basis of that experience, he theorized that leadership could not be exercised by those at the top of a hierarchy solely at their discretion. Rather, leadership depended for its effectiveness largely upon the willingness of others (followers) to accept and respond to it. Barnard maintained that followers (workers, in an organization) had a social-psychological "zone of acceptance" (sometimes referred to as "zone of indifference"), meaning the extent to which a follower is willing to be led, to obey commands or directives from a leader.[13] Barnard was, of course, assuming noncoercive commands, that is, commands not accompanied by the application of brute force. His main point was that those being led have a great deal to do with the nature and effectiveness of leadership over them. Whatever legal, political, or organizational authority leaders possess, followers must "grant" leaders authority over themselves.

Barnard's view of leadership also included the idea that leaders and followers each had something the other sought and could in effect exchange these commodities to their mutual advantage. Organization leaders could offer appropriate incentives to workers, and workers could contribute to the welfare of the organization through improved job performance. This early version of what has come to be known as *exchange theory*[14] reflected Barnard's position that coercive leadership relying on negative incentives (punishments or wage reductions, for example) was less effective than supportive leadership offering positive inducements. In other words, Barnard thought that the "carrot" was more effective than the "stick" as a motivator.

Kurt Lewin, founder of the Group Dynamics School at the University of Iowa earlier in the 1930s, conducted a series of experiments aimed at testing the effects of different types of leaders on the work output and group atmosphere of ten-year-old boys.[15] Lewin and his associates trained adult leaders in three leadership styles, then rotated different leaders among groups of boys making masks. The leadership styles were (1) authoritarian—a threatening, intimidating, coercive leader who permitted "no nonsense" in the work group (thus suppressing the natural high-spiritedness of young boys), who specialized in finding fault with individual workers, and who resorted to "scapegoating" when things went wrong; (2) laissez-faire—a distant, nonthreatening leader who gave no direction, said nothing concerning cooperation among the workers or the need to keep on working, and gave no encouragement to the boys (the French phrase means "hands off," and that was this leader's attitude and bearing toward the work group); and (3) democratic—a leader who stressed the job "we" have to do, maintained a relaxed and informal atmosphere, kept a loose hold on the reins in terms of exercising leadership authority over the workers, was very positive and supportive, encouraged the boys to do their best, lavished praise for work well done, and encouraged those who were becoming proficient at mask-making to assist those still having some difficulty.

The principal findings in the Iowa experiments were revealing, at least insofar as it is possible to draw firm conclusions from a study where ten-year-old boys were the subjects. First, total productivity was greatest under the authoritarian leader, with the democratic leader second, and the laissez-faire leader third. The only exception to this pattern was during "leader-out" periods, when the leader left the group on its own. Groups under democratic leadership maintained highest production in those periods, with authoritarian-led groups falling off sharply without the presence and coercive motivation of the authoritarian leader. Second, interaction among members of the respective groups varied dramatically according to the style of leadership, as did levels of group satisfaction with the work experience. Democratic leadership was clearly most conducive to interpersonal cooperation and group integration, as well as worker satisfaction. Authoritarian leadership led to considerable hostility among some group members and apathy on the part of others, with tensions running very high. Laissez-faire leadership had the least impact on worker behavior and attitudes.

There are limitations on the findings of the Iowa experiments, as on all such research. The major one is the extent to which we can apply these findings to other, more complex situations. Many tasks in business, industry, and government are more complex than making masks; adult workers' personal and psychological needs may be different from those of ten-year-old boys; hierarchical organizations with multiple layers of "leaders" and "followers" present different problems of group motivation; and a work force that is socially, economically, ethnically, and professionally diverse is infinitely more difficult to deal with than a homogeneous group of boys.

Yet the findings of this experiment and the conceptions suggested by Barnard both pointed to the possible importance of leadership as another variable in getting the most and the best out of workers in an organization. Like the concern for working conditions and social interaction, this represented a fertile new field of inquiry in organization theory, with some reason to think that "better leadership" might well help to make a "better" organization. The fact that the Iowa results may not be universally applicable does not offset, by any means, their significance in the study of organizations.

Critiques of the Human Relations School

More recent scholars have devoted some attention to shortcomings in the human relations school of organization theory. The principal criticisms have revolved around three points. First and most commonly noted is failure to take account of the potential for conflict between workers and managers.[16] Critics have pointed out that "good human relations" seemed to be advanced as the remedy for just about any difficulty between employers and employees; yet where basic conflicts exist over such things as long-range goals, work methods, and specific task assignments, it is not enough simply to make the worker feel important. In this respect, human relations proponents were guilty of the same oversight that had been made by formal theorists. That is, neither approach to organizations seemed to acknowledge that conflict was a real possibility, and one that had to be dealt with conceptually as well as in daily practice.

Second, the human relations school seemed to discount almost entirely the effects of formal structure on those in the organization. Also, the "rational-economic" incentives so much in favor with formal theorists were given little if any emphasis in these later formulations. This is not surprising in light of the fact that it was formal theory with which the human relations school was in sharpest conceptual disagreement, and it was, after all, the first body of theory to take issue with the Weber-Taylor-Fayol-Gulick approach. Even so, there is some accuracy in such criticisms.

A study conducted by William F. Whyte in the 1950s found that whether a company had a "flat" or "tall" hierarchy (that is, few or many levels within the formal structure) *did* seem to make some difference in the amount of conflict and tension that existed between labor and management.[17] Whyte also found, in another study, that for some production workers (a relatively small percentage) economic incentive plans served as more effective motivators than did noneconomic incentives, contrary to Mayo's contentions.[18] Other research has pointed to similar conclusions concerning monetary incentives, though with the qualification that it may depend in part on how large a wage or salary differential is offered as an incentive.[19]

Third, it has been contended that the kind and complexity of technologies employed in an organization matter considerably more in shaping informal social structure and human interaction than do the factors which Mayo, Lewin, and others regarded as pivotal. Robert Blauner in particular has made this point persuasively, stressing impersonal factors (that is, technology) as crucial.[20] It is possible, however, that this is not really a contradiction of the human relations findings, since Blauner, writing in the 1960s, was observing an organizational environment in which technology played a much bigger part than it had during the 1930s, when human relations emphases first emerged. Still, this does suggest that as factors in the work situation change, theories previously useful in analyzing organizations may have less applicability.

These are not the first critiques of the human relations approach, however. Another body of research begun in the 1940s and 1950s contributed a different perspective on the worker's place in the organization, and on what satisfactions and motivations existed in the work situation. This approach, known as "organizational" or "industrial humanism," was concerned with what factors in the overall organizational picture contributed to the psychological and psychosocial health of the worker. In particular, it defined the worker's relationship to the *work itself* as an important variable in maintaining motivation and job satisfaction, something quite different from worker-supervisor or worker-worker interactions. Organizational humanism marked a turning point, serving as something of a bridge between the human relations approach and what we refer to as "modern" organization theory.

Organizational Humanism

Organizational humanism was based on several assumptions which differed perceptibly from those of both formal organization theory and the human relations school. First, work held some intrinsic interest, which would itself serve to motivate the worker to perform it well. Second, individuals worked not only to satisfy off-the-job needs and desires, but some on the job as well. This suggested, in effect, that workers sought satisfactions *in the work,* and that achieving those satisfactions was a separate and distinct objective related to the most fundamental reasons for working. Third, work was a central life interest to the worker, not merely something to be tolerated or endured.

A fourth assumption, following directly from the notion of the centrality of work and of on-the-job satisfactions, proved to be a harbinger of things to come in contemporary organization theory. It was that management was better advised to promote positive motivation—through delegating responsibility, permitting discretion and creativity on the job, and involving the worker in important policy decisions affecting the work environment—than to assume that workers were inherently disinterested in the work and would avoid doing it if possible. The latter view of workers was an implicit part of formal theories of organization, and even human relations scholars seemed to share it to some extent. Organizational humanists, however, assumed the opposite. They did so in light of their research findings, which showed that authoritarian management practices designed to control lazy, irresponsible employees were resulting in unhappy and frustrated workers, and poor work performance.

Douglas McGregor was among the pioneers of organizational humanism, arguing that workers could be self-motivating due to their own interest in the work and their own inclination to perform it.[21] McGregor's "Theory Y" was in sharp contrast to what he called "Theory X"—the earlier view that workers were lazy, wanted to avoid doing the work, and needed to be forced to do it (see Table 6–1 for summaries of Theories X and Y). Another major figure among organizational humanists was social psychologist Chris Argyris, whose view of work as a central life interest was fundamental to this approach.[22] Argyris also pointed out the need of workers to identify with their work, a further source of motivation to perform it well.

The writings of Rensis Likert emphasized employee participation in as many phases of management as possible, directed by a leader or leaders in the democratic mold (consistent with Kurt Lewin's findings). And Frederick Herzberg, in a study of over 200 accountants and engineers and some nonprofessional employees in a Pittsburgh firm, found that motivators such as salary, fringe benefits, good lighting, and adequate facilities served only to meet workers' minimum expectations, without producing real satisfaction on the job. What *did* yield personal satisfaction were such things as recognition for good job performance, opportunity to take initiative and exhibit creativity, and responsibility entrusted by management to individual workers and groups of workers. These "intangibles," according to Herzberg's study, proved to be far better motivators than such "tangible" features as salary or fringe benefits because they were the most satisfying aspects of the jobs.[23]

Among the most important research in organizational humanism was the work of Abraham Maslow, who wrote of "self-actualizing" workers

TABLE 6–1
THEORY X AND THEORY Y: A SUMMARY

Underlying Belief System: Theory X

1. Most work is distasteful for most people.
2. Most people prefer close and continuous direction.
3. Most people can exercise little or no creativity in solving organizational problems.
4. Motivation occurs mostly or only as a response to "bread-and-butter" issues—threat or punishment—and is strictly an individual matter.

Underlying Belief System: Theory Y

1. Most people can find work as natural as play, if conditions permit.
2. Most people prefer and can provide self-control in achieving organizational objectives.
3. Most people can exercise significant creativity in solving organizational problems.
4. Motivation often occurs in response to ego and social rewards, particularly under conditions of full employment, and motivation is often dependent upon groups.

Source: Douglas McGregor, "Theory X and Theory Y," in Robert T. Golembiewski and Michael Cohen, *People in Public Service: A Reader in Public Personnel Administration* (Itasca, Ill.: F. E. Peacock, 1970), p. 380.

achieving the highest degree of self-fulfillment on the job through maximum use of their creative capacities and individual independence.[24] Maslow viewed the worker as having what he called a "hierarchy of needs," each level of which had to be satisfied before the individual could go on to the next one. The first level of the "hierarchy" was *physiological needs*—food, shelter, the basic means of survival. Next was *minimum job security*—a reasonable assurance (but not necessarily a guarantee) of continued employment. After these essentials came *social needs*—group acceptance on and off the job and interpersonal relationships that are positive and supportive. *Ego satisfaction and independence needs* represented the fourth step in Maslow's hierarchy, derived from accomplishments in one's work and public recognition of them. (A management practice of some importance in this regard is "public praise, private criticism" for an employee.) Finally, Maslow's highest level was *self-actualization*—feelings of personal fulfillment resulting from independent, creative, and responsible job performance.

As the worker satisfied the needs of one level, he or she was seen as being further motivated to work toward satisfying the needs of the next higher level. Thus Maslow placed his emphasis on interactions among the essential needs of the employee on and off the job, the work being done, the attitude of both management and employee toward work performance, and the relationship among employees in the work situation. In a sense, Maslow incorporated those aspects of the human relations approach centering on interpersonal interactions among workers into a larger and more complex scheme. The "hierarchy of needs," like other formulations in organizational humanism, assumed that worker satisfactions could be affected by many factors in the organization, both close to the work situation itself and more distant from it.

Organizational humanism is not without its critics, however. Robert Dubin found, for example, that fewer than 10 percent of the workers he studied in an industrial work group preferred the informality, job-centeredness, and independence on the job so highly valued in organizational humanism.[25] He suggested that different workers have widely varying needs, and that no *one* approach could successfully meet all of them. Some workers needed strong direction from a leader, not independence; lack of direction caused them to be anxious and frustrated in their work. Some really did work for the money. Some simply did not get along with their coworkers, and to emphasize group interaction would cause additional problems instead of solving existing ones. Some were not especially interested in participation in organizational decision making. Some were content to achieve certain needs in Maslow's hierarchy without continuing to strive for higher-level satisfactions, thus posing motivation problems for managers relying on Maslow's formulations. Dubin, in sum, suggested that placing too much faith in organizational humanism should be avoided. The varied needs of employees in an organization had to be taken into account.

A more recent critique of organizational humanism came from two sociologists who questioned some assumptions about the need for workers to self-actualize in their jobs and to participate in organizational decision making. Writing in the *Public Administration Review,* sociologists H. Roy Kaplan and Curt Tausky maintained that various assumptions of organizational humanism seem to have been grounded more in ideological beliefs than in empirical data, and that there is mounting evidence that they do not stand up to empirical research and testing.[26] According to Kaplan and Tausky, many organizational humanists mistakenly viewed employee motivations and satisfactions in a one-dimensional manner, failing to take account of those for whom work was *not* intrinsically interesting and fulfilling, for whom creativity and independence were not valued features of their work, and for whom monetary and other tangible benefits were of the first order of importance. Theirs is a wide-ranging challenge to orthodox organizational humanism, echoing to some degree Dubin's earlier critique.

Citing their own research and that of numerous other scholars in the 1950s, 1960s, and 1970s, Kaplan and Tausky made the following central points:

1. Professionals (such as scientists in basic research, academics, managers in government and private industry, and research-and-development engineers) are most likely to be intrinsically dedicated to their work, yet they also work in many cases because of extrinsic rewards, such as salary or fringe benefits;[27]
2. Most manual laborers and lower-level salaried workers derive satisfaction off their jobs rather than on the job, a finding made in a 1975 study by Robert Dubin and two associates;[28]
3. The assumption that "participation increases satisfaction and satisfaction is reflected in increased work effort" is "tenuous," since numerous studies fail to reflect expected connections among greater worker participation, job satisfaction, and more (and more cheerful) work;[29]
4. As illustrated in Table 6–2, there is a widespread commitment to work in this country that would appear *not* to depend upon work being intrinsically interesting;
5. People from blue-collar origins often seek different things in and from their work than do middle- and upper-class individuals, being more likely to place their emphasis on extrinsic rewards and, to some extent, on supervision on the job (see Table 6–3 for data on economic incentives). This is consistent with a good deal of sociological literature emphasizing social class as an important determinant of individual attitudes and orientations toward work, and inconsistent with more generalized assumptions of the organizational humanists that self-actualization is a primary need—even a natural instinct—of all or most human beings in a work situation.

In sum, Kaplan and Tausky brought together substantial evidence suggesting that organizational humanism may be more limited in its ap-

TABLE 6-2
COMPARATIVE EXAMPLES OF THE COMMITMENT
TO WORK IN THE UNITED STATES

Item	Response Alternatives	Samples				
		National Sample of 393 Employed Men	National Sample of 274 Male Blue-Collar Workers	151 Middle Managers in 3 Business Firms	1,379 Male Vocational-Technical Students	275 Hard-Core Unemployed
1. If by some chance you had enough money to live comfortably without working, do you think you would work anyway?	I would work anyway	80%	81%	89%	87%	84%
	I would not work	20%	19%	11%	13%	16%
2. If you were out of work, which would you rather do?	Go on welfare	—	9%	9%	16%	29%
	Take a job as a car washer that paid the same as welfare	—	91%	91%	84%	71%

Source: H. Roy Kaplan and Curt Tausky, "Humanism in Organizations: A Critical Appraisal," *Public Administration Review*, 37 (March/April 1977), 175.

plicability than its proponents have believed. By attempting to define where those limits lie, they have helped illuminate both particular difficulties with this theory of organization and the more fundamental necessity to avoid overgeneralizing about ways in which employees react to their work and respond to different motivational approaches.

One further criticism of organizational humanism should be mentioned, though it is implicit in Kaplan and Tausky's commentary. The *kind* of work being done—routine or nonroutine, individualized or small-group or assembly-line—may have a great deal to do with what possibilities exist for motivating and satisfying workers on the basis of intrinsic job interest. There is reason to believe that the more routine the task, the greater the possibility for worker dissatisfaction, or at least for frustration and boredom. That phenomenon alone limits the applicability of organizational humanism.

On the other hand, there may be some ways to combat this problem. One approach is to make more systematic the recognition for employees doing routinized tasks; the "employee of the month" award at McDonald's restaurants, complete with the individual's photograph hung over the counter, is a familiar example. Another device is to alter the

TABLE 6–3
ECONOMIC ORIENTATIONS TO WORK AMONG
WHITE- AND BLUE-COLLAR WORKERS AND STUDENTS

Item	Response Alternatives	Samples		
		National Sample 274 Male Blue-Collar Workers	1,379 Male Vocational-Technical Students	151 Middle Managers in 3 Business Firms
1. Is the most important thing about getting a promotion . . .	Getting more pay	67%	62%*	78%
	Getting more respect from friends and neighbors	33%	33%	22%
2. Which job would you choose if you could be sure of keeping either job?	Better than average pay as a truck driver	73%	77%	67%
	Less than average pay as a bank clerk	27%	22%	32%
3. If you could be sure your income would go up steadily without getting a promotion, would you care about being promoted?	No	74%	60%	29%
	Yes	26%	40%	71%

*Percentages do not add to 100 due to "no answers."
Source: H. Roy Kaplan and Curt Tausky, "Humanism in Organizations: A Critical Appraisal," *Public Administration Review,* 37 (March/April 1977), 177.

routine work situation, such as an auto assembly line, and give workers the opportunity to form their own work groups which proceed to assemble a single automobile (or other product) "from the ground up." This may have the effect of reducing boredom and frustration on the job while increasing the sense of participation in, and identity with, the product being turned out—in the best tradition of Argyris, Likert, and others of the organizational humanism school. Such programs in auto factories are in wider use in parts of western Europe than in the United States; whether they could be put into practice successfully on this side of the Atlantic is not clear. In any event, the nature of particular tasks, taken separately from the kind of supervision or the backgrounds of the workers, appears to have some relevance in explaining the success or failure of organizational humanism in different work situations.

Modern Organization Theory

Modern organization theory differs from all previous approaches in four key respects. First, there is a deliberate effort to separate facts from values and to study organizational behavior empirically. Proponents of earlier approaches made quite a few assumptions grounded in the predominant economic or social values of the time, the perceived needs of management or labor within organizations, or just plain "common sense." In contrast, modern organization theorists make every effort to minimize the impact of their own values on the organizational phenomena under study.

Second, modern organization theorists make extensive use of empirical research methods unavailable even twenty years ago—including statistics, computer simulations, and quantitative techniques—which permit more sophisticated insights into the operation of organizations.

Third, modern organization theory is constructed on an interdisciplinary basis—drawing on the varied approaches of sociology, organizational psychology, public administration, business, and information science. This greatly broadens the perspectives that can be developed concerning organizational behavior and the management of large, complex enterprises.

Fourth, modern organization theory attempts to generalize about organizations in terms sufficiently broad to be applicable to many different kinds of enterprises—private business corporations, hospitals, universities, interest groups of all kinds, labor unions, voluntary agencies, and community-based organizations, for example. To do this it is necessary to deal in abstract formulations accounting for common characteristics among dissimilar organizations. Thus such features as information and its transmission, informal group processes, power relationships, environmental stability or turbulence, and decision making become the "currency," so to speak, of generalized organization theory. We will examine briefly some of the major approaches that have been developed.

A pioneering study which ushered in the modern period of organization theory was done by John Pfiffner and Frank Sherwood.[30] They described organizations as characterized by a series of overlays or networks superimposed on the formal structure, and they discussed, among other features, formal and informal communications systems, group dynamics, relative power of different parts of the organization, and decision processes. Theirs was the first comprehensive effort to integrate a variety of approaches, and it set the stage for a tremendous expansion of information about organizations and of specific approaches to studying them.

One widely employed approach is *open systems theory,* which conceives of organizations as operating in close relation with their external environments.[31] The systems approach, generally, assumes the existence—for any biological, mechanical, or social entity—of *inputs,* some *means of responding* to those inputs, *outputs, feedback* from the environment in response to system outputs, and *further inputs* into the system stemming from feedback. For an organization, inputs might consist of demands for some action, resources with which to pursue organizational objectives, underlying values of those outside the organization (and within it), and support for, or at least passive acceptance of, its essential structure and goals. The means of responding to inputs would include all formal and informal decision mechanisms, judgments about how or even whether to respond to particular inputs, past history of the organization in similar circumstances and the inclination or lack of it to follow precedent, and availability of necessary resources. Outputs could refer to the rendering of services by the organization, production or processing of goods, symbolic steps taken to maintain favorable images of the organization, rules and regulations for which it has proper authority, and adjustments to demands for change or to reallocations of resources (by a legislature, for example).[32]

Open systems theory, in addition, assumes that different parts of an organization or other entity will seek a condition of *equilibrium,* balancing pressures and responses, demands and resources, worker incentives and contributions (to use Barnard's formulation). All this is in the long-term interest of organizational stability, which permits continued functioning in the manner expected by leaders, workers, and external clienteles. In sum, open systems theory—in sharp contrast to Weber's self-contained, "closed" bureaucracy—defines organizations as a great deal more than just formal structure, or interpersonal relations, or worker involvement in the job. It treats organizations as whole beings, complex in their makeup, and constant in their interaction with the surrounding environment.

Other approaches which use the systems framework as a basis deal with organizations in a similarly broad-gauged fashion. *Information theory* is based on the view that organizations require information to prevent their evolving to a state of chaos or randomness in their operations. *Game theory* addresses itself to competition among members of an organization for gains and losses, in terms of resources and access to resources; game theory is distinctly mathematical in orientation and methods. The concept of the self-regulating organization is advanced in *cybernetics,* emphasizing feedback which triggers appropriate adaptive responses throughout the organizational system;[33] a thermostat operates on the same principle.

Mention should be made of some other approaches as well. *Organizational change* concentrates on the characteristics within organizations which promote or retard change in response to, or in anticipation of, change in demands from the external environment, particularly with regard to needs and desires for the products (however defined) of the organization.[34] *Organization development* focuses on analysis of organizational problems and formulation of possible solutions.[35] It is geared to increasing the capacity of an organization to identify, analyze, and solve internal problems as a regular function within its ongoing routines. *Management according to task* conceives of organizations which do not follow a single structure or format, top to bottom.[36] Rather, depending upon the set of tasks in a particular unit of the organization, that unit will be shaped structurally, socially, and technologically in the most appropriate manner. Thus, in a large and complex organization, there is likely to be considerable diversity in the arrangements of different units.

We come, finally, to two approaches which address basic questions about the structures and purposes of primarily hierarchical organizations. The theory of *organizational adaptiveness,* while similar in some respects to organizational change theory, holds that when conditions in the external environment change fundamentally, an organization may have to do the same or else run the risk of becoming progressively less effective. Warren Bennis has argued that Weber-style bureaucratic structure may have been entirely adequate and appropriate for dealing with generally routine and predictable tasks in a stable environment (such as during the early 1900s), but that the unpredictable nature of contemporary organizational life, coupled with a far more turbulent social environment, makes it necessary to develop new forms of organization.[37]

Bennis sees an end to hierarchical leadership because no one leader is capable of mastering the complex and diverse technologies present in so many organizations. Also due to technological needs, managers will increasingly become coordinators, or as Rensis Likert put it, "linking pins,"[38] among teams of experts operating within an almost horizontal chain of command rather than a traditional, vertical one. According to Bennis, this clearly suggests a participative style of management;[39] if the chain of command runs horizontally, it virtually requires a view of organization members as equals, not superiors and subordinates. Such a view of organizations and their future goes against much of what we are accustomed to, but that is true also of the instability and turbulence surrounding many modern organizations.

The other approach raising basic questions related to organization theory is the *New Public Administration.*[40] This contemporary movement in the public administration profession (dating from 1970) focuses on how outputs of public organizations are distributed in society at large, and is keenly concerned with "social equity" as a guiding principle. To the extent that social equity requires change in present patterns of resource distribution, New Public Administrationists are willing to confront the political tension likely to occur. New Public Administration is also concerned with modifying established authority hierarchies because of their negative effects on subordinates and on the work of the organization, seeking instead different ways of integrating and coordinating organizational tasks (through group decision making, decentralization of responsibilities, and so on).

New Public Administration also foresees more direct involvement in public organizations of their disadvantaged-minority clienteles, in the interest of social equity (see the discussion of representativeness in chapter 2), and seeks to change (perhaps dramatically) the "socioemotional" processes which shape internal workings in many organizations. In regard to the latter, emphasis is placed on reducing an individual's reliance on the hierarchy, increasing tolerance for conflict and uncertainty, and making the prospect of taking risks a less formidable one. In sum, the New Public Administration makes social equity a central concern—George Frederickson has called it the "supreme objective" [41]—and encourages organizations to adapt themselves as necessary in order to pursue it.

Organizations: An Overview

The subject of organization theory, for all its intellectual diversity, has been characterized by a unifying theme: the attempt to identify the elements in an organization's existence which are most important to its successfully reaching organizational goals. What those elements are, what the goals are, and indeed what comprises the organization itself, have not been agreed upon. The overlapping series of "schools" or approaches has given us a wide range of ideas from which to choose. The evolution of organization theory, furthermore, has reflected changing emphases in a host of academic disciplines, in business and industry, and in society at large concerning what is important in organizational life and how to go about achieving it.

Organization Theory in Perspective

Several general comments are in order. First, the various approaches have clearly overlapped chronologically and, more to the point, intellectually. The human relations school, while departing significantly from Weber and Taylor, assumed the same formal, hierarchical structure. Organizational humanism borrowed from the human relations approach. The New Public Administration has incorporated some elements of organizational humanism, and so on. Thus various strands of theoretical development have often been woven together as parts of different fabrics, so to speak. Each theory is not self-contained.

Second, although various approaches may fall out of favor among organization theorists of a particular period, that is not to say that their influence disappears. On the contrary, the influence of organization theories generally is cumulative, so that at any given time one may find in existing organizations some offshoots of earlier belief and practice. For example, while Weber's and Taylor's ideas of formal theory are no longer predominant among contemporary scholars, they have had a powerful influence in shaping many public and private institutions and, significantly, are still influential (however indirectly) in the thinking of many people. The same may be said for "principles" of administration and the human relations approach, both of which still carry some weight in theory and practice.

Third, it may be important that a great deal of theory has originated in business and industry, not in public administration. Many of the values, crucial assumptions, subjects and tasks selected for study, and explicit and implicit findings reflect the production mode common to industry and other private-sector enterprises. Indeed, much of the theoretical foundation of public administration was derived originally from business-oriented values. What this means for theories of *public* organizations, as well as their operations in practice, is not altogether clear. Recent theorizing has suggested two points of view—on the one hand, treating problems of all organizations and managers as similar[42]; on the other, an approach intent on addressing problems of public administration as distinct from those of industry, voluntary private-sector organizations, and so on.[43] What directions public organization theory will take remains to be seen.

Organization theory has grown more complex over the years, paralleling what was occurring in real-life organizations throughout modern society. As more knowledge has been brought to bear, it is not surprising that we are presently confronted both by greater diversity of approaches and by less certainty about the nature of large-scale organizations and the people within them. That trend is likely to continue.

The Public Organization in Perspective

Organization theory generally has not drawn sharp distinctions between public and private sectors, tending to treat all organizations, regardless of purpose or context, as though they were "cut from the same piece of cloth." This has resulted in considerable uncertainty about what is required in managing public organizations, and about what features peculiar to government entities may make it necessary to modify general organization theory to adapt to public organizational needs. In recent years a number of efforts have been made in this direction, and some brief comments are in order on the uniqueness of public organizations.[44]

First, most public organizations can survive comfortably even in the absence of highest-quality performance of their functions. They hold a monopoly, for one thing, on providing certain public services which citizen consumers deem necessary, regardless of economic value. This is especially true at the local level, where (as we saw in chapter 5) provision of services is a primary function.

Second, until very recently most government entities lacked performance measures of any kind, and those currently used are not very exact. In the private sector, economic measures are accepted and used widely, but for the most part there is nothing comparable in the public sector. New emphases on efficiency, productivity, and accountability have produced fresh concern for performance measures, but we are still at a very early stage in developing them in most governments.

Third, concerns about achieving results in the public sector must compete for attention with procedural concerns. Values such as participation and public accountability, as well as political influences, make it necessary for public managers to divide their attention between substantive results and how to obtain them. It is difficult to achieve maximum economy and efficiency while keeping a wary eye on possible political repercussions—and this is what many public managers must do in much of their work.

Fourth, in contrast to the profit-oriented concern shared by most of "management" in the private sector, there are often conflicting incentives among citizens, elected representatives, and administrative supervisors and leaders. If agreement is lacking on *what* is to be done and *why* (not to mention the "how" of it, noted above), an organization will not function with the same smoothness as one where incentives are agreed upon. Just as economic measures of performance have no counterpart in the public sector, general economic incentives have no parallel either.

Fifth, most public organizations suffer from diffused responsibility, often resulting in absence of accountability for decisions made. Separation of powers is one factor in this, but a fragmented executive branch in most large governments (including those at the local level) is another. In contrast, centralized executive responsibility is a key feature of many profit-oriented organizations. It should be noted, however, that there are exceptions to this generalization in both types of organization.

Finally, public organizations, unlike private ones, entrust a fair amount of decision responsibility to nonprofessionals—citizen groups, political decision centers, courts, and boards or commissions of various types. Thus a clear chain of command is not possible, because of numerous opportunities for outside pressures to be felt.

The net effect of all this is to produce organizations with operational characteristics quite different from the tightly run "machine model" of organization stressed by Weber, Taylor, and many in the business world today. As we have noted, even the many critics of formal organization theory did not particularly take issue with the implicit assumption of "sameness" in private and public organizations; the distinction simply did not attract interest for many years. As we have become more aware of distinguishing features, the need to develop distinctive approaches to public organization theory has been asserted with increasing frequency. Perhaps the greatest challenge lies in determining just where the lines should be drawn between those organizational characteristics which *are* shared in common and those which are not, between public and private organizations. That effort is just getting under way, and it promises to be a lively one. The first step, however, is the realization that "you cannot manage city hall exactly the way you manage General Motors." [45] If that realization takes hold, it will challenge some of our most commonly accepted beliefs about what makes organizations tick, adding still more dimensions to the turbulence in contemporary organization theory.

SUMMARY

Organization theory is a body of knowledge focusing on the formal and informal structures, internal dynamics, and surrounding social environments of complex human organizations. Spanning several academic disciplines, it has emphasized at different times the needs of management, the needs and motivations of workers, and the relationship between organizations and the stability or turbulence of their environments. Four major areas of organization theory are (1) formal theory, (2) human relations, (3) organizational humanism, and (4) modern organization theory.

Weber's model of bureaucracy incorporated the concepts of vertical hierarchy, division of labor and functional specialization, a formal framework of rules and procedures, maintenance of files and other records, professionalization, and adequate legal and political authority. American public administration, patterned in some ways after the Weber model, differs from it due to the flow of commands from outside the formal hierarchy, the extent of functional overlap among agencies, less than complete operation of merit personnel systems, the diversity of substantive professional expertise, the looseness of requirements for continuing competence, and late development of career emphases.

Taylor's theory of scientific management was geared to the needs of expanding private industry in the early 1900s. The values of efficiency, rationality, productivity, and profit were the foundation of his theory. Authority within the organization was to be concentrated in management's hands, and management was to direct discovery and implementation of the "one best way" to perform each task. In both theory and practice, scientific management encountered some difficulties, though it gained wide acceptance in both private and public organizations.

The "principles" approach so vital to the early development of public administration was strongly influenced by scientific management. Developing a science of management, the effort to discover principles of administration, concepts such as unity of command and functional specialization, and a formal, even mechanistic view of the organization were highly reminiscent of Taylor's writings.

The human relations school, first of the "informal" theories, was launched with the Hawthorne studies in the late 1920s and early 1930s. Mayo and his associates found that an informal social structure, rather than pure economic motivation, greatly affected work patterns. Production target figures were set more effectively by informal agreement within the group than by what management dictated. Also, workers often reacted in the context of the group, as group members, rather than strictly in terms of individual self-interest.

Another major emphasis of the human relations school was how leadership affected worker performance and social interaction. According to Barnard, a worker's "zone of acceptance" defined leadership effectiveness far more than did formal leadership position or hierarchical arrangement. Barnard also viewed the leadership function as one of offering positive incentives to workers in exchange for their contributions to the organization and its work. Lewin studied varying effects of different leadership styles on groups of young boys doing simple tasks and found that work quality and group interaction were generally highest under democratic leadership. Though this study has its limitations, the findings are regarded as significant, and some other evidence exists to support them.

Critical appraisals of the human relations approach have maintained that (1) there was inadequate treatment of the potential for conflict within organizations; (2) the effects of formal structure and of "rational-economic" incentives should not have been discounted to the extent that they were; and (3) the technology utilized in the work situation is important in defining the informal social structure, yet was completely overlooked.

Organizational humanism was founded on four central assumptions: (1) work was, or could be made, intrinsically interesting to the worker; (2) workers sought satisfactions in their jobs; (3) work was a central life interest to the worker, not merely a means to other ends; and (4) greater involvement of the workers by management—through delegation of responsibility, opportunities for creativity and independence, and inclusion in important policy decisions—could promote positive motivation and improve worker performance and satisfaction. McGregor ("Theory X" and "Theory Y"), Argyris, Likert, and Herzberg were foremost among organizational humanists in developing these themes. Maslow analyzed the "hierarchy of needs" of workers, suggesting that as basic needs (food, shelter, job security) were met, individuals strove for social acceptance, ego satisfaction, and (at the top of the "hierarchy") self-actualization through personal fulfillment in one's work.

Critiques of organizational humanism have suggested that not all workers respond to participation, independence, creativity, or motivation in Maslow's terms; some work for money, need decisive direction from supervisors, and do not get along with coworkers. Also, socioeconomic background and the routine or nonroutine nature of work may influence the effectiveness of an organizational humanist approach.

Modern organization theory is characterized by an effort to separate facts from values, utilization of empirical research methods (including statistical data and computers), incorporation of information from diverse sources, and much more complexity in the formulation and application of theory. Major contributions to modern theory have come from the concept of "overlays," open systems theory, information theory, cybernetics, organization development, organizational adaptiveness, and the New Public Administration, among others.

Organization theory of all kinds has sought to identify the elements that are crucial to organizational success. There has been both chronological and intellectual overlap from one body of theory to the next. Most theories have left their imprint upon society even after passing from prominence among theorists. And the majority of theory has had its roots in industry and business, not in public administration. The complexity of modern organization theory parallels real-life organizational complexity, and is likely to continue.

Public organizations have some unique features, setting them apart from private-sector, profit-motivated entities. Their existence does not depend on high-quality performance; measures of performance are largely lacking; procedural concerns tend to be important; "management" suffers from conflicting incentives; responsibility is diffused; and nonprofessionals have considerable influence on decisions. A need is now perceived to begin developing a body of *public* organization theory, though that will challenge widely accepted beliefs.

NOTES

1. H. H. Gerth and C. Wright Mills, *From Max Weber: Essays in Sociology* (New York: Oxford University Press, 1946), pp. 196–203.

2. Julien Freund, *The Sociology of Max Weber* (New York: Vintage Books, 1969), pp. 142–148.

3. Frederick W. Taylor, *The Principles of Scientific Management* (New York: W. W. Norton, 1967). The work was first published in 1911.

4. Ibid., p. 25.

5. Ibid., pp. 43–47.

6. For a humorous, first-person account of life with two other "time and motion" experts, Frank and Lillian Gilbreth, see Frank B. Gilbreth and Ernestine Gilbreth Carey, *Cheaper by the Dozen,* rev. ed. (New York: Thomas Y. Crowell, 1963).

7. See Luther Gulick and Lyndall Urwick, eds., *Papers on the Science of Administration* (New York: Institute of Public Administration, 1937).

8. Ibid., p. 13.

9. Ibid., pp. 1–46.

10. The best source on the Hawthorne experiments is F. J. Roethlisberger and William J. Dickson, *Management and the Worker* (Cambridge: Harvard University Press, 1939). See also Elton Mayo, *The Human Problems of an Industrial Civilization* (Boston: Harvard Business School, 1933), for a statement of Mayo's general approach to his research.

11. Roethlisberger and Dickson, *Management and the Worker*, p. 522.

12. See the summary of findings in Amitai Etzioni, *Modern Organizations* (Englewood Cliffs, N.J.: Prentice-Hall, 1964), at pp. 34–35.

13. See Chester Barnard, *The Functions of the Executive* (Cambridge: Harvard University Press, 1938), especially pp. 92–94.

14. Warren G. Bennis, "Organizational Developments and the Fate of Bureaucracy," in Fred A. Kramer, ed., *Perspectives on Public Bureaucracy* (Cambridge, Mass.: Winthrop, 1973), pp. 167–168. See also James G. March and Herbert A. Simon, *Organizations* (New York: John Wiley and Sons, 1958), pp. 83–88.

15. The following is taken from Ralph White and Ronald Lippitt, "Leader Behavior and Member Reaction in Three 'Social Climates'," in Dorwin Cartwright and Alvin Zander, eds., *Group Dynamics, Research and Theory,* 3rd ed. (New York: Harper & Row, 1968), pp. 527–553. Other studies of leadership include Philip Selznick, *Leadership in Administration* (New York: Harper & Row, 1957); Robert Guest, *Organizational Change: The Effects of Successful Leadership* (Homewood, Ill.: Dorsey and Irwin, 1962); Fred E. Fiedler, *A Theory of Leadership Effectiveness* (New York: McGraw-Hill, 1967); and Fred E., Fiedler and Martin Chemers, *Leadership and Effective Management* (Glenview, Ill.: Scott, Foresman, 1974). See also chapter 8.

16. See, for example, Etzioni, *Modern Organizations,* p. 44.

17. William F. Whyte, "Human Relations—A Progress Report," in Amitai Etzioni, ed., *Complex Organizations: A Sociological Reader* (New York: Holt, Rinehart and Winston, 1961), at p. 112.

18. William F. Whyte, *Money and Motivation: An Analysis of Incentives in Industry* (New York: Harper and Brothers, 1955), as summarized in Edgar Schein, *Organizational Psychology,* 2nd ed. (Englewood Cliffs, N.J.: Prentice-Hall, 1970), at pp. 35–37.

19. See C. R. Walker and R. H. Guest, *The Man on the Assembly Line* (Cambridge: Harvard University Press, 1952), p. 91; cited by Etzioni in *Modern Organizations,* at p. 49.

20. Robert Blauner, *Alienation and Freedom: The Factory Worker and His Industry* (Chicago: University of Chicago Press, 1964).

21. Douglas McGregor, *The Human Side of Enterprise* (New York: McGraw-Hill, 1960).

22. Chris Argyris, *Personality and Organization* (New York: Harper & Row, 1957), and *Integrating the Individual and the Organization* (New York: John Wiley and Sons, 1964).

23. Frederick Herzberg, Bernard Mausner, and Barbara Synderman, *The Motivation to Work* (New York: John Wiley and Sons, 1959), and Herzberg, *Work and the Nature of Man* (Cleveland: World, 1966).

24. See Abraham H. Maslow, *Motivation and Personality,* 2nd ed. (New York: Harper & Row, 1970), pp. 35–58.

25. Robert Dubin, "Industrial Worker Worlds: A Study of the 'Central Life

Interests' of Industrial Workers," *Social Problems,* 4 (May 1956), 136–140. See also Dubin's "Persons and Organization," in Robert Dubin, ed., *Human Relations in Administration, with Readings,* 4th ed. (Englewood Cliffs, N.J.: Prentice-Hall, 1974).

26. H. Roy Kaplan and Curt Tausky, "Humanism in Organizations: A Critical Appraisal," *Public Administration Review,* 37 (March/April 1977), 171–180.

27. Ibid., p. 176.

28. Ibid. The study referred to is Robert Dubin, Joseph E. Champoux, and Lyman W. Porter, "Central Life Interests and Organizational Commitment of Blue-Collar and Clerical Workers," *Administrative Science Quarterly,* 20 (September 1975), 411–421.

29. Ibid., p. 172, et seq.

30. John M. Pfiffner and Frank P. Sherwood, *Administrative Organization* (Englewood Cliffs, N.J.: Prentice-Hall, 1960).

31. Among the leading sources on the topic of systems theory and organizations are Daniel Katz and Robert L. Kahn, *The Social Psychology of Organizations* (New York: John Wiley and Sons, 1966); Walter Buckley, *Sociology and Modern Systems Theory* (Englewood Cliffs, N.J.: Prentice-Hall, 1967); and James D. Thompson, *Organizations in Action* (New York: McGraw-Hill, 1967).

32. A basic source applying systems theory to the political process is David Easton, *A Framework for Political Analysis* (Englewood Cliffs, N.J.: Prentice-Hall, 1965).

33. See Stafford Beer, *Cybernetics and Management* (New York: John Wiley and Sons, 1959); Karl Deutsch, *The Nerves of Government* (New York: The Free Press, 1963); and Katz and Kahn, *The Social Psychology of Organizations.*

34. See, among others, Jerald Hage and Michael Aiken, *Social Change in Complex Organizations* (New York: Random House, 1970).

35. See Larry Kirkhart and Neely Gardner, eds., "Symposium on Organization Development," *Public Administration Review,* 34 (March/April 1974), 97–140; Paul R. Lawrence and Jay W. Lorsch, *Developing Organizations: Diagnosis and Action* (Reading, Mass.: Addison-Wesley, 1969); and Gerald Zaltman, Robert Duncan, and Jonny Holbeck, *Innovations and Organizations* (New York: John Wiley and Sons, 1973).

36. See Harold J. Leavitt, "Unhuman Organizations," and Harold J. Leavitt and Thomas L. Whisler, "Management in the 1980s," in Harold J. Leavitt and Louis R. Pondy, eds., *Readings in Managerial Psychology* (Chicago: University of Chicago Press, 1964); cited by Warren G. Bennis, "Organizational Developments and the Fate of Bureaucracy," in Fred A. Kramer, ed., *Perspectives on Public Bureaucracy,* p. 172.

37. See Warren G. Bennis and Philip E. Slater, *The Temporary Society* (New York: Harper & Row, 1968); Bennis, "Organizational Developments and the Fate of Bureaucracy"; and Buckley, *Sociology and Modern Systems Theory.*

38. Rensis Likert, *New Patterns of Management* (New York: McGraw-Hill, 1961).

39. Bennis and Slater, *The Temporary Society,* p. 6.

40. See Frank Marini, ed., *Toward a New Public Administration: The Minnowbrook Perspective* (Scranton, Pa.: Chandler Publishing, 1971); and H. George

Frederickson, "Organization Theory and New Public Administration," in Kramer, ed., *Perspectives on Public Bureaucracy.*

41. Frederickson, "Organization Theory and New Public Administration," in Kramer, ed., *Perspectives on Public Bureaucracy,* p. 197.

42. See Michael A. Murray, "Comparing Public and Private Management," *Public Administration Review,* 35 (July/August 1975), 364–371.

43. See Nicholas Henry, "Paradigms of Public Administration," *Public Administration Review,* 35 (July/August 1975), especially pp. 384–385.

44. This discussion relies on Brian W. Rapp, "You Can't Manage City Hall The Way You Manage General Motors," *Good Government,* 92 (Summer 1975), 12–15. See also Joseph L. Bower, "Effective Public Management: It Isn't the Same as Effective Business Management," *Harvard Business Review,* 55 (March/April 1977), 131–140.

45. Rapp, "You Can't Manage City Hall The Way You Manage General Motors," p. 15. See also Robert N. Anthony and Regina Herzlinger, *Management Control in Nonprofit Organizations* (Homewood, Ill.: Irwin, 1975).

SUGGESTED READINGS

Argyris, Chris. *Integrating the Individual and the Organization.* New York: John Wiley and Sons, 1964.

Barnard, Chester. *The Functions of the Executive.* Cambridge: Harvard University Press, 1938.

Bennis, Warren G., and Philip E. Slater. *The Temporary Society.* New York: Harper & Row, 1968.

Dubin, Robert, ed. *Human Relations in Administration, with Readings,* 4th ed. Englewood Cliffs, N.J.: Prentice-Hall, 1974.

Etzioni, Amitai. *Modern Organizations.* Englewood Cliffs, N.J.: Prentice-Hall, 1964.

Gulick, Luther, and Lyndall Urwick, eds. *Papers on the Science of Administration.* New York: Institute of Public Administration, 1937.

Kaplan, H. Roy, and Curt Tausky. "Humanism in Organizations: A Critical Appraisal." *Public Administration Review,* 37 (March/April 1977), 171–180.

Katz, Daniel, and Robert L. Kahn. *The Social Psychology of Organizations.* New York: John Wiley and Sons, 1966.

March, James G., and Herbert A. Simon. *Organizations.* New York: John Wiley and Sons, 1958.

Maslow, Abraham H. *Motivation and Personality,* 2nd ed. New York: Harper & Row, 1970.

CHAPTER 7
Decision Making in Administration

The making of decisions is at the heart of public administration, as it is of all organized human behavior. How decisions are made in a bureaucracy, by whom, according to what standards, and for whose benefit are questions of continuing interest as well as occasional controversy. Current quests for influence over decisions, access to decision makers, and accountability of decision makers all attest to the importance attached to the process.

The procedures by which decisions are made and applied, as well as their substance, leave a lasting imprint on administrative politics. We shall discuss the general nature of bureaucratic decision making, the role and impact of different kinds of goals, major features of the surrounding environment which ordinarily enter into the process, the concern for "rationality" in decision making and principal alternatives to the rational model, and the role politics plays in affecting the way many administrative decisions are made.

The Nature of Decision Making

Decision making in an organization involves making a choice to alter some existing condition,[1] choosing one course of action in preference to other possible courses of action, expending some amount of organizational or individual resources to implement the decision, and acting with the expectation of gaining something desirable. This definition suggests that a decision is not a single, self-contained event; rather, it is a *process*—begun when authoritative individuals or groups within an organization see a need to examine alternatives to the status quo, and continuing on through subsequent specific choices and the monitoring of their impacts. Thus "a decision" entails a series of other choices, which may rightly be regarded as part of it.

It is assumed that a decision maker selects the course of action most appropriate to achieving a desired objective or objectives, although deciding what is most appropriate is often difficult. There is some uncertainty regarding the eventual outcome of a decision, and consequently a degree of risk (however small) involved in taking actions decided upon. Concerns central to the decision-making process, therefore, include increasing potential gains, monitoring the ongoing decisional process, and reducing the resource expenditure, uncertainty, and risk involved in achieving whatever gains are made.[2]

The Problem of Goals

Before considering a range of decision alternatives, decision makers must define the goal or goals toward which a decision is directed. They must also understand distinctions among different types of goals and how courses of action and goals are linked. Goals may be very specific or very general, substantive or symbolic, individual or organizational or suborganizational, predominantly for the benefit of those within the organization or those outside. But regardless of their nature, goals usually help shape the decision environment significantly. Agreement or disagreement about a given decision may depend in large part upon agreement or disagreement about the goal—that is, upon goal congruence or goal divergence—among those making and those reacting to the decision. Virtually all decisions have some goal-related content, and evaluations of a decision may depend on how effectively it moves an organization toward a particular goal or, more fundamentally, how strongly the goal itself is supported.

Organizational Goals

An assumption often made by casual observers of government organizations is that they exist to achieve only certain kinds of goals, such as substantive programmatic objectives (for example, adequate health care or safe, reasonably priced air travel), and that they act out of a desire to satisfy a broad public interest. Other observers assume, in contrast, that government bureaucracies are interested only in their own survival and enhancement, taking a most limited view of the public interest. Neither view is totally wrong, but both fail to appreciate the complexity of goals within government agencies.

Survival and maintenance are indeed principal goals of virtually all organizations, governmental or otherwise. (An analogy to individual human behavior can be drawn here, in that survival is a fundamental instinct without being the sole purpose of our existence.) Administrative agencies, like other organizations, have as one of their goals maintenance of their own position. Such inward-oriented goals have been termed "reflexive"[3]; they are supported by those aspects of an organization's behavior and programs which have primary impact internally rather than on the external environment. Agencies pursue such goals by attempting to persuade a significant constituency, by actions and proposals, that their functions are essential either to society at large or to an important segment of society.

Administrative agencies are also concerned with substantive goals. All government organizations work toward accomplishment of programmatic objectives, whether popular or unpopular, visible or obscure, major or minor. Programmatic objectives appear to be the *raison d'être* of administrative agencies, and in many cases they constitute a powerful argument for an agency's existence. This type of goal has been labeled "transitive," in that there is an intended programmatic impact on the environment beyond the organization itself.[4] In advancing its cause through the political process, an agency will emphasize substantive goals—their importance to particular clienteles and to the whole society, and the agency's performance in pursuit of them.

Pursuit of program goals is not without its subtleties or pitfalls, however. In the first place, an agency may have certain substantive goals and others that are largely symbolic.[5] Symbolic goals are most valuable to an agency because of the political support they can attract; in effect, the agency adopts the goals of persons outside it. Frequently an agency goal can be described as both substantive and symbolic, with merit in objective terms as well as beneficial political consequences for the agency. Finally, it is quite common to find agencies suggesting that they are attempting to accomplish a worthwhile but virtually unreachable goal—for example, total eradication of poverty in the United States—yet continued pursuit of that objective yields benefits to both the agency and society. Many citizens and public officials are in favor of trying to wipe out poverty and are willing to appropriate government funds to agencies with jurisdiction to carry on the struggle, which benefits at least some of America's poor.

Another dimension of substantive goals is the tricky question of goal attainment. How do we know when a goal has been met and what happens to the agency in charge of a program when its "goal has been reached"? Achievement of organizational goals can be detrimental to an agency's continued operation. If an agency accomplishes its purposes, some might question the further need for it. On the other hand, if in order to avoid that embarrassing dilemma, an agency does not act vigorously to "solve the problem," it risks the wrath of supporters in the legislative and executive branches, as well as clientele groups. Fortunately for most agencies the dilemma is not insoluble, because of the broadness of many goals and the different dimensions of "goal attainment" situations.

First, many goals are not objectively attainable. It is possible to view a goal conceptually as "a value to be sought after, not an object to be achieved."[6] In this sense, "goals" are sets of broad directions in which organization members seek to move without necessarily expecting to accomplish them, while "objectives" are more limited purposes—related to the larger goals—which are achievable. "Adequate health care," for example, is an abstract goal; "attracting more doctors" and "building another hospital" are concrete objectives which move the organization (a community or state or nation) closer to the goal. Using this example, is it possible to reach the goal of "adequate health care" so that efforts to achieve it may cease? Not really, for two reasons. One is that definitions of what constitutes "adequacy" have to be agreed upon through the political process. There may well be continuing disagreement about what is adequate, and consequently about whether the goal has in fact been achieved. The other reason is that even if it can be agreed that "health care is now adequate," ongoing programs will be required to *keep* it that way. As a result, relevant programs continue to be necessary.

Second, there may be political advantage in deliberately stating agency goals in general terms. The goal of "educational quality in our schools" is far less likely to cause problems for a Department of Education than is a goal of assuring that high school graduates are equipped with specific reading and writing skills, and are qualified for entry into colleges and universities according to a prescribed entrance test score. Also, the more generalized a goal statement, the more widely supported it is likely to be, with less chance of concerted political opposition.

Third, legislative language establishing agency goals can be imprecise. For example, a health program in the Department of Health, Education, and Welfare could have as its overall goal "minimizing heart disease and related ailments among adult Americans." This is a laudable goal; no one would quarrel with it. But who is to say that the "minimum" has been reached, and by what measures? As with "adequate health care," such language is quite common in legislation and administrative rules and regulations. Under these circumstances, all an agency with such responsibilities needs to show is that it has had *some* success in putting across its message (get more exercise, have regular checkups, etc.), with *some* resultant reduction in heart disease and related ailments, and it is likely to be able to sustain itself and its programs.

Fourth, most agencies start with a combination of related goals, which can cushion the effect of one or two no longer requiring significant effort. In addition, many agencies "branch out" from original goals into new but related areas. In the example of an agency combating heart disease, the possibility of combating "related ailments" was raised, and that opens the way to concern for a multitude of cardiovascular and respiratory diseases, provided the agency can obtain necessary political support. To cite a case that is not hypothetical, the Tennessee Valley Authority began its existence with a primary emphasis on flood control through construction of major dams on the Tennessee River and its principal tributaries, and a secondary emphasis on generating electric power. The latter became a major emphasis during World War II because of a decision, made elsewhere, to locate a nuclear research center (the "Manhattan Project'') at Oak Ridge, Tennessee, just twenty miles from TVA head-quarters at Knoxville. The Oak Ridge facility required vast quantities of electricity, and the availability of low-cost TVA electricity was clearly a key factor influencing the location decision. TVA, naturally, responded to the demand. When the war ended, TVA had a far larger power system than it had before the war. As a result the relative standing of the electric power program within TVA's overall framework was dramatically altered.[7] As this example demonstrates, overall agency goals may undergo modification at the instigation of decision makers *outside* the agency—in this instance, defense planners in charge of top-secret nuclear development.

The National Aeronautics and Space Administration (NASA) provides perhaps the best example of what can happen to an agency with explicit goals which have clearly been accomplished. Charged with directing the national effort to land a man on the moon before the end of the 1960s, NASA set about its business and did exactly that. After a series of Mercury, Gemini, and Apollo flights, Neil Armstrong took that "giant leap for mankind" in mid-1969. Mission accomplished—spectacularly! But what then? NASA found itself faced with growing public disenchantment over the billions of dollars spent for space exploration when its primary mission of the decade was fulfilled. Its role consequently diminished, as controversy enveloped discussion of future enterprises. NASA's attempt to generate new programs was less than wholly success-ful. (Plans for a space shuttle, for example, have not moved forward with the same dispatch—or political support—as did the man-on-the-moon effort) Note that the potential scientific value of NASA's space exploration has not had decisive impact on its fortunes, much to the chagrin and frustration of NASA personnel. Other (political) considerations have had much more to do with the agency's fortunes than have its own substantive goals and aspirations. *outdated*

One other major point should be made about organizational goals. When public bureaucracies are repeatedly criticized for ''failure to reach their goals,'' they may develop a tendency to publicly articulate goals they know they can reach. Bureaucracies also know they may suffer politically from excessive attachment, whether in fact or image, to goals which turn out to be unpopular. In short, politics may influence the choice of official or unofficial organizational goals. Quoting political scientist Aaron Wildavsky:

> What we call goals or objectives may, in large part, be operationally determined by the *policies we can agree upon*. The mixture of values found in complex policies may have to be taken in packages, so that *policies may determine goals at least as much as general objectives determine policies*.[8]

An agency, in short, may adopt as official goals only those objectives which, in the judgment of its leaders, will produce the requisite political support for its operations. This does not happen universally, but the fact that it *can* be the case should serve as a warning not to take goal definition too seriously—not to view goals as abstract, permanent, or sacred statements "above" politics or separate from the agencies themselves.

Personal Goals

In addition to organizational goals, there are the personal goals of employees to be considered, since these also play a role in an institution's performance. Most individuals have goals of their own which working within the organization helps fulfill. These might be basic drives for earning a decent living and job security. They might relate to opportunities for professional advancement. Or they could be strong personal feelings about public policy directions the individual believes the organization should be pursuing. Personal goals such as these could affect organizational goals in two ways: individuals might devote more time and energy to pursuing their own goals than those of the organization, and they might come into conflict with others in the organization over such things as advancement through the ranks or policy-related organization activities. Conflict among individuals diverts attention and resources from the effort to attain organizational objectives.

Political economist Anthony Downs has suggested five types of bureaucratic employees, each formed around devotion to a particular combination of goals.[9] Two types, "climbers" and "conservers," act purely out of self-interest. Climbers are interested in increasing their power, income, and prestige, while conservers look first to maximizing their job security and maintaining the power, income, and prestige they already have.[10] The three other types are, in Downs' phrase, "mixed-motive officials, [who] . . . combine self-interest and altruistic loyalty to larger values. The main difference among the three types of mixed-motive officials is the breadth of the larger values to which they are loyal."[11] The three types are "zealots," "advocates," and "statesmen," who focus their energies respectively on relatively narrow policies or concepts, on a set of somewhat wider functions or on a wider organization, and on the general welfare or public interest, broadly defined.[12]

Although Downs' formulation is admittedly hypothetical and ideal-type, he nonetheless focuses on major motivations which relate to actual bureaucratic behavior. The essential point here is that the greater the variety of bureaucratic types and motives, the more difficult it is to attain official organizational objectives, since so many other unofficial objectives are present. Also, potential for internal conflict is increased where there is a variety of bureaucratic types, and a higher level of conflict will inhibit attainment of both official and unofficial goals.

From the standpoint of an organization's being able to fulfill its official objectives and manage its programs effectively, the ideal situation is one in which there is a high degree of *goal congruence* among all organization members. Where leaders, themselves agreed on objectives and priorities, can count on unified support from employees in attaining shared objectives, an organization's chances of success are obviously enhanced. Such congruence, however, is the exception rather than the rule, even within the leadership. Also, within the framework of the organization at large there are likely to be numerous small groups, each with its own particularistic goals, which may be given greater weight than those of the wider organization. The importance of small-group goals has been emphasized by the findings of Elton Mayo and his associates in the Hawthorne experiments, and by John Pfiffner and Frank Sherwood in their studies a quarter of a century later (see chapter 6).[13] All this makes it even less likely that substantial goal congruence will exist.

Decisions in the Balance:
Costs, Benefits, and Consequences

In addition to questions concerning goals, a number of other considerations are involved in reaching decisions. First (and often first in importance) is the matter of the resources necessary to implement a decision. The decision maker must consider both what kinds and what quantity of resources will be expended by pursuing a particular course of action. A decision to take some organizational action may require expenditures of time, personnel resources, money, and what we might call political capital (influence, prestige, and so on). The responsible official must have a reasonably clear idea—the clearer, the better—of just "how much it will cost" in terms of *all* these resources.

Second, decisions are made presumably to obtain some kind of gain or benefit. The potential gain normally is clearly perceived by decision makers, and indeed may be the stimulus for making a decision. The particular kind of gain might be monetary, political, programmatic, or possibly personnel-related, or a combination. The task of the decision maker, in any case, is to assess accurately the probabilities of achieving the desired benefits before going ahead with the effort to secure them. It is never sound policy to pursue the unreachable; thus, it is imperative that an effort be made to determine beforehand that the goal is in fact reachable.

Third, decision makers are faced with establishing whether or not potential benefits are worth probable costs; that is, what the *cost-benefit ratio* is likely to be. This requires answering such questions as these: Do we have sufficient time to devote to this enterprise, given our other responsibilities? Will our political supporters go along with us, or will we encounter pressure to do it differently, or perhaps not at all? Are we sufficiently certain about the probable benefits we can derive? At times, decision makers may have to choose between two mutually exclusive benefits (either this gain or that one, but not both), decide whether to seek something now or later (entailing the risk that it might be difficult now, but impossible later), and (especially in government) weigh the impact of values that are not central to the specific decisional equation (setting a bad political precedent, damaging democratic traditions, inviting a legal challenge in court, and so on).

A corollary concern is how to measure both costs and benefits, or even whether meaningful measures are available. One of the most persuasive measures is in dollar terms, particularly regarding costs. However, there has been considerable debate in recent years, both in the academic community and in government, over different ways to measure costs and benefits, separately and in relation to each other, and over the political implications of using different sets of measures.

Fourth, decision makers may base their decisions on different grounds, singly or in combination. Three such grounds are most prominent. One is substantive grounds—decisions are made "on the merits" of the question. For example, a decision made "on the merits" concerning the design of a highway linking two major cities would focus on the "shortest distance between two points" in terms of mileage, travel time, and construction costs and time. A second basis is political grounds—that is, net gain or loss measured by changes in political support, political resources, or political pressures. Using the example of the highway, the decision as to specific route might be affected by the discovery that following a straight line between the cities would take it across some valuable farmland owned by an influential politician or a contributor to the election campaigns of incumbent officeholders. In this instance the "shortest distance" might well include a generous curve around the perimeter of the farm property, even if this meant that total dollar costs, mileage, and construction time would increase. A third ground for decision is organizational in nature. For example, if the government's highway engineers felt strongly that a detour around the farm property would detract from economy, efficiency, sensible roadway design, and scenic value, the responsible decision maker would have to weigh the possible effect on the engineers' morale of deciding to build the curve anyway.

Note that different decisional considerations produce the need for a prior decision—namely, which factor(s) should be given predominant weight in the final decision. In the highway example, the question would be: Can the organization better afford to have on its hands an angry politician, demoralized professional employees, or displeased consumers (the highway users)? There is no easy or automatic solution to such a dilemma. Other factors would have to be taken into account, such as who else would be pleased or displeased with a particular decision. In hundreds of administrative decisions—some routine, some not—the same sorts of considerations apply. The less routine a decision is, the more carefully such considerations must be weighed.

A comment is in order about the types of official administrative decision makers who are likely to be concerned with the different grounds for decisions. Ordinarily, the experts in an organization (the engineers in the highway example) have as their highest priority the substance of a decision or issue rather than concerns of politics or of the organization as a whole. This is in keeping with the main task of substantive specialists—to concentrate on the subject-matter area of their expertise. Those more highly placed in an organization, however, whether higher-ranking specialists or so-called "political generalists," ordinarily have a different order of priorities, giving greater weight to political and organizational aspects of decision making than do their subordinates. This is not to say that top-level officials are ignorant of, or oblivious to, the merits of a question, as we have used that term, or that specialists care little for politics. It is to say, however, that generalists—in contrast to specialists—are often inclined toward more of a balancing process, weighing and choosing from among a greater number of decisional criteria.

Many generalists are appointed directly through political channels or are otherwise politically connected to a greater extent than are the bulk of the experts; consequently, they are under more constraint to act with sensitivity toward their political mentors (and adversaries). At the same time, their concern for the organization as a whole prompts them to be watchful of the morale of specialists who are likely to be dissatisfied with political decision making which runs counter to their expert opinion and preference. Some pressures and tensions within a bureaucracy are due to these variations in approaches to decision making in different parts of the organization's hierarchy, though such variations are not always present.[14]

The potential dilemma posed by conflicting grounds for decision can be illustrated by an intense controversy which boiled up in Washington politics in 1969 and 1970.[15] Former President Richard M. Nixon's first secretary of Health, Education, and Welfare (HEW) was Robert Finch, a personal friend of Nixon's from his California days, a former lieutenant governor of that state, and a moderate Republican. Prior to the time Nixon took office in 1969, HEW had been a major force in implementing much of Lyndon Johnson's Great Society program, focusing on enforcement of civil rights regulations, most notably in school desegregation. President Nixon, however, took a position in favor of easing requirements for compliance with school desegregation guidelines (which, as it happened, coincided with fairly strong sentiment in Congress). This was a presidential decision, not one made by Secretary Finch. But as a member of the president's cabinet—appointed by him, subject to removal by him, and loyal to him personally—Finch was expected in the normal course of events to direct implementation of this presidential policy. His dilemma was that HEW bureaucrats strongly favored continuation of school desegregation efforts. As the conflict intensified, Finch found himself caught between *political* demands of the Nixon White House and *organizational* pressures from within HEW. There clearly was no easy solution.

Finch had found himself on a political "hot seat" from the beginning of his tenure as HEW secretary. His department was administratively responsible for numerous programs which affected a wide range of social and economic interests, and these programs were under political pressure from the Nixon White House. They also tended to be among the more costly ones in the executive budget, and the administration was intent on reducing federal spending, or at least its rate of increase. Conflict was inevitable between career bureaucrats of HEW and the political leadership of the Nixon administration. Finch, as part of that leadership, initially endeavored to speak for his department while still supporting presidential policy. But as time wore on, this became ever more difficult.

The issue of school desegregation was but one on which Secretary Finch resisted to some extent the policy directions of Richard Nixon. He also opposed retaliating against campus demonstrations by restricting federal funds going to universities, and disassembling the Office of Economic Opportunity (see chapter 3). On school desegregation he "tried to defend Leon E. Panetta for his policies as HEW's Special Assistant to the Secretary for Civil Rights. Panetta had antagonized many in Congress for his aggressive enforcement policies on school desegregation."[16] As conflicting pressures mounted on Finch from his own subordinates, on the one hand, and the president and Congress, on the other, his position became increasingly untenable. Furthermore, because of political conflict between HEW and the White House, morale among department employees sagged badly during 1970, adding to Finch's organizational concerns. However, "some of the department's highly committed civil servants . . . , while increasingly critical of Mr. Finch for his support of Administration policies, . . . sympathized with his plight [having to publicly support the president's positions] and were convinced of his personal commitment and compassionate concern."[17]

Finally, however, Finch tendered his resignation as HEW secretary, leaving behind him a demoralized, bitter, and disorganized bureaucracy.[18] His ability to balance conflicting political and organizational demands allowed him to remain in his position for a longer period than might otherwise have been the case, and it is a tribute to his skills as an administrative leader that he was held in such high regard throughout the episode by most HEW employees, including most of those committed to intensive school desegregation efforts.

In addition to the considerations already discussed, there is normally a time factor in decision making. Time is one of the key resources that must be committed to both making and implementing a decision; accordingly, it is necessary to allow for sufficient time at every stage of deliberation and action. There are, furthermore, two other time considerations. First, the amount of time in which to reach a decision is not unlimited. Time constraints—especially during an emergency or crisis—can profoundly affect the ability of decision makers to gather and analyze information, and to project and compare the consequences of different alternatives, ultimately affecting the course of action selected. Second, decisions can have long-term and short-term consequences which may have to be dealt with. It frequently happens, for instance, that anticipated benefits from a decision are long-term, while costs are short-term; thus in the immediate future costs will outweigh benefits. A case in point is job training for the unemployed; it takes time for them to become fully productive workers (as it does for any new worker on the job), and per-capita costs of training run very high. How quickly and with how much certainty benefits will be derived would have to be considered. Politically, a decision that yields some gain right away and carries with it the promise of better things still to come is the most defensible. The essential point is that time is a relevant consideration in assessing a given course of action's costs and benefits.

Central to all of these decision-making elements is the quantity and quality of information available. All decision makers need enough information to serve as a minimal basis for making reasoned choices, and most try to gather as much information as possible prior to making a final decision. The ideal situation (rarely if ever achieved) would be one in which an official had total access to all quantitative and nonquantitative data (which could be verified for accuracy) directly related to the decisional alternatives under consideration, including comprehensive projections of all possible consequences resulting from each proposed course of action. In practice, decision makers may consciously settle for less than complete information, usually because a decision is needed promptly. Or they may try to postpone a decision, pending the acquisition of more information which will reduce the risk of making mistakes.[19] Even officials or agencies enjoying strong political support seek to accumulate hard data to back their decisions; a recurring pattern of faulty or inadequate data could endanger that support. Information, in sum, is needed to make decisions that are supportable, both objectively and politically.

There are several significant limitations on the acquisition and use of information. Perhaps most important is the fact that we live in a world of imperfect information. It is futile to mount a search for literally *all* the information that might be obtained on a subject, and most decision makers have somewhat more modest ambitions. Compounding that problem is the fact that communication of information is often less than clear, subject to human error both at the point of origin and at the receiving end, even when both parties desire full mutual understanding.[20]

Another crucial limitation on information resources is the cost entailed in obtaining information. Information costs include the personnel and time that must be devoted to its acquisition, organization, and presentation. Acquisition costs in particular can become prohibitive. The greatest value of the computer as an information storage and retrieval system is the enormous saving in time and money it makes possible in obtaining a given quantity of data, compared to the investment necessary to gather the same amount of data by traditional methods.[21]

The last major limitation stems from the conscious and (especially) unconscious biases of those who send, relay, and receive information. We tend to attach high importance to "objective" information, yet there is great difficulty in interpreting all information with complete objectivity. Even the most fair-minded individuals have subjective values which color, however slightly, their perceptions of data, images, or phenomena. Existing preferences can shape responses, or even receptiveness, to particular information. Thus pure objectivity in data interpretation is an impossibility and, consequently, absolutely objective information is beyond our grasp.

Finally, there is the problem of deliberate distortion of information. Information is a source of political power, and it is often in the best interests of an agency or official to provide only that information which will have a positive political effect. We may debate the utility and wisdom of political interference with objectivity in information, but it is undeniably a significant constraint. With enough effort, deliberate distortions can be discovered and corrected, but that effort can require large investments of resources, and consequently is made only irregularly. Self-interest motives, in sum, can seriously impair objective use of data.

Decision makers face three other kinds of problems. First, decision making is strongly affected by previous decisions and policies that have been put into effect. Some decision alternatives, in other words, are not available because of past decision making. Instead of working with a "clean slate," decisions must be made within the confines allowed by past choices. Second, there are frequently unanticipated consequences, in spite of efforts to foresee all the outcomes of each decision. Sometimes the projected outcome fails to materialize; sometimes there are unintended side effects which develop together with the projected outcome; sometimes there are only the side effects. If these unanticipated results turn out to be serious, they can cause intense problems and political repercussions. Third, decision making involves *sunk costs*— certain irrecoverable costs resulting from commitment of resources.

The term "sunk costs" has two meanings. First, a given resource or commodity, once spent, cannot be spent again. For example, a piece of land committed to use as the site of an approach ramp to a superhighway obviously cannot also be used as a hospital site. The realities of "sunk costs" raise the stakes in decision making. Second, "sunk costs" suggests that once a decision has been made to proceed in a particular policy direction, certain costs would necessarily be incurred if that direction were to be reversed later. An analogy would be a motorist at a fork in the road, pondering which one leads to his destination. If he makes the wrong choice, it will take extra time, gasoline, and wear-and-tear on the car to return to the junction and resume the trip, this time in the right direction. In administration, too, investment of extra resources is required to reverse a policy direction, and some political risk is entailed as well. It appears that it is much easier to maintain a given policy direction than to change it, which, if true, would explain why administrative agencies resist having to modify what they are doing.[22] If, however, the costs of *not* changing direction should approach or exceed the costs of changing, the agency would be far more likely to adapt itself.[23] In any event, "sunk costs" represent an additional factor to be taken into account when calculating a cost-benefit equation.

The Quest for Rationality in Decision Making

"Rationality" in decision making must seem at times like the pot of gold at the end of the rainbow. The search for rationality has gone on continually, yet still it frequently eludes its most avid pursuers. The rational model can be described in precise detail, but pure rationality itself seems all but unattainable.

The *rational,* or *rational-comprehensive,* model of decision making is derived principally from economic theories about how to make the "best" economic decisions. The key element in the economic model is the effort to maximize marginal utility—to achieve the highest level of return or satisfaction possible on a given investment of resources.[24] In its noneconomic applications, the rational-comprehensive model calls for diagnosis of the problem; thorough examination of all facets of available alternatives, including definitions of means-ends relationships and comparison of the consequences likely to result from each alternative; and selection of the "best possible" solution to the problem.[25] This suggests that rationality in administrative decision making depends on the following combination of considerations: (1) decisions made strictly "on the merits"; (2) rigorous analysis of how each alternative relates to the desired objective, and assessment of the appropriateness of each alternative; (3) careful cost-benefit analysis, utilizing all possible information about all kinds of costs and benefits; (4) comprehensive investigation of consequences, seeking to assess all possible outcomes in every context, both long term and short term; and (5) comprehensiveness in assumptions, data, and evaluations. The overall objective of the rational-comprehensive decision maker would be to maximize gains, to obtain the largest possible return for a given investment of resources, in any and all circumstances.

Many observers of contemporary public administration feel that pure rationality in decision making is beyond reach, and they question whether it ever was a realistic possibility. According to Anthony Downs, there are a number of serious impediments to the attainment of rationality in decision making. They include (1) time constraints, (2) the ability of a decision maker to handle only a limited amount of information at any one time, (3) an inability to give one's undivided attention to a single problem or decision, (4) failure to secure all possible information, (5) problems of information acquisition costs, and (6) an inability to predict the future, resulting in "some ineradicable uncertainty."[26] To the extent that efforts to overcome these limitations are successful, rationality in decision making is enhanced.

There are, however, other problems as well. Political and organizational grounds for making a decision compete with substantive grounds. Decision makers and agencies compete with one another for resources and gains, preventing any *one* from achieving maximum marginal utility. Errors and misunderstandings in the transmission of information are common. The necessity of dealing with different aspects of the same problem requires simultaneous consideration of shifting and interrelated consequences. As discussed earlier, there is often some uncertainty or ambiguity about goals, making difficult any meaningful analysis of relationships between proposed alternatives and the goals toward which they are directed. Furthermore, there is some inevitable lack of precision in measuring costs, benefits, and side effects. Finally, unpredictable changes in the sociopolitical environment affect both substantive needs and the availability of alternatives.[27] Each of these factors can reduce the degree of rationality attainable in decision making, and in combination they may severely hamper the achievement even of reasonableness and good sense.

With all these limitations, it might seem that the effort to achieve rational decisions is a futile one, and indeed it may be. But even if pure rationality is beyond reach, trying to make rational decisions can itself be a worthwhile endeavor. Attempting to foresee as many of the consequences as possible; to gather as much information as possible in the time available; to be as precise as one can be about goals, costs, benefits, and side effects—in short, to *strive* for rationality—can strengthen decision-making processes and lead to decisions that can better stand the test of time and experience. A willingness to acknowledge limitations on rationality is not the same as saying there is no purpose or gain in trying to be rational.

Alternative Approaches to Making Decisions

Major criticisms of the rational model of decision making have centered on several of its basic assumptions: the quest for maximizing gains, emphasis on long-term consequences at the expense of concern for short-term changes, the focus on the interrelatedness of decisional outcomes and the necessity to take account of these links, and the heavy bias in favor of economic conceptualizations of costs, benefits, and their relationships. A number of scholars and theorists have expanded upon these criticisms and argued that individual decisions, and change in general, come about through an "incremental" process. *Incrementalism,* in contrast to rationality, stresses decision making through a series of limited successive comparisons, with a relatively narrow range of alternatives rather than a determinedly comprehensive range, and seeks to bring about only marginal changes from the status quo. Incrementalism focuses primary attention on short-term rather than long-term effects, on the most crucial consequences of an action rather than all those conceivable, and on less formalized methods of measuring costs and benefits.

The differences between rationalists and incrementalists were (and are) very sharp. First, where the rationalist attempts to maximize the benefits in all phases of decision making, the incrementalist tries to "satisfice," to use Herbert Simon's term.[28] To "satisfice" is to reach a decision which is *satis*factory, yielding benefits that suf*fice* to meet situational needs of the decision maker. The incremental decision maker accepts the fact that it may not be possible to get everything out of a given decision, and that settling for "half a loaf" is not unreasonable. Furthermore, the incrementalist maintains that it may well be *irrational* to "shoot for the moon" each and every time a decision is made, because the risks—and consequences—of failure are far greater, and because resources could be expended too rapidly.

Second, incrementalism, while not dismissing the importance of long-term consequences, emphasizes meeting short-term needs and solving short-term problems. Incrementalists are comfortable as "troubleshooters," responding to immediate pressures and seeking to alleviate the worst of them. Charles Lindblom, perhaps the leading spokesman for the incrementalist school of thought, speaks of serial analyses—that is, repeated and ongoing analyses—rather than one comprehensive analysis, such as points the way down the rationalist's road.[29] Lindblom maintains that continual incremental adjustments in both the definition of a problem and the formulation of solutions is a reasonable and effective method of solving problems and making decisions.

Third, Lindblom and others suggest that the emphasis in the rational model on comprehensive evaluation of how a given decision would affect all other decisions is unrealistic. They contend that it is simply not possible to account in advance for all the ways that a particular course of action will affect other decisional processes and their outcomes.

Most important, those who have advanced the incremental approach reject the notion that economic models of decision making are the only ones that have legitimacy. They argue, at least indirectly, that noneconomic models and modes of decision making have intrinsic value, and that in some circumstances using economic models might well be inappropriate, not rational. Furthermore, the incremental model allows for measures of costs, benefits, and side effects of decisions which are not economic, or even necessarily quantitative. Incrementalists acknowledge that this approach permits subjective values to influence decisions, but find ample justification in the fact that subjectivity plays some role in any case; they maintain that it is better to openly incorporate sound subjective judgment than to self-consciously attempt to exclude on principle all traces of subjectivity. At the same time, incrementalists are quick to endorse the need for adequate information and good-quality data, to voice concern for choosing sound courses of action, and so on. The difference is that they are prepared to make decisions even where the ideal conditions called for by the rationalists do not exist, which they say happens in an overwhelming majority of decision-making situations.

The incremental approach itself has come under fire. Two critics, in particular, stand out—one for identifying a serious shortcoming, the other for elaborating on the criticism of the first and outlining a third approach to decision making. Yehezkel Dror, in a pointed response to Lindblom, emphasized that marginal changes acceptable to incrementalists may *not* suffice to meet real and growing policy demands—that as policy needs change, decision makers may have to develop innovations bolder than those contemplated by the incremental approach.[30] Dror's message was that if the incrementalist focuses solely or even primarily on small-scale changes designed to meet disjointed and short-run needs, larger needs and demands are likely to be overlooked and the decision-making process rendered impotent or, worse, irrelevant.

Dror also criticized incrementalism for making more acceptable the many forces in human organizations which tend toward inertia and maintenance of the status quo, resisting innovation. His comments suggest that one could find in incrementalism considerable justification for the behavior of Downs' "conserver"—the bureaucrat chiefly interested in maintaining power, prestige, and income who takes a cautious, low-risk approach to decision making. Dror clearly leaned to a view of bureaucratic behavior which encourages both responsiveness to larger-scale needs and innovativeness in seeking solutions; he found incrementalism wanting in both respects.

Amitai Etzioni expanded on Dror's criticisms of the incremental model and offered an alternative approach, which he labeled "mixed scanning."[31] Etzioni's chief criticism of the incremental approach was its apparent failure to distinguish between fundamental and nonfundamental decisions. He suggested that for nonfundamental decision making the incremental approach was entirely valid and appropriate, but that in making fundamental decisions a decision maker needed to have wider perceptual horizons in order to appreciate the scope and significance of the choice to be made. More important, he felt that incrementalists tended to decide only nonfundamental matters—stemming from their emphasis on the "trouble-shooter" approach to solving problems—and, as a result, promoted a general aimlessness in overall policy.[32] In preference to pure incrementalism, Etzioni suggested a twofold or mixed approach to decision making which incorporates some elements of both the rational-comprehensive and incremental approaches.

Etzioni's mixed-scanning model can best be understood by using his analogy of a high-altitude weather satellite in orbit around the earth.[33] On board the satellite are two cameras—one equipped with a wide-angle lens which can scan a large area and record major weather patterns, the other equipped with a narrow-angle lens capable of "zeroing in" on turbulence and examining it in much finer detail. Examination by the narrow-lens camera is contingent upon the wide-lens camera first discovering large systems of turbulent weather. Conversely, the wide-lens camera is incapable of detailed analysis of storm centers and other phenomena. In sum, either camera without the other would supply some useful information, but much more can be obtained when they are used in combination. Further, the analysis provided by the narrow-lens camera is more intelligible when meteorologists have some idea of the size, exact location, and boundaries of the total weather system; that is, when they have a meaningful context for the detailed data. So it is also, according to Etzioni, with decision making:

> Fundamental decisions are made by exploring the main alternatives the actor sees in view of his conception of his goals, but—unlike what rationalism would indicate—details and specifications are omitted so that an overview is feasible. *Incremental decisions are made but within the context set by fundamental decisions (and fundamental reviews).* Thus, each of the two elements in mixed-scanning helps to reduce the effects of the particular shortcomings of the other; incrementalism reduces the unrealistic aspects of rationalism by limiting the details required in fundamental decisions, and . . . rationalism helps to overcome the conservative slant of incrementalism by exploring longer-run alternatives.[34]

"Political Rationality": A Contradiction in Terms?

We have been speaking, for the most part, of decision makers in the abstract, and of models of decision making applied to theoretical situations. We now take up a question central to our overall concern in this book: whether or not it is possible to achieve rationality, wholly or in part, in a public administrative system permeated by political influences and pressures. Can administrators who act at least partially in response to political stimuli be said to be acting rationally, in any sense, when they

make decisions? Can "politics" and "rational decision making" be made
to coexist, or at least not be totally contradictory?

Much of the literature on rational decision making in economics and
political science would seem to suggest that the answer to these questions
is an unequivocal "No." Politics is frequently represented as interfering
with rational processes, outweighing more objective considerations, and
overriding "neutral" or "nonpolitical" measurements and data. When
political considerations predominate in decision making, as they
frequently do, the stigma of irrationality is attached to the process and the
outcomes. To dispute this characterization of politicized decision making
requires a significant modification of the meaning of rationality. In
particular, what must be changed is the "currency" of rationality, the criteria by which rationality is defined and measured.

Plainly stated, rationality has traditionally been an economic
measure and the currency implicitly or explicitly quantitative. Most
economists, and many in other disciplines including public administration, have assumed for many years that economic-quantitative rationality
is sufficient as an overall definition of the concept. Recently, however,
the possibility has been raised that there may be other, equally valid,
forms of rationality, specifically *political rationality*.[35] This is to say that
political and economic choices are often conceived in different terms and
directed toward fulfilling different kinds of objectives, and should
therefore be evaluated according to different criteria.

Wildavsky has suggested that in a political setting a decision maker's
need for political support assumes central importance, and that political
costs and benefits of decisions are crucial.[36] Political benefits which might
accrue to a decision maker are self evident: success in obtaining short-
term policy rewards, enhanced power over future decisions, added access
to and/or earlier inclusion in the decision-making process (given that both
access and involvement are meaningful), and so on. Political costs,
however, are less obvious and need more explicit categorization, which
Wildavsky provides:

> *Exchange costs* are incurred by a political leader when he needs the support
> of other people to get a policy adopted. He has to pay for this assistance by
> using up resources in the form of favors (patronage, logrolling) or coercive
> moves (threats or acts to veto or remove from office). By supporting a policy
> and influencing others to do the same, a politician antagonizes some people
> and may suffer their retaliation. If these *hostility costs* mount they may turn
> into *reelection costs*—actions that decrease his chances (or those of his
> friends) of being elected or reelected to office. Election costs, in turn, may
> become *policy costs* through inability to command the necessary formal
> powers to accomplish the desired policy objectives. . . . [We] may also talk
> about *reputation costs*, i.e., not only loss of popularity with segments of the
> electorate but also loss of esteem and effectiveness with other participants in
> the political system and loss of ability to secure policies other than the one
> immediately under consideration.[37]

It is apparent that, as stated here, political benefits are rarely measurable in quantifiable terms. The one set of political costs that might be measurable numerically is reelection costs, but it is difficult to determine from voting data how particular actions by politicians affect the ballot choices of thousands of voters. Their lack of easy measurability, however, does not diminish the impact political costs have on the behavior of governmental decision makers, including those in bureaucracy.

It is possible to argue, in fact, that bureaucratic decision makers tend to behave more and more like Downs' "conservers"[38] at least partly for political reasons. Cautious behavior that minimizes risk, whether individual or institutional, is inherently political. Self-interest motives, which Downs ascribes to "climbers" as well as to "conservers,"[39] are themselves political and bring about bureaucratic behavior patterns which can best be characterized as such. "Mixed" motives of self-interest and altruism are also partly political. Only Downs' primarily altruistic "statesman" seems to have the general good and not "politics" in view, but, as Downs suggests, by his not contesting for organizational resources, the statesman's functions "will probably receive an underallocation of resources."[40] Without being so labeled, that is an argument on behalf of political rationality.

The point of all this is that there is a widespread tendency, even among some political scientists, to scornfully dismiss or downgrade as "irrational" any behavior or decision not clearly directed toward achieving the "best" results. But if criteria of political rationality were to be used—that is, establishing cost-benefit ratios in the "currency" of politics—such behavior and decisional outcomes might be perfectly "rational." Perhaps most important, decisions made and measured even by the most objective economic-quantitative criteria have political implications; for example, an economically "rational" tax reform law will benefit some more than others. The mistake all too frequently made, in and out of government, is ignoring or denigrating those implications because they somehow "pollute" the "truly objective" decisions based on only the most "neutral" of considerations.[41] In every instance, the choice of criteria by which to measure decisional outcomes has political significance because of the ever-present possibility that adherence to a particular set of criteria (including quantitative data) will ultimately favor the political interests of one group over those of other groups.

Another observer who makes a similar point from a different perspective is Martin Landau.[42] He questions the traditional inclination to minimize or eradicate all traces of organizational duplication and overlap in the interests of economy and efficiency, broadly defined, and points out that such practices, contrary to being rational, may prove to be quite irrational. He suggests, first, that duplication of organizational features may make overall performance more reliable, in the event any one part breaks down. As an example, he cites an automobile with dual braking systems; the secondary system may seem to be just so much extra baggage, so uneconomical, so wasteful—until the primary braking system fails![43] Within human organizations, training more than one individual or staff in essentially the same tasks fits the same description of "rational duplication"; the alternative is increased risk of organizational breakdown should any one part fail. Second, Landau asserts that overlapping parts may improve performance by allowing for greater adaptability within the organization as a whole. His examples of "rational overlapping" include, among others, biological organisms which can adapt and survive in the face of a failing part, and, significantly, the Constitution of the United States.

Why the latter as an example of "rational overlap"? Because our framework of government was calculated, from the outset, to be overlapping (and, for that matter, duplicative) in the interest of preventing political tyranny, that most efficient of governmental methods. Separation of powers and checks and balances were both designed to prevent any one branch of government from becoming predominant. And what is checks and balances except *deliberately designed overlap* in the execution of essential government functions? Similarly, our structure of federalism is clearly duplicative, yet the purpose is the same: to prevent undue concentration of power. From Landau we can infer that in working toward the accomplishment of clearly delineated political goals (in this example, preventing concentration of power), some structural and behavioral arrangements may be politically rational and defensible, even though they might appear quite irrational in economic or other "value-neutral" terms. Above all, both Landau and Wildavsky challenge the unthinking application of economic criteria to the measurement of political phenomena, as well as the assumption that economic rationality is, by definition, superior to political rationality.

By the same token, political rationality and all it implies should not be regarded as inherently superior to economic rationality. Landau, Wildavsky, and others have made a case for political rationality by comparing it to its economic counterpart simply because the latter is so deeply imbedded in our general approaches to decision making. None of those who espouse the notion of political rationality would suggest that economic rationality has no place, or that it is detrimental to decision making to employ goal- or cost-related criteria and to view decisional situations with as much objectivity as possible. All they suggest is that the notion of political rationality can have equal validity as a measure of the worth of particular decision processes and their specific outcomes.

In sum, then, "political rationality" is not at all a contradiction in terms. One can accept the propositions that politics is legitimately concerned with enabling the decision processes of government to function adequately, that basing decisions on political grounds is as valid as basing them on other grounds, and that rationality according to the currency of politics is as defensible as rationality according to the currency of economics. Political rationality, when appropriately conceived and applied, can be a useful tool for evaluating both the processes and the outcomes of organizational decision making.

SUMMARY

Decision making involves seeking to bring about a change in order to achieve some gain, by means of a particular course of action involving expenditure of a certain amount of resources. There is some unavoidable uncertainty, and therefore some risk involved, and most decision makers seek to minimize both.

Organizational goals can heavily influence an agency's behavior, and can in turn be influenced by political considerations. Key goals may include agency survival and maintenance ("reflexive" goals), accomplishment of substantive program objectives ("transitive" goals), and symbolic goals. Agencies seek to articulate their goals in relatively general fashion and may be deliberately unclear about some of them to preserve their political support. Efforts to achieve certain kinds of goals may have to be ongoing, due to the nature of the problem. The personal goals of agency employees usually vary considerably, thus making goal congruence between individual and organizational goals difficult to bring about. Finally, some goals may be determined by the extent to which political support can be generated for them.

The major considerations in the decisional process are (1) the goals being sought, (2) the resources necessary, (3) projected benefits, (4) the cost-benefit ratio, (5) substantive, political, and organizational grounds for decisions, (6) the time element, (7) the quality and quantity of information available, (8) past decisions and policies, (9) the prospect of unanticipated consequences and efforts to avoid them, and (10) "sunk costs," that is, resources expended in having made and implemented a decisional commitment and resources which would be necessary to alter it.

Rational decision making suggests a process of identifying goals clearly, gathering maximum information about all possible alternative methods for accomplishing the goals, and selecting the method which will yield the largest benefit at the smallest cost. Pure rationality has been criticized as an unrealistic ideal. A number of serious limitations operate to impede its attainment, including time and information constraints, competing grounds for decisions as well as political competition for some of the same benefits, and difficulties in clearly defining means-ends relationships. However, these limitations should not defeat the *effort* to make rational decisions.

Two major alternatives to the rational model have been proposed. Incrementalism attempts to make only limited changes in the status quo, seeking adequate information about a few possible alternatives as opposed to maximum information about all alternatives, and concentrating on short-term effects of decisions. Critics of incrementalism, distinguishing between fundamental and nonfundamental decisions, have suggested that the "trouble-shooting" approach is not adequate to meet all kinds of decisional needs. Furthermore, incrementalism has been charged with supporting the status quo. An approach which synthesizes some aspects of the rational and incremental models—mixed scanning—suggests that there is value in identifying long-term problem areas while maintaining an organization's capability to meet immediate needs effectively.

Another critique of "rationality" is founded on the premise that economic-quantitative measures may not always be appropriate in determining what is "rational." By using a set of explicitly political measures, cost-benefit analysis in terms of political rationality is possible. What is politically rational may not be economically rational, and vice versa, and applying economic concepts of rationality to political phenomena might be misleading. Both economic and political rationality have validity, and both are useful in evaluating decisions and decision processes.

NOTES

1. Some decisions are made to leave things as they are rather than change them, but theoretically the mere fact that a decision was called for *not* to change something alters the overall situation.

2. An extensive literature has grown up in the area of decision making, including Stephen K. Archer, "The Structure of Management Decision Theory," in Robert Golembiewski, et al., eds., *Public Administration* (Chicago: Rand McNally, 1966); David Braybrooke and Charles E. Lindblom, *A Strategy of Decision* (London: Collier-Macmillan, 1963); William R. Dill, "Administrative Decision Making," in Sidney Mailick and Edward H. Van Ness, eds., *Concepts and Issues in Administrative Behavior* (Englewood Cliffs, N.J.: Prentice-Hall, 1962); William J. Gore, *Administrative Decision Making: A Heuristic Model* (New York: John Wiley and Sons, 1964); William J. Gore and J. W. Dyson, *The Making of Decisions* (New York: The Free Press, 1964); Charles E. Lindblom, "The Science of Muddling Through," *Public Administration Review*, 19 (Spring 1959), 79–88; Martin Shubik, "Studies and Theories of Decision Making," *Administrative Science Quarterly*, 3 (December 1958), 289–306; Herbert A. Simon, *Administrative Behavior*, 3rd ed. (New York: The Free Press, 1976); and Allen W. Lerner, *The Politics of Decision Making: Strategy, Cooperation, and Conflict* (Beverly Hills, Calif.: Sage, 1976).

3. Lawrence B. Mohr, "The Concept of Organizational Goal," *American Political Science Review*, 67 (June 1973), 470–481, at p. 475.

4. Ibid., pp. 475–476.

5. See Murray Edelman, *The Symbolic Uses of Politics* (Urbana: University of Illinois Press, 1964), and *Politics as Symbolic Action* (Chicago: Markham, 1971).

6. Robert C. Young, "Goals and Goal-Setting," *Journal of the American Institute of Planners*, 32 (March 1966), 76–85, at p. 78.

7. More than twenty years ago the power program was described as one in which ". . . a secondary activity, the production and sale of surplus power, has come to overshadow other program goals, some say to the considerable disadvantage of the whole." See Roscoe C. Martin, ed., *TVA: The First Twenty Years* (University, Ala., and Knoxville, Tenn,: University of Alabama Press and University of Tennessee Press, 1956), chapter 17, "Retrospect and Prospect," at p. 267.

8. Aaron Wildavsky, *The Politics of the Budgetary Process,* 2nd ed. (Boston: Little, Brown, 1974), pp. 191–192 (emphasis added).

9. This discussion is taken from Anthony Downs, *Inside Bureaucracy* (Boston: Little, Brown, 1967), chapter 8.

10. Ibid., p. 88.

11. Ibid.

12. Ibid.

13. F. J. Roethlisberger and William J. Dickson, *Management and the Worker* (Cambridge: Harvard University Press, 1939); John M. Pfiffner and Frank P. Sherwood, *Administrative Organization* (Englewood Cliffs, N.J.: Prentice-Hall, 1960).

14. It has been suggested that variations in personal goals may also be related, if indirectly, to hierarchical location. See Downs, *Inside Bureaucracy,* chapter 8, especially p. 89.

15. The following account is based on *Congressional Quarterly (CQ) Almanac,* vol. 25: 91st Congress, First Session, 1969 (Washington, D.C.: Congressional Quarterly, Inc., 1970); *CQ Almanac,* vol. 26: 91st Congress, Second Session, 1970 (Washington, D.C.: Congressional Quarterly, Inc., 1971); and the *Wall Street Journal,* vol. 175, nos. 111 and 113 (June 8, 1970, and June 10, 1970).

16. *CQ Almanac,* vol. 26: 91st Congress, Second Session, 1970 (Washington, D.C.: Congressional Quarterly, Inc., 1971), p. 1185. On at least one occasion Finch appealed publicly to Congress to permit HEW to continue its school desegregation efforts rather than legislating restrictions. See *CQ Almanac*, vol. 25, p. 553.

17. *Wall Street Journal,* June 8, 1970, p. 28.

18. Ibid.

19. See Shubik, "Studies and Theories of Decision Making," for an elaboration of "probable risk" and its minimization.

20. An outstanding analysis of the problem of obtaining reliability in organizational communications can be found in Martin Landau's "Redundancy, Rationality, and the Problem of Duplication and Overlap," in *Public Administration Review,* 29 (July/August 1969), 346–358. The argument that multiple channels of communication can increase the accuracy of messages going to the same receiver has been made by Downs, *Inside Bureaucracy*, chapter 10. Arthur Schlesinger and Richard Neustadt have described persuasively how various American presidents have made use of multiple channels. See Schlesinger's "Roosevelt as Chief Administrator," in Francis E. Rourke, ed., *Bureaucratic Power in National Politics*, 2nd ed. (Boston: Little, Brown, 1972), pp. 126–138, especially pp. 128–132; and Neustadt's *Presidential Power* (New York: John Wiley and Sons, 1960), chapter 7.

21. This, incidentally, is a clear example of long-term benefit making worthwhile a high short-term cost. Installing a computerized information system is very

expensive, but the long-term dollar saving realized through use of the system more than makes up for the initial investment.

22. See Downs, *Inside Bureaucracy,* chapter 14.

23. Ibid., p. 195.

24. Braybrooke and Lindblom, in *A Strategy of Decision,* cite numerous theorists responsible for developing the rational-comprehensive economic model.

25. See John M. Pfiffner, "Administrative Rationality," *Public Administration Review,* 20 (Summer 1960), pp. 125–132.

26. Downs, *Inside Bureaucracy,* p. 75.

27. See Louis C. Gawthrop, *Administrative Politics and Social Change* (New York: St. Martin's, 1971); and Dwight Waldo, ed., *Public Administration in a Time of Turbulence* (Scranton, Pa.: Chandler Publishing, 1971).

28. Herbert A. Simon, *Administrative Behavior* (New York: Macmillan, 1957), Preface to the 2nd ed.

29. Charles Lindblom's principal contributions to decision-making theory appeared in "The Science of 'Muddling Through'," *Public Administration Review,* 19 (Spring 1959), 79–88; *The Intelligence of Democracy* (New York: The Free Press, 1965); and *The Policy-Making Process* (Englewood Cliffs, N.J.: Prentice-Hall, 1968).

30. Yehezkel Dror, "Muddling Through—'Science' or Inertia," in "Governmental Decision Making" (a symposium), *Public Administration Review,* 24 (September 1964), 153–157.

31. Amitai Etzioni, "Mixed Scanning: A 'Third' Approach to Decision Making," *Public Administration Review,* 27 (December 1967), 385–392.

32. Ibid., p. 388.

33. Ibid., p. 389.

34. Ibid., pp. 389–390 (emphasis added).

35. Aaron Wildavsky outlines concisely the nature of political rationality in *The Politics of the Budgetary Process,* 2nd ed. (Boston: Little, Brown, 1974), pp. 189–194. This discussion relies heavily on his writing there and on his critical appraisals of Planning-Programming-Budgeting Systems (PPBS) that have appeared in *Public Administration Review.*

36. Wildavsky, *The Politics of the Budgetary Process,* 2nd ed., p. 192.

37. Ibid. (emphasis added).

38. Downs, *Inside Bureaucracy,* p. 99.

39. Ibid., p. 88.

40. Ibid., p. 111.

41. Wildavsky, *The Politics of the Budgetary Process,* 2nd ed., p. 190, makes a similar point with regard to advocates of budgetary reform in the national government.

42. Landau, "Redundancy, Rationality, and the Problem of Duplication and Overlap," pp. 346–358, especially pp. 350–353.

43. Ibid., pp. 349–350.

SUGGESTED READINGS

Braybrooke, David, and Charles E. Lindblom. *A Strategy of Decision.* London: Collier-Macmillan, 1963.

Downs, Anthony. *Inside Bureaucracy.* Boston: Little, Brown, 1967, chapter 8.

Etzioni, Amitai. "Mixed Scanning: A 'Third' Approach to Decision Making." *Public Administration Review,* 27 (December 1967), 385–392.

Gore, William J., and J. W. Dyson. *The Making of Decisions.* New York: The Free Press, 1964.

"Governmental Decision Making" (a symposium). *Public Administration Review,* 24 (September 1964), 153–165.

Lindblom, Charles E. "The Science of 'Muddling Through'." *Public Administration Review,* 19 (Spring 1959), 79–88.

Mohr, Lawrence B. "The Concept of Organizational Goal." *American Political Science Review,* 67 (June 1973), 470–481.

Pfiffner, John M. "Administrative Rationality." *Public Administration Review,* 20 (Summer 1960), 125–132.

Simon, Herbert A. *Administrative Behavior,* 3rd ed. New York: The Free Press, 1976.

Wildavsky, Aaron. *The Politics of the Budgetary Process,* 2nd ed. Boston: Little, Brown, 1974, pp. 189–194.

CHAPTER 8
The "Tasks" of Administrative Leadership

Leadership functions have attracted great interest in both ancient and modern times from scholars, generals, politicians, and more casual observers. Virtually every social order, from the most primitive society to the most complex industrial and postindustrial nations, has operated within some sort of framework in which leadership functions are differentiated, identified, and exercised by some and not others. Styles of leadership have been studied and restudied; prescriptions for leadership have been written and revised; exercise of leadership has been carefully analyzed and often sharply criticized. Despite all this attention, the question of "what it takes to be an effective leader" is still far from settled. More research has been done in this century, paralleling the expansion of knowledge in related fields such as social psychology, sociology, organization theory, and political science. The subject has taken on a particular urgency in the past two decades, however, as popular discontent has grown regarding existing social institutions, including their leaderships.

In administrative hierarchies, leadership is a multidimensional function, due to multiple levels of organization, wide variation in specific tasks and general functions, and numerous situations requiring leadership of some kind. The "job" of a leader within the administrative framework, therefore, is not constant, in the sense that the particular combinations of needs (organizational, personal, task-oriented, political, and so on) within groups being led are rarely the same from one set of circumstances to the next.

We will discuss traditional approaches to the study of leadership and then examine a number of roles and tasks which are, or can be, a part of the leadership function. To focus our consideration on the exercise of leadership, we make several assumptions. First, it is assumed that the leader attains his or her position through legitimate means and remains the leader through the acquiescence of the "followership." Management psychologist Ralph Stogdill suggests that groups tend to accept more readily leaders whose characteristics and abilities facilitate accomplishment of the group's specific tasks—for example, the captain of a swimming team is likely to be both a good swimmer and a good motivator.[1] It is also assumed, however, that the leader's legitimacy is not automatically continued, that the leader's actions contribute to or detract from the *legitimacy* the group accords him or her (see chapter 1 for a discussion of the same general principle, as it applies to the political system at large).

Second, our principal interest is in leaders within organizations whose members do not have the major voice in selecting the leader originally. This refers to administrative hierarchies where advancement through the ranks or appointment from outside the organization by top-level superiors constitute the main methods of filling leadership slots. Third, we assume that organization members have at least a minimal interest in appropriately carrying out both the organization's overall responsibilities and their own particular responsibilities. Furthermore, we assume that the members' job performance can be affected by the ways in which top leaders and immediate supervisors conduct themselves in the course of discharging *their* responsibilities. There is ample evidence supporting the view that the interaction of leaders and followers, as well as followers' personal feelings about leaders and the way they lead, can have major consequences for work performance and the general work atmosphere.[2]

Finally, the leadership roles and tasks we will be discussing center on leaders who are in a strong position—official or unofficial—to influence significantly what happens within an organization. This is mentioned explicitly because it frequently is *not* the case; that is, some leaders are in a relatively weak position due to group structure and the nature of the work to be done.[3] One example of such leadership would be found in a research team of equally competent and well-known scientists where one member informally assumes overall direction of team tasks. As "first among equals," this leader would have to guide the others through persuasion and participative decision making. Our concern, however, is with leaders who are significantly involved with the totality of the group or organization's existence, activities, and sense of identity, and whose leadership is accepted and acknowledged by group members.

Traditional Approaches to the Study of Leadership

The earliest efforts to analyze leadership employed two principal approaches, which centered on the individual leader and on the leadership situation, respectively. The *traits* approach sought to explain leadership in terms of personality characteristics such as intelligence, ambition, ego drives, and interpersonal skills. Considerable emphasis was placed on leadership traits during the early years of the twentieth century, but in numerous studies since then the traits approach has been found to explain little. Furthermore, contrary to the most basic assumption of this approach, leaders were not found to possess common characteristics. The traits approach was discarded by most scholarly observers (though not necessarily in the "conventional wisdom" about leaders) by the 1950s. Attention shifted to a seemingly more promising avenue of exploration—namely, analysis of leadership situations and how situational factors were related to what was required in a leader in a particular set of circumstances.

The *situational* approach has become the general framework of analysis in most subsequent leadership studies. Rather than trying to explain leadership success or failure, particular styles of leadership, or why one person becomes a leader while another does not in terms of variations in personal skills and character, the situational approach emphasizes leader-follower interactions, needs of the group or organization (or nation) in the time period under study, the kind of work being done, general group values and ethics, and the like. From this, it follows that leaders in one situation may not be cut out to be leaders in other situations.[4] Some years ago a city manager in a midwestern city was asked to serve as president of a university in a neighboring state on the basis of the widespread popularity and respect he had come to have. He took the position, but shortly thereafter the university governing board realized it had made a mistake—the successful city manager was an abject failure as a university president. Not only were the specific duties different; so also were the types of people he encountered, their expectations, and his interactions with university personnel as opposed to government officials. To cite another example, it has been suggested that generals do not make the best civilian political leaders because so many features of military life and leadership conflict with the needs, values, and expectations of civilian (especially democratic) politics.

The point is, variations in the times, in circumstances, and in group characteristics help determine the most appropriate kinds of leadership and, to an important degree, who shall lead. Personality, skills, ambition, and the rest do make some difference, but only in the context of the social environment, setting of leadership, and demands arising from the group. "Personal traits within the situation," with emphasis on the latter, now best describes the most common approach in studying leadership.[5]

Fred Fiedler and his associates at the University of Illinois Group-Effectiveness Research Laboratory have developed a three-part classification of group situations, indicating variations in leader effectiveness.[6] They suggest that group situations vary according to (1) "position power" of the leader, defined as the authority vested in the leader's official position; (2) task structure of the group, that is, the degree to which the group's assignment(s) can be programed and specified in a step-by-step fashion; and (3) leader-member personal relationships, based on affection, admiration, and trust of group members for the leader. Their general conclusion is that "the leader who is liked by his group and has a clear-cut task and high position power . . . has everything in his favor. The leader who has poor relationships with his group members, an unstructured task and weak position power likely will be unable to exert much influence over the group."[7]

But how to choose the particular leadership style most appropriate to a given situation? Fiedler's research suggests that leadership effectiveness is related to a *combination* of interpersonal and group-situational factors. For example, if tasks are clear-cut, relations between leader and members are positive, and official position power is considerable, a leader is best advised to be strongly directive rather than democratic and nondirective. An All-American quarterback at Notre Dame does not call the plays by taking votes in the huddle! By the same token, the chairman of a voluntary committee "cannot ask with impunity that the group members vote or act according to his instructions."[8]

This theory of leadership is important for what it suggests about what can be changed to improve leadership effectiveness—rank, task structure, and concern for followers—as well as what cannot be changed—leader personality, work situation, and organizational characteristics. Fiedler's research reinforces the view that both traits (within limits) and situational dynamics dictate what leadership style will be most effective. This must be determined almost on a case-by-case basis; it is anything but preordained.

Another general dimension of leadership is how specific styles of managerial decision making affect the power, influence, and freedom of action of leaders and followers in an organization. Figure 8–1 illustrates a continuum of leadership behavior, suggesting the range of possibilities open to leaders in choosing management techniques. Such choices, like leadership effectiveness, are conditioned to a considerable extent by the nature of the organization and the work to be done.

We turn now to "tasks" of leadership in an effort to describe the many facets of the leader's role. The intention here is not to make a definitive appraisal of the leader's job but rather to suggest the scope of leadership functions in a way applicable to many different organizational settings. We will consider five such tasks and attempt to suggest very broadly what makes a "good" leader in terms of these tasks.

Figure 8–1
The Continuum of Leadership Behavior: Relations Between Managers and Nonmanagers

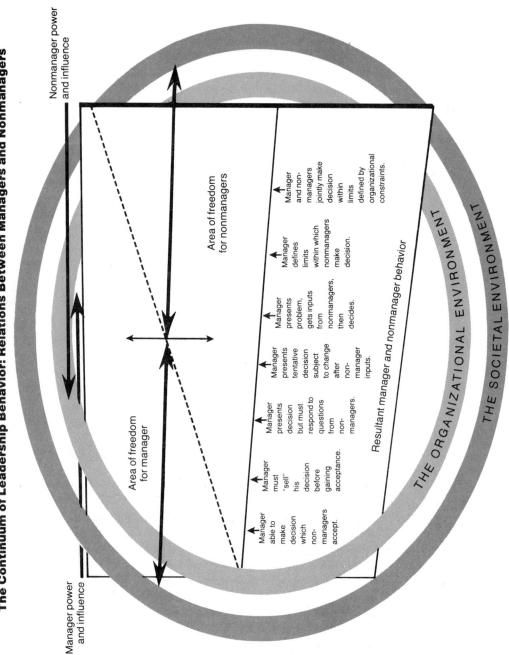

Source: Robert Tannenbaum and Warren H. Schmidt, "How To Choose a Leadership Pattern," *Harvard Business*

Leader as Director: Reconciling Personal and Organizational Goals

An essential function of leadership is to bring some coherence to the multitude of activities within an organization. This is facilitated by persuading those in charge of various activities to emphasize the aspects of their work directed toward common organizational objectives. And this in turn requires reconciling personal and organizational goals, which (as discussed in the preceding chapter) can diverge and even conflict.

The key to a leader's efforts to reconcile personal and organizational goals is to create as much psychological overlap as possible between the two. If a leader is able to induce organization members to internalize (accept as their own) general objectives of the whole, then most of this task will have been accomplished. This might be done by direct and indirect persuasion, by example, or by developing members' understanding of rationales for pursuing particular objectives or adopting specific tactics. To the extent that there is conflict over goals, of course, this task will remain an ongoing one, with considerable potential for difficulty. The optimum situation is one in which members see pursuit of organizational goals as consistent with and supportive of achieving their personal goals.

Goal articulation is a function of leadership, and the manner in which this is done may trigger positive or negative reactions among members. If negative—owing to substantive disagreement, lack of consideration for their views, or inadequate preparation—gaining members' support will be that much more difficult. Leaders often have to devote a significant amount of time, energy, and resources to winning member support for group goals, and they do not always succeed. Very often, they must settle for grudging or reluctant cooperation, which is a far cry from genuine support.

Another difficulty lies in the possibility that members' personal goals may be more important to them, on the job, than the business of the organization. The types of bureaucrats Anthony Downs labeled "climbers" and "conservers"[9]—those interested respectively in achieving and preserving power, prestige, and income—attest to the fact that highly personalized goals may predominate among some organization members. The larger the proportion of total membership which falls into the climber or conserver mold, the more difficult the task of directing the organization's activities toward larger goals. A related problem is determining the true state of affairs in this regard—that is, knowing what members' goals really are.

Besides these problems, there is the possibility that leaders' personal goals might interfere with organizational performance and attainment of group objectives, though leaders tend to be somewhat more committed to group goals than are their followers.[10] (Commitment to achieving organizational goals seems to depend in part on the degree of responsibility for attaining them.[11]) Enlightened leadership requires a clear commitment to organizational goals which outweighs any personal objectives—and which is perceived as such by followers.

To this point we have discussed organizational goals as something separate from personal goals and from the feelings, values, and preferences of an organization's members. From this perspective, goals seem to exist independently of organization members—as something determined by persons outside the organization, as self-defining in the course of organization activities, or as the product of articulation by the leadership.

Lawrence B. Mohr has suggested an alternative conception of organizational goals, which both narrows and sharpens what is meant by the term. In Mohr's view, we may accurately label as "organizational goals" only those on which there is widespread "consensus of intent" (agreement as to purpose) among the large majority of organization members, and which relate to "main streams" of organizational behavior.[12] Mohr maintains that these goals must be identified on the basis of empirical investigation rather than a superficial reading of "official" pronouncements, informal discussion with leaders or members, or intuitive judgments. He raises the possibility, in other words, of being able to identify such organizational goals empirically and precisely and stresses the necessity of doing so. Without identifying goals in this manner, Mohr says, the results of any inquiry into the goals of an organization are likely to be misleading, or at best incomplete. The implication of this conception of goals is simply this: if organizational goals are formulated by "consensus of intent" among the organization's members (including leaders), then by definition there is substantial overlap between personal and organizational goals. Were this the commonly accepted and applied definition of organizational goals, the leader's task in this regard would be virtually nonexistent.

Research in the human relations school of organization theory, as well as later studies, suggests that where there are differences between an organization's official and actual goals, it is group norms among members that both account for those differences and designate *actual* goals. Where leaders rely on member preferences and attitudes as significant factors in goal definition, the chances are greater that personal and organizational goals can be reconciled at least to some degree. This is because the "followership" can be expected to respond favorably to a leadership willing to "include them in" on so basic a question as the goals of *their* organization. Leaders are therefore well advised to focus on the task of goal definition. If the results here are positive, other leadership tasks will be more readily accomplished.

Leader as Motivator: The Carrot or the Stick?

We have already discussed motivation within organizations at some length (see chapter 6). Our purpose here is to review the major themes outlined earlier and put them into perspective as part of the tasks of leaders who seek to motivate their followers in the most positive fashion.

First, if we use the analogy of the "carrot or the stick" to describe one kind of choice to be made in motivating members of an organization, the stick is distinctly second choice. A substantial body of research clearly suggests that coercive measures aimed at motivating employees are not effective in the long run, though they may have some short-term impacts.[13] Far more likely to succeed overall is a combination of incentives and conditions appropriate to the interests of those doing the work. On the basis of research conducted over several decades, there is reason to believe that emphasis should be given to such things as offering attractive salaries, fringe benefits, and working conditions; creating positive social interaction among groups of workers; and making the work as interesting as possible. The problem is that different things work for different people, and leaders face a continuing challenge of tailoring these motivators as closely as they can to the needs, preferences, and attitudes of organization members or member groups. This is important not only for accomplishing immediate goals, but also for building cohesiveness in the organization through member satisfaction. It may not be possible, however, to fully satisfy each and every individual.

A 1975 study by the Society for the Advancement of Management sought to discover what workers in private companies regarded as the single most positive feature in the behavior of their immediate supervisors. The most common response was that the supervisor had been "encouraging" to the employee in work performance. Since there is other evidence suggesting that the interaction between employees and their "first-line" supervisors is of crucial importance to the group's performance, its morale, and individual job satisfaction,[14] a positive and supportive attitude toward employees on the part of the supervisor takes on added importance. It would seem, therefore, that an organization's leaders should take great care in appointing first-line supervisors.[15] More generally, leaders should be concerned about the quality of face-to-face supervision at all levels, as well as tangible benefits, intrinsic work interest, and the like.

Motivation continues to be a complex task of leadership. There appears to be a pattern of member responsiveness to leadership that is clearly defined, and at the same time self-confident, persuasive, fair, and supportive.[16] But no rule is universally applicable; exceptions are frequent, and leaders have to remain alert if they expect to cope with the motivational problems that could arise in their organizations.

Leader as Coordinator/Integrator: Meshing the Gears

A function of steadily rising importance for leaders in complex organizations has been coordinating and integrating the varied functions and tasks of increasingly specialized members. Leaders, themselves usually not as knowledgeable about the specialties found in their organizations as are individual specialists, must rely on the competence of their subordinates at the same time they attempt to organize their efforts into a coherent whole. If the tasks of directing and motivating members have been carried out effectively, coordinating and integrating their efforts should follow naturally, but conceptually there are a number of factors to be considered.

Most important is the tendency for individuals concentrating on their own particular work to develop "tunnel vision," through which they see the importance of their own tasks (or at least feel their work is important), but fail to appreciate the importance of other aspects of the organization's activity. For example, a leader attempting to change the operations of a division, staff, or branch for the purpose of strengthening (in his or her view) the organization's overall capacities and/or performance may encounter resistance from members in that subsection who believe their procedures and output are adequate for their purposes. Their frame of reference, so to speak, is *their* work, defined as work of the subsection, whereas the leadership's responsibilities encompass the work of the entire organization, with a frame of reference to match.

For a leader to successfully overcome member resistance in such a case requires the ability to convey a sense of the larger issues, needs, and contexts which gave rise to the leader's desire for change. In essence, this means "broadening the horizons" of these members to include a fuller picture of the organization in operation. Robert Guest, in a landmark study in the early 1960s, concluded that "for a leader to induce others to act requires that he establish for himself and for others mechanisms that allow both to be continually [accumulating]. . . facts and ideas that have had broad circulation before they are acted upon."[17] That is, by institutionalizing "idea-collecting mechanisms,"[18] a leader can better insure wider exchange of information among organization members. The result, ideally, would be that when actions were proposed affecting specific work units, members of those units—by understanding larger organizational purposes—would be more inclined to accept, and even to take an active part in, what the leadership intended to do.

Such mechanisms for collecting ideas might be regular newsletters, suggestion boxes, question-and-answer sessions, advance communication of proposed actions to members, and so on. This amounts to "regularized brainstorming" for ideas, a process which, by involving members, is likely to make ultimate decisions more palatable to more people in the organization. Circulation of information about actions that already have been taken can also be beneficial. Not circulating information widely can result in built-up resentments, which can linger and affect subsequent organizational affairs.

Even in the best of circumstances, leaders will have to manage diverse operations on a smoothly coordinated time schedule. Personnel, materials, financial resources, services to consumers of the organization's output (however defined), and so on, all have to be integrated as part of the organization's ongoing activities. In this respect, advance planning is a key leadership function, in insuring that the necessary components are on hand as needed. Every organization in existence faces that common need, and the leadership is expected to take responsibility for meeting it.

Another dimension of coordination and integration of organizational activities is the need to mesh the leadership's own tasks with those of the remainder of the organization. The need here is to avoid "working at cross-purposes," making certain that leaders and followers generally share the same understanding of what the organization is about and what the intended end-products are. This ties in with the "leader as director" task in the effort to create psychological overlap among several different sets of goals. It is also linked to "leader as motivator" in the creation of inducements designed to move members in particular directions.

In sum, organizations comprising diverse specialties and functions require efforts at the top, as well as throughout the ranks, to bring about a satisfactory level of coordination and integration. Organization members need some sense that their different functions somehow fit into a larger, rational context. And leaders, being in the best position to do so, must take responsibility for instilling that view.

Leader as Catalyst/Innovator: Pointing the Way

The conception of a leader as a "spark plug," as the "one who makes it happen," that is widespread in the conventional wisdom about groups and organizations (especially sports teams) appears to have some validity. But it is important to note that the particular conditions prevailing in the group situation may strongly affect a leader's opportunities to stimulate group action. Fred Fiedler suggests that the best opportunities occur when the leader has influence in the group, informal support, and a relatively well-structured task at hand—when "the group is ready to be directed, and the members expect to be told what to do."[19] As an example, Fiedler cites the captain of an airliner in its final approach before landing, when his decisions, instructions, and actions are crucial, and no one would realistically want him to discuss or evaluate his options with the flight crew. Other examples of well-structured tasks where a leader is the catalyst for group action include rescue operations after a disaster, a company's efforts to meet a production deadline, and a football team's last-minute drive for the winning touchdown. In these examples, the tasks to be performed are short term; those responsible will succeed or fail within a limited time period.

Many tasks, however, are less structured and more time-consuming. Here, too, a leader may be a successful catalyst, provided that members understand and support general organizational objectives and that the leader has made clear how individual activities help promote those objectives. For example, a university department chairman concerned about financial support for his department from the university administration may actively encourage faculty members to pursue research interests as well as excellence in teaching. Published articles, books, and research papers enhance a department's prestige outside the university, providing a strong argument for continued support internally. Even though such activities are conducted largely on an individual basis, a chairman can relate them to departmental well-being and thus attempt to motivate faculty members in terms of group welfare.

The process of *innovation* is tied to the role of "catalyst" because in many instances an organization's routine operations do not require very substantial leader participation. When normal procedures are all that is required, the leader is ordinarily in the background—in fact, is best advised to remain there so as to permit members to function with some measure of independence. However, changes in routines, temporary or permanent, must usually be initiated outside the group or subgroup, since the routines may well serve a stabilizing function inside the group and have the support of its members (see the earlier discussion in this chapter of "tunnel vision"). Furthermore, routines frequently evolve in a way that reflects the values and preferences of the group, regarding not only the mechanics but also the very purposes of group activities. Thus group members may interpret a proposed change in routine as a comment on their purposes as well as their procedures (which may be true). The challenge to the leader, then, is to justify adequately to group members any proposed change he or she deems necessary in the context of the larger organization.[20] Clearly, the "catalyst" role is important if innovation is to be brought about.

Leader as External Spokesman—and "Gladiator"

One of the most crucial tasks for a leader is to act as representative of the organization's views and interests in the external environment. This involves articulating organizational positions (to the extent that they legitimately represent a consensus of opinion) to those outside the organization. It also ordinarily includes an advocacy role when the organization seeks to secure additional resources or to maintain the resources it has. This "spokesman" task has become more important as organizations have become more complex, particularly so for leaders of the suborganizational units within larger hierarchical structures. The branch chief within a government bureaucracy, the plant manager in a large manufacturing conglomerate, and the academic department chairman within a college structure headed by a dean have in common the periodic need to "go to bat" for "their" organization.

The most common setting for the "spokesman" role is budgetary decision making, where a favorable portrayal of the organization can be decisive in influencing those who hold the purse strings, or make the budget recommendations, for the next fiscal year. This, however, is only the most visible kind of occasion. In fact the "gladiator" task is ongoing, taking the form of standing up for the organization or group and its members when there is some complaint about its operation, anticipating and preparing for changes in the external environment which might adversely affect the organization or group, or simply keeping abreast of developments in the larger organization as they relate to the values, work, and well-being of members of the unit.

There is evidence to suggest that few things are better for group morale than a leader who willingly and effectively defends the group's welfare.[21] Aside from the practical benefits such advocacy can produce, a leader actively supporting and defending the organization represents in a concrete form the faith placed in the members and their work. The leader, in acting as "gladiator," is demonstrating that he or she is a part of the organization, rather than standing aloof. In addition, the "leader as gladiator" is in effect carrying out one of the cardinal principles of good management: bestow praise publicly! Defense or advocacy on behalf of the organization constitutes collective rather than individual praise, it is true, but indicates positive feedback in a strategically important fashion, and that is usually not lost on members of an organization.

What Makes a "Good" Leader?

We come back, then, to the persistent question that is at the core of most inquiries into the subject of leadership. Without claiming to have found the answers, let us suggest a number of general considerations relevant to achieving effective leadership (see Figure 8-2).

First, it appears that a leader is wise to convey to organization members that they are regarded as competent in their work by the leadership. Many *are*, of course, quite competent; but the point here is that competent workers will appreciate the fact that "management" has taken note of their worth, and a less competent worker might work

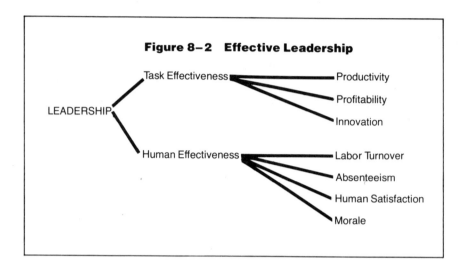

Figure 8–2 Effective Leadership

harder to live up to the leadership's expectations. The expectation of competence, in fact, may be a key factor in developing motivations to *be* competent, at least as that is defined by the leadership.[22]

Second, there is strong evidence that if members of an organization perceive the leadership as receptive to ideas, feedback, comments, even complaints, from "below," they will be far more willing to respond to leaders' directives.[23] For one thing, communications from members give leaders the clearest picture of the things that are important to members, as well as their general attitudes and aspirations. This cannot help but make it easier for the leaders to communicate meaningfully. But more important, the leaders' willingness to hear and, presumably, act upon useful ideas from the ranks builds a sense of cohesiveness among the members that over time is likely to increase each member's commitment to the organization's well-being.

Third, several studies suggest that the "democratic" leader is more effective in the broad view than is any other type.[24] Member satisfaction was clearly higher in democratically led groups, and interaction among group members was distinctly more relaxed and mutually supportive. At the same time, the democratic leaders in these studies did not abdicate leadership functions, but managed them in an open, participative, and supportive way. There is some reason to believe that such a style works more effectively with some types of followers than with others (for example, professionals and some in "flat" hierarchies with less formal structures), and perhaps better for some types of personalities than others. Yet the pattern seems to be one of fairly successful leadership direction under democratic conditions.

Fourth, a 1958 study of a work group in private industry suggests indirectly some of the leadership features to which employees may respond favorably. The study indicated that the more highly employees rated supervisors on a number of key attributes, the less employees expressed a desire for unionization.[25] The attributes mentioned were fairness, authority, ability to handle people, giving credit, readiness to discuss problems, and keeping employees informed. This combination suggests the scope of ability demanded in many leadership situations.

At the risk of oversimplification, it is worth pointing out that several other qualities are also important. (1) Ideally, a leader should be clear, reasonable, and consistent concerning expectations and standards of judgment for member performance. (2) A leader is well advised to deal openly, fairly, and equitably with all members, making distinctions among members only on work-related criteria. (3) A leader should maintain a fairly firm hold on the reins of leadership, while at the same time fostering a genuinely constructive two-way flow of communication by explaining rationales for proposed courses of action and by acting on worthwhile suggestions from members. (4) A leader should move carefully and democratically to secure consensus—more than merely a majority vote—on significant actions. One tactic is to strive for consensus by means of an extensive consultative process which requires formal votes only infrequently. (5) The wise leader will try to prevent "empire-building" and other divisive tendencies within the ranks. The goal is to prevent disunity as one step toward building cohesion within the group. (6) "Cronyism" and favoritism should be absolutely avoided. And (7), perhaps hardest of all, a leader can greatly influence the whole course of events in the organization by "setting the tone" of interactions with the members. While "tone" is admittedly a vague term, the leader sets some behavioral standards which often are imitated, consciously or unconsciously, by other members of the group. This is not to say that such "tone setting" will work completely or in all instances. However, where a leader has in general acted constructively, the chances are greatly improved that members will respond in kind, both in their attitudes and behaviors toward the leader and in their general demeanor toward one another. These generalizations have their exceptions, but as standards for positive and enlightened leadership, they appear to have much to recommend them.

Of course, there are some obstacles to effective leadership. For one thing, the situational potential for leadership may vary according to the organizational level of a particular group leader. It may also vary according to the flexibility which higher-level leaders permit within the rest of the organization. The tighter the rein held on subordinates by superiors, the less chance subordinates will have to exercise leadership within their own organizational bailiwicks. In addition, if an organization is highly structured—some would say "bureaucratized"—the possibilities of leadership in the manner we have described are more limited. This is so because more of the decisions concerning management of organizational affairs are already settled questions, and thus are not ordinarily subject to being reopened. In this sense, bureaucracy is not conducive to leadership.

Second, individual goals may simply remain beyond the reach of the leaders' influence, though cooperation could more easily be induced from less secure members than from those with seniority, tenure, and the like. The leadership will probably have to accept some disparities between what it seeks and what individual members seek.

Third, fighting "tunnel vision" (among both members and leaders) may turn out to be a frustrating job.

Fourth, innovation in highly structured organizations is difficult to manage, and there is a body of professional opinion which holds that traditional management values—of the "scientific management" school and its conceptual descendants—hamper development of conditions conducive to innovation.[26] Additionally, the values and preferences of organization members may prove to be quite enduring, making innovation necessarily a matter of coercion. In the face of stiff resistance, a leader would have to weigh the costs of coercion against the calculated benefits of innovation.

Fifth, a "gladiator" will not always be successful in the external environment, and depending on the mix of failure and success, this could work to the leader's disadvantage both inside and outside the organization. Part of a leader's skill should lie in knowing when to fight and when not to.

Finally, leadership is conditioned by the particular combination of people, tasks, and organizational dynamics which exists in each case. Despite what we do know about leadership, it is still not possible to construct an all-inclusive set of leadership guidelines.

SUMMARY

Leadership is a subject that has aroused interest for many centuries. In the past few decades, however, studies of leadership have become more numerous and cut across a wider span of human knowledge. Our discussion of leadership makes the following assumptions: that leadership is acquired and maintained legitimately; that leaders obtain their positions by some means in which the voice of the membership is not predominant; that members are at least minimally interested in carrying out their responsibilities and that leader-follower interactions can influence their behavior; and that leaders are significant participants in the totality of organizational life.

Traditionally, leadership has been studied through two approaches. The traits approach emphasized the personality and aptitudes of individuals who were leaders, in an effort to isolate "leader" characteristics. This conception was followed by the situational approach, which views all organizational circumstances—structural, interpersonal, task-related, value-related, and so on—as crucial to the kind of leadership that comes to exist. Currently a combination of the two approaches, with emphasis on the situational, is most common in studies of leadership.

Variations in group situation may significantly affect leader effectiveness. Factors in the group situation important in this regard are position power of the leader, task structure of the group, and leader-member personal relationships. Leadership appears to be most effective where a well-liked, well-respected leader occupies high position in a group with clearly structured tasks. Under such circumstances, leaders are best advised to be directive, giving clear instructions, rather than democratic and nondirective. Where position power is weak, tasks not clearly defined, and personal relationships not as positive, leaders should be less directive and more democratic. To be effective, leadership must vary with circumstances in the group and the work situation.

The purpose of examining the "tasks" of leadership is to illuminate the many facets of a leader's role. "Leader as director" refers to the challenge of bringing some unity of purpose to the organization's members. "Leader as motivator" is a key task, centering on devices such as tangible benefits, positive social interaction, work interest, encouragement by job supervisors, and leadership that is self-confident, persuasive, fair, and supportive. "Leader as coordinator and integrator" involves bringing some order to the multitude of functions within a complex organization. "Leader as catalyst and innovator" is a formalized conception of the "spark plug" role in a group setting. As part of the catalyst role, a leader is also expected to introduce innovations into an organization. There are numerous difficulties which limit the leadership's ability to innovate successfully internally.[27] "Leader as gladiator" requires engaging in advocacy for, and defense of, the organization in the external environment.

What makes a "good" leader? Among other things, an effort to convey the leader's respect for members; a manifest willingness to hear and respond to feelings and opinions communicated by members; a "democratic" style and relationship to members; attributes such as fairness, giving credit, readiness to discuss problems, and keeping members informed; consistency and equity in defining standards and judging work performance; and avoidance of such pitfalls as "empire-building" (by either leaders or followers) and "cronyism."

Virtually all of these tasks face obstacles to their full accomplishment—in the organization's dynamics the mix of members, and the nature of the external environment. It is simply not possible to construct leadership guidelines that will cover every conceivable leadership situation.

NOTES

1. Ralph M. Stogdill, *Handbook of Leadership: A Survey of Theory and Research* (New York: The Free Press, 1974), pp. 167–169.

2. See chapter 6 for a summary of several important studies concerning the nature of leadership and its significance. See also Philip Selznick, *Leadership in*

Administration (New York: Harper & Row, 1957); Fred E. Fiedler, *Leader Attitudes and Group Effectiveness* (Urbana, Ill.: University of Illinois Press, 1958); Robert H. Guest, *Organizational Change: The Effects of Successful Leadership* (Homewood, Ill.: Dorsey and Irwin, 1962); Stephen R. Graubard and Gerald Holton, eds., *Excellence and Leadership in a Democracy* (New York: Columbia University Press, 1962); Fred E. Fiedler, *A Theory of Leadership Effectiveness* (New York: McGraw-Hill, 1967); Fred E. Fiedler and Martin Chemers, *Leadership and Effective Management* (Glenview, Ill.: Scott, Foresman, 1974); and Stogdill, *Handbook of Leadership.*

3. Fiedler, in *A Theory of Leadership Effectiveness,* discusses varieties of work situations as they relate to leadership. See, especially, his chapter 7.

4. Stogdill, *Handbook of Leadership,* p. 64.

5. See Fiedler, *A Theory of Leadership Effectiveness,* p. 247.

6. Fred E. Fiedler, "Style or Circumstance: The Leadership Enigma," *Psychology Today,* 2 (March 1969), 39–43.

7. Ibid., p. 41.

8. Ibid., p. 42.

9. See Anthony Downs, *Inside Bureaucracy* (Boston: Little, Brown, 1967), p. 88.

10. Stogdill, *Handbook of Leadership,* p. 271.

11. Ibid., p. 270.

12. Lawrence B. Mohr, "The Concept of Organizational Goal," *American Political Science Review,* 67 (June 1973), 470–481, at p. 474.

13. See, for example, Stogdill, *Handbook of Leadership;* and the discussion of authoritarian leadership style in the Iowa experiment, in Ralph White and Ronald Lippitt, "Leader Behavior and Member Reaction in Three 'Social Climates'," in Dorwin Cartwright and Alvin Zander, eds., *Group Dynamics: Research and Theory,* 3rd ed. (New York: Harper & Row, 1968), pp. 527–553.

14. Fiedler, *A Theory of Leadership Effectiveness,* p. 236.

15. Stogdill, *Handbook of Leadership,* p. 327.

16. Ibid., pp. 327–330.

17. Robert H. Guest, *Organizational Change: The Effects of Successful Leadership* (Homewood, Ill.: Dorsey and Irwin, 1962), p. 131.

18. Ibid., p. 130.

19. Fiedler, *A Theory of Leadership Effectiveness,* p. 147. See the discussion, above, of situational factors.

20. For a case study of the importance of bureaucratic routines, see Graham Allison, *Essence of Decision: Explaining the Cuban Missile Crisis* (Boston: Little, Brown, 1971). Consideration is given to problems of innovation in, among others, Warren G. Bennis, ed., *American Bureaucracy* (New Brunswick, N.J.: Transaction Books, 1970), pp. 111–187, especially pp. 135–164; and Guest, *Organizational Change.* A recent contribution is Ronald D. Hedlund and James Wahner, "Leadership Style as a Catalyst for Legislative Change," paper delivered at the annual meeting of the Midwest Political Science Association, Chicago, April 21–23, 1977.

21. Anthony Downs cites the work of Georg Simmel and Lewis Coser in this regard. See *Inside Bureaucracy,* p. 105.

22. Expectations of authority figures as a key force in determining subordinates' behavior patterns is not a new principle in the literature, but it may have

wider applicability than was once thought. For a discussion of how teacher expectations may shape student performance, see William Ryan, *Blaming the Victim* (New York: Pantheon Books, 1971), chapter 2.

23. See, among others, Peter F. Drucker, *Management: Tasks, Responsibilities, Practices* (New York: Harper & Row, 1974), chapter 38.

24. See Stogdill, *Handbook of Leadership*, pp. 365–370.

25. Ibid., p. 379.

26. Victor A. Thompson, "How Scientific Management Thwarts Innovation," in Warren G. Bennis, ed., *American Bureaucracy*, pp. 121–133, especially pp. 123–124. See also Thompson's *Bureaucracy and Innovation* (University, Ala.: University of Alabama Press, 1969).

27. It should be noted that leadership can just as easily resist innovation desired by members as the other way around. Our focus here on "leader as innovator" presupposes that change can be threatening to members, and as such must be pushed through by the leadership. Under the circumstance of leaders resisting innovation sought by followers, the task of "leader as director" will be considerably frustrated as leadership and followership goals grow further apart.

SUGGESTED READINGS

Drucker, Peter F. *Management: Tasks, Responsibilities, Practices*. New York: Harper & Row, 1974, chapter 38.

Fiedler, Fred E. *Leader Attitudes and Group Effectiveness*. Urbana, Ill.: University of Illinois Press, 1958.

———. "Style or Circumstance: The Leadership Enigma." *Psychology Today*, 2 (March 1969), 39–43.

———. *A Theory of Leadership Effectiveness*. New York: McGraw-Hill, 1967.

———, and Martin Chemers. *Leadership and Effective Management*. Glenview, Ill.: Scott, Foresman, 1974.

Graubard, Stephen R., and Gerald Holton, eds. *Excellence and Leadership in a Democracy*. New York: Columbia University Press, 1962.

Guest, Robert H. *Organizational Change: The Effects of Successful Leadership*. Homewood, Ill.: Dorsey and Irwin, 1962.

Selznick, Philip. *Leadership in Administration*. New York: Harper & Row, 1957.

Stogdill, Ralph M. *Handbook of Leadership: A Survey of Theory and Research*. New York: The Free Press, 1974.

White, Ralph, and Ronald Lippitt. "Leader Behavior and Member Reaction in Three 'Social Climates'." In Dorwin Cartwright and Alvin Zander, eds. *Group Dynamics: Research and Theory*, 3rd ed. New York: Harper & Row, 1968, pp. 527–553.

PART FOUR
ADMINISTRATIVE PROCESSES

This section covers four broad functions central to the conduct of public administration. These are (1) public personnel administration, (2) the budgetary process, (3) the regulatory process, and (4) implementation and evaluation of public policies. Each of these represents a fundamentally important set of activities in administrative practice.

The personnel function, treated in chapter 9, concerns, among other things, criteria and methods for hiring individuals into the public service in national, state, and local government; for promoting and transferring them within the ranks; and, on occasion, for dismissing them from their jobs. Politically charged issues such as patronage, affirmative action, and collective bargaining pose at least some questions which must be answered within the domain of public personnel administration.

The budgetary process, discussed in chapter 10, is obviously important because of rising costs of government and the political conflict over allocation of government funds (to agencies both inside and outside the government). It is important also because control over major aspects of budgeting represents crucial political power. This has always been true, but in the past half-century the political stakes in the budgetary game have risen steadily higher.

The regulatory process (chapter 11) has become one of the most pervasive, complex, and controversial aspects of government activity in recent years. At the heart of the process in the national government are the formally designated independent regulatory agencies, with legal responsibility for setting and enforcing rules and regulations which govern the operations of thousands of private industries and businesses. However, government regulation is now carried on by a host of other agencies as well, with impact on virtually every aspect of American economic and social life.

Finally, chapter 12 examines implementation and evaluation of public policies. These activities have always been important, but in recent years we have developed a greater capacity to examine systematically—and presumably objectively—the extent to which stated policies are carried out, forces which promote or inhibit policy implementation, and ways some policies change in the course of being implemented. At the same time, political pressures have mounted for more careful and systematic evaluation of existing policies. This has coincided with rising public demands for greater responsiveness from government at all levels, particularly a willingness to change those policies which fail to meet public needs and/or expectations.

CHAPTER 9
Public Personnel Administration

From the time the first executive-branch agency opened its doors, even before ratification of the Constitution, the personnel function has been a part of American public administration. It has evolved from a relatively obscure, often routine function of government to a prominent, frequently controversial area of administrative practice. Since the early 1800s there has been considerable variation in the rules and regulations governing personnel practices and policies.

Changes have come in response to shifts in the values and assumptions of society pertaining to "proper" methods of filling government positions. Herbert Kaufman has suggested that three values predominant in our approach to government have had particular impact on personnel practices: (1) the quest for strong executive leadership, (2) desire for a politically neutral, competent public service, and (3) pervasive belief in representativeness in our governmental institutions.[1] Strong executive leadership and representativeness have often been pursued in tandem. More accurately, perhaps, as one has been achieved, the other has also been strengthened. For example, when a strong mayor practices patronage in hiring, it increases political representativeness of the electoral majority at the same time that it adds to the mayor's influence. The quest for politically neutral competence, on the other hand, has usually been carried on in opposition to leadership-and-representativeness advocates. For example, supporters of civil service (merit) reform in the early 1900s harshly attacked both political "bosses" and the system of patronage which enabled them to dominate many states and cities.

Public personnel administration can be defined briefly as "the organizations, policies, and processes used to match the needs of governmental agencies and the people who staff those agencies."[2] Personnel administration in the public sector differs from that in business and industry in important respects, most prominently the necessity of conducting the personnel function within constraints set by other formal political institutions, by agency clienteles, professional associations of employees, and other interest groups, and by political parties and the mass media.[3] Public personnel administration is no longer regarded (as it once was) as something separate from the general processes of public policy making, for two reasons. First, decisions made in the personnel process have a direct bearing on who makes and implements government policies. Second, personnel decisions have themselves become policy matters, reflecting demands for employee rights, affirmative action in minority hiring, and traditional merit reforms, among others. Political scientist Joseph Cayer has noted accurately that "personnel policies and practices are, in part, an expression of political values,"[4] and the political dimension of the field has taken on increasing importance in recent years.

Finally, the sheer size and scope of contemporary government make personnel concerns more important than ever before. It is not size alone, but also the diversity of professional skills and outlooks that pose challenges to personnel administrators. Furthermore, although the issue of "big government" is not directly tied to personnel policies, political pressures for reducing or controlling bureaucratic size inevitably involve personnel administrators and affect some of their decisions. A Gallup poll in June 1977 found that 67 percent of those surveyed felt the national government employs too many people, after an earlier survey had found that just over half of the respondents (53 percent) favored reducing the number of federal employees by 5 percent per year over a three-year period.[5]

The image of a bloated federal bureaucracy, however, is not completely accurate. First, employment in state and local governments increased at a much more rapid rate in the period 1947–1975 than did employment in the national government. Total state-local employment more than tripled, from roughly 3.5 million to just over 12 million, both full-time and part-time; the figure for "full-time equivalent" employees was approximately 10 million. During the same period, the federal bureaucracy grew by some 37 percent, from about 2.1 million to 2.9 million employees (full-time equivalent: 2.7 million). Second, national government employment expressed as the number of employees per 1,000 population has fluctuated considerably during the last thirty years, ranging from a high of 16.3 in 1952 to a low of 12.8 in 1965. Following a sharp rise during the late 1960s, the figure has steadily declined.[6] Thus increases in national government employment have not kept pace with population growth. Still, public concern persists about the size of government bureaucracy, and this can affect personnel administration, at least indirectly.

In state and local governments, the personnel picture is a bit more complicated because of substantial numbers of employees in public education. According to public personnel expert O. Glenn Stahl, in the early 1970s approximately half of all state and local government employees were working in primary, secondary, or higher education.[7] State employees (noneducation) accounted for another 15 percent, and the remaining one-third were noneducation employees in city, county, and other local governments.[8] (See Table 9–1 for a breakdown of state and local "full-time equivalent" employment.) The dramatic expansion of public employment at the state-local level between 1947 and 1975 was due in large part to a sharp rise in educational employment during the 1960s, but other areas of state-local employment have now begun to catch up.

TABLE 9–1
STATE AND LOCAL GOVERNMENT EMPLOYMENT*

Function	Full-time Equivalent Employment	
	Number	Percentage
TOTAL	9,881,000	100.0
Education	4,930,000	49.9
Local schools	3,839,000	38.9
Institutions of higher education	1,005,000	10.2
Other education	86,000	0.9
Hospitals	935,000	9.5
Highways	561,000	5.7
Police protection	532,000	5.4
General control	317,000	3.2
Public welfare	316,000	3.2
Financial administration	242,000	2.4
Local fire protection	211,000	2.1
Correction	185,000	1.9
Local utilities other than water supply	181,000	1.8
Health	179,000	1.8
Natural resources	169,000	1.7
Local parks and recreation	136,000	1.4
Sanitation other than sewerage	124,000	1.3
Water supply	118,000	1.2
Employment security administration	85,000	0.9
Sewerage	78,000	0.8
All other	582,000	5.9

*As of October 1974.

Source: Bureau of the Census, *Public Employment in 1974* (Washington, D.C.: U.S. Government Printing Office, 1975).

Evolution of Public Personnel Administration

The evolution of public personnel administration, from 1789 to the present, did not occur in a social or political vacuum. Rather, development of the personnel function and of specific practices was related to other changes in public administration and society generally. We shall discuss six major phases in the evolution of personnel administration.[9]

Government by "Gentlemen," 1789–1829

The period 1789–1829 was characterized by limited political participation, and consequently those in government service came almost exclusively from the participating (meaning wealthier, propertied) segments of society. Government positions were filled on a basis that blended what later came to be known as "patronage" and "merit" appointment. That is, political loyalty to the chief executive was a major consideration, just as in modern patronage arrangements. But in addition, "proper" social standing and advanced education—what one observer has called being a member of the establishment[10]—were also necessary. Thus in this forty-year period, most government personnel were hired through a "patronage of the elite" system. Both the Federalists and Democratic-Republicans supported this arrangement, and throughout most of the 1820s, "tests of loyalty, regional considerations, preference for veterans, and consultation with Congress remained factors in public service staffing."[11]

Government by the "Common Man," 1829–1883

Political ferment intensified during the 1820s, focusing on greatly expanding the right to participate in processes of government. In this period eleven new states were admitted to the Union—nine in the West—and political parties were being built up in all parts of the country. The traditions of the frontier, where equality was a strong norm and no established aristocracy ruled the political scene, permeated the rest of society.[12] In many states and localities, egalitarianism and an interest in strengthening party organizations merged in the form of extending the right to vote to the "common man." Partisan patronage—blunt, straightforward, without apology—was born in many western state and local governments, and was used deliberately to build up loyal party followings. In the late 1820s this approach spread to the national government.[13]

The individual most commonly associated with this broad movement for democratization was Andrew Jackson. In 1824 Jackson ran for president; he collected the most popular and electoral votes but failed to win a clear majority in the Electoral College and then lost to John Quincy Adams in the House of Representatives. But in 1828 Jackson ran again and won handily, ushering in an era in which "establishment" credentials were not only unnecessary but also an affront to "ordinary citizens," who looked upon the aristocracy in government as hostile to their political interests. This early version of "populist" politics—supporting the "little people" or, simply, "the people" against those with wealth, title, education, and political and economic power—was to be echoed in numerous political movements in subsequent years, in every instance demonstrating the link suggested by Herbert Kaufman between strong executive leadership and some form of political representativeness.

Jacksonian democracy and later populist movements shared a belief that common folk were fully capable of discharging the responsibilities of public office. President Jackson inaugurated a full-scale "spoils system" of personnel appointment, following the principle "to the victors belong the spoils of victory." Government jobs were offered to those whose political loyalties were on the "right" side, without major emphasis on job-related competence since "everybody was competent to perform public service." Jackson is remembered as the "father" of the patronage system, though in reality Thomas Jefferson was the first president to view partisan loyalty as an important criterion in the selection of public servants.[14] Moreover, Jackson insisted on more than a little competence in government employees and was nowhere near as abusive in his patronage tactics as were some later presidents (notably James Buchanan and Abraham Lincoln).[15]

A rising tide of political protest against the spoils system began to make itself felt during the 1860s and 1870s. In the late 1870s civil service reform associations were formed in thirteen states, and in 1881 they banded together as the National Civil Service Reform League. Stahl suggests that four developments were crucial in this period: (1) the persistence of a group of intellectual idealists, led by George William Curtis, who kept up a drumbeat of reform agitation during the 1870s; (2) formation of the National Civil Service Reform League; (3) preparation of a report on the British civil service by Dorman B. Eaton, at the request of President Rutherford Hayes; and (4) the assassination in 1881 of President James Garfield by a frustrated officer-seeker who was also mentally ill.[16]

Garfield's assassination was the catalyst for definitive action, and in 1883 Congress passed the Civil Service (Pendleton) Act. This act created a bipartisan commission, responsible to the president, that was to administer open competitive examinations for civil service positions. The new system was to afford an equal chance for all to compete for government employment, but practical, job-related skill was required to actually obtain a position.[17] That was a far cry from the partisan favoritism of the preceding half-century. It also held out some hope of ending massive turnover of personnel at each change of presidential administration, the exalting of inexperience, and day-to-day partiality in the routine business of government.[18] Finally, in making politically neutral competence a major criterion for government service, the act deemphasized both strong executive leadership and political representativeness.

Government by the "Good," 1883–1906

The period immediately following passage of the Pendleton Act was one of intensive change in public personnel administration, and indeed in all of public administration. The most direct effect was creation of the Civil

Service Commission to oversee the new civil service system under rules and regulations that it established. At first only about 10 percent of those in the public service were subject to provisions of the Pendleton Act, but coverage was gradually expanded by executive order.

In a broader sense, the period 1883–1906 was one of consolidation, when the successful drive for merit reform had to be translated into workable day-to-day arrangements. The moral fervor of the civil service reformers left an imprint in several respects. One was the fact that "efficiency" in government referred less to any systematic managerial concerns than it did to ending corruption in hiring practices (other dimensions of efficiency as a management objective emerged only after 1906).[19] Government "efficiency" came to be viewed as the diametric opposite of government "corruption," and the dichotomy between "politics" (equated with corruption) and "administration" (equated with efficient, nonpoliticized processes) took root. As discussed in chapter 2, this distinction has continued to influence basic perceptions and assumptions concerning American public administration.

Another major emphasis of this period was a self-conscious egalitarianism in the new system. There was an attempt to avoid creation of a distinct "administrative class" in the civil service (in contrast to the British model) and keep the service open to anyone who could pass the competitive entrance examinations. It also involved making no particular provision for those with better education to automatically achieve higher placement in the public service. Not until the 1930s was any major effort made to upgrade the level of education in the bureaucracy, or to insure that educational preparation counted for something in obtaining federal government employment.[20]

Finally, the Civil Service Commission took up the task of insulating the new personnel system against political pressures from Congress and the White House. This meant that the commission itself had to be substantially independent of both the chief executive and the legislature.[21] Initially the commission focused on screening applicants and little else, but as time went on it became active in a wider range of personnel policy making. The presidency of Theodore Roosevelt marked a confirmation of the power and prestige of the commission, and it has continued to increase its role in directing personnel policies for the entire executive branch.[22]

At state and local levels, similar stirrings were evident, but the pace of reform was predictably much more uneven. New York and Massachusetts passed civil service legislation in 1883 and 1884, respectively. During the first decade of this century, four more states—Wisconsin, Illinois, Colorado, and New Jersey—followed suit. And between 1910 and 1920, Ohio, California, Connecticut, and Maryland did the same. The other states did not act for at least another fifteen years, though most now have some kind of civil service system in effect (some systems, admittedly, quite a bit more thoroughgoing than others). At the local level a great deal of controversy surrounded efforts to do away with urban political "machines" (see chapter 3, regarding the politics of organization), but quite a number of municipal governments were successfully "reformed." In county governments and most other rural entities, civil service reform has come much later, if at all.[23]

Government by the "Efficient," 1906–1937

The major focus of public personnel administration from 1906 to 1937 was maintenance of the merit system and political neutrality, as well as pursuit of efficiency in the management of government programs. The doctrine of separation between politics and administration was in full bloom—and indeed was strengthened—and "scientific management" exerted increasing influence on both business and public administration. It has been suggested that efficiency was the major conceptual emphasis within a "package" that included goodness, merit, morality, neutrality, and science—a "somewhat inconsistent but soothing amalgam of beliefs."[24]

The Civil Service Commission and agency personnel administrators concentrated on classifying government positions in a rational relationship to one another, and on writing specific job descriptions and analyses of responsibilities for each position. This made possible extension of merit coverage to a much larger number of positions, the percentage of those covered rising from approximately 46 percent in 1900 to about 80 percent by 1930.[25]

The emphasis on efficiency and neutrality permitted further expansion of seemingly nonpoliticized administrative machinery, which was fully in keeping with prevailing values in both government and society. It also made it possible for Franklin Roosevelt to inherit a government bureaucracy that focused on good, effective management. This was not unimportant, as Roosevelt began increasingly to involve bureaucracy in planning and managing new programs, leading to basic changes in the role of government in American society.

Government by "Administrators," 1937–1955

By 1937 government generally, and public administration in particular, were seen as spearheading dramatic efforts to overcome the effects of the Great Depression. This was a new view of the public service—one of an activist administrative apparatus which was able to respond to Roosevelt's vigorous policy leadership. The enlarged policy-making role of public administrators was directly related to the political initiatives and requirements of the Roosevelt administration. That fact, however, necessitated some change in prevailing thinking about the politics-administration dichotomy. Some began to feel that, under a strong president (whom they liked and supported), political representativeness in government personnel might not be such a bad thing after all. Further, the possibility that politics and administration might mix to some extent without "polluting" the administrative process seemed more legitimate when viewed in the context of the Roosevelt presidency. Some allowance was made, in principle, for overlap between politics and administration without completely letting go of the idea that administration "should" be separated from the political process.

Two major reports to the president marked the beginning and end, respectively, of this period. The first was the so-called Brownlow Report, named after the chairman of Roosevelt's Committee on Administrative Management. The Brownlow Report called on the president to assume greater responsibility and authority for directing executive-branch activities, and for centralization and consolidation of responsibility throughout the executive establishment. It also advocated extension of merit protection and favored administrators with broad, general skills as opposed to narrow, overly specialized bureaucrats. One important consequence of the report was an executive order issued by Roosevelt the following year mandating professional personnel administrators for every agency. Another result was that the president began to pay ongoing attention to matters such as directing the bureaucracy, clarifying lines of authority, and defining relationships among the different parts of the executive structure. Yet another consequence, which took longer to be fully recognized, was the growing need to decentralize management of many personnel responsibilities from the Civil Service Commission to agency personnel officers.[26]

The second of these major reports was that of the second Hoover Commission to President Eisenhower in 1955. Formally known as the Commission on Organization of the Executive Branch of the Government and chaired by former President Herbert Hoover, it followed up on studies conducted by the first Hoover Commission, which had reported to President Harry S Truman in 1949. The second Hoover Commission was appointed partly because after twenty years out of power, the Republicans had captured the White House in 1952 and found themselves facing a bureaucracy founded on principles of political neutrality but populated inevitably by quite a few Democrats. However, the most notable contributions of the commission were only indirectly of value to President Eisenhower as he wrestled with political problems posed by the bureaucracy.

A general section of the commission's report dealt for the first time with relations between political appointees and career public servants. Among the specific recommendations was creation of a "Senior Civil Service" comprised of about 3,000 upper-level career executives serving in administrative positions for which their particular skills and competencies suited them, and from which they could transfer into similar positions in other government agencies. These emphases in the higher career grades marked new directions in personnel administration, and though the idea for a "senior" civil service never became reality, these two elements have been incorporated into general practices of personnel administration in the national government.[27]

The period of government by "administrators," in sum, saw the elevation of public personnel administration to a place alongside other managerial tasks and functions of traditional public administration. Accompanying this development was concern for the manner in which expanding governmental responsibilities were discharged, and, in the early 1950s, a growing interest in the individual skills of bureaucratic employees.

Government by "Professionals," 1955 to the Present

The year 1955 saw establishment of the Federal Service Entrance Examination (FSEE), designed to accomplish several objectives simultaneously. One was to provide a single point of entry into the public service, through a common examination that could be used as a broad basis for personnel decisions. A companion objective was to make it possible for public servants to transfer from one agency to another. As long as each agency had had its own entry and placement tests, it was extremely difficult for a career bureaucrat to be mobile within the public service. Creation of a common entry examination, after which individual agencies could test further for particular skills, increased prospects for mobility. Finally, the FSEE allowed the Civil Service Commission to engage in more systematic recruiting, especially on college and university campuses. Recruitment, in fact, became a conscious activity of the national bureaucracy for the first time in 1955, and has continued to be a prominent concern.

The major development since 1955 has been the rise of widespread professionalism in the public service and a partial shift to a career emphasis which differs in significant ways from the traditional civil service emphasis. It is not surprising that demand for professionally trained employees has risen in the government bureaucracy since it has just about everywhere else. But this development has posed some problems for personnel administration.

For one thing, it has meant that rules and regulations sufficient to cover government employees in the past are no longer flexible enough. As one example, separate salary schedules have had to be established in selected federal personnel grades for professionals in printing management, engineering and architecture, medicine and nursing, metallurgy, petroleum engineering, and veterinary medicine, among others.[28] Another salary issue concerns the fact that although total size of the bureaucracy has stabilized or slightly declined in recent years, the cost (mainly in salaries) of running it has jumped dramatically, by almost 50 percent in the period 1968–1973.[29] Also, diversity of skills and training among government employees makes it difficult to formulate and implement generally applicable personnel procedures, such as job classification and personnel evaluation.

Another effect of professionalism has been establishment of ties with institutions of higher education that can provide training of needed professionals. "Government work" can look attractive to the recent graduate, especially since efforts to boost government salaries have been quite successful. The range of professions the national government now employs is impressive, and the same may be said of state and local governments.

Perhaps the most important impact of professionalism on the public service, however, is a largely conceptual one. The most common emphasis since 1883 has been on developing a system of administrative positions which function in a coherent relationship to one another, and developing in turn necessary procedures for filling those positions on the basis of job-related competence (merit). The emphasis, in other words, has been on the *job,* the position, and formal responsibilities associated with it. With the rise of professionalization in the public service, however, a second emphasis has developed—an emphasis on the *people* filling government posts and on their *career* needs within their professions. This has placed new pressures on personnel administration.

For one thing, personnel (and other) administrators must plan for agency needs at the same time that a growing proportion of their employees are pursuing career interests which may take little account of the agency. For another, professional expertise may be the employee's chief concern rather than performing a job in accord with agency objectives and needs. There is also the strong possibility that loyalty to the ethics of a profession (such as medicine or law) may supersede loyalty to the agency as the principal standard by which professional employees judge their own work and the value of their contributions to the organization.[30] Individual loyalties to widely varying professional standards can create tensions within an agency, and it can be very difficult to deal with these tensions effectively. In sum, contemporary personnel administration must take account of the needs of both government agencies and their professional employees.

Politically, there is an increasingly significant problem posed by the growth of professionalism. Not only have professional standards and ethics loomed larger in the daily activities of thousands of public servants, but professional associations have also become politically active and have come to influence quite strongly the policy-making process in their highly specialized substantive areas. Licensing of insurance agents and realtors at the state level and regulatory processes at the national level are two areas where professional influence is strong—some say, too strong. Professions such as law, medicine, and civil engineering have been described by different observers as enjoying excessive influence in formulating and implementing public policy. The lack of public accountability of such professional associations is central to critiques of their role.[31]

Professionalism, then, is a new feature of bureaucracy which has implications for the general conduct of public affairs and for particular aspects of personnel administration. One indication of its impact was establishment of the federal Professional and Administrative Career Examination (PACE) in 1974, to replace the FSEE. More than just the title of the examination was changed. The content was geared more explicitly to the professional training of prospective employees, though without sacrificing interest in a good general background. Similar developments have taken place, varying in extent, in state and local governments which have strong merit systems. It is likely that the problems discussed here will intensify.

"Merit" and Patronage in Perspective

The merit-versus-patronage debate arouses deep passions in many Americans. The devotion of so many people to what they see as interconnected values of efficiency, economy, political neutrality, and governmental integrity fosters a strong preference for merit system personnel practices, often accompanied by contempt for "political favoritism," or patronage. As we have seen, both have a rich history in American public personnel administration, yet in the past century merit has clearly held favor among middle- and upper-class Americans.

The distinctions between merit and patronage systems can be boiled down to a difference in defining "job qualifications." Those who favor merit are fond of saying that "you don't have to be qualified" to get a patronage job, but that is not really true—the qualifications are political rather than job-related, but they are job requirements, just the same. Put simply, merit judges what you know, while patronage is more interested in whom you know, what you have done or can do, and how you can help politically. Each system has some clear advantages to recommend it, which may be taken as disadvantages of the other.

The most obvious advantage of a merit system is its ability to bring into the public service individuals who are competent to perform the tasks required in a given position. Doing a job well is a strong value in both the private and public sectors, and is the root of the value system favoring merit. There is also some value in having a reasonable degree of continuity and stability in the public service instead of the dramatic (and traumatic) turnovers in personnel experienced at the beginning of every new administration between 1829 and 1881.[32]

On the other side of the coin, a patronage system also affords some advantages. The most important one in terms of executive-branch operations is that the chief executive can command much more effectively the loyalties of bureaucratic subordinates. Every local, state, and national "boss" has had that ability, and the effect in each case has been to buttress chief executive leadership (see chapter 4). It is undoubtedly true that this approach yields a vastly different kind of bureaucracy, and very likely a different set of social, economic, and political priorities in public policies. But to the extent that we value strong leadership (as Herbert Kaufman has suggested we do), we may favor a patronage system as conducive to its existence.

The other principal advantage of patronage is less directly political and administrative and more a matter of social structure and status. In many communities, ethnic minorities were effectively cut off from advancing up the social ladder through business (even labor) or other "rungs" available to the ethnic majority. For them, political power and the ability to share it easily with their cohorts offered the best chance they had to make something of themselves economically and socially. This explains the intense feelings among many ethnic minorities in favor of patronage—and the *social* dichotomy between large groups of Americans on opposite sides of the issue. It appears that merit personnel practices have been supported by *majoritarian* social/ethnic groups—mostly white, mostly Protestant, many of Anglo-Saxon heritage—and strongly opposed by many who are nonwhite, Roman Catholic, of southern or eastern European heritage, or some combination. Merit reform in the late 1800s and early 1900s was, in part, directed toward preventing immigrants of that period from acquiring political power and influence. With this in mind, patronage can be seen as a promising instrument for social as well as political advancement, if enough votes can be gathered to elect a minority ethnic coalition to office.

Are merit and patronage, then, permanent and inevitable opposites in personnel administration? Perhaps surprisingly, the answer is no. In practice, neither merit systems nor patronage exists in a pure form. Some political influence is not unknown in merit selection, though it is ordinarily quite subtle and not very common. In some states and cities, the appearance of a merit system may mask an effectively functioning patronage arrangement. "Knowing someone" is still useful to the candidate for a merit position. By the same token, patronage practices have been affected by governments' having to hire individuals with needed technical skills. The era of the "political hack," if not gone forever, has been significantly transformed by the changing needs of a technological, complex society. In sum, there is overlap in practice between merit and patronage, which is quite consistent with our past history.

Formal Arrangements of Personnel Systems

All civil service systems are not created equal, but the national government arrangements will serve as an illustrative model for discussion of the structure of most merit personnel systems. Many state arrangements, among the nearly forty states that have merit systems, closely resemble the federal format, though with some variations.

Approximately 90 percent of all federal executive-branch employees are presently covered by some merit system, most under the U.S. Civil Service Commission's merit practices. Table 9–2 indicates the growth in the proportion of federal employees subject to merit coverage. It is apparent that merit protection has been steadily expanded.

Partly due to prodding from the national government, state governments have gradually extended (or first established) merit systems in their executive branches. Congress passed several laws in the 1940s and 1950s requiring some merit policies in the personnel systems of governments receiving federal aid (see chapter 5), and the Intergovernmental Personnel Act of 1970 greatly reinforced that requirement, so that most states now have many merit features built into their personnel arrangements. Local governments have been similarly affected, but to a lesser extent.

The system of *position classification* is central to any personnel structuring. In the federal service, jobs are classified according to eighteen *grades,* or levels, which make up the General Schedule (GS). GS-1 through GS-4 are lower-level positions, of the secretarial-clerical-janitorial type. Grades GS-5 through GS-11 cover lower-middle management posts, but are divided into two subschedules: GS-6, GS-8 and GS-10 are for the most part technical, skilled crafts, and senior clerical positions, while GS-5, GS-7, GS-9 and GS-11 are professional career grades. The latter four grades are the most common entry-level grades for

TABLE 9–2
FEDERAL EMPLOYEES SUBJECT TO MERIT PERSONNEL SYSTEMS

Year	Number of Federal Civilian Workers*	Number Under Merit Systems	Percentage Under Merit Systems
1884	131,200	13,800	10.5
1900	208,000	94,900	45.6
1930	580,500	462,100	79.6
1950	1,934,000	1,641,900	84.9
1970	3,000,000	2,675,000	89.1
1977	2,823,300	2,567,600	90.9

*The total number of federal civilian workers includes those in the Congressional Budget Office, General Accounting Office, and Government Printing Office, which are in the legislative branch but are subject to the general merit system.

Sources: Data for the years 1884–1970 are taken from O. Glenn Stahl, *Public Personnel Administration,* 7th ed. (New York: Harper & Row, 1976), p. 48. Data for 1977 were obtained from the U.S. Civil Service Commission, Washington, D.C. All figures are rounded to the nearest hundred.

college graduates. Grades GS-12 through GS-15 are upper-level positions, reflecting career advancement and acceptable job competence. GS-16 through GS-18 are the so-called "supergrades," filled by senior civil servants who serve as bureau chiefs, staff directors, and so on. Their superiors are the political appointees who head most executive-branch agencies. Promotion from one grade to the next is not automatic and, at the outset of one's career, retention in the service itself is not assured. A probation period of six to eighteen months must be served before full merit protection is attained, and not all employees are put under merit. In many instances promotion comes after one year in the service (for example, from GS-9 to GS-11), and in some agencies failure to achieve promotion in that time is tantamount to an invitation to seek employment outside the service.

In keeping with the recent emphasis on general preparation and skills, it is not terribly difficult for an employee in the public service to transfer from one agency to another—or even, in some cases, from one merit system to another. The Civil Service Commission has reciprocal agreements with the Tennessee Valley Authority and Panama Canal Zone, for example, which permits civil service employees to transfer to the other systems, and vice versa, with no loss of career rights such as pension benefits or grade level.[33] This interagency mobility has advantages not only for employees but also for agencies looking for varied combinations of skill and experience.

In some state merit systems it is possible to move up the ladder very rapidly. In Illinois, for example, competitive examinations for higher-level jobs—open only to those already holding state positions—are given with some frequency. A capable individual who has landed a "first job" can take the examinations every time they are administered and, if successful, can achieve significant career advancement in a relatively short time. It is not unknown for an employee to move from an entry-level post to a staff director's job within four years. The federal service does not afford quite that kind of advancement possibility, nor do many other states. But advancement through the ranks—on the basis of competence, time in grade, and so on—is far from an impossible dream for most government employees.

Formal Tasks of Personnel Administration

The formal tasks of personnel administration have traditionally included such things as position classification, compensation, recruitment, examination, and selection. More recently, as management of complex organizations has itself become more complex, administrators (including personnel administrators) have had to become better grounded in counseling, motivating employees, labor relations, and the like.[34] We will briefly discuss major traditional emphases, with some extended consideration of particular topics.

Position Classification

The major purpose of position classification, referred to previously, is to facilitate performance of other personnel functions across a wide range of agencies within the same general personnel system. Many positions in different agencies have similar duties, so it makes sense to group into one classification jobs with essentially the same responsibilities. Otherwise, recruitment and examination would be far more difficult; trying to describe and test for each and every individual position in a system of some 2.9 million is much more complicated than explaining or examining for the general duties and responsibilities of a GS-11 or GS-13. Pay scales, as another example, can only be set up if positions are grouped so that it is possible to award "equal pay for equal work," which has been an underlying rationale of position classification since passage of the Pendleton Act.

A written description of duties and responsibilities involved in a position is the basis for its classification. Analysis of those functions is the basis for distinguishing it from other jobs. But there are obstacles to effective classification. While description of duties is relatively easy, the exact responsibilities of a position—regarding supervisory tasks, evaluation of the work of subordinates, and expectations for initiative, innovation, or suggestions—can be exceedingly elusive.[35] How challenging the duties and responsibilities are is another ambiguous aspect of position descriptions. In an effort to counteract these problems, some weighting of the various features of the job—frequency of supervision, difficulty and complexity of each task, and so on—has been tried, so that classifications reflect as accurately as possible the true nature of each position. But the obstacles are not easily overcome, and many classification systems consequently (perhaps inevitably) contain some flaws and "soft spots" that require continuing attention.

The following aspects of classification deserve some mention.[36] First, while each agency is responsible for classifying, according to existing schedules, the positions in that agency, there is a legitimate interest in maintaining some consistency in classifications from one agency to the next. Consequently, most states and localities as well as the national government provide for reviews and audits by a central personnel office with authority to change, if necessary, agency classifications that are out of line. Second, there is concern that overly narrow specialization in many job descriptions has hampered efforts to attract into the public service qualified individuals who lack *exactly* the right combination of skills for a given position. In this respect, position classification may be said to interfere with the merit principle itself. Third, there is always the possibility that, without adequate monitoring, an existing classification system will become outdated due to rapidly changing job requirements. Fourth, it has been contended that as task-oriented groups become more common, position classification geared to hierarchical organization will itself become obsolete. That is a problem that bears watching, but because most government organizations still are arranged hierarchically, position classification is likely to remain both appropriate and useful.

Compensation

Deciding how much to pay employees is one of the more delicate and occasionally controversial tasks confronting any government personnel system. In one sense the task is made easier by the fact that legislatures almost always must approve pay scales and other rules of compensation, but hard decisions about what to propose remain a central responsibility of personnel administration.

There are several key considerations in determining a reasonable level of compensation. One is the necessity to pay employees enough to fulfill their minimum economic needs. Closely related is the question of compensation in proportion to the work being done in terms of its importance, quality, and quantity. These can be highly subjective measures, permitting considerable disagreement about what is appropriate. A third consideration is comparability of pay scales. This has two dimensions: (1) insuring that wages and salaries for a given classification bear a "reasonable pay relationship to others in terms of complexity, responsibility, and skill,"[37] and (2) maintaining rates of compensation for government employees that are not dramatically different from the wages and salaries paid for similar kinds of work in the private sector.

An issue within the comparability question concerns variations throughout the nation, and even within many states, in wage and salary levels paid in private business and industry, which makes it difficult to align government salaries with them on a truly comparable basis. In the mid-1970s another factor entered into this equation: cost-of-living variations and how these affected compensation. There appears to be a trend emerging—sometimes formalized, sometimes not—to tie wage and salary levels to changes (upward, of course) in the cost of living. As a practical matter, that avoids some tough questions, but the harm it does to the merit principle and to the expectation that more skilled individuals will be better paid is obvious.

In recent times government compensation policies have been questioned from several vantage points. First they came under fire for being too low; critics included scholarly observers, some legislators, some citizens, and (predictably enough) many employees of government. At the national level a concerted effort was made in the 1950s and, especially, the early 1960s to improve the situation. In 1962 President John Kennedy signed the Federal Salary Reform Act, which established the principle of pay comparability to private-sector jobs for all national government positions across the country. And in the Pay Comparability Act of 1970, Congress delegated to the president authority to set the salaries of all General Schedule and Foreign Service employees, subject to congressional disapproval. During the late 1960s and early 1970s, federal salaries rose rapidly, though more so in the middle and lower grades than the upper grades.

Table 9-3 indicates federal salaries for the General Schedule (Grades 1 through 15) as of October 1977; the pay "steps" within each grade show the range of compensation possible without requiring promotion to the next higher grade. Note that the pay steps of one grade tend to overlap the steps of the grades immediately above and below; for example, the top pay step at the GS-14 level is higher than the bottom step at the GS-15 level. That is deliberate, to allow an employee to win some recognition for competent job performance without having to wait for promotion, while promotion still can carry with it a financial award as well—for example, from step 9 at GS-12 to step 4 at GS-13. Increases from one salary step to the next are granted at one- to three-year intervals according to a set formula, and while, theoretically, poor job performance can cause a worker to be denied an increase, at least one researcher, Marjorie Boyd, could find no evidence of this being done. One official told her, "All you have to do is breathe."[38]

As a result of actions taken to raise the salaries of national government employees, the pendulum now has swung the other way. There is some concern among the general public that government employees are being paid *too* well! Certainly the pace of increase has been lively, and as noted earlier, the growing presence of skilled professionals has had the effect of pulling the general salary scale higher. So has inflation, for that matter. But existing concern stems in part from an implicit assumption that salaries were adequate before increases were granted, and that to have salaries rise so rapidly cannot be justified. In contrast, if we assume salaries and wages were lagging badly behind the private sector—for equivalent positions and responsibilities—then recent pay hikes really represent a needed realignment. Most studies have found that public-sector salaries did in fact lag behind, but there remains some unease about the rate of increase, as well as about salary levels themselves. The 1977 Gallup poll referred to earlier found that 64 percent of those surveyed believed government employees were paid more than their counterparts in nongovernmental jobs, and 77 percent believed fringe benefits available to government workers (such as health insurance and vacations) were better than those in similar jobs in the private sector.[39]

TABLE 9–3
FEDERAL GENERAL SCHEDULE SALARIES

Grade	1*	2	3	4	5	6	7	8	9	10
GS–1	$ 6,219	$ 6,426	$ 6,633	$ 6,840	$ 7,047	$ 7,254	$ 7,461	$ 7,668	$ 7,875	$ 8,082
GS–2	7,035	7,270	7,505	7,740	7,975	8,210	8,445	8,680	8,915	9,150
GS–3	7,930	8,194	8,458	8,772	8,986	9,250	9,514	9,778	10,042	10,306
GS–4	8,902	9,199	9,496	9,793	10,090	10,387	10,684	10,981	11,278	11,575
GS–5	9,959	10,291	10,623	10,955	11,287	11,619	11,951	12,283	12,615	12,947
GS–6	11,101	11,471	11,841	12,211	12,581	12,951	13,321	13,691	14,061	14,431
GS–7	12,336	12,747	13,158	13,569	13,980	14,391	14,802	15,213	15,624	16,035
GS–8	13,662	14,117	14,572	15,027	15,482	15,937	16,392	16,847	17,302	17,757
GS–9	15,090	15,593	16,096	16,599	17,102	17,605	18,108	18,611	19,114	19,617
GS–10	16,618	17,172	17,726	18,280	18,834	19,388	19,942	20,496	21,050	21,604
GS–11	18,258	18,867	19,476	20,085	20,694	21,303	21,912	22,521	23,130	23,739
GS–12	21,883	22,612	23,341	24,070	24,799	25,528	26,257	26,986	27,715	28,444
GS–13	26,022	26,889	27,756	28,623	29,490	30,357	31,224	32,091	32,958	33,825
GS–14	30,750	31,775	32,800	33,825	34,850	35,875	36,900	37,925	38,950	39,975
GS–15	36,171	37,377	38,583	39,789	40,995	42,201	43,407	44,613	45,819	47,025

*Pay step 1 is the usual entry-level salary for new employees.
Source: U.S. Civil Service Commission, Chicago, Illinois. These salaries were effective October 1977.

In the federal service at present, positions with salaries most comparable to those in the private sector are in the GS-9 to GS-15 range. Neither the very top nor the very bottom jobs are paid as well as parallel private-sector jobs.[40] The disparity is greatest at the top, where cabinet secretaries and other high-ranking executives almost invariably take substantial pay cuts when entering government service. When William Simon became Secretary of the Treasury, leaving a Wall Street brokerage firm in which he was a senior member, he took a pay cut of about 80 percent from the $200,000 per year he earned on Wall Street. To the average worker (or student), that is not cause for much sympathy, but for the government it poses a major problem in attracting and holding top-level executive talent.

What of state and local government in this regard? Generally speaking, these jurisdictions do not pay their employees as well as the national government. Larger jurisdictions ordinarily do better than smaller ones at the same level of government. To take one example, the state of Illinois, which utilizes a thirty-grade structure in its merit system, with seven salary steps in each grade, pays Grade 1 clerks between $6,048 and $7,644 per year; Grade 12 (college-entry) bank examiners, labor relations specialist trainees, and so on between $10,104 and $13,356; Grade 15 entry-level engineers between $11,940 and $15,924; Grade 18 supervisory personnel between $14,280 and $19,188; and Grade 25 bureau chiefs and division managers between $22,680 and $31,068.[41]

State and local government patterns of compensation differ from those in the national government largely because of two features: (1) the proportion of employees at the local level who work in education, and (2) the much greater impact of public employee unions and collective bargaining on wages and salaries. There appears to be some relationship between size of jurisdiction and salary levels, between degree of professionalization in a given bureaucracy and compensation levels, and between collective bargaining wage settlements and (especially) local government compensation.

Recruitment, Examination, and Selection

Attracting, testing, and choosing those who join the public service have been systematic activities of personnel administration for a relatively limited period of time. The concerns and issues involved in these areas overlap one another to some extent, but deserve discussion separately as well.

Recruitment was something of a problem for far longer than it was recognized as such. During the early decades of this century, a combination of low pay and low prestige—not unrelated—made working for the national government and most other jurisdictions distinctly unattractive. The prestige problem was a matter of public values and attitudes toward government generally; even among those who favored strong administrative capabilities, "politics" was seen as unsavory and something to be tolerated rather than actively joined. While remnants of that attitude persist among quite a number of people, the prestige of government service has increased significantly over the past few decades. Increased compensation has been both cause and effect of the change in prestige. It has therefore become less difficult to arouse the interest of skilled and competent individuals in the possibility of a government service career. But quite an effort had to be made.

The most important developments were the establishment of systematic ties to recruiting services on college campuses, in search of the professionally trained student as well as the liberal arts graduate, and to professional associations. At the same time, a host of requirements (filing fees, residency, and the like) which had acted to constrict access to the public service were dropped, and open competitive examinations were adopted. In a word, the recruitment process was democratized.

Of late, the recruitment picture has changed somewhat, primarily because of the tightening job market in both private and public sectors. In 1973 the Civil Service Commission reported that approximately 459,000 persons applied for 83,000 clerical openings in engineering and scientific jobs.[42] In 1975 222,000 people took the PACE test, and 112,000 passed. Of that number, only 11,180—10 percent—actually got jobs in the bureaucracy. And in 1976 the ratio of applicants to available positions was 30 to 1.[43] Clearly the necessity to go out and "beat the bushes" for prospective employees has all but disappeared, as the government looks more and more attractive to increasing numbers of job seekers.

The *examination* process is a complex one, if for no other reason than that a wide variety of positions stand to be filled by individuals whose first screening is a broad-gauged examination such as the national government's PACE test. Thus an examination must be broad enough to adequately test for skills that will be used in widely varying agencies, yet still precise enough to be meaningful in testing specific skills and competencies. Many federal agencies, as noted earlier, supplement the PACE examination with more specialized tests, interviews, written work submitted by the applicant, and so on. In state and local government, similar sorts of examinations are often used, but not as much attention has been paid in those jurisdictions to problems of testing as part of the personnel process.

Most government entrance examinations are written, though it is becoming more common to incorporate both written and oral portions. Also, most tests attempt to measure both aptitude and achievement (not unlike the standardized college and graduate school entrance exams administered by the Educational Testing Service). As alternative methods of measuring competence, it is common practice to give some weight to education and experience, and in some instances enough of one or both

SAMPLE TEST QUESTIONS DEALING
WITH ADMINISTRATION FROM NEW YORK CITY
POLICE EXAMINATIONS*

1. "Records of attendance, case load, and individual performance are ordinarily compiled for a police department by a records unit." A plan is suggested whereby all patrol sergeants would regularly review summaries of these detailed records, in so far as they concern the men under them. The adoption of such a plan would be
 (A) inadvisable; the attention of the patrol sergeant would be unduly diverted away from the important function of patrol supervision.
 (B) advisable; the information provided by summaries of detailed records would conclusively indicate to the patrol sergeant the subordinates who should be given specific patrol assignments.
 (C) inadvisable; the original records should be reviewed in detail by the patrol sergeant if he is to derive any value from a record review procedure.
 (D) advisable; the patrol sergeant would then have information that would supplement his personal knowledge of his subordinates.

2. In planning the distribution of the patrol force of a police department, the one of the following factors that should be considered first is the
 (A) availability of supervisory personnel for each of the predetermined tours of police duty.
 (B) hourly need for police services throughout the 24 hours of the day.
 (C) determination of the types of patrol to be utilized for the most effective police effort.
 (D) division of the total area into posts determined by their relative need for police service.

3. There are some who maintain that the efficiency of a police department is determined solely by its numerical strength. This viewpoint oversimplifies a highly complex problem mainly because
 (A) enlargement of the patrol force involves a disproportionate increase in specialized units and increased need for supervision.
 (B) supervisory standards tend to decline in an enlarged department.
 (C) the selection and training of the force, and the quality of supervision must also be considered.
 (D) the efficiency of the department is not related to its numerical strength.

*(Correct answers: 1–D, 2–B, 3–C)

Source: Modern Promotion Courses publications, New York City.

can substitute for taking the initial examination. In the great majority of cases, a combination of written and oral examinations, personal interviews, education and experience, and written statements is used as the basis for evaluating prospective employees.

A central concern of the examination process is the *validity* of examinations, that is, how well they actually test what they are designed to test. In the face of changing job requirements, maintaining test validity must be an ongoing concern. Another consideration is whether tests should measure specific work skills or such factors as imagination, creativity, managerial talent, and the capacity to learn and grow on the job. Clearly, for some positions work skills deserve major emphasis, while for others the second set of abilities should also be considered. And of growing concern in recent years is the matter of bias in testing—specifically, whether examinations have exhibited an unintentional cultural bias which unfairly discriminated against members of minority groups. There have been strong pressures for "affirmative action" hiring programs to deal with this problem, in the interest both of redressing past social grievances against members of these minorities and of making the public service more representative of their numbers in the general population.

Selection processes vary widely from government to government, and here as elsewhere the national government has set the pace for developing systematic procedures. There clearly is no overall pattern, since merit systems are not identical and patronage still operates in some state and local jurisdictions. But the situation in the national government suggests what is possible in making selections according to set patterns, and some idea of limitations and weak spots in what is designed to be purely "merit" selection.

The normal procedure runs something like this. After taking the PACE test, or otherwise qualifying through education or experience, an applicant receives a merit rating, qualifying the individual for a GS–7 or GS–9, for example. The applicant's name is also placed on a register, meaning that he or she is officially under consideration for appropriate positions as these become available throughout the federal bureaucracy. At that point it is up to each agency to notify the Civil Service Commission as positions open up. The commission then forwards to the agency names of those it finds qualified on the basis of total points earned on the PACE test or through other qualifications, and the agency takes it from there.

In this procedure there are three general "rules of thumb" which help shape the final decision. The first is called the "rule of three," referring to the Civil Service Commission's practice of sending three names at a time to agencies which have one position to fill; those three individuals are, literally, finalists in the competition. The other two rules of thumb help determine whose names are included in that vital set of three, because they affect total points assigned to each applicant. The more important of these two is veterans' preference. All veterans who achieve the minimum passing score of 70 on the PACE test get a five-point bonus; all disabled veterans receive a ten-point bonus, as do veterans of the Vietnam conflict; and those disabled in Vietnam receive a fifteen-point bonus. In some instances survivors of veterans killed in action receive these bonuses as well. In many state and local jurisdictions, disabled veterans receive an absolute preference, going well beyond even the generous bonus arrangements of the national government. Veterans' preference reflects the political strength of veterans' groups, as well as the generally high regard in which American fighting men (and women) have been held.

The other rule of thumb, somewhat more obscure than either the rule of three or veterans' preference, has to do with one of the earliest requirements under the Pendleton Act—namely, that the federal service was to include employees from the various states of the Union proportionate to each state's population. This affects selection in that some states—notably Maryland and Virginia, where most of those working in Washington, D.C., reside—are overrepresented, while others (for example, Arizona) are underrepresented, compared to their percentage of the nation's population. Thus state of residence cannot help a Marylander or Virginian get a job in the federal service, but residence in Arizona would be an asset, all other things being equal, for an individual seeking a job in Washington or perhaps a federal regional office in Phoenix.

It should be noted that both veterans' preference and the requirement concerning state representativeness do some harm to the principle of pure merit selection. In both instances, as with affirmative action programs, a characteristic of the applicant other than job-related competence is used as a criterion for judging suitability for government employment. Veterans' preference in particular has been a factor of considerable significance in selection of national government employees, and defenders of the merit system are hard pressed to support this kind of generosity, even toward veterans. Alan K. Campbell, appointed by President Carter as chairman of the Civil Service Commission, is on record as favoring sharp curtailment of veterans' preference in selection of merit employees, on the grounds that it "has damaged the quality of the senior civil service, to say nothing of discriminating against women in the federal government."[44] Campbell's proposed changes would require an act of Congress, and veterans' groups would hardly be likely to support them. But if Campbell's views come to be shared by the president, such changes are a possibility. One suggestion is to have a veterans' preference policy in effect for, say, two years after an individual is discharged from the armed forces,[45] but it is by no means clear that this or anything else in the way of modification will actually come about in the near future.

Current Developments in Personnel Administration

Over the years there has clearly been a great deal of ferment and change in the processes of fulfilling government's need for qualified people ("qualified" by whatever criteria). Today public personnel administration is, if anything, even more susceptible to both internal and external pressures for change, and for adaptation to changing values and conditions. By focusing on four of the most important developments of recent times, it is possible to get some understanding of how personnel administration has been coping with an ever more turbulent and unpredictable environment. The four developments are (1) more emphasis on intergovernmental personnel relations, (2) pressures for affirmative action in hiring and promotion on behalf of women and minority groups, (3) collective bargaining in the public service, and (4) proposals for change in requirements of political neutrality.

Personnel Administration and Intergovernmental Relations

The most important development in this area was passage of the Intergovernmental Personnel Act of 1970. The act accomplished a number of objectives sought by civil service reformers. First, it enabled the U.S. Civil Service Commission to assist financially state and local governments seeking to establish merit systems or upgrade existing ones. Second, it permitted expansion of in-service training programs for federal agency employees, and allowed state and local administrators also to take part. Third, it provided for federal funding of state and local in-service training programs. Fourth, it established federal grants for graduate-level education and training for selected state and local personnel, and grants to universities and associations of cities or counties for training of state and local professional personnel.

Finally, the act has made possible personnel exchanges between different levels of government, designed to give employees experience in another setting to deepen their appreciation of problems other governments face. For example, federal employees at the Department of Housing and Urban Development (HUD) have served one- and two-year internship-style appointments with local housing authorities, so as to better understand how their own agency—HUD—looks from the local level. Local officials have served in federal agencies, as well, multiplying opportunities for "expanded horizons." In an era of increased intergovernmental program funding and management, such exchanges may benefit both bureaucrats in charge of collaborative programs and the public served by them.

Affirmative Action

In the public service, as in educational systems and other institutions receiving national government funds, there has been emphasis in recent years on "affirmative action" programs in the hiring and advancement of members of minority groups and of women. The rationale behind the affirmative action movement is that these individuals and groups have been unfairly—in some cases, arbitrarily—discriminated against in the past, and that seeking to bring them into government service is one effective way to redress old grievances. The national government has gone a long way, under provisions of legislation such as the 1964 Civil Rights Act and the 1972 Equal Employment Opportunity Act, to insure that women and minorities are given at least strong consideration, if not outright preferential treatment, in decisions to hire government (and not a few other) employees.

The issues raised by affirmative action programs are weighty ones, and they can generate intense passions on all sides. First, if a merit system is viewed as one which goes strictly according to the applicant's job-related competence, affirmative action conflicts with that objective. This has been the basis of many criticisms of such programs. Those who support affirmative action point out, however, that it is entirely appropriate in light of the long-time lack of access to jobs in the government and elsewhere suffered by minorities and women. They also point to such features as veterans' preference, and failure to enforce standards of competence as vigorously after appointment as before, as evidence of imperfection in existing merit practices. The essence of their contention is that denial of access through accidental or systematic exclusion of certain groups is best remedied by practicing *systematic inclusion* through affirmative action. They claim, also, that this makes the public service more truly representative of different groups in the population, which, in their view, is especially desirable (see chapter 13).

Affirmative action is also said to be needed because of past biases in testing for employment. With some support from scholarly research,[46] it is alleged that competitive examinations have often been discriminatory, above and beyond the *necessary* discrimination (that is, distinguishing) among the various skills of those seeking employment. Advocates of this view argue that tests based on the experience and training of a white, middle-class population will almost inevitably discriminate unfairly against those whose experience and training are very different. There has been quite a bit of attention given to this problem in recent years, and while some grounds for criticism still exist, there have been good-faith efforts to modify competitive examinations to afford a more equitable opportunity to all applicants. This is true in many states and some localities as well as in the national government's testing programs. Still, many support affirmative action to compensate for past bias in testing.

Another major area of controversy regarding affirmative action is the issue of quotas in hiring—setting aside a fixed percentage of all positions for members of certain ethnic groups and for women. Court decisions have alternately supported and rejected this practice, though in 1977 there was some indication that affirmative action plans setting relatively rigid quotas were coming under more rigorous judicial examination in state and federal courts. Congress, too, showed signs of backtracking on previous actions which had opened the way for quota systems. Again, the conflict is between those who see systematic inclusion (which is what quotas really amount to) as a remedial device for decades of exclusion for significant numbers of American citizens, and those who prefer to staff the public service on the basis of job-related competence and other relatively objective criteria, such as education and experience.

The debate over affirmative action and quotas—indeed the whole area of what has come to be called "reverse discrimination"—is likely to continue, regardless of decisions made in legislatures or courts in the immediate future. But what difference has all this furor made? Looking strictly at the numbers in national, state, and local government, it would appear that minorities (more so than women) have made considerable gains in government employment, coming much closer to their proportionate numbers in the general population. But closer investigation raises some doubts—minorities are disproportionately concentrated in the lower grades, GS–1 through GS–4, and distinctly underrepresented in the range GS–12 to GS–18. Women are even less represented in the upper levels of the federal bureaucracy. Much the same situation prevails in many state and local bureaucracies, though the data available are much sketchier than those for the national government.[47] Clearly, affirmative action has not done all its proponents hoped it would do; it is questionable that any single policy step could possibly have tilted the balance as far as some might have preferred.

Collective Bargaining in the Public Sector

One of the most significant developments in public personnel administration in recent years is the tremendous expansion of collective bargaining arrangements between government employers and employees.[48] Public employee associations in some form date back to the mid-1800s, but their rapid expansion and much greater visibility in the personnel process are recent phenomena. Development of public-sector unions and collective bargaining has moved forward at both the national level and in states and localities.

Early versions of public employee unions were the benevolent associations of the 1850s and occasional teacher associations during the same period, but these organizations did not exist for any collective purpose vis-à-vis employers. The first true public unions at the national level emerged in the Post Office, principally as a protest against some of the worst working conditions in the public sector.[49] But there was strong resistance throughout the executive branch and Congress to any real movement toward worker organization (this was true also in many localities and most states). In 1912, however, Congress passed the Lloyd-

LaFollette Act, which authorized federal government workers to join worker associations and to act as a group in their collective interest, though not to bargain. With a few exceptions—notably the pioneering agreement between the Tennessee Valley Authority and its employees organized as the Tennessee Valley Trades and Labor Council in the 1930s—there was little further movement at the national level until 1962, when John F. Kennedy redeemed a 1960 campaign pledge by issuing Executive Order 10988. This order extended to federal employees a limited right to negotiate working conditions, with some mediation and conciliation mechanisms established as well.[50]

In 1969 Richard Nixon responded to rising federal employee discontent with existing procedures by issuing Executive Order 11491, which established stronger machinery for resolving labor-management disputes. That machinery consisted of an Assistant Secretary of Labor for Labor-Management Relations, with responsibility for determining union eligibility, elections, and appropriate units in the bureaucracy for union representation; a Federal Labor Relations Council to decide major policy issues and administer policy, as well as to handle appeals from decisions of the assistant labor secretary; and a Federal Service Impasse Panel to resolve impasses on substantive issues in negotiations.[51] The order did not broaden the area of issues that could be negotiated to include salaries or wages, but the postal workers' strike of 1970 resulted in limited negotiation over those matters. Neither 11491 nor a subsequent executive order (11616) has completely met the demands of federal employees for more comprehensive bargaining.

At state and local levels, unionization and collective bargaining have advanced somewhat more dramatically, and certainly with more controversy. There are at present a number of major unions, the most important being the American Federation of State, County, and Municipal Employees (AFSCME), with 700,000 members in 1975 and still growing (from only 100,000 in 1955); the American Federation of Teachers (AFT), with 444,000 members in 1974, up nearly 200,000 in only two years; the National Education Association (NEA), a union in everything but name, with almost 1.5 million members in 1975; and, a bit surprisingly, the Teamsters Union, with some 200,000 government members, mostly in law enforcement (though some signs of slippage appeared in 1976 and 1977).[52]

Membership in these and other state and local public-sector unions increased nearly 60 percent between 1968 and 1974 (from about 2.5 million to 3.9 million).[53] Membership growth in federal employee unions has also been rapid, but not *as* rapid. The American Federation of Government Employees (AFGE) grew to 325,000 members by 1972, and has continued to gain adherents since then. But that was only a fraction (albeit the largest one) of total union membership in the federal government, which in 1973 stood at 1.6 million, up from less than 700,000 just ten years earlier. Such rapid growth is due in part to stepped-up organizing activities since 1960, especially by private-sector unions seeking new membership; wage and fringe benefit gains registered by private-sector unions, which government employees looked upon with some understandable frustration; and growing acceptance in society at large of more militant means for achieving group objectives.[54]

The collective bargaining issue is controversial because it revolves around several key questions which trouble many observers and some participants in public employee labor-management relations. One question concerns the legal status of government employment, and indeed of the government itself. Traditionally, many people regarded public employment as a *privilege,* not a right; this was the commonly accepted view in the nineteenth century.[55] That older view, however, has clearly given way to an alternative concept of public employment as more of a right, in which case employee participation in personnel decisions is not at all inconsistent.

A second controversial question related to collective bargaining is that of the right to strike—and here public passions have been aroused. The concept of the public servant as both loyal employee and provider of necessary public services is deeply embedded in the national consciousness, so that the prospect of public-sector strikes stirs considerable negative feeling. Those who advocate the right to strike for public employees contend that denial of that right infringes on the First Amendment's guarantee of freedom of association, and draws an arbitrary distinction between public and private employees in that the latter can exercise such a right. Laws on the subject are almost uniform in denying the right to strike (though four states now have granted a limited right to strike for certain employees only—mainly those whose striking would not interrupt provision of essential public services). The fact is, however, that laws prohibiting strikes have not been very effective; Table 9–4 shows the increase in the number of work stoppages, and the number of workers involved in state and local government across the country in the period 1960–1974.

At the state and local level, particularly, the strike question is a difficult one. One reason is that state laws vary considerably in permitting or mandating collective bargaining; another is that, especially during the recent downturn in the national economy, many states and localities have simply not had the money to meet their workers' demands. A third (and related) difficulty concerns the effects of negotiations on the local budgetary process and on the budgets themselves. Protracted negotiations can bring the budget-making process to a grinding halt until agreement is reached—and that works to the disadvantage of the entire local government, regardless of how justified in principle employee claims may be. These problems give no sign of going away, and local officials will probably continue to have to wrestle with them.

TABLE 9-4
STATE AND LOCAL EMPLOYEE WORK STOPPAGES,
1960-1974

Year	State Government		Local Government	
	Number of Stoppages	Workers Involved (thousands)	Number of Stoppages	Workers Involved (thousands)
1960	3	1.0	33	27.6
1961	0	0	28	6.6
1962	2	1.7	21	25.3
1963	2	.3	27	4.6
1964	4	.3	37	22.5
1965	0	0	42	11.9
1966	9	3.1	133	102.0
1967	12	4.7	169	127.0
1968	16	9.3	235	190.9
1969	37	20.5	372	139.0
1970	23	8.8	386	168.9
1971	23	14.5	304	137.1
1972	40	27.4	335	114.7
1973	29	12.3	357	183.7
1974	34	24.7	348	135.4

Source: Bureau of Labor Statistics, U.S. Department of Labor.

One other point should be mentioned. From time to time it has been politically advantageous for a local or state official to "stand up to the unions," and there are signs that it is becoming even more advantageous to do so. In 1977 a number of strikes were unsuccessful in winning any significant gains for the striking employees—a garbage collectors' strike in Atlanta, a maintenance workers' walkout at the University of Michigan, teachers' strikes in Cincinnati and Kansas City.[56] This may portend a major shift from patterns of the late 1960s and early 1970s. The unions and their memberships, sensing this change, are becoming aware there may be a limit to public, as well as public official, patience.

The Coalition of American Public Employees (CAPE) was formed early in 1977 to try to reverse the tide of public opinion that appears to be running against public employees in their wage and fringe benefit demands. Jerry Wurf, head of AFSCME, is among those union leaders who have begun to discourage strikes, concentrating instead on getting the message to the public that employee needs are legitimate and that it is in the public's interest to help them meet those needs, so that public services can be maintained if nothing else.[57] It is probably too early to tell whether this new direction will be sustained, but it may be that union militancy has reached a peak and that a period of some retrenchment is in store.

Political Neutrality of Public Servants

The political neutrality of public servants was a primary objective of merit reformers in the nineteenth century, and was embodied in the Political Activities Act of 1939, more commonly known as the Hatch Act. This legislation, as amended in 1940 and 1966, effectively prohibited any active participation in political campaigns by national government employees, state and local employees working in any federally funded program, and employees of private organizations working with community-action programs funded by the Economic Opportunity Act.[58] But as rights of government employees became more of a concern in the 1960s and early 1970s, efforts were made to limit or overturn the Hatch Act. The reasoning behind these efforts was that provisions barring political involvement were said to constitute an infringement on constitutional rights exercised by others, thus rendering government personnel second-class citizens. The right to vote was not enough, it was argued; government employees should have the right to participate in all aspects of politics.

In a series of court cases in the early 1970s, several state and local versions of the Hatch Act were challenged, some successfully. In 1972 the U.S. District Court for the District of Columbia declared the Hatch Act itself unconstitutional on grounds of vagueness and of First Amendment violations.[59] But in 1973 the Supreme Court reversed that lower court ruling on a 6 to 3 vote, upholding the act and its constitutionality. Since that time, efforts have centered on getting Congress to at least loosen, if not lift, restrictions on political activity by government employees. President Carter's election boosted the hopes of those seeking change, and he supported such legislation in the 95th Congress in early 1977, achieving House passage of a bill that would ease, but not remove entirely, existing restrictions. The bill retained prohibitions against political pressures or intimidation of any kind, soliciting for funds in government buildings, and the like, and focused primarily on preventing abuses of official power for partisan political purposes. However, the legislation would permit civil servants to run for elective office and publicly support partisan candidates of their choice. Senate action was still pending in late 1977, but it seemed certain that if any bill was enacted, it would be at least as specific as the House version in prohibiting political activities that might compromise the effectiveness or impartiality of government employees.[60]

Whether civil servants would in fact become more active under loosened restrictions is open to some question. In a 1975 article, Jeffrey Rinehart and E. Lee Bernick noted earlier findings that 71 percent of federal employees surveyed had refrained from particular political activities because they chose to, not because they were civil servants, and fully 60 percent thought they would not get much more involved if the Hatch Act were liberalized.[61] For all that, efforts to ease these restrictions have continued, and the issue seems likely to be resolved in favor of expanded political participation.

Perspectives and Implications

Of all the areas of public administration in which there has been ferment and change in recent years, public personnel administration is among the most crucial. The federal civil service has existed for nearly a century on a foundation of belief and practice clear in intent and quite consistent in manner of operation. Now, however, all the assumptions underlying past practice have become shaky indeed. The merit system, already modified to a degree to accommodate veterans' preference and regional representativeness, has been subjected to further pressures in support of greater ethnic and sexual representativeness. Political neutrality of civil servants appears to be under pressure also, as efforts to permit greater political involvement have mounted and seem headed for success. Labor relations, including collective bargaining, wage disputes, and public employee strikes, have become steadily more complicated at all levels of government.

In short, change has been both monumental and fundamental. This kind of turmoil in a central area of public administration undoubtedly has an effect on quality of performance and the condition of the public service generally. But the more essential point to consider is the *vast uncertainty* surrounding public personnel functions, triggered by heavy political pressures for different sorts of change. What public personnel administration will look like in the 1980s and beyond is, almost literally, anyone's guess, as basic concepts and their meanings continue to undergo a long-term process of redefinition.

SUMMARY

Public personnel administration has evolved from a fairly routine function of government to a more controversial one. Personnel practices that have been in effect have varied a great deal, reflecting at different times the values of strong executive leadership and political representativeness, on the one hand, and politically neutral competence, on the other.

Public personnel administration is "the organizations, policies, and processes used to match the needs of governmental agencies and the people who staff those agencies." The *public* aspect of public personnel administration reflects the impacts of other political institutions, the politics of interest groups and associations, the political parties, and the mass media.

The size of government bureaucracies is a matter of some concern to personnel administrators, as is the diversity of skills of government employees. A related problem is the apparent public unease about the growth and current size of administrative structures. The greatest increases have come in state and local governments, particularly educational employment.

Public personnel administration has evolved, at the national level, through a series of stages related to changing values in society about government and administration. Government by "gentlemen" (1789–1829) reflected the powerful influence of the American quasi-aristocracy on all of politics. Government by the "common man" (1829–1883) resulted from the movement toward a more egalitarian political system. The public service was democratized, with Andrew Jackson the leader of this "populist" drive. Government by the "good" (1883–1906) focused on efficiency in government, meaning especially elimination of corruption in hiring practices. Emphasis also was placed on maintaining equality of access to competitive entrance examinations. Government by the "efficient" (1906–1937) was characterized by two major themes: maintenance of the merit system and of political neutrality, and the pursuit of efficiency in management. Government by "administrators" (1937–1955) saw the development of an activist role for public administrators in dealing with the crisis of the Depression. Some mixing of politics and administration was evident, and some conceptual accommodation was made by those still favoring separation of the two. Government by "professionals" (1955–present) has been a period of greater concern for recruitment and for testing generalized skills of job applicants. At the same time, there has also been more concern for meeting the challenges as well as the opportunities of increased professionalism in the public service.

Merit versus patronage is an old debate that is still very much with us. Merit systems emphasize competence related to the job; patronage systems favor political connections and loyalties. Merit offers some continuity and stability in personnel, in addition to promoting job-related competence; patronage permits a chief executive to select loyal subordinates. Merit has its social roots in the ethnic majorities and their values; patronage was and is a valuable instrument of social advancement for ethnic minorities. In practice, they overlap.

The formal arrangements of most civil service merit systems are generally similar. In the national government about 90 percent of all employees are under a merit system of some kind. However, there is a great deal of variation in the extent of merit coverage in state and local governments. The federal service is classified into eighteen grade levels, most of which are career positions; the top seven grades are management and "supergrade" levels.

Formal tasks of personnel administration include some traditional and other relatively new functions. Position classification is essential in order to conduct recruitment, administer a broad-gauged entrance examination, and award "equal pay for equal work" in different agencies and positions. Compensation levels are designed to be proportionate to the work being done and comparable to those in the private sector for similar types of jobs. Salary and wage levels have risen rapidly in the national government, to the point that there is now concern that compensation is too generous. State and local compensation tends to be less, ordinarily, than federal pay levels.

Recruitment, examination, and selection all have undergone considerable change in recent times. Recruitment in the 1950s became both more systematic and less restricted; consequently, greater numbers of applicants were recruited. Examination processes are now more complex than before, with applicant qualifications measured by written and oral examinations. Education and experience are also given more weight in current examination processes. Selection in the national government is conducted jointly through the agency which has a position open and the Civil Service Commission, which maintains a list of eligible candidates. An applicant's score on the PACE test, subject to adjustment for veterans' preference and for proportionate state representation, is the principal basis for selection.

Significant current developments in public personnel administration include emphasis on intergovernmental personnel relations, pressures for affirmative action, collective bargaining on behalf of public employees, and pressure for change in restrictions on political activity by merit employees. Intergovernmental personnel relations have included (among others) national assistance for development and upgrading of state and local merit systems, grants for graduate study and training for professionals in states and localities, and intergovernmental personnel exchanges for one or two years. Affirmative action programs seek to compensate for past discriminatory practices against women and selected minorities by affording some preference to members of these groups in government hiring practices. Collective bargaining in the public sector has expanded dramatically in the past twenty-five years. At the federal level, a series of executive orders—chiefly, orders 10988 in 1962 and 11491 in 1969—broadened the range of issues which could be negotiated, and strengthened negotiation and arbitration machinery. In state and local government, unionization and collective bargaining have advanced even more dramatically. Issues in collective bargaining include the right to strike, budgetary impacts, and the political advantage in supporting or opposing union demands. Maintenance of political neutrality requirements for many government employees has lately become a more pressing and heated issue. Some employees have filed suits in federal (and state) courts in an effort to limit or overturn Hatch Act provisions. A 1973 Supreme

Court ruling upheld that act, and it is now up to Congress and the president to decide whether to lift restrictions completely, partially, or not at all.

The most basic beliefs and practices of the federal civil service during the past century have become shaky and uncertain in recent years. The merit system, political neutrality of civil servants, and labor relations are all focal points of controversy and change. While this undoubtedly has had an effect on the work done by civil servants, and on the public service generally, the heart of the matter is continuing uncertainty surrounding public personnel administration. We are still in the midst of redefining basic concepts and exactly what they mean, as well as what they *will* mean in the future.

NOTES

1. Herbert Kaufman, "Administrative Decentralization and Political Power," *Public Administration Review,* 29 (January/February 1969), 3–15. See, also, chapter 2.

2. N. Joseph Cayer, *Public Personnel Administration in the United States* (New York: St. Martin's, 1975), p. 1.

3. Ibid., pp. 3–10.

4. Ibid., p. 12.

5. Gallup poll, published in the Bloomington-Normal, Illinois, *Daily Pantagraph,* June 12, 1977, p. D-2.

6. These data are taken from an article by Suzanne DeLesseps of Editorial Research Reports, which appeared in the Bloomington-Normal, Illinois, *Daily Pantagraph,* October 24, 1976, p. A-5. At the conclusion of World War II, 3.75 million civilian employees worked for the national government, many in war-related jobs. The number of civilian employees had not been that high before nor has it been since.

7. O. Glenn Stahl, *Public Personnel Administration,* 6th ed. (New York: Harper & Row, 1971), p. 14.

8. Ibid. These figures include both full-time and part-time employees.

9. This categorization of time periods is based on Frederick C. Mosher, *Democracy and the Public Service* (New York: Oxford University Press, 1968), chapters 3 and 4.

10. Nicholas Henry, *Public Administration and Public Affairs* (Englewood Cliffs, N.J.: Prentice-Hall, 1975), p. 187.

11. Cayer, *Public Personnel Administration in the United States,* pp. 18–19.

12. Ibid., p. 19.

13. Ibid.

14. Ibid., p. 20.

15. Ibid., pp. 20–21. Lincoln resorted to patronage to assure loyalty to the Union during the Civil War.

16. Stahl, *Public Personnel Administration,* p. 33. See also Henry, *Public Administration and Public Affairs,* pp. 188–189.

17. Stahl, *Public Personnel Administration,* p. 29.

18. Ibid., p. 33.

19. Henry, *Public Administration and Public Affairs*, p. 190.

20. Ibid., p. 189.

21. Ibid., p. 190.

22. Cayer, *Public Personnel Administration in the United States*, p. 28.

23. Stahl, *Public Personnel Administration*, p. 33.

24. Henry, *Public Administration and Public Affairs*, p. 191.

25. Stahl, *Public Personnel Administration*, p. 36.

26. Cayer, *Public Personnel Administration in the United States*, p. 46.

27. Henry, *Public Administration and Public Affairs*, p. 194.

28. This and other salary-related information appearing in this chapter was furnished by the Federal Job Information Center, U.S. Civil Service Commission, Chicago.

29. Henry, *Public Administration and Public Affairs*, p. 196.

30. Cayer, *Public Personnel Administration in the United States*, p. 49.

31. Henry, *Public Administration and Public Affairs*, p. 198. See also Guy Benveniste, *The Politics of Expertise*, 2nd ed. (San Francisco: Boyd and Fraser, 1977), for a careful examination of the role and influence of experts in public policy making.

32. Cayer notes that one reason Congress acted in 1883 to pass the Pendleton Act was a fear by its Republican majority that the Democrats could win the presidency in 1884 and "clean out" the GOP-dominated bureaucracy. By passing the act when it did, Congress made it possible to extend merit protection to incumbents in the bureaucracy. Cayer, *Public Personnel Administration in the United States*, p. 25.

33. Ibid., p. 36.

34. Ibid., p. 56. Much of this discussion relies on Cayer's treatment.

35. Ibid., p. 59.

36. Ibid., pp. 59–64.

37. Stahl, *Public Personnel Administration*, p. 83.

38. Marjorie Boyd, "Inflated Grades," in "What's Wrong with the Civil Service," *The Washington Monthly*, 9 (April 1977), 51.

39. Gallup poll, June 12, 1977.

40. Marjorie Boyd, "Inflated Grades," pp. 52–53.

41. Salary data furnished by the Division of Classification, Department of Personnel, State of Illinois, Springfield.

42. These data appeared in a wire service story carried in the Bloomington-Normal, Illinois, *Daily Pantagraph* of September 17, 1974, p. A-10.

43. Stephen J. Chapman, "Inflated Pay," in "What's Wrong with the Civil Service," *The Washington Monthly*, 9 (April 1977), 60.

44. The quote is taken from David Broder's column about Campbell not long after he became Civil Service Commission head. The column appeared under the headline "New Look in Civil Service," in the Bloomington-Normal, Illinois, *Daily Pantagraph*, May 25, 1977, p. A-4.

45. Cayer, *Public Personnel Administration in the United States*, p. 79.

46. See, among numerous other sources, Ollie A. Jensen, "Cultural Bias in Selection," *Public Personnel Review*, 27 (April 1966), 125–130.

47. See Henry, *Public Administration and Public Affairs*, pp. 213–215.

48. An indication of the interest in collective bargaining is the increasing bibliography available on the subject, including, among others: Frank H. Cassell and

Jean J. Baron, *Collective Bargaining in the Public Sector: Cases in Public Policy* (Columbus, Ohio: Grid, Inc., 1975); J. Joseph Loewenberg and Michael H. Moskow, *Collective Bargaining in Government: Readings and Cases* (Englewood Cliffs, N.J.: Prentice-Hall, 1972); Michael H. Moskow, J. Joseph Loewenberg, and Edward C. Koziara, *Collective Bargaining in Public Employment* (New York: Random House, 1970); Felix A. Nigro, ed., "A Symposium, Collective Bargaining in the Public Service: A Reappraisal," *Public Administration Review,* 32 (March/April 1972), 97–126; Neal R. Peirce, "Employment Report/Public Employee Unions Show Rise in Membership, Militancy," *National Journal,* 7 (August 30, 1975), 1239–1249; Sterling D. Spero and John M. Capozzola, *The Urban Community and Its Unionized Bureaucracies: Pressure Politics in Local Government Labor Relations* (New York: Dunellen, 1973); and Sam Zagoria, ed., *Public Workers and Public Unions* (Englewood Cliffs, N.J.: Prentice-Hall, 1972).

49. Stahl, *Public Personnel Administration,* p. 263.

50. Spero and Capozzola, *The Urban Community and Its Unionized Bureaucracies,* p. 6.

51. Stahl, *Public Personnel Administration,* pp. 265–266.

52. Peirce, "Employment Report/Public Employee Unions Show Rise in Membership, Militancy," pp. 1239–1240.

53. Ibid., p. 1239.

54. Harry P. Cohany and Lucretia M. Dewey, "Union Membership among Government Employees," in J. Joseph Loewenberg and Michael H. Moskow, *Collective Bargaining in Government: Readings and Cases* (Englewood Cliffs, N.J.: Prentice-Hall, 1972), pp. 5–11.

55. This is partly why patronage flourished as long as it did, also. If a job was a privilege, it followed that the party in power could legitimately dispense that "privilege" to those who were deserving—that is, its friends and supporters.

56. "Public Employee Unions Seek to End Role as Whipping Boy," St. Louis *Post-Dispatch,* May 29, 1977, p. 1-B.

57. Ibid., p. 12-B.

58. This description is taken from Philip L. Martin, "The Hatch Act in Court: Some Recent Developments," *Public Administration Review,* 33 (September/October 1973), 443–447, at p. 443.

59. *National Association of Letter Carriers, AFL-CIO* v. *United States Civil Service Commission* (346 F. Supp. 578, 1972).

60. *Congressional Quarterly Weekly Report,* 35 (June 11, 1977), 1146.

61. Jeffrey C. Rinehart and E. Lee Bernick, "Political Attitudes and Behavior Patterns of Federal Civil Servants," *Public Administration Review,* 35 (November/December 1975), 603–611, at p. 609.

SUGGESTED READINGS

Cassell, Frank H., and Jean J. Baron. *Collective Bargaining in the Public Sector: Cases in Public Policy.* Columbus, Ohio: Grid, Inc., 1975.

Cayer, N. Joseph. *Public Personnel Administration in the United States.* New York: St. Martin's, 1975.

Loewenberg, J. Joseph, and Michael H. Moskow. *Collective Bargaining in Government: Readings and Cases.* Englewood Cliffs, N.J.: Prentice-Hall, 1972.

Martin, Philip L. "The Hatch Act in Court: Some Recent Developments," *Public Administration Review,* 33 (September/October 1973), 443–447.

Mosher, Frederick C. *Democracy and the Public Service.* New York: Oxford University Press, 1968.

Nigro, Felix A., ed. "A Symposium, Collective Bargaining in the Public Service: A Reappraisal," *Public Administration Review,* 32 (March/April 1972), 97–126.

Nigro, Felix A., and Lloyd G. Nigro. *The New Public Personnel Administration.* Itasca, Ill.: Peacock, 1976.

Peirce, Neal R. "Employment Report/Public Employee Unions Show Rise in Membership, Militancy," *National Journal,* 7 (August 30, 1975), 1239–1249.

Rinehart, Jeffrey C., and E. Lee Bernick. "Political Attitudes and Behavior Patterns of Federal Civil Servants," *Public Administration Review,* 35 (November/December 1975), 603–611.

Stahl, O. Glenn. *Public Personnel Administration,* 7th ed. New York: Harper & Row, 1976.

"What's Wrong with the Civil Service," *The Washington Monthly,* 9 (April 1977), 50–61.

CHAPTER 10
Government Budgeting

Budgeting in the public sector is a process central to politics, particularly to administrative politics and the operation of government agencies and programs. From a practical standpoint, it is the major formal mechanism through which necessary resources are obtained. In one sense, it is the culmination of other assertions of influence, a major point at which political influence really comes into play and makes a crucial difference to the welfare of an agency. From a theoretical standpoint, budgeting represents a formalized process of allocating resources, of deciding who gets what, when, and how—two essential definitions of politics itself (see chapter 1). It is something of a crossroads in the political process, where all the forces in the political arena converge around one of the most important recurring questions in government: how resources are acquired, and in what quantities.

A number of fiscal, and other, purposes can be served through budgeting, some or all of them simultaneously. At its simplest, a budget can be a device for counting and recording income and expenditures, though this is a minimal purpose. It may not even be appropriate to label such a document as a budget; perhaps "ledger" is better. Budgeting, however, does include this accounting and tabulating purpose. Another function of budgeting is to generate a statement of financial intent, constructed on the basis of anticipated income and "outgo." A closely related function is to indicate programmatic intent, showing both preferences and, more important, priorities in deciding what to do with funds available. This suggests still another function of budgets, intentional or not: they reflect the political priorities of those who formulated and/or approved them.

A government budget—and, in principle, other budgets as well—may be read as something of an index to relative distribution of power in the political and economic system in which the budget was enacted,[1] by examining both how it was made up and what resources were distributed to different participants within that system. This is true whether we are speaking of university decisions to allocate a certain amount for academic scholarships or more faculty, or of national government appropriations for the Pentagon's latest weapons systems. Budgets represent decisions to spend money in certain ways, in preference to others, and such decisions do not just "happen." They are made through a political process in which power is crucial to success.

Foundations of Modern Government Budgeting

Prior to the Civil War, budgeting was rather informal and routine at all levels of government. The national budget was fairly small, amounting to some $63 million in 1860, though it rose sharply during the Civil War and never returned to that modest level.[2] The budgetary process was highly fragmented, with little systematic direction. Beginning with the presidency of Thomas Jefferson, agencies seeking funds dealt more or less on their own with congressional committees having jurisdiction over their respective operations. The president had no authority to amend agency requests and no institutional means of influencing the formulation of requests. Congress made its appropriations very detailed, both to control executive discretion to transfer funds from one appropriation account to another, and to keep spending within appropriations limits.[3]

Starting with the Civil War, some important long-term changes began to affect numerous government practices, and the framework of a truly national economy slowly took shape. The war itself was a watershed in the course of national-state relations, as well as in development of the presidency as a predominant force in national politics. During the 1870s and later, three general patterns of governmental behavior became more prominent—patterns which were to have implications for the rise of the modern budgetary process.

The first of these was growth of the national government's authority with respect to monitoring and regulating the expanding industrial economy, and exercising the war power and related prerogatives in foreign affairs and policy making (especially by the president). At the same time, the tax power was used to a greater degree than ever before. The regulatory power, given institutional form for the first time with creation of the Interstate Commerce Commission (ICC) in 1887, represented a governmental response to the industrial revolution and to emergence of powerful private economic interests. The war power was exercised most visibly in the Civil War and in the Spanish-American War, and U.S. diplomatic involvement was clearly on the rise as well. The tax power was expanded by successful amending of the Constitution in 1913, permitting a graduated income tax. These developments clearly enhanced the general position of the national government.

The second pattern—government involvement in the private economy—meant more than simply regulating the flow of commerce.

Starting in 1864, when the National Banking Act created a single, unified banking system as another step toward a national economy, the government's role in monetary and financial affairs became more regularized. Equally important, the way was paved for further expansion of governmental activity, which in this century has come to include not only increasing regulation of private economic enterprise, but also participation in planning and managing various public enterprises affecting, more or less directly, the course of the national economy.

Two dimensions of government policy have been important in this connection: (1) *monetary policy,* under which the government can influence the economy by regulating the supply of money released into circulation by the Federal Reserve Board (under terms of the Federal Reserve Act of 1913) and by regulating interest rates; and (2) *fiscal policy*—that is, deliberate choices in government spending made in order to accomplish specific economic objectives. Since 1933 and the New Deal, fiscal policy has been the predominant instrument of the national government in influencing the economy, one that presidents of both parties have not hesitated to use when it has suited their economic and political purposes. That being the case, it is not hard to see how budgetary processes and their substantive outcomes have grown in importance, since their consequences now reach far beyond the government itself.

The third pattern was growth in presidential strength and influence, beginning in the last half of the nineteenth century and continuing to the present. As noted in chapter 4, recurrent crisis was a contributing factor in the growth of presidential power. The first enthusiastically activist president was Theodore Roosevelt. Others after him, notably Woodrow Wilson and especially Franklin Roosevelt, made even more dramatic and significant changes in the presidential role. Truman, Kennedy, Johnson, and Nixon all actively supported expansion of presidential prerogatives, albeit for widely varying purposes, and Dwight Eisenhower—though not associated with an activist view of the office—presided over a fairly rapid expansion of the role of the executive branch, generally, and he did little to roll back changes made before he took office. Action by Congress delegating discretionary authority to the president was a recurring feature of these years. Gerald Ford and Jimmy Carter have exercised presidential prerogatives a bit more cautiously, in view of the public's reaction to Watergate, but the office itself remains very strong.

Taken together, these three patterns had several important consequences in the development of modern budgetary practice. First, they raised the stakes of government budgetary decision making by increasing the scope and economic impact of such decisions, and the political interests affected as a result. Second, they created both the possibility and necessity of more effectively coordinating scattered spending activities of the national government—possibility, because of growing capabilities of the presidential office; necessity, because expenditures were rising and some centralization of control seemed appropriate. Third, they prompted the first stirrings of budgetary reform in the early 1900s, which pointed the way toward the assumptions, purposes, and practices of contemporary budgeting. Primary among these was the concept of the *executive budget,* with the chief executive placed in charge of developing and coordinating budget proposals for the entire executive branch prior to their presentation to the legislature.

Government Budgets and Fiscal Policy

Economist Jesse Burkhead has noted the potential importance of government budgets as instruments for managing national economies, pointing out that a budget's impact will depend on the relative importance of the public sector in the total economic picture and on "prevailing attitudes toward the role and responsibility of government."[4] The budget can be regarded as a "tool of *fiscal policy,* that is, as an instrument for consciously influencing the economic life of a nation."[5] Different governments regard this potential budgetary role quite differently. For example, our national government's budget is now consciously shaped with its impact on economic activity firmly fixed as one of its major purposes, while in state and local governments it is rare indeed to find budgets constructed with that same goal in mind. Similarly, the extent to which national budgets in other countries are treated as tools of fiscal policy varies widely. As Burkhead (and we) use the term, fiscal policy refers to government actions aimed at development and stabilization of the private economy— specifically, taxation and tax policy, expenditures, and management of the national debt. Related to fiscal policy—and, ideally, fully coordinated with it—are monetary and credit controls. We shall briefly examine these tools and relate them to the budget process, relying largely on Burkhead's analysis.

Fiscal Policy Tools

Traditionally, *taxation* was viewed simply as a means of raising government revenue and very little more. For the past forty to fifty years, however, taxation and tax policy have also been used to influence the volume of spending by private citizens and organizations. Raising taxes has at times been a weapon against inflationary spending, since it reduces the amount of disposable personal income; conversely, reducing taxes has been viewed as one means of boosting consumer spending. Such policy was relatively clear-cut until the recent wave of worldwide inflation-recession, which seemed to violate the economic principle that *either* inflation *or* recession could cause problems for a national economy, but not both at once. Reducing taxes, for example, to "spend our way out of recession" works very nicely, assuming that such spending will not trigger an inflationary spiral. But if any significant increase in spending is inflationary, then the old rules do not work any more, and tax policy will be decided more on political grounds. The uncertain condition of the economy has clearly raised new questions about how to use tax policy as an instrument of economic management.

As with tax policy, there has been a fundamental change in attitude toward *government expenditures.* The traditional view was that as government spent money, the sums expended were a replacement for private-sector spending, representing a "last resort" action when the private sector could not carry on whatever activities the money paid for. Now, however, the government's spending practices are seen as an essential part of total spending for goods and services, and as having major impact on private-sector expenditures.

As an example, governmental decisions to close or not to close several large military installations in 1975 and 1976—the Boston Navy Yard and the Frankford Arsenal in Philadelphia, for example—carried with them crucial economic implications for those communities and others like them. When the installations were opened, there had been an infusion of new dollars into the local (and state) economies in the form of a *multiplier,* or "ripple effect,"[6] boosting demand for goods and services, increasing tax revenues in all taxing jurisdictions (both state and local), and in general strengthening the localities' financial bases because of new jobs created and increased population. The outcry from local politicians and civic leaders, state officials, and members of Congress from the affected areas was ample testimony that they understood what the impact would be if the installations were closed—that is, a negative "ripple effect." Similar government decisions have the same kinds of wide-ranging economic impacts.

Political influence over such decisions can be valuable to a local community. One classic illustration is Charleston, South Carolina, which benefited hugely from the flow of federal dollars while Representative L. Mendel Rivers, from a district in Charleston, was chairman of the House Armed Services Committee. Another example is the NASA Space Center in Houston—rather far removed from Cape Canaveral in Florida—which was placed in the Texas city during a time when Representative Olin Teague of Texas was chairman of two House subcommittees—Manned Spaceflight and NASA Oversight—and Representative Albert Thomas (from Houston) was chairman of the Independent Offices subcommittee of the House Appropriations Committee, which had jurisdiction over NASA appropriations. No mere coincidence there!

A third fiscal policy tool is *management of the national debt.* Sale of government bonds and other obligations took on fiscal policy overtones only during World War II, when sale of war bonds was touted as another means of holding down consumer spending for scarce goods and services. In selling bonds, "a government changes the composition of privately held assets—converts private assets from money to bonds."[7] This has an impact, though indirect, on the amount and composition of private holdings and on income and spending rates. Furthermore, in recent years government borrowing to finance ongoing and new programs has become a political issue, with many arguing that the national debt ceiling should not be raised any further and that government spending should be reduced. One school of thought holds that large public debt is a cause of inflation; that alone casts questions about existing debt into a political setting. At state and local levels, in contrast, questions concerning debt management rarely arise, since many state constitutions require both state and local governments to operate with balanced budgets.

Monetary and Credit Controls

Monetary controls are ordinarily exercised in three forms by the government. First, the Board of Governors of the Federal Reserve System regulates the supply of money released into circulation. Restricting the money supply has been used to restrain inflation; increasing the supply, to stimulate economic activity. Second, interest rates are subject to regulation, and, as we have seen in recent times, the "prime lending rates" which banks make available to their prime borrowers have a lot to do with business investment, home construction, and financing of home mortgages. Third, government loan programs make a crucial difference in a wide range of activities—crop and seed loans for farmers, disaster loans for victims of flooding and the like, VA and FHA loans for buying or building a house, NDEA loans for college students. Loans are controlled in part by the budgetary process, in the form of initial appropriations and of yearly expenses to continue operation of loan programs.

Economic Coordination

Underlying all goverment activity to influence the private economy is public acceptance, in principle, of governmental responsibility for economic stability and central coordination of policies directed toward broad economic (and socioeconomic) goals. The national government's role in this respect gained wide—though far from universal—acceptance during the Great Depression years and after, marked particularly by passage of the Employment Act of 1946 to combat the postwar recession. This act made promoting maximum employment, production, and purchasing power an ongoing governmental commitment. In addition, the act established the president's Council of Economic Advisors (CEA), discussed in chapter 1. These steps were important both in themselves and as indicators of likely governmental responses to subsequent economic crises.

Central economic coordination has come to mean a considerable, perhaps dominant, role for the president, both in determining the existence of crisis conditions and in directing governmental response to a crisis. Perhaps the most significant step in this respect during the past decade was enactment of the Economic Stabilization Act of 1970, the statutory basis for Richard Nixon's move in August 1971 to impose a ninety-day freeze on prices, rents, wages, and salaries. This intricate and comprehensive program marked "a watershed in economic policy, placing the federal government in *direct control of the economy*, as distinguished from the more indirect methods utilized in fiscal and monetary policy."[8]

In 1974 Gerald Ford added another coordinative instrument to the president's arsenal, the Economic Policy Board (EPB). The EPB, and particularly its nine-member executive committee, served as "the central clearinghouse for Presidential policy on all economic and financial matters, a broad range that cuts across spending, taxes, agriculture, labor, business, and international economic issues."[9] Arthur Burns, former chairman of the Federal Reserve Board, called the EPB "the best system for coordinating economic policy he had seen since he had been in government,"[10] dating back to the Eisenhower administration, when Burns was chairman of the Council of Economic Advisors. Though not very widely known, the EPB rather rapidly became a focal point of economic policy development. As part of a White House reorganization, however, Jimmy Carter abolished the EPB in 1977.

In sum, we now have not only a "mixed economy" in which the public and private sectors overlap considerably, but also a mixed set of economic controls available to the national government with vast potential for influencing decisively virtually every kind of economic activity.

Links to Government Budgeting

All federal government instruments to influence the national economy as well as state and local economies are connected to budgeting directly or indirectly. Debt management as well as monetary and credit controls have only incidental relationship to the budgetary process—the former in that debates over budget allocations may hinge in part on whether adequate revenues are available to finance proposed programs without increasing the debt, the latter in that appropriations are needed to pay expenses of ongoing loan programs. Of much more direct consequence to budgeting are tax policy, expenditures, and economic coordination.

Tax policy obviously influences how much revenue is available to disburse in government programs. Tax decisions, however, are normally made outside the direct focus of budget making, and involve a somewhat different set of participants both on Capitol Hill—the House Ways and Means Committee and the Senate Finance Committee, primarily—and in the executive branch. Tax policy impacts on the taxpayer, while significant, lacked any direct relation to the federal government's budget until the mid-1970s.

Expenditure policy *is* budget making when all is said and done. The effects on the national economy of government spending decisions can be very dramatic—as in the case of federal installations—or hardly visible. But large or small individually, their cumulative consequences act to shape or reshape economic activity in significant ways. A case can be made for the position that the federal budget is as important for its effects on the nation's economy as for how it affects the operations of government agencies funded through direct budgetary allocations.

Finally, economic coordination in the broad sense is tied closely to budget making, since the budget is a major instrument of government— especially presidential—economic policies. The budget is related to economic coordination not only because it reflects chosen courses of action in existing fiscal policy, but also because it can be a major battleground in determining the shape of that policy, and consequently economic activity in both public and private sectors. This is why the budgetary process is so heavily laden with political conflict: control over the content of budgets means the ability to allocate resources to some and not others. The president has other means at his disposal to use in economic coordination, but the federal budget remains an instrument of the highest importance.

Budget Making in the Executive Branch

The rising importance of the executive budget has been a hallmark of American national politics throughout this century. As the federal budget became an instrument of national economic policy, it became steadily more important to have a central budget mechanism that could respond to changing economic conditions and needs. Various efforts at reforming the executive budget have been made, dating from the early 1900s. Budget reform, in fact, has been a recurrent theme, at first stressing control of expenditures, then performance measures aimed at improving program adequacy. Prior to 1960 these two emphases dominated the reform movement.

The first actions for budget reform were taken at the local level as part of a larger movement for general local government reform, including especially the drive to establish the city-manager form of government.[11] By the mid-1920s, most major American cities had adopted some form of budgeting system, in most cases strengthening the chief executive's budgetary role. At the state level a strong movement for reform was under way between 1910 and 1920, centering on making "the executive accountable by first giving him authority over the executive branch."[12] By 1920 budget reform had occurred to some extent in forty-four of the (then) forty-eight states, and by 1929 all the states had central budget offices.

Action was also being taken at the national level throughout this same period, triggered by President William Howard Taft's Commission on Economy and Efficiency, which was established in 1909 and made its final report to the president three years later. That report recommended that a budgetary process be instituted under direction of the president, a proposal greeted by considerable skepticism from those who feared any such grant of authority to the chief executive. One who felt that way was Woodrow Wilson, who as president vetoed legislation in 1920 that would have set up a Bureau of the Budget in the executive branch and a General Accounting Office as an arm of Congress. One year later, President Warren Harding signed virtually identical legislation into law, and a formalized executive budget system was instituted. The 1921 act vested in the president "sole authority to consolidate agency budget requests and to present to Congress an overall recommendation."[13]

The central purpose in all these developments was control of expenditures, with emphasis on accounting for all money spent in public programs. This emphasis on budgetary control was the first modern budget concept to gain currency, and it remained the predominant approach to budgeting through the mid-1930s. In this period budgets were constructed on a *line-item,* or *object-of-expenditure,* basis, indicating very specifically items or services purchased and their costs. "The hallmark of control was the detailed itemization of expenses, by means of which central supervision was maintained over purchasing and hiring practices, and agency spending was closely monitored."[14] The focus was on *how much* each agency acquired and spent, with an eye to completeness and honesty in fiscal accounting.

The next broad phase of reform involved a conceptual change that brought about further structural adjustment. Beginning with the New Deal, when management of national government programs became centrally important, the line-item budget went into something of a decline, to be replaced by a managerial concept which came to be known as *performance budgeting.* Performance budgeting differed from the previous control orientation in several ways. First, it was directed toward promoting effective management. Second, it dealt not only with the quantity of resources each agency acquired, but also—more important— *what was done* with those resources. Third, it called for "redesign of expenditure accounts, the development of work and cost measures, and adjustments in the roles of central budgeters and in their relationships with agencies."[15]

Performance budgeting demanded a greater degree of centralized coordination and control. In that connection, the Bureau of the Budget

(BOB) was transferred from the Treasury Department, where it had been lodged by the Budgeting and Accounting Act of 1921, to the newly established Executive Office of the President (EXOP) in 1939. (EXOP was itself a product of the movement for consolidation of executive control over administrative activities.) Ironically, under performance budgeting procedures, control and planning functions were dispersed to agency heads rather than being retained in BOB. Alleged agency failures to maintain control and to plan adequately for future activities later led to proposals for centralization of these functions within BOB.

During the performance budgeting era, which spanned approximately twenty-five years (1935–1960), there were a number of noteworthy developments contributing to more systematic executive budget making. The major one was World War II, during which both presidential powers and the scope of the federal budget expanded markedly. In 1940 the total federal budget was just over $9 billion; only five years later it was nearly $98.5 billion, or roughly eleven times as large. As happened following the Civil War, the budget total dropped sharply after its wartime peak, but it remained substantially higher than prewar levels.[16] A second step was enactment of the Employment Act of 1946, discussed previously, which signaled governmental intent to utilize fiscal policy and economic planning to an unprecedented degree. A third development at about the same time was the first Hoover Commission's report to President Truman in 1949 on improving federal government management practices. The report made clear that performance budgeting was more coherent and illuminating than line-item budgeting, indicating more clearly what agencies were actually doing. The report also recommended expansion of BOB's role in budget and management coordination, again emphasizing growing presidential influence in both aspects of administrative operations.

In 1950 Congress passed the Budget and Accounting Procedures Act, which mandated performance budgeting for the entire national government. Aiming at developing work-load and unit-cost measures of activities, it appeared to do much more than simply control and record aggregate expenditures. But as it turned out, though performance budgeting was very good at measuring *efficiency* of government programs, it did little or nothing to measure *effectiveness*. "The efficiency of a school district, for instance, might be measured in terms of the cost per student, but the effectiveness might be measured by whether graduates can read and write, are accepted into universities, or obtain and retain well-paying jobs."[17] The difference is between assessing programs in terms of their operations as such, and assessing them in terms of end-products, the results and impacts, of program activities. Nowhere was this difficulty more pronounced than in the Defense Department, where, for example, data on training soldiers expressed in per-unit cost told little about whether the "right" things were being taught or the "right" number of soldiers were in training.[18] Little wonder, then, that the next movement for executive budget reform centered on the Defense Department. We will take up that phase of reform—known as planning-programming-budgeting systems (PPBS)—following a review of the budget-making process.

The Process of Budget Making

The Constitution vests the "power of the purse" in the legislative branch, a pattern repeated in all state and local governments, and that power has been jealously guarded over the years. Conflict between executive and legislature over spending purposes and control of expenditures is frequent and quite often intense. But the conflict is as much a product of the way Congress itself is organized to review the budget as it is an inherent aspect of a separation-of-powers system. Much of this discussion applies to state government as well.

Nowhere does the fragmented nature of American political decision making have more of an impact on the complexity of the process than in budget making.[19] In addition to institutional conflict between president and Congress, the House and Senate often treat legislation, including money bills, differently. Committees within the two chambers guard *their* respective jurisdictions and are sensitive to any perceived "invasion of their turf" or prerogatives. In addition, revenue and spending bills are handled by different committees on both sides of Capitol Hill: tax bills are handled by the House Ways and Means Committee and the Senate Finance Committee; appropriations bills, by the respective Appropriations Committees. What results is an imperfect look, at best, at how expenditures and revenues are related over time. This is made more complicated by the fact that in any given fiscal year, perhaps 70 percent of expenditures result from new obligational authority (NOA) to spend money, with the remaining 30 percent paying for obligations incurred in earlier years. In sum, federal budget making is characterized by both institutional and political fragmentation, opening the way for influence to be exerted at multiple points during the process—a system that virtually requires compromise as the ultimate basis for most budgetary decisions.

The national government budgets on an *annual* (twelve-month) basis for the most part, though some funds are allocated over multiyear periods. The budget covers a *fiscal* year rather than the calendar year that runs from January 1 to December 31; presently the federal fiscal year runs from October 1 to September 30. (In many state and local governments, the fiscal year begins on some other date, most commonly July 1.) Each stage of budget making is predominantly under auspices of either the executive or legislative branch, though few functions in budgeting are *exclusively* the responsibility of either one. In addition, because budget making for a given fiscal year begins before the year's start and continues after it ends, budgeting is an ongoing process, with budgets of as many as four fiscal years commanding attention at any given time.

The federal budget progresses through five broad stages. In sequence, they are (1) *preparation*, which is almost wholly internal to the executive branch; (2) *authorization*, principally a function of Congress; (3) *appropriations*, a legislative function; (4) *execution* (implementation), mainly—but by no means entirely—an executive function; and (5) *audit*, carried out by both legislative and executive entities, but ordinarily independently of one another. We will examine each of these budgeting stages more closely.

OMB and Budget Preparation

Preparation of the budget begins when the Office of Management and Budget (OMB),[20] having made some preliminary economic studies and fiscal projections, sends out a "call for estimates" to all executive agencies. This occurs some fifteen to nineteen months before the fiscal year begins—that is, in late spring of the previous calendar year. The call for estimates is a request for agencies to assemble and forward to OMB their projections as to funding they will need for ongoing and new programs in that fiscal year. This requires heads of agencies and of their subordinate units to develop program and fiscal data which make it possible to formulate an estimate of overall agency needs. This information is sent on to OMB together with supporting memoranda and analytic studies, especially with regard to proposals for new or expanded programs.

OMB next calls on individuals bearing the title of "budget examiner," about 300 in all, each one of whom is assigned on a regular basis to an agency or agencies for the purpose of becoming thoroughly acquainted with agency activities and expenditure needs. The examiners are, in effect, OMB's "field workers," holding hearings with agency representatives on programmatic, management, and budget questions.[21] The agency's representatives normally include unit heads and agency budget officers, though others may be included. While budget examiners work regularly *with* agencies, they most definitely work *for* OMB; their job is to probe and question every major expenditure proposal which agency leaders have felt worthwhile enough to include in a budget estimate.

When this process is completed, the examiners make their recommendations to OMB. In the meantime, the director of OMB and the president work out general budget policy, major program issues, budgetary ceilings, and other fiscal projections, ultimately developing ceilings for each agency. The examiners' recommendations are incorporated into reviews of each agency's estimates, and are often the basis for revision ordered by OMB. After a process that usually takes from four to six months, original agency estimates are generally trimmed somewhat, and all agency requests are assembled into a single budget document running to several hundred pages. This becomes the president's budget message, which is submitted to Capitol Hill shortly after the first of the (calendar) year.

Congress and Authorization

The authorization stage[22] involves congressional determination of maximum spending levels for each program approved by Congress. This is the responsibility initially of subject-matter standing committees in each chamber, such as the Senate Committee on Banking, Housing, and Urban Affairs, and the House Committee on International Relations. The committees make recommendations to the full chambers for the agencies under their respective jurisdictions. After chamber approval a bill is normally considered by a House-Senate conference committee, which irons out differences in amounts authorized by each chamber. Assuming that agreement is reached (which is almost always the case), the authorization bills are forwarded to the president for his signature.

Appropriations Politics in Congress

The appropriations stage is one of the most crucial to budget making. "Appropriations, as distinguished from authorizations, grant the money to spend or [the power] to incur financial obligations, and the Appropriations Committees in the two houses play the major role in this phase of the budgetary process."[23] According to existing rules of procedure, no appropriation may be voted until after an authorization has been approved for a particular program. But it has been known to happen otherwise. Reporter John Hart of "NBC-TV News" reported in late June of 1977 that the House had appropriated funds for development of the controversial neutron bomb—a weapon said to kill by radiation without destroying neighboring populations or property—before any formal authorization had been made. It was a bomb, some said, that nobody knew we had, and the appropriation had been "buried" in a $10.4-billion water, power, and energy research appropriation bill.[24] This can work the other way as well: some substantive legislation leaves the Appropriations Committees little discretion on spending matters and sometimes bypasses the appropriations process altogether. This practice has come to be known as "back-door financing," and not surprisingly it is a source of considerable irritation to members of the House and Senate Appropriations Committees.

The House of Representatives is the first stop for all money bills—by tradition in the case of spending bills, and by constitutional requirement in the case of tax proposals—and the House Appropriations Committee (HAC) has wielded tremendous influence over the federal budget for quite a number of years. Political scientist Richard Fenno, in appraising both chambers' committees on appropriations, has said that the House committee, rather than its Senate counterpart, "dominates appropriations politics in Congress."[25] The HAC, numbering fifty-five members, is the largest committee on Capitol Hill, containing more than one-eighth of the total House membership of 435; perhaps more important, it contains one-fourth of the number needed to pass legislation in that chamber (218, assuming everyone votes).

Fenno's classic study of HAC[26] focused on how committee members defined their roles and the role of the committee, and the relationship between their self-perceptions and the success they enjoyed. He found one major substantive norm, or role, and three procedural norms which loomed large in committee operations. The committee's principal role, as defined by its members, was that of "guardian of the Treasury," as if all other participants in budget making—agencies, OMB, the president, even (perhaps especially) the Senate—were the worst kind of free-wheeling, profligate spenders. A virtual motto of committee members was "there's no budget that can't be cut." Procedurally, Fenno found the committee members followed the norms of unity, specialization, and reciprocity. These norms facilitated completion of committee tasks by use of agreed-upon paths of action, while making it possible for members to remain united in defense of committee decisions after the hard deliberations were concluded. By following these norms the committee was able to maximize its influence—and its power—in appropriations decisions.

Unity meant that within the committee's executive (closed) sessions, and within each subcommittee, there could be as much argument and disagreement as time—and diplomacy—allowed, but when decisions were made and it was time to go before the full House, all the members stood as one. This made it very difficult for outsiders to find support for alternative points of view, thus reinforcing committee or subcommittee influence. Fenno found that during the period 1947–1957, 132 out of 141 committee reports—that is, recommendations on appropriations to the full House—were unanimous, with no minority reports filed, reflecting the members' belief that "the greater their internal unity, the greater the likelihood that their recommendations will pass the House."[27]

Specialization, a practice of no little importance in the Congress generally, was particularly emphasized in HAC. Since its subject-matter subcommittees were largely autonomous in their deliberations, it was considered obligatory for every member to become a specialist in the area dealt with by the subcommittee on which he or she served. This promoted two positive objectives: (1) individual influence over a narrow area of policy, and (2) better guardianship of the Treasury, since specialists would be sufficiently familiar with their areas to screen budget requests intelligently.[28]

Reciprocity was closely related to both unity and specialization. It derived from specialization, because specialists could agree to defer to, and support, each other's judgments about recommended appropriations amounts. In practice, members of subcommittees were given virtually a free hand to make recommendations in their respective areas, as long as they in turn respected decisions made by other subcommittees. For that to work, of course, subcommittee members had to remain united. But if it did work, then the committee as a whole was able to present that all-important united front to the full House of Representatives.

A different pattern characterizes Senate action. The Senate Appropriations Committee usually acts as a sort of "court of appeals" for agencies seeking to have restored some or all of the funds cut out by the "guardians of the Treasury" over on the House side. Many times the Senate acts favorably on those pleas, raising funding levels and thereby necessitating a conference of senators and representatives to iron out differences. Conferees normally include the elected leaderships of the two chambers, the chairmen and ranking minority party members of the two Appropriations Committees, and other chairmen and minority members from committees with jurisdiction over the particular agencies affected. The agreed-upon compromise bill needs approval in both chambers (which is almost always routine) before it is sent to the president for his signature.

The budgetary process described here is, as indicated previously, highly fragmented. As Aaron Wildavsky has assessed it, it is also incremental, specialized, conducted with an eye to past budget allocations for the same program or agency, and approached (at least in the House Appropriations Committee) with a primary concern for making "marginal, monetary adjustments to existing programs so that the question of the ultimate desirability of most programs arises only once in a while."[29] A very important feature is the pattern of regarding the previous year's allocation as the "base" for each appropriations process. Most decisions have revolved around what increase over the base amount should be allocated. Thus, budget formation as viewed from both the executive branch and Congress has involved a vast series of rather narrow decisions, focusing on individual programs within individual agencies and only occasionally being reviewed in its totality—and then usually on the expenditure side only. Prior to the mid-1970s, the closest thing to a comprehensive budget review came during OMB's assembling of executive budget proposals before they were sent to the Capitol. But once that was done, OMB officials had no further part in defending the requests—agencies were on their own—and specialized consideration of specialized requests was not only the rule, it was nearly universal.

Execution of the Budget

Budget execution is the process of spending money appropriated by Congress and approved by the president. As a process it is indistinguishable from administering the programs the funds support. Money is apportioned from the Treasury, covering three-month periods beginning October 1, January 1, April 1, and July 1. Spending of funds is monitored by an agency's leadership, OMB, standing committees of Congress with jurisdiction over the agencies, and (periodically) the General Accounting Office (GAO), the auditing and investigative arm of Congress.

Two procedural elements resulting from this quarterly apportionment arrangement should be noted. First, most agencies will try not to spend all their quarterly allotment in that quarter, in order to maintain something in reserve—for emergencies, unforeseen expenses, or simply because costs are higher during some parts of the year than others. (For example, the National Park Service's expenses in the spring and summer are far greater than during the dead of winter.) In the last quarter of the fiscal year, however, this reserve buildup can lead to a strange phenomenon. Agencies do not want to turn money back to the Treasury at the end of the year; thus in the last few weeks they will attempt to spend all but a small portion of their quarterly allotment plus any reserve accumulated through the first three quarters. The reason for reluctance to return money to the Treasury is that agencies fear being told the next time they go before an appropriations subcommittee, ''Well, you didn't need all we gave you last year, so we'll just reduce your appropriation accordingly this year.'' Whether that *would* happen in every instance is not clear, but the fear is strong enough to produce behavior that is a bit surprising; one might think that agencies would be proud of demonstrating their concern for the tax-payer's dollar. But it is not to be, most times.

The other procedural element, which we shall discuss more fully shortly, is the possibility the chief executive might attempt to *impound* (withhold) some of the funds appropriated rather than approving each quarterly allocation. The reasons for doing so are varied, but in most cases *impoundment* is a last-ditch instrument of fiscal control for the chief executive. As we shall see, its legality has also been questioned.

Auditing the Budget

The audit stage really involves several functions divided among different auditors and carried out during different time periods. Informal audits are ongoing within agencies—they have to be to generate fiscal data necessary to demonstrate proper spending of funds and programmatic efficiency. Formal audits are under the direction, at various times, of agency auditors (or of private auditing firms with which agencies contract), OMB, and the GAO. In some states an Auditor General or Auditor of Accounts is responsible, full-time, for maintaining a check on expenditures of all agencies. Also, legislative oversight amounts to an ongoing informal legislative audit, though for somewhat different purposes—programmatic as well as expenditure control. A full-scale, formal, publicized audit indicates trouble for an agency, but otherwise auditing is routine—though no less important—for every agency.

In summarizing the five stages, it should be noted that at any given time, an agency head or budget officer can be giving attention to as many as four fiscal years. By way of illustration, in the late spring of 1977 (during the third quarter of fiscal 1977) routine audits of fiscal 1976 were nearing conclusion, expenditures in fiscal 1977 were well under way, budget submissions for fiscal 1978 had already occurred, and preliminary preparation of estimates for fiscal 1979 had begun. Another point worth noting is that despite some major modifications in budgetary procedures in the 1960s and 1970s—to be taken up in the following sections—much of what has been described here is still applicable to budget making. However, enough dissatisfaction with some of these arrangements developed in the late 1950s and early 1960s to bring about some changes intended to be fundamental. We shall focus on three major developments: (1) the executive budget tool known as PPBS, (2) debates about Congress's budgetary role and the steps taken toward revising it, and (3) growth of zero-base budgeting (ZBB) and "sunset" laws, which are the latest devices designed to control not only agency expenditures but also the operations, indeed perhaps the very existence, of agencies themselves.

The 1960s: PPBS

Planning-programming-budgeting systems (PPBS or, sometimes, PPB), was an instrument of budgeting designed to alter processes, outcomes, and impacts of government budgeting in significant ways.[30] As the label implies, it was aimed at improving the planning process in advance of program development and before budgetary allocations were made. It was designed also to allow budget decisions to be made on the basis of previously formulated plans.

Second, PPBS was intended to make programs, rather than agencies, the central focus of budget making. Incremental budgeting focused on programs to a degree, but there was no expectation or objective that called for choosing one and only one program of a particular type. By budgeting incrementally it was possible for two or more similar programs to be approved by Congress. PPBS was seen as a device for reducing duplicative and overlapping programs, but it was necessary to study programs more or less in isolation from their agency "homes" in order to select the optimum one.

Third, PPBS was designed to foster a budgetary process in which it was possible to relate budget decisions to broad national goals. In the words of one observer, "the determination of public objectives and programs became the key budget function."[31] Put another way, PPBS represented an effort to incorporate *rationality* in budgetary decision making, in place of existing (and well-entrenched) incrementalism. The language and logic of systems theory, systems analysis, and budgetary rationality were employed as part of the effort to introduce PPBS into federal (and some state and local) budget processes.

Fourth, PPBS was designed to make it possible to take account not only of agency resources and activities (as under line-item and performance budgeting), but also of actual external effects of those activities. To accomplish that, it was necessary to design new information systems and, more important, to obtain new and objective information that would demonstrate on a firm factual basis which programs were most likely to achieve their programmatic objectives. Part of this effort was directed toward identifying possible alternatives to existing programs which might be more effective. Systematically evaluating programs, and budgeting for them, in terms of their actual consequences had been suggested on occasion previously,[32] but it had never been tried in the federal budgetary process.

Finally, PPBS contained a distinct economics emphasis. Implementation of PPBS in budget formulation depended on the presence in the bureaucracy and in BOB (and later, OMB) of individuals skilled in economic analysis—specifically, cost-benefit analysis of federal programs. Furthermore, in assessing consequences of federal budget decisions, advocates of PPBS called for examination of their economic impacts on society.

PPBS was not a brand-new phenomenon at the time it was first introduced into the Defense Department in 1961. An early version of it had been utilized by the General Motors Corporation in the mid-1920s, and during World War II another version of it had been employed by the War Production Board in one of its programs. A turning point came in the 1950s when the RAND Corporation, an Air Force–sponsored "think tank" for defense planning, recommended "program packages" as the basic units of budgeting in Air Force planning.[33] It was not until 1961, however, that PPBS actually came to Washington under the stewardship of Defense Secretary Robert McNamara and Assistant Secretary Charles J. Hitch. The latter, formerly with the RAND Corporation, was instrumental in developing applications of systems analysis in planning and evaluating defense programs.

One other aspect of PPBS should also be noted. Though there is informed opinion to the contrary,[34] it seems apparent that to make PPBS work for the entire executive branch would require centralized control over composition of executive budget proposals, as well as over planning, determination, and evaluation of goals, and so on. This, in fact, was one of the arguments made in support of PPBS: that it would bring some coherence, consistency, and rationality into a budget picture that was said to be notably lacking in those characteristics. But depending on one's point of view, increased centralization could be an argument against PPBS as well—and, indeed, that argument was used during the early hectic days of the 1960s.

PPBS in the National Government

Shortly after John Kennedy's inauguration and Robert McNamara's appointment as defense secretary, PPBS was established in the Defense Department. In that setting, unlike most of the rest of the executive branch, it was not a major break with past practice; efforts to install performance budgeting, to make more informed choices, and to evaluate military operations more systematically had gone on for close to twenty years, at that point. Yet these efforts had not been successful. "The lack of clear-cut missions for the specific services intensified the need for a management approach that would consider the defense system as a whole."[35]

Other pressures also existed for tighter control over military budgets and programs: increasing costs of weapons systems, which made errors correspondingly more expensive; the greatly reduced lead time available to plan responses to new situations, owing to new weapons systems capable of striking in minutes, not weeks or months; and program needs determined only after dollar limits were placed on Pentagon spending. Secretary McNamara and other top aides sought to remedy this situation by linking planning with budgeting within the Pentagon; prior to that time they had been independent functions, managed by separate staffs. By firmly linking them, and by promoting use of a five-year defense plan, McNamara sought to organize all defense activities on a multiyear basis within a mission context, permitting incremental decision making but tying such decisions to clearly defined long-range program goals.

Lyndon Johnson, pleased with what he saw of PPBS in the Pentagon, ordered in August 1965 that it be applied to all civilian agencies. It was assumed—some say wrongly—that what worked in the Defense Department could be adapted for use elsewhere. The agencies were to submit to BOB, with their budget requests, a multiyear Program and Financial Plan (PFP); they were to request changes subsequently in the PFP through detailed Program Memoranda; and they were to support their documents with Special Analytic Studies—all of which were aimed at the same objectives of consistency and rationality that had been part of Pentagon budget changes four years before.

Expectations ran high for PPBS in its early stages. Some thought it would reform budgeting in the national government so as to bring about greater rationality, less "politics," better and more informed decisions, and so on. But for a variety of reasons, PPBS failed to gain a permanent place in federal budget making. That may be because expectations were inflated, or because PPBS was flawed, or because those who were to implement it were not sufficiently knowledgeable or motivated to make it work (and some actively resisted it). Most likely, all these explanations have some validity.

Several different kinds of problems plagued the effort to implement PPBS. Federal civilian agencies, for one thing, lacked the background in planning and analysis which the Pentagon had had prior to PPBS, and also lacked adequate staffing for planning and analysis; for them, the change was more of a revolution in management than it was for the Pentagon. Second, it proved far more difficult than anticipated for most civilian agencies to operationalize their program goals. Third, it turned out that what PPBS was, as a process, was not clear to many in the bureaucracy. Instead of serving as a decision framework within which incremental adjustments could be made without losing sight of broader objectives (a sort of "mixed scanning" model adapted to the budgetary process), what happened in many instances was that PPBS amounted to more analysis in budget making rather than a reformulation of the entire decision-making process. Finally, it was evident early on that BOB (and subsequently OMB) was not taking charge of government-wide development of PPBS (note the similarity to performance budgeting decentralization to the agencies). That being the case, PPBS came to mean different things in different agencies, with widely varying degrees of application, thoroughness, and effect.

There was one other major source of resistance to PPBS for much of this period: Congress, especially the Appropriations Committees. Members of Congress, who in some instances had spent years building up their contacts, understanding, and knowledge of agency budgets, were not favorably disposed toward a new budgeting system which in their view threatened to disrupt their channels of both information and influence. Even at its peak, budgets were not sent to Congress solely in the PPBS arrangement. Agencies and OMB were told to submit budgets in the old agency format as well as the new program format, and to indicate by means of a "crosswalk"—illustrated hypothetically in Figure 10–1— where an individual expenditure proposal fit into each. More important, Congress did not change its appropriations practices to accommodate PPBS. Many legislators regarded McNamara, Hitch, David Novick, and others at the Pentagon—the modern pioneers of PPBS—as "whiz kids," a label not meant to be complimentary. Also, Congress objected to the im-

Figure 10–1 The "Crosswalk" between Organization Structure and Program Structure

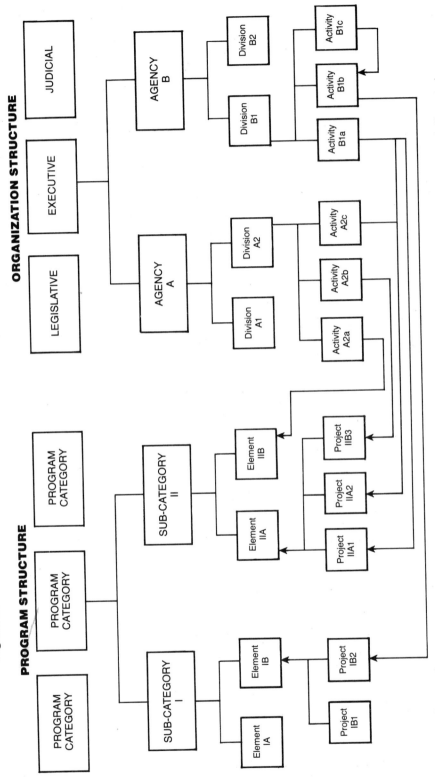

Source: Jack Rabin, "State and Local PPBS," in Robert T. Golembiewski and Jack Rabin, eds., *Public Budgeting and Finance: Readings in Theory and Practice*, 2nd ed. (Itasca, Ill.: Peacock, 1975), p. 437.

plication that it was up to the executive branch, by whatever method, to determine what the nation's programmatic goals were and what programs were satisfactorily directed toward achieving those goals. Finally, a Congress in which "political rationality" and political consequences of spending were at least as important as economic, cost-effectiveness criteria; where simplifying complex budget choices—rather than seeking comprehensive analyses of alternative courses of action—was a way of life; and where consensus and compromise were preferred to direct conflict over choices among alternatives, was not a Congress likely to be very receptive to a budget system seeming to stress the latter over the former in each case.[36]

The reaction to PPBS from different groups and coalitions in national politics varied according to its perceived impact on their success in securing budgetary resources. To the extent that PPBS strengthened objective assessment of budgetary requests without as much regard for political strength or weakness in the budgetary process, it posed something of a threat to those groups that were already strong. Conversely, it held out some hope for agencies and their constituencies which had previously lacked the strength to win some of their budget battles. One assessment of PPBS's failure to be sustained in the federal budget process suggests that "however ineffective, PPBS was *too* effective for the groups presently dominating the budgetary process."[37] It is a mark of their political strength that these groups (primarily dominant subsystems) succeeded in sharply limiting the impact—and the duration—of federal PPBS.

Budget expert Allen Schick wrote in 1973 that PPBS had not worked, and that in fact OMB had signaled its demise by lifting requirements for submission of PFPs, Program Memoranda, and Special Analytic Studies.[38] Schick did not say PPBS had had no impact on federal budgeting, but did say that it had not achieved its primary goal—"to recast federal budgeting from a repetitive process for financing permanent bureaucracies into an instrument for deciding the purposes and programs of government."[39] Schick attributed its failures to the following problems.

First, PPBS had been introduced into the bureaucracy across-the-board in 1965, without much advance preparation anywhere except in the Pentagon, where it had already been in use for four years. Second, those who pushed for its implementation were, in Schick's words, "arrogantly insensitive to budgetary traditions, institutional loyalties, and personal relationships."[40] Third, PPBS suffered from inadequate support and leadership at the very top, with woefully inadequate resources invested in its behalf. Fourth, good analysts and data were in short supply, and not enough time was allowed to close the gap. Fifth, PPBS ran roughshod over some important American political values, such as representation of diverse political interests and noncentralization of the decision-making process. Finally, PPBS did not work out because those already in charge of budget making were not willing to make so substantial and significant a switch, and those supporting PPBS could not overcome the resistance they met.[41]

Schick's catalogue of shortcomings should not be taken to mean that PPBS or its residual effects have totally disappeared, however. As John A. Worthley pointed out just over a year after Schick's "obituary" for PPBS appeared, much of the PPBS "package" may have been dismantled, but some components live on and in some cases are thriving. Worthley mentioned the following: (1) a basic focus on information, (2) concern with the impact of programs, (3) emphasis on goal definition, and (4) a planning perspective. Furthermore, Worthley suggests that the emphasis on rationality characteristic of PPBS may be a healthy counterweight to "less ordered techniques such as confrontation and participation" in policy making, and that government is strengthened by the interaction of both kinds of processes. Summing up, Worthley claims that PPBS "is alive and well, though it has new names and wardrobes."[42] He notes particularly that implementation of PPBS has gone forward in several states and a number of local governments, many of which tried it in the wake of the federal government experience. A brief look at state and local PPBS will help to round out the picture of this important budgetary phenomenon.

PPBS in State and Local Government

General budgetary development in state government prior to 1960 had followed roughly the same path as in the national government, but with some important differences. The major one was much later adoption of the executive budget concept, under which the governor is responsible for coordinating budget proposals from the executive branch to the state legislature.

Before 1947, the year the first Hoover Commission was established, virtually all the states had used a line-item budget approach, faithful to the control orientation of the previous thirty years.[43] In the wake of the commission's report, some states began moving toward performance budgeting, but unlike the national government, most tried to retain elements of the line-item approach as well. The result was what Schick has called the "hybridization" syndrome—mixed usage of line-item and performance budgeting, with some, but not all, the trappings of performance measurements. During the 1960s only twenty states included work-load data and only ten included per-unit cost data—both key measures of performance—in their budget documents. Hybridization "weakened the application, and complicated the study, of performance budgeting" in state government.[44]

Performance budgeting in the states seemed to be tied, in Schick's view, to the fate of administrative reorganization; when enthusiasm for that died down, the impulse to push for performance budgeting waned also. Neither governors, legislators, nor budget officers seemed particularly enthusiastic about performance budgeting, though in some instances their position was one of neutrality rather than of outright opposition. For that reason, some who wanted limited adaptation of performance budgeting were successful in bringing about small changes while potential opponents remained neutral. If they tried to go too far or too fast, however, opposition appeared, and in at least one state—Ohio—that opposition caused performance budgeting to be dropped altogether.[45]

Thus when efforts were made in the late 1960s to implement PPBS in state government, existing foundations of the budgetary process were rather different from those prevailing in the national government, making introduction of PPBS far more difficult. In addition, many state legislatures had few of the institutionalized procedures, norms, and expectations that characterized congressional appropriations. All in all, state budgetary processes were a great deal more routinized, less complex, and more predictable than was the national budget process.

It appears that the nature of state budgeting has been changed minimally, if at all, by the coming of PPBS. With a few notable exceptions—such as Pennsylvania, California, and Hawaii—efforts to incorporate PPBS (or an equivalent under some other name) have either been unsuccessful or limited in their practical impact. For the most part, PPBS has failed to penetrate decision-making arenas of state government.[46] One major consequence that PPBS *has* had is to facilitate efforts to finish installing performance budgeting, by providing more complete information about operations of state agencies. That represents, however, only a partial application of PPBS, since in most instances neither program units nor state objectives are a prominent part of the information systems. It appears that one reason for the slow, rather tentative movement toward PPBS in many states is that it is difficult to move from a "pre-performance budgeting situation" to PPBS.[47] Apparently, quite a few states stopped along the way and have never finished the job. A few which moved early to implement PPBS, such as New York, were also among the first to abandon it in the early 1970s in favor of some other (not dissimilar) planning-programming approach to budget making.

Two states with notable successes in incorporating PPBS are Hawaii and Pennsylvania. Hawaii is noteworthy not only for the extent of PPBS—it is the only state to have "fully incorporated PPB into its budget law and legislated the form in which PPB is to be developed"[48]—but also for the fact that the impetus for installing PPBS came from the state legislature, the only time that has happened. In Pennsylvania, PPBS took root after top state officials, including a new governor in 1967, became interested in its potential. The key to success in Pennsylvania apparently was that PPBS was not simply an "add-on" to existing budget arrangements; rather, it gradually replaced old budget forms and procedures. Most important, major budgetary decisions were made by using the new procedures instead of bypassing them, as happened in numerous other states. Under the direction of Professor Robert Mowitz of Penn State, Pennsylvania's PPBS system is now the most fully developed of any in the fifty states.[49]

At the local level, budget making has been highly varied, ranging from a fragmented and uncoordinated process in very bureaucratized settings (such as New York City) to a relatively simple and centralized procedure in smaller cities and towns. PPBS has been tried in some communities, but with very limited impact. The major effort to provide a focal point for state and local budget reform was the State-Local Finances Project of George Washington University, established in 1967. Nicknamed the "5-5-5" project because it included five states, five counties, and five cities, the project attempted to provide direct advisory assistance to participant governments and to serve as a nationwide clearinghouse for information pertaining to PPBS. Neither of these functions was fully carried out due to understaffing, but the symbolic importance of "5-5-5" as a rallying point had some impact. A 1968 survey taken under the auspices of the project indicated, however, that PPBS affected only a few city halls across the country, and not all the cities in the project had fully implemented PPBS.[50]

Only one major urban government—Philadelphia—has gone very far toward implementing PPBS with tangible effect. Local budget officials were instrumental in its introduction in December 1966, and "constant effort was made to gain and retain agency acceptance of the new system of budgeting. In fact, only after an agency had accepted the idea of budgeting by program structure were efforts made to introduce further PPBS procedures, such as cost-benefit analysis."[51] Philadelphia was also the first to have orientation programs for local officials. Agency cooperation was the key to successful implementation of PPBS in the Quaker City, and this cooperation has been attributed to several factors: making agency personnel, not the chief executive, responsible for introducing PPBS; gaining agency acceptance one step at a time for each component of the new procedure; and avoiding creation of a large new staff capability at the beginning, which enabled city officials to minimize interagency rivalry.[52]

PPBS, then, made quite a splash at the start of the 1960s, but its actual impacts at all three levels of government were a great deal more modest than some early claims for it might have suggested. With the coming of the 1970s, different sorts of concerns began to emerge which caused attention to shift away from PPBS as such and toward different issues in the budgetary process.

The 1970s: Ferment, Reform, and More Reform

Our discussion of the 1970s will concentrate on three areas. First, we shall examine the conflict between Richard Nixon and Congress over presidential impoundment of funds. Second, we will look at the new budgetary role of Congress in its efforts to establish and maintain a *legislative* budget. Third, we will consider the latest budgeting device—zero-base budgeting, or ZBB—which some say holds promise as an instrument of chief executive control over the operations, even the very existence, of government agencies.

President Versus Congress

The theme of Richard Nixon's presidency was a general moderating of certain government practices and policies, most notably government's expanding role in economic regulation and social programs. Fiscally conservative and regarded as moderate-to-conservative on social questions, Nixon not surprisingly tried to reduce spending—or at least the rate of increase in government expenditures—with emphasis on trimming programs established and/or expanded during the years of Lyndon Johnson's "Great Society." Trying to limit or undo some of the Johnson legacy brought Nixon into inevitable conflict with liberal (and other) Democrats in Congress and across the country, and with many in the bureaucracy (see chapter 7 for an account of how some HEW employees reacted). Vietnam was still a deeply divisive issue, campus disorders shocked the country, and civil rights issues had not exactly disappeared. Vice-President Agnew courted the "silent majority" and baited the press (which took the bait), thus opening up another battleground. All in all, political life in the nation's capital and elsewhere during Richard Nixon's first term was anything but tranquil.

Nowhere was the battle between president and Congress joined more vigorously or more significantly than in the fight over Nixon's efforts to restrain congressional spending by impounding funds after they had been authorized and appropriated. Impoundment is something of a "super item veto," not subject to a congressional override, as is the case with the formal veto power. Nixon was not the first president to impound funds. Indeed, the practice of establishing reserves or administratively withholding spending authority from some programs dated back at least a century. "What made the situation critical in the early 1970s (beyond the general political climate) was the number and magnitude of the funds impounded on the orders of the chief executive, especially funds for those programs that had grown out of the Great Society of the Johnson years."[53] The Nixon administration impounded increasing amounts of appropriated funding in this period, culminating in a total of about $15 billion in 1973.

Members of Congress, and others, complained about this practice in speeches and press releases. Some were moved to file suit against the president, claiming among other things that impoundment was not authorized by the Constitution and that, while precedents existed, these were not constitutionally sanctioned. In twenty-two separate court tests in 1973, Nixon won one and lost twenty-one.[54] The most dramatic of these involved funding for construction of a stretch of interstate highway in Missouri; seventeen of the (then) eighteen U.S. Senate committee chairmen joined in the suit as ''friends of the court''—a rare display of unity among those individuals. But Congress, growing increasingly impatient with lengthy court proceedings, took action early in 1974 to halt impoundment through statutory provision.

The Congressional Budget and Impoundment Control Act of 1974 abolished an earlier limited authorization for a president to withhold funds. It also sharply limited permissible grounds for deferring spending of appropriated funds, required positive action by both House and Senate to sustain an impoundment beyond a period of forty-five days, required monthly reports from either the president or comptroller-general (head of the GAO) on any deferred spending, and made it possible for the comptroller-general to go to court for an order to spend impounded funds in the event a president failed to comply with any of the preceding.[55] These provisions seemingly restored a considerable measure of congressional control over appropriation and expenditure of federal dollars. While Gerald Ford also engaged in some impounding, it was not on a scale to resemble that done by Richard Nixon. In the wake of Watergate, Ford had much higher political standing in Congress, and consequently the impoundment issue was much less controversial. With other developments in Congress's budgetary role, impoundment has moved off center stage as a key question in legislative-executive relations, but it remains to be seen whether it will crop up again despite efforts to settle it in 1974 and since.

Congress's New Budgetary Role

In the confrontation between President Nixon and Congress over impoundment, another crucial issue had been raised that was also dealt with in the 1974 legislation. That was whether Congress had the institutional capacity to monitor its own actions approving expenditures, and to put a brake on rising spending totals. Some observers believe the 1974 act was at least as important for the new congressional budgetary procedures it instituted as for the restrictions it established on presidential authority to impound funds.

The appropriations procedures previously followed, described earlier in this chapter, left Congress open to the kinds of criticisms Richard Nixon had found effective in justifying greater presidential impoundment authority to control federal spending: fragmented consideration of and action on the budget, failure to consider financial implications of future expenditure obligations, willingness to enact supplemental and deficiency appropriations, and so on.[56] In addition, two other factors had contributed to growing difficulties in maintaining control over expenditures.

First, very often a subsystem alliance—a program manager, an interested subcommittee chairman in either the standing committee or possibly the Appropriations Committee, and outside interest groups—united "to thwart the will of the President and of the Congress as a whole"[57] through its capacity to effectively control financing and administering of particular programs. Second, two of the most important norms discussed earlier in connection with the House Appropriations Committee—guardianship of the Treasury and reciprocity among members—were in noticeable decline during the 1960s and 1970s. In the past, Congress had "cut requests the President made on behalf of the spending agencies," but it gradually came to cut less, and less regularly, than it once had.[58] Appropriations subcommittees, well known for assuming that "there is no budget that can't be cut," were becoming more likely merely to "hold the line" at the level requested by the president than to assume that cuts would or should be made. Reciprocity, also, was waning. There was less willingness, generally, to defer to the judgments of specialized subcommittees, and in the appropriations process subcommittee and committee recommendations were being overturned on the floor of the House and Senate much more frequently—usually in the direction of higher, not lower, amounts.[59]

The combined effect of these changes was considerably higher appropriation levels in legislation passed by both House and Senate. More important, there was growing realization by observers in and out of Congress that little if any meaningful legislative control existed over the *totality* of the federal budget. No one argued that individual portions of the budget were outside the effective influence of individual substantive committees and subcommittees of Congress, but that was just the point: control was piecemeal and (again) fragmented, with few having any idea what "whole" was the end-product of the "parts." The 1974 Congressional Budget and Impoundment Control Act attempted to deal with these problems. The new budget procedures mandated by the act can be analyzed in five segments.[60]

First, each chamber established a Budget Committee—twenty-five members in the House, sixteen in the Senate—which would consider annual budgets in their entirety, not broken up for consideration as in the past. Committee membership, particularly in the House, overlapped with membership on the Appropriations and Ways and Means Committees (five from each of those committees serve on the House Budget Committee), thus insuring some integration of effort among those three key entities.

Second, the act established the Congressional Budget Office (CBO), with a professional staff and a director appointed jointly by the speaker of the House and the president pro tem of the Senate for a four-year term.

CBO was to assist the Budget Committees and Congress as a whole in analyzing and projecting from budgetary proposals. It was to serve both as a provider of "hard, practical economic and fiscal data from which to draft spending legislation," as the House wanted, and as something of a "think tank" with a more philosophical approach to spending and an interest in examining national priorities, thus satisfying the Senate.[61] Whether CBO has succeeded, or could have, in both endeavors is not clear. Some critics in Congress thought CBO should have been able to get itself organized and functioning more rapidly and effectively than they say it did.[62]

Third, the act established a procedure whereby Congress would enact at least two concurrent budget resolutions each year, one in the spring and the other in the fall, for purposes of setting maximum spending levels for itself during the appropriations process. The spring resolution (which must be approved by May 15) sets targets for spending, revenue, public debt, and the annual surplus or deficit, while the fall resolution (with a September 15 deadline) sets the final figures for each. Congress may enact more than two resolutions if it deems necessary, but revenue and expenditures must be in accord with whatever the last resolution provides.

Fourth, a new timetable was put into effect which added a step to the stages of the budget cycle described earlier (with the fiscal year beginning on October 1 instead of July 1). Table 10–1 outlines this new congressional budgetary timetable, and Figure 10–2 illustrates the major steps in the new budget process.

Fifth, most new "back-door" spending programs—authorization bills with mandated expenditures—have been placed under the appropriations process, thus extending congressional control of the budget even further, though by no means has back-door spending been eliminated.

Has the new budget procedure worked? Has it done what it was supposed to do? There appears to be some consensus that it has, although there have clearly been some problems. Compared to an earlier congressional attempt in the late 1940s to establish a legislative budget and a spending ceiling—an attempt which proved to be unwieldy and woefully understaffed—this effort has been a sparkling success.

The 1974 statute did nothing less than make it possible for Congress "to participate, on an equal footing with the President, in the formulation of national economic and fiscal policy."[63] It allowed Congress to establish its own budgetary priorities, set spending limits, and enforce restrictions on presidential impoundment. The key to its application—which was widely recognized when it was first passed—was whether Congress would be capable of the procedural and policy discipline the act required of it. The view from Washington, at least, is that Congress thus far has acquitted itself well.

TABLE 10–1
CONGRESSIONAL BUDGETARY TIMETABLE*

Action Required	Final Date	Explanation
President submits current services budget	Nov. 10	The "current services budget" indicates what would be necessary to maintain existing programs at current levels
Joint Economic Committee submits economic evaluation	Dec. 31	
President submits his budget	15th day after Congress meets	
Standing Committees, Joint Economic Committee, and Joint Committee on Internal Revenue Taxation submit reports to Budget Committees	Mar. 15	These reports recommend authorization levels; they represent the essential step added to the budget cycle
Congressional Budget Office submits report on fiscal policy and national budget priorities to Budget Committees	Apr. 1	
Budget Committees report first concurrent resolution to their Houses	Apr. 15	
Standing Committees report bills and resolutions authorizing new budget authority to full chambers	May 15	
Congress completes all action on first concurrent resolution	May 15	
Congress completes action on all bills and resolutions providing new budget and new spending authority	7th day after Labor Day	
Congress completes all action on second required concurrent resolution	Sept. 15	
Congress completes action on reconciliation bill or resolution, or both, implementing second required concurrent resolution	Sept. 25	Final spending recommendations must be reconciled with budget ceiling adopted in second concurrent resolution
Fiscal Year begins (beginning in 1976)	Oct. 1	

*In accordance with the Congressional Budget and Impoundment Control Act of 1974 (Public Law 93–344).
Source: Adapted from James J. Finley, "The 1974 Congressional Initiative in Budget Making," *Public Administration Review,* 35 (May/June 1975), p. 272.

Figure 10–2 Major Steps in the Budget Process

PERIOD BEFORE THE FISCAL YEAR

FISCAL YEAR

BEYOND FISCAL YEAR

MARCH   NOVEMBER   JANUARY   OCTOBER   SEPTEMBER 30   NOVEMBER 15

Formulation of president's budget
(beginning 19 months before fiscal year)[a]

Congressional budget process
including action on appropriations and
revenue measures (beginning 10½
months before fiscal year)[b]

Execution of enacted budget
(during fiscal year)

Final data available

[a] The president's budget is transmitted to Congress within fifteen days after Congress convenes.

[b] If appropriation action is not completed by September 30, Congress enacts temporary appropriation (i.e., continuing resolution).

Source: Executive Office of the President/Office of Management and Budget, January 1977.

A major factor in the success of the new procedures has been development by CBO of "objective, open, and timely cost analysis data on congressional legislation," thus contributing to a minimization of the "'budget numbers game' among the administration, agencies, lobbyists, and Hill staff that formerly accompanied legislative bargaining." [64] There has been some disagreement about CBO's data from time to time, but it certainly is an improvement over the fluid situation of the past, where whom to believe in forecasting or analysis was itself a big concern.

Another important factor has been effective monitoring by both Budget Committees and CBO of Congress's revenue and spending actions. "The Budget Committees, aided by the CBO, produced weekly scorekeeping reports from June through September [1976] to inform the members of how each spending or revenue bill reported by each committee compared with congressional budget targets [for that committee]." [65] The Budget Committees, through their initial responsibility for determining total federal revenues, the annual deficit, and level of the national debt, could also monitor broad-gauge effects of individual committee and floor actions, and duly inform the members. They were even successful in defeating a tax proposal favored by Senator Russell Long, the influential chairman of the Senate Finance Committee, because it would have fallen far short of the revenue target set by the two Budget Committees.

Other factors in this early record of success included the severe recession of 1974–1975, which coincided with the backlash (in Congress and in the country) against presidential excesses and the resulting opportunity for Congress to assert itself; general public concern over growth of government spending; partisan jockeying during an election year, especially in the wake of the presidential traumas of 1972–1974; provisions of the Budget Act itself which provided for adequate staff assistance, enforcement mechanisms for various deadlines in the new budget cycle, and structural coordination among key committees; the determined leadership of Budget Committee chairmen Brock Adams in the House and Edmund Muskie in the Senate; and a great deal of plain hard work by Budget Committee members in both chambers. [66]

Is there more to be done? It would seem so. Congress has yet to tackle the job of setting priorities with quite the same gusto as it did the issues involved in fiscal policy making. Also, there are twenty-three government-owned or -sponsored agencies which for various reasons are not included in the unified federal budget; some attention has already been given to their possible inclusion. There is renewed attention to so-called "uncontrollable" spending—federal outlays mandated under existing law that require no further action by Congress in each new fiscal year—for example, interest on the national debt, Social Security payments, unemployment insurance, farm price supports, and revenue-sharing. [67] In fiscal 1977 these "uncontrollables" amounted to approximately *75 percent* of all federal expenditures (compared to about 60 percent in fiscal 1967),[68] so that concern about them is surely warranted. Finally, more interest is being shown in zero-base budgeting as a device for bringing government spending under still firmer control.

Zero-Base Budgeting (ZBB) and "Sunset" Laws

Activities of government, in virtually every respect, have come under increasing pressure in the 1970s for a combination of reasons. Clearly, one reason is growing public restlessness about particular policy directions, such as the war in Vietnam, civil rights enforcement, and some regulatory activities of the national government. A second reason is the tightening fiscal crunch in which many governments, if not most, increasingly find themselves, necessitating a more careful choosing among competing interests of what will be funded and what will not be. Third, there has developed a general feeling, reflected in public opinion polls, that the public is not getting its money's worth from more costly government programs, and that a harder look needs to be taken at what is working and what isn't.

Problems of financing activities and evaluating their effectiveness are not confined to government. Business and industry also have had to confront these issues and try to deal with them. It is no accident that zero-base budgeting developed in industry during the same period when some in government—notably state government—were installing elements of it there. *Zero-base budgeting* (ZBB) got its start at Texas Instruments, Inc., under the guidance of Peter Pyhrr, who later helped implement it in Georgia during the administration of Governor Jimmy Carter (1971–1975). It is from this base that ZBB has been launched in about a dozen other states, numerous industries, some local governments, and (on a selective, trial basis) in the federal government. At the same time, so-called "sunset" laws, designed to require some kind of positive legislative action to continue government agencies in operation, have attracted increasing interest as another (and related) method of exerting meaningful control over government bureaucracies.[69]

ZBB involves three basic procedural elements within each administrative entity. The first is identification of "decision units," the lowest-level entities in a bureaucracy for which budgets are prepared—staffs, branches, programs, functions, even individual appropriations items. Second is analysis of these decision units and formulation of "decision packages" by an identifiable manager with authority to establish priorities and prepare budgets for all activities within the administrative entity. The analysis begins with basic questions about the consequences if the decision unit were eliminated (or given a "zero" dollar allocation) and about cost-effectiveness and efficiency of the unit, then proceeds to formulation of decision packages. The third procedural element is ranking of decision packages in an order from highest to lowest priority. Higher-level agency officials next establish priorities among all packages from all units, with the probable available funding in mind. The high-priority packages that can be funded within the probable total dollar allocation are then included in the agency budget request, and the others are dropped.[70]

An important aspect of the whole process is that each manager prepares several different decision packages pertaining to the same set of activities, so as to allow those conducting higher-level reviews to select from alternative sets of proposals for essentially the same program or function. Packages receive higher priority as their cost declines, again assuming the same activity or set of activities.[71]

ZBB as it has been put into operation in the private sector and in government has not had the effect of literally reducing budgetary allocations to zero before analysis of activities is begun, or of reallocating funds on a large scale from some policy areas to others.[72] While ideally it calls for reexamining every item in the budget periodically—every one, two, or five years, for example—realistically this would not be workable; "it demands too much budgetary upheaval without equipping budget makers with the tools to redirect budgetary outcomes."[73] An experiment during fiscal 1964 in the U.S. Department of Agriculture (USDA) attempted just this kind of examination "from the ground up," and after considerable effort had been expended, little change could be discerned in the budget which was actually submitted to BOB and to Congress. Old issues already settled (they thought) had had to be rehashed, with little benefit, while some expenditures were mandated under law and consequently beyond the discretion of anyone at USDA.[74] If ZBB were implemented in the manner USDA adopted, it would not work at all. (It has been suggested, however, that USDA's experiment was poorly conceived and executed.)

In practice, according to Allen Schick, zero-base budgeting is "more a form of marginal analysis than a requirement that the budget be built up from scratch each year. It is a device for shifting some budget attention from increments above [additions to] the base to decrements below [subtractions from] the base."[75] The "zero" in ZBB could be misleading if one takes it literally as a statement of intent, but it has proved useful nevertheless.

In Georgia, where ZBB has been in use since fiscal 1973, three advantageous results have been development of a planning phase prior to the budget's preparation, better management information, and more involvement by lower management personnel in the budget-making process. (Only the last of these is, in Schick's words, "uniquely attributable" to zero-base budgeting.) ZBB also has apparently succeeded in encouraging agency officials to examine the productivity of their activities and to shift from less productive to more productive ones.[76] In New Jersey in the mid-1970s, there was some feeling that ZBB helped in assessing competing demands for funds and in determining the most appropriate level of program and expenditure. And in Texas during the same period, there was considerable agreement on the proposition that evaluating current-level funding was useful in and of itself; it was deemed important to know what "current dollars would produce in the future and what it would cost to produce the current output in the future."[77] In all three states there was improved management information capability under ZBB. That alone was a worthwhile contribution.

Will ZBB work in the federal budget process, as President Carter seems to want? There is some question about that, not least of which concerns the scope and particular mechanics that accompany its introduction. Schick believes the "big payoff" in the federal government will come, if at all, in facilitating presidential and department-level choices among broad policy alternatives.[78] Another observer suggests implicitly that success will depend on ZBB's being viewed as an *approach* to resource allocation rather than as a fixed set of procedures, applicable across the board.[79] A third observer feels that the necessity, under ZBB, of articulating unambiguous and relatively fixed goals and objectives could reduce the flexibility necessary for the "political public executive"; however, ZBB could enhance the president's ability to take policy initiatives and secure cooperation of career bureaucrats in support of them.[80]

Several trial runs of ZBB in selected federal agencies have already begun. The Consumer Product Safety Commission and the National Aeronautics and Space Administration undertook ZBB experiments in the fall of 1976 under guidance of a House appropriations subcommittee. Early results included considerably more paperwork (apparently an inevitable early-stage feature of ZBB) and the feeling among those involved that it would be extremely difficult to implement ZBB across the board in the federal government and receive great results the first year.[81] One influential House committee chairman—Jack Brooks (D–Texas) of the Government Operations Committee—indicated, early in President Carter's term, strong personal reservations about introducing ZBB into the federal government. Significantly, it is Brooks's committee which has jurisdiction over budget and accounting measures and "overall economy and efficiency of government."[82] Thus incorporation of ZBB into the federal budget process will require considerable political skill on the part of the president, as well as extensive adaptation of existing practice to needs and procedures of ZBB itself.

In principle, a *sunset law* would require that all government programs be renewed periodically through legislative action or else cease to exist. Presumably, if agencies and programs were subjected to periodic review and were forced continually to justify their activities—perhaps their very existence—they would be prevented from falling into patterns of complacency and routine behavior which have been said to make them less accountable to the legislature and, in turn, to the public.

As described by an early proponent, sunset laws should operate according to the following essential guidelines.[83] In addition to provision for automatic termination of programs and agencies unless affirmatively reestablished by law, sunset laws should mandate periodic evaluations—for example, every five, seven, or nine years—to institutionalize the program evaluation process. The sunset mechanism should be phased in gradually, with recognition of the need to learn both why and how to use it. Programs and agencies in the same policy area should be reviewed simultaneously, to encourage and facilitate coordination, consolidation, and responsible trimming of existing entities. Preliminary evaluation work should be done by agencies such as OMB, CBO, and GAO (and their state-level counterparts), but their staff capacities for evaluation should be strengthened.

In addition, sunset proposals should establish general criteria for evaluation, to make the process meaningful. Evaluation information should be presented to top decision makers in a form which aids their understanding of actual program or agency performance. Significantly, substantial reorganization of legislative committees, including adoption of a system of rotation of committee members, is deemed necessary for purposes of more meaningful legislative oversight. Such reorganization, it is felt, would sharply reduce subsystem influences and limit the impact of self-serving evaluations. Sunset mechanisms should contain safeguards against arbitrary terminations and should provide for displaced agency personnel and any remaining financial obligations. Finally, public participation should be incorporated as part of the sunset process, in the form of access to evaluation information, and public hearings held only after due notice is given as to time and place.

The political appeal of sunset laws grew very rapidly in the second half of the 1970s. By early 1977 several states had enacted sunset legislation—for example, Colorado—and nearly a dozen others were considering it.[84] President Carter had advocated similar legislation for the federal bureaucracy, and both chambers of Congress had bills in committee. The federal proposal would require that program funding authorizations be reestablished periodically, but would not require legislative renewal of agency existence. Such legislation would require examination of an agency's operations and effectiveness over a period of years, an advantage over ZBB's focus on annual budget cycles. In combination, however, ZBB and sunset laws could in some ways complement one another's effectiveness.

The objective of increasing bureaucratic accountability and responsiveness, by reducing the degree of assured agency and program permanence, seems to be well served by enactment of sunset legislation. Yet political supporters of an agency would be unlikely to permit it to expire without a fight; thus it is safe to assume the level of political tension and conflict would rise, at least as an expiration date approached, and probably earlier as well. Further, it is not clear from past experience that either sunset laws or zero-base budgeting significantly alters agency operations or budgetary allotments, though it is far too soon to draw reliable conclusions from either national or state experience. However, it does appear there is strong public support for steps such as these, and it is likely we will see more of them in the immediate future.

SUMMARY

Budgeting is a process central to politics. It is the formalized means of allocating resources, of deciding who gets what, when, how. Budgets can serve a variety of purposes, such as recording income and expenditure, indicating political priorities, or reflecting political and economic influence in fiscal decision making.

Before 1860 government budgeting was quite simple and routine at all levels. After the Civil War, changed conditions gave rise to modern budgeting. Three fundamental patterns emerged which set the stage: (1) growth of national government authority, (2) growing government involvement in the economy, and (3) growing presidential power.

Government budgets can be, but are not always, tools of fiscal policy—actions aimed at development and stabilization of the private economy. The major instruments of fiscal policy are taxation and tax policy, expenditure policies, and management of the national debt. Other related tools are monetary controls and credit controls. These are all related to budgeting, but in varying degrees; the most directly related are tax policy, expenditures, and the broad function of economic coordination.

Growth of the executive budget is linked to successive periods of budgetary reform in which two key concepts were major focal points. The first budgetary reform—line-item budgeting—had as its central purpose maintenance of *control* over expenditures. The second reform—performance budgeting—began in the national government during the New Deal and was addressed to problems of management and questions of how agencies put their resources to use. Performance budgeting was associated with a period of considerable change in federal budget making.

The budget-making process prior to 1960 was fragmented between president and Congress, between the House and Senate, and among substantive and appropriations committees in both chambers. Political party differences and conflicts contributed to budgetary process fragmentation, as did the separate handling of revenue and spending bills. Budgeting was (and still is) an ongoing process spanning more than just the single fiscal year for which a budget is prepared.

Budget preparation involves an OMB "call for estimates," followed by investigation of agency budget proposals by the OMB staff of budget examiners. The president and the director of OMB develop broad budget guidelines, issuing dollar ceilings for each agency, within which agency budget requests are finalized. The president's budget message, compiled from agency requests, is then forwarded to Congress.

Authorization involves congressional determination of maximum possible spending levels for all agencies and programs. Approval at this stage means money may be spent when appropriated; it does not confer spending power.

The appropriations stage involves granting of authority to spend money or to incur financial obligations under authorizations previously approved. Central to this process is the House Appropriations Committee, the largest and one of the most powerful committees on Capitol Hill. Prior to 1960, the committee operated on the basis of its being "guardian of the Treasury," and attempted to maximize its influence in the full House of Representatives through observing the norms of unity, specialization, and reciprocity. The Senate Appropriations Committee, by contrast, viewed its function as something of a "court of appeals." The process was fragmented, but also specialized, incremental, and concerned with the amount of additional funding to be allocated over the previous year's "base" figure. At virtually no point during the appropriations stage was a comprehensive review of the budget carried out.

Execution of the budget involves expenditure of appropriated funds, which are apportioned on a quarterly basis. Auditing is divided among several auditors and time periods. Routine audits are an expected part of agency operations, but a formal, full-scale audit can be a source of major difficulty.

Several major developments of the 1960s and 1970s have been addressed to making the budgetary process more systematic and rational. These are (1) PPBS, (2) the changing budgetary role of Congress, and (3) the rise of zero-base budgeting (ZBB) and so-called sunset laws.

Planning-programming-budgeting systems (PPBS) had several major objectives: (1) to improve planning as a basis for compiling budgets, (2) to emphasize programs, (3) to relate budget decisions to broad national goals, (4) to carefully consider effects of government activities and possible alternatives to those in operation, and (5) to utilize cost-benefit analysis in assessing government program activities.

The Defense Department was the first federal agency to adopt PPBS. Its effectiveness at the Pentagon prompted President Johnson to extend PPBS to all civilian agencies in 1965. But PPBS's success was limited, for a number of reasons—an inadequate background in planning and analysis in many agencies, difficulty in operationalizing goals, uncertainty about what PPBS itself involved, an absence of OMB leadership in implementing it, and resistance from Congress. Some residual effects of PPBS remain—a focus on information and on program impacts, an emphasis on goal definition, and a planning perspective. While not as lively as it once seemed to be, PPBS has not altogether disappeared.

In state and local governments, PPBS was introduced on a much less firm foundation of budgetary experience—executive budgets had been introduced much later than at the national level, and in most states even performance budgeting was not well established. PPBS did not fare well in most states, though Pennsylvania, Hawaii, and California (which adopted it under another label) are notable exceptions. PPBS has had only limited impact in local government. The "5–5–5" project served as an information clearinghouse, but even some cities participating in the project failed to implement PPBS. Few cities were affected, and only one major urban government—Philadelphia—has implemented PPBS with tangible effect. Attention, particularly at state and national levels, has shifted to other instruments of budgetary reform in the 1970s.

Conflict between Richard Nixon and Congress led to a major confrontation over presidential impoundment of appropriated funds, and ultimately to a new congressional role in the federal budgetary process. Nixon lost all but one court contest concerning impoundment in 1973, and lost again when Congress passed the 1974 Congressional Budget and Impoundment Control Act, sharply restricting his authority to impound. Nixon, however, accused Congress of being unable to monitor its own spending (an important rationale for his impounding "excessive" expenditures), and this led to a significant change in congressional budget roles.

Entering the 1970s, Congress's ability to exercise broad control over its own spending activities clearly had deteriorated. Subsystems were able to dominate specialized policy areas, and norms of guardianship and reciprocity were in decline—both resulting in higher appropriations year after year. The 1974 act established Budget Committees in each chamber; set up a Congressional Budget Office (CBO) to act as a data gatherer and analyst regarding budgets and fiscal policy, and as an examiner of national priorities; mandated enactment of budget resolutions setting target maximums and firm budget ceilings on annual appropriations; reordered the budget cycle timetable, changing the start of the fiscal year from July 1 to October 1 and fixing deadlines for particular congressional actions on the budget; and placed most new "back-door" spending under the appropriations process.

The procedures set up by the 1974 act offered an opportunity—but no guarantees—for Congress to participate more fully and equally with the president in the formulation of national economic and fiscal policy. The discipline needed was maintained, surprising many both in and out of Congress. The initial success of the new budget procedures was due to development of very useful data by CBO, CBO's "scorekeeping" on revenues and expenditures, the 1974–1975 recession, which focused attention on better fiscal management by Congress, public concern over rising government spending, strong leadership by Brock Adams and Edmund Muskie, and hard work by members of the budget committees. More, however, remains to be done.

Zero-base budgeting (ZBB) and sunset laws are the most recent devices applied to problems of government spending, program efficiency, and agency accountability. ZBB has been utilized in industry, state governments, some local governments, and—on a trial basis—the federal government. Sunset laws have been passed in several states and have received serious consideration in others, as well as in Washington. It has been suggested that for sunset laws to work effectively, particular steps should be taken and guidelines followed. These include, among others, a gradual "phasing in" of sunset processes, strengthening and institutionalizing of evaluation procedures, reviewing programs in the same policy area simultaneously, and incorporating public participation. Both ZBB and sunset laws are likely to have more limited impact than their respective labels might suggest, though their effects may indeed be useful to strong presidents interested in securing bureaucratic cooperation, and to legislators seeking to strengthen their control of bureaucracies under their jurisdiction. Public support is evident for measures such as these.

NOTES

1. Jesse Burkhead, *Government Budgeting* (New York: John Wiley and Sons, 1956), p. 59.

2. Robert D. Lee, Jr., and Ronald W. Johnson, *Public Budgeting Systems* (Baltimore: University Park Press, 1973), p. 36.

3. Charles L. Schultze, *The Politics and Economics of Public Spending* (Washington, D.C.: The Brookings Institution, 1968), p. 8. Schultze notes (pp. 7–8) that when Alexander Hamilton was George Washington's treasury secretary, he had established a central executive budget which gave broad discretion to the executive and "contained the potential for development of a centrally planned budget and a deliberate allocation of resources among competing agencies." Jefferson, however, ended that practice, opposing Hamilton's preferences for a strong central government and a strong executive within it.

4. Burkhead, *Government Budgeting*, p. 59.

5. Ibid., p. 60 (emphasis added).

6. See David J. Ott and Attiat F. Ott, *Federal Budget Policy*, rev. ed. (Washington, D.C.: The Brookings Institution, 1969), pp. 72–75.

7. Burkhead, *Government Budgeting*, p. 63.

8. Lee and Johnson, *Public Budgeting Systems*, pp. 64–65 (emphasis added).

9. *Congressional Quarterly Weekly Report*, 34 (February 28, 1976), 475.

10. Ibid.

11. Lee and Johnson, *Public Budgeting Systems*, p. 7. This description of early local, state, and national reform efforts relies on their treatment found on pp. 7–9.

12. Ibid., p. 8.

13. Linda L. Smith, "The Congressional Budget Process: Why It Worked This Time," *The Bureaucrat*, 6 (Spring 1977), 88–111, at p. 89.

14. Allen Schick, *Budget Innovation in the States* (Washington, D.C.: The Brookings Institution, 1971), p. 6.

15. Ibid., p. 7.

16. Lee and Johnson, *Public Budgeting Systems*, p. 36.

17. Ibid., p. 108.

18. Ibid., p. 113.

19. This discussion relies extensively on Lee and Johnson, *Public Budgeting Systems,* chapter 9, and Aaron Wildavsky, *The Politics of the Budgetary Process,* 2nd ed. (Boston: Little, Brown, 1974).

20. Formerly the Bureau of the Budget (BOB), reorganized in 1970.

21. Wildavsky, *The Politics of the Budgetary Process,* p. 245.

22. Under new congressional procedures established in the Congressional Budget and Impoundment Control Act of 1974, there is an intervening step of some importance prior to completion of authorization deliberations—namely, setting of *target maximums* for congressional spending for the fiscal year under consideration. This is taken up later in the chapter, after the basic, long-standing framework of congressional deliberations is outlined.

23. Lee and Johnson, *Public Budgeting Systems,* p. 204.

24. Reported on "NBC Nightly News," June 24, 1977.

25. Richard F. Fenno, Jr., *The Power of the Purse: Appropriations Politics in Congress* (Boston: Little, Brown, 1966), p. 503.

26. Richard F. Fenno, Jr., "The House Appropriations Committee as a Political System: The Problem of Integration," *American Political Science Review,* 56 (June 1962), 310–324, and incorporated in *The Power of the Purse.*

27. Fenno, "The House Appropriations Committee," p. 317.

28. Ibid., p. 316.

29. Wildavsky, *The Politics of the Budgetary Process,* chapter 2. The passage quoted appears on page 60.

30. The literature on PPBS is quite extensive. Among the most useful sources are Charles J. Hitch and Roland N. McKean, *The Economics of Defense in the Nuclear Age* (Cambridge: Harvard University Press, 1967); David Novick, ed., *Program Budgeting: Program Analysis and the Federal Budget,* 2nd ed. (New York: Holt, Rinehart and Winston, 1969); Schultze, *The Politics and Economics of Public Spending;* Dwight Waldo, ed., "Planning-Programming-Budgeting System: A Symposium," *Public Administration Review,* 26 (December 1966), 243–310; and, "Planning-Programming-Budgeting System Re-examined: Development, Analysis, and Criticism: A Symposium," *Public Administration Review,* 29 (March/April 1969), 111-202. Critical appraisals of PPBS can be found in Leonard Merewitz and Stephen H. Sosnick, *The Budget's New Clothes: A Critique of Planning-Programming-Budgeting and Benefit-Cost Analysis* (Chicago: Markham, 1971), and Wildavsky, *The Politics of the Budgetary Process,* chapter 6.

31. Schick, *Budget Innovation in the States,* p. 7. See also his "The Road to PPB: The Stages of Budget Reform," *Public Administration Review,* 26 (December 1966), 243–258.

32. See, for example, Wylie Kilpatrick, "Classification and Measurement of Public Expenditures," *Annals of the American Academy of Political and Social Science,* 183 (January 1936), 19–26.

33. Nicholas Henry, *Public Administration and Public Affairs* (Englewood Cliffs, N.J.: Prentice-Hall, 1975), p. 163.

34. See, for example, William M. Capron, "The Impact of Analysis on Bargaining in Government," in James W. Davis, Jr., ed., *Politics, Programs, and Budgets: A Reader in Government Budgeting* (Englewood Cliffs, N.J.: Prentice-Hall, 1969), pp. 253–267.

35. Lee and Johnson, *Public Budgeting Systems,* p. 125. The following discussion relies on Lee and Johnson's treatment, at pp. 125–138.

36. Ibid., pp. 220–222. Some in and out of Congress, however, felt PPBS might make available much better information with which Congress could judge performance of executive-branch agencies, thus working to the advantage of the legislative oversight function.

37. Stanley B. Botner, "PPB Under Nixon," *Public Administration Review,* 32 (May/June 1972), 255.

38. Allen Schick, "A Death in the Bureaucracy: The Demise of Federal PPB," *Public Administration Review,* 33 (March/April 1973), 146–156.

39. Ibid., p. 146.

40. Ibid., p. 148.

41. Ibid., pp. 148–149.

42. John A. Worthley, "PPB: Dead or Alive?" *Public Administration Review,* 34 (July/August 1974), 392–394. The passage quoted appears on p. 393. Worthley notes that the notion of PPBS as a counterweight to confrontation was first suggested by Frederick C. Mosher.

43. This discussion of state budgeting relies primarily on Schick, *Budget Innovation in the States,* chapters 3–5.

44. Ibid., p. 54.

45. Ibid., pp. 64–69.

46. Ibid., p. 86.

47. Ibid., pp. 106–107.

48. Ibid., p. 153.

49. Ibid., pp. 145–153, and Lee and Johnson, *Public Budgeting Systems,* pp. 145–147.

50. Lee and Johnson, *Public Budgeting Systems,* pp. 140–143.

51. Jack Rabin, "State and Local PPBS," in Robert T. Golembiewski and Jack Rabin, eds., *Public Budgeting and Finance: Readings in Theory and Practice,* 2nd ed. (Itasca, Ill.: Peacock, 1975), pp. 427–447, at p. 444.

52. Ibid., pp. 444–445.

53. Ernest C. Betts, Jr., and Richard E. Miller, "More About the Impact of the Congressional Budget and Impoundment Control Act," *The Bureaucrat,* 6 (Spring 1977), 112–120, at p. 114.

54. St. Louis *Post-Dispatch,* August 5, 1973, p. 19A.

55. *Congressional Record,* H5180–5182 (Daily Record, June 18, 1974); *Congressional Quarterly Weekly Report,* 32 (June 15, 1974), 1594.

56. See Joseph P. Harris, *Congressional Control of Administration* (Washington, D.C.: The Brookings Institution, 1964), pp. 115–116.

57. Betts and Miller, "More About the Impact of the Congressional Budget and Impoundment Control Act," p. 114.

58. Wildavsky, *The Politics of the Budgetary Process,* pp. 213–214.

59. Ibid., p. 214.

60. The following description is based on *Congressional Quarterly Weekly Report,* 32 (June 15, 1974), 1590–1593; *Congressional Record,* H5180–5293 (Daily Record, June 18, 1974); *Congressional Record,* S11221–11243 (Daily Record, June 21, 1974); *National Journal Reports,* 6 (May 18, 1974), 734–742; and *National Journal Reports,* 7 (September 28, 1974), 1445–1453. I am indebted to P. David Sawicki, a graduate student at Illinois State University, who assisted with research on the act and on CBO.

61. *Congressional Quarterly Weekly Report,* 34 (June 5, 1976), 1430.

62. Ibid., pp. 1430–1432.

63. Linda L. Smith, "The Congressional Budget Process: Why It Worked This Time," p. 91.

64. Ibid., p. 96.

65. Ibid., p. 103.

66. Ibid., pp. 106–107.

67. The examples cited are taken from Betts and Miller, "More About the Impact of the Congressional Budget and Impoundment Control Act," p. 119.

68. James Davidson, "Sunset—A New Challenge," *The Bureaucrat,* 6 (Spring 1977), 159–164, at p. 161.

69. This discussion of ZBB and sunset laws relies on the following sources: *Congressional Quarterly Weekly Report,* 35 (March 12, 1977), 441–443; Thomas D. Lynch, "A Context for Zero-Base Budgeting," *The Bureaucrat,* 6 (Spring 1977), 3–11; Peter A. Pyhrr, "The Zero-Base Approach to Government Budgeting," *Public Administration Review,* 37 (January/February 1977), 1–8; Allen Schick, "Zero-Base Budgeting and Sunset: Redundancy or Symbiosis?" *The Bureaucrat,* 6 (Spring 1977), 12–32; and Graeme M. Taylor, "Introduction to Zero-Base Budgeting," *The Bureaucrat,* 6 (Spring 1977), 33–55.

70. Taylor, "Introduction to Zero-Base Budgeting," pp. 36–37.

71. Schick, "Zero-Base Budgeting and Sunset," p. 14.

72. Ibid., p. 18.

73. Ibid., p. 13.

74. Lee and Johnson, *Public Budgeting Systems,* pp. 108–109.

75. Schick, "Zero-Base Budgeting and Sunset," p. 16.

76. Ibid., pp. 16–19.

77. Ibid., pp. 19–22. The quote is from a master's thesis on Texas' ZBB system cited by Schick.

78. Ibid. p. 30.

79. Taylor, "Introduction to Zero-Base Budgeting," p. 55.

80. Walter D. Broadnax, "Zero-Base Budgeting: New Directions for the Bureaucracy?" *The Bureaucrat,* 6 (Spring 1977), 55–66, quotation at p. 62. Similar goals-related problems plagued PPBS during the 1960s.

81. *Congressional Quarterly Weekly Report,* 35 (March 12, 1977), 441–443, at p. 441.

82. *Congressional Quarterly Weekly Report Supplement,* 35 (April 30, 1977), 27.

83. The following is taken from Bruce Adams, "Sunset: A Proposal for Accountable Government," *Administrative Law Review,* 28 (Summer 1976), 511–542, especially pp. 527–541.

84. David Broder, Washington *Post* political columnist, in his column of February 28, 1977.

SUGGESTED READINGS

Adams, Bruce. "Sunset: A Proposal for Accountable Government," *Administrative Law Review,* 28 (Summer 1976), 511–542.

Fenno, Richard F., Jr. *The Power of the Purse: Appropriations Politics in Congress.* Boston: Little, Brown, 1966.

Golembiewski, Robert T., and Jack Rabin, eds. *Public Budgeting and Finance: Readings in Theory and Practice,* 2nd ed. Itasca, Ill.: Peacock, 1975.

Lee, Robert D., Jr., and Ronald W. Johnson. *Public Budgeting Systems.* Baltimore: University Park Press, 1973.

Pressman, Jeffrey L. *House vs. Senate: Conflict in the Appropriations Process.* New Haven: Yale University Press, 1966.

Reagan, Michael D. *The Managed Economy.* New York: Oxford University Press, 1963.

Schick, Allen. *Budget Innovation in the States.* Washington, D.C.: The Brookings Institution, 1971.

———. "A Death in the Bureaucracy: The Demise of Federal PPB," *Public Administration Review,* 33 (March/April 1973), 146–156.

Wildavsky, Aaron. *Budgeting: A Comparative Theory of Budgetary Processes.* Boston: Little, Brown, 1975.

———. *The Politics of the Budgetary Process,* 2nd ed. Boston: Little, Brown, 1974.

"ZBB" (a symposium), *The Bureaucrat,* 6 (Spring 1977), 1–120.

CHAPTER 11
Government Regulation

Regulating various aspects of our economic and social life is a long-standing part of the administrative scene at all levels of government, especially the national level. As suggested in the preceding chapter, much of what the national government does has an impact on individual citizens, private corporations and other business enterprises, agricultural producers and marketers, labor unions, and state and local governments. But some functions are explicitly regulative in nature, setting "ground rules" for many private—especially economic—activities. The first steps at the national level in this regard were taken in the late 1800s and were aimed at punishment for, then prevention of, abuses in the marketplace—prosecuting antitrust violations and price-gouging, for example. In this century government regulation has become more far-reaching, focusing not only on preventing certain kinds of practices but also on requiring that certain operating standards and requirements be met. In recent years Congress has passed more and more regulatory legislation, and part of the public "backlash" against government has its roots in a growing feeling the government now may be doing and requiring too much. Certainly, regulatory actions touch virtually every part of our lives—our transportation (seat belts, air bags, bumper guards, airline routes, no-smoking rules), the food we eat, what can or cannot go into our beverages (for example, saccharin), medications that may be used to treat disease (the controversy over giving Laetrile to cancer patients), chemicals used to treat clothing and furniture and paints, and the like. It is estimated some fifty agencies—regulatory and otherwise—employ 100,000 people and currently spend more than $3 billion annually for government regulatory programs.[1]

The whole subject of government regulation in a "free enterprise" economic system is a bit complicated. Some economists and others contend that the most effective regulator in the marketplace is *competition* among those seeking to attract the buying public, and argue that government regulation, by interfering with free-market mechanisms, works to the ultimate disadvantage of both consumers and producers. Advocates of government regulation, however, see greater need to monitor and guide the course of competition, believing that a completely unrestrained market will lead to monopoly practices and a lower quality of goods and services. In the twentieth century, the national government has tried increasingly to strike a balance between regulating producers and permitting, indeed encouraging, competition in the marketplace, supporting both the right of consumers to products that meet certain standards of safety and effectiveness, and the right of producers to a decent profit.

The *independent regulatory agencies* of the national government, numbering about a dozen, combine features of legislative, executive, and judicial bodies and consequently are organized somewhat differently from most other federal agencies. We will discuss their origins, both societal and political; analyze the formal and political setting in which they operate, and with what consequences; and discuss some of the most volatile issues concerning government regulation in the past twenty years.

The Rise of Government Regulation

Historically, government regulatory activities have taken one of two forms: (1) putting certain limits on prices and practices of those who produce commercial goods; and (2) promoting commerce through grants or subsidies, on the theory that such payments are a public investment that will yield greater returns for the consuming public in the form of better goods and services. A prime example is airline subsidies.[2] The first of these has a longer history than the second.

Regulation of interstate commerce under Congress's direction was a constitutional power of the national government (in Article I, Section 8) right from the start. Yet for virtually all of our first century as a nation, responsibility fell to the states to carry on most of whatever regulation existed. This included, among others, transportation tolls on and across rivers, prices farmers had to pay to grist mills and cotton gins, water rates, and railroad fares. In the period of industrialization after the Civil War, the national government gradually assumed more responsibility for both controlling and promoting commerce, though the states still played an important role in developing and testing ways of controlling prices and commercial practices. As the emerging national economy grew and flourished, however, pressure began to mount for the national government to enter more extensively into the regulatory arena. It stemmed from strong demands that abusive practices of the railroad industry, in particular, be brought under control. State regulatory agencies, some of which were quite active, lacked jurisdiction to deal with enterprises such as rail companies that crossed state lines. Beginning with the New Deal, the national government came to exercise primary governmental responsibility for both controlling and promoting economic activity. Though the states still are primary regulators of a few industries such as insurance, and secondary regulators of industries such as banking, the national government now is the center of regulatory activity.[3]

Making government policy has been regarded as a legislative power under the Constitution, derived principally from Article I, Section 8.[4] Yet Congress and most state legislatures have found it difficult to write all the varied and detailed provisions which are necessarily part of governing a dynamic and complex society. There are two dimensions of the problem for a legislative body. First, most legislatures lack the time and technical expertise required to establish detailed rules and regulations on such complex subjects as atomic energy, monetary policy, air safety, or exploration for and marketing of natural gas. As these and other areas of policy became important, it was increasingly necessary for Congress to create agencies able to deal with them. Second, even if Congress had the time and skills, a large, collective decision-making body lacks the flexibility needed to adjust existing rules and regulations to changing conditions, again justifying creation of other entities to concentrate on each area. Thus, even in the nineteenth century, it was apparent it would be necessary to delegate legislative authority to administrative agencies (regulatory and otherwise), with Congress monitoring their operations and adjusting their legislative charters, but doing little actual regulation.

The first major institutional development in the national government was creation in 1887 of the Interstate Commerce Commission (ICC), in response to public disenchantment with the railroads, especially in the Mississippi Valley and the West. Unlike the eastern portion of the country, where numerous rail lines were engaged in vigorous competition, the nation's midsection and expanding West were served by a small number of railroads, which were thus able to engage in near-monopoly practices. Establishment of the ICC signaled a clear change from the prevailing notion of governmental action taken to punish unlawful acts after they had occurred. This was the first step to prevent such acts from occurring, and to do so by laying down rules which applied to a *class* of industries and actions, relieving the government of the need to proceed on the previous case-by-case basis in federal courts.

Public pressure for controlling industry became stronger in the late 1800s and early 1900s, led by men such as James Weaver of the Greenback party in the 1888 presidential election, and especially William Jennings Bryan. The great "trust-buster," Theodore Roosevelt, was followed into the White House four years later by Woodrow Wilson; both men favored government measures to maintain economic competition and fair trade practices. Franklin Roosevelt, of course, opened the way for even more stringent and far-reaching regulation in the wake of the stock market crash of 1929 and other economic woes of the Great Depression. In this period of about fifty years, six agencies were created (in addition to the ICC) which greatly increased the scope of national government regulation.

The Sherman Antitrust Act of 1890 made it illegal to conspire to fix fares, rates, and prices, and to monopolize an industry, though enforcement mechanisms were not provided for in the original act. In 1903 the Antitrust Division of the Justice Department (not an independent regulatory agency) was created to direct enforcement of the Sherman Act. Again, this proved difficult due both to unclear language in the law and to lack of delegated authority to the division. The result was increasing reliance on the courts to interpret legislative language and, some said, an inappropriate and perhaps excessive involvement of courts in direct policy making. With delegation of authority to the ICC as a precedent, Congress attempted to solve the problem by creating another independent regulatory agency modeled after the ICC.[5] In 1914 the Federal Trade Commission (FTC) was established to assist in antitrust enforcement, principally by interpreting and enforcing provisions of the Clayton Act (passed the same year), which prohibited price discrimination if the purpose or effect of such discrimination was to lessen competition or create a monopoly.[6] The FTC's involvement eased the burden on federal courts, though it did not remove it entirely; the courts have been active continually over the years in settling antitrust and other regulatory questions. The FTC also was responsible by law for controlling deceptive trade practices, but until 1938 this was not in fact its primary function.

During this half-century, other regulatory agencies modeled after the ICC and FTC were also established. The Federal Power Commission (FPC) was created in 1920 to regulate interstate sale (wholesale) of electric energy, and the transportation and sale (including rates) of natural gas. The Federal Communications Commission (FCC), established in 1934, regulates civilian radio and television communication (except for rates), as well as interstate and international communications by wire, cable, and radio (including rates). The FCC assigns frequencies and licenses operators of radio and television stations, and has become more involved lately in issues concerning cable television franchises and pay TV. The Securities and Exchange Commission (SEC), also founded in 1934, was one means used by the government to try to prevent a repetition of the 1929 stock market crash. The SEC regulates stock exchanges and over-the-counter securities dealers, requires disclosures about securities offered for sale, and regulates certain practices of mutual funds and other financial investment concerns. The National Labor Relations Board (NLRB), established in 1935, regulates labor practices of employers and unions, and conducts elections to determine union representation when requested to do so. Finally, the Civil Aeronautics Board (CAB), created in 1938, regulates airline passenger fares and freight rates, promotes and subsidizes air transportation, and awards passenger service routes to commercial airlines.[7]

These seven regulatory agencies are among the most prominent government entities having regulatory authority under congressional statute, but there are numerous others, each of them important. The game of "Washington alphabet soup" (ICC, FTC, NLRB, and so on) is playable not only with regulatory agencies, but also with other government offices having regulative responsibilities: FDIC (Federal Deposit Insurance Corporation), FDA (Food and Drug Administration), FRB (Federal Reserve Board), FAA (Federal Aviation Administration), and CPSC (Consumer Product Safety Commission), to name only a few (see Table 11–1).

TABLE 11–1
SOME MAJOR FEDERAL REGULATORY AGENCIES

Interstate Commerce Commission (ICC) Founded in 1887
Regulates routes, rates, and operations of interstate rail, trucking, bus, inland waterway, and oil and pipeline companies.
Budget: $51 million[a]   Personnel: 2,067[b]

Federal Reserve Board (FRB)   Founded in 1913
Makes and administers credit and monetary policy, and regulates commercial banks in the Federal Reserve System.
Budget: $43 million   Personnel: 1,488

Federal Trade Commission (FTC)   Founded in 1914
Regulates business competition, including some antitrust enforcement, and acts to prevent unfair and deceptive trade practices.
Budget: $47 million   Personnel: 1,622

Federal Energy Regulatory Commission (FERC)   Founded in 1920 as FPC
Since late 1977, located in Department of Energy; regulates the rates and other aspects of interstate wholesale transactions of the electric power and natural gas industries.
Budget: $37 million   Personnel: 1,316

Food and Drug Administration (FDA)   Founded in 1931
Located in HEW; sets standards of purity for some foods and drugs, and licenses drug manufacturers and distributors.
Budget: $222 million   Personnel: 6,500

Federal Communications Commission (FCC)   Founded in 1934
Regulates interstate and international radio, television, telephone, and telegraph communications; licenses U.S. radio and television stations.
Budget: $51 million   Personnel: 2,060

Securities and Exchange Commission (SEC)   Founded in 1934
Regulates issuance and exchanges of stocks and securities; also regulates investment and holding companies.
Budget: $49 million   Personnel: 1,959

National Labor Relations Board (NLRB)   Founded in 1935
Conducts elections to determine labor union representation in the private sector; prevents and remedies unfair labor practices.
Budget: $70 million   Personnel: 2,404

Equal Employment Opportunity Commission (EEOC)   Founded in 1964
Investigates and rules on charges of racial (and other) discrimination by employers and unions, in all aspects of employment.
Budget: $65 million   Personnel: 2,220

TABLE 11–1 (Cont.)

Environmental Protection Agency (EPA)   Founded in 1970
   Issues and enforces pollution-control standards in the areas of air, water, solid waste, pesticides, noise, and radiation.
   Budget: $860 million   Personnel: 11,208

Occupational Safety and Health Administration (OSHA)   Founded in 1971
   Located in Department of Labor; develops safety and health standards for private business and industry; monitors compliance and proposes penalties for noncompliance.
   Budget: $118 million   Personnel: 1,885

Consumer Product Safety Commission (CPSC)   Founded in 1972
   Develops and enforces uniform safety standards for consumer products, and can recall hazardous products.
   Budget: $42 million   Personnel: 1,098

Nuclear Regulatory Commission (NRC)   Founded in 1975
   Issues licenses for nuclear power plant construction and operation, and monitors safety aspects of plant operations.
   Budget: $222 million   Personnel: 2,141

ᵃApproximate fiscal year 1976 budgets.
ᵇPersonnel figures are as of June 30, 1975.
Sources: Regulatory Reform: A Survey of Proposals in the 94th Congress (Washington, D.C.: American Enterprise Institute for Public Policy Research, 1976), pp. 47–48; and *U.S. Government Manual, 1977–78* (Washington, D.C.: Office of the Federal Register, National Archives and Records Service, General Services Administration, 1977).

Mention should be made, also, of the complex of state regulatory agencies, many of which are patterned after those at the national level, and local regulatory activities which have an impact on certain local economic enterprises. As noted previously, states have primary responsibility for regulating insurance, and are involved secondarily in regulation of banks. States also examine and license physicians, insurance agents, and real estate agents, and certify those qualified to practice law. In highly technical and professional fields, such as medicine and law, the respective professional associations—usually well organized at the state level—have a key role in setting state standards for entry into the profession. Indeed, in some instances formal state decisions amount merely to, ratifying standard-setting actions taken by a professional association.

Other state entities also have regulative impact. Public utility commissions have a great deal to do with setting retail rates for electricity and natural gas sold within a state, and some also have investigative capacities. An example of the latter function was an inquiry by the New York State Public Utility Commission into operations of Consolidated Edison, which provides electricity to New York City, after the blackout in July 1977. Additional state requirements were imposed on "Con Ed" as a result of that investigation. State commerce commissions regulate commercial activity occurring entirely within state boundaries (*intra*state, not *inter*state), and can have an influence on shipping rates and other shipping practices, particularly. Liquor control boards (in some states there are state-run liquor outlets), recreation departments, and environmental protection agencies are further examples of state entities that affect private economic enterprise. These all can act on their own authority and initiative without being subject to decisions made at the national level. However, in some areas of regulation, state and national agencies have collaborated on standard-setting, accounting systems, and the like, contributing to the patterns of specialized intergovernmental contacts discussed in chapter 5. Examples include cooperation between the ICC, FDIC, FDA, FCC, FPC, and FTC, and their respective state counterparts,[8] and in recent times, between state and national environmental protection agencies.

At the local level, regulatory activity most frequently involves granting licenses for establishments such as taverns or theaters. Regulatory functions are most likely to be related to the local police power, rather than standing on their own as is the case with national and state regulation. There has been little research on local regulation, which may be an unfair reflection on its scope and significance. In general, however, local regulation is neither as visible nor as far-reaching as regulation at other levels of government.

Structures and Procedures of Federal Regulatory Agencies

The national government's independent regulatory agencies have certain features in common with other administrative entities, but differ in important respects. One similarity is that agencies operate under authority delegated by Congress, and they must therefore be aware of congressional sentiment about their operations. On occasion, Congress as a whole has been persuaded to restrict regulatory activities in some way. A second similarity is that there can be functional overlap between or among regulatory agencies, just as with other agencies. For example, during the controversy over cigarette smoking and public health in the mid-1960s, one question was whether allegedly deceptive radio and TV advertising of cigarettes was properly under jurisdiction of the FTC (responsible for controlling deceptive trade practices) or the FCC (which generally regulates radio and TV advertising).[9] A third similarity is found in the fact that politics is as important in the regulatory process as in other aspects of public administration—maybe more important. While the design of government regulation seems to assume some separation between "regulation" and "politics," in truth there is considerable effort expended by interested groups and individuals to influence regulatory activity, giving rise to a number of issues we will consider later in this chapter.

Differences between regulatory agencies and others are significant, however. Most obvious is the nature of their work. Regulatory agencies are not direct federal program managers. Rather, they take charge of setting out rules and regulations governing private-sector economic activity. A second, crucial difference is in the structural design of these agencies. This design warrants further discussion because of what it indicates about the nature and underlying assumptions of agency regulation.

Regulatory Structures

The structural design is a reflection of the basic premise that these are to be "independent" regulatory agencies—more independent of presidential control and influence than other administrative entities, more independent of congressional direction in day-to-day operation (though not in their ultimate accountability to Congress), and significantly, independent of the businesses and industries they are to regulate. We shall discuss later the degree to which operating realities match this design, particularly regarding those who are regulated, but for now it is important to understand why the formal arrangements exist as they do.

First, regulatory agencies have a plural rather than an individual leadership, with the most common practice before 1950 being to rotate the chairmanship annually among members of the board or commission, with everyone participating in the selection of important staff people. In the wake of a reorganization plan proposed by President Truman and accepted by Congress in 1950, chairmen of all regulatory agencies except the ICC have been appointed to multi-year terms by the president, subject to Senate confirmation, and given authority to choose key staff people. Truman's intent was to pinpoint responsibility for efficiently managing agencies' operations, reducing their backlogs, and making them more effective. One result, however, has been to increase the importance of patronage considerations in staffing the agencies, contrary to what Truman said he wanted and to the original design of the agencies. The chairman also presides over commission or board meetings, has greater public visibility than other members, and, on occasion, possesses considerable influence.

Second, commissioners or board members do *not* serve "at the pleasure of the president," as do cabinet secretaries and other top-level political appointees, and presidential powers to remove them are sharply curtailed. Their terms of office are fixed, and are often quite long—for example, the fourteen-year terms of Federal Reserve Board members. Also, terms of office are staggered—that is, every year or every other year only one member's term expires. Consequently, no president is able to bring about drastic shifts in policy by appointing several board members at once, nor is policy within the agency likely to change abruptly because of membership turnover. Third, each commission or board has an odd number of members, ranging from five to eleven, and decisions are reached by a majority vote. Finally, by law there must be a nearly even partisan balance among the members, meaning, for example, that a five-member board must be either 3 to 2 Republican or 3 to 2 Democratic, a seven-member commission must be 4 to 3 one way or the other, and so on.

The combined effect of these provisions is (or at least was intended to be) a greater degree of "insulation" from political manipulation of these agencies than of others in the executive branch. In particular, it was deemed centrally important to prevent presidential interference with regulatory processes, and to make the agencies answerable to Congress. The effectiveness of "political insulation" can be questioned, however. Decisions clearly favoring some interests over others are not uncommon, though most decisions have substantive as well as political roots. The larger purpose behind organizing the agencies in this manner is to protect the "public interest" in preference, and sometimes in opposition, to private economic interests. But where and how to draw the line between them is frequently decided through the political process rather than as a result of clearly defined boundaries.

Regulatory Procedures

Procedures used by federal regulatory agencies fall into two broad categories, one much larger than the other.[10] Agencies are empowered under the Administrative Procedure Act of 1946 to engage in *rule making,* an action quasilegislative (in the manner of a legislature) in nature. Rule making involves issuing a formal rule or standard of operation which covers a general class of happenings or enterprises. It has about the same effect as a law passed by Congress or another legislature. For example, a rule passed by the ICC might limit the width of tractor-trailers on interstate highways or require lower shipping rates for products made from virgin materials than for those made from recycled material (as in the case of many paper products). Such rules apply to all individual operators, shippers, and others who come under their provisions. Rule making is characterized by its general applicability and by its uniformly affecting all within a given category.[11]

The other procedure is known as an *adjudicatory proceeding,* and such proceedings constitute approximately 90 percent of some agencies' actions.[12] Adjudicatory proceedings are quasijudicial (court-like), in that rulings are made on a case-by-case basis and procedural requirements resemble to some extent those observed in a court of law. In a majority of cases there is no formal proceeding prior to the decision. The agency routinely settles the question, such as FCC renewal of radio station licenses when they expire, or CAB permission for airlines to pool their baggage facilities at a major airport.[13] In such instances an agency is likely to follow informal precedents set in earlier agency rulings involving similar circumstances, though regulatory agency precedents do not carry the same legal force as do court precedents in judicial decision making.

On some occasions, however, adjudicatory proceedings become quite formalized. This usually occurs when major interests are affected, involving thousands of people or millions of dollars, or when a case is contested, or when there is no applicable precedent.[14] Under such circumstances, the rules followed represent an adaptation of courtroom procedures and congressional hearing requirements, including rules governing attorneys, testimony, and so on.[15] Some agencies make use of a *public counsel,* who argues the consumer's point of view at public hearings. A much more common figure in adjudicatory proceedings is the *administrative law judge*—formerly known as hearing examiner—who acts for commissioners or board members in conducting public hearings, taking testimony, and subsequently writing a preliminary recommendation which is the basic factual summary presented to the full commission or board. This procedure greatly reduces the time it takes for an agency to reach its decision.

Administrative law judges, of whom there are now about 800, are among the most highly specialized of all federal employees and occupy a unique niche in the federal service: they are career employees assigned to regulatory agencies, yet very independent of their "bosses" and with a degree of job security unusual even among "merit" employees. The nature of adjudication requires this; they are expected to avoid being arbitrary and unfair, while exercising sufficient freedom to write their recommendations on the basis of information received and interpretation of those data.[16] Though their recommendations do not carry final authority and can be appealed to the full board or commission, administrative law judges have nevertheless come to enjoy considerable prestige, and their recommendations are commonly accepted. In fact, in one instance—the National Labor Relations Board—findings of the administrative law judge may not be appealed to the full board unless a review is specifically requested by the side that lost out in the decision.[17] These, then, are influential individuals whose labors are of considerable benefit to commissioners or board members.

The change of title in 1972 from hearing examiner to administrative law judge is indicative of another change of some importance in the regulatory process. Because of the growth of government regulation and an increasing tendency to contest claims before regulatory agencies, the body of legal doctrine known as *administrative law* has grown by leaps and bounds. Decisions of regulatory agencies, which can be appealed to the U.S. Circuit Court of Appeals in the District of Columbia, have mapped out what amounts to new terrain in the law, and they have come by the hundreds.

One observer has even suggested that the Court of Appeals has been a more effective reformer of regulatory agencies than members of Congress, Ralph Nader, the U.S. Chamber of Commerce, and Presidents Ford and Carter.[18] The comment came after the Appeals Court had overturned three decisions of the FCC in 1976 and 1977, with far-reaching consequences. The first decision threw out an FCC ruling permitting "cross-ownership" (common ownership) of local newspapers and television stations. The second held that the First Amendment prohibited the FCC from regulating broadcast content, as it had tried to do regarding the broadcast by a New York radio station of a comedy routine containing seven "dirty words." The third found the FCC had exceeded its authority in limiting cable television airing of certain programs, principally feature films and sports events. Unless appealed to the Supreme Court and overruled there, these Court of Appeals rulings effectively define regulatory policy in three important areas of broadcasting. This may be consistent with the principle of checks and balances, but it does have certain implications for regulatory policy making. Also, the three decisions illustrate how important the field of administrative law has become. Among other things, it is now the area of law with the largest number of cases recorded, a result of more frequent and more vigorous litigation.[19]

Apart from rule making and adjudicatory procedures, regulatory agencies frequently attempt to resolve disputes or disagreements by encouraging informal, voluntary compliance with agency requirements. The Federal Trade Commission, for example, employs three principal devices to secure voluntary cooperation. The first is issuance of an *advisory opinion,* indicating clearly how the FTC would decide a particular question if it were to come before the agency formally. Regulatory agencies, unlike federal courts, are permitted to issue such opinions on questions which might, but have not yet, come before them. The second is convening of a *Trade Practices Conference,* to which all or most members of an industry are invited for a general airing of their regulatory problems and, it is hoped, for promoting better understanding on all sides of the problems discussed. The third is a *consent order,* representing an agreement voluntarily reached between the FTC and an industry before, or possibly during, an adjudicatory proceeding. (It is sometimes said that consent orders constitute a promise by an industry to stop doing something it hasn't admitted doing in the first place![20]) Without devices such as these, regulatory agencies would have an even more difficult time keeping up with their case loads than they do now.

The Politics of Regulation

Regulatory politics is only rarely the partisan politics of Democrats and Republicans. Rather, it is the politics of patronage, in the appointment of commissioners, board members, legal counsels, and staff personnel; and of privilege, in terms of gaining preferred access to decision makers by economic interests with a definite stake in these agencies' regulatory policies. It is also a many-sided game played by the regulators themselves, who are not insensitive to political pressures placed on their agencies and who are aware that reappointment may depend on political forces; by White House aides and members of Congress, because businesses, industries, and labor unions subject to regulation are important constituents; and by those regulated, who cannot afford not to play. One observer commented in 1969 that the only ones who seemed to be excluded were consumers, though that has changed decisively in less than a decade; now, consumers play the game hard, and well.[21]

Erwin Krasnow and Lawrence Longley, in their study of the FCC and broadcast regulation, suggested that in addition to Congress there are five major institutional influences on broadcast regulatory policy: the FCC itself, the broadcasting industry, citizens' groups, federal courts, and the White House.[22] It is an indication of the nature of regulatory politics, however, that the focal point of Krasnow and Longley's discussion was Congress. The relative political strength of these participants in broadcast regulation, their respective abilities to make Congress act, and rules Congress writes for the FCC and the courts (regarding access to judicial review of FCC decisions) all play a part in ultimately shaping broadcast policy. Regulatory policies in other areas result from similar configurations of institutions and political power.

The political setting of regulation includes many of the same features that apply to all other administrative agencies: legislative oversight by committees of Congress; appropriations concerns centering on congressional Appropriations Committees, OMB, and the new Budget Committees; an increasing focus on potential effects of zero-base budgeting and sunset laws; and attention to a political clientele—which for a regulatory agency is frequently *the very industry or industries it is responsible for regulating*. In addition, though the agencies are nominally bipartisan and thus seemingly removed from the hurly-burly of party struggles, the fact remains that business and corporate interests generally have their own partisan leanings. It follows that there might well be partisan undercurrents in regulatory politics, partly depending on which party holds the White House.

Furthermore, the degree of *independence* possessed by an agency may fall short of that apparently conferred by the statute which created it. For as already noted, the president, Congress, and powerful economic interests frequently interact with a regulatory agency, thereby affecting what it does. Critics of regulatory agencies have charged that they often protect the industries they are supposed to regulate more effectively than they regulate them—a charge not without some foundation. At the same time, however, another set of criticisms has begun to be heard, accusing some regulatory bodies of overdoing it, so to speak, in the exercise of their discretionary authority. Thus, regulatory agencies are increasingly "caught in a squeeze."

Independence from the President

Regulatory agencies are designed to answer to Congress's direction and to be shielded from presidential influence. Commissioners cannot be fired by the president; staggered terms inhibit presidential ability to "sweep out the old and bring in the new"; partisanship is limited by law in the makeup of the agencies. At the same time, however, a president who serves two full terms—or even part of a second term, as in the case of Richard Nixon—can have a powerful impact on agency composition, and therefore policy directions. Former President Nixon, during five and one-half years in the White House, appointed or reappointed the *full* membership of eight regulatory agencies, including the FCC, CAB, FPC, and SEC, and most of the members of all other regulatory bodies.[23] One congressional study in 1973 found that eighty-four individuals previously employed by the Committee to Re-elect the President, the White House, or executive-branch agencies under Nixon had gone on to work for agencies with regulatory functions, including two who were appointed as agency heads—FTC Chairman Lewis Engman and Federal Aviation Administration head Alexander Butterfield. The study was intended to show the extent of executive control or influence over federal regulatory activities, in the regulatory agencies and elsewhere.[24]

There have been other instances of presidential intervention—personally or through White House aides—in regulatory matters, besides simply appointing agency members. For example, in the 1950s Dwight Eisenhower's personal assistant, Sherman Adams, had to resign because of a scandal involving his having intervened on behalf of a friend, industrialist Bernard Goldfine, with the SEC and the FTC.[25] Jimmy Carter, in his 1976 presidential campaign, proposed that the chairman of the Federal Reserve Board (then Arthur Burns, a strong fiscal conservative) serve at the pleasure of the president, in order to enhance presidential control over national economic policy. In making his proposal, Carter may have been aware of the confrontation during the 1960s between another Democratic president—Lyndon Johnson—and another conservative FRB chairman—William McChesney Martin.[26] Though nothing came of Carter's idea, it indicates some of the problems in the independent status of these agencies, especially those with real influence in areas of major policy concern to a president and to Congress (such as the FRB).

The Nixon administration ran afoul of some people's expectations regarding agency hiring when, in late 1973, it was challenged publicly by the Senate Commerce Committee and the Consumer Product Safety Commission (CPSC), one of Washington's newest regulators. The CPSC alleged the White House had interfered in personnel choices of some staff members (under what is known as "Schedule C," applying to about 2,500 senior federal employees who are either designated as "policy makers" or are political appointees under presidential authority). The commission charged that approval by the chairman of the Civil Service Commission, usually routine, was in this case dependent on clearance given by the White House personnel office, before appointments could be confirmed. Four of the five commissioners, including the chairman, wrote to the Civil Service Commission head complaining of the "system of political clearance." They were joined by three members of Congress who had been the principal sponsors of the bill creating the CPSC.[27]

One other aspect of presidential influence in the realm of appointing and reappointing board or commission members deserves mention. The most common practice, it appears, is for presidents to avoid if possible any appointment that will generate controversy. The most convenient method is to allow leaders of regulated industries an informal voice in the selection process.[28] Not all presidents give equal weight to these informal recommendations, but rare indeed is the president who goes ahead with an appointment publicly and vigorously opposed by an industry.

There are two reasons for this presidential deference to industries. First, all presidents—regardless of political party—count on significant support from business and industrial leaders, and it is just common courtesy to one's supporters to "touch base" on a matter of considerable interest to them. Second, a president runs the risk of shaking business confidence and, in the long run, continued economic vitality by setting himself in perpetual opposition to the nation's business and financial communities. Consequently, most presidents take care to "keep their fences mended" with business and industry. What effect that has on a process of regulation assumed to be objective and detached is another matter, but it is the president's political needs which may account for some of the gap between promise and performance of regulatory bodies.[29]

Independence from Congress

From the standpoint of Congress as a whole, regulatory agencies have a great deal of independence. After an agency is established and processes of regulation begun, the main contact members of Congress collectively have with it is in reviewing and voting on annual appropriations. Where Congress does exercise considerable influence, however, is through committee oversight of regulatory agencies, particularly if complaints have been received about the activities of a given agency. Because the agencies operate under delegated legislative authority, it is the prerogative of Congress to review—and possibly modify—the authority which was granted, and agencies are cautious about offending powerful interests in

Congress which could trigger committee action to "rein them in." This does not happen often, but the very possibility is enough to restrain some of the more ambitious impulses.

Under some circumstances, individual members of Congress have indirect influence. Senator Warren Magnuson (D–Washington), a part-owner of radio and TV corporations in his home state, always seemed to have willing listeners at the Federal Communications Commission, who went out of their way to deal with large and small matters as they thought Magnuson wanted them dealt with. The fact that the senator sat on the Senate Commerce Committee certainly did not hurt his standing with FCC staffers or commissioners. Note, however, there is no evidence at all that Magnuson ever intervened directly on behalf of the companies (in which he was never more than a minority stockholder), or that he ever even played a part in managing the broadcast outlets. The important point is that people at the FCC did *what they thought* Magnuson wanted them to do, and certainly acted toward him, his stations, and his requests in a manner calculated to please him. It is not uncommon practice for a government administrator to try to anticipate what powerful members of Congress (or the executive branch) want, so that no favors ever have to be requested directly. The FCC treated in the same way others who were both influential in Congress and connected with broadcasting corporations—for example, Lyndon Johnson, who owned radio and TV stations in Austin, Texas—and other agencies have tended to follow the same pattern of behavior. Again, it's "good politics."[30]

At times, however, Congress's interaction with, and influence over, a regulatory agency is quite direct and occasionally forceful. An example concerns the controversy that raged during the 1960s and into the 1970s over health hazards said to be involved in smoking cigarettes. This involved efforts by several agencies—among them the FTC—to counter tobacco industry advertising that depicted smoking in a very favorable light. The story of this conflict highlights the problems and possibilities for a regulatory agency which takes the initiative in expanding the scope of regulation over a particular industry.[31]

There had been efforts to combat the alleged evils of cigarette smoking dating back many decades, but with a singular lack of success. Any concentrated attempt by concerned members of Congress or citizen groups to challenge the growth, marketing, advertising, or use of tobacco products was rebuffed by a tobacco subsystem. That subsystem included several bureaus in the Department of Agriculture; tobacco growers, manufacturers, and marketers; and Southern members of Congress, among them the chairman of the House Agriculture Committee, which had jurisdiction over tobacco questions. Tobacco was (and is) big business in half a dozen Southern states, and any challenge was a threat to their economic vitality, particularly in North Carolina, Virginia, and Kentucky.

But challenges to existing tobacco policy became more frequent during the 1950s as medical research indicating that smokers were more susceptible to respiratory and other diseases than were nonsmokers began to capture public attention. Families of lung cancer victims sued in some cases to recover damages from cigarette manufacturers, arguing that tobacco products were an immediate cause of their late relatives' deaths. Trial judges, however, were extremely reluctant to award damages, suggesting that they were not qualified to assess medical evidence and that the link between smoking and fatal illness was not sufficiently established to warrant requiring the companies to pay. During this same period, governmental attention was increasingly drawn to possible health hazards of smoking; interest grew particularly within the U.S. Public Health Service of HEW, headed by the surgeon general. Data gathered in the 1950s led to increasing certainty in the 1960s that smoking was indeed hazardous to one's health. A new public health subsystem was created, and pressures mounted on the tobacco lobby—still, however, without notable success.

In the early 1960s the FTC got into the fray for the first time. If Congress was unwilling to legislate any limitations on the tobacco industry, the FTC through its rule-making power was both willing and able to do so. The commission was responsible for controlling deceptive trade practices, among which was deception in advertising. A plan was proposed to require disclosure by cigarette companies of *all* effects of smoking, not just those which helped to sell their product. The FTC proposed rules in 1964 that said cigarettes had to be labeled as a health hazard, and that advertising had to include mention of those health hazards.[32] The FTC held hearings on the rules, but the tobacco industry's main effort to stem the tide of public health concern was directed toward Congress, particularly both chambers' committees on Interstate and Foreign Commerce. By attempting to have Congress decide the issue, the industry was signaling its clear understanding of political realities: the tobacco subsystem was much stronger on Capitol Hill than it was in the Public Health Service (spearhead of the drive for health warnings) or the FTC. Congress's response was to pass the Cigarette Labeling and Advertising Act of 1965, which established the National Clearinghouse for Smoking and Health as part of the Public Health Service, but also suspended FTC rule-making power over cigarette advertising for four years. A bill enacted under the banner of a public health measure was, in reality, more of a victory for the tobacco lobby than it was for the public health interests. The alternative for the industry was the far more threatening FTC rules, and the implicit possibility of further FTC action in the public health controversy.[33]

The role played by Congress and its relation to the regulatory agency in the cigarette controversy is indicative of the way regulatory politics can unfold. Both the tobacco and public health lobbies knew full well where their respective interests were most likely to be favorably regarded and treated; both attempted to maneuver the decision before the particular governmental entity which would best serve their interests; and neither scored a total victory. The cigarette interests got the FTC out of the rule-making—and therefore, the policy-making—arena for four years, during which time they hoped public attention would diminish and pressures for health warnings would ease. The public health subsystem, on the other hand, had succeeded in having a health warning placed on cigarette packages as of January 1, 1966 ("Caution: Cigarette Smoking May Be Hazardous to Your Health"), and the National Clearinghouse for Smoking and Health afforded those interests a first-rate opportunity to coordinate nationwide research and to publicize the results. Both sides also took something of a calculated risk that public opinion would turn their way, and in the end it was the public health interests that won more of that particular gamble.

Congress was not immune to change in public sentiment about cigarettes during the latter part of the 1960s (rarely is it totally immune to widespread public feeling), so that as the tide of public opinion began to run in favor of health considerations, congressional resistance to the FTC and the rest of the health lobby moderated noticeably. With the FTC on the sidelines, other agencies and many private research organizations continued to accumulate health data on cigarettes, and to exert political pressure on the tobacco industry. During this period, the Vietnam War and urban unrest tended to dominate public attention, allowing the health interests to work quietly at reinforcing their case about the ill effects of cigarette smoking. By the time the moratorium on FTC rule making expired in 1969, the balance of power between the two subsystems had changed markedly. Many in and out of Congress were ready to go further in requiring disclosures about health effects of smoking, and the tobacco lobby was much less able to resist those moves.

A related factor during the same period was a major thrust for reform within Congress, in which the seniority system—and, by extension, those chairmen who had risen to power through its use—became a key issue. When seniority itself came under fire, tobacco interests became somewhat less crucial relative to the need, as committee chairmen saw it, to save the system which had made them powerful in the first place.

Since 1969 a new balance of power has been struck between those who might long for the "good old days" of pre-health-lobby success and those who would be perfectly happy to place a far tougher warning on packages, limit sales of cigarettes, and ban smoking entirely in all public places. The establishment of "No Smoking" areas in many restaurants and different seating sections on airliners are clear evidence that antismoking forces continue to exercise considerable influence—indeed, that they have expanded their influence to embrace not only the FTC but also the Civil Aeronautics Board, HEW as a whole, and so on.

With this conflict in mind, we can ask if the regulatory agencies are truly independent of Congress. The answer is "No," but a word of caution is in order. They were never designed to be *completely* independent, after all, and they are not now independent by definition. But they can gain some measure of independence if their political support is strong enough—including, ironically, that in Congress. An "essential characteristic of independent regulatory commissions is their need of political support and leadership for successful regulation in the public interest."[34] It is the exception rather than the rule to find an agency that is truly an "independent operator," since neither Congress nor industry is likely to consent willingly to such an arrangement. Agencies which try to act independently, as the FTC did on cigarettes, find themselves "reined in" by congressional committees or Congress as a whole far more often than they are "turned loose." It is the nature of the game, depending on the balance of political forces at work. But a balance of *some* kind there almost always is, and agencies have to adapt to this, insuring if possible that their support is always stronger than their opposition.[35]

The question of agency independence from the president and from Congress is one with no final answer. William Cary, onetime chairman of the Securities and Exchange Commission, once described regulatory agencies as "stepchildren whose custody is contested by both Congress and the Executive, but without very much affection from either one."[36] Instead of independence, that sounds more like being caught in a crossfire between the White House and Capitol Hill—a situation in which regulatory agencies often find themselves. If neither the president nor Congress regularly lends support to agencies, and support is still needed, that creates a dilemma from which one escape seems most promising. They can try to reach acceptable operating understandings with the industries they regulate in exchange for *their* support—which poses a whole new set of problems for agency "independence."

Independence from Those Regulated

Among the most intense criticisms of regulatory agencies over the years has been the charge that they are "owned," are unduly influenced, or have been co-opted by the industries they are supposed to regulate. This charge has been heard lately with more regularity. The most devastating critiques in recent years probably were those of "Nader's raiders," associated with consumer advocate Ralph Nader, aimed at such venerable agencies as the ICC and FTC. Charges of the regulators' lack of experience, unfamiliarity with problems of particular industries, political cronyism in appointments, and lack of initiative and vigor in pursuing violators of regulatory requirements are the most common ones made. The central theme underlying such allegations is that the regulatory agencies do more to protect and promote "their" industries than to regulate industry activities in the public interest.

Nader and his associates have concentrated on uncovering what they claimed was widespread collaboration, if not downright collusion, between regulators and those regulated. In a series of reports by different "Nader study groups," a number of agencies were held up for spirited, pointed, and well-documented criticism. One of the best-known reports took the ICC to task for failing to enforce many of its own regulations and for bowing to pressures from the trucking industry and railroads on many, if not most, regulatory issues of importance to the carriers.[37] Another study, this one of antitrust enforcement, charged the government with failing to prevent development of monopolies in many industries, resulting in a "closed enterprise" system rather than healthy economic competition.[38] A third report alleged that the FTC did far too little to prevent or even control deceptive trade practices, as it was legally responsible for doing.[39]

In perhaps their most sweeping indictment, "Nader's raiders" characterized the entire system of government regulation as being "monopoly makers."[40] In his introduction to that work, Nader charged that "government economic regulation has frustrated competitive efficiencies and has promoted monopolistic rigidities advocated by the regulatees themselves."[41] In addition, he deplored what he called "corporate socialism, a condition of federal statecraft wherein public agencies control much of the private economy on behalf of a designated corporate clientele,"[42] and called the consumer the "first victim" of such an arrangement between government and corporate power. These allegations were made in connection with attempts to reform the government institutions responsible for economic regulation. While not entirely successful, they have changed the face of regulation considerably and influenced the course of the consumer movement.

However, the fact remains that those serving on regulatory agencies are not expected to isolate themselves personally from those with whom they deal—as, for example, judges are expected to do. On the contrary, some degree of interaction is considered necessary in order for those in the regulatory agency to fully understand the workings of the regulated industry. How to maintain that interaction and still keep an acceptable degree of detachment and objectivity is the central question.

Regulators have all kinds of direct social and professional involvement with individuals in the industries they regulate.[43] Frequently contact occurs in private, informal rule-making and adjudicatory proceedings, where problems can be addressed without all the trappings of a formal regulatory action. Just what comes out of such meetings in terms of protecting the public interest is not easy to determine (if the "public interest" itself can be defined), and the private nature of the conferences is one irritant to observers such as Nader and the "public interest" lobbying group Common Cause. A 1977 decision by the District of Columbia Court of Appeals, however, held that once a government agency asks for public comment on a proposed rule, its officials should refrain from discussing the proposal privately with interested parties. If such discussions do take place, full memoranda on what was said must be put in the public record of the agency. Many agencies have routinely written such memos about formal meetings with outsiders trying to influence the shape of a rule, but they seldom have been placed in public files. The court ruling would change that, putting industry lobbying into a "fishbowl" of public scrutiny.[44]

Furthermore, regulatory agency members routinely attend industry conferences, where they are frequently the main speakers, and some friendly conversation during the social hour is not at all out of place under such congenial circumstances. Then there are private chats in agency offices, out-of-town visits to companies by agency members, and luncheons and dinners where regulators and industry representatives are part of a larger social gathering.

Three things should be emphasized. First, these are routine occurrences, and not inconsistent with the job of regulation. Second, private industries have a legitimate economic self-interest to uphold, and there is a fear among industry executives that if they do nothing to present their case to government regulators, their competitors will. Third, out-and-out industry pressure on a regulator is rare—bribery is almost nonexistent, as are blatant attempts to intimidate or otherwise pressure regulatory officials. Direct exchanges of views, combined with the indirect pressure that can be placed on an agency through the president and Congress, usually are enough to insure industries of a fair hearing for their views and preferences.

The fact that regulatory agencies and their members are expected to be expert as well as detached raises yet another problem: How does one become knowledgeable about an industry without also coming to share that industry's values and outlooks? Appointees to regulatory agency positions often come from industry backgrounds, a natural training ground for acquiring relevant expertise but also a likely place to acquire perspectives favorable to industry interests. Other agency appointees have backgrounds which hardly equip them to deal with the industries— some are named as political favors, others simply because they are non-controversial appointees (sometimes both). In either instance, the industry has an advantage; commission or board members are likely to be sympathetic to—or else largely ignorant of—the industry's problems, and consequently reluctant to intervene in industry affairs.

Sometimes an industry "maverick" is named to a regulatory agency, someone who does not share the predominant economic or social outlook of the industry, although he or she has been a part of it. Former FCC Commissioner Nicholas Johnson, for one, fits this description; during his term of office he was often openly critical both of the broadcast industry and of the FCC itself.[45] But such appointments are exceptions to the rule; Johnson himself was frequently a dissenting minority of one in FCC decisions on everything from radio and TV license renewals to public participation in making broadcasting policy. The pattern of appointing people with industry backgrounds is so well entrenched, however, it is considered news when someone is rejected by the Senate for that reason.

In 1973, when relations between the Nixon White House and the Senate were becoming progressively more strained, the nomination of Robert H. Morris to the Federal Power Commission was defeated on a 50-to-43 vote. Morris, a lawyer who represented Standard Oil of California, fell victim to the growing uneasiness in Congress about industry domination of the regulators (a spinoff effect of the consumer movement). During Senate debate, Commerce Committee Chairman Magnuson warned the president against such nominations, but it was how he phrased his warning that was particularly revealing:

> . . . the Senate is *again* asked to accept, for an independent regulatory agency with vast powers over an industry which affects vital national interest, *yet one more* nominee whose professional career has been dedicated to the furtherance of the private interests of that industry.[46]

The need for both expertise and detachment in regulatory agencies clearly presents a problem not easily solved.

Consumers, Consumerism, and Regulation

The consumer movement of the 1960s and 1970s has had significant impact on government regulatory activity. Prior to the rise of consumerism, almost all major economic interest groups represented producers—those involved in growing, processing, shipping, and selling products in the marketplace. These groups naturally sought to shape market regulation in favor of producer needs and preferences. Consumers were largely unrepresented in any organized fashion. However, major conflicts over cigarettes and public health, and over auto safety (the latter led by Ralph Nader, with the Chevrolet Corvair as its focus), began to change that situation in the 1960s.

Leaders of the budding consumer movement looked to regulatory agencies and other administrative bodies to promote and protect consumer interests. They apparently placed little faith in Congress, reasoning that legislators would be far more likely to respond to producers' wishes than to contrary pressures applied by consumer groups. Rightly or wrongly, they chose to make use of administrative weapons in fighting their political battles, which of course brought them into conflict with both producers and Congress. Advocates of change, such as the Nader organizations, saw in addition a need to reform administrative regulation in order to maximize consumer gains. While not all consumer groups agreed with that view, they generally supported such efforts.

There is little question that consumerism has changed the face of government regulation, both because of new political pressures applied and because of primary reliance on regulatory agencies. "The consumer movement that began in the 1960s has given greater force to administrative law as a tool of social change. The procedures and the laws that agencies use for policy making are not new for the most part. What is new is their use by organized, professionally staffed consumer groups."[47] A study of consumer protection in the early 1970s noted that "the administrative process has proved to be the key element in consumer protection policy . . ."[48] Pressure was placed on Congress, with some success, not only to respond directly to consumer demands but also to increase access to agencies themselves and to federal courts for redress of consumer grievances. Congress's record in these respects is a mixed one, but even that represents an improvement over the past, when consumer groups were much weaker and less organized, and could point to only a handful of gains over long periods of time.

The Nader phenomenon and the rise of consumerism are not unrelated. There is informed opinion that without the Nader organizations— their expertise, full-time commitment, and vigorous criticism of both corporate power and regulatory efforts—the consumer movement would not enjoy the influence it does. By awakening consciousness of "consumer" interests among the general public, Nader and others strengthened, perhaps created, a constituency with sufficient political power to contest the influence of long-established producer groups. Consumer pressure clearly accounts for much of the increase in government regulation during the 1970s, and for increased political conflict over regulation.

The past few years have seen some change in patterns of regulatory interactions with industry. Government regulatory pressures have become more consistent and intense in response to better organized consumer interests, some change in the makeup and policy leanings of congressional membership, and continuing scientific research into health and safety dangers previously taken less seriously.

The Scope and Impact of Government Regulation

It was reported in mid-1977 that if basic federal regulations were compiled into a book, a shelf fifteen feet long would be needed to hold the 60,000 pages of fine print, and that fiscal 1977 expenditures of $3.5 billion represented an increase over fiscal 1976 of 21 percent![49] But the scope and impact of regulative activity goes even beyond that, for congressional statutes, presidential executive orders, judicial decisions, and edicts from other agencies all combine to shape, in subtle but important ways, the kinds of lives Americans lead.

Some actions seemingly unrelated to regulating private lives in fact do so. Prominent examples include local zoning laws; federal housing loan programs which have an income minimum, effectively cutting off many poorer citizens from a chance to buy homes in the suburbs; school desegregation guidelines; the whole complex of equal opportunity requirements in employment, housing, and education; minimum wage laws; and tax policies at all levels of government. Federal energy policies touch many areas of our lives—auto fuel economy, home insulation, energy conservation, and so on. These are broad-sweep actions, whereas our concern is with the multitude of more narrowly focused regulative activities stemming from specific legislation passed by Congress.

When a regulatory agency takes any steps, it must have a firm legislative basis for doing so, representing a majority coalition in Congress at least at the time the law was passed. Some laws are very specific, leaving little room for administrative discretion, and that can cause awkward political problems later on. A prominent recent example is the brisk activity of the Food and Drug Administration (FDA), a part of HEW, in moving to ban various products and substances said to endanger human health, either because they were unsafe or ineffective, or both. Table 11–2 lists some of the products taken off the market in recent years by the FDA. FDA officials have said more than once that the agency, under existing legislation, has had no choice but to remove a product from the market when its potential disease-causing properties are demonstrated under controlled laboratory conditions. This was an especially important position, politically, in the controversy over the FDA's proposal in 1977 to ban saccharin—the only remaining mass-marketed artificial sweetener since cyclamates were taken off the market by the FDA in 1970—which in a number of Canadian tests was linked to cancer, first in laboratory rats, then in human males.

The FDA's stand caused a rather powerful coalition in Washington to question the basic law which required FDA action against carcinogens (substances linked to cancer). Key elements in that coalition were food companies, manufacturers of soft drinks (including diet soft drinks), and perhaps most important, an aroused group of citizens—for example, diabetics—who for various reasons needed or wanted sugar-free beverages available for sale and consumption. Pressure was applied on both sides of the issue, with some arguing that suspected carcinogens should be banned as required by law, regardless of public outcry, and others arguing that it was time to update 1958 legislation requiring FDA action, to permit the FDA to examine potential benefits in relation to the cancer risk.[50] Any time a federal agency receives 40,000 angry letters over a single issue there is reason for it to reconsider its decision, which the FDA did. Its

TABLE 11–2
SELECTED PRODUCTS BANNED
BY THE FOOD AND DRUG ADMINISTRATION
(as of January 1, 1978)

Product	Date*
P-4000— artificial sweetener	1950
Safrole— flavoring compound in food	1960
Cobaltous salts— additive to fermented malt beverages	1966
Calamus— flavoring compound in food	1968
Cyclamate— artificial sweetener	1969
Red Dye No. 2— food and cosmetics coloring	1976
Red Dye No. 4— coloring for maraschino cherries	1976
Chloroform— additive to drug products (such as cough syrup, liniments, and toothpaste)	1976

*Date order was published in the *Federal Register*.
Source: *U.S. Code of Federal Regulations, 1977* (Washington, D.C.: General Services Administration, 1977).

course of action has been affected, however, more by congressional pressure for a delay in the effective date of a saccharin ban than by either direct industry or public pressure. The latter has to be "translated" into congressional action to be truly effective.

The proposed saccharin ban and public reaction to it were just the latest episodes in an unfolding series where the general public has been critical of regulatory action. One such case involved Congress itself mandating an auto ignition interlock system requiring drivers to "buckle up" before they could start their cars. Public response was so intense that it did not take long for a bill repealing the requirement to be introduced and passed. Significantly, it was cosponsored in the Senate by a liberal Democrat (Eagleton of Missouri) and a Conservative-Republican (Buckley of New York).[51] As one observer put it, "Congress learned . . . that the public tolerance for forced regulation is low."[52]

Two other examples serve to illustrate the point. The Occupational Safety and Health Administration (OSHA) in the Department of Labor, created in 1971, has focused on guarding on-the-job safety of workers in thousands of business enterprises. In many instances, the requirements have meant added costs for the employer as well as added paperwork in reporting job conditions to OSHA. One step taken by OSHA in 1976 would have required agricultural employers to install sanitary facilities in their fields so that no employee would be more than five minutes' walk from one of them. This "field privy" requirement set off intense reaction among large agricultural and agribusiness concerns. Their reaction, together with strong pressures from other sectors of the business community, eventually caused Secretary of Labor F. Ray Marshall to publicly redirect OSHA's efforts toward what he called *major* safety and health concerns. Marshall cited regulations requiring a place to hang one's coat in rest rooms and specifying exact dimensions for exit signs in work areas as the sort of detail with which OSHA should be less concerned in the future.

The other recent issue highlighting growing public frustration and disenchantment with federal regulation was the controversy over Laetrile as a treatment for cancer patients. Laetrile—a substance extracted from apricot pits and said by some to be effective as a cancer treatment—has not been an approved drug on the FDA lists. Yet during 1977 demands became more insistent that those who wanted to be treated with Laetrile should have the chance, FDA approval or not, with some arguing that this was an issue of freedom versus government control. The respective points of view have been summed up as follows:

> Freedom is the issue. The American people should be allowed to make their own decisions. They shouldn't have the bureaucrats in Washington, D.C. trying to decide for them what's good and what's bad—as long as it's safe. . . . The FDA is typical of what you get in regulatory agencies—a very protective mentality in bureaucrats who want to protect their own jobs and their own positions. It's easier for them to say "No" to a product—Laetrile or anything else—than it is to say "Yes." . . . The simple fact is that stringent drug regulation for society as a whole limits therapeutic choice by the individual physician who is better able to judge the risks and benefits for the individual patient. I think the whole argument centers on FDA's intervention on the basis of a product's efficacy. . . . I agree that no one should be allowed to defraud the public, but you don't need to rely on the FDA. . . . The real question is: Should the government be protecting you from yourself?[53]

And, on the other side of the Laetrile/FDA question:

> I believe in a society that protects the consumer from the unscrupulous vendor. There was a time in America when we gave free rein to the philosophy of *caveat emptor:* let the buyer beware. We abandoned that a couple of generations ago, and now we have all kinds of consumer protections built into our society.[54]

> . . . instead of freedom of choice, it could be freedom of the industry to defraud the consumer. With the tremendous number of drugs available, it is not possible for the physician and the consumer to really have the information necessary upon which to base an informed judgment in regard to the safety and effectiveness [of a drug].[55]

These statements reflect the two principal approaches to government regulation generally. If public and congressional reaction to the Laetrile controversy is any indication, the dispute is likely to become more heated in the immediate future (on this and other issues).

Regulatory agencies and others in government do not appear to be slacking off in their activities. A sampling of news stories in the spring and summer of 1977 indicated that on many fronts, in a short period of time, a lot was going on.

Item: The Consumer Product Safety Commission banned use of a flame retardant called Tris, used in children's sleepwear, found to be a carcinogen affecting laboratory animals.[56]

Item: The Environmental Protection Agency (EPA) announced plans to require noise labels on a variety of products, including air conditioners, dishwashers, garden equipment, hair dryers, power lawn mowers, and shop tools.[57]

Item: An EPA official indicated some 300 industries and 100 local communities would be prosecuted for failing to meet the July 1, 1977, deadline for reducing water pollution.[58]

Item: On CBS-TV's "Face the Nation," Transportation Secretary Adams announced standards for fuel mileage in automobiles manufactured in the 1981 through 1984 model years. Congress already had set mileage standards for model years 1978, 1979, 1980, and 1985.[59]

Item: Assistant Secretary of Agriculture Carol Foreman directed that foods the federal government buys for schools and other feeding programs be labeled with more complete information about ingredients and additives they contain.[60]

Item: Transportation Secretary Adams ordered air bags or automatic seat belts on all luxury and full-size cars beginning with the 1982 model year, and the same protection built into all cars by the 1984 models. A Gallup poll taken a month after Adams' announcement indicated that the public, by 46 to 37 percent, supported the decision.[61]

Whether such activity is perceived by most consumers as being in their ultimate interest appears to be at the core of current controversies surrounding government regulation. Clearly, not all consumers share the values and objectives of consumer groups, contributing to the "squeeze" on regulatory agencies and others such as the Department of Transportation which have been increasingly active in regulation. It has been well known for some time, for example, that many people do not use their auto seat belts, despite impressive statistical evidence that use of seat belts can greatly reduce risk to life and limb in case of an accident. General Motors at one time offered air bags as an option on its cars, but claimed buyers did not want them. Many people also resent mandatory pollution-control devices on their automobiles. The auto ignition–seat belt interlock system was defeated rather handily in Congress, once the public's sentiments became evident. That could happen again—in auto safety, effectiveness of medicines, the safety of food products, and other areas.

Most of us, given the *abstract* choice between clean or polluted air, pure or impure food and drugs, and so on, would clearly select the former. But how to insure and maintain such conditions is what the current controversies are all about. And what may be happening is simply a shift in prevailing political views about what constitutes appropriate regulation of particular products. Perhaps the best way to view such controversies is that this is a cyclical process, with the tide of public opinion ebbing and flowing on behalf of vigorous government regulation.

While we have dwelled at some length on direct regulative impacts, it should be noted that indirect effects are no less important, even though it may be more difficult to identify their links to our daily lives. When the CAB deliberates about "deregulation" of airlines, including allowing the five largest carriers one new 2,000-mile route per year, permitting freer entry by charter air companies into scheduled air travel, and possibly other steps to encourage airline competition; when the ICC considers giving permission to railroads to abandon thousands of miles of little-used, poorly maintained, and unprofitable rural tracks; when the ICC makes decisions on truck shipments in metropolitan areas that result in reduction of shipping rates—these decisions and others like them inevitably affect the prices we pay for various goods and services, and perhaps their quality as well. Questions that seem to be rooted in distant economic and political considerations eventually come home to roost.

Government regulation clearly has an immense impact on the citizens and economic enterprises of this country. Where we go from here is an important question, one that seems to be arousing the interest of more and more people. We turn now to consideration of the future of regulation, including the possibility of reform.

The Future of Government Regulation

Regulatory reform has been a recurring theme over the years, with various reports to the president making a number of recommendations about how to deal with different regulatory problems. Others have also put forward proposals which have become part of the reform literature. In the recent past, both Presidents Ford and Carter made regulatory reform a matter of high priority, and the issue has taken on greater urgency in and out of government. A brief review of the major reform proposals of the past two decades will be useful.

In 1960 President-elect Kennedy received the Landis Report,[62] which emphasized concerns about agency domination by the regulated industries, failure to move vigorously to promote competition, and lack of independence from the relevant committees and subcommittees of Congress. The report proposed creation of an executive office with a single administrator responsible for all regulatory policy; regulatory agencies would operate under the direction of this regulatory "czar." In 1962 another observer proposed "continuing reevaluation," a procedure whereby regulatory agencies would prepare regular reports on existing policies and their effectiveness in each area of their responsibilities.[63] Political scientist Theodore Lowi proposed in 1969 that the legislation which established regulatory agencies be rewritten to delineate their responsibilities and authority more clearly.[64] And in January 1971 President Nixon received the report on regulatory agencies of his Advisory Council on Executive Organization, known as the Ash Council because of its chairman, industrialist Roy L. Ash.

The Ash Council identified the following as major regulatory problems: (1) lack of accountability to either Congress or the president and lack of coordination between regulatory activities and national policy goals; (2) deficiencies inherent in the commission form of organization; (3) excessive reliance on adjudicatory proceedings instead of rule making; and (4) fragmentation of responsibilities among several agencies (for example, responsibility for transportation divided among the ICC, CAB, and the Federal Maritime Commission) and conflicting responsibilities within the same agency (for example, both antitrust enforcement and consumer protection in the FTC). The Ash Council report made a number of recommendations, such as assigning regulatory responsibility in transportation, power, securities, and consumer protection to agencies headed by single administrators appointed by the president; grouping fragmented agency responsibilities into a single set of functions administered by one agency; and creation of an Administrative Court of the United States to hear appeals from final agency decisions.[65]

Economist Roger Noll criticized the Ash Council for its failure to support most of its conclusions about both the principal failings of regulation and the cause of these failings. Noll also took the council to task for failing to mention that agencies may pay too much attention to industry wishes or act to restrain competition; for ignoring instances of what he called "unwarranted interference" by Congress and the executive in regulatory decisions; for not evaluating the performance of agencies such as the NLRB, FAA, and FDA, for which it offered no reform proposals; and for not indicating why it concluded that greater presidential authority, rather than greater congressional authority, would increase regulatory agencies' sensitivity to the general public interest.[66] Some of the Ash Council suggestions may have been worthwhile, but Noll's critique centered on what was omitted in the council's deliberations.[67]

Noll himself proposed among other things that the president be given authority to issue executive orders establishing general, not case-by-case, regulatory rules and policies, subject to Senate or House countermanding within a specified time (a "legislative veto"); better planning studies conducted by the agencies themselves; and a system of "constituent representatives," that is, reserving seats on boards and commissions for individuals from specific regulated industries, which would formally recognize the reality of interest group influence in the appointment of commissioners and board members.[68] Of all these recommendations and proposals, only those regarding "continuing reevaluation" and better agency planning appear to have been implemented. The others are still on the agenda, however, any time a president or Congress chooses to bring them up again.

Presidents Ford and Carter both addressed themselves to reform, with somewhat different emphases but some similarities as well. They shared concern for reducing economic costs of regulation while boosting efficiency and effectiveness, for enhancing competition and the opportunity to start and maintain one's own business, and for limiting governmental intervention in the marketplace.[69] The Carter administration in 1977 seemed to be emphasizing reducing "nonproductive" activities and increasing "useful" intervention. Carter himself appeared to have something of the businessman's aversion to "excessive" regulation (assuming that can be defined), and apparently was searching for ways to improve the effectiveness of regulatory activities.

In his first three months in office, for example, President Carter called for significant cutbacks in federal regulation of the airline and trucking industries, a reduction in federal paperwork, closer agency review of the manner in which they issue their rules, and greater government responsiveness to the interests of businesses being regulated.[70] In a March 1977 message to Congress, the President urged that the effects of regulation be carefully examined, industry by industry, and promised that "whenever it seems likely that the free market would better service the public, we will eliminate government regulation."[71] And Charles L. Schultze, chairman of the Council of Economic Advisors, has indicated repeatedly that he believes federal regulation contributes to inflation. Testifying before the Senate Commerce, Science, and Transportation Committee's aviation subcommittee in March 1977, Schultze made his position clear:

> We pay a price when we substitute bureaucratic decisions for private initiative—excessive rigidity, inability to deal with very particular needs and circumstances, delays, legal formalism, the temptation to abuse power for political reasons, and sheer unwillingness to take any risks.[72]

With Schultze, Treasury Secretary Michael Blumenthal, and other top officials seemingly in agreement about cutting back on regulation, the direction of federal regulatory policy appears to be changing.

It is clear, finally, that growing debate over government regulation is inevitable in the years ahead. With regulatory activity strongly supported by some as a means of insuring fairness and equity in the marketplace—as well as good product quality—while equally strongly opposed by others on the grounds it constitutes unwarranted interference and a potential threat to individual economic and social freedoms, any conflict is bound to be intense. Regulation is at a crossroads, given continuing governmental, industry, and public ferment. Much more is at stake than a rule here or a regulation there—the nature of our economy and government's relation to it is also.

SUMMARY

Government regulatory activity dates back to the 1800s. In this century, regulative actions have been aimed at requiring compliance with standards set by government, in a widening variety of private economic activities. Both independent regulatory agencies and other government entities have engaged in regulation.

Government regulation most often has been a mix of two main approaches: regulating producers on the one hand, and encouraging competition in the marketplace on the other. More specifically, regulating prices and practices of producers while promoting commerce through grants and subsidies have been common approaches of regulatory agencies. The focal point of regulatory activity has shifted steadily over time from the states to the national government.

As problems of government became more complex in the nineteenth century, Congress and state legislatures found it necessary to delegate legislative authority for regulation to agencies created specifically for that purpose. Public pressure for controlling emerging industrial giants led to creation of several federal agencies during the period 1887–1938, all of which dealt with problems of monopoly, fair pricing, and various commercial trade practices.

State and local regulation is not unimportant. In addition to regulating insurance and banking, state agencies examine and license physicians, lawyers, insurance agents, real estate agents, and so on. Professional associations are usually involved in setting state standards. State public utility commissions have influence on electricity and natural gas rates, and can act with some discretion of their own. Other examples include commerce commissions, liquor control boards, and recreation departments. Local regulation consists primarily of licensing certain businesses, and generally is less significant.

Independent regulatory agencies are similar to other administrative entities in operating under delegated legislative authority, exhibiting functional overlap, and being affected by political considerations. They differ in the kind of work for which they are legally responsible and in structural design. Though designed to be somewhat more "insulated" politically than other agencies, there is reason to believe the insulation is thin at best.

Regulatory procedures fall into two categories: rule making and adjudicatory authority. The increase in regulatory decisions, particularly in adjudication, has meant a substantial increase in the importance of administrative law judges (formerly, hearing examiners). The growth of administrative law itself has been a major phenomenon of the regulatory process. In addition, many agencies encourage voluntary compliance with agency rules and standards.

Regulatory politics is not usually partisan. Rather, it is politics of patronage and privilege. The political setting, here as elsewhere in administration, involves legislative oversight, politics of appropriations, concern about new developments such as zero-base budgeting and sunset laws, and attention to political clienteles. For regulators, constituency support can create an awkward and sensitive problem: they are likely to find such support among those in the industries they regulate.

Regulatory agencies' independence from the president is far from absolute, though structural features do shield agency members from some presidential influence. Presidential appointment power, with Senate consent, is substantial, and other forms of White House intervention are not unknown. Proposals to make certain appointees more responsive to presidential leadership have been heard.

Independence from Congress is limited, though agencies have more to do with individual committees and subcommittees (for purposes of routine legislative oversight) than with Congress as a whole. However, agencies occasionally become more involved with the whole Congress, and with individual committees, if there is adverse public or industry reaction to proposed agency actions. The question of agency independence seems to have an ironic answer: agencies are independent to the extent they have adequate political support to insure freedom of action.

Independence from "their" industries is a major problem for regulatory agencies. It has also been the focal point of a number of critical reports prepared by Ralph Nader and his associates, in which they charged widespread collaboration between regulators and those regulated. "Nader's raiders" also accused government regulators of being "monopoly makers," promoting and protecting industry rather than truly regulating in the public interest.

Regulators are in frequent contact with industry leaders both professionally and socially. Much of this is routine. Industries have a legitimate self-interest to uphold, and direct pressure is the rare exception, not the rule. Another problem is that individuals having the kind of expertise needed in, and sought by, the agencies often received their training and experience in the industries themselves, and thus bring with them a not unnatural "industry slant" on problems and needs. An alternative is to appoint someone with no expertise, which breeds another kind of problem.

Consumerism has had major impact on government regulation. Beginning with concern for health hazards of cigarette smoking and for auto safety, the consumer movement has grown to the point that it now wields considerable political influence. Consumer leaders have relied more on administrative regulators than on Congress for registering consumer gains, while attempting to reshape regulation itself. The Nader phenomenon and consumerism are not unrelated; a consumer constituency now exists, accounting for increased regulation. The fact that not everyone supports "consumerism" as a movement—meaning that many who are consumers oppose the "consumerists"—poses political difficulties of major proportions for regulatory entities. Some agencies have begun to adapt to the political squeeze in which they find themselves.

The scope and impact of regulation are immense. Some decisions and actions of government have regulatory effects even though their primary purpose is something else. More narrowly focused regulative activities are numerous, stemming almost entirely from authorizations granted by congressional statute. There have been many controversial regulatory actions.

Regulatory reform has received increasing attention in the 1960s and 1970s. The Landis Report, the Ash Council report, and academic observers such as Friendly and Lowi have all attempted to analyze regulatory problems and offer possible solutions to them. Noll's critique of the Ash Council report included some recommendations based on his own examination of regulatory agencies. President Carter's apparent emphasis has been on more "useful" intervention and on determining actual effects of regulation on how well the public is being served.

We can expect opposing views on regulation to become more intense. Many continue to support regulation in the interest of fairness, equity, and product quality in the marketplace, while others oppose what they see as unwarranted government interference. Government regulation is now at a crossroads.

NOTES

1. *U.S. News and World Report,* May 9, 1977, p. 61.
2. Much of the background information on regulatory activity is derived from the treatment by Louis M. Kohlmeier, Jr., in *The Regulators: Watchdog Agencies and the Public Interest* (New York: Harper & Row, 1969), chapters 1 and 2.
3. Ibid., pp. 9–11.
4. This discussion of policy making and delegation of authority relies on A. Lee Fritschler, *Smoking and Politics: Policy Making and the Federal Bureaucracy,* 2nd ed. (Englewood Cliffs, N.J.: Prentice-Hall, 1975), pp. 54–69, especially pp. 54–59.
5. Ibid., pp. 60–63.
6. Ibid., p. 63.
7. See Kohlmeier, *The Regulators,* pp. 307–309.

8. Morton Grodzins, *The American System: A New View of Government in the United States* (Chicago: Rand McNally, 1966), pp. 75–80.

9. Fritschler, *Smoking and Politics*, p. 91.

10. This description is derived from Kohlmeier, *The Regulators*, chapter 3, and Fritschler, *Smoking and Politics*, chapter 5.

11. Fritschler, *Smoking and Politics*, p. 71.

12. Kohlmeier, *The Regulators*, p. 31.

13. Ibid.

14. Ibid.

15. Fritschler, *Smoking and Politics*, p. 82.

16. Ibid., pp. 100–101, and Kohlmeier, *The Regulators*, p. 32. Administrative law judges are the subject of an entire issue of *Administrative Law Review*, 25 (Winter 1973).

17. Kohlmeier, *The Regulators*, p. 33.

18. Richard E. Cohen, "Taking the FCC to Court," *National Journal*, 9 (April 2, 1977), 522.

19. Two leading sources in administrative law are Kenneth Culp Davis's *Administrative Law and Government*, 2nd ed. (St. Paul, Minn.: West Publishing Company, 1975), and *Discretionary Justice: A Preliminary Inquiry* (Urbana, Ill.: University of Illinois Press, 1971).

20. Fritschler, *Smoking and Politics*, pp. 73–74.

21. Kohlmeier, *The Regulators*, pp. 34–35.

22. Erwin G. Krasnow and Lawrence D. Longley, *The Politics of Broadcast Regulation* (New York: St. Martin's, 1973), chapter 2.

23. As reported in the Bloomington-Normal, Illinois, *Daily Pantagraph*, September 1, 1974, p. A-5, quoting from *Congressional Quarterly Weekly Report*.

24. St. Louis *Post-Dispatch*, July 19, 1973, p. 2A. The study was authorized by Harley Staggers (D–West Virginia), Chairman of the House Committee on Interstate and Foreign Commerce.

25. Kohlmeier, *The Regulators*, pp. 44–45.

26. Members of the FRB serve fourteen-year terms, so that neither Johnson nor Carter could necessarily expect to appoint a new chairman—and, of course, they could not fire the incumbent. As it happens, Burns' term expired January 31, 1978, and Carter did not reappoint him.

27. St. Louis *Post-Dispatch*, December 24, 1973, p. 7B.

28. Kohlmeier, *The Regulators*, pp. 48–50.

29. Ibid., p. 50.

30. Ibid., pp. 65–67.

31. The full story is recounted comprehensively in Fritschler, *Smoking and Politics*, from which the following account is taken.

32. Kohlmeier, *The Regulators*, p. 56.

33. Fritschler, *Smoking and Politics*, pp. 88–139.

34. Krasnow and Longley, *The Politics of Broadcast Regulation*, p. 24.

35. See Samuel P. Huntington, "The Marasmus of the ICC: The Commissions, the Railroads, and the Public Interest," *Yale Law Journal*, 61 (April 1962), 470.

36. William L. Cary, *Politics and the Regulatory Agencies* (New York: McGraw-Hill, 1967), p. 4.

37. Robert C. Fellmeth, *The Interstate Commerce Omission: Ralph Nader's*

Study Group Report on the Interstate Commerce Commission and Transportation (New York: Grossman Publishers, 1970).

38. Mark J. Green, with Beverly C. Moore, Jr., and Bruce Wasserstein, *The Closed Enterprise System: The Nader Study Group Report on Antitrust Enforcement* (Washington, D.C.: Center for the Study of Responsive Law, 1972).

39. Edward F. Cox, Robert C. Fellmeth, and John F. Schulz, *The Nader Report on the Federal Trade Commission* (New York: R. W. Baron, 1969).

40. Mark J. Green, ed., *The Monopoly Makers: Ralph Nader's Study Group Report on Regulation and Competition* (New York: Grossman Publishers, 1973).

41. Ibid., p. ix.

42. Ibid.

43. See Kohlmeier, *The Regulators,* chapter 6.

44. "The Fishbowl Approach to Agency Lobbying," *Business Week,* May 23, 1977, pp. 31–32.

45. Krasnow and Longley, *The Politics of Broadcast Regulation,* pp. 8, 25, 34, 36, 40, and 117–124; "Attack on FCC Pushed by Nicholas Johnson," St. Louis *Post-Dispatch,* July 29, 1973, p. 20A.

46. Quoted in "Regulatory Agencies Being Studied Anew," Bloomington-Normal, Illinois, *Daily Pantagraph,* January 20, 1974, p. A-5 (reprinted from *Congressional Quarterly Weekly Report* [emphasis added]).

47. Fritschler, *Smoking and Politics,* p. 147.

48. Mark V. Nadel, *The Politics of Consumer Protection* (Indianapolis: Bobbs-Merrill, 1971), p. 29; quoted by Fritschler, *Smoking and Politics,* p. 148.

49. *U.S. News and World Report,* May 9, 1977, p. 61.

50. *U.S. News and World Report,* March 28, 1977, p. 49.

51. James Buckley served one term, 1971–1977, after being elected on the Conservative party ticket in New York state in a three-way race in November 1970.

52. Linda E. Demkovich, "Saccharin's Dead, Dieters Are Blue, What Is Congress Going to Do?" *National Journal,* 9 (June 4, 1977), pp. 856–859.

53. Interview with Representative Steven D. Symms (R–Idaho), in *U.S. News and World Report,* June 13, 1977, pp. 51–52.

54. Interview with Dr. David T. Carr, Associate Director for Cancer Control, Mayo Comprehensive Cancer Center, in *U.S. News and World Report,* June 13, 1977, pp. 51–52.

55. Donald Dalrymple, assistant counsel to the House Interstate and Foreign Commerce Subcommittee on Health and the Environment, quoted in *Congressional Quarterly Weekly Report,* 35 (July 2, 1977), 1348.

56. "Flame-Retardant Ban Dishevels an Industry," *Business Week,* April 18, 1977, pp. 45–46.

57. Bloomington-Normal, Illinois, *Daily Pantagraph,* June 23, 1977, p. A-1.

58. Ibid., June 25, 1977, p. A-3.

59. Ibid., June 27, 1977, p. A-6.

60. Ibid., June 28, 1977, p. B-4.

61. Ibid., June 30, 1977, p. A-1, and July 24, 1977, p. B-15.

62. James M. Landis, *Report on Regulatory Agencies to the President-Elect,* published as a committee print by the Subcommittee on Administrative Practice and Procedure of the Senate Committee on the Judiciary, 86th Congress, 2nd Session (Washington, D.C.: U.S. Government Printing Office, 1960).

63. Henry J. Friendly, *The Federal Administrative Agencies: The Need for Better Definition of Standards* (Cambridge: Harvard University Press, 1962).

64. Theodore J. Lowi, *The End of Liberalism: Ideology, Policy, and the Crisis of Public Authority* (New York: W. W. Norton, 1969). This description of the Landis, Friendly, and Lowi recommendations is taken from Roger G. Noll, *Reforming Regulation: An Evaluation of the Ash Council Proposals* (Washington, D.C.: The Brookings Institution, 1971), p. 14.

65. Noll, *Reforming Regulation*, pp. 113–115.

66. Ibid., pp. 12–13.

67. Other critiques of the Ash Council report can be found in Roger C. Cramton, "Regulatory Structure and Regulatory Performance: A Critique of the Ash Council," *Public Administration Review*, 32 (July/August 1972), 284–291, and, in the same issue, John E. Moore, "Recycling the Regulatory Agencies," 291–298.

68. Noll, *Reforming Regulation*, pp. 92–95.

69. See, for example, "Text of President's Message on Regulatory Reform," *Congressional Quarterly Weekly Report*, 34 (May 22, 1976), 1311.

70. Richard E. Cohen, "Carter Has Landed Running on Regulatory Reform Issues," *National Journal*, 9 (April 16, 1977), 592; "Where Carter's Team Wants to Intervene," *Business Week*, April 4, 1977, p. 63. The *Business Week* issue contained a series of articles under the title "Government Intervention" examining likely directions of the Carter administration, pp. 42–95.

71. Cohen, "Carter Has Landed Running on Regulatory Reform Issues," p. 592.

72. Ibid., p. 593.

SUGGESTED READINGS

Cary, William L. *Politics and the Regulatory Agencies.* New York: McGraw-Hill, 1967.

Davis, Kenneth Culp. *Discretionary Justice: A Preliminary Inquiry.* Urbana, Ill.: University of Illinois Press, 1971.

Fritschler, A. Lee. *Smoking and Politics: Policy Making and the Federal Bureaucracy,* 2nd ed. Englewood Cliffs, N.J.: Prentice-Hall, 1975.

"Government Intervention" (a symposium), *Business Week,* April 4, 1977, pp. 42–95.

Green, Mark J., ed. *The Monopoly Makers: Ralph Nader's Study Group Report on Regulation and Competition.* New York: Grossman Publishers, 1973.

Kohlmeier, Louis M., Jr. *The Regulators: Watchdog Agencies and the Public Interest.* New York: Harper & Row, 1969.

Krasnow, Erwin G., and Lawrence D. Longley. *The Politics of Broadcast Regulation.* New York: St. Martin's, 1973.

Nadel, Mark V. *The Politics of Consumer Protection.* Indianapolis: Bobbs-Merrill, 1971.

Noll, Roger G. *Reforming Regulation: An Evaluation of the Ash Council Proposals*. Washington, D.C.: The Brookings Institution, 1971.

Redford, Emmette S. *The Regulatory Process*. Austin: University of Texas Press, 1969.

Wiesen, Jeremy L. *Regulating Transactions in Securities*. St. Paul, Minn.: West Publishing Company, 1975.

CHAPTER 12
Implementing and Evaluating Public Policies

To speak of "government policy" in areas such as agriculture, environmental quality, foreign affairs, health, transportation, or land use planning somehow conveys an impression of well-defined purposes—carefully mapped out, the necessary resources marshaled and at the ready, with consistent support through the political process. But reality is usually very different from this conception. In a complex system such as ours, there is no *one* political majority capable of determining policy in every instance. Congressional voting coalitions are usually quite temporary, changing from one issue to the next; presidential election majorities are often fashioned out of very diverse groups in the population, each with its own policy interests, which can conflict with one another; court rulings may or may not coincide with public sentiment; administrative agencies are not permanently tied to any one political coalition. The combined impact of these institutions and of a very heterogeneous population on formulating, implementing, and evaluating public policy tends to blur rather than clarify policy objectives and content. Instead of being clear and unmistakable government commitments, many policies are "mixed bags" of programs which represent a variety of past actions and declarations, *ad hoc* responses to contemporary situations, and considerable uncertainty about future policy directions.

In this chapter we will examine the nature of public policies; the policy-making process, particularly as it involves administrative entities; goal setting in public programs; analysis of possible options in program planning; implementation, including how and to what extent some policy directions are altered in the course of implementing individual programs; how programs are (or could be) evaluated and what is done with those evaluations; and the problem of productivity. Our ultimate purpose is to understand how public policies evolve as they do, and the role of administrative politics in this process.

The Nature of Public Policies

What precisely is "public policy"? It has been defined as "whatever governments choose to do or not do,"[1] and also as the organizing framework of purposes and rationales for government programs which deal with specified societal problems. Most people regard public policies as fairly deliberate responses to problems and needs systematically defined or identified by some legitimate means. And it is commonly assumed that governmental policies are addressed to solving—or at least coping with—major social and economic problems. However, there may be some disparity between what the average citizen believes about policy processes and outcomes, and the realities of policy making in America.

Let us consider some of the most common popular assumptions about government policy in general. First, many people seem to assume that governments have clearly defined policies, well thought out in advance, on all or most major issues and problems in the political arena. Second, many believe these policies are established deliberately, through some kind of rational choice made by political leaders and others. Third, some think—logically enough—that everything we then do about a problem or issue follows those policies. Fourth, it is often assumed that the policies of government are clearly perceived and understood by citizens. And fifth, it is commonly assumed that government policies are widely agreed upon and supported—otherwise, how could they remain in force? As appealing or logical as these ideas might seem, however, the fact is that *every one of them is a myth.*

First, public policy in American government is *not* clearly defined in the sense that major problems are anticipated and the machinery of government geared up to meet them before they get out of hand. That would require the kind of centralized leadership resisted, for many reasons, by most participants in the political system. Some processes designed to foresee future developments and prepare for them, such as planning and PPBS, have not accomplished all they were intended to, and "circumstances beyond our control" often prevail. Also, governments do not have policies on all issues, through either inaction or a decision *not* to have a policy. Thus policies tend to be quite a bit less consistent and coherent than many might like.

Second, policies are much more the product of responses to particular sets of circumstances or individual problems than they are of deliberate establishment. They frequently result from decisions made at many levels, at different times, and in all probability by officials and others who see only some parts of the overall problem. Rational policy choice implies a decision-making capacity largely lacking in our noncentralized government institutions.

Third, many government programs and activities do not follow official policy directions or support official goals. Political party platforms, pronouncements by top executives, even resolutions of Congress are often a better reflection of intent than of reality in policy making. What actually takes place may well differ from official definitions of what was supposed to take place.

Fourth, many policies are not clearly perceived and understood by the general population. We tend to pay attention to government activity likely to have a tangible impact on our lives, but otherwise it is unusual for large numbers of people to fully comprehend the intricacies of public policy. A good example is foreign policy. Different nationality groups are sensitive to even small changes in what the government does or contemplates doing regarding "their" mother country, but most citizens have only a generalized awareness of U.S. foreign policy—detente with the Soviet Union, relations with mainland China, peace efforts in the Middle East, and so on. Many domestic policies, such as farm or transportation policy, are also understood only in broad outline. It is not accurate, in short, to assume that most Americans are knowledgeable in detail about individual public policies.

Finally, it is not true that there is widespread, *active* support for existing public policies, although it can be said that most policies have at least *passive* backing. Policy directions which offend basic values of large numbers of people are not likely to be sustained for very long without at least being challenged. Examples of sharp public reaction to unpopular policies include flagrant violations of Prohibition in the 1920s, opposition to the 1973 Supreme Court ruling on abortion which permits women to terminate their pregnancies in the first three months without interference from government, and strong resistance to judicial and legislative enactments mandating school busing to desegregate public schools. In one sense, policies that exist without widespread challenge may be taken as a sort of "barometer" of public feeling about what is acceptable. Few policies survive which offend either powerful political interests or large numbers of ordinary citizens, or both. In sum, while support for what government does is not necessarily active or enthusiastic, public policies have to have a certain amount of *acceptability*.

A few other observations are in order. For one thing, it makes a difference what situations are defined as "problems" and thus deserving of attention in the policy process. Poverty, for example, was part of the American scene for years before it was identified as a problem of high priority by Presidents Kennedy and Johnson in the 1960s. Women's rights, Indian affairs, consumer protection, and hunger are other examples of current issue areas which required political definition as policy problems long before any action was taken. Also, policy initiative can come from many parts of the body politic—the president, Congress, interest groups, the mass media, state or local government, and so on. Perhaps the only policy maker prohibited from initiating policy changes on its own is the judiciary. While chief executives are usually in the best position to take the initiative in developing policy, they have no monopoly on attempting to raise issues for public and governmental attention. Furthermore, most policy changes come about slowly, since it is far easier to resist change then to bring it about. American government tends to move in evolutionary, not revolutionary, fashion; incrementalism is the order of the day, most of the time. Finally, many policy actions are more symbolic than real, especially those with the appearance of change. Symbolism is not without value in politics, but it should be understood for what it is and not confused with substantive change.[2] Because most citizens lack comprehensive familiarity with policy, symbolic actions are often sufficient to satisfy calls for change without threatening the status quo. The passing of public attention from an issue ogten signals a slowdown in dealing with it, even where many in government would prefer to move more rapidly. Organized group support and opposition make a major difference in how substantive—or simply cosmetic—policy changes are.

Public policies, then, tend to be unsystematic, situational rather than deliberate, not widely understood or actively supported, and often inconsistently applied. Not all situations in society which might be defined as problem areas are in fact so defined. Sometimes an unspoken policy exists to take no action on a problem, and most changes in policy are rather slow and unfocused. The wonder is that any coherent policies exist.[3]

The Policy-Making Process

The policy-making process involves all the demands, pressures, conflicts, negotiations and compromises, and formal and informal decisions which result in given policies being adopted, by law or other rules, and pursued through actions of government. This is obviously a broad definition, and deliberately so, for making policy is not the exclusive province of any one branch of government or indeed of any one level of government in the federal system. Political scientist Charles O. Jones has emphasized the complexity of making public policy in American government, focusing not only on interactions of national, state, and local governments but also on involvement of private interests pressing government to respond to their specialized concerns.[4]

Other authors as well have noted the intricate and complex nature of policy making, which little resembles the formal structure laid out by the framers for deciding what government does, let alone matches expectations of coherent, rational, comprehensive, and well-coordinated policy.[5] If, as some contend, there are "policy-making systems" in American government, it seems safe to say they are not very *systematic* systems. Most policies, as noted earlier, are not created whole, successfully mapped out ahead of time, or even put into effect exactly as their architects had intended. The policy-making process is characterized by a lack of centralized direction at every level of government; it is complex, very loosely coordinated, highly competitive, fragmented and specialized (like budgeting), and largely incremental.

Policy making is also an interdependent and overlapping process within the machinery of government, with only bits and pieces of a policy being made in any one place, and others in the process frequently holding an informal veto over actions taken. As one example, environmental policy emerges out of activities conducted by the national Environmental Protection Agency, the President's Council on Environmental Quality, at least three standing committees apiece in the House and Senate, the federal courts, and state and local environmental agencies. To expect consistency in all the decisions of such an amalgam is to expect too much. Prevailing views and doctrines regarding environmental policy are likely to be as diverse as the number of majority coalitions represented in each of these decision-making arenas. For instance, regulating strip mine reclamation is likely to be handled very differently in a state with limited coal reserves than it is in Pennsylvania or West Virginia, where coal operators with considerable political influence can weaken the regulations, or enforcement, or both.

This pattern is repeated in virtually all major policy areas affecting large economic and social interests: agriculture, business, labor, consumers, racial and other ethnic groups, and so on. Also, it is possible for groups frustrated in attaining their policy objectives at one level of government to turn elsewhere and receive some measure of satisfaction. This tactic was used successfully by civil rights groups which sought national government action to overturn state resistance to legal equality for blacks.[6] Thus the policy-making process is not a smoothly functioning, ongoing sequence where one phase predictably follows another. It responds, rather, to pressures placed upon it at many points along the way, so that policy usually reflects the influence of diverse political forces.

Where administrative agencies have a central role in the policy process, as they do now in most instances, policy making is best described as occurring in four stages.[7] The first is a legislative stage involving both Congress and the president, in which basic legislation is drawn up, considered, and approved as law. The second and third stages, primarily administrative in nature, involve writing by the agency of detailed regulations and rules governing application of the law, followed by actual implementation. The fourth is a review stage, by the courts or Congress or perhaps both, during which modifications of existing policy are possible for legal, substantive, or political reasons. As one observer has noted, "problems and demands are constantly being defined and redefined in the policy process."[8] This suggests these stages are part of policy *cycles,* with incremental adjustments in existing policies a routine phenomenon.

One further aspect of policy making worth mentioning is the extensive impact of intergovernmental relations and of intergovernmental policy development. As we discussed in chapter 5, many facets of both program funding and administration are tied closely either to intergovernmental collaboration or competition, or to parallel activities of some kind, as in the case of environmental policy. This serves to complicate both policy making and any effort to trace the roots of a particular policy direction. Legislative and administrative mechanisms at each level of government are fairly complex, affording numerous opportunities for interested parties to have some say in the policy-making process. Slight alterations in policy are possible each time influence is exerted, and their cumulative effects at the same level of government can be significant. It is not difficult to imagine what multiplying these patterns by three levels of government can do to the shape of policy. Intergovernmental dimensions, then, are an important contributing factor to the overall policy process.

In sum, the policy-making process helps account for the disjointed nature of most public policies. An absence of centralized direction and the opportunity for influence to be exerted at multiple points characterize many phases of policy making, producing policies which look—accurately—as though they were arrived at from many directions at once. It is not difficult for a chief executive, for example, to *define* a formal policy intention, but it is another matter altogether to put it into effect. On one occasion John F. Kennedy signed a bill into law, then turned to his aides and remarked: "We have made the law. Now it remains to be seen whether we can get our government to do it."[9]

From the earlier discussion regarding myths about public policy, it is clear "policy" refers both to *intentions* and to actual *results* of governmental activity. One must be careful, therefore, about the sense in which the term is used. Results, however, are normally sought and evaluated in the context of specific government programs rather than broad policies. Programs, in turn, can be further divided into projects dependent for their completion on individual performance on the job. The interrelationships among what might be called the "four *P*s"—policy, program, project, and performance—are crucial to ultimate outcomes of government operations. From a managerial standpoint, no one of them stands in isolation from the other three; each is affected by the others. Figure 12–1 schematically represents linkages among the "four *P*s."[10]

The linkage uniting policies, programs, projects, and individual performance is an important one. Policies are put into effect only to the degree program objectives related to them are met; programs in turn are the sum totals of supporting projects; and each project represents the labors of individuals within the responsible agencies. Discussion of public policy in a "management" sense must focus, then, on *programs* and *projects,* the essential building blocks of what government does. While there are some differences between the two in terms of organizing and di-

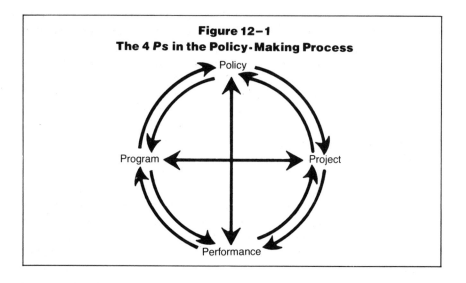

Figure 12–1
The 4 Ps in the Policy-Making Process

recting them, we will emphasize a number of management concerns common to both. They are (1) goal setting, (2) processes of analysis and choice in deciding on courses of action, (3) implementation, (4) evaluation, and (5) productivity.

Goal Setting in Public Programs

Charles O. Jones has defined a government *program* as "a concrete proposition about solving a public problem—that is, somebody's estimate of what will work."[11] Program goals, then, are clearly problem-related; programs themselves are proposed or attempted solutions. Many problems, in fact, are never fully solved—merely addressed—through government action.[12] The choice of goals can make a major difference in shaping policy generally, as well as specific program and project activities managed by an agency.

Public management, in contrast to that in much of the private sector, is characterized by managers who are *not* the principal decision makers about their organization's goals.[13] Executives, interest groups, and especially legislatures have much more to do with defining program and organization goals, creating at least the possibility of goal ambiguity or inconsistency within given programs. Often administrators have discretion in establishing an order of priority among sets of goals and determining the methods used in pursuing them. While that can mean considerable influence over programs or projects, it is not the same as control of goals.

Figure 12–2 is a basic planning guide which could be used by public managers in determining a course of action, beginning with preliminary consideration of goals. (It will be useful to refer to Figure 12–2 throughout this discussion of policies and programs.) Essential steps are identifying desired outcomes, predicting what will actually take place, and assessing probabilities of achieving desired outcomes. Depending on the results of such deliberations, goals can be selected, perhaps modified, and ultimately agreed upon by those involved in pursuing them. The point is, however, that in one form or another this *must* be done early in the life cycle of a project or program, and done periodically throughout its existence, to make any sense out of varied support activities. For example, it would be considered careless policy making to spend program funds for "improving education" without a clear idea of specific project goals—remedial reading instruction, additional equipment and materials, more counseling services, or better testing methods and devices. These are demonstrably related to the broader program goal of "improving education," which in turn may be part of an urban policy designed to "improve the quality of urban life." Certainly at the project level, and most probably for programs and policies, goal definition is a key step.

However, as noted in chapter 7, goals are not simply "there." They must be arrived at in deliberate fashion, and can reflect varying combinations of substantive and political judgments about the need to pursue them. Program and project managers contribute to shaping goals but, as mentioned above, ordinarily are not official goal setters. Thus goal definition for the middle-level manager is a shared process, one in which dominant voices are often those outside the agency. Yet an effort to delineate goals must be made *inside* the agency as well.

Analysis and Choice: Deciding What Actions to Take

Agency performance frequently depends on the quality of prior analysis regarding projected impacts of activities on the problem at hand. Politically, the old adage "good government (that is, performance) is good politics" has never been more true. For agencies with strong political backing, a solid foundation of objective program analysis adds strength to strength. For weak agencies, careful and thorough analysis of their options before selecting the most appropriate one(s) might make the difference between organizational vitality and decay. Gordon Chase, former administrator of the New York City Health Services Administration, has commented on the political importance of analysis:

> In my view, politics happens very often when there is a vacuum, when there is no real analysis. Then resource allocation decision is usually based on who has more clout or who screams louder. . . . [I]f you don't have the analytic talent and if important decisions are up, they'll be made, but they'll be made by another process than analysis.[14]

Figure 12–2
PLANNING GUIDE

I. *What precisely do I want to accomplish?*

    A. First attempt to predict what will occur.

    B. Plan and implement only if
        1. Disaster appears likely (possible);
        2. Substantial improvement is likely.

    C. Identify precisely the outcome I seek.

    D. Why do I seek it?
        1. Good in itself given my values. (If so, do I wish to reconsider my values?)
        2. I believe it will lead to a further outcome which I value. (If so, can I state the causal chain so I can retest?)
        3. I believe it will lead to behavior by other governments. (If so, consider that the other government is not a unitary actor and that its bureaucracy will do only what is in their interest in their own terms. Influence is most likely to take the form of altering incentives and power. Consider also how reliable my information is about the other government.)

    E. How likely am I to get the outcome as I desire it?
        1. Withhold judgment until working out paths to action and strategy.
        2. Consider relevant programs and standard operating procedures.
        3. Consider internal and external biases.

    F. How important is this outcome to me as compared to others?

II. *Alternative paths to action*

    A. Map out alternative routes to the desired outcome.

    B. Recognize that a change in policy may be neither necessary nor sufficient.

    C. Seek to change policy only if
        1. Necessary to remove an absolute barrier to changing action;
        2. Useful as a hunting license;
        3. Necessary given my access to those who must perform the action;
        4. Likely to lead easily to a change in action.

    D. Consider how high I need to go. (Do not involve the President unless necessary or he is likely to be sympathetic, i.e., unless he has a problem this may solve.)

    E. If seeking a change in policy, plot the action path from there to changes in actions.

    F. Consider for each path who will have the action. (Is there any path in which I will have the action?)

    G. Specify the formal actions which are necessary.

    H. What resources do I have to move action along each path with success? (Re-judge after considering tactics.) Relative advantages of each path.

    I. How will resources expended to get to one way-station outcome affect ability to get to further stations?

    J. What additional information will help? Can I get it? At what cost?

Figure 12–2
PLANNING GUIDE

III. *Framing tactics—maneuvers and arguments—to move along a path*
  A. Identification of the participants and their interests, including those beyond the executive branch.
    1. Who will inevitably be involved according to the rules of the game?
    2. Who might seek to play but could be excluded?
    3. Who might not seek to play but could be brought in?
    4. What are the likely interests of the various participants, what face of the issue will they see, how will they define the stakes? Consider organization, personal, political, and national interests.
    5. Who are natural allies, unappeasable opponents, neutrals who might be converted to support, or opponents who might be converted to neutrality?
  B. How can I lead a participant to see that the outcomes I desire are in his interest as he sees it?
  C. How can I change the situation to have an outcome conflicting less (or not at all) with participants' interests as they see them?
  D. Do I have the resources for this purpose? If not, can I get others to use theirs?
  E. What specific maneuvers should I use at what stages?
  F. What arguments should I use:
    1. In general?
    2. On a discriminatory basis?
  G. If I must get a large organization to change its behavior, I must consider the interests, standard operating procedures, and programs of that organization.
  H. Should I try to bring in players outside the executive branch? If so, how?
  I. How can I tell how well I am doing?

IV. *Gauging costs and benefits*
  A. Reconsider all phases from time to time. Specifically:
    1. How high up should one seek a decision?
    2. How should the decision sought relate to the change desired, i.e., should it be a decision to change policy, to change patterns of action, or to take a single particular new step (or to stop an on-going action)?
    3. By what means will the initial decision which is sought be converted into the desired action?
  B. Plan of action.
    1. How to move the action to the way-station and final outcome desired.
    2. What maneuvers and arguments to use on or with the other participants.
    3. A time sequence.

(continued)

Figure 12–2
PLANNING GUIDE

C. To what extent is this process consciously duplicated by participants seeking a change? Are some participants more likely to plan than others? To plan effectively?

D. How is the choice of way-station outcomes and route action made?

Source: Graham T. Allison and Morton H. Halperin, "Bureaucratic Politics: A Paradigm and Some Policy Implications," in *Theory and Policy in International Relations,* ed. by Raymond Tanter and Richard H. Ullman (Princeton: Princeton University Press, 1972), pp. 77–79.

The purpose of analysis is to facilitate the reaching of sound decisions by establishing relevant facts about a situation before attempting to change it in some way, and by determining if possible the respective consequences of different courses of action. The nature of a given problem is not always clear—for example, in the area of education, poverty, military preparedness, or energy—and analysis can help sharpen the focus of decision makers as they consider various objectives and options. Several kinds of analysis might be used; we will review each one briefly.

Policy analysis can be defined as "the systematic investigation of alternative policy options and the assembly and integration of the evidence for and against each option."[15] While activities suggested by such a definition have long been a part of the governmental process, only in the past four decades has a distinct analysis function become *formally* associated with public decision making. A key emphasis in policy analysis is on explaining the nature of problems, and how policies addressed to those problems are put into effect. Some observers believe, however, that an equally legitimate function is to improve, in some sense, processes of policy making as well as policy content.

In its broadest sense, policy analysis makes it possible to investigate policy outcomes in interrelated fields, examine in depth the causes of societal and other problems, and establish cause-and-effect relationships among problems, the contexts in which they occur, and potential solutions. Figure 12–3 is a model of the complex relationships within the overall policy-making process (though most program or project managers would concentrate on analyzing only those considerations most relevant to their immediate responsibilities).

Since problems vary widely in their scope and complexity, policy analysis needs to be flexible enough to permit selection of analytical approaches and techniques appropriate to the particular problem under study. One proposal (among many others) for dealing with this dimension of policy analysis suggests four types of analysis suitable to four different

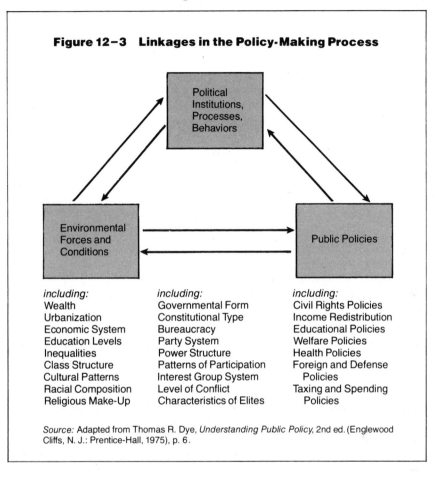

Figure 12–3   Linkages in the Policy-Making Process

Political Institutions, Processes, Behaviors

Environmental Forces and Conditions

Public Policies

including:	*including:*	*including:*
Wealth	Governmental Form	Civil Rights Policies
Urbanization	Constitutional Type	Income Redistribution
Economic System	Bureaucracy	Educational Policies
Education Levels	Party System	Welfare Policies
Inequalities	Power Structure	Health Policies
Class Structure	Patterns of Participation	Foreign and Defense
Cultural Patterns	Interest Group System	Policies
Racial Composition	Level of Conflict	Taxing and Spending
Religious Make-Up	Characteristics of Elites	Policies

Source: Adapted from Thomas R. Dye, *Understanding Public Policy,* 2nd ed. (Englewood Cliffs, N. J.: Prentice-Hall, 1975), p. 6.

sets of circumstances.[16] They are (1) *issue analysis,* where there is a relatively specific policy choice (for example, whether a particular group of businesses or industries should receive a tax reduction) and a highly politicized environment of decision making; (2) *program analysis,* involving both design and evaluation of a particular program (for example, a manpower-training program); (3) *multi-program analysis,* in which decisions must be made concerning resource allocation among programs dealing with the same problem (for instance, different manpower-training programs); and (4) *strategic analysis,* where the policy problem is very large (for example, an economic development strategy for a depressed region). Clearly, different types of problems require analytic approaches tailored to their particular dimensions.

Policy analysis faces some obstacles, however. For one thing, it is not clear what kind of analysis can be done, and what uses can (or should) be made of the results, where negotiation and bargaining among competing political forces are the most common means of carving out policy. Furthermore, as was demonstrated during recent attempts to install and implement PPBS (see chapter 10), adequate numbers of skilled analysts have to be trained—and sufficient resources spent on doing so—before analysis can reach its full potential. Some efforts to cope with these problems, especially the latter, are under way. And, increasingly, policy analysis is becoming better established as a concrete function of governmental decision making.

Systems analysis, a second major analytical approach, is usable (in principle) for comprehensively diagnosing how *all* elements of a political, social, economic, or administrative system might affect—and be affected by—a given project or program. Managers utilizing systems analysis need to be aware of overall systemic objectives and performance (assuming these can be identified and measured), the surrounding social environment, available resources, system components (such as individual programs within a governmental system), and how the system is managed.[17] The overriding objective of systems analysis is to produce greater rationality in management decision making, and efficiency and effectiveness in actual program operations. In terms of the discussion of decision making in chapter 7, systems analysis is devoted to the *rational* approach. The comments made there about seeking comprehensiveness, coping with information needs, and maximizing return on a given investment of resources also apply to systems analysis.

A strength of systems analysis is its permitting a broader view of constraints and consequences relating to an individual program. A weakness, besides those associated with rational decision making, is the possibility that trying to achieve rationality within a single system will cause decision makers to ignore other systems that might also be relevant. An example would be an effort to analyze political factors influencing federal grants-in-aid to states and localities without also analyzing the nation's economy, which ultimately provides the tax base for raising necessary revenues. Systems analysis, then, must be used with care, to avoid seemingly rational "tunnel vision" concerning variables relevant to decision making.

Cost-benefit analysis is a means of measuring relative gains and losses resulting from alternative policy or programmatic options. Usually referred to in quantitative terms and with an assumption of implicit objectivity, it can greatly assist decision makers and program managers in determining the most beneficial path of action to follow. A cost-benefit analysis seeks to identify the actions with the most desirable ratio of benefit to cost, in whatever terms deemed appropriate. Given adequate information, cost-benefit analysis can be very useful in narrowing a range of choices to those most likely to yield desired gains for an affordable cost.

In sum, analysis is a key managerial support activity. As noted earlier, knowledge is power in administrative politics, and analysis greatly enhances a manager's ability to obtain, organize, and apply relevant information in the course of choosing desirable program options.

Program Implementation

In speaking of implementation, we shall adopt Charles Jones's definition of the term, as well as his elaboration of it:

> Let us say simply that by implementation we mean *those activities directed toward putting a program into effect*. Three sets of activities, in particular, are significant: *interpretation*—the translation of program language into acceptable and feasible directives; *organization*—the establishment of units and methods for putting a program into effect; and *application*—the routine provision of services, payments, or other agreed-upon program objectives or instruments.[18]

By taking legislative language and transforming it into clear administrative guidelines, by developing necessary arrangements and routines, and by actually furnishing mandated services, programs are carried out and, ultimately, policies implemented (see Figure 12–4).

All that sounds rather routine. Many citizens apparently *expect* program implementation to be relatively easy under normal conditions. We therefore seek to explain programmatic failures in terms of conflict, extraordinary events, or unexpected circumstances which develop in the course of implementation. However, failure to implement programs in accord with our expectations can often be explained by looking at less dramatic factors in the situation. For example, major difficulties were encountered in putting into effect a much-heralded program of the federal Economic Development Administration (EDA) in Oakland, California, designed to provide permanent jobs to minorities through economic development:

> The evils that afflicted the EDA program in Oakland were of a prosaic and everyday character. Agreements had to be *maintained* after they were reached. Numerous approvals and clearances had to be obtained from a variety of participants. . . . [T]hese *perfectly ordinary circumstances present serious obstacles to implementation. . . .* If one is always looking for unusual circumstances and dramatic events, he cannot appreciate *how difficult it is to make the ordinary happen.*[19]

Thus, even under normal circumstances, it is not routine at all to implement a program or a policy. Few things can be taken for granted in implementation, least of all that participants in a program will automatically "fall in line" in trying to make a program or policy work. Not that they harbor suspect or devious motives; it is simply a case of cooperation hav-

Figure 12−4
A Simplified Representation of the Implementation Process

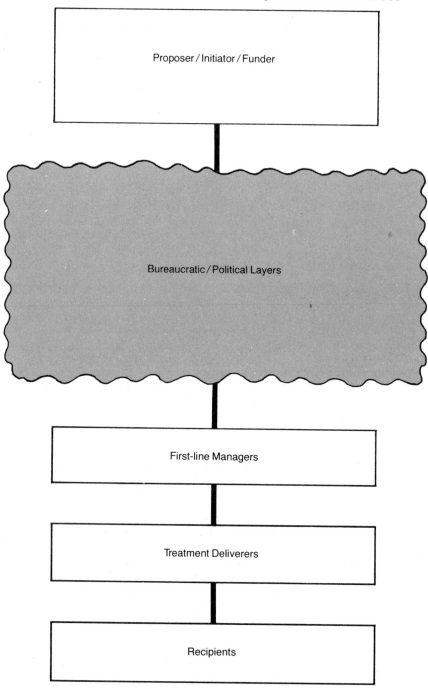

Source: Walter Williams, "Implementation Analysis and Assessment," *Policy Analysis,* I
(Summer 1975), p. 546.

ing to be *induced* on a routine basis rather than being *assumed*. Virtually everyone participating in management of a program has other responsibilities, causing some diverting of attention among even the most conscientious individuals. In sum, a concerted effort is required simply to manage the most minimal aspects of program implementation successfully.

Clearly, what applies to implementing individual programs also applies to policy implementation, perhaps even more so. One policy area may contain numerous programs, all directed toward attainment of broad policy objectives, each one confronted with ordinary problems of program management. Programs which seem to duplicate each other are not uncommon, and not surprisingly they may compete and interfere with one another in operation. It is no wonder, then, that so many policies are said to be only partially implemented—contrary to legislative mandates, executive orders, and public expectations. The essential point, however, is this: failures in implementation are traceable far more often to these rather unexciting obstacles than to anything more dramatic.[20]

Dynamics of Implementation

On occasion it is necessary to create a separate organizational unit to implement a new program or pursue a new or redefined policy direction. This can happen in a number of ways. One is creation of a totally new agency, such as the national Environmental Protection Agency. Another is consolidation, upgrading, or division of existing agencies, as in the case of splitting the Atomic Energy Commission into the Energy Research and Development Administration and the Nuclear Regulatory Commission. More often, however, programs are assigned to existing agencies, which must still interpret and apply the laws as well as develop appropriate methods of implementation.

In most legislation, Congress's intentions regarding program implementation are stated very broadly, such as carrying out a program in a "reasonable" manner, or—to cite a phrase commonly incorporated in federal laws—"in the public interest, convenience, and necessity."[21] Thus the responsible agency has a great deal of discretion in developing operating guidelines and substantive details. This can result in a key agency role in molding and shaping legislated programs, and possibly *modifying* congressional intent. Political pressure on agencies responsible for implementing congressional directives is both real and constant. If it is true, as Jones suggests, that "programs often reflect an attainable consensus rather than a substantive conviction,"[22] it follows that if the *political* consensus changes in the course of implementing a law, chances are good that its implementation will also be modified to accommodate the change.

Since congressional language is so often vague, interpreting legislative intent can present pitfalls for an agency. Representatives and senators themselves, and their state and local counterparts, frequently cannot comprehend all the implications of their enactments. A classic illustration of that was legislation creating the Office of Economic Opportunity (OEO) and undertaking a seemingly comprehensive war on poverty. Members of Congress and many others had difficulty defining precisely what the legislative mandate to OEO really was.[23] Without clear guidance, an agency may be left to fend for itself in the political arena, and—worse—be caught up in disputes over just what the legislature meant (as happened with OEO). Not only is it difficult to make interpretations of initial legislative intent; it is also a tricky business to keep abreast of changing legislative intent after passage of the original law and in the absence of formal amendments to it. We will deal more extensively below with that aspect of implementation.

Many times authorizing legislation represents the best available compromise among competing forces in the legislative process rather than an enactment enthusiastically endorsed by all. Under those circumstances it is nearly certain that conflicts avoided or diluted in the course of formulating a law will crop up in the processes of interpreting and implementing it. Such controversy is not likely to do the responsible agency any good in the political process.[24] Thus interpretation, while necessary, is potentially burdensome.

Application of legislation follows from its interpretation by an agency, and represents more often than not a further series of compromises and accommodations. Applying a law is complicated by the likelihood that other agencies at the same and other government levels also have an interest in the policy area and may well have programs of their own, by difficulties in determining optimum methods for carrying out legislative intent, and even by continuing uncertainty about the nature of a problem or program goals. Many programs are put into operation without full appreciation of a problem's dimensions; political needs to "do something" can outweigh careful and thorough consideration of what is to be done.[25] One example of this phenomenon is the poverty program, referred to previously. Another is funding made available to local law enforcement agencies through the federal Law Enforcement Assistance Administration (LEAA). In the latter case, public concern about rising crime rates prompted Congress to allocate funds for more (and presumably better) crime-fighting hardware, police officer training, and so on. But in retrospect, though there have been improvements in fighting crime, it is not clear that LEAA has done what it was supposed to—partly because there is less than universal agreement on just what that was, and partly because the problem of crime has many more facets to it than simply ability of the police to control it. Similar obstacles hamper application of other policies and programs as well.

It is necessary, then, for agencies to determine the limits to which they can go in applying or enforcing a policy. Usually informal under-standings are reached between program managers and persons or groups outside the agency about what will and will not be done. The danger here, of course, is co-optation of the program by external forces. Depending on the balance of forces, programs may be more or less vigorously pursued; the more controversial a program, the more likely there will be resistance to it.

Support for an individual program is also affected by other programs an agency is responsible for managing, and the order of priority among them within the agency. Still another factor affecting program application is the values and preferences of agency personnel concerning individual programs, as well as their own role and function. Two examples illustrate these points. The first is the response of the Economic Development Administration, particularly its Seattle regional office serving the San Francisco–Oakland area, when the head of EDA formulated a program for promoting minority hiring in Oakland. An Oakland task force was also es-tablished, bypassing normal organizational channels. Many in EDA felt more comfortable working with its traditional concern, that of *rural* eco-nomic development, and after departure of the person who had set up the Oakland program and task force, pressure grew for greater involvement of EDA regional office personnel. At the same time, the Oakland project was treated with far less urgency by EDA, a reflection of its standing in the eyes of most EDA employees working with it.[26]

The second example concerns the educational aid program directed toward disadvantaged students under Title I of the Elementary and Secondary Education Act of 1965 (ESEA). The U.S. Office of Education (USOE), responsible for administering Title I, had spent much of its existence providing technical help to state education agencies and local school districts, taking what one observer called "a passive role with respect to the states," with little insistence on monitoring state activities to be sure they were in compliance with federal law.[27] Title I, by breaking new ground in federal aid to education, called on USOE to administer much larger amounts of federal money and direct much of it into pre-viously uncharted areas, especially aid to culturally and economically disadvantaged school children.[28] Some of the problems said to exist under Title I are traceable to USOE's institutional inertia, stemming from unfa-miliarity with, and reluctance to enter into, new policy directions staked out for it by education reformers in Congress and national educational interest groups. In sum, factors internal as well as external to an agency determine just how far, how fast, and how enthusiastically a program is implemented.

Techniques of Implementation

There are numerous program management techniques that might be used in carrying on agency activities. Traditionally, little attention was paid to this aspect of administration. It was apparently assumed that once a program was in place with adequate funding and political support, writing of operating rules and regulations and actual administering of the program followed routinely. However, specific management techniques which apply to tasks of program operation have evolved since World War II. We will examine two of the most important: Program Evaluation and Review Technique (PERT), which can include a related device known as Critical Path Method; and Management by Objectives.

PERT is a management technique founded on the belief that it is necessary to map out the *sequence* of steps taken in carrying out a program, or project within a program. The steps involved normally include: (1) deciding to address a given problem; (2) choosing activities necessary to deal with all relevant aspects of the problem; and (3) drawing up estimates of the time and other resources required, including minimum, maximum, and most likely amounts.[29] These help the administrator determine what needs to be done and—more important—in what order, as well as time and resource constraints in completing various steps in a project, or projects within a program. Ideally, a PERT chart should indicate how various activities are related to one another in terms of their respective timetables, sequence of execution, and relative resource consumption.

A PERT chart can also be useful in calculating the amounts of time, funding, personnel, and materials which will be necessary, and how much *extra* the agency might have of each of those. For this reason PERT charts are often used to calculate probable resource and time requirements for alternative paths of action. Such charts enable a program manager to see which path of action represents the best choice in terms of having "margins of safety," as well as to evaluate alternative paths. The smaller the surplus of time, money, and other resources, the more critical an individual path of action is. The path with the smallest margins of extra resources with which to complete all assigned program activities is the *critical path*—thus, the Critical Path Method—because any small breakdown in program management, for whatever reason, then becomes critical in determining success or failure of the program. Advance knowledge of such possibilities is clearly in the best interests of the manager, program, and agency.

Despite increasing sophistication in methods such as PERT and Critical Path, there remains a large component of human calculation in determining optimum paths of action to follow. While activities are interdependent and must therefore be planned with an eye to step-by-step execution, there are no assurances that calculations will be accurate.[30] The point is, "best estimates" are often the most reliable data available in projecting into the future. They can be very educated guesses, it is true, but there are risks in placing too much stock in them. Yet often that is all a program manager has to go on.

regarded by some as one of MBO's most important elements; this aspect has been described as one of employee *commitment* to organization objectives, in addition to participation in determining them.[36] (Note, by the way, the similarity between this view of necessary personal commitment and Lawrence Mohr's view of organizational goals discussed in chapter 7.)

The various phases and features of MBO have considerable appeal to those seeking to strengthen management; however, as with other approaches to improving management, there are obstacles to MBO's full realization (some of which we discussed earlier in reference to goals). One observer has noted that agencies often have no *unambiguous* goals, and that it is difficult to make operational the ones they do have.[37] Another dimension is that an organization's stated objectives may not be the real objectives. Furthermore, there are *"no commonly accepted standards for monitoring performance or measuring achievements of many public objectives."*[38]

If, however, objectives can be defined and operationalized, MBO can be a useful management instrument. It is capable of coexisting comfortably in the short run with PERT, and in the longer run with PPBS, zero-base budgeting, and sunset laws. While its application in the national government already appears to have waned somewhat,[39] its residual effects seem destined to take their place alongside those of PPBS and become part of the foundation for further management developments, such as ZBB. MBO may have value, together with ZBB, in helping decision makers choose which programs to postpone, and in effect, abandon.[40] In a time of great concern about priority setting, MBO may prove to have been a harbinger of things to come.

Problems of Implementation

Despite availability of numerous techniques of implementation, problems common to many managerial situations persist. It is appropriate to treat briefly three of the most important ones.

First, management control is a continuing challenge. This problem has two dimensions—an internal one relating to management's ability to secure subordinates' cooperation in program activities, and an external one concerning the agency's ability to cope with individual situations and with the surrounding environment. The more pressing of the two, from a manager's standpoint, is the internal challenge. Control of staffing, allocation of fiscal resources, designation of work assignments, and delegating discretionary authority are potentially useful devices for enhancing management control. Even these, however, do not guarantee effective managerial direction of internal activities.

Related to management control is the challenge of developing harmonious, productive, and beneficial working relationships within an agency.

The other major technique for implementing a program or p(
Management by Objectives, or MBO.[31] First outlined explicitly a (
of a century ago,[32] MBO has been put into practice in national an(
governments as a fairly flexible approach to defining long- and shor
agency objectives, and to keeping a "finger on the pulse" of (
program results and effectiveness. MBO is another in a succession
forts to achieve improved governmental effectiveness and is relat
some respects to performance budgeting, PPBS, and other recent m
ments toward "better management." It appears MBO is more effe(
when integrated into a broader management approach than when stan
alone.

Chester Newland has described the essentials of MBO as it unfol
within the federal government in particular, but with applicabi
elsewhere. He lists the following:

1. Setting goals, objectives, and priorities in terms of results to be accc
   plished in a given time;
2. Developing plans for accomplishment of results;
3. Allocating resources (manpower, money, plant and equipment, and i
   formation) in terms of established goals, objectives, and priorities;
4. Involving people in implementation of plans, with emphasis on con
   munications for responsiveness and on broad sharing in [setting] author
   tative goals and objectives;
5. Tracking or monitoring of progress toward goals and objectives, witl
   specific intermediate milestones;
6. Evaluating results in terms of effectiveness (including quality), efficiency, and economy;
7. Generating and implementing improvements in objectives and results
   (increasing productivity through improved technology, better utilization
   of people, and so on).[33]

Newland points out that no single agency utilizes all seven of these MBO
elements, and the fourth—which is considered by some to be an essential
element indeed—is observed least often. *"At their simplest, the elements
of MBO in actual practice are these: setting objectives, tracking
progress, and evaluating results."*[34] MBO was not applied in the federal
bureaucracy with the same emphasis on uniformity as was PPBS, resulting in greater adaptability to different agency situations.

Some important features of MBO, at least in the abstract, include the
possibility of making objectives explicit, recognizing the multiple-objec-
tive nature of administration, identifying conflicting objectives and dealing with them, providing opportunities for employee involvement in defining organization objectives, and providing for feedback and measurement
of organizational accomplishment.[35] If, as suggested here, MBO makes it
possible to pinpoint conflicting objectives before efforts begin to pursue
them, it renders a significant service in organizational management. And
involvement of employees in "participative management" has been

---

RESISTANCE TO CHANGE: ONE EXAMPLE

Inglewood, California, has used one-man refuse trucks for more than a decade at significantly reduced cost and with fewer injuries and greater satisfaction for personnel.

Informed of the one-man trucks, the sanitation director in an eastern city using four men to a truck said he did not believe it. Having confirmed that they were in use, he opined that Inglewood's streets and contours were different from his city's. Convinced that conditions in both places were generally the same, he lamented that his constituents would never accept the lower level of service. Persuaded that the levels of service were equal, he explained that the sanitation men would not accept a faster pace and harder work conditions. Told that the Inglewood sanitation men prefer the system because they set their own pace and suffer fewer injuries caused by careless co-workers, the director prophesied that the city council would never agree to such a large cutback in manpower. Informed of Inglewood's career development plan to move sanitation men into other city departments, the director pointed out he was responsible only for sanitation.

Source: Improving Productivity in State and Local Government (New York: Committee for Economic Development, March 1976), p. 46.

Lessons of the "human relations" school of organization theory and of organizational humanism, and concerns about effective leadership (see chapters 6 and 8, respectively), enter into the organizational life of both manager and employee in this regard. Of central importance are vertical (leader-follower) and horizontal (follower-follower) relationships, in all their forms. Meeting ego needs, regularizing on-the-job recognition for excellence, developing appropriate opportunities for employee independence or creativity, and facilitating communication among employees represent possible ways of creating and maintaining the kinds of relationships sought. And managers should be alert to the possibilities in their respective work situations.

Finally, a problem associated in the public mind with bureaucracy—namely, resistance to change—is indeed an operating problem of some importance. Any time an organization is called on to undertake a task, the potential for change is present. Pressures for change can be real and direct, prompting employee reluctance to go along. The "conserver" in Anthony Downs's typology of bureaucrats may not be the only one within an agency to exhibit a degree of conservatism; others of every type and description may at times resist change and even the prospect of change. Overcoming such resistance is often a delicate managerial task. It is made more complicated by the fact managers themselves may fear "upsetting the applecart" in their existing situations. Much of the time (though not always) this is due to a survival instinct, which can be difficult for outsiders to understand. Nonetheless, the problem is real. It can, for example, hamper development of new activities, adaptation of existing operations to new circumstances or challenges, and maintenance of sufficient flexibility to meet emergencies. Whatever the causes, costs of resisting change can be substantial, and constant effort is frequently necessary to gain support for many kinds of change in administrative behavior.

Politics of Implementation

In the midst of criticism concerning the failure of so many government programs to live up to their promise, a little-noticed aspect of implementation deserves attention. That is the real possibility that agency implementation of a law may entail actually changing its purpose(s) in order to satisfy shifting political demands. The administrative process is, in this sense, an extension of the legislative arena, where those defeated in the lawmaking process can shift their attention to influencing administration—that is, implementation. If the legislative coalition that was strong enough to pass a law does not continue to support the agency in charge of implementation, it may turn out on later examination that effects of the law were different from those envisioned for it. It is not uncommon for those who failed to "carry the day" in the legislative struggle to recover some of their losses by applying pressure on administrative agencies, thus altering the nature of the program the majority thought it was adopting. Sometimes administrators are willing allies in this effort, sometimes not. Either way, the outcome is the same: *substantive modification* of programs (or policies).

Two examples illustrate this point. Title I of the Elementary and Secondary Education Act of 1965 was a landmark federal law which greatly increased the national government's presence in many phases of education nationwide, most of all in funding local school districts and, to a lesser extent, state education agencies.[41] Title I of ESEA "dictated the use of massive federal funds for the general purpose of upgrading the education of children who were culturally and economically disadvantaged," while leaving considerable discretion in the hands of local education agencies to develop local programs for achieving that goal.[42] "If there was a single theme characterizing the diverse elements of the 1965 . . . Act, it was that of *reform*. . . . ESEA was the first step toward a new face for American education."[43] The key emphasis of Title I was infusion of federal aid to school districts in which there were large numbers of poor children, with the idea that education could contribute to ending poverty for these students, at least in their later adult years. The national government's prevailing political focus in the mid-1960s was on combating poverty, and educational aid allocated as "special purpose" funding under Title I was viewed by many as an essential element in the antipoverty effort.

There were, however, other purposes of Title I which, though not conflicting with aid to disadvantaged students, make it more difficult to determine what its central purpose really was. These included breaking the federal aid barrier, raising achievement levels, pacifying the ghettos, building bridges to private (sectarian) schools, and providing fiscal relief to school districts.[44] Depending on which of these was to receive the greatest emphasis in Title I implementation, it would be possible to draw varying conclusions about whether or not "the" purpose of Title I was in fact being fulfilled.

The point to be made here, however, does not concern evaluations of Title I implementation; we shall deal with that subject shortly. Rather, it is that actual congressional intent—as distinguished from the legislation's stated purpose—may have changed during the first decade of the law's operation (1965–1975), until the only form of aid to education which could gain majority support in Congress was general purpose aid, not special purpose. As the political scene changed in the late 1960s and early 1970s, support for Title I in its original, legislated form apparently changed also. As a result, funding under Title I has come increasingly to be general purpose aid. This matches long-standing preferences of traditional bureaucrats in the Office of Education. But more significantly, Congress itself has in effect broadened Title I aid categories to include general purpose aid. What the most powerful education subsystems wanted, they got—and poverty-related education aid was not their highest priority.[45]

The other example of substantive modification of programmatic intent involves Public Law 480—the Agricultural Trade Development and Assistance Act of 1954, commonly referred to as P.L. 480.[46] This act authorized sale of surplus agricultural commodities to other countries for bargain-basement prices, payable in foreign currencies—an attractive arrangement for hungry nations. It was originally conceived by powerful agricultural interests in this country as a means of reducing growing farm surpluses. These were a source of political embarrassment to farm interests, in light of generous government price supports keeping prices for farm products high. Surpluses could have had the effect of lowering prices in an open market, and agricultural groups feared price supports might be reduced if surpluses continued to accumulate. P.L. 480 sales could serve a useful purpose, in their view, by preventing further accumulation of farm products and cutting back existing surpluses.

In the minds of its proponents, then, P.L. 480 had a rather narrow, modest aim: to hold farm surpluses down. However, because it encompassed overseas sales, administration of the act involved State Department personnel, as well as agricultural attachés at U.S. embassies around the world and some members of Congress. In this group were those who came to see potential foreign policy value in selling food to developing nations, and they viewed the program with a somewhat different perspective. State Department attitudes, in particular, were couched in the broader context of meeting foreign policy objectives. Gradually, foreign policy and agricultural interests came into conflict.

An early disagreement centered on the State Department's reluctance to vigorously pursue food sales in countries where America's allies had legitimate markets for their food exports. Complaints were heard in the mid-1950s from, among others, Australia, Burma, Canada, Argentina, and the Netherlands concerning declines in their exports resulting from our sales under P.L. 480, particularly since prices charged under the program were so low. As the State Department gained influence over administration of P.L. 480 (partly at the initiative of foreign policy–minded members of Congress), it tried to restrain sales somewhat, so as not to risk cordial relations with allied nations—to the dismay of farm interests. Bending of P.L. 480 sales policies in this limited respect represented some modification of its original, non–foreign policy orientation. Farm interests resented what they regarded as "intrusion" of diplomatic considerations into what they saw as a simple sales matter.

Beginning in the late 1950s, however, a more significant modification of initial legislative intent occurred. After amendments to the law were adopted (for foreign policy reasons) easing financial requirements on nations making food purchases, the State Department began to see much greater possibilities in P.L. 480 as an instrument of foreign policy. Specifically, it was assumed that by feeding hungry peoples under the program, this country could limit the appeal of communism in those nations, giving them time (and additional resources) to undertake development. This integration of P.L. 480 into American foreign policy was an even more radical departure from its original legislative moorings. Like Title I of ESEA, P.L. 480, when administered, fulfilled its stated legislative purposes only in part. In the course of implementation, both laws ultimately emerged as something different, in form and content, from what they were at their beginnings.

Program Evaluation

In recent years evaluation of programs has become a central concern to virtually all administrative policy makers, most political executives, legislators, and the public. Like other aspects of policy making, evaluation can be either objective and seemingly value-free, or subject to political influences and the desire to appear to be "doing the job." We will examine evaluation from both perspectives, particularly with regard to how they affect one another.

Evaluation Procedures

Evaluation in an abstract sense requires certain preconditions and a series of steps. The most important preconditions are, first, an understanding of the problem toward which a government program or policy was directed, and second, clarity of goals which the program or policy was designed to achieve. It makes no sense to evaluate "in a vacuum"—that is, without some conception of what was supposed to be accomplished. Evaluation deliberately related to program goals has grown out of recent developments in the budgeting process, where cost-efficiency criteria had told little about what an enterprise was actually doing. Performance budgeting, too, fell short in this regard, though not by as much. For example, a study of per-capita expenditures in a government program might tell us something about political influence and governmental commitment, but not much about the effects of money being spent.[47] Only with increasing concern for program impact and effectiveness could the process of evaluation as a distinct function really come into its own. Instruments such as PERT, PPBS, MBO, ZBB, and sunset laws all share a common focus: to make it possible to *judge the merits* of programs and policies in terms of what is being accomplished, relative to goals set for them.[48]

Steps to be taken in an evaluation include at least the following.[49] First, there must be *specification* of what is to be evaluated, regardless of how narrow and precise or broad and diffuse the object of evaluation is. A nationwide program to immunize children against measles and one to reduce illiteracy among poor adults both can be specified adequately for purposes of evaluation. The second step is *measurement* of the object of evaluation, by collecting data which demonstrate the performance and effect of the program or policy. There are several possibilities, ranging from highly systematic, empirical data and methods such as quantitative techniques, to casual, on-the-scene observation by an untrained observer. The third step is *analysis,* which can similarly vary in the rigor with which it is carried out. How each of these steps is defined and executed affects the final evaluation product.

In order to make a coherent and rational evaluation of program or policy effectiveness, a clear cause-and-effect relationship has to be established between given actions by a government (or private) agency and demonstrated impacts on a societal problem. For example, FBI crime data in mid-1977 indicated that during the cold winter months of 1976–1977, the number of crimes usually committed out-of-doors dropped dramatically—muggings, assaults, and so on. Some might have argued that this was due to beefed-up police patrols or larger local and federal expenditures in law enforcement. Yet the bitter cold weather seems to have played a bigger part than any of these. The crux of the matter, however, is that if police patrols *had* been beefed up or if expenditures *had* been up sharply, then it might have been easy—and politically profitable—to conclude that these factors, not the weather, caused the drop in crime, thereby demonstrating program effectiveness. Simply because an intended result materializes is no guarantee that the relevant program caused it to materialize. Certainly, the chances are that a cause-and-effect relationship does exist, but it is useful to confirm that fact before making judgments based on it.

The opportunities for and methods of evaluation are numerous. Charles O. Jones has suggested various institutionalized evaluation procedures, including legislative oversight, the budgetary process (especially PPBS), and presidential commissions—none of which, according to Jones, is adequate by itself to evaluate systematically or in detail the myriad government programs. Other, informal sources of evaluation are the mass media, interest groups, private individuals, and various scholarly groups and organizations.[50] These help call attention to problems of program operations and effectiveness, but in a relatively unsystematic fashion. Among the more systematic evaluation methods are controlled policy experiments with carefully calculated procedures and observed consequences, comparative evaluations, replication (repeating) of experimental programs, longitudinal analysis (studies over a period of time), and cost-benefit analysis.[51] How thoroughly, systematically, and carefully evaluations are carried out makes a major difference in results obtained. More to the point, how the methods used are regarded by those who must act on the results will largely determine the consequences of evaluation.

Problems and Politics of Evaluation

If the fundamental purpose of evaluation is to assess program performance and accomplishment objectively, it is evident there are numerous difficulties involved in fulfilling that purpose. Some concern problems of performance measurement—the nature of evaluation data, criteria of evaluation, information quality, and the like. Others pertain to political factors which can be injected into an evaluation process, changing the nature—even the very purpose—of a program evaluation. In many instances, the two types of difficulties overlap, compounding the problems which exist.

Perhaps the central problem in evaluating public programs is considerable uncertainty about the reliability of performance indicators. The available indicators of accomplishment, which have been used extensively, are widely regarded as inadequate. It has been difficult to develop measures with enough objective precision to produce meaningful evaluative results. In part, this is a matter of deficiencies in obtaining necessary information, although in recent years more sophisticated management information systems have been designed and put into operation. Improved information capability should enhance the total process of evaluation as an objective function of public administration.

Another dimension of the problem of performance indicators is the fact that the same data can often be manipulated and interpreted in different ways to produce seemingly different results. For example, educational information is quite confusing—few can be certain how well our educational systems function and perform. Yet we have hundreds of studies of educational attainment, test scores, measures of test validity, and much more. What does it all mean? A dozen different experts might give a dozen different answers. Thus development of improved evaluation instruments, by which to make reliable judgments about program performance, remains very much on our agenda of unfinished business.

Two other basic difficulties are the frequently ambiguous nature of the problem which is a program's target and the vagueness of many program goals. Evaluation of a program undertaken with neither a comprehensive understanding of the problem nor a set of well-defined goals can be an unpredictable affair—and, significantly, can become largely politicized. Such an evaluation is unlikely to reveal very much about a program's true effectiveness.

Another factor is whether there are major disparities between the official goals of a program and those of the program's key implementers. This seems to have occurred to some extent in the case of ESEA. One of the harshest evaluations of Title I implementation came in the so-called Martin-McClure Report in 1969, which accused the federal Office of Education of not fulfilling the mandates of Title I—specifically, of not insuring that money intended for educating poor school children was actually being spent by state and local school officials for that purpose. The problem, according to one observer, was that the reformers and implementers were different people, and that the Office of Education staff did not regard itself as investigation-oriented and had no particular inclination to monitor state agencies in their expenditure of Title I funds.[52]

One other problem is the time frame in which programs operate, and how much time is required before a meaningful appraisal can be made of program results. Since no program works perfectly, it is natural for those in charge to seek more time than others might desire in order to correct shortcomings and produce positive results (another instance where political considerations overlap). But even in purely objective terms, required time frames of different programs vary—if Rome wasn't built in a day, neither could man land on the moon in a matter of weeks nor polio be eradicated in a month or two. Reasonable time requirements have to be taken into account—assuming that "reasonable" can be defined to the satisfaction of those concerned.

The politics of evaluation raises different kinds of issues, though not entirely unrelated to those already discussed. Evaluations are used, in the most general sense, to determine *whether there is justification* for continuing a program to the same extent, in the same manner, and for the same cost.[53] But "justification" is a tricky term, and it raises a fundamental issue in the evaluation process. On the one hand, evaluation in an ideal sense is designed to be value-free and objective. On the other hand, "justification" is a value-loaded term, since in order to "justify" something, a context of values must be present. That is, nothing is ever simply "justified"; it is only *"justified in terms of . . ."* Thus an evaluation to determine whether such-and-such a program is justified necessarily becomes bound up with different sets of values about what constitutes adequate justification. This is clearly a political question, in the sense that determining whose values are to prevail must be settled through the political process.

The usual pattern seems to be that evaluations carried out by those in charge of a program or policy are more favorable to its continuation in substantially the same form than are evaluations carried out by independent third parties, especially those who are skeptical of the given program or policy. It is not unduly cynical to suggest that an agency will almost always be kinder in judging its own data, defining the time frame most likely to produce the intended program effect, and taking account of other variables that could produce the desired effect(s), than will others who do not have the same stake in the agency's activities.[54] Since program, and even agency, survival may depend on whether evaluations are positive or negative, a process which many see as value-free and therefore politically neutral is, like so many other things in public administration, weighted down with political implications. That is why internal evaluations so often point up program successes, while external evaluations tend to emphasize deficiencies and ways to improve program management.

Perhaps the mix of factors frustrating truly objective evaluations can best be summed up by the following description of Title I evaluation by the Office of Education:

> Since the beginning of the program, evaluation has been high on the list of federal rhetorical priorities, but low on the list of actual USOE priorities. The reasons for this are many. They include fear of upsetting the federal-state balance, recognition of [the fact] that little expertise exists at the state and local levels to evaluate a broad-scale reform program, and fear of disclosing failure. *No administrator is anxious to show that his program is not working.*[55]

There is another important dimension to the politics of evaluation, namely, how politics affects the uses made of evaluation results. Even when evaluations produce entirely objective data (which, as noted earlier, is infrequent), there is no assurance that they will become the basis of efforts to bring about significant change—whether in program goals, in the way program activities are carried on, or in ultimate performance. Concentrated and effective political support for or opposition to a given program can render evaluations of that program virtually irrelevant, whether they are favorable or unfavorable. Three federal programs illustrate what effects, if any, evaluations might have.

The federal housing program, particularly public housing, has consistently fallen far short of its projected goals, according to a number of separate evaluations. A great national goal, established in 1949, was construction of 810,000 housing units for low-income families over a period of six years—and thirty years later, that number still has not been reached. Regardless of the many critiques of federal housing efforts, those who favored the housing program could not generate the necessary political support for reaching its goals; the interests served by building low-income public housing (the urban poor, primarily) were severely outweighed by the influence of other interests for whom public housing was a low priority—banks, contractors, real estate brokers, and the great majority of the population which was not low-income. Since criticism of the program's alleged failures did not sway its opponents, the program has continued as merely a shadow of what it was supposed to be.[56]

A second example involves ESEA. One observer describes ESEA as having been a "nonprogram": "few activities in school systems can be identified as educational services sponsored by Title I and delivered to poor children. To be sure, the school systems expended Title I funds, but in ways that are hard to relate to specific services."[57] This may be due to the fact that local school districts—interested in general aid, not poverty-related aid—exercised near-total control over Title I funds. Those districts have been described as the Office of Education's "major constituency," one which was able to pressure the Office to respond to its preferences more fully than to those of any other interests—notably, those of the poor![58] Careful evaluation of actual management of Title I seems to indicate that a societal problem considered by many to be of major magnitude in the mid-1960s spawned a program with two essential features: (1) it never really was addressed to the problem of concentrated educational aid to poor school children, and (2) it turned out to be a very different program from the one Congress enacted in 1965, primarily because those in charge could afford to ignore criticisms from those whom Title I was originally intended to serve.

One last policy area bears mentioning in connection with the uses of evaluation, that of so-called "new communities" or "New Towns."[59] New Town policy was one federal response to growing problems in urban areas, particularly the quality of life in cities. The Advisory Commission on Intergovernmental Relations (ACIR) described a New Town as:

> an independent, relatively self-contained, planned community of a size large enough to support a range of housing types and to provide economic opportunity within its borders for the employment of its residents [and] to support a balanced range of public facilities and social and cultural opportunities. . . . New Towns are started on previously undeveloped land and are built by staged development over a period of time.[60]

It is, in essence, a *planned* community, brought into being through a complex intergovernmental web of activity centering on the individual New

Town developer and local units of government in the area (nearby communities and the county, primarily). The best-known of the early New Towns are Reston, Virginia, and Columbia, Maryland, both products of the 1960s; more recently, eleven others in six states have been undertaken.

Despite high hopes for New Towns, they have not become the model communities some had thought they would—yet the program has continued to exist. A thorough evaluation of new communities under this program found that planned New Towns were not appreciably better than unplanned communities, according to opinions of the respective sets of residents and to more objective measures.[61] Services such as transportation, recreation, and health care were at least somewhat better in New Towns; schools and shopping facilities were only marginally better. A slightly larger proportion of New Town residents regarded their communities as excellent places to live, but there was virtually no difference in the proportion who were satisfied with their life as a whole.[62] Because this has been something of a pilot project, however, and because *no major political interests have been threatened,* the unspectacular results of New Towns policy have not become grounds for a concerted political effort to put an end to it.

Government Productivity

Within a framework of concern for productivity in the economy generally, the productivity of government programs has taken on increasing political, economic, and social significance in the 1970s. A brief look at key elements of productivity will indicate where scholarly observers and others have placed most emphasis.[63]

Productivity and efforts to achieve it are lineal descendants of concern for efficiency in government, yet they encompass a broader area than traditional efficiency norms. Productivity, unlike its forerunner, focuses on both efficient use of governmental resources and actual impacts of what government does—that is, on efficiency and effectiveness. It springs also from efforts to identify specific program objectives and measure progress toward achieving them. The task is made more difficult by the fact, mentioned earlier regarding evaluation, that measures available to public managers and their overseers are less precise than we might like, and are less simple than economic measures employed in the private sector. As one example, much of what government tries to do involves *preventing* various social ills—crime, disease, destruction by fire of lives and property. How does one measure productivity of such functions? There is no easy answer. Yet it has been possible to develop some measures useful in assessing performance of individual agencies.

The first approach to measuring productivity deals with programs in which output is easily measurable—for example, number of tons of refuse collected per sanitation truck shift—and the goal is to reduce the unit cost while improving responsiveness in government operations. Urban problem areas such as cleaning and maintaining park facilities, patching streets, and maintenance of sanitation vehicles lend themselves to unit-cost measurement of productivity.

The second approach concerns programs or functions in which output is very hard to measure—for example, provision of police or fire protection. Here the intent is to improve deployment of resources by assessing probable needs, so as to insure as much as possible that resources will be available when and where they are needed most. In addition to police and fire departments, this approach could be usefully employed in sanitation departments, rescue services, and civil defense offices.

But efforts to improve productivity, however measured, may encounter obstacles. Table 12–1 lists common problems at the local level, with possible ways to overcome them. Two general approaches to solving productivity problems have been used. One stresses improving organizational and processing procedures, particularly through imaginative use of computers. Government agencies extensively involved in provision of social services, with attendant record-keeping needs, may find this approach especially beneficial in increasing cost efficiency in a wide variety of programs. Data-processing improvements can make a noticeable difference in areas such as large education systems, large welfare programs, monitoring of capital construction programs, and payments to those who provide goods and services to a government or individual agency. The other approach calls for developing new technological devices which result in more efficient use of human resources—for example, polymerized water for better and less expensive fire-fighting. Though relatively little has been done in this regard, especially in urban governments where the need is great, the possibilities are impressive: improved techniques for combating air and water pollution, construction of low-cost modular housing, use of closed-circuit television for simple medical tests of government employees or prisoners, and many others.

Productivity concerns will continue to be important, if for no other reason than growing awareness of limited financial (and other) resources available. It is becoming more widely accepted, in government and elsewhere, that more and more we may have to "make do with what we have." The promise of productivity efforts lies in the fact that technology has not yet been fully applied to this area, and there is a growing "track record" of successes in various governments, which should encourage similar efforts elsewhere.

SUMMARY

Realities of policy and policy making in American government often differ from the expectations many citizens hold about them. Several popular (but inaccurate) beliefs persist about policy and policy making. They are

TABLE 12–1
SOME COMMON PROBLEMS OF LOW PRODUCTIVITY IN LOCAL GOVERNMENT AND SUGGESTIONS FOR CORRECTIVE ACTION

Problem	Possible Corrective Action	Illustrative Examples
Sufficient work not available or workloads unbalanced	Reallocate manpower	Housing complaint bureau schedules revised and temporary help employed during peak winter season.
	Change work schedules	Mechanics rescheduled to second shift when equipment is not in use.
	Reduce crew size	Collection crew size reduced from 4 to 3 men.
Lack of equipment or materials	Improve inventory control system	Inventory reorder points revised to reduce stock-out occurrences.
	Improve distribution system	Asphalt deliveries expedited to eliminate paving crew delays.
	Improve equipment maintenance	Preventive maintenance program instituted.
	Reevaluate equipment requirements	Obsolete collection trucks replaced.
Self-imposed idle time or slow work pace	Train supervisors	Road maintenance foremen trained in work scheduling, dispatching, and quality-control techniques.
	Use performance standards	"Flat rate" manual standards adopted to measure auto mechanics' performance.
	Schedule more work	Park maintenance crews mobilized and work scheduling system installed.
Too much time spent on non-productive activities	Reduce excessive travel time	Permit expiration dates changed to reduce travel time of health inspectors.
	Reevaluate job description and task assignments	Building inspectors trained to handle multiple inspections.
Excessive manual effort required	Mechanize repetitive tasks	Automatic change and toll collection machines installed and toll collector staffing reduced.
Response or processing time too slow	Combine tasks or functions	Voucher processing and account posting combined to speed vendor payments.
	Automate process	Computerized birth record storage and retrieval system installed.

(continued)

TABLE 12–1 (Cont.)

Problem	Possible Corrective Action	Illustrative Examples
	Improve dispatching procedures	Fire alarm patterns analyzed and equipment response policies revised.
	Revise deployment practices	Police patrol zones redefined to improve response time.
	Adopt project management techniques	Project control system installed to reduce construction cycle.

Source: So, Mr. Mayor, You Want to Improve Productivity . . . (Washington, D.C.: National Commission on Productivity and Work Quality, 1974); and Center for Productive Public Management, John Jay College, New York.

(1) governments have clearly defined policies, well thought out in advance, on most problems; (2) policies are established deliberately; (3) all actions relating to a particular problem are in accord with existing policies; (4) policies are clearly perceived and understood by the general public; and (5) there is active, widespread agreement on and support for existing policies.

The policy-making process involves all sources, procedures, and outcomes leading to adoption and pursuit of particular governmental policies. The process is complex, very loosely coordinated, highly competitive, fragmented, specialized, and largely incremental. It is also interdependent and overlapping, and reflects the varying influence of many groups at many points along the way. The result is a great deal of inconsistency in the policies adopted, and sometimes outright contradictions.

Administrative policy making occurs in four stages: (1) drafting and enactment of basic legislation; (2) writing of rules and regulations governing application of the law; (3) implementation of the law; and (4) review of application and implementation, involving Congress, the courts, or both. Problems and demands "are constantly being defined and redefined in the policy process," suggesting a policy *cycle* which repeats these four stages more than once. Intergovernmental relations also figure prominently in the making of public policy. These and other factors in the policy process help account for the disjointed nature of most public policies.

Policies, programs, projects, and individual performance—the "four *Ps*"—are interrelated, with central importance to outcomes of government operations. Programs and projects are the building blocks of policy, and from a "management" standpoint require particular attention in five areas: goal setting, analysis and choice in deciding on courses of action, implementation, evaluation, and (most recently) productivity.

Goal setting for programs involves accepting goals at least partially defined by forces outside the agency in charge. Goal ambiguity and inconsistency are not unusual.

Analysis in advance of selecting program options can be crucial for an agency, whether strong or weak politically. While rigorous analysis is not a guarantee of mastery over pertinent facts, it is preferable to an absence of analytic capacity.

Implementation refers to those activities directed toward putting a program into effect. It is necessary for agencies in charge of implementation to *interpret, organize,* and *apply* programmatic or policy directives contained in the authorizing legislation. While that sounds routine, in fact it is not. Interpreting ambiguous mandates of a law opens the way for political pressures from those trying to shape a policy as they would prefer. Controversy over legislative intent makes interpretation a difficult task. In addition, program application often takes place through a series of compromises and adjustments. Other factors affecting application include the limits on an agency's activities agreed upon informally, the possibility of co-optation, controversy surrounding a given program or activity, agency priorities with regard to its other responsibilities, and values and preferences of agency personnel concerning individual programs and their own general role and function.

Among the most important methods of program and policy implementation are Program Evaluation and Review Technique (PERT)— which can include Critical Path Method—and Management by Objectives. PERT involves mapping out the sequence of steps necessary to carry out a program or project. It also permits comparisons among different paths of action, each of which has a different "margin of safety" available in its projected resource requirements. The path with the smallest margin of extra resources is the *critical path*. Despite the sophistication of PERT and Critical Path, much of the calculation depends on human judgment, thus leaving its accuracy somewhat uncertain. Management by Objectives (MBO) represents a fairly flexible approach to setting long-term and short-term goals while monitoring actual programmatic results and effectiveness. Among its potential benefits are helping administrators to recognize conflicting objectives and deal with them, providing opportunities for employee participation in defining objectives, and providing feedback and measurement of organizational accomplishment.

A number of implementation problems confront many managers. Management control involves (1) obtaining the cooperation of subordinates, (2) developing good working relationships among followers and between leaders and followers, and (3) overcoming resistance to change. The last poses numerous difficulties for managers; "conservers" are often not the only ones who are reluctant to change their activities, meet new challenges, or respond to emergency situations.

One subtle, yet crucial, aspect of implementation is the possibility that legislative purposes may change during the course of a law's implementation. Examples of this phenomenon are found in the histories of Title I of the ESEA and P.L. 480.

Evaluation of public policies has become increasingly important in recent years, as well as more systematic. In order to conduct an evaluation, it is necessary to specify what is to be evaluated, measure the object of evaluation by collecting useful data of some kind, and analyze data collected. A cause-and-effect relationship must also be established between specific program activities and apparent results (which might be due to other factors).

Methods of evaluation vary widely, from institutionalized procedures and informal evaluation devices to more formalized techniques. The rigor of evaluation methods and uses made of the results will determine the value and impact of the evaluation process.

A central problem in evaluating public programs is lack of adequate indicators of performance and accomplishment. Other difficulties include defining problems, identifying specific goals, dealing with disparities between official goals and those of key program or policy implementers, and properly defining the time frame necessary to "give the program a chance to work."

In theory, evaluation should be objective and value-free, yet evaluations are designed fundamentally to show whether there is justification for continuing an activity, program, or policy in much the same form as before. And "justification" is a value-loaded term, raising political questions and implications. Political factors can also affect the uses made of evaluations.

Concern for government productivity is on the rise. There are several approaches to measuring productivity, and to improving productivity levels. Under conditions of limited resources (of all kinds), productivity in government and elsewhere will continue to be important.

NOTES

1. Thomas R. Dye, *Understanding Public Policy*, 2nd ed. (Englewood Cliffs, N.J.: Prentice-Hall, 1975), p. 1.

2. See Murray Edelman, *The Symbolic Uses of Politics* (Urbana, Ill.: University of Illinois Press, 1964).

3. See Charles O. Jones, *An Introduction to the Study of Public Policy,* 2nd ed. (North Scituate, Mass.: Duxbury, 1977), chapter 1, especially pp. 8–9.

4. Ibid., chapter 1.

5. See, among others, Morton Grodzins, *The American System: A New View of Government in the United States* (Chicago: Rand McNally, 1966); Richard I. Hofferbert, *The Study of Public Policy* (Indianapolis: Bobbs-Merrill, 1974); Charles O. Jones and Robert D. Thomas, eds., *Public Policy Making in a Federal System* (Beverly Hills, Calif.: Sage, 1976); Roscoe C. Martin, *The Cities and the Federal System* (New York: Atherton, 1965); and Peter Woll, *Public Policy* (Cambridge, Mass.: Winthrop, 1974). See also chapter 5.

6. See, among others, Theodore H. White, *The Making of the President 1964* (New York: Atheneum Publishers, 1965), chapter 6.

7. A. Lee Fritschler, *Smoking and Politics: Policy Making and the Federal Bureaucracy,* 2nd ed. (Englewood Cliffs, N.J.: Prentice-Hall, 1975), p. 56.

8. Jones, *An Introduction to the Study of Public Policy,* p. 8.

9. Quoted in Peter H. Rossi and Sonia R. Wright, "Evaluation Research: An Assessment of Theory, Practice, and Politics," *Evaluation Quarterly,* 1 (February 1977), 5–52, at p. 23.

10. The concept of the "four *Ps*" was suggested by the late Roscoe C. Martin of Syracuse University.

11. Jones, *An Introduction to the Study of Public Policy*, p. 139.

12. Ibid., p. 8.

13. Joseph L. Bower, "Effective Public Management: It Isn't the Same as Effective Business Management," *Harvard Business Review,* 55 (March/April 1977), 131–140, at p. 134.

14. Ibid., p. 139.

15. Jacob B. Ukeles, "Policy Analysis: Myth or Reality?" in Norman Beckman, ed., "Symposium on Policy Analysis in Government: Alternatives to 'Muddling Through'," *Public Administration Review*, 37 (May/June 1977), 223–228, at p. 223. See, in the same issue, Selma J. Mushkin, "Policy Analysis in State and Community," 245–253. See, also, Dye, *Understanding Public Policy*, pp. 5–7.

16. Ukeles, "Policy Analysis: Myth or Reality?" pp. 226–227.

17. See Nicholas Henry, *Public Administration and Public Affairs* (Englewood Cliffs, N.J.: Prentice-Hall, 1975), chapter 6, especially pp. 127–130.

18. Jones, *An Introduction to the Study of Public Policy,* p. 139.

19. Jeffrey L. Pressman and Aaron Wildavsky, *Implementation: How Great Expectations in Washington Are Dashed in Oakland; or, Why It's Amazing That Federal Programs Work at All, This Being a Saga of the Economic Development Administration as Told by Two Sympathetic Observers Who Seek to Build Morals on a Foundation of Ruined Hopes* (Berkeley: University of California Press, 1973), p. xii (emphasis added).

20. Jones, *An Introduction to the Study of Public Policy*, pp. 149–150.

21. Fritschler, *Smoking and Politics*, pp. 55–56.

22. Jones, *An Introduction to the Study of Public Policy*, p. 8.

23. Ibid., pp. 162–167.

24. Ibid., pp. 151–152.

25. Ibid., p. 8.

26. Pressman and Wildavsky, *Implementation*, pp. 99–100.

27. Jerome T. Murphy, "Title I of ESEA: The Politics of Implementing Federal Education Reform," *Harvard Educational Review*, 41 (February 1971), 35–63, at pp. 41–42.

28. Stephen K. Bailey and Edith K. Mosher, *ESEA: The Office of Education Administers a Law* (Syracuse, N.Y.: Syracuse University Press, 1968), p. 3.

29. The broad outlines of this discussion are drawn from Henry, *Public Administration and Public Affairs,* Appendix A.

30. Ibid., p. 343.

31. This discussion of MBO is taken from Bruce H. DeWoolfson, Jr., "Public Sector MBO and PPB: Cross Fertilization in Management Systems," *Public Administration Review*, 35 (July/August 1975), 387–394; Jong S. Jun, ed., "Symposium on Management by Objectives in the Public Sector," *Public Administration Review*, 36 (January/February 1976), 1–45; and Richard Rose,

"Implementation and Evaporation: The Record of MBO," *Public Administration Review*, 37 (January/February 1977), 64–71.

32. Peter F. Drucker, *The Practice of Management* (New York: Harper & Row, 1954).

33. Chester A. Newland, "Policy/Program Objectives and Federal Management: The Search for Government Effectiveness," in Jong S. Jun, ed., "Symposium on Management by Objectives in the Public Sector," p. 26.

34. Ibid.

35. DeWoolfson, "Public Sector MBO and PPB," pp. 388–389.

36. Peter F. Drucker, "What Results Should You Expect? A Users' Guide to MBO," in Jong S. Jun, ed., "Symposium on Management by Objectives in the Public Sector," pp. 12–19, at p. 18.

37. Ibid., p. 13.

38. Frank P. Sherwood and William J. Page, Jr., "MBO and Public Management," in Jong S. Jun, ed., "Symposium on Management by Objectives in the Public Sector," pp. 5–12, at p. 9.

39. Rose, "Implementation and Evaporation: The Record of MBO."

40. Drucker, "What Results Should You Expect? A Users' Guide to MBO," pp. 14–16.

41. See, among others, Bailey and Mosher, *ESEA: The Office of Education Administers a Law;* Marilyn Gittell and Alan G. Hevesi, eds., *The Politics of Urban Education* (New York: Praeger, 1969); Milbrey W. McLaughlin, *Evaluation and Reform: The Elementary and Secondary Education Act of 1965/Title I* (Cambridge, Mass.: Ballinger, 1975); Philip Meranto, *The Politics of Federal Aid to Education in 1965* (Syracuse, N.Y.: Syracuse University Press, 1967); and Murphy, "Title I of ESEA."

42. Bailey and Mosher, *ESEA*, p. 3.

43. Murphy, "Title I of ESEA," pp. 35–36 (emphasis added).

44. Ibid., p. 43.

45. Floyd R. Stoner, "Implementation of Federal Education Policy: The Role of Local Resources," paper delivered at the annual meeting of the Midwest Political Science Association, Chicago, Illinois, May 1–3, 1975.

46. This discussion relies on David S. McLellan and Donald Clare, "Public Law 480: The Metamorphosis of a Law," *Eagleton Institute Cases in Practical Politics* (New York: McGraw-Hill, 1965).

47. Dye, *Understanding Public Policy*, p. 328.

48. See Jones, *An Introduction to the Study of Public Policy,* chapter 8. See also Edward A. Suchman, *Evaluative Research* (New York: Russell Sage Foundation, 1967); and Carol H. Weiss, *Evaluation Research* (Englewood Cliffs, N.J.: Prentice-Hall, 1972).

49. Jones, *An Introduction to the Study of Public Policy*, pp. 174–175.

50. Ibid., pp. 180–186.

51. Ibid., pp. 186–189.

52. Murphy, "Title I of ESEA," pp. 41–43.

53. Jones, *An Introduction to the Study of Public Policy*, p. 177.

54. James Q. Wilson, "On Pettigrew and Armor," *The Public Interest*, 31 (Spring 1973), 132–134, cited by Dye, *Understanding Public Policy*, pp. 333–334.

55. Murphy, "Title I of ESEA," p. 43 (emphasis added). Murphy also describes USOE's political position as weak, which may have been a contributing factor.

56. Jones, *An Introduction to the Study of Public Policy*, pp. 193–199. See also Charles Abrams, *The City Is the Frontier* (New York: Harper & Row, 1965).

57. Rossi and Wright, "Evaluation Research: An Assessment of Theory, Practice, and Politics," p. 24.

58. Murphy, "Title I of ESEA," p. 51.

59. The following summary description relies largely on John Rehfuss and Eric Stowe, eds., "A Symposium: The Governance of New Towns," *Public Administration Review*, 35 (May/June 1975), 221–262. See also Martha Derthick, *New Towns In-Town* (Washington, D.C.: Urban Institute, 1972).

60. Quoted in Eric Stowe and John Rehfuss, "Federal New Towns Policy: 'Muddling Through' at the Local Level," in John Rehfuss and Eric Stowe, eds., "A Symposium: The Governance of New Towns," pp. 222–228, at p. 223.

61. Raymond J. Burby III, Shirley F. Weiss, and Robert B. Zehner, "A National Evaluation of Community Services and the Quality of Life in American New Towns," in John Rehfuss and Eric Stowe, eds., "A Symposium: The Governance of New Towns," pp. 229–239.

62. Ibid., pp. 230–237.

63. This discussion relies on the useful overview in Edward K. Hamilton, "Productivity: The New York City Approach," in Chester A. Newland, ed., "Symposium on Productivity in Government," *Public Administration Review,* 32 (November/December 1972), 784–795. See also *Improving Productivity in State and Local Government* (New York: Committee for Economic Development, March 1976).

SUGGESTED READINGS

Bailey, Stephen K., and Edith K. Mosher. *ESEA: The Office of Education Administers a Law.* Syracuse, N.Y.: Syracuse University Press, 1968.

Dye, Thomas R. *Understanding Public Policy*, 2nd ed. Englewood Cliffs, N.J.: Prentice-Hall, 1975.

Jones, Charles O. *An Introduction to the Study of Public Policy,* 2nd ed. North Scituate, Mass.: Duxbury, 1977.

Jun, Jong S., ed. "Symposium on Management by Objectives in the Public Sector," *Public Administration Review,* 36 (January/February 1976), 1–45.

Murphy, Jerome T. "Title I of ESEA: The Politics of Implementing Federal Education Reform," *Harvard Educational Review*, 41 (February 1971), 35–63.

Newland, Chester A., ed. "Symposium on Productivity in Government," *Public Administration Review*, 32 (November/December 1972), 739–850.

Pressman, Jeffrey L., and Aaron Wildavsky. *Implementation.* Berkeley: University of California Press, 1973.

Rehfuss, John, and Eric Stowe, eds. "A Symposium: The Governance of New Towns," *Public Administration Review*, 35 (May/June 1975), 221–262.

Rossi, Peter H., and Sonia R. Wright. "Evaluation Research: An Assessment of Theory, Practice, and Politics," *Evaluation Quarterly*, 1 (February 1977), 5–52.

Weiss, Carol H. *Evaluation Research.* Englewood Cliffs, N.J.: Prentice-Hall, 1972.

PART FIVE

PUBLIC ADMINISTRATION AND THE FUTURE

In this concluding section we shall examine how public administration and democratic government interact, and consider the past and present in public administration as well as look to the future. The discussion of bureaucracy and democracy in chapter 13 focuses on selected current issues which pose difficult problems for a society professing to be democratic but becoming increasingly bureaucratized. These issues include bureaucratic credibility, access, representativeness, and accountability; citizen participation in bureaucratic decision making; and morality and ethical behavior in administrative practice, including the significance of political corruption. Chapter 14 addresses the implications of, and continuing questions arising from, the totality of public administration in American government.

CHAPTER 13
Public Administration and Democratic Government

Popular control of government has always been a matter of considerable importance in American politics. As we saw in chapter 2, the founding fathers emphasized those branches of government—legislative (especially) and executive—which in principle could be held directly accountable to voters through periodic elections. In recent decades, however, this relatively simple and clear-cut arrangement for accountability and popular control has become less workable. Many important decisions are now made by government officials and agencies not subject to direct electoral control and resistant to other kinds of political pressure. Thus it is not surprising to find fresh concern about public access and influence with respect to what government does. Similarly, millions of Americans seek to reassert their control over agencies of government which have major impact on their daily lives.

Bureaucracy has become a focal point of discontent because of its obvious influence, its relatively obscure decision processes, and the degree to which it is insulated from direct (elective) political controls. Investigations of the CIA and FBI, protests against the Nuclear Regulatory Commission and Environmental Protection Agency, complaints about the welfare bureaucracy, reactions to Watergate, and public response to proposed FDA actions all testify to the intensity of feeling about specific actions and the manner in which they were decided upon. More generally, they indicate a growing sense of *distance* between the people and their governing institutions. Public trust has become an issue of major proportions in recent times, and the level of trust has declined measurably.

Out of all this has come a renewed interest in democratic values, particularly as they pertain to public impact on and control over government institutions. With the tremendous expansion of government bureaucracies, differences have become clearer between political values such as representation, participation, and political accountability, and administrative values such as political neutrality and insulation, economy, efficiency, rationalism, and faith in science and expertise. As always when fundamentally different values clash, sparks have flown, and are still flying. But some light also has been shed on the nature of problems we face in trying to reconcile democratic values and practices with politically neutral public bureaucracy. In this chapter we will briefly review those value conflicts, then deal more extensively with specific problems in this area.

Democratic Government: Needs and Constraints

Democratic government (discussed in chapter 2) requires at least the following: (1) some mechanisms through which citizens can participate in policy making, (2) machinery for holding government accountable for its decisions, (3) an independent judiciary, and (4) regular, free elections to maintain participation and accountability.[1] The meaning and/or scope of these values, however, has varied over time.

Participation in the 1700s referred to voting and holding public office and was limited by such qualifications as land or other wealth, education, social status, "race," and sex. Beginning in the 1830s, eligibility for participation has been broadened, so that now virtually every citizen eighteen years of age or older can vote and otherwise become involved in politics. Lately, however, participation has taken on another, more controversial dimension—*mandatory inclusion* of various population groups in governmental decision making.

Accountability once meant holding officials generally responsible for their actions through direct elective mechanisms, as in the case of legislators, or through indirect machinery in which elected officals held others to account on behalf of the public. Now, however, the meaning of accountability is less clear. As discussed in chapter 3, to whom officials are *actually* accountable is a complex issue, making it difficult to determine whether they can in fact be made to answer for what they do.

Representation once referred to a general principle of legislative selection based on the number of inhabitants or amount of territory in a legislative district. But adequate representation has become a major objective of many who feel they were denied it in the past and are now seeking greater influence, particularly in administrative decision making. Closely related is *representativeness,* taken to mean that groups which have been relatively powerless should be represented in government positions in proportion to their numbers in the general population (see chapter 2).

The cumulative effect of the changes in meaning has been to make it more difficult to determine whether these values are being maintained. Conceptual uncertainty about a given value makes it much harder to either prove or disprove accusations that we are not living up to our own standards of democratic government. For example, defining representativeness a particular way might in effect include one group while excluding another from decision making, and the latter might well dispute whether representativeness in fact exists.

It sometimes seems that these concepts are defined in terms of *policy success*—that is, in self-serving terms—rather than in terms of whether or not groups have had a fair opportunity to state their case. Frequently those affected adversely by a major decision tend to blame the processes and institutions which produced it, labeling them not merely as "politically hostile" but as "undemocratic" or "unrepresentative." Clearly, if people feel that "their side" has to win in decision making before they are willing to concede that decision-making processes are "democratic" or "representative," then such terms have lost all objective meaning. Such self-serving definitions may have contributed to recent conflicts over what constitutes accountability, representativeness, and so on.

The larger concern, however, is for maintaining democratic norms and practices in a complex governmental system, within a complex society. Today many fear that democratic values, however defined, are endangered by government which may be moving beyond popular control. Government institutions clearly are under pressure "from the people"—left, right, and center—to stay within the public's political reach. The difficulties in maintaining democracy, however, are hardly new. Assuming that democracy implies fairly equitable access to decision makers, widespread opportunity to exert influence in the political process, and clear public preferences about public policy, the realities of American democracy have fallen short of the ideal for some time.

Access has been unevenly distributed throughout the population, with the wealthy having a better chance than the poor to gain a hearing in official channels. Theodore H. White notes that the one thing most contributors seek by giving money to candidates and political parties is access to those in office after the electoral decisions are made.[2] Similarly, influence in the political process (partly dependent on having access in the first place) is clearly enjoyed by some more than others. Besides money, a key factor seems to be organization, and well-organized groups have long been acknowledged as having the advantage in exercising political influence. Theodore Lowi has even suggested that the dominance of organized over unorganized interests constitutes "the end of liberalism," arguing that it is impossible to sustain a claim of comparable influence among different groups in a system where organization and political power go hand in hand.[3]

Finally, clear public preferences on policy questions simply do not exist in many cases. Contrary to popular belief, voters usually do not confer *policy mandates*—clear statements of policy preference—when they go to the polls. Voting results can be safely interpreted in terms of only the most general policy directions. The Johnson landslide over Goldwater in 1964 and Nixon's triumph over McGovern in 1972 were overwhelming, but many of those voting for the winners clearly did not agree with their every policy position. And both presidents later came into sharp conflict with millions of citizens, including many former supporters. Narrower electoral victories, such as Jimmy Carter's defeat of Gerald Ford in 1976, may be even more ambiguous as to their policy meaning.

If policy mandates are vague, the nature of the "public interest" is even more so While it is possible to argue that the public is the "owner" of government institutions and that those institutions should serve the owner's interest—the public interest[4]—defining what that is as a practical matter is not easy. Various contesting forces in politics claim to be acting in and for the public interest, and each may have a legitimate case. Also, it is not clear whether the public interest represents some generalized view of societal good, or the sum total of all private interests, themselves inconsistent with one another. Just as there are limits on our knowledge of "what the public wants," there are limits on our ability to define just what *is* in the public interest.

Democracy and Public Administration

Democracy, as we have noted, requires mechanisms for both participation and accountability, insured by an independent judiciary and free elections. Public administration, however, poses troublesome problems for any such system. It does not accord with the notion of elected public officials, since most bureaucrats are not elected, and it has emphasized expertise and knowledge over citizen participation. Growing societal complexity and increasing administrative responsibilities have virtually required more specialization and larger numbers of bureaucratic professionals. At the same time, disadvantaged groups and others have turned to government bureaucracy more frequently for various kinds of aid—ironically, while often voicing grievances against many of the same agencies—and to demand a greater role in making policies which affect them. The result has been a head-on collision between the need for professionalism and technical competence on the one hand, and insistent demands for citizen participation in policy making on the other.[5] Bureaucratic accountability in such a system was to be achieved largely if not entirely through *indirect* popular influence, through the legislature and chief executive. Lee Fritschler notes that "it is difficult, though far from impossible, to build both accountability and participation into the policy-making process when administrative agencies are the chief policy makers."[6]

The role of public administration within a constitutional and democratic framework is not clearly defined. This is partly due to continuing debate over the role of government itself in American society; how one regards government bureaucracy is obviously tied to the broader question.[7] If, for example, one accepts the view that ours is a system of limited government, then administration, like all other functions of government, must clearly be responsive to the public's will, in the interest of promoting majority rule and securing individual liberty. Such an approach subordinates other considerations to the primary purpose of keeping government—including bureaucracy—under popular control. If, however, one takes the position that the proper role of government is a more activist one, promoting and protecting the general "public interest" as economically and efficiently as possible, then administration is regarded very differently. A major requirement is then to *insulate* bureaucracy from the political process, rather than *including* it in that process for purposes of control and accountability.

The concerns which have come to center on bureaucracy include, foremost, issues of accountability and participation. Other important issues are representativeness and the whole problem of ethics and "morality in government." In addition, the general disposition of bureaucrats and bureaucracies to operate behind a veil of secrecy, in the best tradition of Max Weber, has sparked efforts to open their activities to public scrutiny. Two such efforts are state and national freedom-of-information laws, and so-called "sunshine" laws that require that public business be conducted in open forums. Congress passed a Freedom of Information Act in 1966 which increased the access of individual citizens to a wide variety of government records and files. While consequences of the act are still debated, there have been definite gains in information acquisition by private citizens.[8] Sunshine laws, which have been passed at all levels of government and apply mainly to legislative proceedings, have given rise to the possibility—and at times the reality—that a similar requirement would be imposed on bureaucracy. Regulatory agencies at the national level are already subject to such a rule, though it was the result of judicial rather than legislative action (see chapter 11).

There is growing insistence, also, that government and bureaucracy do more to protect individual privacy and to insure that government records concerning affairs of private citizens are fair and accurate. This is a particularly sensitive issue in view of computer information capabilities. It is perhaps ironic that the right of privacy was given constitutional protection by the U.S. Supreme Court, in the 1965 case of *Griswold* v. *Connecticut,* during the same period that governmental ability to intrude on that privacy increased rapidly. Prior to the 1960s, information might have been available to government, but it was costly and time-consuming to have it on hand or to organize it. Computers, however, make retrieval and cross-referencing of information not only possible but very convenient. A principal concern is the extent and diversity of personal information which is now stored on computers of public and private organizations—

social security data, credit ratings and transactions, drivers' license information, medical records, income figures, and so on.[9]

Both national and state governments have taken action during the 1970s to better safeguard an individual's right to privacy. Legislation at the national level includes the Freedom of Information Act, Fair Credit Reporting Act, Family Educational Rights and Privacy Act, Privacy Act of 1974, and Fair Credit Billing Act. Congress also established the Privacy Protection Study Commission to look into intrusions on individual privacy by agencies outside the federal executive branch. Over half a dozen states have enacted privacy laws, and an even larger number have adopted their own versions of the Fair Credit Reporting Act.[10] In short, there has been considerable governmental activity in this area, but concern persists that "big brother" may still have too much access to personal records.[11]

Problems of Democratic Administration

In the remainder of this chapter we will examine in more depth selected areas in public administration that pose particular difficulties for the maintenance of democratic norms and practices. We will consider each of the following: (1) citizen participation, (2) bureaucratic representativeness, (3) bureaucratic responsiveness, (4) bureaucratic accountability, (5) ethics and morality in government, (6) administrators' beliefs in the values of democracy, and (7) administrative effectiveness as a threat to personal freedom.

Citizen Participation

The movement for greater citizen participation in government decision making was born in the 1960s out of related movements for civil rights, black liberation, and decentralization of urban government structures. It originated in demands by nonwhites for a larger voice in determining policies and programs directly affecting them. The urban poor, at least during the 1960s, concentrated on organizing themselves and confronting those in power with demands for changes in the way things were. Their participation was formally incorporated in federal Model Cities and Community Action programs, and in others since then. In the 1970s many other groups—white as well as nonwhite, more affluent as well as less—have come to demand participation not only in program implementation but also in program planning.[12] The ideology of citizen participation has developed firm roots in our political values, to the point that it is now a routine expectation for many.

The concept of participation has been applied in different ways to varying problems. "Community control" focused on neighborhood management of schools and delivery of other essential urban services, principally in nonwhite ghetto areas of major American cities.[13] In other places, neighborhood and citizen action organizations sprang up for purposes which came under the heading of "preserving neighborhood character," and sometimes physical structures in the neighborhood. For example, there were concerted efforts to prevent construction of federal interstate highway projects which would cut through, or perhaps level, parts of established urban neighborhoods. One such conflict occurred in northeast Philadelphia, where citizen groups permanently blocked construction of a portion of Interstate 95 through a largely residential section of older, middle-class homes. A similar case involves a continuing conflict in Memphis, Tennessee, over construction of a portion of Interstate 40 through Overton Park, one of the city's oldest park and recreation areas. The proposed stretch of road would almost certainly have an adverse impact on the inhabitants of Overton Park Zoo, not to mention residents in the surrounding neighborhood. A series of court injunctions has halted construction, though no end to the conflict is in sight—after nearly two decades of controversy. Another case centered on a proposal to construct a bridge between the communities of Rye and Oyster Bay, New York, across Long Island Sound. In this case a coalition of citizen action groups succeeded in defeating the proposal, which had the backing of powerful interests and individuals such as Governor Nelson Rockefeller, New York Port Authority head William Ronan, and Robert Moses, long-time power behind the scenes in New York City.[14] These relatively large-scale efforts have been echoed in hundreds of smaller enterprises, from restoring usable buildings and neighborhood landmarks to preserving residential character against incursions of commercial enterprise, multifamily dwellings, and so on.

Citizen participation has also been incorporated into formal mechanisms for decision making. At the national level, for example, public participation in regulatory agency proceedings has been increasing since the late 1960s, though with considerable variation in agency responses and opportunities provided to citizen groups such as consumer organizations. While agencies undoubtedly have legal discretionary authority to decide just how much public participation to permit, particularly whether and how to finance participation by those with limited resources, nonetheless there has been considerable frustration on the part of so-called "public interest" groups which have been slow to gain access to regulatory proceedings. Two observers have noted recent improvements in agency receptivity, with more of them willing to grant direct financial aid as well as facilitate access. Not surprisingly, most of the problems have been over funding. Agencies with consumer protection high among their priorities are most likely to offer assistance, while those in highly technological fields are most likely to resist—but even they have begun to soften their stance.[15]

At the local level, participation is now more regularized, particularly in planning. Programs in urban renewal, Model Cities, and other poverty-related areas have for some time included much greater involvement of affected citizens. As another kind of illustration, the Metropolitan Seattle Transit Planning Study was deliberately designed to include a citizen participation component.[16] Systematic efforts were made to attract "consistent voters" in King County to public discussion meetings arranged specifically to hear citizen views. Most of those attending had been active previously in local area organizations or on particular issues; thus, there was minimal representation of those who had not ordinarily participated in local civic affairs.[17] Citizens and planning professionals attended the public forums, and both agreed that the citizens had had an impact on planning the rapid transit system.

The professionals and citizens were asked to assess the role played by citizen participants in the planning process. Their perceptions, as registered on a "ladder of citizen participation" (see Figure 13-1), were not identical, but both groups felt there had been fairly significant involvement. Seventy percent of the professionals and 44 percent of the citizens indicated a consultative role, while 30 percent of the professionals and 19 percent of the citizens indicated a partnership role.[18] Analysis of the recommendations to the Metro Council indicates the citizens did affect the proposals substantially, though far from totally.[19] For example, citizen preferences were followed on expanding bus service, the design of specific bus routes, and emphasizing speed, low cost, and convenience over facilities such as heated shelters and food service in bus stations. However, other citizen preferences—for buses with nonpolluting engines, expansion of the existing electric trolley fleet, and financing the system through gas tax revenues—were not incorporated in the consultants' report to the council.[20]

Some other aspects of citizen participation deserve mention. First, participation can mean a number of different things. It could mean simply giving advice when asked (or before one is asked); holding jobs in a program; making decisions within an administrative framework; or having effective control. Different advocates, and opponents, of the concept have meant different things by "participation."

Second, the matter of *who* is to participate, and to what extent, is not always clear. In federal antipoverty programs of the mid- and late 1960s, "maximum feasible participation of the poor" was called for, but there was vast uncertainty about what that meant, especially just who was meant by "the poor," and how they were to be selected and incorporated into program operation.[21] Furthermore, in almost all studies of citizen participation, it was found that:

> groups or individuals active in such programs (1) represent organized interests likely to have been previously active in agency affairs, (2) include a

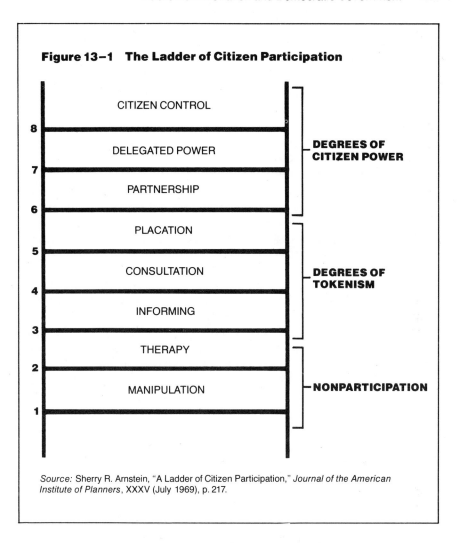

Figure 13–1   The Ladder of Citizen Participation

CITIZEN CONTROL

8

DELEGATED POWER

7

PARTNERSHIP

6

PLACATION

5

CONSULTATION

4

INFORMING

3

THERAPY

2

MANIPULATION

1

DEGREES OF
CITIZEN POWER

DEGREES OF
TOKENISM

NONPARTICIPATION

Source: Sherry R. Arnstein, "A Ladder of Citizen Participation," *Journal of the American Institute of Planners*, XXXV (July 1969), p. 217.

large component of spokesmen for other government agencies, (3) represent a *rather limited range* of potential publics affected by programs, and (4) tend toward the well-educated, affluent middle- to upper-class individuals. Viewed in terms of the ideological program goals, programs seldom appear to . . . produce a great socioeconomic diversity among participating interests.[22]

Third, there is a distinct possibility that official groups and agencies will co-opt citizen action groups. On more than one occasion, what began as a conscientious effort to build greater participation into a decision-making process ended up as more show than substance, with the newer (citizen) groups occupying a place of greater visibility but little increased power. Officially sponsored citizen participation tends to be co-optation rather than representation, more often than not.[23] A study of federal community action programs in the late 1960s indicated great variety in the relationships between neighborhood resident organizations (NROs) and city halls. Some NROs were clearly co-opted; others represented neighborhood interests to which city hall was hostile; still others established a negotiation relationship that facilitated interaction as equals.[24] In sum, nothing was automatic about the manner in which participation and representation were practiced.

Fourth, decentralizing and localizing control over government programs has not been a guarantee of either increased participation at the local level[25] or a more democractic manner of operation. The late political scientist Roscoe Martin observed some years ago that government at the "grass roots" may indeed be *less* democratic than in a larger and more diverse political system.[26] The dangers of co-optation and of domination by a minority of local citizens—perhaps a numerical minority of an ethnic minority—are very real, regardless of official mandates or unofficial expectations.

Fifth, if citizen participation is designed to help keep bureaucracy responsible to the general public, it has had only a mixed record of success. Citizen groups seem to have greatest impact when they have the political power to make bureaucrats listen, and when group values most nearly match those of the bureaucracy. Because of impediments such as expertise, time, and access, citizen inputs are likely to have limited effect in attaining bureaucratic responsibility.[27]

Sixth, citizen participation and its impact will be affected by the degree to which contacts with those in government are characterized by confrontation as opposed to negotiation, by a sense of "we versus they" as opposed to a perceived community of interests. Tension in a political system is not uncommon, but a democratic system virtually requires that tension not be constant. Barring fundamental shifts in the locus of power in a particular decision-making system, continuous confrontation will soon reach a point of diminishing returns for those seeking access to and influence in the decision-making process.

Seventh, a concept quite widespread in the area of participation is "input" from citizens, about which a cautionary note is in order. Many people seem to assume that what they should be seeking by increasing their participation is "greater input" into the mechanisms of decision making. The term is borrowed from computer science, where "input" makes a major difference in results. However, the concept of input carries with it an implicit acknowledgment that somebody else is "running the machine." Those who seek "input" are admitting to a *subordinate* position in the decision process. As Figure 13–1 indicates, there are other possibilities—partnership and full control, for example—for which "input" is an inappropriate concept. To think only in terms of "input," in short, serves to limit the variety of ways that participation can occur, and to confirm the power of those already holding it.

Citizen participation, in sum, has dramatically modified the "usual" methods of making decisions in a host of policy areas, and has taken its place as a major feature of democratic administration. While those in positions of power often have yielded grudgingly to citizen groups, it is unlikely that the gains made will be rolled back. If anything, the near future seems to hold promise for those advocating still further direct citizen involvement.

Representation and Representativeness

Democratic government in practice has meant representative democracy rather than direct democracy, for the most part. The concept of representation may appear clear cut, but there are a number of questions to be answered and problems to be dealt with. Representativeness, a companion but not identical concept, will be discussed subsequently.

There are, first of all, several approaches to representation.[28] Should constituents' opinions and preferences be conveyed to other government officials and reflected faithfully in legislative voting, or should a representative exercise independent judgment and individual conscience in making decisions? The former, which has been labeled the "delegate" role, maximizes the public's impact on decision making but does not take advantage of the representative's potentially superior knowledge of details and of subtleties in making choices. The latter, labeled the "trustee" role, emphasizes the representative's capabilities and the public's trust that their interests will be faithfully served (thus the label of trustee). In both instances, the people are depending on their representatives to somehow serve the "public interest." Unfortunately, it is rarely clear how our elected representatives make their decisions, and to *whose* voices they listen when they do act as delegates. Thus, in its most basic dimension, there is ambiguity concerning representation.

Most legislative bodies operate according to various rules and procedures which further diffuse the representational qualities of their decisions. As just one example, Congress has operated for years under a fragmented committee system in which power is acquired by *seniority* (though somewhat modified among House Democrats since 1975). Thus, in the distribution of power internally—a crucial variable in determining ultimate policy directions and actions—some are better represented than others because seniority is more easily acquired by "safe-seat" legislators than by those who may lose an election periodically. Also, committee chairmanships always go to a member of the majority party, and since 1933 both chambers have been Democratic-controlled with the exception of only four years (1947–1948 and 1953–1954). Congress, then, is loosely representative of the nation, but is far from being perfectly representative—a situation that is not all that surprising, given the nature of politics and power.

An essential difficulty in representation concerns the delegation of authority. In a fundamental sense, we delegate our authority to Congress and to state and local legislatures to make our laws, knowing as we do that representation of our every view is imperfect. Legislatures, in turn, have delegated vast amounts of authority to bureaucracies (and to chief executives), further removing decision-making power from the source of authority—that is, the people. When authority is delegated, it must be either very precisely defined and limited, which tends to be impractical and defeats the purpose of delegating, or else *discretionary*, with those who exercise it deciding how it should be used.

Once discretion enters the picture, which it does very early in administrative decision making, the representational quality of decisions may be diminished. This is particularly true where expertise, technical skill and competence, and rationality are highly prized values, as they are in much of our bureaucratic structure. We come back, then, to a dilemma which troubles much of democratic administration: *the conflict between professionalism and democratic participation/representation*. As in the Seattle transit study, citizens and professionals approach most decisions from different perspectives, particularly what is likely to be "best for the people." Another case where this was the central issue was the Ocean Hill–Brownsville school confrontation in Brooklyn in the late 1960s, when white teachers and educational professionals clashed with black parents, students, and community organizations over what constituted "quality education" in the public schools (and over who would have the power to decide that). Increasingly in recent years, "the people" have grown to resent somebody else making a judgment about what is best for them. Most of the time, that "somebody" was a professional operating from within bureaucracy. Thus, discretionary authority exercised by bureaucratic "trustees," so to speak, increases the chance that the general public's feelings will not be as well represented as they might be under conditions of less (professional) discretion. Popular election is one means of controlling discretion, but as we have seen, that device is not readily applicable to public bureaucracies.

Another aspect of administrative discretion should be noted. If, in the words of one observer, "good administration consists of making [bureaucracy] *predictably and reliably responsive*" to the wishes of the public,[29] then large areas of discretionary authority rather clearly get in the way of predictability. In fact, this is a key dilemma for President Carter and others who have articulated a desire to make the bureaucracy and government in general operate in ways that are more predictable. The only way to accomplish that, given our past history of delegating authority, is to tighten up dramatically on how much discretion technical experts in the bureaucracy are permitted to exercise, and that would require a fundamental reassessment of the kind of bureaucracy—and expertise—we want. Discretionary authority, in short, conflicts directly with a desire for predictability except within very broad limits.

Finally, representation by the bureaucracy is inhibited by long-time practices insulating administrative personnel from direct political pressures. Conceptually, "politics" and "representation of the public's feelings" are virtually synonymous, and to hamper political interchange is to place limits on popular representation.

Representativeness of the bureaucracy has been a focal point of controversy in the 1960s and 1970s, though that is not the first time attention has been paid to it. Political scientist Norton Long observed in 1952 that in terms of age, income, education, and father's occupation, the federal bureaucracy was broadly representative of the population as a whole, and more so than Congress.[30] More recently Samuel Krislov and Kenneth John Meier, in separate studies with differing interpretations, dealt with how to define representativeness in government bureaucracy, and with measuring its extent in a number of countries, including the United States.[31]

Krislov argues that classical political neutrality sacrifices some of the skills and assets which bureaucrats bring with them to government employment, including social representativeness. He sums up his case this way:

> What is really sought is not cold-fish indifference but responsiveness to political direction, an acknowledgment of democratic political supremacy. . . . The qualities of judgment, information, and fervor that bureaucrats do bring as they aid decision makers are in fact resources of immense social advantage, not merely weaknesses men are heir to. In particular, the bureaucrats' affinity for the population has great potential advantage for social stability and increased bureaucratic responsiveness.[32]

Krislov's general point is that by incorporating the skills, viewpoints, and judgments of government bureaucrats, effectiveness *and* representative qualities of the bureaucracy will be enhanced. His is clearly an unorthodox view of bureaucratic neutrality when compared to the likes of Weber, Herbert Simon, and others of traditional bent, but he provides an intellectual foundation for the position that representativeness is a value to be prized and pursued in the civil service. (In the 1960s the value of representativeness began to receive increased emphasis, with the value of administrative neutrality—as outlined by Max Weber and Woodrow Wilson—declining in importance.)

Krislov and Meier both deal with the question of whether or not the U.S. federal service is in fact representative, and arrive at somewhat different answers. Citing data from the mid-1960s comparing general federal employees and the "general employed public," Krislov notes a fairly close parallel between public employees and the general public in four social characteristics: religious preference, race, age, and partisan identification (see Table 13–1). Note, in particular, the comparative nonwhite proportions of each: 21 percent in the federal service to 11 percent overall. Krislov also notes that the percentage of blacks employed in the federal civil service increased slightly in the period 1962–1971, from 13.5 percent to 15 percent of the total. During the same period, the proportion of black employees at different levels within the civil service grade structure also changed. In 1962, 60 percent of all black employees were in grades GS-1 through GS-4, at the bottom of the ladder; by 1971, 43 percent of all blacks remained there. The proportion of blacks in GS-5 through GS-8 positions increased from 28 percent to 39 percent; in GS-9 through GS-11 positions, from 8.5 to 12.3 percent; and in GS-13 through GS-18 positions, from 2.7 to 5.9 percent. These figures indicate some change, but most of all they indicate a continuing concentration of black employees in the lower personnel grades.[33] That was a key point of

TABLE 13–1
FOUR SOCIAL CHARACTERISTICS OF GENERAL FEDERAL EMPLOYEES AND THE GENERAL EMPLOYED PUBLIC

Social Characteristic	General Federal Employees (N = 948)	General Employed Public (N = 1,142)
Religious Preference:		
Protestant	61%	69%
Catholic	31	25
Jewish	5	4
Other or none	4	2
Race:		
White	79	89
Nonwhite	21	11
Age:		
Under 20	0	2
20—24	3	8
25—34	18	22
35—44	37	29
45—54	27	25
55 and over	15	13
Identification:		
Democrat	55	48
Republican	17	26
Independent	23	17
No choice	5	9

N = Number of people in sample.
Source: Samuel Krislov, *Representative Bureaucracy* (Englewood Cliffs, N.J.: Prentice-Hall 1974), p. 106; originally from *Public Administration Review*, 27 (December 1967), 399.

contention in the early 1970s, when minority employment in the federal government became a pressing social and political issue. How much that has changed is still open to some question (see chapter 9).

Kenneth John Meier's study found some representativeness in the U.S. federal service, viewed as a whole, in terms of general values and social origins.[34] Table 13–2, based on survey data compiled by the University of Michigan Survey Research Center, indicates respective issue positions taken by public employees and the general population. Of the eight issue positions shown, public employees and the general population are very close to one another on three (voting for Nixon, Republican party identification, and withdrawal from Vietnam) and fairly close on four others (increasing taxes on high-income people, legalizing marijuana, protecting rights of the accused, and providing government help for minorities). Only on the issue of trading with Communist nations are the two groups apart by more than nine percentage points.

Also of significance is Meier's finding that in terms of fathers' occupational status, the civil service is more representative of the general population than is the foreign service or politically appointed executives.[35] This is not to say, however, that it is in fact representative, only that it is more so than some other sets of government officials. Finally, Meier states unequivocally that while the civil service as a whole is fairly representative of the population at large, the upper grades—where major decision makers are concentrated—are much less representative than the lower grades.[36] This is largely consistent with the comments made in chapter 9 concerning the underrepresentation of women and minorities in upper grades of the federal civil service.

The call for representativeness of minorities, in particular, sparked major changes in the early 1970s. Ethnic minorities took the virtually

TABLE 13–2
ISSUE POSITIONS OF PUBLIC EMPLOYEES
AND THE GENERAL PUBLIC

Issue	Public Employees Favorable	N	Population Favorable	N
Vote for Nixon	61.0%	128	64.6%	1,411
Republican party identification	32.3	130	34.6	2,482
Withdraw from Vietnam	47.6	63	43.7	1,133
Trade with Communists	83.3	48	64.1	840
Increase taxes on high incomes	60.0	50	52.8	922
Legalize marijuana	31.9	113	23.7	2,105
Protect rights of the accused	50.7	77	43.1	1,478
Government should help minorities	51.4	74	44.1	1,431

N = Total number of respondents to each issue question.
Source: Kenneth John Meier, "Representative Bureaucracy: An Empirical Analysis," *American Political Science Review*, 69 (June 1975), 541.

unanimous position that greater ethnic representativeness was needed to enhance general understanding within the civil service of problems peculiar to minority groups. Furthermore, theirs was a call for *advocacy* of their cause, as a central activity of minority administrators.[37] In general, the effort to increase ethnic representativeness was founded on the belief—perhaps quite valid—that government would otherwise continue to ignore minority concerns for which the federal government, especially, managed hundreds of programs. Political activism to bring this about has been intense, and pressure is still on from within government as well as outside.[38]

Responsiveness

Responsiveness on the part of public officials to popular sentiments depends upon several factors being present in the governmental process. For one thing, it depends in a fundamental sense on the people's assumptions about what *is* and what *should be* in the conduct of government and public policy making. It is not only a matter of what we establish, very loosely, as our governmental and societal objectives—it is also very much a matter of what we take for granted in our expectations about governmental activity.

Second, responsiveness requires meaningful access to the *right* decision makers, and at least a legitimate opportunity to be heard. Access is a key step in the policy process, and without it responsiveness cannot be assured.

Third, agencies and the government at large have to be *able* to respond to policy and program demands, even assuming that they are willing to do so. Politically, financially, and administratively, agencies must be equipped to deliver services or otherwise satisfy public demands placed on them.

Fourth, a vital aspect of responsiveness is that government, in all its dimensions, meets enough basic needs of enough people in society. The question is, of course, "how much (many) is 'enough'?" There is considerable uncertainty in this regard, although there are many institutional devices for ascertaining public wants and needs as well as what must be done to fulfill them. No government does a perfect job of meeting *all* public expectations. The task ours has faced lately is to improve on its record in trying to do so.

There are two major constraints on responsiveness. The first concerns public *expectations*. Ideally, public expectations should be realistic, reasonable, and manageable. Admittedly, there is potential for anyone in government to hide behind excuses of unrealistic, unreasonable, or unmanageable public desires to avoid tackling hard problems that may objectively need attention. But the point here is that there may actually be conditions which for legitimate reasons are difficult to deal with—for example, environmental pollution, housing problems, poverty, or nuclear waste disposal. If people assume that a problem can be solved, and it is not solved, the government may be accused (not entirely fairly) of being unresponsive to public wants. Despite our skepticism, inability to act *can* be an operating reality for a government agency—perhaps due to lack of jurisdiction, limited funds, political opposition, or merely difficulties in "making the ordinary happen" (see chapter 12).

The second constraint on responsiveness is the fact that government agencies cannot—or, at least, do not—respond equally to different societal interests. Inevitably, some groups view government as unresponsive because it does not respond to *them*. And they are often correct in that assessment. The main point, however, is that government is not simply "responsive," only "responsive *to*" interests and preferences which exist in society at large. Especially in the context of limited resources (fiscal and otherwise), government cannot be responsive to each and every interest or need, and is rarely able to satisfy fully those interests to which it does respond.

Accountability

Holding government officials to account for their actions is crucial to democratic government, and even more so when substantial responsibility is entrusted to nonelected (administrative) personnel. "Governmental openness to public scrutiny is a key to accountability for official conduct,"[39] in principle. This rationale underlies freedom-of-information laws and "sunshine" (open meeting) laws, both of which increase the public's ability to inquire successfully into the activities of bureaucracy and other branches of government. The glare of publicity has long been known as one means of enforcing accountability, by making possible a better informed citizenry which can then act more intelligently and purposefully. "Sunset" laws (discussed in chapter 10) add another dimension to accountability. By requiring positive legislative action to renew agency mandates, there is a virtual guarantee that some examination of agency performance will take place. It should be emphasized, however, that merely routine reviews and near-universal renewals of agency authorizations will not serve the purposes of sunset legislation. Only careful, thorough, and demanding examinations will do.

The use of sunset laws, in particular, as an instrument of accountability is part of a widespread resurgence of legislative efforts to hold executives accountable.[40] Other institutional devices include the congressional budget procedure, involving CBO and two Budget Committees on Capitol Hill. The public once again seems to be looking to its legislative representatives to lead the way toward greater popular control over what executive-branch agencies do, in the best tradition of those who first shaped the political system. In both state and national government, increasing numbers of legislators seem inclined to respond positively to public pressures, and in some cases to lead public opinion as well as follow it.

Accountability is hampered by the prevalence of technical subject matter in government decision making. In many respects this limits the potential for accountability to those who are able to understand the nature of an issue and the implications of different proposed solutions. A case in point is the energy situation, where the one thing that stands out amid a chorus of problems and solutions is a need for more and better information, for decision maker and citizen alike. Few among us comprehend all the intricacies of natural gas pricing, the politics of supply here and abroad, and so on. If we, the people, are not in a good position to monitor government decisions in a knowledgeable way, how are we to assure that those who made them can be held to account for them? There is no easy answer. It remains to be seen whether rising public demand for accountability can be met.

Ethics, Morality, and Corruption

Public insistence in recent years on a greater degree of ethical and moral behavior in government has been principally a reaction to the traumas, untruths, and tensions of the Nixon administration, epitomized by the Watergate scandals. Yet problems of ethics and morality in government are not new, and devising methods for insuring ethical and moral behavior, and for reducing the incidence of corruption among government officials, is a continuing task.

As with other aspects of politics and public administration, there seems to be some public feeling that it should be easy, even routine, to deal with problems of ethics and morality in the conduct of government. There are those who firmly believe there are moral and ethical absolutes which should be followed regardless of circumstance, in public affairs as well as private life. Simply define the standards of conduct, some say, and then let the bureaucrats adhere to them in their work. But it is not that easy.

Virtually every major commentary on government ethics and morality in the literature of public administration in recent years has noted the *basic moral ambiguity* of public choices and policies.[41] Few, indeed, are the decisions in which one alternative, and one only, is clearly the most moral and ethical. How, then, can we deal meaningfully with the problem of ethics and morality without turning it simply into a matter of "situation ethics," depending largely or entirely on particular issues and circumstances?

Fortunately, there are answers to that question. Some years ago political scientist Stephen K. Bailey suggested that people need certain attitudes and moral qualities in order to behave ethically in the public

PRESIDENTIAL COMMENTS ON ETHICS
IN GOVERNMENT

"Tis substantially true, that virtue or morality is a necessary spring of popular government."
George Washington, 1796

"The whole art of government consists in the art of being honest."
Thomas Jefferson, 1774

"While the people retain their virtue and vigilance, no administration, by any extreme of wickedness or folly, can very seriously injure the government in the short space of four years."
Abraham Lincoln, 1861

"The man who debauches our public life . . . is a greater foe to our well-being as a nation than is even the defaulting cashier of a bank. . . . Without honesty popular government is a repulsive farce."
Theodore Roosevelt, 1910

"When people are dishonorable in private business, they injure only those with whom they deal or their own chances in the next world. But when there is a lack of honor in government, the morals of the whole people are poisoned."
Herbert Hoover, 1951

"The stewardship of public officers is a serious and sacred trust."
Franklin D. Roosevelt, 1938

"In world opinion and in world effectiveness, the United States is measured by the moral firmness of its public officials."
Dwight D. Eisenhower, 1958

"No President can excuse or pardon the slightest deviation from irreproachable standards of behavior on the part of any member of the executive branch. For his firmness and determination is the ultimate source of public confidence in the government of the United States."
John F. Kennedy, 1961

"And let us begin by committing ourselves to the truth, to see it like it is, to tell it like it is—to find the truth, to speak the truth and to live the truth—and that's what we will do."
Richard M. Nixon, 1968

Source: Library of Congress and *CQ Guide to Current American Government* (Washington, D.C.: Congressional Quarterly, Inc., Spring 1974), p. 28.

service.[42] The first attitude is an *awareness* of moral ambiguity in decision making. The second is appreciation of the contextual forces at play in decision situations.[43] The third attitude is a conception of the "paradox of procedures," that is, an understanding of the need for orderly and rational procedures balanced against an understanding that procedures ("red tape") can sometimes be an impediment to responsiveness and public accountability. The three moral qualities are optimism, including a willingness to take risks; courage, including the courage to avoid special favors, to make decisions that are unpopular, and to be able to decide under pressure; and charity, being fair and placing principle above personal needs for recognition, status, and power.[44]

Another aspect of ethics and morality is the question of internal (personal) versus external (legal-institutional) checks on the behavior of the individual administrator. Over the years, a debate has gone on over whether one or the other type of controls is more effective in insuring ethical behavior, accountability, and responsibility. Recent commentaries seem to be inclined toward the position that *both* types are needed. One central point made by a number of observers can be summed up as follows: "The public has to be able to rely on the self-discipline of the great majority of public servants. Otherwise the *official restraints and sanctions must be so numerous and so cumbersome* that effective public administration is impaired greatly."[45] The essential point is that while there may be some things we can—and perhaps must—do to try to insure ethical actions in the public service, the ultimate safeguard is in the character and inclinations of bureaucrats themselves.

In addition, there are some other considerations to bear in mind. *Practical* ethical problems vary widely from agency to agency; they are very different, for example, at the State Department, Department of Energy, and Community Services Administration. Furthermore, there is a basic problem in "how to grasp the true meaning of ethics and morality—what it is from day to day and situation to situation—within a societal framework."[46] There is also the difficulty posed by changing public attention to ethics and morality, and even different definitions of what is or is not acceptable behavior. It should not be forgotten that many citizens have a definition of acceptable conduct clearly at variance with the traditional concept of what is strictly ethical. And even where most of us agree on a definition, there remains the discomfiting fact that in different eras, different definitions have prevailed. In sum, though a "situation ethic" is not inevitable, standards of ethics and morality are not constant, universal, or applicable to all situations.

A crucial distinction in this area is between private and public morality. "John Courtney Murray, the great American Jesuit philosopher, wrote that one of the most dangerous misconceptions of the modern world is the idea that the same standards that govern individual morality should also govern national morality."[47] Behavior that offends private morality, that is, could conceivably be moral according to standards of public morality. But what *is* "public morality"? For an answer we must look back to a basic distinction drawn in chapter 1 between those clothed with the authority of official position and all others; we said then that a crucial difference is to be found in the fact that government has a monopoly on the legitimate use of force. This means, for example, that government may use force when necessary to apprehend suspected criminals, that it may utilize the death penalty as long as it is constitutional to do so, and that it may order its soldiers to kill those of another country in wartime. We judge these acts by standards very different from those applied to our neighbors and ourselves, because the contexts of governmental versus individual actions are different. With power, of course, should go responsibility—some sense that there are different sorts of limits on behavior because of one's *public* obligations.

Some examples will illustrate the point. Private morality, for instance, was violated when the office of Daniel Ellsberg's psychiatrist was burglarized in 1971; private morals tell us that it is wrong to steal that which is not ours and to damage another's property. But this burglary also violated public morality, for several reasons. First, it was supervised by E. Howard Hunt and G. Gordon Liddy, two of the so-called "plumbers" working for the White House, who were attempting to obtain information on Ellsberg, the man who leaked the Pentagon Papers to *The New York Times*.[48] Second, they were acting under the indirect authority of the president of the United States in doing so. Third, illegally obtaining confidential information from a doctor's files was the only way they could learn anything about Ellsberg from his psychiatrist, since the law considers such information "privileged" (protected against forced revelation in police interrogation or courtroom testimony). If one believes that national security considerations represent the highest public morality, these acts might have been justified. Otherwise, the violations of law involved suggest public *im*morality.

Joseph Califano, now HEW secretary, provided another Watergate-related example in a 1973 article:

> Patrick Gray can equivocate in statements to the press, campaign while Acting FBI Director for the Republican Presidential candidate and destroy "politically dynamite" documents, but his Catholic upbringing and schooling did not permit him to lie under oath because that involves personal morality and perhaps serious sin. The Haldeman and Ehrlichman letters of resignation pay lip service to public morality, but protest their private morality as though *that were the ultimate standard* by which their *exercise of the public trust* should be judged.[49]

And that is the point: the public trust and its exercise add a completely different dimension to what individuals do in official capacities, or in matters related to government decisions. The public trust imposes obligations on public officials over and above those arising from private moral codes.

One other example further illustrates confusion of public and private morality. The case involved the late Mayor Richard J. Daley of Chicago and two of his sons who were employed by an insurance firm in suburban Evanston. It became known that the firm had been awarded millions of dollars' worth of Chicago city government insurance contracts, without competitive bidding. When questioned by reporters about this, Daley paused and then explained that any father would do what he could to help his sons! True enough, and by Daley's strict personal moral code, entirely appropriate. But because of his public position and power, there were some, at least, who regarded this as a breach of public trust, in that other insurance firms were also (corporate) citizens of Chicago, and that public morality requires a government to deal equitably with all its citizens. And that, Daley clearly had not done.

Perhaps the most difficult aspect of this subject is that there is no *universal* definition of public morality, and attempts to arrive at one inevitably end up in the rough-and-tumble of the political process. An awareness that there even *is* such a thing as public morality must come before we can engage in the process of deciding what it is—and even then we might fall short. In the case of Richard Nixon, however, enough people agreed on what it was *not* to force his premature exit from the White House in the traumatic summer of 1974. Maybe that sort of negative definition is the best we can do.

What, then, of political corruption? Corruption is offensive to many traditions of private morality, yet rooting it out seems so very difficult. There is one overriding truth about corruption that must be emphasized. According to the standards many of us apply to it, *corruption is universal*, in the sense that virtually every political system known to humanity has had its share of political favoritism, private arrangements between public figures, and out-and-out thievery and bribery. We find this offensive to our Western standards; but without trying to justify it, we should note that not everyone reacts the way we do. In many parts of the world, what we call corruption is part of the routine expectations of politics—and of business and other enterprises, for that matter. Yet it is appropriate to combat it, if in fact corruption violates our expectations of what *our* officials should and should not do.

Corruption is a commonplace in many states and localities. Deals are made quietly, contracts awarded, jobs created, votes bartered for (and occasionally stolen), offices bandied about, power exerted, contributors rewarded, and so on, all on the basis of patronage and other forms of favoritism. The battle over municipal reform (see chapter 3) has centered on making it possible to stamp out corruption in government. Our image of corruption seems to emphasize big-city politics, but the fact is that in rural America there is the same kind of favoring friends and rewarding political loyalty as there is in the city. Patronage is rampant in some states, merely visible in others. The remarkable thing is that so much *has* been done to make the conduct of government more honest and open.

One other observation is in order. Corruption, as a practical matter, is a form of *privilege,* indulged in by those in positions of power, wealth, and influence for their mutual gain. As such, corruption is inherently antidemocratic in nature, since it concentrates power and its benefits in relatively few hands. If democracy is founded in large part on a premise of equality in the political system, corruption is offensive to *that* value as well as to moral and ethical ones. Ultimately, this is another good reason for being concerned with corruption in a democratic government, one at least as relevant as moral and ethical considerations.

Public Administrators and Democratic Values

If we are to be able to practice democratic administration, those who occupy bureaucratic positions clearly must have a commitment to the norms and values of democracy. Unfortunately, we know only a little about administrators' attitudes toward democracy, though the ground has been broken in researching this area, notably by Bob L. Wynia.[50]

Wynia's study involved 405 federal bureaucrats, mainly in Grades GS-13 through GS-15. Participants were given a list of forty-two statements distinctly antidemocratic in tone, and asked to indicate whether they agreed or disagreed with each. There was considerable variation in the percentages agreeing with different statements. However, anywhere from one-tenth to one-third of the respondents agreed with each antidemocratic position. Table 13–3 indicates eight of the items and the

TABLE 13–3
FEDERAL BUREAUCRATS' ATTITUDES TOWARD DEMOCRATIC IDEAS: SELECTED ITEMS

Item	Percentage of Bureaucrats Who Agree with Item
There are times when it almost seems better for the people to take the law into their own hands rather than wait for the machinery of government to act.	31.9
We might as well make up our minds that in order to make the world free a lot of innocent people will have to suffer.	31.0
We have to teach children that all men are created equal but almost everyone knows that some are better than others.	37.5
If congressional committees stuck strictly to rules and gave every witness his rights, they would never succeed in exposing the many dangerous subversives they have turned up.	28.0
To bring about great changes for the benefit of mankind often requires cruelty and even ruthlessness.	27.0
The true American way of life is disappearing so fast that we may have to use force to save it.	18.6
A person who hides behind the laws when he is questioned about his actions doesn't deserve much consideration.	24.8
When the country is in great danger, we may have to force people to testify against themselves even if it violates their rights.	24.6

Source: Bob L. Wynia, "Federal Bureaucrats' Attitudes Toward a Democratic Ideology," *Public Administration Review,* 34 (March/April 1974), 158–159.

proportion of respondents agreeing with them. Wynia then examined the bureaucrats' responses in relation to three factors—agency affiliation, number of years of education, and number of years in public service—and drew the following conclusions.

First, agency affiliation is an important correlate of an individual's attitude toward a democratic philosophy. Grouping career executives into three categories—"social" agencies, "defense-related" agencies, and "other"—Wynia found that those in defense agencies were more antidemocratic in their orientations and general attitudes than those in the other two categories.

Second, the more years a bureaucrat spends in the public service, the more antidemocratic his or her attitudes become. Wynia attributed this to a learning process, particularly of the values peculiar to individual agencies. This form of long-term socialization into an agency is coming to be regarded as being at least as important as one's early learning of political values.

Third, the more formal education a bureaucrat has, the stronger his or her democratic beliefs and habits. This offsets to some degree the effects of longer-term public service, though precisely in what way is not clear. Table 13–4 illustrates some of the patterns Wynia found.

In sum, there is evidence suggesting that bureaucrats in positions of authority in the federal civil service may entertain norms and values that

TABLE 13–4
CORRELATES OF FEDERAL BUREAUCRATS' ATTITUDES TOWARD A DEMOCRATIC IDEOLOGY: SELECTED ITEMS

| | Percentage of "Agrees" | | | | | | | | | | |
| | Average | Agency | | | Years of Education | | | Years in Service | | | |
Item		Social	Defense	Other	0–12	13–15	16+	1–5	6–15	16–25	26+
When the country is in great danger, we may have to force people to testify against themselves even if it violates their rights.	24.6	25.3	30.9	20.4	25.6	26.3	22.5	15.2	23.3	24.6	28.8
Any person who hides behind the laws when he is questioned about his activities doesn't deserve much consideration.	24.8	19.0	29.3	24.4	41.0	26.6	19.1	12.1	16.5	24.6	37.5

Source: Bob L. Wynia, "Federal Bureaucrats' Attitudes Toward a Democratic Ideology," *Public Administration Review,* 34 (March/April 1974), 159.

contradict a democratic philosophy. Since these data were gathered (1969–1970), some change may have occurred, given significant infusions of "new blood," as well as heightened public attention to the ways bureaucrats conduct their business. To the extent such values persist, however, there is cause for concern that democratic administration will be impeded.

Administrative Effectiveness and Personal Liberty

One other topic deserves brief treatment: the possibility that as government machinery is made stronger, it acquires additional potential for diluting individual liberties. This does not necessarily occur as the product of deliberate decision in the highest councils of government. It can result simply from zealous implementation of perceived mandates by an individual agency or bureaucrat. It is even more of a possibility when strong public sentiment exists in support of particular agencies doing a job that inherently poses dangers to individual liberties.

A leading example is law enforcement agencies. In their zeal for "fighting crime" there is danger that the FBI, state law enforcement agencies, or local police may infringe on Bill of Rights protections. This is a serious concern of many people, and involves such issues as search and seizure procedures, wiretapping, the death penalty, and priorities of national security versus individual privacy, among many others. The essential point is that as the machinery of government grows stronger— whether or not it is supported by particular popular majorities—the *potential* for infringement of all sorts of individual rights grows apace. This causes operating problems for those in public administration, but all of society is ultimately involved because of the basic values at issue.

SUMMARY

Public administration poses particular difficulties for those seeking to maintain control over instruments of government. Bureaucracy's influence, coupled with its relative obscurity and political insulation, has caused it to become a focal point for many different pressures. Interest in "democratic" values has increased, as has political activity aimed at increasing governmental responsiveness, particularly to those previously underrepresented in administrative politics.

Democratic government presumes participation and accountability, with an independent judiciary and free elections as essential safeguards. The meanings of those values have changed over time, and have been significantly expanded in recent decades. Two related concepts—representation and representativeness—have taken on new meanings also. For each of these values, there is some definitional uncertainty.

We have long known that problems exist in maintaining democratic norms and practices, and have been aware of difficulties with particular aspects of democracy: unequal access to decision makers, the impact of effective organization and adequate funding, and problems in determining what it is "the people" want. Defining "the public interest" is, if anything, even more difficult.

Public administration is particularly troublesome for a democratic system, for several reasons. Most bureaucrats are not elected. Expertise and knowledge are emphasized over participation. Specialization is valued, as is professionalism. Participation and professionalism conflict frequently, and it is difficult to incorporate both accountability and participation into policy making when administrative agencies are the chief policy makers. How one views bureaucracy and its social/political role is primarily dependent on one's larger view of the role of government itself.

Concerns about public administration and democratic government include the following. Administrative secrecy is a traditional feature of Weberian bureaucracy, though it has been weakened through the use of freedom-of-information laws and sunshine laws. Another recent emphasis is on the need to protect individual privacy against government invasion and misuse of personal information. The computer and its capabilities have made this a vital issue.

Major problems of democratic administration include: (1) citizen participation, (2) bureaucratic representativeness, (3) bureaucratic responsiveness, (4) bureaucratic accountability, (5) ethics and morality in government, including corruption, (6) administrators' beliefs in democratic values, and (7) administrative effectiveness as a threat to personal freedoms.

Citizen participation originated with efforts on the part of the urban poor (and some others) to obtain a greater voice in government decisions affecting their lives. It has now been adapted to the purposes of many other groups, white as well as nonwhite, more affluent and less affluent. Citizen participation has taken many forms: "community control" in the 1960s, preserving neighborhood character—and sometimes neighborhoods themselves—in the 1970s. It also has been incorporated into formal mechanisms for decision making. Citizen participation is limited by the following factors, among others: (1) some uncertainty as to its exact meaning, about who is to participate, and to what extent; (2) the possibility of co-optation of citizen participants; (3) the likelihood that insufficient power, incongruent values, and impediments of expertise, time, and access will hamper citizens' ability to achieve bureaucratic responsibility; and (4) the conceptual implications of merely "seeking input." The outlook is for continued citizen participation in numerous forms.

Representation and representativeness in government generally and public administration specifically have recently been given more attention. The representational qualities of our institutions—Congress, other legislative bodies, and so on—are affected by various rules and procedures followed. Further complicating representation is delegation of authority. Most delegated authority becomes discretionary in its use, limiting its representational qualities. Another dimension of discretion is its effect of diminishing bureaucratic predictability. Finally, traditional political insulation of administrative agencies places limits on representation.

The representativeness of governmental bureaucracy is not a new concern. It was asserted a quarter-century ago that the federal bureaucracy was more representative of the general population than was Congress in terms of age, income, education, and father's occupation. Representativeness has been said to enhance bureaucratic effectiveness and responsiveness. A key finding of recent research is that civil servants in the upper grades—the decision makers—are much less representative than the civil service as a whole. Representativeness of minorities, emphasized since the late 1960s, may have increased in the civil service, though that is not entirely clear.

Bureaucratic responsiveness depends upon popular assumptions about what *is* and *should be* in the conduct of government, meaningful access to decision makers, agencies' ability to respond to public demands, and government meeting enough basic needs of enough people. Public expectations can affect how responsive the government is thought to be. Also, government cannot or will not respond equally to every interest or preference that exists in society.

Accountability requires government openness to public scrutiny. In this connection, freedom-of-information laws and "sunshine" laws have been enacted increasingly in the 1970s. "Sunset" laws help legislative bodies hold executive-branch agencies accountable. Accountability is made more difficult by the technical subject matter in so much government activity.

Ethics and morality in government, as well as corruption, have received much attention in the 1970s. For some, it is a simple matter of government officials behaving "properly," by fixed and clear standards. However, ethics and morality are more likely to be achieved in the public context if bureaucrats are aware of the moral ambiguities in decision making, if they appreciate contextual forces in decision situations, and if they understand that while orderly and rational procedures are important, they should not become ends in themselves. Optimism, courage, and charity are moral qualities which contribute to ethical behavior. But while the character of bureaucrats is a crucial factor, legal-institutional checks are also needed to promote morality in the public service. Practical ethical problems vary from agency to agency, situation to situation, and time to time. No universal or constant standard of ethics and morality exists. In addition, there are differences between private and public morality. The latter is based on the idea that special responsibilities accompany exercise of the public trust and legitimate use of force.

Corruption, often defined in terms of private moral standards, is a widespread if not universal phenomenon. Much of the effort to reform politics has as its principal focus a Judaeo-Christian moral emphasis. Another reason for opposing political corruption is the fact that it is a form of privilege, and as such is inherently antidemocratic in nature, since it normally favors relatively few at the expense of the many.

Federal bureaucrats' attitudes toward democracy, as documented in one important study, vary according to a number of factors. Agency affiliation was found to have an impact, with those in defense-related agencies distinctly more favorable to antidemocratic statements than those elsewhere. Long service also seemed to contribute to antidemocratic sentiment. Education, however, tended to strengthen democratic beliefs and habits.

Finally, strong government machinery—even for legitimate and popularly supported purposes—is a potential threat to individual liberty. As an operating problem, striking a balance between governmental strength and individual liberty is particularly important for public administration; as a value question, it concerns the whole of society.

NOTES

1. A. Lee Fritschler, *Smoking and Politics: Policy Making and the Federal Bureaucracy,* 2nd ed. (Englewood Cliffs, N.J.: Prentice-Hall, 1975), p. 13.

2. Theodore H. White, *The Making of the President 1972* (New York: Atheneum Publishers, 1973), pp. 299–300.

3. Theodore J. Lowi, *The End of Liberalism: Ideology, Policy, and the Crisis of Public Authority* (New York: W. W. Norton, 1969).

4. Victor A. Thompson, "Bureaucracy in a Democratic Society," in Roscoe C. Martin, ed., *Public Administration and Democracy* (Syracuse, N.Y.: Syracuse University Press, 1965), pp. 205–226, at p. 207.

5. William B. Eimicke, *Public Administration in a Democratic Context: Theory and Practice* (Beverly Hills, Calif.: Sage, 1974), p. 17.

6. Fritschler, *Smoking and Politics,* p. 13.

7. This discussion is derived from Eimicke, *Public Administration in a Democratic Context.*

8. See, among others, Lloyd Nurick, "Access to Public Records: Strengthening Democracy," *The Bureaucrat,* 4 (April 1975), 34–44. Congress first attempted to open the bureaucracy to the public in the 1946 Administrative Procedure Act, which encouraged distribution of information on a "need to know" basis.

9. See Willis H. Ware and Carole W. Parsons, "Perspectives on Privacy," *The Bureaucrat,* 5 (July 1976), 141–156.

10. Ibid., pp. 144–148.

11. See, also, Frank G. De Balogh, "Public Administrators and 'The Privacy Thing': A Time to Speak Out," *Public Administration Review,* 32 (September/October 1972), 526–530; E. Edward Stephens, "Legal Invasions of Our Right of Privacy," *The Bureaucrat,* 4 (October 1975), 290–292; Edmund Dwyer, "The Right of Privacy versus Technological Advances," *The Bureaucrat,* 4 (October 1975), 293–298; Hugh V. O'Neill, "The Privacy Act of 1974: Introduction and Overview," *The Bureaucrat,* 5 (July 1976), 131–140; Robert P. Bedell, "The Privacy Act: The Implementation at First Glance," *The Bureaucrat,* 5 (July 1976), 157–170; and Hugh V. O'Neill and John P. Fanning, "The Challenge of Implementing and Operating under the Privacy Act in the Largest Public Sector Conglomerate—HEW," *The Bureaucrat,* 5 (July 1976), 171–188.

12. Walter A. Rosenbaum, "The Paradoxes of Public Participation," *Administration and Society,* 8 (November 1976), 355–383, at pp. 362–363.

13. See, among others, Alan Altshuler, *Community Control: The Black Demand for Participation in Large American Cities* (New York: Pegasus, 1970); Milton Kotler, *Neighborhood Government: The Local Foundations of Political Life* (Indianapolis: Bobbs-Merrill, 1969); and Joseph Zimmerman, *The Federated City: Community Control in Large Cities* (New York: St. Martin's, 1972).

14. For an incisive, in-depth study of the Rye–Oyster Bay Bridge controversy emphasizing the role of citizen organizations, see Thomas A. Droleskey, "The Politics of the Proposal to Construct a Bridge Crossing from Oyster Bay to Rye, New York: A Study of Group Politics and Public Policy Decision Making," unpublished Ph.D. dissertation, Graduate School of Public Affairs, State University of New York at Albany, 1977.

15. Max D. Paglin and Edgar Shor, "Regulatory Agency Responses to the Development of Public Participation," *Public Administration Review,* 37 (March/April 1977), 140–148.

16. Adepoju G. Onibokun and Martha Curry, "An Ideology of Citizen Participation: The Metropolitan Seattle Transit Case Study," *Public Administration Review,* 36 (May/June 1976), 269–277.

17. Ibid., p. 271.

18. Developed by Sherry Arnstein, "A Ladder of Citizen Participation," *The Journal of the American Institute of Planners,* 35 (July 1969), 216–224, cited in Adepoju G. Onibokun and Martha Curry, "An Ideology of Citizen Participation: The Metropolitan Seattle Transit Case Study," *Public Administration Review,* 36 (May/June 1976), 269–277, at p. 273.

19. Onibokun and Curry, "An Ideology of Citizen Participation: The Metropolitan Seattle Transit Case Study," p. 273.

20. Ibid., p. 274.

21. These questions are suggested by John H. Strange, "The Impact of Citizen Participation on Public Administration," *Public Administration Review, Special Issue,* 32 (September 1972), 457–470, at pp. 460–461.

22. Rosenbaum, "The Paradoxes of Public Participation," p. 273 (emphasis added).

23. James A. Riedel, "Citizen Participation: Myths and Realities," *Public Administration Review,* 32 (May/June 1972), 211–220, at p. 212.

24. James L. Sundquist, with the collaboration of David W. Davis, *Making Federalism Work: A Study of Program Coordination at the Community Level* (Washington, D.C.: The Brookings Institution, 1969), pp. 94–101.

25. Riedel, "Citizen Participation: Myths and Realities," p. 212.

26. Roscoe C. Martin, *Grass Roots* (University, Ala.: University of Alabama Press, 1957).

27. Robert W. Kweit, "Bureaucratic Decision Making: Impediments to Citizen Participation," paper presented at the 1977 annual meeting of the Midwest Political Science Association, Chicago, April 21–23, 1977.

28. This discussion relies in part on Eimicke, *Public Administration in a Democratic Context,* pp. 33–44.

29. Thompson, "Bureaucracy in a Democratic Society," p. 207 (emphasis added).

30. Norton E. Long, "Bureaucracy and Constitutionalism," *American Political Science Review,* 46 (September 1952), 808–818.

31. Samuel Krislov, *Representative Bureaucracy* (Englewood Cliffs, N.J.: Prentice-Hall, 1974); Kenneth John Meier, "Representative Bureaucracy: An Empirical Analysis," *American Political Science Review,* 69 (June 1975), 526–542.

32. Krislov, *Representative Bureaucracy,* p. 81.

33. Ibid., p. 113.

34. Meier, "Representative Bureaucracy: An Empirical Analysis," p. 526.

35. Ibid., p. 539.

36. Ibid., p. 541.

37. Armando Rodriguez, "A Chicano Looks at the Bureaucracy," *The Bureaucrat,* 2 (Summer 1973), 170–172, at p. 172.

38. See Cleveland L. Dennard and Carl Akins, eds., "Public Policy Forum: Minority Perspectives on Bureaucracy," *The Bureaucrat,* 2 (Summer 1973), 127–191.

39. Justice Bertram Harnett of the New York State Supreme Court, quoted in Nurick, "Access to Public Records: Strengthening Democracy," p. 40.

40. Bruce Adams, "Sunset: A Proposal for Accountable Government," *Administrative Law Review,* 28 (Summer 1976), 511–542.

41. See, for example, Susan Wakefield, "Ethics and the Public Service," *Public Administration Review,* 36 (November/December 1976), 661–666.

42. Stephen K. Bailey, "Ethics and the Public Service," in Roscoe C. Martin, ed., *Public Administration and Democracy* (Syracuse, N.Y.: Syracuse University Press, 1965), pp. 283–298.

43. Ibid., p. 291.

44. Ibid., p. 293.

45. DeWitt C. Armstrong III and George A. Graham, "Ethical Preparation for the Public Service," *The Bureaucrat,* 4 (April 1975), 6–23, at p. 6 (emphasis added).

46. Ersa Poston and Walter D. Broadnax, "Ethics and Morality in Government: Introduction," *The Bureaucrat,* 4 (April 1975), 3–4, at p. 3.

47. Cited by Joseph A. Califano, Jr., "Richard Nixon: The Resignation Option," *The Bureaucrat,* 2 (Summer 1973), 222–231, at p. 225.

48. Carl Bernstein and Bob Woodward, *All the President's Men* (New York: Simon and Schuster, 1974), p. 343; White, *The Making of the President 1972,* p. 308.

49. Califano, "Richard Nixon: The Resignation Option," p. 226 (emphasis added).

50. Bob L. Wynia, "Federal Bureaucrats' Attitudes Toward a Democratic Ideology," *Public Administration Review,* 34 (March/April 1974), 156–162.

SUGGESTED READINGS

"Citizens Action in Model Cities and CAP Programs: Case Studies and Evaluation," *Public Administration Review, Special Issue,* 32 (September 1972), 377–470.

"Curriculum Essays on Citizens, Politics, and Administration in Urban Neighborhoods," *Public Administration Review, Special Issue,* 32 (October 1972), 565–738.

Eimicke, William B. *Public Administration in a Democratic Context: Theory and Practice.* Beverly Hills, Calif.: Sage, 1974.

Krislov, Samuel. *Representative Bureaucracy.* Englewood Cliffs, N.J.: Prentice-Hall, 1974.

Lowi, Theodore J. *The End of Liberalism: Ideology, Policy, and the Crisis of Public Authority.* New York: W. W. Norton, 1969.

Martin, Roscoe C. *Grass Roots.* University, Ala.: University of Alabama Press, 1957.

Martin, Roscoe C., ed. *Public Administration and Democracy.* Syracuse, N.Y.: Syracuse University Press, 1965.

Meier, Kenneth John. "Representative Bureaucracy: An Empirical Analysis," *American Political Science Review,* 69 (June 1975), 526–542.

Poston, Ersa, and Walter D. Broadnax, forum editors. "Ethics and Morality in Government: A Public Policy Forum," *The Bureaucrat,* 4 (April 1975), 3–65.

Rosenbaum, Walter A. "The Paradoxes of Public Participation," *Administration and Society,* 8 (November 1976), 355–383.

Wynia, Bob L. "Federal Bureaucrats' Attitudes Toward a Democratic Ideology," *Public Administration Review,* 34 (March/April 1974), 156–162.

CHAPTER 14
Public Administration in a Time of Uncertainty

Our examination of public administration in the United States is now completed. From treatment of various topics in this text—values, executive leadership, intergovernmental relations, organization theory, personnel and budgeting, government regulation, and the rest—several impressions should have emerged clearly. Most important is that the current state of public administration is characterized by considerable uncertainty and change, by dramatic developments in and out of the field affecting what it presently is and does and the likely shape of its future.

Another impression is (or should have been) that while it might be desirable to maintain various features of governmental and administrative practice—such as efficiency, accountability, participation, and strong leadership—it is difficult, if not impossible, to achieve all or even most of them simultaneously. This poses hard questions for us. On which feature(s) do we place greatest value? Which are we willing to forego in order to achieve another? Who benefits and who loses from choosing one over another? In short, intricate and perplexing questions abound in public administration—questions from which there is no escape. We must contend with ambiguities and inconsistencies if we are to comprehend the present and future in this area.

In this chapter we will discuss public administration in the context of continuing uncertainty. We will look first at the social and governmental environment, building on the discussion presented in chapter 2. Then we will consider growing ferment and change in concepts and practices of governmental administration, review evolving issues and challenges in its study and teaching, and conclude by noting several continuing features—and questions—in the field.

The Social and Governmental Environment

For the past quarter century social and political struggles have taken new forms in this country, imposing great pressures on our values and institutions. A central reason for rising social tension and value conflicts is *social and economic diversity.* Societal relations directly affect political interests and competition. If those relations are tense and competitive among a large number of groups, as they have been recently, that will be reflected in political values and procedures, including those in administration.

There is much more to the social and governmental environment than simply diversity, however. Recent turbulence surrounding public administration in theory and practice has resulted from a host of changes, paradoxes, and conflicts. Chief among them is *rapid social change,* not only in population growth and geographic distribution but also in economic instruments, evolving governmental roles, and technological developments. Our capacity for booming economic growth is seriously hampered by limits on access to needed raw materials—chiefly oil, but also metals from other countries—as well as limits resulting from depletion of the earth's natural resources.

Another factor is the so-called "knowledge explosion" of the past forty years, which carries with it "increasing potential for human intervention and control both good and bad."[1] Growth of knowledge, science, and technology is closely linked with changes in the nature of society and in human capabilities, values, and behavior.[2] As one example, scientific explanations about origins of the universe and of life on this planet may profoundly affect traditional religious beliefs; as another example, consider the implications of unlocking the mysteries of human genetics and of death. If these were at one time the stuff of dreamers or science fiction writers, they are no longer.

Such developments have an ironic twist. We have had faith for decades that expanding our knowledge would make our world both more secure and more predictable, and that science would help us answer age-old questions with much more precision and certainty. Yet we have found just the opposite: the more we have learned, the *less* certain everything seems. Many people are disturbed by all this uncertainty, and it is possible that expanded knowledge contributes to *social instability,* with many seeking to return to a less unnerving past.

A further dimension of the present social and governmental environment is a focus on social problems and the need to solve them. A direct link exists between this emphasis and public administration, since "on virtually every major problem and every major challenge and opportunity we turn to government"—control of the weather, exploring outer space, controlling population growth, eliminating racial or sexual discrimination, guaranteeing safety and effectiveness of drugs, or rescuing a bankrupt railroad.[3] In terms of a balance between public and private sectors in dealing with society's problems, the public (governmental) side of the scale now receives much greater weight. Furthermore, "as the range of public problems and programs broadens, and as knowledge relevant to each grows and deepens, it becomes less and less possible for politically elected representatives to get a handle on more than a few of the significant issues."[4] Thus the role of expert administrators to whom responsibility for program management is delegated becomes ever larger. This is reinforced by the challenges of urban problems, domestic violence, economic recession, consumerism, and environmental pollution, among many others.

All this is occurring, however, in the context of more fundamental value changes in society. A wide range of beliefs and institutions is under attack from new and competing ideologies. Central to change at this basic level is decline of authority: traditional sources and centers of authority—including family, religion, and law—exert diminishing influence.[5] Decline of authority across the board suggests changing institutional patterns. The ability of government to govern may well be compromised, to say nothing of how other institutions such as churches, universities, and businesses will be affected. Current (worldwide) unrest within the Roman Catholic church illustrates the decline of authority within that system. Others are experiencing similar breakdowns.

Social and Governmental Paradoxes

Contributing still further to uncertainty in public administration is a series of paradoxical developments, some within this country alone and others worldwide in their scope. We shall consider eight of these paradoxes, keeping in mind their potential and actual impact on administrative theory and practice.

First, there is a blurring of distinctions between public and private sectors in this country,[6] contrary to a widespread public perception that they are separate and distinct. While the line between them never has been clear and simple, the degree of overlap in a public-private "gray area" has sharply increased in this century, especially in the last five decades. Every important program to raise income, employment, and productivity, relieve social distress, correct abuses, and protect rights has "entailed the creation of new and complex arrangements in which the distinction between public and private has become more blurred."[7] Examples are numerous: Amtrak, the Corporation for Public Broadcasting, and programs in urban renewal, national defense, space exploration, and health care delivery. Increasing mention has been made recently of a "Third Sector" in public administration, in which public and private entities collaborate on new and uncharted ventures.[8]

Second, we are confronted by the legacy of a "revolution of rising expectations" which still dominates politics in developing nations and some portions of our own population. At the same time, a cry has gone up from others for a lowering of our expectations. Both refer to expectations for economic development, industrialization, increased productivity, acquisition of material possessions, and a rising standard of living.[9] In this country, rising expectations and government's responses to them centered on the poor, in particular racial and ethnic minorities who have by no means given up their aspirations to the "good life." The countering trend toward lowering expectations reflects concern for environmental quality, finite resources, population growth, and "quality of life" as against "standard of living."[10] Since both rising expectations and the perceived need to lower our expectations stem from deeply held human values—albeit contradictory ones—it can be assumed that as they come increasingly into conflict, pressures will be generated for conflicting actions and programs by government. Political controversies of recent years over "economy versus ecology" and over nuclear power plants illustrate this point.

Third, a paradox exists between continuing emphasis on industrialism (closely linked to economic development and rising expectations) and the emergence of what has been called the "postindustrial society."[11] Postindustrialism refers to a socioeconomic order in which there is a relative decline in importance of production, land, and labor as economic forces, and a relative upsurge in importance of knowledge, new technologies, rendering of services (as against production of goods), and available leisure time. It is an established fact the U.S. economy has already become more service-oriented and less "goods"-oriented in recent years. Accompanying that change has been pressure on manufacturers and factory labor (including automation and computerization), chronic unemployment in a number of industries, discussion of reduced work weeks, and considerable labor-management friction in adjusting to the changes. This is not a forecast of industry's death, but it *is* a prediction of vast transformations in it. Implications for government and administration are immense: changes in revenue patterns, service needs, political demands, and so on. Elements of the postindustrial society are inexorably creeping into the fabric of social and economic life, and therefore into the complex of forces pressing on government and administration.

Fourth, forces of nationalism still run strong in many parts of the world, while conflicting currents of "postnationalism" have arisen and are gaining strength.[12] In some of the older nation-states, nationalism— identity with a national unit of government, patriotism, observance of duties of citizenship, pride in one's country—seems to be in decline. "Postnational" cynicism toward patriotism and political symbols such as anthems and flags, and growing alienation from—if not outright hostility toward—government institutions, all mark this decline. Postnationalism could mean one of two things: either an awakening of feeling for "world community," for organizing political arrangements which would strengthen international bonds of cooperation and respect (such as the European Economic Community), or a trend toward emphasizing individual *group* identities within nations at the expense of established political entities. Tribalism in African nations, the Quebec separatist movement, language rivalries in Belgium, and racial separatism in the United States are examples of the latter, which currently seems to have the edge over the former.

A fifth paradox involves tendencies toward violence and nonviolence.[13] The former is no stranger to either world affairs or our own domestic scene. Huge stockpiles of nuclear weapons in the United States and Soviet Union, with the prospect of other countries such as Israel and South Africa joining the "nuclear club," create potential not only for violence but for worldwide holocaust. Nonnuclear wars are fought between or within nations—Northern Ireland, Ethiopia, the Middle East, South Africa, and Rhodesia, to name a few—reminding us almost constantly of how far we are from a world order characterized by the peaceful rule of law. On the other hand, there is rising sentiment for nonviolent resolution of disputes, with considerable organizational sophistication in some instances—the United Nations and its complex of organizations is the best-known example. Martin Luther King patterned his nonviolent civil rights movement after the example of Mohandas Gandhi, leader of India's independence movement against Britain in the 1940s; efforts to find a formula for peaceful transition from white to black rule in southern Africa were intense throughout 1977; the antiwar movement trying to stop our involvement in Vietnam during the late 1960s and early 1970s was generally (though not entirely) nonviolent. Another irony is present, however, in that "some movements for peace and brotherhood take violence as a *means*."[14] Perhaps that is the best example of paradox concerning these phenomena.

Sixth, as noted in chapters 2 and 12, the value of limited government continues to exert a hold on our thinking in this country, yet many government programs and activities seem to conflict with it. Government regulation is a prime example. To the extent we look to government to protect us from market abuses and related ills, we create potential for government to regulate more than economic behavior. How limited we want our government to be will continue to be an issue in politics and administration for the foreseeable future, with no clear sign now of which way it will be resolved—if in fact it *can be* resolved.

Seventh, a paradox similar to the one just noted exists in dual tendencies of many people to regard government with hostility at the same time they want it to satisfy their demands.[15] A prevailing attitude appears to be one of "I want mine" from government, while not respecting or trusting government institutions very much. This attitude contributes to general political tension and to pressure on administrative machinery.

Finally, multiple meanings of "representation" and "representative" pose an important paradox. Throughout our discussion we have referred to the calls for "representativeness" as meaning inclusion in decision-making processes of those whose interests are affected by decisions made, especially those previously excluded. An older, more traditional meaning of "representation" refers to "overhead democracy"—that is, majority control through political representatives, "wherein administrative officers are primarily responsible and loyal to their superiors for carrying out the directions of the elected representatives."[16] Old and new meanings of representation have collided in theory and practice during the past two decades, and no slackening of the conflict between them is in sight. Ultimately, it is a conflict between concepts stressing, respectively, *majoritarian* and *minoritarian* political representation—that is, generalized majority rule versus systematic inclusion of social, political, and economic minorities.

These eight paradoxes have a number of aspects in common. Where our values have changed—for example, raised and lowered expectations of economic development, or nationalism and postnationalism—it is impossible to pinpoint just when the emphasis shifted from one to the other or, for that matter, just how far it has moved. Also, divergent tendencies present in all eight paradoxes are related to one another in some instances—for example, in federal antipoverty programs where rising expectations, public/private overlap, violence/nonviolence, and postnationalism come together; or in the federal highway program, where many people want to facilitate auto travel but worry about air pollution and, most of all, do not want highways built through their neighborhoods (see chapter 13).

Most important, these paradoxes have certain crucial implications for public administration as a whole. Administrative machinery is "government's central instrument for dealing with general social problems" and consequently "it is located in or between" whatever paradoxes exist in the surrounding society. "It is affected by whatever forces and turbulence there are; and it attempts also to *act,* to restrain or to increase the direction or degree of change."[17] Because of public expectations that government *will* act, administrative agencies and personnel *must* do so, even when choices are unclear, consequences only dimly perceived, and political pressures arising from these paradoxes troublesome and unyielding. Responding to public expectations is likely to become more difficult in years ahead.

In sum, the existing social and governmental environment, with its turbulence and paradoxes, poses many challenges to public administration. Since the outlook is for even more societal complexity in the future, the prognosis for public administration based on its external environment alone would be that it will experience continued pressures—for service delivery, adaptation to new needs and challenges, and political responsiveness to this or that interest. As noted in chapter 2, however, administration already has changed in response to social turbulence, in ways that may foretell future development. Administrative problems are already very different from those even one generation ago, and the rate of change promises to accelerate.

Ferment and Change in Public Administration: Concepts and Practices

This discussion of ferment and change in "practical" public administration will cover some of the same ground explored in earlier chapters. However, it is appropriate here to reexamine the contours of change in the context of what it may portend for the future.

First, bureaucracy as Max Weber defined and described it has changed considerably in the past quarter century. "The old Weberian description of bureaucracy, with its emphasis upon formal structure, hierarchy, routinization, and efficiency in its narrow sense, is rapidly becoming obsolete in many organizations."[18] It is especially inadequate, some say, for agencies operating within a turbulent environment, facing increasing complexity in their programs, and staffed heavily with highly professional or scientific personnel. Such organizations, in order to maintain needed flexibility, creativity, and innovativeness, must be structured around projects or problems to be solved rather than as permanent hierarchies. The latter will remain for various administrative purposes, such as record keeping and auditing, and for fixing final responsibility, but "work itself will be organized more collegially on a team basis. Generalist decisions will be reached through the pooling of the perspectives and techniques of a variety of specialists. Leadership will be increasingly stimulative and collaborative rather than directive."[19] This assessment is in keeping with those we encountered in chapter 6, referring to emerging bureaucratic forms quite different from the ones of Weber's and Taylor's conceptions.

A dramatic change in Weberian *practices* as well as structures is already detectable. Among the most basic functions in Weber's model of bureaucracy were orderliness, predictability, and control[20], each of which has been profoundly affected by contemporary turbulence in and around public administration. Another irony is evident: many people longing for bureaucratic predictability are among the harshest critics of Weberian bureaucracy, which highly values that very thing; furthermore, increased citizen participation has reduced predictability somewhat. The control function has been redefined a number of ways. Much more complex and elaborate leader-follower relations have been prescribed by the human relations school, organizational humanists, scholars of leadership such as Fred Fiedler, and advocates of "organization development" who emphasize democratic leadership and employee participation. Also, the control function is disrupted by subsystem politics, discussed in chapter 3, wherein administrators develop foundations of power *outside* traditional vertical bureaucratic channels of command and responsibility. All of this has some impact on bureaucratic orderliness.

Finally, bureaucratic secrecy, which Weber saw as a protection for bureaucrats, has been diminished considerably by efforts to gain public access to records and decision processes—what one observer calls "watchdogging functions."[21] Such functions have expanded significantly under prodding from the Nader organizations and groups such as Common Cause. The seemingly permanent movement away from Weberian formalism, toward much less structured and more diversified bureaucratic forms, indicates that Weber's influence lingers, but decreasingly.

Other major changes have occurred in public administration in the 1960s and 1970s.[22] First is a far wider range of participation and demands for new forms of it. From what is usually known as the "liberal" side of the political spectrum have come calls for greater *internal* participation in decision making by employees of government agencies, and *external* participation by affected clienteles. But participation has two other dimensions as well. One is *devolution* (transfer) of national government functions "back to states and local governments," which is advocated by many political conservatives. Both demands for greater participation and for devolution "are responses to a feeling of powerlessness, even alienation; both manifest a distrust of bigness and distance; both represent an attempt to gain control of decisions affecting vital personal concerns."[23]

The other dimension of participation is structural in nature, but reflects the same sort of impulse for greater popular control over government. Regional associations of governments, economic development commissions, and community action organizations have sprung up, partly at the behest of federal planners but also in response to identifiable local sentiments. Elements of both "participation" and "devolution," as well as specific administrative and economic considerations, have played a part in developing such organizations. The point here is that various steps already have been taken to translate existing preferences for participation and devolution into organizational reality (for example, citizen action groups).

A second significant change has been development of management techniques which have contributed mightily to more sophisticated and systematic administration. One dimension involves the growing use of quantitative methods and computers—in short, "management science." Another is development of "operations research," used most fruitfully to solve repeating problems—for example, determining most efficient transportation routes, allocating resources for particular tasks, and reducing costs of auditing and inspecting.[24] Others include "project management," a package of techniques designed to move individual projects along paths set out for them, and the practice of "contracting out," under which private contractors provide designated goods or services to government agencies for an agreed-upon fee. Note that contracting out is an obvious example of overlap between public and private sectors, one which has grown considerably in recent years.

A third development is public employee unionization and collective bargaining, treated in chapter 9. Underlying this development is the rise of a service-oriented economy (postindustrial), with a far larger proportion of the work force engaged in public employment. Also, general social and ideological ferment has contributed to a relaxation of laws and regulations restraining public-sector unionization. Economic recession in the mid-1970s was a factor, though that came after the drive for unionization was well under way. These developments bear directly on personnel management in the public service, but also on government's role in economic and social affairs and on the status and nature of government itself as an employer.

A fourth development is emphasis on evaluation and productivity, treated in chapter 12. Efforts are going forward to improve our capabilities in both of these areas, and some results are encouraging. Two problems, however, deserve-mention here, in addition to those treated earlier. One is so-called "Lockheed" issues—that is, those arising from demands for government to subsidize corporate enterprises (such as Lockheed Aircraft) that have become closely government-related, if and when they find themselves in financial difficulty. How one evaluates government's participation in "rescuing" such corporations is a complex question. The other problem is whether unionization and collective bargaining in the public sector will help or hinder efforts to increase productivity and improve job performance. The latter issue will hinge on whether or not union leaders and members are as concerned about these challenges as are employers. Both problems indicate the kinds of crosscurrents confronting public administration in at least the near future.

Finally, other developments should be noted. Continuing specialization and professionalization raise the challenge of bridging gaps among specialists in different professions. The decline of PPBS as an instrument of budget making and program evaluation marks the end of a period of feverish experimentation, especially in the national government. Yet ZBB promises in some respects to pick up where PPBS left off, possibly utilizing parts of the earlier budgetary approach. Executive reorganization, both as a potential and actual tool of bureaucratic control, promises to receive wider use in years ahead; more states allow their governors to submit "package" proposals to their legislatures, and President Carter has made reorganization a major priority of his administration. Reforms in fiscal federalism, particularly general revenue sharing, will continue to affect state and local administration in a host of programmatic areas; it is not to be assumed, however, that Congress will automatically renew revenue sharing in the same form each time the program expires. Also, public administration will be affected by efforts to "debureaucratize" organizational life in the public service—by deemphasizing credentials of public servants, broadening decision making, decreasing rigidities, and increasing lateral (not vertical) communication within bureaucracy.

Paradoxes in Concept and Practice

Just as there are paradoxes in the environment surrounding public administration, so also in concept and practice. Let us consider them individually.

First, the quest for administrative rationality—for example, PPBS—is frustrated by at least three countercurrents. One is *incrementalism,* which relies on an avowedly "political" assessment of costs, benefits, and program feasibility.[25] The second is *organization development* ("OD"), noted in chapter 6 and referred to earlier in this chapter; "OD" places other values above rationality, including sensitivity to employee preferences and needs and participative decision making. Third is the *politics of confrontation.*

In the 1960s and 1970s, the confrontation approach stressed moral imperatives in public policy, demanding that government address itself to social and economic problems which by some people's definition were "evil." By following a set of values measuring social phenomena according to standards of "good" and "evil," those engaging in confrontation politics crowded out alternative approaches to policy questions and solutions which attempted to deal more objectively with reality. The "confronters" defined reality according to the evils *they* perceived, and little else mattered. Ideological politics may be the "wave of the future," but it threatens any enterprise in or out of government which resists being defined according to *only one* set of moral values. Public administration is a likely battleground in any future conflict over "good" and "evil" in public affairs because of its prominent role and its tradition (itself now under attack) of seeking rationality and efficiency in a presumably value-free manner.

A second broad paradox revolves around impacts of participation in administrative decision making, by divergent—and frequently conflicting—groupings of "participants." These include program clienteles (as, for example, under terms of the Economic Opportunity Act of 1964 and the call for "maximum feasible participation" of the poor), public employee unions, and agency personnel seeking "participative management" consistent with values of organization development. All three kinds of participation offer potential opposition to the values of rationality, professionalism, leadership, and accountability.

Participation can conflict with rationality because the former is based on political inclusion of new and varied interests, while the latter presumes to identify objectively the most favorable cost-benefit ratios without regard to particular political interests or impacts on them.

Participation can conflict with professionalism because, as noted in earlier discussions, its advocates seek to have decisions framed in terms of their impacts on those affected rather than on the basis of what professionals think is "best" for the people (see discussion of the Seattle transit study in chapter 13).

Participation can conflict with leadership by acting as a constraint on leaders' ability to set the direction of organizations or political systems. Participation is a potential counterweight to what leaders desire, though in some instances it can be a source of leadership support. It comes down to a question of what views and interests are *added* to the decision-making process by expanding participation.

Finally, participation can conflict with accountability. Since the former is specifically designed to promote the latter, how can this statement be justified? The answer is this: by increasing participation in decision making, it becomes more difficult to pinpoint just who was responsible for initiating and enforcing a decision, and therefore to hold those persons to account for their actions. A skillful leader may be able to guide the participatory decision-making system along lines he or she prefers, with no one the wiser; such a technique camouflages where responsibility for a given decision really lies. Thus, though intended to promote accountability, participation carries with it the potential for doing precisely the opposite.

Emphasis on participation reflects a strong faith in *process* leading to "correct" (optimum, appropriate) results. Americans have a reputation for being pragmatic, practical people with concern for *how* things get done. Yet this discussion of participation points up an increasingly important lesson, in and out of public administration. It is that casually assuming a relationship between "doing it the right way" and getting the desired results can be risky. It may be necessary to examine precisely what is produced through given procedures—for example, in a decision-making process—to determine whether that is the way participants or clienteles wish to continue operating. Concern with consequences, as opposed to simply "perfecting the machinery," is growing, though it is to be hoped the pendulum will not swing too far the other way, ignoring means and concentrating *only* on results.

A third broad paradox involves contradictory tendencies toward centralization and decentralization. The 1960s, in particular, saw considerable centralization in and out of government, because of factors nobody could fully control. Population growth and mobility, as well as technology, produced extensive geographic interdependence in this country, and:

> interdependence forces centralization in public (as well as private) policy. The people of California have a stake in the educational standards of Mississippi, as do those of Buffalo in the waste disposal practices of Cleveland, those of New York in the economic and manpower situation in Puerto Rico, and all of us in the antipollution devices put on new cars in Detroit.[26]

Superior fiscal capacities of the national government and some state governments also encourage centralization because these governments simply can do more than others.

At the same time, it is clear that since World War II public opinion has increasingly demanded decentralization of administrative machinery, linked in many cases to the desire for expanded participation. How to accomplish that in the face of centralizing forces (in addition to the influence of some who may prefer centralization, for whatever reasons) is a key challenge—how to move in "both directions at the same time."[27] One possibility appears in recent proposed changes in metropolitan area government. In 1970 the Committee for Economic Development (CED), a business-sponsored research organization, proposed a two-level form of government for large metropolitan areas; this would consist of a powerful metropolitan-wide unit and semiautonomous community units, existing in a federal relationship to one another.[28] Since only a few essential services—such as land-use planning, utilities, transportation, and water supply[29]—need areawide coordination, this arrangement could conceivably be applied in many different places. Federation experiments in the Toronto and Miami areas[30] suggest the possibilities for practical application of this idea, though Toronto's experience more closely resembles the CED proposal than does Miami's.

Another paradox relates to a need for greater intermingling of diverse professionals, in the face of continued emphasis on professional specialization. It is not merely a matter of teams of professionals being assembled to work on specific projects. Rather, many problems in today's society have so many dimensions to them that "crime is no longer a problem for the police alone nor health for doctors alone nor highways for engineers alone nor justice for lawyers alone."[31] Growing professional interdependence, in short, will of necessity characterize public administration in the future much more than in the past.

Some other general comments should be made. First, those who advocate greater creativity, initiative, innovation, and experimentation in organizational life see emphasis on careerism in the public service as an impediment to those goals. This view is based on the assumption that careerism limits one's options for doing innovative work or otherwise "going out on a limb" because of real or imagined potential for harming one's career aspirations.[32] A related implication is conflict between individual talents such as creativity and initiative, and effective, coordinated organizational leadership. Obviously, that would depend on situational factors, primarily on whether tasks and leadership of an organization are conducive to allowing, perhaps encouraging, innovation by group members. There is little question, however, that often leaders regard themselves as custodians of the organization's mission, thus discouraging both member participation *and* creativity. In many cases, the pattern appears to be one of conflict between central, coordinated, directive leadership and flexible, creative, participative organizational operation.

FUNNY BUSINESS

Second, administrative discretion has become an issue and is likely to remain one for some time. While it is true discretionary actions by professionals in public administration may not promote *representational qualities,* nevertheless discretion does not necessarily interfere with achieving *accountability.* We might legitimately try to achieve one or both, but they must be understood properly as separate and distinct features of administrative politics in order to sensibly pursue either of them.

Finally, it would appear that as a nation we are a bit uncertain about how to achieve accountability. The original design of our political system as well as later evolution of it stressed accountability to "the people" through a complex, interrelated web of institutional channels. However, current efforts seem to focus on making all of government accountable to all of the people. It is difficult to see how that can be done. Direct accountability "to the people" is an appealing idea, but it may also be said that if officials are accountable to everybody, they are accountable to nobody! It requires careful structuring of mechanisms of accountability to maximize the chances of attaining it. Can we, then, rely on a *single* mechanism? Probably not; that would result in an excessive endowment of power in too few hands. The next best thing would seem to be a variety of mechanisms, each acting as a channel for public control but also held to account for what *it* does. There is a label for such a complex of mechanisms: "checks and balances." We may simply need to gain better control over them—again—in order to assure accountability to public interests.

Ferment and Change in Public Administration as a Field of Study

Given the wide-ranging change in concepts and practices of public administration, it is not surprising the field of study known by the same name is subject to considerable turbulence as well. Again, some of these areas were discussed previously, particularly in chapter 1, but we will deal with them as interrelated factors helping to shape the future of the academic discipline.

First, a fundamental change in mood enveloped public administration during the 1960s and 1970s.[33] One element was a cry for "relevance" in teaching curricula, paralleling similar calls throughout the academic community connected with the civil rights movement, urban unrest, and the Vietnam War. What was meant was teaching socially and politically meaningful material addressed to what were defined as major problems of the day. Closely related was pressure for dealing with *applied* problems rather than abstract theoretical problems, and for interdisciplinary efforts to address them (note the parallel to interprofessional linkages in administrative practice). As a result, an "altered academic-intellectual environment" emerged on the campus and in public administration,[34] stressing different values and priorities to be conveyed to students of the discipline.

Second, movement away from political science—its ancestral home, so to speak—characterized much of public administration and its academic professionals. As discussed in chapter 1, developments in both fields after World War II led to increasingly divergent emphases, with political science stressing behavioral research of a type which many in public administration found uncongenial in their work. The latter often was treated as an academic "second class citizen," giving rise to pressure for separation, which has taken the form of interdisciplinary programs in public administration and growing numbers of independent academic programs and departments. Yet "postbehavioral" changes in political science, beginning in the 1960s, raise the possibility that the two may be closer together now than at any time in the past twenty years. "A political science concerned deeply with public policy and not disdainful of the means by which policy is effectuated would be much more attractive to public administrationists than has been the political science of recent decades."[35]

Third, there has been some movement toward an integrated discipline known as "political economy." This would join political science and economics "in the interest of greater theoretical coherence and better policy guidance."[36] Two examples of a budding political economy may be cited, both with relevance to public administration. One is the work of Anthony Downs, originally an economist, whose *Inside Bureaucracy*[37] is one of the leading theoretical studies of public bureaucracy. The other is PPBS, founded on themes related more to economics than to politics and focused on dimensions of government—budgeting, fiscal policy, program evaluation—with *both* political and economic implications.

Fourth, schools of management and business administration have inaugurated distinct "public-sector" management portions of their course offerings, recognizing both the growing importance of education in public-sector-related fields for business graduates and the intentions of larger numbers of their students to work in the public sector upon graduation.

Fifth, there has been a proliferation of schools, programs, and institutes of public administration in the 1960s and 1970s, with a number of distinctive features. They generally are separate from political science departments, as already implied. They tend to be graduate-level rather than undergraduate programs, building on a base of a good general education. And they clearly reflect a flexible, heterogeneous approach to the subject matter taught. Labels such as "public administration," "public policy," "public affairs," "management," and "management science" abound. A directory published in 1974 by the National Association of Schools of Public Affairs and Administration listed more than 100 institutes and programs, featuring a tremendous variety of available courses and curricula.

Sixth, the "New Public Administration" has had some influence in the discipline and promises to have more. This movement, based on the value of "social equity" (see chapter 6), calls for more explicit involvement by activist administrators on behalf of clienteles previously underrepresented, inadequately served, or both, by existing administrative entities. Precisely how this movement will relate to other currents in the discipline is not clear, but one effect already noticeable is modification of curricula to reflect greater social concern.

Seventh, organizational humanism and organization development have continued to exert an influence in public administration. The former, stressing increased self-realization and greater organizational democracy, has found some response within public administration, especially in those organizations with less structured tasks permitting greater creativity and initiative. The latter has evolved from early emphasis on hardware and systems—with no great concern for interpersonal relations—to a more widely supported focus on human components of the organization and concern for normative organizational goals (what *should* be done). OD includes, among other internal techniques, consultation, survey feedback, team building, and human relations training.[38] While both approaches have had only limited impact in the great mass of public (and private) organizations, their influence appears to be on the rise.

In sum, traditional approaches in the very framework of ideas about public administration have been altered or discarded. All manner of social science research has had major impact on assumptions, forms, and behaviors in teaching public administration and on endeavors in the field. It is unlikely, in Dwight Waldo's view and that of others, that any *"single* school of philosophy, academic discipline, or type of methodology—or combination of these—would . . . persuade public administration to march under its banner."[39] This may not be altogether a bad thing. "An untidy, swiftly changing world may be better addressed by an enterprise which contains many facets, perspectives, interests, and methodologies: one which is eclectic, experimental, open-ended."[40]

A number of other observations merit inclusion here in assessing the academic field of public administration. One of its most important functions has been professional training—in programs that offer a Master's of Public Administration or Public Affairs (MPA)—of those who go on to take positions in civil service systems at all three levels of government. Some observers are concerned about the kind of training available, stressing particularly that programs should not turn out narrowly specialized individuals who "can't see past the end of their noses." These observers advocate well-trained professionals who also have perspective on themselves and their work, and on social and political contexts in which they will find themselves working.[41] Professor Frederick Mosher has noted that universities are "equipped to open the students' minds to the broader value questions of the society and of *their professions' roles in that society."*[42] What Mosher and others fear most is continuation of an educational pattern in which professional specialists "have little systematic study beyond the high school level about the society and culture in which they will live and practice their trades."[43]

The academic discipline of public administration is likely to continue to change rapidly. The state of learning is in flux, with new theories and findings appearing in great numbers, and this field, like all others, will be affected. If diversity and uncertainty characterize the discipline at the end of the 1970s, they will be ever more characteristic of it in the decades immediately ahead. Of course, that is true of the "practical" side of the discipline as well. The interchange between the two also will prove lively and unpredictable, contributing to general ferment in the profession.

Further Thoughts and Observations

In this closing section, the author will take the opportunity to add a few comments which seem important in the overall scheme of things in public administration. They are intended to supplement what has been said earlier in this chapter and to mark out significant areas in the field for future consideration by the reader.

First, interest in maintaining leadership, politically neutral competence, and representativeness will continue to exist, but tensions among them may take a different form. Whereas previously the first and third of these were linked through elective politics, and leaders clearly represented a majority coalition which had put them in office, now what is sought in each case differs somewhat. Leaders are not as widely respected or trusted; political scandals, mounting social problems and failure to deal with them, and a general atmosphere of political cynicism have contributed to that development. Simultaneously, representativeness for many is no longer the type achieved through winning elections; it has been replaced (though clearly not for everyone) by a preference for *enforced* representativeness, by means of legal inclusion in decision making of a host of interests which often are in the political (and other) minority.

Thus, contrary to Herbert Kaufman's description, leadership and this kind of representativeness have been separated, with neither dependent on the other for its existence. It is probably too early to tell, but this may portend an era of politics in which leaders are not responsible to any discernible political coalition, seeking instead to answer to a generalized "people" or "public," the specific identity of which may be hard to discover. Leaders, in other words, may represent increasingly diverse coalitions of interests, so that representation may become less meaningful. This raises the possibility, mentioned earlier, that they will be responsible to everybody—and nobody! Depending on how such leadership regards bureaucracy, this could greatly expand administrative discretion or sharply restrict it. Of course, at the same time political neutrality will also have declined in importance as a value of bureaucracy. As a result, the political setting of public administration will have been changed significantly.

Second, chief executive control over bureaucracy will continue to be balanced by the latter's information capabilities, substantive specialization in a complex world, and discretionary decision making. If impersonal bureaucracy is to be a political target, those taking aim would do well to have pertinent "ammunition" at their disposal. Total control over bureaucracy is unlikely, and in a checks-and-balances system, undesirable. It should not be forgotten that a few short years ago, parts of the bureaucracy acted as a check on a president who left office in disgrace. Control, in short, is—and should be—a two-way street.

Third, it is likely there will be continued ambiguity concerning goals in politics and administration, as well as performance. Efforts to define "what our goals are" will probably continue, but goals will also continue to be only partially agreed upon. With goals vaguely defined or even in conflict, measuring performance against "common goals" is, of course, impossible. Nevertheless, developing improved performance indicators within specific programs and projects will yield some benefits incrementally, in the form of improved planning and direction of those programs on which we *can* agree.

Fourth, it must be borne in mind, as we refine our theories of organization, leadership, and management control, that there are limits on how widely such theories can be applied. The nature of work, workers, and organizations affects applicability of theories such as organizational humanism, of leadership styles, and of methods of management control (see chapters 6, 8, and 12, respectively). These limitations must be respected to avoid problems resulting from over-eager, wholesale acceptance of any theory.

Fifth, there is some irony in current pursuit of such administrative values as greater efficiency, rationality, and productivity, which were three major elements in Frederick Taylor's theory of scientific management. This is not to say we have returned to his values, with nothing else changed. However, we may be in a cycle in which these norms once again appeal to us due to our perceiving an absence of one or more of them in the bureaucracies around us.

Sixth, some favorite terms and concepts we apply to public administration may require rethinking. We tend to speak of a *leader;* Fred Fiedler's research suggests we should be concerned instead with a *leader of,* defining effective leadership much more explicitly in terms of that which is led. In the same way, we may need to speak of politicians and administrators who are *accountable to,* not just accountable; *responsive to,* not simply responsive; bureaucracies *efficient at,* not merely efficient; and organizations *productive in terms of,* not just productive. We must bear in mind that these values are most important as means of achieving other, higher ends—not as ends in themselves. Yet all too often we treat them as the latter. For example, *why* is it important to be efficient? Is it *always* desirable? One might argue, for example, that less, not more, efficiency might have benefited thousands or millions of people in the context of the Nazi death camps during World War II. The norm of "efficiency" is not a truly neutral standard; one can *only* be efficient *at* something, and some sort of value system is involved almost always. Further, can we clearly define efficiency? Many doubt that we can. These kinds of admittedly troubling considerations should give us pause, and encourage us to think through our own assumptions about such values and norms. Clear heads and careful thinking are advantageous, especially in a time of turbulence.

Seventh, there are political implications in various areas of public administration that should be reemphasized. Some of the most important are the politics of structure, bureaucratic neutrality versus increasing nonneutrality, significance of "overhead" control of bureaucracy (president and Congress as a whole versus subsystems), changed budget procedures involving Congress as well as the president, and changes in behavior of the House Appropriations Committee in its seemingly looser control of expenditures. Other areas might also be named: ferment in intergovernmental relations, government regulation, and public personnel administration come to mind readily. The *politics* of public administration, in short, promises to be every bit as turbulent as any other area.

Eighth, after two decades of sharp disagreement over how to make the "best" decisions in administration, questions on the subject are still numerous, and though we have several major devices and systems at hand—PPBS, ZBB, and "mixed scanning," among others—the turmoil goes on unabated. We seem, in this observer's view, to be heading toward an administrative/political process where incremental decision making will still be strong, but based on information superior to that in the past and more explicitly concerned with system impacts and consequences. Though PPBS is no longer formally in effect in the national government, its influence remains. Pure incrementalism is unlikely to make a comeback; pure rationality, equally unlikely to take command. The upshot: more turmoil in store.

Ninth, government generally—indeed the entire political system—faces a challenge usually referred to as a "crisis of confidence." In the 1960s and 1970s,

> the American public began to see in the political rhetoric, the technical jargon, and the bureaucratic double-talk an uncomfortable pattern which seemed disturbingly similar to what they had learned to call propaganda. And along with propaganda, they began to identify another phenomenon—the coverup: the My Lai coverup, the Cambodian bombing coverup, the Watergate coverup, and so on. . . . [Together with private-sector scandals such as those involving ITT, Lockheed, and the Penn Central debacle] the revelations of the past ten years clearly threaten to turn the characteristic American streak of cheerful skepticism into a darker sort of general suspicion.[44]

It would appear that this is a possibility—and worse, that many citizens are assuming the worst about their government in any given situation. We may have lost not only the "cheerful" aspects of our skepticism; we may also have reached a point where we prejudge officials and, in effect, find them "guilty until proven innocent" of real or imagined misdeeds in public office.

Part of this problem runs deeper than public suspicion of government officials. There is evidence suggesting that many in this country are seeking something approaching perfection when setting about to correct perceived social, political, or economic ills. When things do not go "right," there seems to be an increasing tendency to pass a law, go to court, or otherwise keep trying to make them right—until they *are* right. The problem with that is not the effort itself—without the ability to try setting things right, much of the point of a free society, broadly defined, would be lost. The problem, rather, is the expectation that everything *can* be made "just so," meeting standards we set for things we regard as important, irrespective of how realistic or unrealistic some of our perceptions may be.

In this regard, Vice-President Mondale said something critically important in the television debate with Republican candidate Robert Dole during the 1976 national election campaign. Mondale observed that while what we *do* in government policy is important, even more crucial is what we *try to do,* the policy directions we seek to pursue. The remark is noteworthy not only for what it says directly, but for what it implies: that we may *not* achieve everything we would like to, but the effort is itself worthwhile and should be sustained even in the face of less-than-perfect results. Unfortunately, too many people are demanding much more than that before they are willing to declare themselves satisfied with the workings of the political system. If something does not work out just as we might want it, more and more frequently we blame "crooked politicians," "incompetent bureaucrats," or that most convenient of targets, a "conspiracy." Diminished public trust does not bode well for maintenance of either democratic processes or effective government.

Finally, and ironically, the dark mood of mistrust is if anything *unwarranted.* Scholarly studies of public opinion, both of recent vintage and in earlier periods, have indicated that the public's voice is heard by those in government—including those in bureaucracy—if that voice is clear in what it is saying and forceful in its expression. The "voice of the people" is really many voices, saying many things—about particular policies, conduct of government generally, public ethics, and much more. Yet it has been demonstrated that when public opinion is generally united on a position, and feelings run strong on the matter, government's response is *nearly always* in the direction desired by the majority. Does that mean we should just "take a poll" and then do what it says? No, because public opinion is more complex than that, as is governmental machinery. It *does* mean, however, we can afford a somewhat more optimistic view of governmental responsiveness to majority preferences than many seem to hold at this point. As one knowledgeable observer has put it: "In the long run, the public almost always gets its way."[45]

What, then, is the prognosis for public administration? There is no brief answer to that. Without question public administration will continue to be a focal point of concern, with controversy encompassing every major policy area and every political interest with a stake in administrative operations. Since that description applies to a multitude of coalitions and interests, it suggests comprehensive societal interaction with the whole of administration. In the words of political scientist Carl Friedrich, public administration is "the core of modern government." There can be little doubt, therefore, that public administration "is and will be a focal area for change and transformation in society generally."[46] Virtually the only thing *certain* in all this, in closing, is the *uncertain* directions public administration will take.

NOTES

1. Frederick C. Mosher, "The Public Service in the Temporary Society," *Public Administration Review,* 31 (January/February 1971), 47–62, at p. 48. The quote is originally from Paul T. David, "The Study of the Future," *Public Administration Review,* 28 (March/April 1968), p. 193.

2. Mosher, "The Public Service in the Temporary Society," p. 48.

3. Ibid., p. 49.

4. Ibid.

5. Dwight Waldo, "Developments in Public Administration," *Annals of the American Academy of Political and Social Science,* 404 (November 1972), 217–245, at p. 245.

6. Ibid., p. 219.

7. Ibid.

8. See Michael E. McGill and Leland M. Wooton, symposium editors, "Management in the Third Sector: A Symposium," *Public Administration Review,* 35 (September/October 1975), 443–477.

9. Waldo, "Developments in Public Administration," pp. 219–220.

10. Ibid.

11. Ibid., pp. 220–221.

12. Ibid., p. 221.

13. Ibid., pp. 221–222.

14. Ibid., p. 221 (emphasis added).

15. See Theodore H. White, *The Making of the President 1972* (New York: Atheneum Publishers, 1973), p. 165.

16. Mosher, "The Public Service in the Temporary Society," p. 51. The phrase was used originally by Emmette Redford in *Democracy in the Administrative State* (New York: Oxford University Press, 1969), p. 70.

17. Waldo, "Developments in Public Administration," p. 222.

18. Mosher, "The Public Service in the Temporary Society," p. 54.

19. Ibid.

20. David P. Snyder, "The Intolerant Society: An Assessment of Our Evolving Institutional Environment," *The Bureaucrat,* 3 (October 1974), 247–269, at p. 256.

21. Ibid.

22. The following relies on Waldo, "Developments in Public Administration," pp. 225–232.

23. Ibid., p. 226.

24. Nicholas Henry, *Public Administration and Public Affairs* (Englewood Cliffs, N.J.: Prentice-Hall, 1975), pp. 134–135.

25. This discussion rests on the treatment by Mosher, "The Public Service in the Temporary Society," pp. 49–52.

26. Ibid., p. 51.

27. Ibid.

28. See *Reshaping Government in Metropolitan Areas* (New York: Committee for Economic Development, 1970).

29. See the testimony of William L. Slayton, Executive Vice-President, Urban America, Inc., in *Creative Federalism:* Hearings before the Subcommittee on Intergovernmental Relations, Committee on Government Operations, U.S. Senate, 89th Congress, 2nd Session, on the Intergovernmental Cooperation Act of

1967 and related bills, November 1966 and February 1967 (Washington, D.C.: U.S. Government Printing Office, 1967), p. 874.

30. See, for example, Edward Sofen, *The Miami Metropolitan Experiment* (Bloomington: Indiana University Press, 1963).
31. Mosher, "The Public Service in the Temporary Society," p. 52.
32. Ibid., p. 58.
33. Waldo, "Developments in Public Administration," pp. 232–241.
34. Ibid., p. 233.
35. Ibid., p. 235.
36. Ibid.
37. Anthony Downs, *Inside Bureaucracy* (Boston: Little, Brown, 1967).
38. Waldo, "Developments in Public Administration," p. 240.
39. Ibid., p. 243 (emphasis added).
40. Ibid.
41. Mosher, "The Public Service in the Temporary Society," p. 56.
42. Ibid., p. 60 (emphasis added).
43. Ibid.
44. Snyder, "The Intolerant Society," p. 253.
45. Alan D. Monroe, *Public Opinion in America* (New York: Dodd, Mead, 1975), p. 292.
46. Waldo, "Developments in Public Administration," p. 244.

SUGGESTED READINGS

Lambright, W. Henry. *Governing Science and Technology*. New York: Oxford University Press, 1976.

Meade, Marvin. " 'Participative' Administration—Emerging Reality or Wishful Thinking?" In Dwight Waldo, ed., *Public Administration in a Time of Turbulence*. Scranton, Pa.: Chandler Publishing, 1971, pp. 169–187.

Miller, S. M., and Martin Rein. "Participation, Poverty, and Administration," *Public Administration Review*, 29 (January/February 1969), 15–25.

Mosher, Frederick C. "The Public Service in the Temporary Society," *Public Administration Review*, 31 (January/February 1971), 47–62.

Ostrom, Vincent. *The Intellectual Crisis in American Public Administration*. University, Ala.: University of Alabama Press, 1973.

Redford, Emmette S. *Democracy in the Administrative State*. New York: Oxford University Press, 1969.

Rivlin, Alice M. *Systematic Thinking for Social Action*. Washington, D.C.: The Brookings Institution, 1970.

Snyder, David P. "The Intolerant Society: An Assessment of Our Evolving Institutional Environment," *The Bureaucrat*, 3 (October 1974), 247–269.

Waldo, Dwight. "Developments in Public Administration," *Annals of the American Academy of Political and Social Science*, 404 (November 1972), 217–245.

Weidenbaum, Murray. *The Modern Public Sector: New Ways of Doing the Government's Business*. New York: Basic Books, 1969.

White, Orion F., Jr. "The Dialectical Organization: An Alternative to Bureaucracy," *Public Administration Review*, 29 (January/February 1969), 32–63.

GLOSSARY
ACKNOWLEDGMENTS
INDEX

GLOSSARY

accountability a political principle according to which an agency or organization, such as those in government, is subject to some form of external control, causing it to give a general accounting of and for its actions; also, the ability of those outside an organization to maintain some check on it.

adjudicatory proceeding a regulatory agency procedure involving case-by-case resolution of regulatory questions; when a formal proceeding is held, court-like rules of procedure are followed, with an administrative law judge presiding and later making preliminary recommendations to the board or commission.

administrative discretion the ability of individual administrators in a bureaucracy to make significant choices affecting the management and operation of programs for which they are responsible; particularly evident in separation-of-powers systems; related terms: *discretionary authority, discretionary power*.

advisory opinion one means used by some federal regulatory agencies to secure voluntary compliance with agency requirements; involves issuance of a memorandum indicating how the agency (for example, the FTC) would decide an issue if it were presented formally.

advocacy in the context of public administration, a function of actively pursuing particular policy goals while seeking to uphold well defined sets of social-political values; in general, seeking to persuade others to adopt a particular point of view.

affirmative action program in the context of public personnel administration, a program designed to bring into public service larger numbers of citizens that were largely excluded from public employment in years past; applied especially to women, to blacks, and to other minorities.

authority power that has been defined according to a legal and institutional framework, and vested in a formal structure (a nation, organization, and so on); power exercised through legitimate channels and for valid purposes.

bloc grant a form of grant-in-aid in which the purposes to be served by the funding are defined very broadly by the grantor, leaving considerable discretion and flexibility in the hands of the recipient.

bureaucracy (1) a formal organizational arrangement characterized by division of labor, job specialization with no functional overlap, exercise of authority through a vertical

445

hierarchy (chain of command), and a system of internal rules, regulations, and record-keeping; (2) in common usage, the administrative branch of government (national, state, or local) in the United States; also, individual administrative agencies of those governments.

bureaucratic neutrality a feature of bureaucracy whereby it carries out directives of other institutions of government (such as executive or legislative), without acting as a political force in its own right; a traditional notion concerning bureaucratic behavior in Western governments.

capitalism a major economic doctrine that emphasizes maximum freedom for private entrepreneurs, opportunity to acquire private profits, minimal involvement of government in the private economy, and general economic growth.

categorical grant-in-aid a form of grant-in-aid with purposes narrowly defined by the grantor, leaving the recipient very little discretionary choice as to how the grant funding is to be used.

confederation a government system in which constitutional authority is vested in regional units of government (such as states), which have a high degree of autonomy and which may delegate some authority to a central government; also, a loose governmental alliance or league, such as the Confederate States of America.

consent order one means used by some federal regulatory agencies to secure voluntary compliance with agency requirements; involves a formal agreement between the agency and an industry or industries, in which the latter agree to cease a practice in return for the agency's dropping actions brought against it or them.

constituency any group or organization interested in the work and actions of a given official, agency, or organization, and a potential source of support for it; also, the interests (or sometimes geographic area) served by an elected or appointed official.

co-optation a process in organizational relations whereby one group or organization acquires the ability to influence activities of another, usually for a considerable period of time; involves a surrender by a weaker entity to a stronger one of some ability to influence the former's long-term activities.

cost-benefit analysis a technique designed to measure relative gains and losses resulting from alternative policy or program options; emphasizes identification of the most desirable cost-benefit ratio in quantitative or other terms.

cost-benefit ratio the proportional relationship between expenditure of a given quantity of resources and the benefits derived therefrom; a guideline for choosing among alternatives.

"creative" federalism a label developed during the presidency of Lyndon Johnson to describe his approach to intergovernmental relations; involved, in principle, wide-ranging interactions among all levels of government as well as the private sector, with a focus on alleviating urban poverty.

Critical Path Method (CPM) a management technique of program implementation (related to PERT) in which a manager attempts to assess the resource needs of different paths of action and to identify the path with the smallest margin of extra resources needed to complete all assigned program activities (the "critical path").

cybernetics a modern theory of organization that treats organizations as self-regulating; emphasizes interactions between feedback (both internal and external) that trigger adaptive mechanisms within the organization; a nonorganizational example of the cybernetic principle is the thermostat.

decision making a process in which choices are made to change (or leave unchanged) an existing condition, to select a course of action most appropriate to achieving a desired objective, and to minimize risks, uncertainty, and resource expenditures in pursuing the objective.

"dual" federalism a label applied to one type of national-state relations in the United States, said to have existed in the 1800s, whereby the functions and responsibilities of different levels of government were theoretically clearly distinguished from one another; also called "layer-cake" federalism.

economic democracy a social and political belief in equal distribution of wealth throughout a society, with few very rich or very poor; believed by some to be a key prerequisite of true political democracy.

egalitarianism a philosophical concept stressing individual equality in political, social, economic, and other relations; in the context of public personnel administration, the conceptual basis for "government by the common person."

exception principle an assumption in traditional administrative thinking that chief executives do not have to be involved in administrative activities unless some problem or disruption of routine activity occurs—that is, where there is an exception to routine operations.

federalism a constitutional division of governmental power between a central or national government and regional governmental units (such as states), with each having some independent authority over its citizens.

"first-line" supervisor a worker's immediate superior on the job; the focus of research on how superiors influence workers and the work situation.

formal theories of organization theories stressing formal, structural arrangements within organizations and/or "correct" or "scientific" methods to be followed in order to achieve the highest degree of organizational efficiency; examples include Weber's theory of bureaucracy and Taylor's "scientific management" scheme.

formula grant a type of federal grant-in-aid available to states and localities for purposes that are ongoing and common to many government jurisdictions; distributed according to a set formula that treats all applicants uniformly, at least in principle.

freedom of information law an act passed by the national and some state legislatures establishing procedures through which private citizens may gain access to a wide variety of records and files from government agencies; a principal instrument for breaking down bureaucratic secrecy in American public administration.

functional overlap a phenomenon of contemporary American bureaucracy whereby functions performed by one bureaucratic entity may also be performed by another—conflicts with Weber's notions of division of labor and specialization.

game theory a modern theory viewing organizational behavior in terms of competition among members for resources; based on distinctly mathematical assumptions, employing mathematical methods.

general revenue-sharing one type of revenue-sharing adopted during the first Nixon administration, designed as a supplement to existing grant funding in order to meet rising costs of government; nearly $7 billion is available annually under this program.

goal articulation a process of defining and clearly expressing goals generally held by those in an organization or group; usually regarded as a function of organization or group leaders; a key step in developing support for official goals.

goal congruence agreement on fundamental goals; in the context of an organization, refers to agreement among leaders and followers in the organization on central objectives; in practice, its absence in many instances creates internal tensions and difficulties in goal definition.

grant-in-aid a money payment furnished by a higher to a lower level of government to be used for specified purposes and subject to conditions spelled out in law or administrative regulation; the dominant form of national aid to state and local governments.

Hatch Act a law (formally known as the Political Activities Act of 1939) that prohibits active political campaign participation by national government employees, state and local employees working in federally funded programs, and private-sector employees working with community action programs; target of reform efforts in the 1970s.

hierarchy a characteristic of formal bureaucratic organizations; a clear vertical "chain of command" in which each unit is subordinate to the one above it and superior to the one below it; one of the most common features of government and other bureaucracies.

hierarchy of needs a psychological concept formulated by Abraham Maslow which holds that workers have different kinds of needs that must be satisfied in sequence—basic survival needs, job security, social needs, ego needs, and personal fulfillment in the job.

human relations theories of organization theories stressing workers' non-economic needs and motivations on the job; sought to identify these needs and how to satisfy them; focused on working conditions and social interactions among workers.

impoundment in the context of the budgetary process, the practice by a chief executive of withholding final spending approval of funds appropriated by the legislature in a bill already signed into law.

incrementalism a model of decision making stressing consideration of only limited changes from the status quo, focusing on short-term rather than long-term consequences.

individualism a philosophical belief in the worth and dignity of the individual, particularly as part of a political order; holds that government and politics should regard the well-being and aspirations of individuals as more important than those of the government.

information theory a modern theory of organization that views organizations as requiring constant input of information in order to continue functioning systematically and productively; assumes that a lack of information will lead to chaos or randomness in organizational operations.

interest group a private organization representing a portion (usually small) of the general adult population, which exists in order to pursue particular public policy objectives and seeks to influence government activity so as to achieve its objectives.

intergovernmental fiscal relations the complex of financial transactions, transfers of funds, and accompanying rules and regulations (or lack thereof) which increasingly characterizes national-state, national-local, and state-local relations; also known as fiscal federalism.

intergovernmental relations all the activities and interactions occurring between or among governmental units of all types and levels within the American federal system.

item veto a constitutional power available to approximately half of America's governors, under which they may disapprove some provisions of a bill while approving the others.

"knowledge explosion" a social phenomenon of the past forty years, particularly in Western industrial nations, creating new technologies and vast new areas of research and education; examples include space exploration, mass communications, nuclear technology, mass production, and energy research.

legislative intent the purposes and objectives of a legislative body, given concrete form in its enactments (though actual intent may change over time); bureaucratic behavior is assumed to follow legislative intent in implementing laws.

legislative oversight the process by which a legislative body continually supervises the work of the bureaucracy in order to insure its conformity with legislative intent.

legitimacy a characteristic of a social institution (such as government) whereby it has the right—as well as the legal authority—to make laws and other rules for the people who belong to it; such a right is, in effect, granted to the institution by the people, and is not automatic.

liberal democracy a fundamental form of political arrangement, founded on the concepts of popular sovereignty and limited government.

limited government a central concept of American politics, holding that because government poses a fundamental threat to individual liberties, it must be carefully limited in its capacity to act arbitrarily; the Founders believed it was to be achieved through separation of powers, checks and balances, federalism, and judicial review.

line-item budgeting the earliest approach to modern executive budget making, emphasizing control of expenditures through careful accounting for all money spent in public programs; facilitated central control of purchasing and hiring and completeness and honesty in fiscal accounting.

management according to task a modern theory of organization that conceives of the internal units of an organization as structured in a manner most appropriate to their particular tasks; assumes great diversity within an organization in terms of suborganizational structures (formal, social, technological).

Management by Objectives (MBO) a management technique designed to facilitate goal- and priority-setting, development of plans, resource allocation, monitoring progress toward goals, evaluating results, and generating and implementing improvements in performance.

"marble-cake" federalism a label applied to cooperative relationships among different units and levels of government, resulting in an intermingling of functions and responsibilities; said to exist in the twentieth century, and (by some) in the nineteenth century as well; the opposite of "dual" federalism; also called "cooperative" federalism.

"Miranda Rule" a principle of constitutional law established by the U.S. Supreme Court in the case of *Miranda* v. *Arizona* (1966), holding that criminal suspects must be advised of their rights prior to questioning by the police.

mixed scanning a model of decision making that combines the rational-comprehensive model's emphasis on fundamental choices and long-term consequences with the incrementalists' emphasis on changing only what needs to be changed in the immediate situation; emphasizes short-term decisions.

modern organization theory a body of theory emphasizing empirical examination of organizational behavior, interdisciplinary research employing varied approaches, and attempts to arrive at generalizations applicable to many different kinds of organizations.

New Public Administration a movement among public administration professionals during the 1970s that advocates "social equity" as a central guiding principle for administrative decision making with regard to allocation of resources; also concerned with how decisions are made within organizations.

Office of Management and Budget (OMB) an important entity in the Executive Office of the President that assists the president in assembling executive branch budget requests, coordinating programs, developing executive talent, and supervising management processes in government agencies.

OMB Circular A–95 a 1969 directive designed to implement provisions of the Model Cities and Intergovernmental Cooperation Acts requiring evaluation and review by state, regional, and local "clearinghouses" of all applications for federal grants-in-aid, especially those from local governments.

open systems theory a theory of organization that views organizations not as "closed" bureaucratic structures separate from their surroundings, but as operating constantly in interaction with their environment; assumes that organizational components will seek an "equilibrium" among the forces pressing on them and their own responses to those forces.

organization development a theory of organization that concentrates on increasing the ability of an organization to solve internal problems of organizational behavior as one of its routine functions; concerned primarily with identification and analysis of such problems.

organizational adaptiveness a theory of organization (similar in some respects to organizational change), that emphasizes the need for fundamental reordering of structures and functions when the external environment changes in fundamental ways; holds that failure to change can greatly reduce effectiveness.

organizational change a theory of organization that focuses on those characteristics of an organization that promote or hinder change; assumes that demands for change originate in the external environment, and that the organization should be in the best position to respond to them.

organizational humanism a set of organization theories stressing that work held intrinsic interest for the worker, that workers sought satisfaction in their work, that they wanted to work rather than avoid it, and that they could be motivated through systems of positive incentives (such as participation in decision making).

participatory democracy a political and philosophical belief in direct involvement by affected citizens in the processes of governmental decision making; believed by some to be essential to the existence of democratic government; related term: *citizen participation.*

Pendleton Act a law, formally known

as the Civil Service Act of 1883 (sponsored by Ohio Senator George Pendleton), establishing job-related competence as the primary basis for filling national government jobs; created the U.S. Civil Service Commission to oversee the new "merit" system.

performance budgeting an approach to modern executive budget making that gained currency in the 1930s, emphasizing not only resources acquired by an agency but also what it did with them; geared to promoting effective management of government programs in a time of growing programmatic complexity.

"picket-fence" federalism a term describing a new dimension of American federalism—intergovernmental administrative relationships among bureaucratic specialists, and their clientele groups, in the same substantive areas; suggests that allied bureaucrats exercise considerable power over intergovernmental programs; related term: *vertical functional autocracies*.

planning-programming-budgeting system (PPBS) a system widely applied in the 1960s, designed to link planning and program development to the budgetary process; emphasized budgetary rationality, determining budget impacts, cost-benefit analysis, and expanded budgetary information.

pluralism a social and political theory stressing the appropriateness of group organization, and diversity of groups and their activities, as a means of protecting broad group interests in society; assumes that groups are good and that bargaining and competition among them will benefit the public interest.

policy analysis the systematic investigation of alternative policy options and the assembly and integration of evidence for and against each; emphasizes explaining the nature of policy problems, and how public policies are put into effect.

policy development a general political and governmental process of formulating relatively concrete goals and directions for government activity and proposing an overall framework of programs related to them; usually but not always regarded as a chief executive's task.

policy implementation a general political and governmental process of carrying out programs in order to fulfill specified policy objectives; a responsibility chiefly of administrative agencies, under chief executive and/or legislative guidance; also, the activities directed toward putting a policy into effect.

political rationality a concept advanced by Wildavsky, suggesting that behavior of decision makers may be entirely rational when judged by criteria of political costs, benefits, and consequences, even if irrational according to economic criteria; emphasizes that political criteria for "rationality" have validity.

politics (1) the pursuit and exercise of power; (2) competition and conflict over scarce resources; (3) the authoritative allocation of resources; (4) deciding "who gets what, when, how."

popular sovereignty government by the ultimate consent of the governed, implying some degree of participation by the people in choosing government officials and in carrying on other political activities (though not necessarily mass participation).

position classification a formal task of American public personnel administration, intended to classify together jobs in different agencies that have essentially the same types of functions and responsibilities, based on written descriptions of duties and responsibilities.

postindustrialism a social and economic phenomenon said by some to be emerging in many previously industrialized nations; characterized by a relative decline in the importance of production, labor, and durable goods, and an increase in the importance of knowledge, new technologies, the provision of services, and leisure time.

Professional and Administrative Career Examination (PACE) the federal general entrance examination for civil service applicants, established in 1974; emphasizes both broad training and background and professional specialties; replaced the Federal Service Entrance Examination (FSEE).

Program Evaluation and Review Technique (PERT) a management technique of program implementation in which the sequence of steps for carrying out a project or program is mapped out in advance; involves choosing necessary activities and estimating time and other resources required.

project grant a form of grant-in-aid available to states and localities, by application, for an individual project; more numerous than formula grants, with more funding available as well.

public administration (1) all processes, organizations, and individuals (the latter acting in official positions and roles) associated with carrying out laws and other rules adopted or issued by legislatures, executives, and courts; many activities are concerned also with formulation of these rules; (2) a field of academic study and professional training leading to public service careers at all levels of government.

"public interest" group a group organized to gain influence, in the name of the "public interest," over decisions and activities of government agencies; dedicated to advancing its view of the general public's well-being, as opposed to that of individual group interests; examples: Common Cause, Public Citizen.

public policy (1) the organizing framework of purposes and rationales for government programs that deal with specified societal problems; (2) whatever governments choose to do or not do. (3) the complex of programs enacted and implemented by government.

rational-comprehensive model of decision making derived from economic theories of how to make the "best" decisions; involves efforts to maximize returns on a given investment of resources by a comprehensive analysis of alternatives and a rigorous analysis of the costs, benefits, and consequences of each.

reflexive goal a goal of an organization or individual that is related primarily to survival and maintenance; "inward-oriented" as opposed to one focusing on external impacts.

revenue-sharing a form of national government aid to states and localities, distributed without application according to a fixed formula; use of funding is determined largely, if not entirely, by recipient governments; a major political program of the Nixon years, offered as an alternative to federal grants.

"revolution of rising expectations" a social phenomenon of the period since World War II, affecting many nations, in which people who have been relatively poor have sought to increase their level of prosperity both as individuals and as groups; related in part to faith in technological and social advances.

rule making a regulatory agency procedure involving issuance of a formal rule or standard of operation covering a general class or category of events and enterprises, and affecting all uniformly; said to be quasi-legislative.

"rule of three" a procedure usually followed by the U.S. Civil Service Commission in narrowing the list of people most qualified for a particular job opening in a federal agency; three names are sent to the agency, which then makes the final selection, based on PACE test scores and other considerations.

salience the degree to which an issue is directly meaningful (salient) or significant to an individual; usually determined by how much impact the individual believes the issue has on his or her life.

scientific management a formal theory of organization developed by Frederick Taylor in the early 1900s; concerned with achieving efficiency in production, rational work procedures, maximum productivity, and profit; focused on management's responsibilities and on "scientifically" developed work procedures.

seniority system in Congress, the method used for selecting House and Senate committee chairmen; the individual who has served the longest time, in years of *consecutive* service in Congress and on a committee, becomes chairman; favors members from "safe" districts or states.

"situational" approach to leadership a method of analyzing leadership in a group or organization that emphasizes factors in the particular leadership situation such as leader-follower interactions, group values and needs, and the work being done.

special revenue-sharing a political program of the Nixon administration which, if enacted, would have replaced existing federal grant programs with virtually unrestricted funding for many of the same overall purposes; defeated by Congress in the early 1970s and never revived.

spoils system a system of hiring personnel based on political loyalty and connections; can also extend to government contracts and the like; usually takes the form of rewarding party supporters with government jobs.

substantive goal an organizational goal focusing on the accomplishment of tangible programmatic objectives.

subsystem in the context of American politics (especially at the national level), any political alliance uniting some members of an administrative agency, a legislative committee or

subcommittee, and an interest group according to shared values and preferences in the same substantive area of policy making.

sunk cost in the context of organizational resources committed to a given decision, any cost involved in the decision that is irrecoverable; resources of the organization are lessened by that amount if it later reverses its decision.

"sunset" law a law designed to increase accountability and control over administrative agencies by requiring: (a) automatic termination of programs and agencies unless specifically reestablished by the legislature, and (b) periodic evaluations of programs and agencies prior to a termination date.

"sunshine" law an act passed by the national Congress, and by some states and localities, requiring that various legislative proceedings (especially those of committees and subcommittees) be held in public rather than behind closed doors; one device for increasing visibility and accountability.

systems analysis an analytical technique designed to permit comprehensive investigation of the impacts within a given system of changing one or more elements of that system; in the context of analyzing policies, emphasizes overall objectives, surrounding environments, available resources, and system components.

systems theory a theory of social organizations, holding that change in any one part of a group or organization affects all other parts; a key conceptual assumption behind planning-programming-budgeting systems (PPBS) and efforts to install PPBS in federal, state, and local budget making.

"traits" approach to leadership a traditional method (now used less widely by scholars) of analyzing leadership in a group or organization;

assumes that certain personality characteristics such as intelligence, ambition, tact, and diplomacy distinguish leaders from others in the group.

transitive goal an organizational goal that, if achieved, would have an impact on an organization's external environment; a goal concerned more with external than with internal consequences of organizational actions.

zero-base budgeting (ZBB) a technique designed to permit top executives to base budgetary decisions on assessments of agency and program effectiveness/efficiency, assuming allocations of "zero" dollars and higher amounts; used in industry and some states, including Georgia under Governor Jimmy Carter.

ACKNOWLEDGMENTS (continued from page iv)

Table 4–1   From Charles E. Jacob, "The Quest for Presidential Control: Innovation and Institutionalization in the Executive Branch," Paper prepared for the Annual Meeting of the American Political Science Association; Jung Hotel, New Orleans, Louisiana, September 4–8, 1973. Reprinted by permission of the American Political Science Association.

Figure 4–2   From Peter L. DeGroote, "Recognizing Professional Positions," *Public Management*, LV (March 1973), p. 7. Reprinted with permission from the March 1973 issue of *Public Management*. Copyright © 1973, The International City Management Association.

Figure 5–2   From Deil S. Wright, "Intergovernmental Relations: An Analytical Overview," *Annals of the American Academy of Political and Social Science,* 416 (November 1974), p. 15 © 1974 by The American Academy of Political and Social Science. All rights reserved.

Table 6–1   From Douglas McGregor, "Theory X and Theory Y," in Robert T. Golembiewski and Michael Cohen, *People in Public Service: A Reader in Public Personnel Administration* (Itasca, Ill.: F. E. Peacock, 1970), p. 380. Reproduced by permission of the publisher, F. E. Peacock Publishers, Inc., Itasca, Illinois.

Table 6–2   From H. Roy Kaplan and Curt Tausky, "Humanism in Organizations: A Critical Appraisal," *Public Administration Review,* 37 (March/April 1977), p. 175. Reprinted from *Public Administration Review.* © 1977 by American Society for Public Administration, 1225 Connecticut Avenue, N.W., Washington, D.C. 20036. All rights reserved.

Table 6–3   From H. Roy Kaplan and Curt Tausky, "Humanism in Organizations: A Critical Appraisal," *Public Administration Review,* 34 (March/April 1977), p. 177. Reprinted from *Public Administration Review.* © 1977 by American Society for Public Administration, 1225 Connecticut Avenue, N.W., Washington, D.C. 20036. All rights reserved.

Figure 8–1   From Robert Tannenbaum and Warren H. Schmidt, "How to Choose a Leadership Pattern," *Harvard Business Review,* May–June 1973. Copyright © 1973 by the President and Fellows of Harvard College. All rights reserved.

Table 9–2   After table, "Federal Employees Subject to Merit Personnel Policies," p. 48, in *Public Personnel Administration,* 7th edition by O. Glenn Stahl. Copyright © 1976 by O. Glenn Stahl. By permission of Harper & Row, Publishers, Inc.

Figure 10–1   From Jack Rabin, "State and Local PPBS," in Robert T. Golembiewski and Jack Rabin, eds., *Public Budgeting and Finance: Readings in Theory and Practice,* 2nd ed. (Itasca, Ill.: F. E. Peacock, 1975), p. 437. Reproduced by permission of the publisher, F. E. Peacock Publishers, Inc., Itasca, Illinois.

"Sample Test Questions Dealing with Administration from New York City Police Examinations," reprinted courtesy of Modern Promotion Courses, Fresh Meadows, New York.

Table 10–1   From James J. Finley, "The 1974 Congressional Initiative in Budget Making," *Public Administration Review,* 35 (May/June 1975), p. 272. Reprinted from *Public Administration Review.* © 1975 by American Society for Public Administration, 1225 Connecticut Avenue, N.W., Washington, D.C. 20036. All rights reserved.

Table 11–1   Budget and Personnel figures from *Regulatory Reform: A Survey of Proposals in the 94th Congress* (Washington, D.C.: American Enterprise Institute for Public Policy Research, 1976), pp. 47–48. Used with permission.

Table 12–1   From *So, Mr. Mayor, You Want to Improve Productivity . . .* (Washington: National Commission on Productivity and Work Quality, 1974), and Center for Productive Public Management, John Jay College, New York.

Figure 12–2 From Graham T. Allison and Morton H. Halperin, "Bureaucratic Politics: A Paradigm and Some Policy Implications," in *Theory and Policy in International Relations* by Raymond Tanter and Richard H. Ullman (eds.), pp. 77–79. Copyright © 1972 by Princeton University Press. Reprinted by permission of Princeton University Press.

Figure 12–3 From Thomas R. Dye, *Understanding Public Policy,* Second Edition, © 1975, p. 6. Reprinted by permission of Prentice-Hall, Inc., Englewood Cliffs, New Jersey.

Figure 12–4 From Walter Williams, "Implementation Analysis and Assessment," *Policy Analysis* (Summer 1975), p. 546. Reprinted by permission.

Table 13–1 From Milton C. Cummings, Jr., M. Kent Jennings, and Franklin P. Kilpatrick, "Federal and Non-Federal Employees: A Comparative Social Occupational Analysis," *Public Administration Review,* 27 (December 1967), p. 399. Reprinted from *Public Administration Review.* © 1967 by American Society for Public Administration, 1225 Connecticut Avenue, N.W., Washington, D.C. 20036. All rights reserved.

Figure 13–1 Redrawn and reprinted from Sherry R. Arnstein, "A Ladder of Citizen Participation," *Journal of the American Institute of Planners,* XXXV (July 1969), p. 217. Copyright © 1969 American Institute of Planners.

Presidential Comments on Ethics in Government From Library of Congress and *Congressional Quarterly Guide to Current American Government* (Spring 1974), p. 28. © 1974 Congressional Quarterly Inc.

Table 13–2 From Kenneth John Meier, "Representative Bureaucracy: An Empirical Analysis," *American Political Science Review,* 69 (June 1975), p. 541. Reprinted by permission of the American Political Science Association.

Table 13–3 From Bob L. Wynia, "Federal Bureaucrats' Attitudes Toward a Democratic Ideology," *Public Administration Review,* 34 (March/April 1974), 158–159. Reprinted from *Public Administration Review.* © 1974 by American Society for Public Administration, 1225 Connecticut Avenue, N.W., Washington, D.C. 20036. All rights reserved.

Table 13–4 From Bob L. Wynia, "Federal Bureaucrats' Attitudes Toward a Democratic Ideology," *Public Administration Review* 34 (March/April 1974), p. 159. Reprinted from *Public Administration Review.* © 1974 by American Society for Public Administration, 1225 Connecticut Avenue, N.W., Washington, D.C. 20036. All rights reserved.

"Funny Business" Cartoon. Reprinted by permission of Newspaper Enterprise Association (or NEA).

INDEX